Makers of Modern Korean Buddhism

SUNY Series in Korean Studies

Sung Bae Park, editor

Makers of Modern Korean Buddhism

Edited by

Jin Y. Park

SUNY PRESS

Published by State University of New York Press, Albany

Printed in the United States of America

For information, contact State University of New York Press, Albany, NY
www.sunypress.edu

Production by Eileen Meehan
Marketing by Michael Campochiaro

Library of Congress Cataloging-in-Publication Data

Makers of modern Korean Buddhism / edited by Jin Y. Park.
p. cm. — (SUNY series in Korean studies)
Includes bibliographical references and index.
ISBN 978-1-4384-2921-2 (hardcover : alk. paper)
ISBN 978-1-4384-2922-9 (pbk. : alk. paper)
1. Buddhism—Korea—History. I. Park, Jin Y.

BQ658.M35 2009
294.309519—dc22 2009005247

10 9 8 7 6 5 4 3 2 1

Contents

PART TWO
Revival of Zen Buddhism in Modern Korea

PART THREE
Religion, History, and Politics

Acknowledgments

I would like to express my sincere appreciation to Professor Sung Bae Park for his support for this project and for making this volume a part of SUNY Series in Korean Studies. I would like to thank Steven Heine for his support for this project and acknowledgment of the importance of this volume. I also thank Professor John Gould for his critical reading of the essays in this volume and helpful comments on each essay. I thank all the contributors for their participation, patience, and support for this volume. I also thank Nancy Ellegate at SUNY Press for her help throughout the process of the publication of this volume. Christopher Frascella, Jeff Epstein, and Juliet Mohnkern helped me at the different stages in the preparation of this volume. I thank them for their time and efforts.

An earlier version of Chapter 1 was originally published in *Korea Journal* 45, no.1 (Spring 2005): 29–63 under the title "A Monk of Mukti and Karma: The Life and Thought of Baek Yongseong."

An earlier version of Chapter 2 was originally published in *Seoul Journal of Korean Studies* 20, no. 1 (2007): 21–44 under the title "A Korean Buddhist Response to Modernity: The Doctrinal Underpinning of Han Yongun's (1879–1944) Reformist Thought."

An earlier version of Chapter 5 was originally published in *Korea Journal* 45, no. 1 (Spring 2005): 114–141 under the title "Gendered Response to Modernity: Kim Iryeop and Buddhism."

An earlier version of Chapter 6 was originally published in *Korean Studies* 7 (1983): 9–33 under the title "The Life and Thought of the Korean Son Master Kyongho."

An earlier version of Chapter 11 was originally published in *International Journal of Buddhist Thought & Culture* 4 (February 2004): 7–49 under the title "The Japanese Missionaries and their Impact on Korean Buddhist Developments (1876–1910)."

An earlier version of Chapter 13 was originally published in *Korea Journal* 45, no. 1 (Spring 2005): 5–28, under the title "The Formation of Modern Buddhist Scholarship: the Case of Bak Jong-hong and Kim Dong-hwa."

Abbreviations

C	Chinese pronunciation
CN	The Canon in the *Scripture of Won Buddhism*
CS	*Chogyejong sa: Kŭn.hyŏndae p'yŏn* 曺溪宗史: 근현대편
HIBL	*Hanam Ilballok: Hanam taejongsa pŏbŏrok* 漢巖一鉢錄: 漢巖大宗師法語錄
HPC	*Han'guk Pulgyo chŏnsŏ* 韓國佛教全書
HYC	*Han Yongun chŏnjip* 韓龍雲全集
J	Japanese pronunciation
K	Korean pronunciation
KP	*Kyŏnghŏ pŏbŏ* 鏡虛法語
PCHC	*Pak Chonghong chŏnjip* vol. 4. 朴鍾鴻全集
SC	*Sŏnmun chŏngno* 禪門正路
Sk	Sanskrit
SS	The Scripture of Sot'aesan in the *Scripture of Won Buddhism*
T	*Taishō shinshū daizōkyō* 大正新修大蔵経
YTC	*Yongsŏng taejongsa chŏnjip* 龍城大宗師全集
ZZ	*Dai Nihon zokuzōkyō* 大日本続蔵経

Introduction

Buddhism and Modernity in Korea

Jin Y. Park

Buddhism's encounters with modernity appear in different forms, depending on the regional specifics and historical contexts in which these encounters took place. In the West, the encounter resulted in the introduction of Buddhism to the Western world, which was followed by the emergence of a modern style of Buddhist scholarship and of new forms of Buddhism. In the context of Asia, Buddhism's encounters with modernity have been frequently discussed in relation to political situations including nationalism, colonialism, and communism; and their socio-religious manifestations have been characterized by, among others, mass-proselytization, lay Buddhist movements, institutional reform, and the emergence of socially engaged Buddhism.

Buddhism in modern Korea also experienced the phenomena identified above, but in their responses to modernity, Korean Buddhists had to deal with their unique socio-historical and political situations. In this context, three aspects are especially noticeable in Korean Buddhism's encounters with modernity. I will identify them as Buddhist reform movements, Zen/Sŏn revivalism, and the Buddhist encounter with new intellectualism. In this introduction, I will discuss the major issues in these three aspects of modern Korean Buddhism and close this essay by proposing three issues that need reconsideration for a better understanding of the evolution of Buddhism in modern Korea.

Buddhist Reform Movements

At the end of the nineteenth and the beginning of the twentieth centuries, Korean Buddhism faced a dual challenge generated by the legacy of its past and the prospects for its future. Most urgent was the recovery of its dignity after centuries-long persecution under the neo-Confucian Chosŏn dynasty (1392–1910).

Beginning in the mid-fifteenth century, Buddhist monks and nuns were prohibited from entering the capital city; this ban remained effective until 1895. The ban is a concrete example of the severe persecution Korean Buddhists experienced for more than 400 years prior to Korea's opening to the modern world. As Korea made the transition from a pre-modern to a modern society, Korean Buddhists were hoping to exploit this opportunity to regain the dignity of Buddhism in Korean society. This hope was also charged with the urgent need to renovate the religion so as to prove that the Buddhism, which had a 1,500-year history in Korea, was still relevant in the modern world.

The dual task of Korean Buddhism in reestablishing its status as a major religio-philosophical system on the one hand and demonstrating its relevance in modern society on the other was further complicated because of the political situation of colonialism. Korea was annexed to Japan in 1910, beginning a 35-year colonial period. Colonialism is one of the shared aspects that Buddhism had to deal with in Asia in its encounter with modernity. However, Korean Buddhist colonial experiences were unique in that Korea was colonized not by a non-Buddhist Western country but by an Asian country in which Buddhism had long been a dominant religion. This situation caused conflicting and sometimes contradictory responses of Korean Buddhism to Japanese Buddhism and Japanese colonial policy.

At the initial stage of Korean Buddhism's encounter with modernity, Korean Buddhists considered Japanese Buddhism a model to follow for the revival of Korean Buddhism. Some Buddhist intellectuals also considered the possibility of employing Buddhism for the modernization of Korea. As early as the late 1870s, Japanese Buddhist missionaries arrived in Korea for the purpose of proselytization, and in exchange, progressive-minded Korean monks traveled to Japan in order to learn what they considered an advanced form of Buddhism. A representative case during the initial stage of the encounter between Buddhism and modernity is that of a monk named Yi Tongin (1849?–1881?). Yi introduced techniques of modern education to Buddhist lecture halls and traveled to Japan to learn about its civilization and progress in an effort to use them as models for reform in both Korean Buddhism and Korean society.[1] His reform movement, however, faced an early death amidst social and political turbulence in Korea.[2] Despite the premature death of Yi Tongin's project, and of Yi himself, his case demonstrates that the reformist spirit was already in the process of making changes in Korean Buddhism during the late nineteenth century. The appearance of publications demanding the reformation of Korean Buddhism during the early twentieth century is visible proof of this spirit.

Starting from the early 1910s and continuing until the late 1930s, a series of treatises containing the reform agenda of Korean Buddhism appear. Kwŏn Sangno (1879–1965), who was not a favorite of Korean Buddhist scholars because of his collaboration with the Japanese colonialists, published a treatise titled *Chosŏn Pulgyo kyehyŏk ron* (Treatise on the Reformation of Korean Buddhism, 1912–1913). *Chosŏn Pulgyo yusillon* (Treatise on the Revitalization of Korean Buddhism) by Han Yongun (1879–1944), the most well-known figure in this group, was published in 1913. Yi Yŏngjae's (1900–1929) *Chosŏn Pulgyo kaehyŏksillon* (A New Treatise on the Reformation of Korean Buddhism) appeared in 1922, and *Chosŏn Pulgyo hyŏksillon* (Treatise on the Renovation of Korean Buddhism) by Pak Chungbin (1891–1943), the founder of Won Buddhism, was published in 1935. These treatises share a number of agendas they proposed for the renovation of Korean Buddhism. Depending on the time the treatises were written, each holds different positions as to Japanese colonial policy and Korean Buddhism's relation to Japanese Buddhism.

One of most emphasized issues at the early stages of Buddhist reform movements was education. Kwŏn Sangno especially focused his reform agenda on the issue of education, including the creation of educational institutions for Buddhists and the general public. Han Yongun's treatise also proposed the education of clerics as one main agenda for the reformation of the Buddhist community (saṅgha). Other issues that Han Yongun emphasized for that purpose include the unification of the doctrinal orientation of the saṅgha, the simplification of Buddhist practices, and the centralization of the saṅgha administration by reforming its policies and customs. Han's proposals became a framework for subsequent saṅgha reformation.

Buddhist concern for the general public, or *minjung* (the masses), was another visible aspect of the reform agenda. Paek Yongsŏng (1864–1940) was a pioneer in expanding the audience of Buddhism beyond the Buddhist clergy. He contended that reaching out to the public was the very way to realize the original teaching of Śākyamuni Buddha and developed his idea into a movement called *Tae'gakkyo undong* (the Great Enlightenment Movement).

The concern for the public made the Buddhist reformists aware of the importance of translation projects. Buddhist literature at the time was mostly written in classical Chinese, with which the majority of Korean people were unfamiliar. Thus, translating Buddhist scriptures into the Korean language was one of the first steps to make Buddhism accessible to the public. Paek Yongsŏng was especially keen on the importance of translating Buddhist scriptures, being influenced and alarmed by the existence of the Korean version of the Bible introduced by Christian missionaries.

The creation of city-center gathering places for Buddhists was another project to which Buddhist reformists paid close attention. Traditionally, Korean Buddhist monasteries were mostly located on the mountainside. However, Buddhist reformists found the remote location of Buddhist monasteries to be an obstacle for the growth of Buddhism in modern society, both practically and philosophically. In terms of practicality, the remote location of Buddhist temples made it difficult for people to frequent them, which naturally created a gap between the religion and the people. Philosophically, the spatial distance between Buddhist monasteries and society was considered a visible sign of the religion's incapacity to deal with issues relevant to modern society. Han Yongun was vehemently vocal about the issue, writing,

> What happens when a temple locates itself on a mountain? First of all, progressive thoughts will disappear . . . And adventurous ideas will vanish. . . . Then a liberating element will evaporate . . . And then a resistant spirit will cease to exist . . . Located on secluded mountains, [Buddhist] temples do not recognize upheavals in the world. As a result, although anti-religious sounds of drums and trumpets disturb the earth, Buddhism never wages war against them. Nor does it console the defeated warriors. Despite the commanding banners in the Buddhist castle, the religion is so helpless and powerless that it cannot raise a flag of resistance.[3]

As the reformists endeavored to bring Buddhism closer to people's lives, the traditionally rigid demarcation between the ordained and lay practitioners blurred. This does not mean that the ordained monks were laicized, as in the case of Japan during the modern period.[4] Instead, in Korea, the traditional emphasis on the privileged position of the ordained monks was gradually replaced with mutual recognition of the ordained and lay circle in an effort to bring both Buddhism and Buddhist community into the milieu of daily life. Lay Buddhist movements that emerged in the first half of the twentieth century reflect this aspect of modern Korean Buddhism. Yi Nŭnghwa (1869–1943), a lay practitioner, scholar, and intellectual, was a notable figure in this context. Yi launched a lay Buddhist movement (K. *kŏsa Pulgyo*) and proposed a reform agenda focusing on the laity.

The modern period also witnessed the emergence of new forms of Buddhism. By creating a new Buddhist order, the founders of these new forms had more flexibility in renovating Buddhism without being constrained by tradition. Won Buddhism, founded by Sot'aesan Pak Chungbin (1891–1943) in 1916, offers a good example. Pak's idea was to create a form of Buddhism that fit into the modern lifestyle: Won Buddhist scripture was written in the Korean language (not in classical Chinese), its gathering places were located in village centers in the milieu of people's everyday lives instead of on a remote mountainside, sophisticated Buddhist doctrines were reinterpreted to make them more easily understood by commoners, and the lay and ordained distinction was underplayed in Won Buddhist doctrine. In the *Chosŏn Pulgyo hyŏksillon* (Treatise on the Renovation of Korean Buddhism, 1935), Sot'aesan succinctly summarizes the objectives of his Buddhist reform as the change of Korean Buddhism "from the Buddhism of abroad to Buddhism for Koreans [. . .]; from the Buddhism of the past to the Buddhism of the present and future [. . .]; from the Buddhism of a few monks residing on the mountain to the Buddhism of the general public."[5]

Korean Buddhist efforts to bring Buddhism to the milieu of people's daily lives by actively engaging themselves in the social and political situations of the time re-emerged in the 1970s and 1980s in the form of Minjung Buddhism. The term "minjung" (the masses) was used during the first half of the twentieth century by Buddhist reformists, as they emphasized the importance of the religion's rapport with society and the people. Minjung Buddhism during the second half of the twentieth century takes visibly political stances, directly responding to the military dictatorship in Korea. By its founding principles, Minjung Buddhism is Buddhism for the politically oppressed, economically exploited, and socio-culturally alienated. Philosophically, Minjung Buddhists appeal to the bodhisattva ideal and compassion. Adherents of Minjung Buddhism emphasize the liberation from all forms of oppression including social and political constraints.

Part One of this volume discusses the major Buddhist reformers. In Chapter 1, Woosung Huh examines Paek Yongsŏng's Buddhist reform movement, focusing on the balance between individual practice and bodhisattva activities of helping sentient beings. American Buddhist scholarship has been keen on the relationship between wisdom and compassion, or between Buddhist practice and Buddhism's social engagement, in relation to Buddhism's potential as social theory. Huh's essay offers an example of a Korean Buddhist stance on the issue at the beginning of the twentieth century. In Chapter 2, Pori Pak investigates Han Yongun's Buddhist thoughts with a focus on the integration of doctrinal study (K. *kyo*) and Zen meditation (Sŏn). Chapter 3 discusses Won Buddhism. In this chapter, Bongkil Chung offers a detailed explanation of the structure of Won Buddhism and its relation to Korean Buddhism. Yi Nŭnghwa's contribution to Korean Buddhism is the theme of Chapter 4, in which Jongmyung Kim offers a critical assessment of Yi Nŭnghwa's lay Buddhist movement and Yi's efforts to utilize Buddhism for the modernization of Korea. Two chapters in Part Three are also relevant to the theme of Buddhist reform. In Chapter 11, Vladimir Tihkonov addresses in detail Yi Tongin's activities and Korean Buddhism's initial encounter with Japanese Buddhist missionaries during the period from 1876, the year Korea opened her door to the outside world, until 1910, when Korea was annexed to Japan. In Chapter 12, John Jorgensen offers an in-depth exploration of the history and philosophy of Minjung Buddhism together with his critique.

Revival of Sŏn/Zen Buddhism

While the reform-minded Buddhists endeavored to renovate Buddhism so as to make it fit into the social and cultural milieu of modern life, another form of renovation was also underway: that is, Sŏn/Zen revivalism. On the surface, Buddhist reformism and Sŏn revivalism seem to pull Buddhism in opposite directions: the former trying to take Buddhism into the future and the latter attempting to revive the past. On a deeper level, we find that they were both attempts to reconstruct Buddhism, but with different focuses. Sŏn revivalists sought to reinstate the quality of Sŏn practice and the training at the Sŏn monasteries, whereas Buddhist reformists emphasized the religion's rapport with society.

In the course of its history, Korean Buddhism developed a strong Sŏn Buddhist tradition. Within Sŏn Buddhism, the Kanhwa Sŏn (C. Kanhua Chan) tradition, which was consolidated by the thirteenth century National Master Pojo Chinul (1158–1210), dominated Korean Buddhism. During the Chosŏn Dynasty, Sŏn Buddhism suffered from neo-Confucian anti-Buddhist policy together with other Buddhist schools. At the beginning of the Chosŏn period, Buddhist schools were merged or abolished according to government policy, and as a result, starting from the mid-fifteenth century onward, no Buddhist sectarian identity was allowed. This is called the period of mountain Buddhism, when Buddhism sustained itself on the remote mountainside. Centuries later, this resulted in an identity crisis for Sŏn Buddhists.

Around the beginning of the nineteenth century, attempts were made to overcome the decline of Buddhism by critically exploring the identity of Sŏn Buddhism. In the debate known as the Debate on the Types of Sŏn (K. *yijong Sŏn-samjong Sŏn nonjaeng*), Paekp'a Kŭngsŏn (1767–1852) proposed a systematization of Sŏn Buddhist teachings in his *Sŏnmun su'gyŏng* (Hand Mirror of Sŏn School, 1820), and Ch'oŭi Ŭisun (1786–1866) critically responded to Paekp'a's theory in his *Sŏnmun sabyŏn manŏ* (Talks on the Four Divisions of Sŏn School).[6] The debate on the identity of Sŏn Buddhism revived the scholastic zeal for Sŏn Buddhism and opened a way for Sŏn revivalism, but in order to fully re-establish the Sŏn tradition, one had to wait for the appearance of a radical practitioner of meditation who could confirm the efficiency and relevance of Sŏn meditation in the path to one's enlightenment.

In this context, Kyŏnghŏ Sŏngu (1849–1912) is considered the revivalist of Korean Sŏn Buddhism in modern time. Kyŏnghŏ joined the monastery when he was nine and was appointed as a *sūtra*-lecturer at the young age of 23, which earned him national fame. A dramatic incident in his life, however, became a turning point for Kyŏnghŏ to condemn the doctrinal approach to Buddhism and wholeheartedly devote himself to the practice of *huatou* (K. *hwadu*) meditation, through which he had an awakening experience.

By setting a model for Sŏn practitioners at a time when the tradition was at its lowest point in the history of Korean Buddhism, Kyŏnghŏ set the foundation for Sŏn revivalism. In an effort to revive Sŏn tradition, Kyŏnghŏ created compact communities at Hae'in Monastery in 1899 and at Pŏmŏ Monastery in 1902. Kyŏnghŏ's contribution to modern Korean Sŏn tradition is also demonstrated by the fact that his disciples, especially Suwŏl (1855–1928), Hyewŏl (1861–1937), Man'gong (1871–1946), and Hanam, played a significant role in modern Korean Buddhism, and by so doing, they re-established the Sŏn lineage.

In a literary work dedicated to the creation of the compact community at the Hae'in Monastery, Kyŏnghŏ admonishes those who underestimate their capacity for Buddhist practice and abandon efforts to attain Buddhahood. He also criticizes the premature declaration of awakening among the practitioners of meditation. With these warnings, Kyŏnghŏ invites everyone to seek to attain Buddhahood by focusing on real practice, which Kyŏnghŏ, following the Sŏn school's premise, defines as being none other than finding one's own nature.[7]

In order to reinstate rigorous Sŏn practice at monasteries, Sŏn revivalists offered new versions of Sŏn monastic regulations. Traditionally, the first guidelines of the Chan monastery known as Pure Rules (C. *qinggui*; K. *ch'ŏnggyu*) were formulated by Chinese monk Baizhang Huaihai (721–814). Baizhang's Pure Rules were introduced to Korea during the Koryŏ dynasty (918–1392) and subsequently served as guidelines for practitioners in Sŏn monasteries. Sŏn revivalists introduced their versions of Pure Rules, and three are the most notable. The first was composed by Kyŏnghŏ in 1902 at Pŏmŏ Monastery.[8] Kyŏnghŏ's disciple Pang Hanam introduced two sets of Sŏn monastic regulations: "Sŭngga och'ik" (Five Regulations for the Saṅgha) and "Sŏnwŏn kyurye" (Regulations of Sŏn Monastery) in 1922 at Kŏnbong Monastery.[9] The third was known as "Kongju kyuyak" (Community Regulations), written by T'oe'ong Sŏngch'ŏl (1912–1993) together with Ch'ŏngdam (1902–1971) and several other Sŏn masters at Pongam Monastery.[10] Pure Rules are not administrative regulations; they are rules aiming for guiding Sŏn practitioners in their spiritual cultivation, and in this sense, the three versions of Pure Rules that I listed above distinguish themselves from the institutional reform agenda that Buddhist reformists introduced to renovate Korean Buddhism.

Another notable aspect of Sŏn revivalism is the emergence of a training system for nuns. Kyŏnghŏ's disciple Song Man'gong is credited as being the first to support and guide nuns' meditation practice in modern time. Man'gong's disciple Myori Pŏphŭi (1887–1975) is known as a pioneer of the Sŏn lineage of nuns in modern Korea. Together with Pŏphŭi, Mansŏng (1897–1975), Iryŏp (1896–1971), and Pon'gong (1907–1965) were all influenced and supported by Man'gong and set the models for nuns' Sŏn practice.[11] The opening of Kyŏnsŏng Hermitage at Sudŏk Monastery in 1928—the first meditation hall for nuns—made a significant contribution to the promotion of Sŏn practice for nuns. Immediately after its opening, Kyŏnsŏng Hermitage became a center for revitalizing the Sŏn tradition among Korean nuns. In addition, the first modern seminary for nuns opened in 1935 at Po'mun Monastery in Seoul.[12]

Korean nuns receive training in two ways: Seminaries (K. *kangwŏn*) offer basic education, and meditation practice is done at the meditation hall (K. *sŏnwŏn*). With the opening of Kyŏnsŏng Hermitage as nuns' meditation hall, and the seminary at Po'mun Monastery for nuns' education, the primary foundations for nuns' training were set up. In the second half of the twentieth century,

Daehaeng (1927–) was recognized by her activities of founding Hanmaŭm Sŏnwŏn in 1972.

Kyŏnghŏ's disciple Man'gong was a leading Sŏn master during the colonial period, whose challenge to Japanese colonial officials left behind various legends and Sŏn stories. Another of Kyŏnghŏ's disciples, Pang Hanam, was appointed as the first Patriarch of the Chogye Order, established during the colonial period. The Chogye Order (Jogye Order) is currently the most dominant Buddhist order in Korea. The revival of Sŏn Buddhism culminated in T'oe'ong Sŏngch'ŏl, a renowned Sŏn master during the second half of the twentieth century. Well-known for his relentlessly strict Sŏn practice, Sŏngch'ŏl demanded that fellow Sŏn practitioners return to the "original teachings of the Buddha and the Patriarchs" (K. *ko-Pul kojo*) in every detail of monastic life including the material of monks' bowls and robes, and the relationship of the monastic community with the lay circle.[13]

During the 1990s, Sŏngch'ŏl's publications on Korean Buddhism kindled a debate which later developed into the Sudden-Gradual Debate. Sŏngch'ŏl criticized Chinul for allowing gradualism in Sŏn practice and accused him of being a heretic in the Sŏn School. After criticizing Chinul as the origin of the inauthentic practice of Korean Sŏn Buddhism, Sŏngch'ŏl proposed his subitist theory as the orthodox way for Sŏn practice.[14] Regardless of one's position concerning the subitist and gradualist theories, the debate can be understood in the context of Sŏn revivalism in modern Korea and its efforts to bring back the authentic form of Sŏn practice in modern times, which culminated in Sŏngch'ŏl's claim of subitism as the "purist" Sŏn practice.

Chapters in Part Two of this volume discuss Sŏn revivalism, focusing on individual figures. In Chapter 6, Henrik Sørenson examines the life and thoughts of Kyŏnghŏ Sŏngu through a close reading of Kyŏnghŏ's writings in *Kyŏnghŏ pŏbŏ* (Dharma Talks of Kyŏnghŏ). In Chapter 7, Mu Seong offers life stories of Man'gong, mostly based on the collections of the orally transmitted anecdotes related to him. In Chapter 8, Patrick R. Uhlmann examines Pang Hanam's Buddhism with a close analysis of his Five Regulations for the Saṅgha (K. *sŭngga och'ik*). In Chapter 9, Woncheol Yun presents T'oe'ong Sŏngch'ŏl's theory of Sŏn practice based on Sŏngch'ŏl's *Sŏnmun chŏngno* (Correct Path of the Sŏn School). Finally, in Chapter 10, Chong Go discusses Daehaeng's teaching known as "Doing without Doing."

Buddhist Encounter with New Intellectualism

During the first half of the twentieth century, both Buddhist reformists and Sŏn revivalists were actively promoting Buddhism. In addition to these two aspects, I propose Korean Buddhism's encounter with what I would call new intellectualism as the third characteristic of modern Korean Buddhism. New intellectualism does not refer to a specific movement; it is a term I employ here to denote intellectual orientations of those whose thought was significantly influenced by modernity and by the modern mindset. One characteristic aspect of modernity is an effort to break away from traditional modes of thinking. The new intellectuals, who challenged the status quo of their society in the spirit of modernity, more often than not came from the middle class or socially marginalized groups. The reformist intellectuals from the late eighteenth to late nineteenth centuries were one such group. The New Woman, the first generation of Korean women who received modern-style education and demanded gender equality during the 1920s and 1930s, was another such group. Yi Tongin's Buddhist thought and Reform Party members' Buddhism can be included in the category of Korean Buddhism's encounter with new intellectualism.[15] The Buddhism of New Woman Kim Iryŏp (1896–1971) exemplifies female intellectuals' reinterpretation of Buddhism. Kim Iryŏp was a writer and leading female intellectual before she joined a monastery. In her search for identity and freedom in a patriarchal society, Kim Iryŏp resorted to Buddhism, in which she explored the idea that the great "I" (K. *taea*) earned through Buddhist awakening liberated the small "I" (K. *soa*) of the daily life.

Another aspect of Buddhism's encounter with new intellectualism is the emergence of a modern-style Buddhist scholarship. Yi Nŭnghwa is credited with setting the foundations of Korean Buddhist scholarship and Korean Studies. Along with the appearance of Buddhist scholarship, publications on the history of Korean Buddhism emerged as well. Yi Nŭnghwa's *Chosŏn Pulgyo t'ongsa* (A Comprehensive History of Korean Buddhism), the first in its kind, appeared in 1918.[16] Buddhist journals also began to appear during the 1910s, providing a forum for discussion of Buddhist philosophy, reform ideas, and literature by Buddhist intellectuals.

The emergence of new interpretations of Korean Buddhism reflecting the social and political situation and the intellectual orientation of the time is yet another result of Buddhism's encounter with new intellectualism as well. Ch'oe Namsŏn (1880–1957), a writer and historian, defined Korean Buddhism as ecumenical Buddhism (K. *t'ong Pulgyo*) in his essay "Chosŏn Pulgyo: Tongbang munhwasasang e itnŭn kŭ chiwi" (Chosŏn [Korean] Buddhism: Its Place in Oriental Cultural History).[17] In his efforts to find the identity of Korean Buddhism in the milieu of foreign cultures rushing into Korea, Ch'oe underscored the importance of the seventh-century monk-scholar Wŏnhyo's (617–686) Buddhism. Ch'oe characterized Wŏnhyo's Buddhist thought as ecumenical and contended that Wŏnhyo's ecumenical Buddhism was the culmination of Buddhist teachings not only in Korea but in Eastern Buddhism in general. In doing so, Ch'oe suggested the prominent position of Korean culture in the intellectual history of East Asia. Ch'oe's theory of ecumenism as the identity of Korean Buddhism continues to influence Korean Buddhist scholarship today, if not without being challenged.[18]

Three essays in this volume address Korean Buddhism's encounter with new intellectualism. In Chapter 4, Jongmyung Kim offers a critical evaluation of Yi Nŭnghwa's Buddhism and his contribution to the construction of Korean Buddhist scholarship during the first half of the twentieth century. In Chapter 13, Sungtaek Cho discusses another aspect of modern Korean Buddhist scholarship, focusing on Pak Chonghong and Kim Tonghwa, two leading figures of Korean Buddhist scholarship during the second half of the twentieth century. In Chapter 5, Jin Y. Park discusses Kim Iryŏp's Buddhism. Park emphasizes the search for identity as a theme running through Kim Iryŏp's philosophy from her feminist writings as a New Woman to her Sŏn essays as a Buddhist nun and contends that woman's experiences of modernity and modern Korean Buddhism are significantly different from those of male practitioners.

Reconsidering Buddhism and Modernity in Korea

I have identified three characteristics of modern Korean Buddhism as Buddhist reform movements, Sŏn revivalism, and Buddhism's encounter with new intellectualism. Needless to say, these three are closely related to one another, and the figures discussed in this volume demonstrate, one way or another, that the three issues are intricately interwoven in their Buddhism. In exploring these themes, one finds the need to reconsider some aspects of the scholarship of modern Korean Buddhism that are taken for granted. I will point out three such issues as starting points to be re-examined for a better understanding of Buddhism in modern Korea.

The first is the issue of periodization. The most commonly used date as the beginning of the modern period in Korean Buddhism is 1895, when a ban on monks' and nuns' entering the capital city was repealed.[19] Another historical date used for this purpose is 1876, when Korea opened its door to foreign power. This relatively simple way of employing historical dates to identify the time line separating the pre-modern and modern periods in Korean Buddhism can be an easy way of dealing with the issue of periodization, but not without problems. As we investigate changes in Korean Buddhism during this period, a question arises: How was it possible that Korean Buddhism, which allegedly reached its lowest point by the end of the nineteenth century, was able to reemerge so quickly?

In order to answer this question, let us go back to the beginning of the modern period of Korean Buddhism and examine the situation at the time.[20] As we have discussed, during the late nineteenth century, when Korea was in the process of transforming into a modern society, Yi Tongin and other reform-minded Korean Buddhists considered the social and political changes an opportunity for Buddhist revival. Yi Tongin had a close relationship with members of the political party known as the Reform Party (K. *kaehwadang*). It has been claimed that Yi was not just an acquaintance of the reformist intellectuals at that time, but actually taught Buddhism to those intellectuals.[21] In addition, Yi Nŭnghwa writes in his *Chosŏn Pulgyo t'ongsa* (A Comprehensive History of Korean Buddhism) that during the second half of the nineteenth century, there was a boom in Sŏn studies among reform-minded intellectuals who gathered together in the capital city to study Buddhism and practice Sŏn meditation.[22] Referring to Yi Nŭnghwa's description of the temporary resurgence of the interest in Sŏn meditation among Korean intellectuals, Korean Buddhist scholar Kim Kyŏngjip mentions that the trend was especially influenced by Yu Taech'i, a member of the Reform Party. Yu Taech'i evaluated Confucianism as the ideology of the ruling class that fell short of functioning as a religion. Kim Kyŏngjip proposes that Yu Taech'i's reformist consciousness challenged the stratified social system of the ruling ideology and that Buddhism with its egalitarian doctrines made an appeal to him in this context.[23]

Yi Nŭnghwa's discussion of the tradition of lay Buddhists in China and Korea helps us further expand the scope of this encounter between Buddhism and reform-minded intellectuals. In his *Chosŏn Pulgyo t'ongsa*, Yi Nŭnghwa offers a list of thinkers and writers who were influenced by the Chan/Sŏn spirit, and the list expands all the way to the Tang-Song poet-intellectuals in China.[24] In the context of our discussion, it is worth noting that Yi Nŭnghwa pays special attention to Kim Chŏnghui (1786–1856, courtesy name, Ch'usa), a renowned calligrapher who frequented Qing China to learn about new ideas. Yi Nŭnghwa identifies Kim Chŏnghui as one of the immediate influences on the lay Buddhist movement in Yi's time and on Reform Party members' interest in Buddhism. A full-scale examination of the intellectual history of the evolution of Korean Buddhism from the pre-modern to modern periods would require a separate project. For now, I would like to propose the following hypothesis as one paradigm to understand the transition from the pre-modern to the modern period of Korean Buddhism. During the Chosŏn dynasty, neo-Confucianism was a dominant ideology; as the society searched for reformation, Buddhism offered an alternative to neo-Confucian ruling ideology, especially to reform-minded intellectuals and underprivileged groups. The question remains as to whether this dual paradigm of neo-Confucianism as a religion and ideology for the privileged and Buddhism for underprivileged and marginalized groups was simply a result of social and historical situations, or whether it had to do with philosophy represented by these two traditions. Without answering this question, we can still say that the root of Buddhist reform movements, Sŏn revivalism, and Buddhism's encounter with new intellectualism in modern time can be traced further back to the late eighteenth and early nineteenth centuries. This suggests us that, in order to better understand modern Korean Buddhism, instead of merely relying on the convenience of historical markers, we need to pay closer attention to the evolution of Buddhism from the pre-modern to the modern periods. Such a project will not only enable us to understand what we now consider modern Korean Buddhism, but also reveal to us potentials and possibilities that could have been modern Korean Buddhism, but that have failed to be recognized as such because of social, political, historical, or other factors that contributed to the process of modernization of Korea.

The second issue is to reconsider the nature of colonial modernity and its impact on modern Korean Buddhism. As the expression "colonial modernity" suggests, modernity in Korea cannot be understood without considering colonial experiences. However, the colonial and postcolonial reality has often excessively influenced both scholars and Buddhists in Korea, to the extent that binary postulations are uncritically accepted. As a result, most Buddhist activities during the colonial period have been evaluated through the lens of whether certain activities were patriotic, or collaborating with Japanese colonialists. The nationalist tendency in understanding modern Korean Buddhism has reduced the religious and philosophical identity of Buddhism to purely political issues. If we look into the situation more closely, however, we find that such dualism does not always work. One example that demonstrates the complexity of the situation can be found in the practice of monks' meat-eating and clerical marriage. Married monks among Koreans began to appear at the beginning of the twentieth century, before colonization, and the number of married monks rapidly increased during the 1910s and 1920s. Having maintained the tradition of celibacy and vegetarianism, many Korean Buddhists strongly disapproved of the practice of meat-eating and clerical marriage as a form of monkhood contaminated by Japanese Buddhism. The conflict between celibate and married monks continued in postcolonial space, creating one of most devastating internal conflicts in Korean Buddhism during the 1950s and 1960s.

To group celibacy with religious purity, Korean national identity, and patriotism on the one hand, and to set them against married monks, stigmatizing them as religiously impure, Japanese invaders, and traitors on the other hand, would oversimplify the situation. Paek Yongsŏng, a leading Buddhist reformer during the colonial period, submitted a petition to the Governor-General requesting a prohibition of monks' marriage, which did not produce visible results. Meanwhile, Han Yongun, another leading Buddhist during the same period who is still a national hero for his anti-Japanese activities, filed a petition in the early 1910s requesting that monks be allowed to marry. In 1926, monks' marriages became officially allowed in Korea. Both Paek Yongsŏng and Han Yongun are still considered to have played significant role in modern Korean Buddhism, but they took opposite positions on the question of clerical marriage. The incident demonstrates that the binary postulation of pure Korean Buddhism versus contaminated Japanese Buddhism, and further elaborated binary sets of celibacy-Korean patriots versus clerical marriage-colonial collaborators, oversimplify the situation. A crucial re-examination of binary postulations is necessary in order to understand the complexity involved in Korean Buddhism's encounters with modernity.

The third issue is related to another form of binary postulation. This time the binary postulation takes the form of modernity versus tradition. Modernization in Korea has come to denote Westernization. This tendency of conceptualizing modernity with the civilization and culture of the West has created the assumption that the modern is equated with the West and the pre-modern with traditional Asia. Buddhism being part of traditional Korea, in the process of modernization, the idea that tradition is something to leave behind if Korea is to develop into a "modern" nation fostered an environment that considered Buddhism as having nothing to offer in the nation's path to a modern and advanced society. The case of the Buddhist encounter with new intellectualism suggests that this did not have to be the case.

When we consider modernity from its functional aspects, including institutional efficiency, consideration for the general public, and the new role of religion, Korean Buddhism did need reformation. The activities of Buddhist reformists reflect this aspect of the Buddhist encounter with modernity. On the other hand, if we consider the philosophy and spirit of modernity that has been characterized as the individual's search for self, freedom, and equality, one can argue that Buddhism has much to offer in the shaping of modernity in Asia. Our discussions in this volume on Buddhism and modernity in Korea suggest that we need to move beyond modernization of Buddhism and conceive a vision of Buddhist modernity which will help us to understand new aspects of modernity itself. Such an effort might help us shed light on certain aspects of Buddhism that have been suppressed or forgotten in our race toward modernization.

This volume consists of three parts. The first two parts comprise ten chapters, each of which discusses individual figures in modern Korean Buddhism. Three chapters in Part Three take a thematic approach to some of the major issues in modern Korean Buddhism. Throughout this volume the words Chan/Zen/Sŏn have been used interchangeably. The following Sanskrit words are not italicized: nirvāṇa, saṃsāra, dharma, samādhi, prajñā, and saṅgha. Asian names in this volume appear in the Asian tradition of the family name placed before the given name, unless the Asian name has appeared in English publications, in which case the name will follow the precedent of the previous publications.

Notes

1. See Kim Kyŏngjip, *Han'guk kŭndae Pulgyo sa* (History of Modern Korean Buddhism) (Seoul: Kyŏngsŏwŏn, 1998), pp. 50–65. On Yi Tongin, also see Kim Kyŏngjip, "Kŭndae kaehwasŭng ŭi hwaldong kwa hyŏnsil insik" (Activities of Modern Reformist

Monks and Their Reality Consciousness), *Pojo sasang* 25 (Feb 2006): 463–490; Sin Pongsŭng, *Yi Tongin ŭi nara* (Yi Tongin's Country), 3 vols. (Seoul: Tongbang midia, 2001).

2. See Kim Kyŏngjip, *Han'guk kŭndae Pulgyo sa*, pp. 59–60. Yi Tongin is believed to have been murdered for political reasons, but whether he was assassinated by his political opponent or by one from his own group is unclear.

3. Han Yongun, *Chosŏn Pulgyo yusillon* (Treatise on the Revitalization of Korean Buddhism), *Han Yongun chŏnjip*, vol. 2 (Seoul: Sin'gu munhwasa, 1974), pp. 33–125, 66–68. This issue is also emphasized repeatedly by Sot'aesan Pak Chungbin in his reform agenda through Won Buddhism. See Chapter 3 of this volume for details.

4. Following the 1872 edict, modern Japanese Buddhism allowed monks to marry, eat meat, and abandon tonsure. An in-depth study on the issue is found in Richard M. Jaffe, *Neither Monk nor Layman: Clerical Marriage in Modern Japanese Buddhism* (Princeton and Oxford: Princeton University Press, 2001).

5. Wŏnbulgyo kyo'go ch'onggan, vol. 4, *Ch'ogi kyosŏ* (Collections of Early Teachings) (Chŏnbuk, Korea: Wŏnbulgyo chŏnghwasa, 1970), pp. 96–105.

6. Paekp'a identified the three phrases of Linji with the three types of Sŏn—Patriarchal Sŏn, Tathāgata Sŏn, and Theoretical Sŏn—and he understood their relationship as hierarchical. Paekp'a also identified the first phrase in the Linji's three phrases with live words (K. *hwalgu*) and with Patriarchal Sŏn, whereas the third phrase was identified with that of dead words (K. *sagu*) and with Theoretical Sŏn. (See *Sŏnmun sugyŏng, HPC* 10.514c–527c.)

Ch'oŭi warned that Paekp'a's theory of the three types of Sŏn could distort Sŏn teachings. Ch'oŭi argued that neither the Linji's three phrases nor the four classifications of Patriarchal Sŏn, Tathāgata Sŏn, Outside-formal Sŏn (K. *kyŏgoe-Sŏn*), and Theoretical Sŏn formed a hierarchical order. Ch'oŭi considered all four types of Sŏn to be skillful means of Buddhist teachings in which different methods could and should be used according to the different levels and characters of practitioners. (See *Sŏnmun sabyŏn manŏ*, *HPC* 10.820b–830b.)

Ch'oŭi is also well known for the idea of the oneness of Sŏn and tea (K. *ta-Sŏn ilmi*) and has been credited as a revivalist of tea-culture (K. *tado*) in modern Korea. For his thoughts on tea, see *Tasinjŏn* (Story of Tea-Spirits, *HPC* 10.871a–873b) and *Tongdasong* (Songs of Eastern [Korean] Tea *HPC* 10.873–876b).

7. Sŏk Myŏngjŏng, ed., *Kyŏnghŏ chip* (Collected Works of Kyŏnghŏ) (Korea: Kŭngnak sŏnwŏn, 1990), pp. 86–117; *HPC* 11.601b–607b.

8. Sŏk Myŏngjŏng, ed., *Kyŏnghŏ chip*, pp. 74–78; *HPC* 11.599c–600a.

9. Pang Hanam, *Hanam ilballok: Hanam Taejongsa pŏbŏrok* (Hanam's One Bowl of Records: The Recorded Dharma-lectures of Great Patriarch Hanam), ed., Hanam Taejongsa Munjip P'yŏnch'an Wiwŏn Hoe (Seoul: Minjoksa, 1996), pp. 27–36.

10. See Kim Kwangsik, "Yi Sŏngch'ŏl ŭi Pulgyo kaehyŏngnon" (Yi Sŏngch'ŏl's Theory of Buddhist Reform) in Sungtaek Cho, ed., *T'oe'ong Sŏngch'ŏl ŭi kkaedarŭm kwa suhaeng* (Seoul: Yemun sŏwŏn, 2006), 216–265, pp. 224–227.

11. For a study of major figures among Korean nuns in the modern period, see Ha Ch'unsaeng, *Kkadarŭn ŭi kkot: Han'guk kŭnserŭl pitnaen kŭnse pi'guni* (The Flowers of Enlightenment: Buddhist Nuns in Modern Times Who Have Lightened Up Korean Buddhism), 2 vols. (Seoul: Yŏrae, 1998–2001).

12. See Su'gyŏng, "Han'guk pi'guni kangwŏn paltalsa" (History of the Evolution of Bhikkhuni Seminaries in Korea), in Chŏn'guk pi'gunihoe, ed., *Han'guk pi'guni ŭi suhaeng kwa salm* (The Practice and Life of Korean Buddhist Nuns) (Seoul: Yemun sŏwŏn, 2007), 15–51.

13. T'oe'ong Sŏngch'ŏl, "Pongamsa kyŏlsa" (Compact Community at the Pongam Monastery), in *Cha'girŭl paro popsida* (Let's Look at Ourselves Clearly) (Seoul: Changgyŏnggak, 1987), 220–235.

14. Sŏngch'ŏl, *Sŏnmun chŏngno* (Correct Path of the Sŏn School) (Seoul: Pulgwang, 1981), pp. 201–209. On the debate, see Kang Kŏn'gi and Kim Hosŏng, eds., *Kkadarŭm: tono tonsu in'ga, tono chŏmsu in'ga* (Enlightenment: Is it Sudden Awakening and Sudden Cultivation or Sudden Awakening and Gradual Cultivation?) (Seoul: Minjoksa, 1992).

15. I will further discuss this issue in the next section.

16. Kwŏn Sangno's *Chosŏn Pulgyo yaksa* (An Abridged History of Korean Buddhism) was published in 1917.

17. Ch'oe Namsŏn, "Chosŏn Pulgyo: Tongbang munhwasasang e itnŭn kŭ chiwi" (Chosŏn Buddhism: Its Place in Oriental Cultural History), in *Pulgyo* 74 (1930): 1–51, p. 17.

18. Robert E. Buswell claims that the concept of national identity of Buddhism is purely a modern invention. In his essay "Imagining 'Korean Buddhism': The Invention of a National Religious Tradition," Buswell contends: "It would be going much too far to posit that there was any independent sense of a "Korean" national tradition of Buddhism, distinct from the broader Sinitic tradition, during the premodern era" (Hyung Il Pai & Timothy R. Tangherlini, eds., *Nationalism and the Construction of Korean Identity* [Institute of East Asian Studies, University of California, Berkeley, 1998], 73–107, p. 74). Eunsu Cho also discusses the limits of Ch'oe Namsŏn's definition of Korean Buddhism as "ecumenical Buddhism" in her essay "T'ong Pulgyo tamnon ŭl t'onghae pon Han'guk Pulgyosa insik: Han'guk Pulgyo rŭl tasi saenggak handa" (The Understanding of the History of Korean Buddhism Seen through the Lens of the Theory of Ecumenical Buddhism: Re-thinking Korean Buddhism), *Pulgyo p'yŏngnon* 6, no. 4 (Winter 2004): 30–51.

19. For example, Kim Kyŏngjip, *Han'guk kŭndae Pulgyo sa*, p 21; Kang Sŏkchu and Pak Kyŏnghun, eds., *Pulgyo kŭnse pangnyŏn* (Recent Hundred Years of Buddhism) (Seoul: Minjoksa, 2002), p. 8.

20. Throughout this introduction, I use the term modern or modern period in reference to the time period of the late nineteenth century, based on Korean Buddhist scholarship's common use of either 1876 or 1895 as .the beginning of modern period in Korean Buddhism.

21. Kim Kyŏngjip, *Han'guk kŭndae Pulgyo sa*, p. 51.

22. Yi Nŭnghwa, *Chosŏn Pulgyo t'ongsa* (A Comprehensive History of Korean Buddhism), vol. 2 (Seoul: Sinmun'gwan, 1918), p. 899.

23. Kim Kyŏngjip, *Han'guk kŭndae Pulgyo sa*, pp. 91–94.

24. Yi Nŭnghwa, *Chosŏn Pulgyo t'ongsa*, vol. 2, p. 897.

Part One

Modernity, Colonialism, and Buddhist Reform

1

Individual Salvation and Compassionate Action

The Life and Thoughts of Paek Yongsŏng[1]

Woosung Huh

Historical Background

The late nineteenth and early twentieth centuries were a troubled period in Korean history marked by the political failure of the Chosŏn dynasty (1392–1910) and Japanese oppression and colonialism (1910–1945). For modern Korean Buddhists in general, and for Paek Yongsŏng (1864–1940) in particular, this period represents a time when freedom, independence, purity, vigor, and sensitivity to changing times gave way to restraint, submission, corruption, powerlessness, and backwardness because of the seizure of national identity that arose from colonization. Along with the loss of the Korean people's freedom and independence, the decline in vitality of Buddhist organizations and their lack of relevance with the realities of ordinary people (K. *min*), as well as the absence of purity among professional Buddhist practitioners, are the primary context within which we should understand Yongsŏng. The Buddhism of the period had been severely weakened by 500 years of oppression under the Chosŏn dynasty's "anti-Buddhist, pro-Confucian" policy. Buddhism had little social influence and was barely able to sustain itself. Monasteries were forced to retreat deep into the mountains and were subject to exploitation by officials. Monks were despised as members of the lowest stratum of society and often abused by people; they were even strictly forbidden from entering the capital city and from engaging themselves in missionary activities. Buddhists were unable to attain any social standing or to establish organizations. Buddhism survived mainly through private practice, which was frequently combined with Shamanism, Daoism, and folk beliefs. Both before and after the liberation of Korea from Japanese occupation, the idea persisted that the Chosŏn dynasty's continuous suppression of Buddhism was responsible for the reduced influence of Buddhism in modern times.

An even greater problem for Korean Buddhism was the invasion of Japanese Buddhism and the introduction of Christianity. The latter quickly grew in popularity. The time period between the invasion of Japanese Buddhism in 1870 and the proclamation of the 1911 Temple Ordinance (K. *sach'alryŏng*) can be divided into two stages. During the first stage, prior to the annexation, Japanese Buddhism laid the groundwork for the assimilation of Korean Buddhism into Japanese Buddhism. During the second stage, dating from the Japanese annexation of Korea in 1910 to the proclamation in 1911, Japanese Buddhism solidified its control over Korean Buddhism. Paek Yongsŏng's and Han Yongun's subsequent opposition to the ordinance and their advocacy for the separation of state and religion in 1912 represented a struggle against the control and constraints of the colonial government. One of the most problematic results of the invasion of Japanese Buddhism was the appearance of married monks and their rise to power. Korean Buddhism had traditionally prescribed that monks and nuns maintain celibacy. The existence of clerical marriage aroused the opposition of celibate monks, and this issue led Yongsŏng to distinguish himself from more liberal Buddhists like Han Yongun, who supported open marriage of monks. Aside from this issue, Yongsŏng shares with Han Yongun the basic ideas of what Korean Buddhism should be in his time.

The introduction of Christianity and its growing popularity is an aspect of Korean history that cannot be ignored in order to understand modern Korean Buddhism.[2] Yongsŏng exerted a great deal of energy to revitalize Buddhist organizations and reinvent the Buddhist view of the "world-arising" (K. *segye kisi*) in order to prevent the spread of Christian evangelism. Many of his writings, including *Kwiwŏn chŏngjong* (Returning to True Religion, 1913), *Simjo manyuron* (Treatise on Mind Creating All Things, 1921), and *Kakhae illyun* (Enlightenment Ocean Like the Sun, 1931) contained numerous passages that were intended to replace the existence of God and the creation narrative with his interpretation of the Buddhist version of the "world-arising," which was based on his adaptation and reinvention of the traditional Buddhist theory of the "Mind-Only" (K. *yusim*).

Yongsŏng was keenly aware of Korean Buddhism's serious predicament in his time, and he eventually joined Han Yongun in the March First Independence Movement in 1919. This action can be interpreted as an explicit expression of his nationalist sentiment. Upon his release from prison in 1921, Yongsŏng set aside his political concerns and redirected his energy to Buddhist issues. The *Taegakkyo* (Great Enlightenment) movement was an indirect manifestation of his political concerns through Buddhist activities.

In Mahāyāna Buddhism, the aim of Buddhist practice is often expressed in the phrase "seeking enlightenment above" (K. *sanggu pori*) and "transforming sentient beings below" (K. *hahwa chungsaeng*). The first phrase is related to individual salvation, and the second involves compassionate actions to save others. Distancing himself from many of the other monks of his time, Paek Yongsŏng chose a middle way between individual salvation and compassionate actions. In this context, Yongsŏng became one of the most important figures in modern Korean Buddhism in that he was able to achieve and maintain a balance between the two paths. This essay demonstrates how Yongsŏng's life reflects his belief in the importance of this balance, and contends that the balance of life and thoughts in Yongsŏng should become a model for Korean Buddhists.

The Awakening Experiences

Yongsŏng, which is his dharma name, was born in Chŏlla province in 1864. His secular name was Sanggyu. Yongsŏng was on the one hand a traditional monk who emphasized the importance of practicing meditation and preserving the precepts. On the other hand, he was a reform-minded revolutionary who tried every method to popularize Buddhism and to establish and strengthen Buddhist organizations. By taking measures that were considered revolutionary at the time, he subjected himself to a great deal of criticism from his contemporaries.[3]

Most scholars of Yongsŏng agree that his mendicant life can be divided into two periods. Han Pogwang, for example, draws a dividing line at the age of 47 (1910). Han identifies the first half as "the period of ascetic practice on the mountain" (K. *sanjung suhaenggi*), which lasted nearly thirty years, beginning at the time he joined monastery in 1879 at the age of 16, and the second half as "the period of transforming the masses" (K. *taejung kyohwagi*).[4] The first half was mainly devoted to "seeking enlightenment above," and the second half to "transforming sentient beings below." The year 1910 may be considered a watershed in Yongsŏng's career. Up until that year, he almost exclusively devoted his life to learning, practicing, and transmitting Buddhism, living mostly in hermitages on the mountain.[5]

If we understand that "transforming sentient beings below" requires strong determination, energy, passion, courage, and forbearance, as well as compassion, and if cultivating all of these qualities requires a long period of time, the entire scope of the first half of his life was preparation for Yongsŏng to be able to move toward the second period. In approximately 30 years of his mendicant life, the only radical action in which Yongsŏng was involved was his participation in the March First Independence Movement (1919). Many contemporary scholars credit Yongsŏng with reinventing and repopularizing Sŏn Buddhism among the general public. It is also to his credit that Korean people became familiar with the expression "*ch'amson*" (Zen meditation). Yongsŏng was determined in his emphasis on the importance of Sŏn meditation and made it clear that observing the precepts was a prerequisite for keeping Buddhist organizations pure and healthy.

As he put an end to his hermitic life in mountainside retreats, Yongsŏng began to devote his time to practicing what he called a "revolutionary people's religion" (K. *hyŏngmyŏngjŏk minjonggyo*), which aptly characterizes the second half of his life. The term "revolutionary people's religion" was first used around 1927 in his letter to Master Kyŏngbong (1892–1982), in which Yongsŏng also mentioned his Great Enlightenment Teaching.[6] The idea of the "revolutionary people's religion" began to take shape in his mind far earlier, immediately after his first visit to Seoul in 1905, and became concretized during his imprisonment. Since then, the "revolutionary people's religion" remained the major concern of his Buddhist activities. After his release from prison, he considered the translation of Buddhist scriptures into the Korean language to be the most suitable way of spreading Buddhism.

From the perspective of the "revolutionary people's religion," traditional teachings cannot remain great unless they respond in some way to the problems of the time. Yongsŏng believed that working for the survival of Korean Buddhism was a worthy cause for him. He also believed that in order for traditional Korean Buddhism to survive in the new era, it needed to be revitalized so that it could be understood and practiced by the general public of his time. Yonsŏng emphasized the importance of economic independence of Buddhist organizations and disapproved of the centuries-old practice of monks' begging. The goal of his Great Enlightenment Movement was to find a way for Buddhism to go back to the general public, which he considered the way of returning to the original teachings of Śākyamuni Buddha. Yongsŏng believed that this became possible by reinventing traditional Sŏn Buddhism.

Yongsŏng undertook various ascetic practices through which he wanted to reduce himself to the state of zero or emptiness. Zero represents emptiness, a void, blankness, and impracticality; but, at the same time, it represents the possibility of producing all things, and it becomes the necessary condition for non-dual experiences with other beings and compassionate actions toward them. These practices continued throughout the first half of his life, from the ages of 16 to 47. His practices during this period included the recital of dharani or mantras, examination of the "wu kongan" (K. *muja kongan*), and scripture readings.

Yongsŏng had five awakening experiences; the most significant of these took place in relation to the recitation of the mantra of Great Compassion in the *Ch'ŏnsugyŏng* (Thousand Hands Sūtra). According to Han Pogwang, Yongsŏng began the recitation of the *Thousand Hands Sūtra* soon after he joined the monastery. Master Suwŏl Yŏngmin (1817–1893) told the 16-year-old Yongsŏng, "The Sage has been gone for too long. Demons are strong, and the dharma is weak. Thus karmic obstructions are heavy, so it is difficult to cultivate [your mind]. If you wholeheartedly take refuge in Buddha, dharma, and the Buddhist Community (*saṅgha*) and diligently recite the spell of Great Compassion, then, your karmic obstructions will spontaneously dissolve, your mind will dawn brightly, and your afflictions will be penetrated."[7] The spell referred to here is the passage "*sinmyo changgu tae darani*" (great mantra of marvelous passage) from the *Thousand Hands Sūtra*, which culminates in the spell of six syllables: "om ma ni pad me hum." After a six-day-long devoted recitation of this sacred spell, his mind was awakened. He was 21. This first awakening experience was symbolically expressed by the phrase, "A thought is experienced, as if the bottom lid of a bucket suddenly fell off" (*YTC* 1:10). The expression "the bottom lid of a bucket suddenly fell off" has been frequently used in Sŏn tradition to show that one's mind becomes brighter with the removal of karmic obstructions that have accumulated for eons.

Another form of recitation that Yongsŏng practiced throughout his life was the presentation of the name of Avalokiteśvara bodhisattva (K. *Kwanŭm posal*), who was Yongsŏng's favorite bodhisattva figure. Through the simple repetition of the name, he could express his earnest devotion and prayer to the bodhisattva. Yongsŏng's devotion to Avalokiteśvara bodhisattva was further manifested through the establishment of the Kwanŭmchŏn (the Hall of Avalokiteśvara) in 1905 on Po'gae Mountain in Kangwŏn Province. Yongsŏng also translated the *Thousand Hands Sūtra* into Korean in 1938, two years before his death. It appears that, throughout his life, Yongsŏng regularly recited the passage in the *sūtra*: "We invoke the vast, consummate, unimpeded, great compassionate, great dharani of the thousand-handed, thousand-eyed Avalokiteśvara bodhisattva" (K. *ch'ŏnsu ch'ŏnan kwanchaje posal kwangdae wŏnman mu'ae taejabi taedarani kyech'ŏng*). Note that this phrase is followed by "I bow to the great compassion of Avalokiteśvara" (K. *kyesu kwanŭm taebiju*). This passage is followed by the ten vows, each of which begins with the phrase "Homage to the greatly compassionate Avalokiteśvara" (K. *namu taejabi kwanseŭm*). By repeating the name of Avalokiteśvara and utilizing the power of the vows, Buddhists express their yearning to be saved from suffering. In the same process, they also transform their selfish minds into compassionate ones, which, in turn, become foundations for saving other sentient beings. Thus, in this *sūtra*, we find the phrase that enumerates various places to which the sentient beings should go during the process of realizing their vows. Those places include the Mountain of Swords Hell, the Boiling Fire Hell, the realm of the hungry ghosts, and the realm of the Asuras. Upon their arrival in these places, all kinds of suffering will immediately end.

At the age of 20, Yongsŏng began to take the *mu kongan* as a subject of meditation under the guidance of the Sŏn Master Muyung.[8] The following year, Yongsŏng allegedly had another awakening experience. The verse symbolizing this second awakening reads:

> Dispersing clouds and grasping mists, I found Mañjuśri Bodhisattva,
> Once attaining him, he was totally empty.
> Form is emptiness, but emptiness again becomes empty;
> Emptiness is form, and this process is endless (*YTC* 1:379).

Mañjuśri Bodhisattva represents the perfection of wisdom. But attaining this perfection does not make that perfection graspable; instead, it makes the practitioner realize the emptiness of things and the emptiness of emptiness. Yongsŏng's verse signifies the non-duality of form and emptiness, an important realization that Yongsŏng was to abide by for the next fifty years. In relating this experience of non-duality to the aspiration of helping others, the first awakening achieved by repeating "om ma ni pad me hum" may be understood as a prerequisite for the non-duality of form and emptiness. For Yongsŏng, the realm where sentient beings reside cannot be one of nihilistic emptiness; instead, if one fails to exercise one's compassion for others, the person, even though claiming to be enlightened, falls into the pitfall of the false emptiness. Yongsŏng severely criticized this false concept of emptiness, or, in his words, the "bad attachment to emptiness" (K. *akch'wi gonggyŏn*).

Yongsŏng's third awakening experience took place while he was reading a passage from *Chuandeng lu* (The Transmission of the Lamp). The passage reads: "The moon is like a curved arrow; it rains only a little, but the wind is very strong." This experience was symbolically expressed by the following phrase: "As my nostrils were beaten up, the sun Buddha and the moon Buddha, and the meaning of the nothingness *kongan* were shining brightly, leaving no trace of doubt" (*YTC* 1: 379).[9]

In the autumn of 1886, at the age of 23, near the Naktong River, Yongsŏng had the fourth awakening experience. He described this experience in a poem: "In Kŭmo mountain, a thousand-year old moon rises;/Waves rise for ten thousand miles in the Naktong River./Where has the fishing boat gone?/I dream in a field of reeds as in the old days" (*YTC* 1: 380). On first reading, the poem does not seem to entail much of Buddhist enlightenment, but Yongsŏng refers to this poem when he declares the tenets of the Great Enlightenment Movement.[10] After these four awakening experiences, Yongsŏng practiced *kongans* and tried to confirm his awakenings by perusing Buddhist scriptures including *The Platform Sūtra of the Sixth Patriarch* and *The Record of Transmission of the Lamp*. We have no record of Yongsŏng's whereabouts for the seven years (1893–1900) following his fourth awakening experience. According to Han Pogwang, Yongsŏng seemed to have inner struggles during this period.

The first four awakenings did not seem to be sufficient for Yongsŏng to begin to lead the Great Enlightenment Movement. His fifth awakening, the only one not mentioned in his *Yongsŏng sŏnsa ŏrok* (The Sayings of Sŏn Master Yongsŏng), was also needed. This was the awakening of his sensitivity to the changing milieu of his country and the suffering of the people. This awakening emerged slowly, beginning with his first short visit to Seoul in 1905, and it took shape through his participation in the March First Independence Movement in 1919 and his subsequent imprisonment.

In a short remark entitled "Yŏkkyŏng ŭi ch'wiji" (The Significance of Translating Scriptures) attached to his translation of *The Brahmajāla Sūtra* (The Sūtra of Brahma's Net) (1933), he said, "as I 'calmly perceived' (K. *chŏnggwan*) the trend of thought in the world and the change of literature in 1921, I immediately started to translate scriptures and published forty-five thousand volumes" (*YTC* 3:7). This "calm perception," which might have led him to understand the realities of Korean people, amounts to what I call the fifth awakening. It can be argued that all five awakenings were needed for Yongsŏng to finally direct his activities to the Great Awakening Movement. Through the first four awakening experiences, Yongsŏng consolidated his vows for compassionate actions to help sentient beings; through the fifth awakening experience, he turned the vows into concrete action to transform Korean Buddhism.

In a short essay, "Chesul kwa pŏnyŏk e taehan yŏn'gi" ("Reasons for Writings and Translations") attached to *Chosŏn'gŭl Hwaŏm kyŏng* (The Korean Avataṁsaka Sūtra) (1928), we have the following key paragraph:

> As one of the representatives of the Declaration of Independence, I suffered bitterly in the Sŏdaemun prison for three years. There were numerous political prisoners like me, though belonging to different religions. Each of them asked to bring in their own religious texts, and continued to learn and pray. When I perused their books, I found that they were all translated into Korean. There were almost no books printed in Classical Chinese. I felt that this was most deplorable. Thus, I took a great vow [to translate Buddhist scriptures into Korean]. . . . Today when there are so many things to learn, such as philosophy, science, and mechanics, spending several decades learning Chinese characters is not only a stupid act but is also an obstacle to the development of civilization. . . . Just as Chinese people are fond of the Chinese scripts, so the Korean language is suitable for Koreans. Men and women of all social classes can easily understand writings in Korean when they begin to learn how to read, and the language is also easier to propagate. I made up my mind that once I was released from prison, I would immediately muster men under my banner and make every effort to translate Buddhist scriptures into Korean. I regarded this task as my compass for truth searching. Sometime after my release from prison in March 1921, I discussed the matter with several people. There was none who agreed with me, but there were many who scorned me (*YTC* 12: 987).

This paragraph shows that, in addition to the realization of his calling and the real condition of the people, the prison experience awakened Yongsŏng to the following beliefs: Learning about Buddhism should not be limited to educated people, but extended to include those who are uneducated; in order to accomplish that goal, it is absolutely necessary to translate Buddhist scriptures into Korean; and finally, Buddhists should pay more attention to other branches of study, including philosophy, natural science, and mechanics or they will fall behind.

Upon his release from prison, Yongsŏng began the translation of Buddhist scriptures. In April 1921, within a month of his release, Yongsŏng established the Samjang (Tripiṭaka) Translation Society. His fellow monks, however, greeted this project with disapproval. The ulterior motive behind Yongsŏng's participation in the March First Independence Movement may have been his hope for national independence, a goal that was certainly political. That political motivation, however, did not continue with the same direction and with the same intensity after his release. Instead of fighting directly against Japanese colonial rule, Yongsŏng began to focus on transforming and popularizing Buddhist teachings to the Korean people.

Great Enlightenment Movement: Its Social and Spiritual Dimensions

Yongsŏng's desire to balance individual awakening with compassionate actions for others was well demonstrated in the Great Enlightenment Movement. Considering the first use of the term *taegak* (great enlightenment), which appeared in *P'alsangnok* (Record on Eight Phases of the Buddha's Life) published in 1922, Han Pogwang has claimed that the Great Enlightenment Movement seems to have begun when Yongsŏng was 59, in 1922.[11] Since the term "great enlightenment" was simply Yongsŏng's translation of Buddha (*YTC* 9: 729), the literal meaning of the Great Enlightenment Movement is the movement of Buddhism. Yongsŏng believed not only in the teaching of Śākyamuni Buddha, but also in its transmission to Mahākāśyapa. Yongsŏng also made it clear that he believed the Buddhist narrative, which describes how, during his sermon on Vulture Peak, the Exalted One held up a golden lotus blossom to all those assembled and that only Mahākāśyapa understood and smiled in response (*YTC* 9: 725–885). This element of the story is an important aspect of mind-to-mind transmission of the Buddha's teaching in the East Asian Zen Buddhist tradition. Yongsŏng fully accepted the succession of the Sŏn lineage, although he attempted to reinvent and rediscover it whenever he felt the need to do so. Asked how a Buddhist should accumulate merits, in *Enlightenment Ocean Like the Sun*, Yongsŏng described his view of an authentic Buddhist as follows:

> There is no place where you cannot create merits (K. *pokjitki*): if you are filial to your parents and respect your teachers and elders; if you are friendly to your brothers and harmonize your family; if you keep your residence clean; if you work for the public good according to your ability and keep clear of private desires; if you propagate the truth of Great Enlightenment to all the people in the world (K. *ch'ŏnha taejung*) so that they can remove superstition, and tread a righteous path; if you are pleased with the fact that you see other people go well; if, when you offer holy food to the Buddha, you wish that all sentient beings, beginning with human beings, should be freed from the suffering of the triple worlds and that each of them should become a Buddha; if you relieve a person from poverty and disease; and if you do not commit any evil and instead practice good deeds, then you will create merits (*YTC* 6: 329).

In this passage, Yongsŏng teaches that merits should be earned through diverse activities in life, and this teaching constitutes the core of his Great Enlightenment Movement. Yongsŏng started making substantial efforts to expand the Great Enlightenment Movement by opening Great Enlightenment Sunday School in 1928 and holding Sŏn meetings at the Great Enlightenment Temple. The Great Enlightenment School building, which Yongsŏng constructed in Manchuria, was the first Korean Buddhist propagation center in a foreign country. Moreover, he opened an orchard named Hwagwawŏn in Kyŏngsang Province, declaring it a productive form of Buddhism, which he named "Sŏn-Agriculture Buddhism" (K. *sŏnnong Pulgyo*). Yongsŏng also created Buddhist rituals that are unique to the Great Enlightenment Movement, as well as new forms of precept-receiving rituals for lay practitioners.

Yongsŏng was twenty-one when he received *bhikṣu* (Buddhist monk) and bodhisattva precepts at the T'ongdo monastery in Kyŏngsang Province. Even at that time, Yongsŏng was aware that the tendency of not observing precepts had been damaging the root of Korean Buddhism. For him, receiving precepts was not a matter of mere formality. To Yongsŏng, observing precepts was not only at the core of monkhood but vital to keeping the monastic community healthy. Observing precepts was also the essential feature of being an authentic human being. Yongsŏng even argued that only with the observance of five precepts could we be reborn as human beings (See *YTC* 6:286). Without observing these precepts, there is no way to return to the true religion, to Śākyamuni Buddha, and to the Great Enlightenment.

The Sunday school founded at the Great Enlightenment Center and the textbooks compiled especially for children demonstrate Yongsŏng's interest in training the younger generation. Yongsŏng also published a Korean version of the *Huayan sūtra* and retranslated its Korean-Chinese bilingual version through the Samjang Translation Society, which served as the headquarters for the Great Enlightenment Movement.

The movement's spiritual level is as important as the social aspects discussed above and enabled Yongsŏng to be awakened to the non-duality of binary postulations in one's thoughts and to further transform that awakening into compassionate activities for sentient beings. In the *Treatise on Mind Creating All Things*, he discusses his experience of one true mind as the source of all things. He contends that the "one true mind, greatly shining substance" (K. *ilchinsim taegwangmyŏngch'e*; Vairocana Buddha) is the common source for numerous things in the world including heaven, earth, and "me" (*YTC* 4: 13–14). The identity of myriad elements in the world and "me" becomes the foundation of compassion toward all living beings. One of the most important aspects of non-dual experiences for social activities is the non-duality of the ultimate (K. *chin*) and the conventional (K. *sok*) levels. In *Enlightenment Ocean Like the Sun*, Yongsŏng states, "One is called a Hinayanist when one does not realize that the ultimate and conventional levels are 'completely merged' (K. *yungt'ong*) so that all dharmas eternally exist, neither arising nor disappearing" (*YTC* 6: 378). When one is awakened to the complete merging of these two levels, one is a Mahayanist, and he or she embraces any and all dharmas, all kinds of actions, including various kinds of merit-producing activities.

Yongsŏng's understanding of the merging of the ultimate and conventional levels is reminiscent of his denial of empty emptiness. In a letter to Sŏn Master Kyŏngbong dated 1928, Yongsŏng criticizes a negative attachment to emptiness by emphasizing the idea that "emptiness itself is empty":

> In the case of present-day monks who are said to realize the Way (C. *dao*), what they have realized is nothing more than emptiness. Both emptiness and non-emptiness (K. *pulgong*) are empty, and emptiness is also empty. Though emptiness is empty, they cannot see their true nature (K. *chinsŏng*) even in dreams. Emptiness is empty, and emptiness is still empty. Though emptiness is empty in this manner without an ending, it is difficult to leave behind emptiness. Though one may express the fact that one has attained self-realization through long-standing silence, it is not appropriate. For religious masters, emptiness without words cannot be called the Way, since emptiness is neither the Way nor the principal nature (K. *sŏngni*). Just as an empty space is not in itself myriad forms, so is the principal nature of Enlightenment.[12]

Yongsŏng's critical stance toward the empty emptiness and long-standing silence (K. *yanggu muk'ŏn*) needs to be understood in the context of his notion of "revolutionary people's Buddhism." For Yongsŏng, the non-duality of ultimate and conventional levels of truth demands that practitioners be actively engaged in worldly affairs including constructing buildings, managing businesses, writing, or translating scriptures. In this context, Yongsŏng's critical attitude toward the empty emptiness and the practice of long-standing silence in solitude parallels that of Manhae.[13] Both Yongsŏng and Manhae believe that Buddhism's ultimate objective is neither merely practicing dharma in the remote mountains nor transcending the secular world to become an enlightened individual. Religion, to them, must lead one to authentic existence, and authentic existence is possible by being authentically engaged in the activities in the world. Without social engagement, emptiness cannot mean anything but literal blankness without form, which Yongsŏng criticizes as meaningless emptiness. In this sense, Yongsŏng's vision of the "revolutionary people's religion" shares its principles with that of Manhae's Minjung Buddhism (people's Buddhism).

Christianity and the Mind-Only Theory

Yongsŏng's first defense of Buddhism against the rapid growth of Christianity is found in the second volume of *Returning to True Religion*. After enumerating the ten commandments of the Old Testament, Yongsŏng quotes the first passage of Pojo Chinul's (1158–1210) *Kwŏnsu chŏnghae kyŏlsamun* (Encouragement to Practice: The Compact of Samādhī and Prajñā Community):

> A person who falls to the ground gets back up by using that ground. To try to get up without relying on that ground would be impossible. Sentient beings are those who are deluded in regard to the one mind (K. *ilsim*) and give rise to boundless defilements. Buddhas are those who have awakened to the one mind and have given rise to boundless sublime functions. Although there is a difference between delusion and awakening, both essentially derive from the one mind. Hence, to see Buddhahood apart from the mind is impossible.[14] (*YTC* 8: 843)

Yongsŏng goes on to say, "Bodhidharma said that those who sought Buddhas and patriarchs apart from the mind of sentient beings were 'heavenly demons and heretics' (K. *ch'ŏnma oedo*) . . . There are people who seek Heaven (K. *ch'ŏn*) apart from mind-nature (K. *simsŏng*) and worship it, and there are those who say that Heaven is creating [something], but they are all deluded" (*YTC* 8: 844).

Yongsŏng was convinced that the Christian doctrine of God and its creation theory was deluded and false; however, he continued to be greatly impressed with and alarmed by the persuasive force of the Christian narrative of creation.

He seemed to think that one of the most efficient ways of protecting Buddhism against Christian evangelism was to offer a Buddhist narrative on the arising of the world and humanity. It is important to note that the word "arising" (K. *ki*), not creation (K. *ch'angjo*), was used. In *Returning to True Religion* and *Record on Eight Phases of the Buddha's Life*, Yongsŏng gave a detailed Buddhist counterpart to the Christian narrative of creation.

Yongsŏng highly relied on the *ālayavijñāna* (storehouse-consciousness) theory of the Yogācāra school in constructing the Buddhist version of the Christian creation story. One of early versions of such a theory can be found in the *Treatise on the Mind Creating All Things*.[15] The first section of the *Treatise* is titled the "World-Arising" (K. Segye kisi), in which Yongsŏng tries to establish the mind as the origin of all dharmas including the four great elements of earth, water, fire, and wind. In the same section, he also enumerates ten causes for human life: (1) "the essence of the true mind" (K. *chinsim sŏngch'e*); (2) "non-enlightenment" (K. *pulgak*, that is, ālaya-consciousness); (3) "thought-arising" (K. *yŏmgi*); (4) "view-arising" (K. *kyŏn'gi*); (5) "object appearance" (K. *kyŏnghyŏn*); (6) "grasping dharmas" (K. *chippŏp*); (7) "grasping ego" (K. *chib'a*); (8) "greed-anger-delusion" (K. *t'amjinch'i*); (9) "creating karma" (K *cho'ŏp*); and (10) "receiving results" (K. *subo*). Yongsŏng states:

> Buddhism is a religion which teaches about the mind, but which does not worship Heaven or God, the sun, the moon, or stars. There is no Buddha except the mind, and there is no mind except the Buddha. Buddha is another name of the true mind (K. *chinsim*). Buddhism is not theism but atheism. It makes us directly perceive the human mind and be awakened to the "true nature." It brightens the one mind (K. *ilsim*) through myriad dharmas. It is true that our original true nature (K. *ponwŏn chinsŏng*) creates heaven, earth, and myriad things, but it is not true that Heaven (*ch'ŏn*) or God (*sin*) created heaven, earth, all things, and the self. All things in the triple worlds are created by the mind only (*YTC* 4: 14–15).

Yongsŏng further elaborates his theory of the "World-Arising" in *Enlightenment Ocean Like the Sun*, in which he explains the myriad things in the world resulting from the function of the mind.[16] In this work, Yongsŏng employs a number of different expressions to describe the ultimate experience, which transcends all forms of dualities. This experience eventually turns into the beginning point of "various arisings," (*YTC* 6: 262) and included in the "various arisings" are heaven and earth, human beings, and animals.

Yongsŏng describes the ultimate experience, which is the beginning point of the world-arising through the use of various expressions including original enlightenment, the nature of mysteriously perfect enlightenment, true enlightenment, the nature of greatly perfect enlightenment, and the mysteriously bright true mind. From this mysteriously bright true mind, Yongsŏng contends, a thought "suddenly" arises. This thought is identified as *ālayavijñāna,* which is the first moment of the "world-arising" (*YTC* 6: 262). However, Yongsŏng claims that this suddenly arising eighth consciousness, or storehouse consciousness, is deluded. Hence, we read in the *Treatise on the Mind Creating All Things*, "The 'ignorance-wind,' which moves and turns itself into the *ālayavijñāna*, is non-enlightenment" (*YTC* 4: 20).

Yongsŏng also employs the concepts of male and female energies in his efforts to offer Buddhist explanations of natural phenomena including seasonal changes, the blooming of flowers, the ripening of fruit, and the alternations of day and night. He criticizes both Christian and so-called scientific explanations of such natural phenomena: "All these things are not the work of the Lord of Heaven (K. *okhwang sangje*) or some ghosts (K. *kwisin*)" (*YTC* 6: 265). He asserts that there is neither God nor ghosts behind all these natural phenomena, since phenomena arise and cease based on conditions (K. *yŏn*).

A short chapter entitled "Explaining World Creation" in *Enlightenment Ocean Like the Sun* discusses in detail the process of the world-arising (*YTC* 6: 269–273). It begins with the mysteriously bright true mind (or the pure great enlightenment). When this true mind moves very subtly, "storehouse consciousness" occurs. Once storehouse consciousness starts to move, it internally obstructs the true mind and externally causes all kinds of forms to arise. This obstruction is so subtle that it cannot be grasped by ordinary people. Only the Buddha, in his "great calm illumination of samādhi," (K. *taejŏkkwang sammae*) can grasp it.[17] As the storehouse consciousness evolves, Yongsŏng contends, it divides itself into two—stubborn, evil emptiness and perceptive knowledge. From the stubborn, evil emptiness arises the world of non-sentient beings, and from the perceptive knowledge arises the world of sentient beings. When the world of non-sentient beings arises from stubborn and evil emptiness, various kinds of energies emerge. The interactions of these energies create all things (*YTC* 6: 271–272). Interestingly enough, for Yongsŏng, social phenomena such as empires, republics, labor, and communism are also part of this world-arising through the mind. Hence, he asks, "You insist materialism and deny the mind with an assumption that material controls the world. Your mind is like a tree or a rock and does not discriminate; what then is it that makes discrimination? Does material outside one's mind discriminate?" (*YTC* 6: 291).

In Part II of *Enlightenment Ocean Like the Sun*, Yongsŏng categorizes different existences through the use of Buddhist terms. The categories of existence include those that were "womb-born" (K. *t'aesaeng*), "egg-born" (K. *nansaeng*), "moisture-born" (K. *sŭpsaeng*), and "born by transformation" (K. hwasaeng); and "beings with form" (K. *yusang chungsaeng*), "beings without form" (K. *musaek chungsaeng*), "beings without form but with thought" (K. *musaek yusang chungsaeng*), "beings without thought," (K. *musang chungsaeng*) and so on. Human beings are womb-born; the Christian God (K. *Hanŭnim*) belongs to beings without form (*YTC* 6: 355–356); mountain deities and tutelary deities are idols with form. In later sections of *Enlightenment Ocean Like the Sun*, Yongsŏng replaces the Christian Heaven with the Buddhist realm of non-form (K. *musaekkye chŏn*; Sk. *arūpāvacara*), which can be attained by cultivating the four emptiness meditations. Yongsŏng did not forget to emphasize the difference between the Christian concept of Heaven and the Buddhist concept of the realm of non-form: "Our Great Enlightenment teaching is intended not to lead one to Heaven (K. *ch'ŏndang*), but to liberate one forever from the suffering of the world of life and death by awakening all sentient beings to their perfect Buddhahood."[18]

When and how does storehouse consciousness occur? Why does a deluded thought suddenly occur from perfect enlightenment, which is, by definition not deluded? Who or what gives rise to delusion, and for what purpose? Why suddenly? Yongsŏng does not ask these questions. Instead, he just assumes that the evolution of the corrupted world "naturally" proceeded (*YTC* 6: 263–264). By perceiving the corrupted situation of the world as a "natural" phenomenon, Yongsŏng avoids the necessity of answering those questions. This seems to demonstrate the burden of modernity that Yongsŏng had to face as he dealt with the challenge of defending Buddhism against the rapidly growing power of Christianity. From the very beginning of *Returning to True Religion* and throughout *Enlightenment Ocean Like the Sun*, Yongsŏng attempts to reformulate the Buddhist concept of mind-only theory in response to the creation theory of Christianity.

Responses to Confucianism

Yongsŏng found Confucianism less intimidating than Christianity, but still felt the need to criticize it in order to protect Buddhism. The first section of *Returning to True Religion* offers what Yongsŏng considered to be Confucian critiques of Buddhism (*YTC* 8: 763–784). One question that Yongsŏng raised was: "Śrāmaneras [mendicants], those sons of Śakyamuni, do not observe the 'three bonds and five relationships' (K. *samgang oryun*) but enjoy solitude in deep mountains, and have no concern for other human beings. What use are they for the world?" Yongsŏng's answer was: "You do not know the core of the Sage's teaching. Our Buddha, the World-Honored One, is empowered to make all forms empty in order to establish the knowledge of all dharmas, and to save sentient beings according to their conditions" (*YTC* 8: 763). Yongsŏng argues that the core of Confucian teachings is already embedded in the Buddha's teachings. Through the use of somewhat far-fetched reasoning, Yongsŏng draws parallels between Confucianism and Buddhism in their doctrines only to demonstrate the superiority of the latter. In an essay entitled "Discussions of Confucian Scholars in the Song Dynasty Are Not as Profound as the Teachings of Confucius," Yongsŏng argues that benevolence (K. *in*) in Confucianism is equivalent to the mind (K. *sim*) in Buddhism. He then makes a rather sharp distinction between Confucius and neo-Confucians, especially the Cheng brothers, and criticizes the latter, arguing that they did not understand the way of Confucius, nor did they reach the level of Confucius in their philosophy (*YTC* 1: 434ff). While criticizing neo-Confucianism, Yongsŏng also claims the unity of the teachings of Buddhism, Confucianism, and Daoism, and supports this claim by citing passages from Hamhŏ Tŭkt'ong (1376–1433), a Buddhist monk during the Chosŏn dynasty (*YTC* 1: 435), who is well-known in the Korean philosophical tradition for his efforts to harmonize the three traditions.

Yongsŏng is also critical of Zhuxi (1130–1200), whom he considers to have made wrong assumptions about Buddhism. Zhuxi mistook Buddhism for nihilism; Zhuxi also misunderstood Buddhism and thus contended that Buddhism had neither practical applicability nor real substance as a philosophical system. In response to Zhuxi's criticism, Yongsŏng argues that the Buddha's talk of annihilation indicates the annihilation of the deluded mind, not of the "true mind and its mysterious function" (K. *chinsim myoyong*) (*YTC* 8: 790). Yongsŏng supports this idea by citing a passage from the *Holy Teachings of Vimalakīrti*: "You should absorb yourself in contemplation in such a way that you can manifest all ordinary behavior without cessation."[19] Yongsŏng asks, "How is it possible that essence (K. *ch'e*) exists without function (K. *yong*)?" (*YTC* 8: 790). Yongsŏng argues that as long as one maintains one's true mind, this mind should also function in the ethical realm of what Confucians identify as the "three bonds and five relations." Yongsŏng's efforts to find room for the function of the true mind in the social realm that is familiar to Confucians well reflects his vision of Buddhism and true religion, which, for Yongsŏng, includes, among other aspects, active involvement with society. Eventually, Yongsŏng finds it unnecessary to criticize Confucianism. In *Enlightenment Ocean Like the Sun*, he casually refers to Confucius in his discussion of causality, but no direct attack on the Cheng brothers is found. Obviously, he comes to be aware that Confucianism has lost its influence on Korean society, and, thus, no longer poses threats to Buddhism.

The Decline of the Great Enlightenment Movement

Yongsŏng devoted more than ten years to the promotion of the Great Enlightenment Movement. However, by the 1930s, the movement had begun to decline. Han Pogwang offers three reasons for this decline: First, there was insufficient support for the movement. At times, the Korean Buddhist Order itself obstructed the movement. Second, there was the intervention of the Japanese colonial government. The pressure from the Japanese colonial government made it difficult to maintain the assets that Yongsŏng had left in trust to a bank in Pusan. In 1936, he entrusted it to the Kyŏngsŏng Propagation House of Pŏmŏ Monastery. Financial insecurity inevitably weakened the movement. Third, the movement failed to train individuals who could continue the movement.[20]

There was a time when Yongsŏng was proud of his achievements. When he began the Sŏn movement in Seoul in 1912, he wrote a short note titled "On Establishing the One Thousand Sŏn Meditation Society," in which he said, "I had three thousand believers after three years' propagation. Due to my work, the words 'Sŏn meditation' began to be known to the people" (*YTC* 1: 546). Three thousand is no small number for three years of work, even by today's standards. His pride in this feat was completely legitimate, but this sense of pride and contentment was rare for him. He often felt disappointed, and faced various adversities. In one of his letters to Sŏn Master Kyŏngbong, written in 1928 at the age of 65, Yongsŏng lamented:

> This year, I have fulfilled my responsibility for the Sŏn monasteries, but I am unable to give further assistance. I have struggled with my bare hands to manage business on the Northern Jiandao and in the city of Nanam in Hamgyŏng Province in order to keep the house in Seoul. In addition to this, I have just embarked on the translation of *Huayan Sūtra*, yet, sometimes, I have no will to carry on, nor do I feel like having the capacity for the work. Furthermore there is no single monk suitable for the Sŏn monasteries. Is this the problem of our time or is this my fate? What can be done about it? I am afraid that Buddha's dharma disappears by itself . . . I am getting old, my energy dissipating, and it is difficult even to walk. My body and mind are exhausted. This is because I was born in the time when the Buddha's teaching is dead (K. *pulpŏp myŏlmang sidae*), which is due to my sin. The current situation of Buddhism is devastating, but no monks in Seoul pay attention to this situation; they just get together to greedily satiate their appetite. In the midst of this danger, I am left with various bills that need to be paid. Therefore, even the word "Buddha" has become a pain to me. It was said that Zhaozhou (778–897) said: "I do not want to hear the word Buddha." This saying is indeed a truthful one.[21]

This letter reveals the depth of Yongsŏng's sorrow, despair, and exhaustion. However, as if battling his own sin and destiny, Yongsŏng continued to publish his works, including "Imjonggyŏl" (One's Last Words) in 1936, "Odo ŭi chilli" (The Truth of My Way) in 1937, and "Odo nŭn kak" (My Way is Enlightenment) in 1938. He also translated the *Thousand Hands Sūtra* into Korean and published it in 1938.

Yongsŏng, Manhae, and Sŏngch'ŏl

Where should we place Yongsŏng's life and thoughts in the history of modern Korean Buddhism? One of the best ways of determining this is by comparing his life and thoughts to those of other contributors to modern Korean Buddhism. In this context, Manhae and Sŏngch'ŏl (1912–1993) can serve as good references for comparison because both greatly influenced modern Korean Buddhism. Manhae is well-known for his *minjung* Buddhism,[22] and Sŏngch'ŏl for his purist and absolutist approach to Buddhism, as well as his strict observance of precepts.

Yongsŏng shares with Manhae several agendas in his proposals to revive Korean Buddhism. However, Yongsŏng was more traditional than Manhae in insisting on the absolute importance of celibacy in the monastic life, and in emphasizing the observance of precepts as a key difference between human beings and animals. A rather liberal interpretation of precepts has been one of the salient features of Japanese Buddhism. For many Japanese Buddhists and Korean sympathizers, not strictly observing precepts is fully compatible with practicing Buddhism. Yongsŏng was strongly against this trend, and submitted two petitions to the Japanese colonial authorities in 1926 requesting that the colonial government purge temples of those monks who broke precepts through such unbecoming behaviors as clerical marriage and meat eating. In the first paragraph of his first petition (1926), Yongsŏng criticized those who violated the precept of maintaining celibacy, and he demanded the revision of the Temple Code (K. *sabŏp*), which allowed those who breached these precepts to become temple abbots:

> These days, a group of shameless demons have soiled their minds with the five desires, destroyed the Buddha's True Law, dared to have wives and eat meat, and turned pure temples into dens of demons, while having totally forgotten Sŏn meditation, invocation of the Buddha's name, and the reading of scriptures. For this reason, all the Heaven-Gods weep and the Earth-Gods become angry (*YTC* I: 550).

Despite his efforts, the Japanese colonial authorities did nothing. Considering his critique of the Temple Code and the Japanese Buddhist attitude on precepts, one may interpret his emphasis on precepts as an indirect attack on Japanese imperialism. We cannot find Yongsŏng's criticism specifically addressing Manhae, who had a positive view of clerical marriage. However, it is quite possible that Yongsŏng demonstrated his disapproval of Manhae when he submitted the two petitions to purge the Buddhist Order of those behaving in violation of priesthood.

Yongsŏng opposed external, political interference in religious matters, including the 30 Head Temple System established by the Japanese colonial government.

After his prison experience, however, he developed distaste for politics and departed from the political realm, something which Manhae would not condone. His departure from politics was already evident, as he revealed his motive for participating in the independence movement to the Japanese prosecutor: "Having nothing to do with politics, I have nothing to complain about nor to be satisfied with, but I thought it was better for Chosŏn to become independent."[23] His statement here is ambiguous, evasive, or even self-contradictory. Thus, Yongsŏng's "revolutionary people's Buddhism" can be subject to criticism that it was not revolutionary enough to make changes in the lives of people who suffered from the deprivation of rights as a result of Japanese colonial rule in Korea.

The record of Yongsŏng's response to the Japanese prosecutor illustrates a stark contrast to that of Manhae, of whom a Japanese prosecutor asked, "Are you going to commit yourself to the Chosŏn independence movement from this moment on?" Manhae replied, "Certainly. I will not change my mind. Even if my body perishes, I will maintain this spirit for eons."[24] The religious-political characteristic of Manhae's Buddhism, and his firm belief in the inseparability of politics and religion, were even more conspicuous in one of his short essays, "Nanŭn wae chung i toeŏttna?" (Why Did I Become a Monk?), which expresses Manhae's reflections on his imprisonment, and which was written eight years after his release in 1922. "Even so, shall I finish my life as a man and as a monk?" he wrote. "Isn't there a political forum in front of us? Didn't I become a monk because no such forum existed?"[25] Manhae does not answer these questions, but his essay demonstrates that, for Manhae, his prison experience could not make him withdraw from the political realm.

Sŏngch'ŏl also expressed his assessment of Yongsŏng's Buddhism. In the following passage, the core of Sŏngch'ŏl's own view of Buddhism is evident:

> When the long night of darkness has fallen over the modern history of Buddhism, how greatly our deceased teacher [Yongsŏng] presented the "eternal, true dharma" (K. *manse chŏngbŏp*); his activities were like a shower of compassion over fallen weeds! Though they can turn the sun cold and the moon hot, no demon can destroy the "true words" (K. *ch'amdoen malssŭm*) of Śākyamuni Buddha. No one in modern times was superior to our deceased teacher [Yongsŏng] in promoting the "treasury of the eye of the true dharma" (K. *chŏngbŏp anjang*) . . . He became the model for his juniors through his observance of pure precepts. Like the wind and moon seen outside a beaded hanging screen, he is as bright at night as it is by day. And just like the flowers growing in front of the withered tree-rock, it always represents spring. [26]

These words are, of course, not a systematic, full-scale assessment of Yongsŏng's achievements, but they sufficiently convey Sŏngch'ŏl's view of the history of modern Korean Buddhism and of what he considers to be genuine Buddhist enlightenment. From Sŏngch'ŏl's perspective, compassion, true Dharma, and observance of pure precepts are the features that deserve praise and admiration in Yongsŏng's life. But Sŏngch'ŏl failed to point out Yongsŏng's political engagements, his response to the needs of the time and the cries of people in pain, and his sensitivity to the changing times. The most significant part of Yongsŏng's Buddhism lies in the very notion of revolutionary people's Buddhism, and S'ŏngch'ŏl failed to see that.

We may, then, place Yongsŏng's Buddhism in the middle point between the far-left "people's Buddhism" of Manhae and the far-right elitist, purist Buddhism of Sŏngch'ŏl. Yongsŏng's Buddhism was so revolutionary that Sŏngch'ŏl turned his back on Yongsŏng's most important endeavor, which was to expand the scope of Buddhist compassion. Yet, Yongsŏng withdrew himself from social and political engagements after his prison experience, which put significant limits on the realization of his "revolutionary people's religion," which became less revolutionary than the "people's Buddhism" of Manhae.

Conclusion

This essay began with the statement that Yongsŏng's Buddhism is characterized by his efforts to maintain the balance between "seeking enlightenment above" and "transforming sentient beings below." The balance, demonstrated in the 30 years of his second mendicant life, which included more than ten years of involvement with the Great Enlightenment Movement, offers a valuable example to future generations in the history of Korean Buddhism. The balance between "seeking enlightenment" and "helping sentient beings" can also be understood as a balance between the true mind and mysterious function, between contemplation and ordinary activities, and between essence and function. Keeping these balances in mind, this essay can be closed with some reflections drawn from Yongsŏng's life and thoughts.

First, as one of the influential founders of modern Korean Buddhism, Yongsŏng demonstrated that individual salvation should always be accompanied by action for other people. Yongsŏng's admonition, which I summarized as "earning merits through diverse activities for sentient beings," contends that enlightenment without compassionate action makes Buddhism a less than perfect teaching.

Second, Korean Buddhism must seek alternative training methods to help sentient beings awaken to their minds and become sensitive to the rapidly changing milieu of the twenty-first century. The exclusive usage of the *kongan* method, or overemphasis on "no-reliance on words and letters" (K. *pullip munja*), can put limits on Buddhism. The *kongan* practice should be supplemented by other means, such as scripture reading, prayers to bodhisattvas, exercising concern for the secular world, serving social needs, enhancing one's sensitivity to the changing world, and cultivating a compassionate mind to help sentient beings.

Third, Yongsŏng opposed the political intervention of Japanese imperialism in Korean Buddhism. However, he was less revolutionary and less political than Manhae, and, thus, left the following questions with us: "How much should Buddhists engage themselves with political matters?" and "What would be a proper Buddhist reaction to political situations, especially when the failure of politics results in tragedies with such a magnitude as the fall of a dynasty and colonization as seen in the pre-modern and modern history of Korea?" In response to these questions, Yongsŏng does not tell us exactly how we should maintain the balance of personal practice and compassionate actions for others. Instead, he demands that we strike our own balance according to our compassionate insight in reference to sentient beings.

Notes

1. An earlier version of this essay appeared in *Korea Journal*, vol. 45, no. 1 (Spring 2005): 29–63, under the title "A Monk of Mukti and Karma: The Life and Thought of Baek Yongseong."

2. Han Pogwang, a well-known scholar-monk of the twentieth century, painfully observes that the propagation of Buddhism to Seoul has a history that is less than a century old, a far shorter period than that of Catholicism and Protestantism. See Han Pogwang, "Yongsŏng sŭnim ŭi chŏnban'gi ŭi saengae—sanjung suhaengi rŭl chungsim ŭiro" (The First Half of Master Yongsŏng's Life: Focusing on the Period of Ascetic Practices in Mountains), *Taegak sasang* (Journal of Maha Bodhi Thought), vol. 1 (1998): 27–50, pp. 29–30.

3. For more details, see Sŏk Taeŭn, "Ko Paek Yongsŏng daejongsa ŭi ch'umo" (In Memory of the Late Sŏn Master Paek Yongsŏng), quoted in Han Pogwang, "Yongsŏng sŭnim ŭi huban'gi ŭi saengae (2): Taegak kyose ŭi hwakjang kwa haesan" (The Second Half of Master Yongsŏng's Life, 2: the Expansion of the Great Enlightenment Movement and its Dispersion), *Taegak sasang*, vol. 4 (2001): 9–72, pp. 66–69.

4. Han Pogwang, "Yongsŏng sŭnim ŭi chŏnban'gi ŭi saengae," 27–50.

5. Yongsŏng spent the last seven years (1903–1910) of his ascetic period in Sŏn meetings of the monks, which may be seen as the first preliminary practice of "transforming below."

6. Myŏngjŏng, *Samsogul sosik* (News from the Samsogul Hermitage) (Yangsan, Korea: Tongdosa Temple Kŭngnak Sŏnwŏn, 1997), p. 175. The text does not indicate in what year this letter was written, but it should be dated, according to its content, after the introduction of Great Enlightenment Teaching in North Jiandao in 1927.

7. Paek Yongsŏng, *Yongsŏng taejongsa chŏnjip* (Complete Works of the Great Master Yongsŏng), 18 vols. (Seoul: Taegaksa, 1991), vol 1, p. 378. Henceforth, citations from this collection will be noted in the text with the abbreviation *YTC*, followed by the volume and page numbers.

8. No information is available other than his name, Sŏn Master Muyung.

9. Interpreting this phrase, Han Pogwang says: "This refers to the fact that Yongsŏng attained the stage where the five aggregates disappear, and where the wu kongan, sentient and non-sentient beings, and mundane and supra-mundane worlds are all empty." Han Pogwang, "Yongsŏng sŭnim ŭi chŏnban'gi ŭi saengae," p. 39.

10. Kim Kwangsik made a brief comment on this somewhat enigmatic poem: "This verse shows his last awakening, and the state of rising above the world." See Kim Kwangsik, *Yongsŏng* (Seoul: Minjoksa, 1999), p. 40. Of course, his "rising above the world" cannot mean leaving the world behind.

11. Han Pogwang, "Yongsŏng sŭnim ŭi chŏnban'gi ŭi saengae," p. 26.

12. Myŏngjŏng, *Samsogul sosik*, pp. 185–186.

13. Woosung Huh, "Manhae's Understanding of Buddhism," *Korea Journal*, vol. 40. no. 2 (2000): 65–101. Especially see the section on "The Goal of Buddhism and the Two Worlds."

14. English translation quoted from Robert E. Buswell, Jr., *The Korean Approach to Zen* (Honolulu: University of Hawai'i Press, 1983), p. 93.

15. See *YTC* 4: 13ff. As far as this work is concerned, Yongsŏng seemed to have read various Mind-Only literatures and the *Awakening of Faith* attributed to Aśvaghoṣa, as he used the words, the true mind, one mind, "ignorance-wind" (K. *mumyŏngp'ung*), as well as the notion of causality (K. *yŏn'gi*), the harmony of the non-phenomenal mind, and the phenomenal consciousness. It clearly reminds one not only of the *Awakening of Faith* but also of Wonhyo's commentary on it.

16. In this work, Yongsŏng even composed what may be called a "Verse of Creation" (*YTC* 6: 273–280).

17. His explanation of the "world-arising," based upon Great Enlightenment and ālaya-consciousness, reminds us of the Samkhyan; Sāṃkhya philosophy explains the evolution of the world by postulating the independent existence and movement of the primal matter (Sk. *prakṛti*); the role of *prakṛti* is similar to the role of store-consciousness in Yongsŏng's elucidation of the "world-arising," realizing Puruṣa (primal person) may be likened to realizing Great Enlightenment. However, the fundamentally dualistic philosophy of the Sāṃkhya can not explain *prakṛti* in terms of *puruṣa* as Yongsŏng would have done it.

18. Similarly, in "Odo ŭi chilli" (The Truth of My Way), in which Yongsŏng argues against the Christian doctrine that when people die they go to heaven or hell, he puts forward a Buddhist version of life and death: "The birth of a man is to give rise to 'function' (K. *yong*) from 'substance' (K. *ch'e*); and the death of a man is to gather 'function' into substance, that is, going back to the origin (K. *panbon hwanwŏn*). Thus, there is no need to mention heaven or hell" (*YTC* 4: 959–960). It is interesting to note that Yongsŏng did not say that the Christian concept of heaven or hell is either absurd or useless. Instead, he accepted the usefulness of talking about heaven; although he gave a Buddhist version of heaven in order to compete with the Christian Heaven. The reason may be that an outright dismissal of Christian Heaven could have offended many people.

19. English translation by Robert A. F. Thurman, *The Holy Teaching of Vimalakirti: A Mahayana Scripture* (University Park and London: Pennsylvania State University Press, 1976), p. 24.

20. Han Pogwang, *Yongsŏng sŏnsa yŏn'gu* (A Study of the Sŏn Master Yongsŏng), (Seoul: Kamnodang, 1981), pp. 108–111.

21. Myŏngjŏng, *Samsogul sosik*, pp. 183–184.

22. For details, see Woosung Huh, "Manhae's Understanding of Buddhism."

23. Han Pogwang, *Yongsŏng sŏnsa yŏn'gu*, p. 175.

24. Han Yongun, *Han Yongun chŏnjip* (Collected Works of Han Yongun), vol. 1 (Seoul: Sin'gu munhwasa, 1980), vol. I, p. 372

25. Han Yongun, *Han Yongun chŏnjip*, vol. I, p. 412.

26. T'oe'ong Sŏngch'ŏl, "Introduction," in Paek Yongsŏng, *Yongsŏng sŏnsa ŏrok* (The Sayings of Sŏn Master Yongsŏng) (Seoul: Samjang yŏkhoe, 1941), p. 3.

2

A Korean Buddhist Response to Modernity

Manhae Han Yongun's Doctrinal Reinterpretation for His Reformist Thought[1]

Pori Park

Introduction

During the first half of the twentieth century, Korean Buddhism had to deal with two challenges: It had to overcome the effect of the anti-Buddhist policies of the Confucian Chosŏn dynasty (1392–1910), under which Buddhism had suffered institutionally, doctrinally, and socially; at the same time, it also had to transform itself into a religion that was compatible with the new society under Japanese colonial rule (1910–1945). The outset of opening of the nation to foreign powers was regarded by most Buddhist clerics as an opportunity for change (K. *yusin*) and progress (K. *chinbo*). The old Buddhist ways had to give rise to "enlightened" (K. *kaemyŏng sidae*) and "civilized" times (K. *munmyŏng sidae*).[2] Korean Buddhists accepted a melioristic view of history, sharing the views of the majority of contemporary Korean intellectuals, who were greatly inclined toward Spencerian social Darwinism[3] and who viewed the activities of Japanese Buddhism and Christianity as advanced forms of religion. The arrival of these religions provided Korean Buddhists with both challenges and a frame of reference for their idea for modernity.

The utmost interest of Korean Buddhists during the first half of the twentieth century was to present a socially viable form of Buddhism. The main areas of the reforms, designed to make the saṅgha accessible to the public, were cleric education and methods of proselytization. The curriculum included secular subjects designed to make Buddhist clerics conversant with society. The saṅgha co-opted the social activities of Christian missionaries and attempted to develop a sense of connection among the clerics, the laity, and society. As such, these early reforms were not politically oriented, but rather had the prime goal of survival of the saṅgha and protection of the institution's interests.

Manhae Han Yongun's (1879–1944) ideas for reform typified those of his time by subsuming other reform ideas. His first reform proposal, *Chosŏn Pulgyo yusillon* (Treatise on the Reformation of Korean Buddhism), criticized the mild and gradualist approaches proposed by Kwŏn Sangno (1876–1965), a monk-scholar. Manhae proposed radical reformation, and his reform ideas became the main source of reference for the reformation of the saṅgha. Manhae shared ideas with other reform-minded monks, Paek Yongsŏng (1864–1940) and Pak Hanyŏng (1870–1948), and provided leadership and inspiration to young Buddhist clerics.

After the March First Independence Movement of 1919, a nationwide movement, Korean Buddhists shifted the reforms in political directions and joined the nationalist march for the restoration of sovereignty. Buddhist youth launched the youth movement, claiming the separation of religion from politics and the abolition of the "temple ordinance" (K. *sach'allyŏng*) by which, they thought, the Japanese government had stripped the saṅgha of its independence.[4] They criticized bureaucratic Buddhism (K. *kwanje Pulgyo*; Buddhism for the rulers) that was subservient to the Japanese regime. Along with Manhae, young Buddhist clerics instead promoted *minjung* Buddhism (Buddhism for the masses) as a means to sever the ties of saṅgha from the powerful Japanese state and to serve the general public. In this sense, *minjung Pulgyo* was not only a way of socially reaching out to people, but also a way of resisting state intervention.

The mere adoption of social involvement by Buddhist clerics, however, prompted confusion and posed major challenges. The reforms required that Buddhists seriously reflect on the ways to render social engagement congruent with the Buddhist system of thought. Without giving much thought to the fundamental soteriological difference, Buddhists superficially imitated the social welfare activities of Christianity, but never fully incorporated them into Buddhism. More specifically, their changes were regarded as only *upaya* (expedient means), so that the core of Buddhist teachings would remain relevant in Korean society at the time. Accordingly, *upaya* was not the ultimate concern for Buddhist clerics and, despite their sense of urgency about modern change, they showed a lack of interest in or passion for social involvement. The lackluster pursuit of social involvement, in turn, produced adverse results, including helping to sustain the status quo or collaborating with the colonial regime. More seriously, it created an opportunity for Buddhist clerics to be affected by worldly values, while increasingly violating the monastic rules and forgetting their vows of voluntary poverty.

Manhae was a unique figure in Korean Buddhism in that he attempted to overcome this Buddhist impasse in dealing with social salvation. He treated the social involvement not as a temporary cure, but as something fully ingrained in the main Buddhist system of thought. He juxtaposed social involvement and the pursuit of the Buddhist awakening with his non-dual approach of Kyo (doctrinal teachings) and Sŏn (meditation). In this way, the social dimension would no longer be alienated from the mind of Buddhists and the clerics would no longer be lost in their involvement in social activities.

This essay examines how Manhae doctrinally supported his reform ideas and resolved the Buddhist impasse in dealing with social salvation. The paper begins with a discussion of his ideas on reformation and then focuses on his doctrinal presentation.

Reform Buddhism

Manhae's early social awareness came from his upbringing in Confucian education. As a prodigy praised by local villagers, he is said to have mastered Confucian classics, such as *Analects*, *Mencius*, *The Great Learning*, *Doctrine of the Mean*, *Book of Poetry*, *Book of History*, and others in his teens. Manhae left his village after both his father and brother were killed by the court army while involved in one of the "righteous army" (K. *ŭibyŏng*) movements, which occurred frequently after the Tonghak Peasant Uprising in 1894. Manhae recalled the moment he headed for Paektam Monastery on Mount Sŏrak in Kangwŏn Province, where he was ordained as a novice monk and later took the full ordination:

> Isn't our life transient? What could be left when we were to face our final moment [death] after all those days of struggling? Could it be honor or wealth? Couldn't all that is left be ephemeral? Everything, after all, becomes empty, intangible, and nothing. My skepticism was getting worse and made me deeply troubled. I concluded that I should first find out what life was and then do some worthy work [for the troubled nation]. I changed my route to Seoul and headed for Paektam Monastery of Mount Sŏrak where I had heard a renowned Buddhist master resided.[5]

Manhae took Buddhist training to explore the meaning of life and to prepare himself for devoting his life to society. This complementary purpose of his life remained a tension throughout his Buddhist career.

As a Buddhist reformer, Manhae first addressed the issue of the religious instinct in human beings, explaining why human beings turn to religion as a last resort (*HYC* 2: 278–79). He believed that people are bound to have fear and dissatisfaction because human existence is confined in time and space. They seek comfort and safety from these existential limits and exhaust their minds in an effort to overcome their psychological anxiety, the physical dangers of life, and their fear of death. People get easily entangled in suffering and affliction due to these facts of human nature. Misery and social conflict, however, cannot be eased simply by the advancement of science, law enforcement, social charity, or the Socialist ideal of economic equality. As such, Manhae believed that people need religion.

Manhae singled out Buddhism as a religion par excellence for leading the future civilization of humanity. Buddhist practice enables people to overcome such afflictions and to attain the ultimate joy of truth. Buddhism teaches that human beings are endowed with every faculty needed to expand the mind to become one with the universe and to realize the universe inside the mind (*HYC* 2: 288). Manhae thus stated that the strong point of Buddhism is its religious aspiration for the awakening of innate Buddha-nature and its self-reliant practices.

Manhae further attempted to show the relevance and prominence of Buddhism in modern life by using Western concepts of religion and philosophy. As a religion, Buddhism gives people a hope for life by leading them to a state beyond birth and death (*HYC* 2: 36–38). He contrasted Buddhism with Christianity, claiming that the former is a religion of wisdom and the latter a superstitious belief; Christianity forces devotees to have blind faith in God and heaven while Buddhism allows them to become awakened to their own minds. There is nothing apart from the mind, and forced faith puts unnecessary limits on people's wisdom. He also advocated Buddhism as philosophy (*HYC* 2: 38–43). He defined philosophy as a discipline that tries to attain universal and thorough knowledge by inquiring into the nature of things. Buddhism is thus philosophical because it leads people to omniscience once they have been awakened to the mind. He argued that both Eastern and Western philosophies were nothing but footnotes to Buddhist teaching. He concluded that Buddhism would be necessary for the future ethics and culture of human society.

Manhae embarked on his journey of reformation of Buddhism as a way of preparing the religion to fulfill its function for the Korean people. He believed that, through reformation, the saṅgha could actively intervene in people's lives by restoring the religious prestige of Korea. The long period of stagnation and deterioration of its religious status, due to the oppression of Buddhism in the Chosŏn dynasty, had produced daunting negative effects on Korean Buddhism. Chosŏn persecution left Buddhism lacking a function in society. Buddhist monasteries were hidden and scattered in the mountains; the members of the saṅgha lacked social status.

Manhae first called for reformation in response to these effects by publishing the *Chosŏn Pulgyo yusillon* in 1913, three years after he had finished a first draft. The treatise consists of seventeen chapters that cover various aspects of the saṅgha reforms. Throughout his life, Manhae maintained the ideas proposed in this treatise and expanded them a little further in his later article "Record on the Reformation of Korean Buddhism" (Chosŏn Pulgyo kaehyŏk an), written in 1931.

Manhae contended that, despite of its strength, Buddhism had accumulated wrong practices over its long history (*HYC* 2: 47). Old Buddhist practices that could not be resonant with a new era should thus be abandoned. He thought that religion that cannot satisfy the development of human intellect and human civilization is destined to die out.[6] Any established religion should willingly reform the practices that cannot meet the expectations of human development. His remedy was to reform Buddhist practices so as to function in society, developing a socially conscious Buddhism.

As shown in the *Chosŏn Pulgyo yusillon*, Manhae was exposed to the thoughts of Western philosophers, such as Rene Descartes, Francis Bacon, and Immanuel Kant, through the writings of Liang Qichao (1873–1929) (*HYC* 2: 38–42). He learned about Western civilization from *Yinbinshi wenji*, Liang Qichao's encyclopedic book on Western knowledge of political thought, history, and philosophy.[7] Early Japanese Buddhist experiments with Western ideas must also have provided a frame of reference. For example, in 1908 Manhae had an opportunity to go to Japan which he believed to have emerged as a new center of modern civilization at that time. He was assisted by monks of the Sōtō sect during his stay at Sōtōshū (now Komazawa) University from May through August, 1908. He also made a tour to various Japanese cities, such as Tokyo, Kyoto, Shimonoseki, and Nikkō. He returned to Korea after staying eight months in Japan.[8]

Manhae was also sympathetic to the Socialist goal of social equality, which reflected his advocacy of *minjung Pulgyo* (Buddhism for the masses). In an interview in 1931, conducted by a magazine called *Samchŏlli*, he said that he was planning to write about Buddhist Socialism (*HYC* 2: 292). He asserted that Buddhism does not support the possession of personal wealth and economic inequality, yet he did not develop any further aspects of Buddhist Socialism. Despite this sympathetic attitude, at the same time he emphasized the importance of religion over the Socialist attack on religion (*HYC* 2: 278–81). Because religion was the only means for the oppressed proletariat to receive comfort in their economic suffering, he thought that religion should be an important part of life for the proletariat. He further believed that since people are innately endowed with a religious mind, a temporary ideological or belief system cannot replace religion.

Manhae regarded Buddhist practices as the products of historical developments, which were thus subject to change. He offered the following rationale to support his proposal for Buddhist reformation: "It is said that if one returns to the way of ancient times while living in the present time, disasters will inevitably prevail upon the person. Today's stage is not that of the past; one can no longer dance properly without changing the long-sleeved dress to the short-sleeved one" (*HYC* 2: 119).

The main purpose of *Chosŏn Pulgyo yusillon* is to reform the saṅgha. Manhae assessed the present situation of the sṅgha and criticized the practices that he thought had contributed to the decline of Buddhism. He provided a detailed blueprint of the kind of changes that were needed for the enhancement of Buddhism in society. The *Chosŏn Pulgyo yusillon* is the first and most comprehensive systematic writing on Buddhist reformation that appeared in Korea during this time. Areas of changes included cleric's education, proselytization, rituals, and the saṅgha's policies regarding monasteries and clerics. He proposed reforms in order to prepare the saṅgha to have easy access to the laity and the public. His reform ideas can be divided into four major groups: unification of doctrinal orientation of the saṅgha, simplification of practices, centralization of the saṅgha administration, and reformation of the saṅgha policies and customs.

Manhae attempted to awaken the saṅgha, which was lacking structure and regulations. He tried to establish an order both in doctrine and practice so that a sense of religious identity could emerge. To do this, he proposed drastic changes in many aspects of Buddhist practice. But the focus of the *Chosŏn Pulgyo yusillon* was reform of saṅgha practices; it lacked concern for the laity. Manhae's later writings, such as *Pulgyo taejŏn* (Great Canon of Buddhism), fill the gap. Also, the treatise lacked political awareness because the draft was completed before the annexation, and thus we have to wait for his later writings to investigate his attitude concerning the political situation. Another oversight of this treatise emerged later. In order to overcome the isolation of Buddhism at the time, Manhae emphasized the opening and outreach of the saṅgha to society, proposing moving monasteries into cities and villages, engaging clerics in production, and adopting cleric marriage. But the social contact did not enhance Buddhist influence in society as much as expected; on the contrary, the saṅgha rapidly came under the influence of the secular society. In this treatise Manhae was not fully aware of the importance of the issue with regard to how the existential orientation of Buddhism could be combined with social involvement.

The reform ideas proposed in the *Chosŏn Pulgyo yusillon* provided the main frame of reference for the subsequent saṅgha reformation. The saṅgha adapted Manhae's ideas on education and proselytization in particular. It began to change the education system for clerics and proselytization policies. As Manhae suggested, the saṅgha became interested in providing clerics with a general education and in establishing a teacher's college. Young clerics were sent to foreign countries, mostly to Japan, to study. Branch temples (K. *p'ogyoso*) were built in villages and towns to increase contact with the people. The Conference Office of the Abbots of the Thirty Main Monasteries (K. *Samsip ponsa chuji hoeŭi-so*) decided to convert Chanting Halls (K. *yŏmbultang*) of all monasteries to Meditation Halls (K. *sŏndang*), excepting that of Kŏnbong Monastery.[9] The saṅgha, however, faced many difficulties in implementing its reform ideas. The financial limits and the state control were the major obstacles.

Manhae himself worked as a propagator (K. *p'ogyo-sa*) around 1916 at the Central Propagation Office of Korean Sŏn Buddhism (Chosŏn Sŏnjong chung'ang p'ogyo-dang), which was built in 1912 as one of the central propagation temples in Seoul. He published his own magazine *Yusim* (Mind-Only), but only for a short period of time, from September to December of 1918, due to the lack of funds.[10] He served as an editor-in-chief of *Pulgyo* (Buddhism) from 1931 to 1933; and contributed articles to *Pulgyo* (*Sin*) (Buddhism: New Edition) from 1937 to 1940 and to *Sŏnwŏn* (Sŏn Collection) from 1931 to 1935.[11] He presented his reform ideas and Buddhist thought in those magazines.

While the *Chosŏn Pulgyo yusillon* focused exclusively on reforms of the saṅgha without mentioning state policies, Manhae later developed his reform ideas in response to Japanese policies on Buddhism.[12] He shared his insight with the Buddhist youth, providing leadership to them. In the 1920s young Buddhist clerics began to raise their voices against the "temple ordinance" and embarked on the Buddhist youth movement. They formed the Buddhist Youth Association in 1920 and its branch associations in local monasteries. They also formed the Buddhist Reformation Association as advocates of the Buddhist Youth Association in December 1921. During this time Manhae was incarcerated for his involvement with the March First Movement from 1919 to 1922. After his release from imprisonment, the Buddhist Youth Association elected Manhae to be its director in 1924, but by this time this association had become inactive. The secret Buddhist society, *Mandang* also sought advice and inspiration from Manhae by having him as its figurehead leader. Manhae embraced the major goals of these youth associations: the separation of religion and state with the abolition of the "temple ordinance"; centralization of the saṅgha administration; and the practice of *minjung Pulgyo*.

When Manhae took the job of editor-in-chief of the combined 84th/85th edition of Pulgyo in 1931, the content had changed drastically. The magazine contained articles that criticized the administration of the saṅgha and the colonial regime's intervention in Buddhist affairs. The frequent contributors were young clerics, most of whom had studied in Japan, such as Kim Pŏmnin, Kim T'aehŭp, Hŏ Yŏngho, Im T'aekchin, Kim P'ogwang, and Cho Chonghyŏn. The special centennial edition of 1932, in particular, was a comprehensive review of issues of Korean Buddhism, including government policies of religion, analysis of education and propagation reforms, financial reviews, Buddhist identity issues, and internal conflicts. Manhae also involved himself in the operation of the magazine, since the central administration office, Kyomuwŏn, refused to run it.[13] He ran *Pulgyo* until the 108th edition, issued in July 1933. After the 108th edition, *Pulgyo* was discontinued from 1933 to March 1937 because of financial difficulties and its disfavorable content, which was critical of the policies of both the saṅgha and the Japanese regime.[14] The clerics of Kyomuwŏn did not favor the criticism laid out by the articles of *Pulgyo*. The new edition of *Pulgyo*, *Pulgyo (Sin)* succeeded in 1937, and Manhae continued until 1940 to contribute articles but to a lesser degree.

Manhae considered the "temple ordinance" to be a major obstacle to Korean Buddhism and insisted on the self-management of the saṅgha. The "temple ordinance" forced the administration, the management of properties, and the whole system of the saṅgha to be under the Japanese regime's control. Manhae stressed that this violated the principle of the separation of religion and state, and ran counter to the spirit of the constitutions of many foreign countries. Even within the Korean peninsula, only Buddhism was under this law, so that the Buddhist community was subject to suspicion and disgrace. He further pointed out that the general public and other religions disdained Buddhism by the use of the term *kwanje Pulgyo* (bureaucratic Buddhism).[15] This term was used in a negative sense to mock the close ties between the saṅgha and the colonial regime. He insisted in 1920 that Buddhism should reorganize itself with *minjung*:

> Does Buddhism reside in monasteries? No. Does Buddhism reside in clerics? It does not, either. Does Buddhism reside in its canons? The answer is also "no." Buddhism resides indeed in every individual's mental awareness. There are many ways to recognize the dignity and insight of each person. I sincerely wish for Buddhism to reflect this great truth and make connections with the *minjung* and live with the *minjung* (*HYC* 2: 133).

Manhae argued that everything had to be changed for the *minjung*, including the doctrine, system, and properties of the saṅgha (*HYC* 2: 133-134). Buddhist doctrines and canons should be made easy and simple so as to be accessible to the *minjung*.[16] Buddhist institutions and properties had to be open to, and used for the benefit of, the *minjung*. In his article, "Record on the Reformation of Korean Buddhism" (Chosŏn Pulgyo kaehyŏk an) published in 1931, Manhae asserted that Buddhism should be involved in making secure the lives of the *minjung*. By investing Buddhist properties to run factories, the saṅgha could generate income to support the poor and the needy. By comparison, Manhae had previously proposed in the *Chosŏn Pulgyo yusillon* the same commercial operation of the saṅgha, but to achieve economic self-sufficiency of the saṅgha and thus enhance the status of Buddhist clerics. He later expanded the profit to the lay people, stating that the essential meaning of religion was to increase people's happiness.[17] He showed a pragmatic approach to religion. Like secular ideologies, such as Socialism and Capitalism, he believed that Buddhism should be functioning in the daily lives of people in addition to taking care of spiritual concerns. He defined *minjung Pulgyo* as follows:

> *Taejung Pulgyo* [*minjung Pulgyo*] means to practice Buddhism for *minjung*. Buddhists neither abandon human society nor deny close, loving relationships with people. They instead attain enlightenment through defilement and achieve nirvāṇa in the midst of the stream of life and death. Being aware of this truth and getting involved in action are the practices of *Taejung Pulgyo*.[18]

Thus, Buddhists should participate in social activities by establishing Buddhist libraries, welfare institutions for laborers and farmers, and educational facilities for the general public.[19] Manhae attempted to construct a socially sensitive Buddhism, letting Buddhist practices take root in a concrete place.

Manhae also pursued his initial ideas for the centralization of the saṅgha. In the *Chosŏn Pulgyo yusillon* he laid out two steps of the centralization: sectional unification (K. *kubun t'onghal*) and complete unification (K. *honhap t'onghal*).[20] The former was intended to accomplish partial centralization by establishing independent regional centers while the latter consisted of only one central system to govern the entire saṅgha. Manhae admitted that the thirty-one *ponsan* (main monastery district) system through the "temple ordinance" was a sort of *kubun t'onghal*. But he criticized the fact that each *ponsan* established its own independent system under its abbot. He argued that political intervention in Buddhist affairs was the main obstacle to unification. The separation of religion and state, that is, securing the independence of the saṅgha in its operation, was thus an ideal step for the unification of saṅgha.[21] He compromised, however, with the political situation in which no changes of colonial rules were attainable. Given that situation, he suggested the establishment of a central organ in the present system as an alternative:

> The unification of monasteries means to change the monastic system fundamentally by separating religion from the state. This will be the ultimate ideal form of unification. But until the ultimate stage is attained, the next best is to establish the central organization for the current monastic systems so that the saṅgha could perform its activities uniformly under the unified regulations.[22]

As a way to unify the saṅgha, Manhae supported the revision of temple laws (K. *sabŏp*). Manhae contends that the central organization of Korean Buddhism should have the power of appointing abbots and the temple law should be unified so that all monasteries in Korea follow the same policies.[23] Manhae envisioned that all main monasteries would have the same temple laws, which includes the establishment of the central organization and its related regulations.[24] The existing temple laws at the time limited the qualifications of main monastery abbots as follows: The candidates had to have the same dharma lineages with the majority of the main monastery clerics and had to be older than forty years. Manhae insisted that the election of abbots should include those who were qualified regardless of their lineages and who were younger, beginning at thirty years.

Manhae's reform ideas are primarily centered on the saṅgha reformation in order to secure the survival of the religion in a modern context. His later reform ideas were presented as a form of resistance against the state intervention. He tried to sever the saṅgha's dependence on the powerful and attempted to establish direct contact between the religion and the people. In this pursuit of self-government, unlike most other clerics, Manhae made clear his position toward the Japanese colonizers.

Manhae's reform activities, however, mainly consisted of writings and lectures. He was critical of the saṅgha reform policies, but failed to produce a grassroots movement of his own that would test his new ideas. His idea of *minjung* Buddhism was thus not carried out in any specific form in the Buddhist community.

The Integration of Sŏn and Kyo

Manhae finds the doctrinal basis for his Buddhist reform in two major principles of Buddhism. In his *Pulgyo yusillon*, he divided the quintessence of Buddhist teachings into two aspects: the principle of equality (K. *p'yŏngdŭng chuŭi*) and the principle of saving the world (K. *kuse chuŭi*) (*HYC* 2: 104). The principle of equality refers to the absolute, universal, and impartial nature of the Buddha and of truth. In this absolute point, both sentient and insentient beings have the Buddha-nature that has never been deluded by phenomenon. The latter *kuse chuŭi* refers to the compassion and vows of buddhas and bodhisattvas to save all beings from their suffering. Manhae interprets this principle of saving others in light of the principle of equality by building a dialectical tension between the two principles. Applying the fundamental nature of equality to a way of living, Manhae states that the major goal of Buddhism is to love and save all beings equally (*HYC* 2: 288). Similarly, Manhae emphasizes the non-dual aspect of "mind-only" (K. *yusim*); the mind (equality) includes the material world, and the mind is no different from matter. Mind and matter depend upon each other for their existence. The absolute truth and the phenomenal world are thus coexistent, making a harmonious whole. Manhae explains this dialectics of mind and matter as follows: "Buddhism is a way of transcending this world (K. *ch'ulsegan*), but it teaches us to transcend the world by entering the world, not by avoiding it" (*HYC* 2: 167). He argues that Buddhism is to be practiced through active participations in the society. One attains enlightenment through predicaments and achieves nirvāṇa without leaving behind the stream of life and death (*HYC* 2: 167). The salvation of one's own existence and a full scale engagement in the affairs in this world are to be fulfilled simultaneously.

By juxtaposing the principle of saving the world with the principle of absolute equality, Manhae was able to demonstrate social salvation as a fundamental principle of Buddhism not as its contingent aspect. Moreover, this juxtaposition aimed to prevent Buddhist social involvement from being affected by secular values by balancing the social involvement with the absolute truth. By bridging social salvation with existential freedom, Manhae was also able to offer a

Buddhist concept of social engagement, which was not to be misunderstood as a Buddhist imitation of Christian view of social engagement.

As a means of fulfilling the major goals of the principles of equality and of saving the world, Manhae presents an approach which unifies Sŏn (meditation training) and Kyo (Buddhist doctrines). Through meditation (Sŏn), Manhae emphasizes internal concentration, whereas through the doctrinal teachings, Manhae suggests the ideas for concrete social involvement. The absolute truth, for Manhae, lies in active social engagement, not in the practice isolated from society. In his vision, active involvement with society does not hinder existential freedom; instead, it renders each moment the perfect manifestation of the absolute. In this sense, the simultaneous practice of meditation and doctrines constitutes the core of Buddhism for Manhae. He writes:

> We cannot talk about Buddhism apart from Sŏn and Kyo, so that Sŏn/Kyo is Buddhism and Buddhism is nothing but Sŏn/Kyo. Sŏn (or meditation) is Buddhism's metaphysical truth; and *kyo* (or doctrinal teaching) is Buddhist teachings in writings. We acquire prajñā (wisdom) from the doctrinal teaching and samādhi (meditative concentration) from Sŏn. With the attainment of samādhi, we can reach nirvāṇa passing over the turbulent sea of life and death; and by doctrinal teaching we can acquire the wisdom of saving sentient beings (*HYC* 2: 168).

Manhae epitomized the entire Buddhist teachings into Sŏn and Kyo. Sŏn and Kyo are in dialectical tension, influencing one another. Sŏn provides the solid basis for the ultimate deliverance from entanglements while Kyo offers specific guidance on how to live together with others. Thus, Sŏn and Kyo constitute a complementary whole. Manhae states, "not depending upon words and letters" (Sŏn) is a way to see one's own nature and attain Buddhahood (*HYC* 2: 304). On the other hand, "not leaving behind words and letters" (Kyo) consummates one's nature and also provides a great means to save all beings. One should thus be able to see "words and letters" in Sŏn and attain Sŏn through "words and letters."

Unification of Sŏn and Kyo had been one significant agenda of major Buddhist thinkers in Korea before Manhae, including Pojo Chinul (1158–1210) and Ch'ŏnghŏ Hyujŏng (1520–1604). Chinul, a Sŏn apologist during the Koryŏ dynasty (918–1392), faced disharmony among the Buddhist practitioners who split themselves between Sŏn and Kyo. Chinul integrated Sŏn and Kyo from the point of Sŏn praxis. He introduced doctrinal understanding into Sŏn by advocating the sudden awakening/gradual cultivation (K. *ton'o chŏmsu*). Doctrinal understanding could spur the initial sudden awakening to the inherent Buddha-nature and thus help complete Sŏn training proper. This sudden/gradual schemata reconciled Sŏn with the teachings of the *Avataṁsaka Sūtra*. The fifty-two stages in the bodhisattva development became possible through the sudden awakening in the beginning of the path.[25] Due to the initial awakening to the mind-essence, this long process became bearable to practitioners who understood the non-dual aspects of practice and the realization of innate purity. Chinul's approach stemed from his concern for presenting a workable Sŏn soteriology to his fellow practitioners while coming up with a doctrinally-based rationale for this system. Chinul focused on the restoration of the proper sense of monastic order by establishing a concrete mode of praxis to which his fellow practitioners could resort.

Similarly, Hyujŏng, a leading Sŏn master during the Chosŏn dynasty, tried to harmonize Sŏn and Kyo in order to subdue the conflict between the two schools. He taught that both Sŏn and Kyo originated from the Buddha, "Sŏn being the Buddha's mind and Kyo his words."[26] Sŏn is a way to attain the ultimate state that is beyond words (enlightenment) by means of no-words, while Kyo is a way to reach the state through words. For Hyujŏng, Kyo is necessary to teach the differences of all dharmas to people of ordinary faculty before showing them the ultimate truth, that is, emptiness.[27] But Sŏn training, from the outset requires complete renunciation of Kyo, because Sŏn teaches one to see, at each thought-moment, one's own nature, which is beyond thought and understanding in words. Hyujŏng thus lay more significance on Sŏn than Kyo, encouraging the shortcut investigation of live-words (K. *hwalgu*), which are beyond the reaches of reason, meaning, mind, or words.[28] In contrast, he regarded Kyo as ratiocination in association with meaning, mind, and consciousness.

In comparison, Manhae's Sŏn and Kyo integration provided the doctrinal foundation for the unification movement of the saṅgha during the colonial period. The Korean saṅgha at the time struggled to establish a central organization. Manhae proposed a centralization of the saṅgha in order to utilize the human and financial resources of the institution. Equally important to Manhae was to bring about a socially viable Buddhism. However, Manhae was aware that, as Buddhism expands its interests to social problems and interacts with wider society, the dangers of secularization could increase. Hence, Manhae's emphasis on Sŏn practice was intended to counteract inner disturbances caused by such involvement in social activities.

Manhae defined Sŏn as a way to find out the nature of one's mind (*HYC* 2: 52–53). Once the mind is illuminated, all mysteries of life will be solved. If nothing blocks the brightness of the mind, the mind can reflect all objects on its surface in every detail. He further elaborated: "There is nothing but the mind, so that no independent, objective things could exist without any relation to the mind. Only the mind is able to give rise to the existence of history and myriad things in space. Nothing exists outside the mind" (*HYC* 2: 52). The mind is the key behind all things and troubles, and its cultivation thus reigns in Buddhist practice. The mind is accountable, Manhae believed, for every aspect of human life (*HYC* 2: 311). In order to lead a good life, one should cultivate the mind. Perceiving the mind from the absolute point of view, it is originally empty, being neither existent nor nonexistent (*HYC* 2: 312). From sentient beings's viewpoint, however, all dharmas are constantly arising and ceasing. Cultivating the mind is to preserve the original essence of emptiness. Manhae recommended Sŏn practice to people in every walk of life for the cultivation of the mind. He delineated Sŏn practice as follows: "Sŏn is neither religious faith nor the object of academic inquiry. It is something that no one can avoid practicing. It is an easy and necessary practice for everyone. It provides solid foundation for one's character, and it is a supreme hobby and an ultimate art on Earth" (*HYC* 2: 311). Manhae depicted Sŏn as an integral cultivation that provides a sense of completeness in human life. Sŏn is not only a means of salvation, but also provides a foundation for living without being entangled in the cycle of life and death.

Sŏn practice, Manhae stated, help practitioners not to be disturbed by any external circumstances (*HYC* 2: 318). The "real person" (K. *ch'am saram*) never loses the original self (K. *chin'a*) no matter what happens. The eye faculty is not affected by objects that it sees, and the ear faculty is not disturbed by sounds when it hears. Because of the power of samādhi, one is not agitated by any aspect of life, including sadness, irritation, or pleasure. Also, the mind is not swayed by either danger or comfort. Manhae epitomizes the spirit of Sŏn as follows:

> Sŏn [that I refer to] is not "dead Sŏn" (K. *sa-Sŏn*) that clings to quiet calmness. It is "live Sŏn" (I. *hwal-Sŏn*) that could make use of the Sŏn spirit: you soar as you please, and as you please you soar (K. *imun dŭngdŭng*). Sŏn can get rid of danger and fear, and it repels sorrow and pain. And it eventually leads one to transcend life and death (*HYC* 2: 317).

One enters into the world of life and death with the mind that has already overreached the boundary of phenomenon. There is no death to overcome because the adept has already died. Manhae mentioned that great-life (K. *taehwal*) is possible by great-death (K. *taesa*) (*HYC* 1: 240). A trivial life that has indulged in selfish desires is nothing but death. Life in a real sense begins when one disregards death. For Manhae, then, death, which is an experience of disregarding one's own self, paradoxically saves the life of the person. Accordingly, Manhae regarded Sŏn as the best form of art in the world.

For Manhae, Sŏn is the essence (K. *ch'e*) of Buddhism and Kyo, its function (K. *yong*); also Sŏn, to Manhae, implies sudden awakening (K. *tono*) whereas Kyo means gradual awakening (K. *chŏmo*) (*HYC* 2: 54). For Manhae, the mind is beyond the reach of human wisdom and thought. The only plausible way to gain access to the mind is to let the mind shine by itself by revealing its essence calmly. The mind is like muddy water: It will become clear as soon as one lets the dirt submerge by itself (*HYC* 2: 312). The mind is originally pure and calm, and yet it becomes like a burning house or hell because of deluded thoughts. As in the case of the water, the mind manifests its original nature only if one lets one's deluded thoughts calm down. However, deluded thoughts never stop if one wills to stop them, and even good thoughts adversely affect Sŏn practice.

While traditional Sŏn focused on individual liberation, Manhae extended the area of Sŏn practice beyond the religious pursuit of enlightenment. He brought Sŏn down to people's daily life. He believed that anyone could practice Sŏn, and that it is a necessary part of living. Sŏn could provide not only inward peace for this death-bound existence, but also give poise and courage for daily life. He coined the expression "live Sŏn" (K. *hwal-Sŏn*) in order to emphasize its active involvement in life; in contrast he called the meditation, when it seeks only an individual's inner quietude, "dead Sŏn" (K. *sa-Sŏn*). Manhae's main interest lay in the social functions of Sŏn. In comparison, traditional *kanhwa* Sŏn advocated "live words" to warn against the intellectual endeavor to attain awakening. The whole Buddhist thought of Manhae is directed to two major problems in life, namely existential and social sufferings. To Manhae, the salvation to this death-bound existence and the alleviation of social predicaments are coexistent.

Non-dual philosophy, seen in the *zhong* (center) and *pian* (off-center) of the Caodong school and the *li* (principle) and *shi* (phenomena) of the Huayan system, was an attempt to show the possibility of Buddhist practice in the temporal world. By positing the identity between the absolute and the relative, it propounds that Buddhist enlightenment is attainable without departing the social life. In other words, according to these doctrines, the temporal world could be the foundation of Buddhist practice. The ultimate goal of this non-dual world is enlightenment, which is beyond thought and conceptualization. This non-dual philosophy is not a way of improving and developing the social world. The social world, as it is, is a place for attaining enlightenment. Careless identification between this Huayan universe and the human world could thus create a potential danger of totalitarian and antinomian tendencies. The undifferentiated non-dual world does not discriminate between the natural world and the world of history. It could help maintain the status quo since anything could be acceptable under the rubric of non-duality.

Manhae attempted to resolve this impasse by introducing a value system into the world of enlightenment. Manhae drew social values—freedom, equality, and peace—from absolute equality. He interpreted absolute equality as being fundamentally free as he states: "What is the position of equality? It refers to truth [tathatā] which does not have any obstructions because it is free from time and space" (*HYC* 2: 44). Manhae translated this absolute sense of freedom and equality into social terms.[29] He regarded social equality as the social manifestation of tathatā. Manhae mentioned that contemporary liberalism and cosmopolitanism could have derived from the absolute truth (*HYC* 2: 44). As previously mentioned, by respecting the freedom of others as that of one's own, liberalism would epitomize the ideal of equality. Cosmopolitanism (K. *segye chuŭi*) would also reflect absolute equality by seeing the world as one house and all people as one's own brothers and sisters. It thus discourages competition and military conquest of other countries. The practice of social equality is possible by the realization of the absolute. In other words, for Manhae the fundamental awareness of the absolute is the key to social justice.

A value system, which is based on discrimination between higher and lower values, is not compatible with the world of enlightenment, which is beyond any traits of thought or judgment. The world of value, which is in the realm of thought, could go along with the world of enlightenment only with an attitude of no-self. Activities without ego consciousness are thus highly valued. For example, Manhae suggested "a man of purpose" (K. *chisa*) as an ideal type. The will and determination for social justice become feasible modes of life only because of the *chisa's* resolution. The *chisa's* determination goes beyond his own self-interests. The *chisa* makes a strong resolution for society and the country in place of his own well-being. Manhae idealized *chisa*:

> However treacherous mountains and waters may be, there is no place that could block *chisa* from going forward. However rapidly changing circumstances may be, there is no time period that could inhibit *chisa* from carrying out his work. The resolution itself becomes his time and space which are in turn his life and world. No hells, heavens, battleships, and weapons could obstruct his path (*HYC* 1: 224).

In order to live up to the resolution, this man of principle does not mind facing his own death, let alone temporary difficulties of life (*HYC* 1: 273). The principle never changes its course by selfish interests or external circumstances, including threats of death. Manhae noted that it is changed only by his own conscious, progressive decision. He compares this kind of person with a plum blossom that blossoms most beautifully amidst snow and bitter-cold wind (*HYC*, 2: 352). This ideal man, Manhae promotes, resembles in many ways the ideal figure of neo-Confucianism, which emphasizes the righteous ways of living. Manhae seemed to incorporate this Confucian belief into Buddhism in his exploration of the functioning of the absolute in concrete reality. With the attitude of no-self, no dangers, no personal adversities, or no destitution could inhibit that person's life. This lifestyle also epitomizes the bodhisattva ideal in which personal interests are dissolved into compassion for the suffered beings. Like the *chisa*, bodhisattvas make vows to rescue people in pain and danger, laying aside their egoistic pursuits.

Manhae thus envisaged an active mode of life. In order to realize the absolute equality in concrete social environments, Manhae contends that the mind should resist any social inequality and be willing to take risks in order to protect social justice:

> Liberty is the life of all beings and peace is the happiness of life. So a person without liberty is like a dead body and a person deprived of peace is the one who suffers the greatest pain. . . . Therefore, in order to obtain liberty and secure peace, one must regard life as lightly as a strand of hair and be willing to sacrifice (*HYC* 1: 346).

Needless to say, Manhae was critical of colonialism and militarism in addition to social inequalities, all of which he considered as counter to the values of liberty and equality. He opposed Japan's coercive annexation of Korea in the sense that, with the invasion, Japanese violated Korean people's rights for liberty and equality. He believed that relationship among nations as much as among individuals should be based on truth, not on exploitation, for the goal of the latter is a pursuit of power. Manhae focused much of his energy on the modernization and centralization of the saṅgha. At the same time, he criticized the saṅgha-centered operation, which resulted in heavy emphasis on monastic training of clerics at the expense of their social responsibilities. He encouraged active participation of lay Buddhists and interaction between clerics and laypeople with a hope that they can eventually work together on equal terms.[30] He published the *Pulgyo taejŏn* as a guidebook for lay Buddhists. The advocacy of *minjung* Pulgyo was also derived from his concern for the laity.

Conclusion

As a Buddhist reformer and philosopher, Manhae strove to solve two major problems doctrinally. First, he had to present a socially active Buddhism for the saṅgha so that Buddhism could survive the challenges of modernity. In this context, Manhae made a conscious effort to promote Buddhism's place in a society. Manhae realized that, with the traditional image of Buddhism as being aloof from society, the very existence of Buddhism became questionable in a country rapidly being westernized. As such, Manhae believed that Buddhism needed to demonstrate its utility in this process of modernization. His challenge was to show the social dimension of Buddhism as an essential part of the religion, not as its appendage. Social salvation needed to be in harmony with the existential salvation of the Buddhist tradition. This incorporation of the two also made social involvement uniquely Buddhist, not a mere imitation of Christianity. By connecting the two, he was hoping to ameliorate Buddhist lack of social concern and thus their lack of passion in social engagement.

Second, Manhae had to prevent the negative concomitants of the social engagement of Buddhist clerics. At first, Buddhist monks showed a reluctance to take full responsibility for social involvement, but once they became involved in social activities, they were easily affected by the worldly values of society. Their social involvement blurred the distinction between a religious career and a lay livelihood, and monkhood was thus becoming a worldly profession. As the clerics began to be affected by worldly values, the maintenance of a monastic community became questionable.

To resolve these two problems concurrently, Manhae proposed his unified philosophy of Buddhist teachings. Manhae presented the principle of equality and the principle of saving the world as the core of Buddhism. He attempted to place a social ethic within Buddhist teachings. He emphasized the principle of "saving the world" as a fundamental teaching of Buddhism, interpreting the absolute sense of equality and liberty in social terms. The absolute world of enlightenment thus became no different than its realization in the social world. Manhae encouraged Buddhist active social involvement to cure social ills and injustice, which he believed impeded the ultimate Buddhist goal of attaining enlightenment.

By establishing a dialectical tension between Sŏn and Kyo, Manhae incorporated social salvation into the Buddhist existential system. For Manhae, Buddhist social engagement cannot disturb their inner pursuit of salvation because, in both cases, Buddhist working principle is based on the doctrine of no-self and equanimity drawn from the absolute world of enlightenment. And Sŏn cultivation is a way through which the absolute manifests in the relative.

Notes

1. A version of this paper appeared under the title "A Korean Buddhist Response to Modernity: The Doctrinal Underpining of Han Yongun's (1879–1944) Reformist Thought," *Seoul Journal of Korean Studies* 20, no. 1 (2007): 21–44.

2. One example of this trend was: O Chaeyŏng, "Pulgyo po'gŭp e taehan ŭigyŏn" (My Thoughts on the Promulgation of Buddhism), *Haedong Pulbo* 7 (1914): 562–571.

3. Starting in the late nineteenth century, Korean Buddhists adopted the notion of "modernism" from Western liberalism. Korean intellectuals were heavily influenced by late-Qing intellectuals because of their shared political experiences as victims of colonialism. The "modern" thought of Yen Fu (1853–1921) and Liang Qichao, especially, had a great influence on Korean intellectuals and particularly Korean Buddhists regarding the notions of "modernization." These Chinese intellectuals advocated the concepts of Spencerian social Darwinism. Liberalism in this context was a movement that would create conditions allowing individuals to fulfill their own interests and perform to their utmost abilities. "Modernism" here meant constant evolution and progress in which only the fittest and the strongest survived. Most of initial reform ideas of the Korean Buddhists were presented along these lines. Benjamin Schwartz, *In Search of Wealth and Power: Yen Fu and the West* (Cambridge, MA: Harvard University Press, 1964), pp. 42–90.

4. The Japanese colonial government announced the "temple ordinance" in 1911 and placed Korean saṅgha under its direct control by making each of the 30 main monasteries an independent administrative system.

5. Han Yongun, "Siberia kŏch'ŏ Sŏul ro" (To Seoul via Siberia), *Han Yongun chŏnjip* (Collected Works of Han Yongun) I (Seoul: Shn'gu munhwasa, 1980), p. 255. Henceforth, this is indicated as *HYC* and marked in the text followed by volume and page numbers.

6. Han Yongun, "Pan chonggyo undong e taehayŏ," *HYC* 2: 279.

7. Ko Ŭn, *Han Yongun p'yŏngjŏn* (Seoul: Minŭmsa, 1975), pp. 140–141. The *Yinbinshi wenji* influenced Manhae in his writing of *Chosŏn Pulgyo yusillon.*

8. Beongcheon Yu, *Han Yong-un and Yi Kwang-su: Two Pioneers in Modern Korean Literature* (Detroit: Wayne State University Press, 1992), p. 182.

9. *Haedong Pulbo* 4 (1914): 325.

10. For the table of contents of *Yusim*, see *Pulgyo kwan'gye tosŏ mongnok* (Seoul: Taewŏnjŏngsa, 1986), pp. 258–259.

11. For the list of Buddhist journals during the Japanese occupation and their contents, see *Pulgyo kwan'gye tosŏ mongnok* pp. 207–279.

12. This is because the *Chosŏn Pulgyo yusillon* was completed in 1910 before the Japanese developed its religious policies.

13. Han Yongun, "Pulgyo sokkan e taehayŏ" (About the Continuation of the Publication of *Pulgyo*), *Pulgyo* (*Sin*) 1 (1937): 3–4, p. 3.

14. Han Yongun,"Pulgyo sokkan e taehayŏ," pp. 3–4.

15. Han Yongun, "Chŏnggyo rŭl pullip hara" (Do Separate Religion from Politics), *HYC* 2: 144–145; *Pulgyo* 87 (1931): 425.

16. We can see Socialist influence in the term *minjung* (the masses). Kang Man'gil of Koryŏ University notes that the first usage of *minjung* as the leading group of the nationalist movement appeared in Sin Ch'aeho's "The Declaration of the Korean Revolution" ("Chosŏn hyŏngmyŏng sŏnŏn sŏ") written in 1923. Kang infers that Sin's *minjung* may refer to the proletariat of the oppressed colonial nations in Asia. It is said that movements of peasants and laborers became rampant during the mid-1920s. Prior to Sin's usage, the term *minjung*, which appeared in the latter half of the nineteenth century, simply indicated the general populace. See Kang Man'gil, "Contemporary Nationalist Movements and the Minjung," in *South Korean's Minjung Movement: The Culture and Politics of Dissidence*, ed., Kenneth Wells (Honolulu: University of Hawai'i Press, 1995), pp. 32–34.

Buddhists used the concepts *minjung* and *taejung* interchangeably: *minjung* thus probably referred to wider range of people who are the governed in contrast to the governing. During the later parts of the 1920s, the term *minjung* seemed to have been used widely by society and also among Buddhists. In 1928, a monk stated that at that time no one failed to mention *minjung*: *Pulgyo* 43 (1928): 9. The term *minjung Pulgyo* was also used by the Buddhist counterparts in Japan. It was widely spread by the introduction of democracy during the Taishō era (1912–1925), referring to the larger segment of the general populace: Tamamuro Taijō, ed., *Nihon Bukkyō shi*, vol. 3 (Kyoto: Hozokan, 1967), pp. 399–406.

17. Han Yongun, "Chosŏn Pulgyo ŭi kaehyŏk an" (Record on the Reformation of Korean Buddhism"), *HYC* 2: 164–165; *Pulgyo* 88 (1931): 490–491.

18. Han Yongun, "Chosŏn Pulgyo kaehyŏk an," *HYC* 2: 167; *Pulgyo* 88 (1931): 492–493.

19. Han Yongun, "Chosŏn Pulgyo kaehyŏk an," *HYC* 2: 167; *Pulgyo* 88 (1931): 492-493.

20. Han Yongun, *Chosŏn Pulgyo yusillon*, *HYC* 2: 124-25.

21. Han Yongun, "Chosŏn Pulgyo rŭl t'ong'il hara" (Unify Korean Buddhism), *HYC* 2: 146–147; *Pulgyo* 84/5 (1931): 215–216.

22. Han Yongun, "Chosŏn Pulgyo rŭl t'ong'il hara," *HYC* 2: 147; *Pulgyo* 84/5 (1931): 216.

23. Han Yongun, "Chosŏn Pulgyo kaehyŏk an," *HYC* 2: 162; *Pulgyo* 88 (1931): 488.

24. Han Yongun, "Sabŏp kaejŏng e taehayŏ" (Regarding the Revision of Temple Laws), *HYC* 2: 150–151; *Pulgyo* 91 (1932): 3–4.

25. Robert E. Buswell, Jr., *Tracing Back the Radiance: Chinul's Korean Way of Zen* (Honolulu: University of Hawai'i Press, 1991), p. 51.

26. Hyujŏng, *Sŏn'ga kwigam*, *Han'guk Pulgyo chŏnsŏ* (Seoul: Tongguk taehak ch'ulp'anbu, 1984), 7: 635b. Hyujŏng quoted this phrase from Zongmi's Preface to the *Collections of the Origin of Various Chan Teachings* (*Chanyuan zhuquan jidu*) 1, *T* 2015.48.400b.10–11.

27. Hyujŏng, *Sŏn'ga kwigam*, *HPC* 7:636b.

28. Hyujŏng, *Sŏn Kyo kyŏl* (Secrets of Sŏn and Kyo), *HPC* 7:658a.

29. An Pyŏngjik, "Manhae Han Yongun ŭi tongnip sasang" (Manhae Han Yongun's Thoughts on Independence), in *Han Yongun sasang yŏn'gu* (Studies on Manhae's Thought), ed. Manhae Sasang Yŏn'guhoe (Seoul: Minjoksa, 1980), p. 73.

30. Han Yongun, "Chosŏn Pulgyo rŭl t'ong'il hara," *HYC* 2: 148; *Pulgyo* 84/5 (1931): 217.

3

Sot'aesan's Creation of Won Buddhism through the Reformation of Korean Buddhism

Bongkil Chung

This chapter attempts to clarify the relationship between Won Buddhism and Korean Buddhism by discussing (1) a history of the foundation of Won Buddhism, (2) Sot'aesan's reformation of Korean Buddhism, (3) the four platforms of Won Buddhist teaching, and (4) its central doctrines.

Historical Background

The root of Won Buddhism (K. Wŏnbulgyo) is traced back to a seven-year-old boy who wondered about the mystery of the world. The boy's name is Pak Chungbin (1891–1943), later known by his cognomen Sot'aesan. He was born to a poor family in a remote village with a tidal river running through mountains along the southwest coast of the Korean peninsula. As there was then no elementary school like that of today, there was no one to answer this inquisitive boy's questions concerning the mystery of nature. He was grabbed by such questions as why there arose clouds out of the blue sky, why his parents were so kind to each other, and so on. The only education he received was about two years of learning Chinese classics of the Confucian teaching.[1] If he had entered a Buddhist order as a Buddhist acolyte, he might have found answers to his questions. Instead, he tried to solve the questions by praying for about four years to a mountain god, who he was told could answer his questions. When he was fourteen, now married in accordance to the Korean tradition, his devotion to meet a mountain god, who had not responded to him after all, changed to a desire to meet an enlightened wizard who, as he learned from a Korean classical fiction, might offer answers to his questions. He met some alleged wizards only to find that they were not really enlightened mentors. Since his father passed away in 1910 leaving the household affairs with heavy debt on Pak's shoulder, the state of the household fell into destitution while he could not free himself from the insoluble doubts. By the time he reached age 25, his body was covered with blotches. He was regarded as a pitiful lost soul by the villagers.

It was at dawn on April 28, 1916, six years after Korea lost inpendence because of Japanese colonialism that, at age twenty-five, Pak Chungbin finally had an enlightenment experience and awakened from a long absorption. With this experience, Sot'aesan recovered his health with radiance on his countenance; his awesome appearance impressed his villagers so forcefully that he had over forty followers in a couple of months thereafter, most of them his seniors. He formed a body of ten members, choosing eight of them, but leaving the center position vacant, which was filled by his successor Song Kyu (1900–1962).[2] Sot'aesan gave a name to this ten member body, "the savings union," for the new life movement, which became the first order of the new religion he was about to establish. At the beginning, this order had nothing to do with Korean Buddhism.

Upon his enlightenment he had a precognition that human beings were in danger of being enslaved to the material power. He felt it urgent to strengthen the spiritual power of humankind in order to help protect them from the formidable material power. He believed that the only way for humans to enhance their spiritual power was by having faith in truthful religion and by cultivating sound morality. Thus, the motto with which he opened the new religious order was: "Since material power is unfolding, let us unfold the spiritual power accordingly." It goes without saying that his precognition was veridical, for the formidable power of material civilization has been threatening the very survival of human race.

In order to check his enlightenment against those of ancient sages, Sot'aesan perused some of the basic scriptures of Buddhism, Confucianism, Daoism, Ch'ŏndogyo, and Christianity.[3] Upon reading the *Diamond Sūtra*, Sot'aesan declared that Śākyamuni Buddha was the sage of all sages and that he would take the Buddha's teaching as the central tenet of the doctrine of the new religion he was planning to establish. He did so because he realized that the Buddha's teaching was the best in explicating the fundamental truth of the universe. However, he could not mention Buddhism to his disciples because Buddhism in Korea at that time had been ostracized for 500 years by the Chosŏn dynasty's national ideology of neo-Confucianism, and Buddhist monks were treated as the lowest of Korean society's eight low classes. Buddhism as practiced in Korean society at the time was not in a state to be the source for the spiritual power for the new era. Sot'aesan thus said, "When the world enters into the degenerate and troublesome era, a great savior sage comes of necessity with a truthful doctrine potent enough to rule the world, rectifies the world and harmonizes the spirit of mankind by redirecting the numinous power of heaven and earth" (*SS* 14: 1).

Because the spiritual lights of ancient sages had been dimmed for a long time, they were not bright enough for the spiritual darkness of the new era. Sot'aesan, however, incorporated some of the relevant tenets of the ancient sages into the doctrine of the new religious order, taking the Buddha-dharma as the central tenet. The doctrine of his new religious order should be simple enough for everyone to practice and yet potent enough for anyone to realize Buddhahood and nirvāṇa in this troubled world.

Before mentioning anything about Buddhism to his disciples, the young Sot'aesan accomplished two things as examples of a new religious life. First, in order to show the way of transforming the old world into a new one, Sot'aesan set up guiding precepts emphasizing diligence and frugality, abolition of empty formalities, doing away with superstition, and abstinence from alcoholic drink and smoking. Second, he ordered his nine disciples to erect an embankment to stop the sea water in front of his village so that the tidal land could be reclaimed as a farmland. In March 1918 he commenced the project and had it completed after one year of hard labor. Although the land reclaimed was only 25 acres, Sot'aesan set an example of the new religious life and created part of the financial foundation of the new religious order.

Upon completing the embankment project, he ordered his nine disciples to offer special prayers, saying that some ancient sages who wished to save the world had offered prayers to heaven and earth in order to obtain the authentication of their sincerity. The prayers began on the 26th day of the third month (lunar calendar) of 1919 and continued until October.[4] During that period there occurred a miraculous event. As there was no sign that the numinous spirits of heaven and earth were moved by their prayers until mid-August, Sot'aesan introduced the old saying, "One sacrifices oneself in order to preserve one's integrity." The nine disciples decided to sacrifice their lives for the well-being of all sentient beings. When they resolved to do so, their sincerity moved the numinous power of heaven and earth and they received the authentication of their sincerity with miraculous signs. As the nine disciples were about to leave for their prayer sites on the mountain tops where they planned to commit suicide at the same time, Sot'aesan saw nine bloody fingerprints under the nine names on the sheet of white paper where they had pressed their bare thumbs as the signature of acceptance of the injunction: "Sacrifice with no regret." Taking this sign as an authentication of their selfless devotion, Sot'aesan called them back and told them that they did not have to carry out their sacrifice because the numinous power of heaven and earth was moved by their selfless sincerity and devotion. This became the spiritual foundation of the new religious order and the standard of the Won Buddhist priesthood for future generations: A Won Buddhist priest ought to serve selflessly for the well-being of all sentient beings.

In the tenth month of 1919 with the dual foundations of the new religious order completed, Sot'aesan, together with a few disciples, moved to Pongnae

Cloister located on Mt. Pongnae, in Puan County, North Chŏlla Province. There he spent five years warding the enlightened mind, avoiding the public during the turbulent times, and crystallizing his ideas of the doctrine and system for the new religious order to be opened. In 1920 Sot'aesan announced the outline of the doctrine for the new religious order. Its contents consisted of two ways: the way man *qua* man ought to follow, and the way of moral cultivation.

In 1924 Sot'aesan temporarily rented Pogwang-sa in Iri (now Iksan). The tentative name of the order was Pulbŏp yŏn'gu hoe (The Society for the Study of Buddha-dharma). The name was used until the order was renamed Wŏnbulgyo (Won Buddhism) by his successor Song Kyu (1900–1962) in 1947, two years after Korea was liberated. In the autumn of 1924, two straw-thatched houses were built at Sinyong-dong, Iri, North Chŏlla Province, which marked the beginning of the construction of the general headquarters. This was eight years after Sot'aesan's great enlightenment. At the beginning of the construction, the communal life of the devotees began. The nine disciples as well as other disciples of the earlier years were mostly poor farmers; hence, their communal life during the construction was a continuation of poverty and hardship. However, they found their life rewarding as they were trained in the doctrine of the new religious order.

In 1935, the dharma hall, Taegakchŏn (Great Enlightenment Hall), was built in the precinct of the general headquarters, and *Irwŏnsang* (unitary circular form) was enshrined there as the symbol of the object of religious worship and the standard of moral cultivation. With the enshrinement of *Irwŏnsang,* Sot'aesan completed the foundation of the new religious order. With the new doctrine, Sot'aesan taught his disciples the way toward the realization of Buddhahood, and his disciples were sent to branch temples to introduce Sot'aesan's new religion to the public.

Reformation of Korean Buddhism

Sot'aesan's affinity with Śākyamuni Buddha and Buddhism goes back to the time of his enlightenment, although he attained it with no relationship to the Buddhist tradition. Not long after his enlightenment, the *Kŭmganggyŏng* (*Diamond Sūtra*) was introduced in his dream, which he consequently obtained from Pulgapsa, a Buddhist temple, and read it. Upon perusing the basic scriptures of other religions to check his enlightenment, he thought that his search for truth and essence agreed with that of the Buddha, and he declared that Śākyamuni Buddha is the sage of all sages. Sot'aesan made up his mind to take the Buddha-dharma as the central tenet of the doctrine of the new religion he was establishing. He was aware of the condition of Korean Buddhism after five centuries of persecution by the Chosŏn dynasty's pro-Confucian national ideology. He thought, nevertheless, that the best way to save the world was hidden in Buddha-dharma, but in order to have more relevance for the secular world, its method of edification should be reformed. He declared categorically that Buddha-dharma is superior to any other ethico-religious system (*CN*, pt. 1, chap. 2). He made it clear to his disciples in the inchoate stage of the order that what should be learned, taught, and practiced in his new religious order was Buddha-dharma. He made this declaration when the general populace of the Korean society had been following the Confucian morals for five centuries and when any Buddhist idea was a taboo in the society. However, he was clearly aware of the necessity to reform Korean Buddhism if it was to be used as a means to deliver sentient beings.

While staying at Pongnae Cloister, Sot'aesan exchanged his ideas for Buddhist reformation with Buddhist monks. In 1920, he drafted the *Chosŏn Pulgyo hyŏksillon* (Treatise on the Renovation of Korean Buddhism), which was published in 1935. The *Chosŏn Pulgyo hyŏksillon* contains the following seven themes: (1) past Korean society's opinion of Buddhism, (2) the lifestyle of Korean monks, (3) the wisdom and ability of the Buddha Śākyamuni, (4) from foreign Buddhism to domestic Buddhism, (5) from the Buddhism for minority to that for majority, (6) unifying the separated Buddhist curricula, and (7) from the Buddha-statue worship to Irwŏnsang (unitary circular form) worship. When the *Pulgyo chŏngjŏn* (The Correct Canon of Buddhism) was published in 1943, *Chosŏn Pulgyo hyŏksillon* was included as the part one of this scripture.[5] The following is the core of Sot'aesan's reform agenda as discussed in the *Chosŏn Pulgyo hyŏksillon*:

> The doctrine and system of traditional Buddhism were structured mainly for the livelihood of the bonze priests and, hence, were unsuitable for those living in the secular world. Accordingly, the laity was not of primary but of secondary importance, so that none of the laity could stand in the lineage of the direct disciples of the Buddha or enter as a patriarch except for those who made an unusual material contribution, or attained extraordinary spiritual cultivation. The aim of a religion lies in delivering sentient beings; however, the Buddhist temples are located in deep mountain valleys remote from the secular world. How could people, busy with secular life, leave the mundane life behind in order to find the leisure for learning Buddha-dharma? The Buddhist scriptures are written in Chinese compound words and nouns which are too difficult to understand and learn, and too difficult to teach to the public, learned or ignorant, men or women, old or young. As the Buddhist monks, having no occupation of scholar-officials, farmers, artisans, or merchants, depended on the laity's offerings to the Buddha statue, donations, and alms for food and clothing, this life style could not be for the public. Monks were

strictly prohibited from marrying. They articulated various forms for Buddhist offering, but did not provide the rules of rite and propriety for the secular world. Thus, the livelihood of the monks cannot be followed by the public. In this order, therefore, these matters shall be reformed.

(1) There shall be no discrimination between priesthood and laity as to the question of primary and secondary status; distinctions will only be recognized in the degrees of practice and public service.

(2) There will be no discrimination between priesthood and laity in the lineage of Dharma succession.

(3) The temples for Buddhist cultivation shall be established wherever the laity resides.

(4) The scriptures shall include only the most essential ones, and be written in an easy language that the public can learn.

(5) Priests shall be allowed to have suitable occupations in accordance with circumstances.

(6) Marriage of the priests shall be left to the wish of each priest.

(7) Complicated and useless formalities shall be abolished from the rituals of Buddhist offering and the new rules of rite shall be formulated with emphasis on realistic rituals that will be appropriate and useful to the secular life.

(8) As to the course of a priest's life, one shall acquire, except for special circumstances, general education during childhood, train oneself in practice, and exert oneself for the work of deliverance during the prime of life. During senescence one will stay in a scenic and quiet place, severing the worldly attachments of love and desire, and meditating and drilling oneself to become emancipated from the grave matter of birth and death. In spring and autumn, the old priest will visit temples, one after another, and in the secular world render help in the task of deliverance. In winter and summer one will concentrate on spiritual cultivation [sitting in meditation and intoning the name of Buddha]. In this way the life of the priest can be well rounded, lacking nothing.[6]

Sot'aesan said that the order, which will execute this doctrine and system, shall be made perfect for the times and the public morals (*SS* I: 18). In his view, the subjects taught in the traditional Buddhist sects were not comprehensive enough because each sect was focusing exclusively on one of the following: (a) scriptures, (b) *kanhwa* meditation,[7] (c) intoning the name of a Buddha, (d) incantation, or (e) Buddhist offering. Sot'aesan emphasized the need to integrate different practice method for a Buddhist practice to be complete.

> The laity must learn all of these subjects. Traditionally, different sects attached themselves to one or two of them with partial practice, arguing against one another, thus, impeding the faith and practice of the believer. Our intention is to integrate all these practices under one soteriological principle after we examine all *kongan*s [public documents] of the Zen school and all scriptures of the doctrinal schools. Leaving out the complicated *kongan*s and scriptures, we will choose as follows. As the training subjects for attaining the power of inquiry into facts and principles, those *kongan*s and scriptures which explicate the most essential principles of Buddha-dharma will be used. As the training subjects for spiritual cultivation, intoning the name of Buddha, sitting in meditation, and incantation will be used. And as the training subjects for careful choice in *karmic* action, a number of precepts, explanations of the principle of *karmic* retribution, and the moral duties to the fourfold beneficence [*CN* pt. 2, chap. 2], which are suitable for secular living, will be used (*SS* I: 19).

The Four Mottoes of Reformation

The main points of reformation were expressed in four mottoes in the frontispiece of the *Pulgyo chŏngjŏn*: 1. Everywhere is the Buddha-image. Do all things as making an offering to Buddha. 2. Timeless Zen and placeless Zen. 3. Maintain One Suchness in motion and at rest. Perfect both soul and flesh. 4. Buddha-dharma is daily life; daily life is Buddha-dharma. These mottoes clearly represent the direction of Sot'aesan's reformation.

1. Everywhere is the Buddha-image (K. *ch'ŏch'ŏ pulsang*). Do all things as making an offering to Buddha (K. *sasa pulgong*).

The first motto reflects Sot'aesan's spirit of a drastic change of the Buddhist religious worship. For Sot'aesan, all things in the universe are manifestation of the cosmic body of Dharmakāya Buddha, which he categorized as the fourfold beneficence (heaven and earth, parents, brethren, and laws) and as the ultimate source of life. To a disciple's question concerning the difference between the worship of the statue of the Buddha and that of *Irwŏnsang* Sot'aesan answered,

> The worship of the statue of the Buddha, being limited to his personality, has no more significance than the commemoration and

> veneration that we, as late disciples, pay to him; whereas the worship of *Irwŏnsang* has a great significance. Instead of limiting the object of worship to the personality of the Buddha, we treat and worship all things in the universe as the Buddha and seek thereby the source of blessings and punishment in them. Furthermore, one should cultivate one's personality to be as perfect as *Irwŏnsang* by taking it as the standard of practice. In general these are the differences (*SS* II: 12).

This view of Sot'aesan is not completely new in Buddhist tradition. In the metaphysics of Huayan Buddhism it is referred to as Vairocana Buddha, which is identified with the universe itself.[8] Thus, by such a motto, the traditional Buddhist ritual of making an offering to the Buddha statue for blessings is abolished and a new way of receiving Buddha's blessing is suggested as, in Sot'aesan's view, everything in the universe is the manifestation of the cosmic body of Buddha, and everything has the power and authority to bless or punish. More realistic and practical ways of making offerings to living Buddhas are spelled out in terms of awareness and requital of the fourfold beneficence to which one owes one's existence. Sot'aesan shows his disciples an example of effective Buddha offerings in the following episode.

One day, while Sot'aesan was residing at Pongnae Cloister, an old couple passed by and said that they were on their way to Silsangsa to make an offering to the Buddha statue in the temple so that their daughter-in-law, ill-natured and extremely unfilial to them, might be changed for the better. Hearing this, Sot'aesan said, "You know that you will be helped if you make an offering to the Buddha statue, but you don't know that you will be better helped by making offerings to a living Buddha" (*SS* II: 15). The couple asked, "Where is the living Buddha?" Sot'aesan said, "Your daughter-in-law in your home is a living Buddha. She is the one who has the authority to be filial or unfilial to you. So, why don't you try to make an offering of worship to her first?"[9] The couple returned home and did as was advised. Their daughter-in-law changed herself to be very filial to them. So, the old couple paid a visit to Sot'aesan and expressed heartfelt appreciation. Sot'aesan said to his disciples beside him, "This is an example of the realistic worship of Buddha offered directly to the actual source of misery and blessedness" (*SS* II: 15). In Sot'aesan's view the new era needs a new form of Buddhism that can be of true service to the realization of a limitless paradise in the mundane world.

2. Timeless Zen and Placeless Zen. (K. *musisŏn much'ŏsŏn*)

With this motto Sot'aesan intended to secularize the secret teaching of Zen, making it relevant to the daily life of the laity in rural and urban areas. One should maintain the Zen mind anytime and anywhere, aiming at realizing enlightenment in daily mundane life. What is assumed in this practice is that in one's mind is hidden the original enlightenment covered up with defilement. Hence, by practicing Zen, one can see into one's own nature of the enlightenment, or what Chinul (1158–1210) called "the mind-essence of void and calm, numinous awareness." There are still unsettled controversies over whether one can ever experience enlightenment without years of strenuous Zen practice, whether enlightenment comes gradually or suddenly, and whether one can finish cultivation of mind suddenly or gradually after enlightenment.[10] Sot'aesan's view on this issue is as drastic as his view on the object of Buddhist worship: He claims that, from now on, awakening to one's own nature will be practiced at home (*SS* VII: 23). As the essence of Zen practice in daily life, he should be able to maintain concentration (*samādhi*), wisdom (*prajñā*), and morality (*śīla*) to balance the disturbance, delusions, and errors, respectively, as they arise in one's mental spheres (*CN* pt. 3, chap. 1). This is Sot'aesan's way of putting into practice the three aspects of *Dharmakāya* of one's own nature as taught by Huineng in the *Platform Sūtra*.[11]

3. Maintain One Suchness in motion and at rest (K. *tongjŏng iryŏ*). Perfect both soul and flesh (K. *yŏngyuk sangjŏn*).

With this set of mottoes Sot'aesan aimed at correcting the ills of the traditional religious mind by requiring the Buddhist practitioners to maintain One Suchness of Buddha's enlightened mind not only in quiet mountain valleys but also in the noisy, hustling, and bustling urban life. It also requires the practitioner to improve both spiritual and physical life in good balance. This requirement implies a sharp criticism of the century-old Buddhist saṅgha system, reminding one of Baizhang's (720–814) rules, "A day without work—a day without eating."[12] In Sot'aesan's view, this rule should be applied in the secular world that suffers from the moral defilement of greed, hatred, and delusions. He encouraged his followers to eliminate poverty, ignorance, and disease by having a sound occupation while putting the doctrine into practice in daily life. He exemplified the spirit of these mottoes when he performed a year of hard labor on the embankment project. This happened even before he mentioned anything about Buddhism to his disciples. By having his followers take a daily vow to maintain and use their mind and body perfectly, Sot'aesan placed utmost importance on the balanced perfection of the mental and physical life.

4. Buddha-dharma is daily life (K. *pulbŏp si saenghwal*); daily life is Buddha-dharma (K. *saenghwal si pulbŏp*).

In this set of mottoes, too, Sot'aesan shows his intention to make Buddha-dharma relevant to the daily life in the secular world. Sot'aesan believed that Buddhism offers a very effective cure for the ills of the world in general and

Korean society in particular. The cause of the human predicament, individual or collective, ultimately lies in the three poisonous elements of human mind, viz., greed, anger, and delusion. These poisons can be best removed by Buddha-dharma. One's knowledge of Buddha-dharma, no matter how extensive it may be, will be of no use unless one can realize its goals in daily life as an individual, a member of a family, a society, a state, and the world. While Confucianism was concerned exclusively with the importance of the secular world of human affairs, Buddhism was concerned with its unimportance, which became one cause for the neo-Confucians in China and Korea to judge Buddhism as evil teachings. Envisioning a new era, Sot'aesan was as much concerned with the importance of the mundane world as Confucius, saying that benevolence and righteousness are the main principles of morality (*SS* I). To most people in Korea during Sot'aesan's time, Buddhism fell short of offering social norms, whereas, Confucianism had been the dominant culture for centuries. By emphasizing these four mottoes, Sot'aesan demonstrated that Buddhism for the new world should be different from the Buddhism practiced by monks and nuns in the remote mountain valleys. In Sot'aesan's view, Buddhism and Confucianism can be synthesized into a sound religious and moral system. This can be seen from Sot'aesan's response to a new Confucian convert who was worried about the Confucian masters' condemnation of Buddha-dharma. He said,

> It was the Buddha's original intention to open the gate of deliverance for innumerable parents and children throughout his many incarnations for many *kalpas*. It has occasionally happened, however, that his later disciples did things against his original intentions. You do not have to worry about abnegation of parents and sovereignties since the future doctrine will be made suitable for the times so that faith in Buddha-dharma will improve family life as well as social and national affairs. . . . However, if you end up with emptiness and ultimate quiescence, you cannot become a superior man of the way. In order to practice the perfect and great way, you should be able to apply the truth to all human affairs, taking emptiness and ultimate quiescence as the substance of the way, and *ren* (benevolence), *yi* (righteousness), *li* (propriety), and *zhi* (wisdom) as its function."[13]

The attempt to synthesize Buddhism with Confucianism was not new in Buddhist tradition. Zongmi (780–841), for instance, argued that the five Confucian constant virtues of *ren* (benevolence), *yi* (righteousness), *li* (propriety), *zhi* (wisdom), and *xin* (trustworthiness) are just the Buddhist five precepts of no killing, no stealing, no adultery, no lying, and no drinking wine and eating meat, respectively.[14]

The Four Platforms

The goal of Sot'aesan's new religion lies in "deliverance of sentient beings" and "curing the world of moral ills." The whole doctrine of Won Buddhism is structured as a means to the realization of these two goals. For the former, Sot'aesan adopts some elements of Buddha-dharma and Daoist practice, and for the latter, those of Confucianism, through a creative synthesis, which he used to form a new religious doctrine. Sot'aesan expressed his plan for a grand synthesis of the three East Asian religions as follows:

> In the past, the founders of various religions came in accordance with the call of the times and taught what humankind ought to do. However, the doctrines with which they edified people varied depending on the times and districts. . . . Buddhism takes as its central tenet the emptiness of the ultimate reality of all things in the universe and teaches the truth of neither arising nor ceasing and the causal law of karmic retribution. Thereby, Buddhism mainly explicates the path for changing the deluded into the enlightened. Confucianism takes as its main tenet the reality of all things in the universe and teaches the three duties, the five human relations, the four constant virtues of benevolence [*ren*], righteousness [*yi*], propriety [*li*], and wisdom [*zhi*]. Thereby, it mainly explicates the ways of personal moral cultivation, regulation of household affairs, governing a state, and realizing peace in the world. Taoism takes as its main tenet the way of naturalness manifested in all things in the universe and teaches how to nourish one's nature. It thereby explicates the path of purity, tranquility, and not doing unnatural things. Now, these three paths are different from one another in what they take as the essence of their doctrines; however, they agree in their purposes, namely, to correct the ills of the world and help all sentient beings. . . . In the future the world cannot be delivered by any one of them, hence we intend to unify the three doctrines (*SS* II: 1).

However, Sot'aesan made it very clear that the Buddha-dharma should be the central doctrine of his new religious order. He said,

> From now on, what we should learn is Buddha-dharma and what we should teach our followers is Buddha-dharma. . . . If the fundamental truth is to be discovered and if sentient beings are to be led to the gate of blessings and wisdom through correct practice, then Buddha-dharma should be taken as the main doctrine. Moreover,

> Buddhism will be the major religion of the world. However, the Buddha-dharma of the future will be different from that of the past. The Buddha-dharma of the future will be practiced by all walks of life. . . . The worship of the Buddha shall not be limited to taking refuge in the statue of the Buddha. One will realize that all things in the universe and the dharma realm of empty space are none other than the Buddha. Buddha-dharma will not be separated from daily work. . . . The ritual of making offerings to Buddha for blessing should be reformed so that Buddha and place for making offerings are not set aside in a particular place; they are wherever one works and wishes for blessings (*SS* I: 15).

Sot'aesan's attempt to bring Buddha-dharma from the mountain valleys to the urban and rural areas needed a clear doctrinal structure that was simple but potent enough to save the sick world. Thus the doctrine of the new religious order he was establishing was to be used as a means to the dual goals of "delivering the sentient beings" and "curing the world of its illness." The first goal is to be achieved by the tenet of the religion of self-reliance and the second by that of the other-power. The essence of the former is correct enlightenment and right practice, and that of the latter is awareness of beneficence and its requital. Thus, the whole doctrine of Won Buddhism is structured to provide for the ways to realize these goals. The general direction of the Won Buddhist religious faith and practice is outlined in the following four platforms (*CN* pt. 1, chap. 3).

The first is "Correct Enlightenment and Right Practice" (K. *chŏnggak chŏgnhaeng*). This platform requires one to be enlightened to one's own nature or Buddha-nature as symbolized in the circular form, *Irwŏnsang*, so that one can practice the dharma correctly in using one's body, mouth, and mind. It is also the mind-seal that buddhas and patriarchs correctly transmit from one to the other. It is presupposed in this injunction that one's mind creates a paradise or a hell depending on whether or not one is enlightened to one's own Buddha-nature. Sot'aesan accepts the Mahāyāna Buddhist tenet that the whole world is the creation of one's own mind (*SS* II: 27). In his view, the cause of suffering lies in the deluded mind of sentient beings. Thus, correct enlightenment and right practice is a necessary condition for delivering sentient beings from suffering. The way of correct enlightenment and right practice is spelled out in the tenets of *Irwŏnsang* and the threefold practice (*CN* pt. 2, chaps. 1 and 4).

The second of the four platforms is "Awareness and Requital of Beneficence" (K. *chiŭn poŭn*). This platform requires one to be aware of and requite the fourfold beneficence (heaven and earth, parents, brethren, and laws) to which one owes one's existence. This reflects Sot'aesan's prescription to cure the world of ills and the essence of the Won Buddhist religious faith. In Sot'aesan's view, the main cause of social ills is resentment and grudges among individuals, families, societies, and nations. The cause of resentment in turn lies in the ignorance of one's indebtedness to the sources of one's existence: the universal beneficence of the cosmic Buddha body (*Dharmakāya* Buddha). Since the world full of resentment is a hell, and conversely a world full of gratitude is a paradise, Sot'aesan expounded the doctrine of beneficence, in which is explained how one is indebted to the fourfold beneficence and how one should requite them. Since the cosmic Buddha body (*Dharmakāya* Buddha) is none other than the essence and the fundamental sources of the fourfold beneficence to which one owes one's existence, one should requite their beneficence with the spirit of making an offering to the Buddha. This is the heart of the Won Buddhist religious worship (*CN*, pt. 2, chap. 2; pt. 3, chap. 10).

The third platform is called "Practical Application of Buddha-dharma" (K. *pulbŏp hwaryong*). It requires one to make practical applications of Buddha-dharma in daily life so that the Buddha-dharma can be made relevant to the secular world as expressed in the motto: "Buddha-dharma is daily life; Daily life is Buddha-dharma." Sot'aesan's central idea of Buddhist practice lies in the dictum that one should peruse many teachings only to enlighten the One Mind in one's own nature (*SS* VII: 5). For this purpose, Sot'aesan proposed a combined training of Zen meditation, chanting, and study of basic Buddhist scriptures and treatises. The goal of this guidline is to make Buddhism available to the general public, as he states:

> The teachings of the Buddha embody supreme truth. As the truth and expediencies of his teachings are boundless, numerous Buddhist priests of high virtue have taken them as the basis of their schools and sects of Buddhism thereby opening the gates of propagation and teaching countless people. . . . The Buddhist system in particular was mainly formed for the life of monks in a monastic order and was not suitable for people living in the secular world. Anyone who wished to be a true Buddhist under such a system, had to ignore one's duties and obligations to the secular life and give up one's occupation. Under such a system, the Buddha-grace, no matter how good Buddha-dharma may be, cannot reach the numberless sentient beings of the world. How could such a system be the great and perfect way? (*CN* pt. 1, chap. 2)

The last platform states "Selfless Service for the Public" (K. *mua ponggong*). This platform advocates altruism, the ideal of bodhisattvas who find the true meaning of existence only in delivering sentient beings from suffering. Sot'aesan suggested four essentials for social ethics (*CN* pt. 2, chap. 3). In order to be of any service to the public one should first not be a burden to anyone. Thus, the first of the four essentials for social reformation requires one to cultivate self-reliance. For the well-being of the public, one should be ready to follow the lead of the wise; hence, the second of the four essentials requires one to follow the lead of the wise ones. The third requires one to practice the spirit of universal education, encouraging one, if possible, to educate the children of others who are without resources for education. The fourth is to develop the public spirit by duly honoring those who selflessly dedicate themselves to the public well-being. For the general well-being, it is not enough for the state and laws to punish those who cause pains to the public; it should produce as many altruists as possible. These are the four essentials for social reformation, and they constitute prerequisites for the realization of the ideal, selfless service for public well-being (*CN* pt. 2, chap. 3).

The Central Doctrines

In January 1943, Sot'aesan released the doctrinal chart and said, "the quintessence of my teaching lies herein; but how many can understand the true essence of my intention?" (*SS* XV: 7). The doctrinal chart that Sot'aesan himself composed as printed in the *Pulgyo chŏngjŏn* provides a bird's-eye view of the structure of the central doctrine of new Buddhism for the new era. However, the doctrinal chart in the *Wŏnbulgyo kyojŏn* (Scriptures of Won Buddhism) (1962) is significantly different from Sot'aesan's original composition. The alteration through the redaction process is comparable to a bungled arrangement of a musical masterpiece.[15] The alteration was done against Sot'aesan's warning, "In the doctrine I have formulated, the fundamental principles of the doctrine with *Irwŏn* as the essence, viz., threefold practice and eight articles, and fourfold beneficence, shall not be altered in any country and at any time. However, the remaining sections and systems may be changed to fit the times and the country" (*SS* XV: 16).

In the doctrinal chart can be seen a circular form, *Irwŏnsang*, like the head of a turtle and the four platforms as four legs supporting the central doctrine spelled out in three columns of a rectangle (the back shell). In the middle column is expressed the meaning of *Irwŏnsang*. In the left column is spelled out the path of practice approaching *Irwŏnsang*; on the right is shown the path of faith in *Irwŏnsang*.

The meaning of *Irwŏnsang* is that it is *Dharmakāya* Buddha, the noumenal nature of all beings in the universe, the mind-seal of all buddhas and sages, and the Buddha-nature of all sentient beings. Sot'aesan expressed its ontological principles as a *gāthā*: "Being turns into nonbeing and nonbeing into being, turning and turning; then both being and nonbeing are ultimately void, yet the void is also complete."

The path of practice aims at perfecting the three aspects of *Dharmakāya* of one's own nature, viz., precepts (*śīla*), concentration (*samādhi*), and wisdom (*prajñā*), which are achieved by following, nourishing, and seeing the nature, respectively. Sot'aesan's method of achieving them is by the practice of careful choice in karmic action, cultivation of spirit, and enquiry into facts and principle, respectively. Prerequisites for the threefold practice are faith, zeal, doubt (*ŭi*), and devotion. The threefold practice is pursued by timeless Zen, the fundamental principle of which is: When the six sense organs are free from work, cultivate One Mind by eliminating worldly thought; and when they are at work, cultivate justice and forsake injustice.

The path of faith in *Dharmakāya* Buddha is approached through the requital of four beneficences of heaven and earth, parents, brethren, and laws to which one owes one's existence. The essence of the Won Buddhist ethics lies in following the general principles of beneficence requital, which are the ways of no thought after rendering favors, of protecting the helpless, of benefiting oneself by benefiting others, and of doing justice and forsaking injustice, respectively. Making offerings to Buddha is none other than requiting the four beneficences.[16] Thus, the whole doctrine of Won Buddhism is epitomized in terms of *Dharmakāya* Buddha, *Irwŏnsang*, the threefold practice, and the fourfold beneficence.

In Sot'aesan's view, various names are used to refer to what the circular form *Irwŏnsang* does. This can be seen in his answer to a question concerning the relationship between *Irwŏnsang* and humanity.

> *Irwŏnsang* is enshrined in this order in a similar way as the statue of the Buddha is enshrined in the traditional Buddhist order. However, the statue of the Buddha is the symbol of the Buddha's bodily appearance, whereas *Irwŏnsang* is the symbol of the essence of the Buddha's mind. The bodily appearance is merely a doll, whereas the essence of mind, being vast, great, and infinite, includes both being and nonbeing and penetrates the three periods of past, present and future. It is the fundamental source of all things in the universe and the realm of samādhi that cannot be expressed in words. It is called *Tai-chi* [the great ultimate] or *Wu-chi* [the ultimate of nonbeing] in Confucianism; Nature, or *Tao* [the Way] in Taoism; and pure *Dharmakāya* Buddha in Buddhism. However, one and the same principle is called by these different names. No matter which of these directions one takes, one will eventually return to the truth of *Irwŏn* (*SS* II: 3).

This view is not new with Sot'aesan; for Yefu's (1127–1130) *Yuanxiang song* (Eulogy to the Circular Form) includes the same idea.

> . . . Of all the dharmas, pure or impure, in the four dharma realms of three worlds, not a single dharma arises outside of this circle. In

> Chan it is called the first phrase; in *jiao* (scriptural teaching) it is called the pure dharma realm. Among the Confucians it is called *taiji*, the one pervading substance; in Taoism the mother of all things under heaven. In truth, all these names refer to this. So someone in the past said of this: "Before the birth of past Buddhas existed one circle; even Śākyamuni could not understand it, how could Kāśyapa transmit it"?[17]

Whether Sot'aesan read this is not known; however it is highly probable that he might have read this version of the *Diamond Sūtra*, to which he was introduced in his dream after the enlightenment. The circular symbol, *Irwŏnsang*, is well-known because it was used as the Mind-seal in the Guiyang sect of Chan Buddhism. Nanyang Huizhong (675–775), one of the five chief disciples of the Sixth Patriarch Huineng (638–713), is said to have used the perfect sign for the first time as the sign of the nature of the enlightened mind.[18] In Korea, the circular symbols were introduced by Sunji (fl.858), who studied under Yangshan Huiji (803–887) in China, cofounder of the Guiyang sect of the classical Chinese Chan tradition.[19] What is new with Sot'aesan is the idea to make it the object of religious worship and the standard of practice, abolishing the practice of the Buddha statue worship. Furthermore, the *Irwŏnsang* doctrine in Won Buddhism has its root in Sot'aesan's enlightenment in 1916. Sot'aesan asked his disciple Chŏngsan to compose a verse using two Chinese characters meaning "one" and "circle." Chŏngsan composed two lines: "The noumenal essence of all things is unitary; the whole universe is an immense circle."[20] In August 1919, Sot'aesan drew a circle on the door lintel in a room of Kŭmsansa as the symbol of the truth to which he was enlightened.

This does not mean that Sot'aesan severed himself from the Buddhist tradition. To the question of which of the traditional buddhas in the line of the dharma transmission was his ancestral master, Sot'aesan answered, "Though we are at the juncture of transition from the old to a new era, Śākyamuni Buddha is my ancestral master" (*SS* VI: 21). Moreover, he had *Irwŏnsang* enshrined as the symbol of Mind-Buddha (K. *simbul*), which can be seen in the title: "The Details of Mind-Buddha *Irwŏnsang* and Vow."[21] In the canonized version "the Mind-Buddha" has been replaced with "*Dharmakāya* Buddha" (K. *pŏpsinbul*). *Irwŏn* (unitary circle) and *Irwŏnsang* (unitary circular form) have been used without due distinctions in the scriptures of Won Buddhism causing significant confusion. However, Sot'aesan made it very clear at least once, "However, I do not mean that the senseless *Irwŏnsang* drawn on the wood-board owns such truth, power, and the way of practice. *Irwŏnsang* is a model that is used to let you know the true *Irwŏn*; this is analogous to when you point at the moon with your finger, the latter is not the former. Hence, the practitioner must discover the true *Irwŏn* by means of *Irwŏnsang*."[22] However, what Sot'aesan means by "true *Irwŏn*" remains a question unless it is just another name of *Dharmakāya* Buddha.

It is noteworthy that *Irwŏnsang* was enshrined in 1935 in the Dharma halls, that Chŏngsan wrote the essay "On *Irwŏnsang*" (Irwŏnsang e taehayŏ) in 1936, and that Sot'aesan wrote the "Vow to *Irwŏnsang*" in 1937. In Chŏngsan's essay, the central tenets of the doctrine of Won Buddhism are outlined in relation to *Irwŏnsang*.[23] Chŏngsan's ideas in the essay have formed the central tenets of the doctrine of Won Buddhism systematized in the *Pulgyo chŏngjŏn* of the 1943 edition, which was redacted as the *Chŏngjŏn* (*Canon*) of the *Wŏnbulgyo kyojŏn* (Scriptures of Won Buddhism) of 1962 edition. When the former was compiled, the sections of the truth, faith, and practice of *Irwŏnsang* were written by Chŏngsan.[24] The following is a paraphrase of Chŏngsan's view on the truth of *Irwŏnsang*.

Chŏngsan first states that *Dharmakāya* Buddha, referred to as *Irwŏn* (unitary circle with no circumference), is the noumenal essence of all things in the universe, the original nature of all buddhas and patriarchs, the Buddha-nature of all sentient beings. This reflects the Mahāyāna Buddhist tenet that all things are nothing but *Dharmakāya* Buddha. Chŏgsan then states that the realm of *Dharmakāya* Buddha is devoid of such characteristics as the differentiation of noumenon from phenomenon, being from nonbeing, the change of arising and ceasing, or going and coming, the retribution of good and evil karma, and the linguistic, audible, and visible characteristics. Chŏngsan then writes that it is due to the light of the mind-essence of empty and calm, numinous awareness[25] that the differentiation of noumenon from phenomenon and being from nonbeing appears. And thereby the distinction between good and evil karmic retribution comes into being, and the linguistic, audible, and visible characteristics become clear and distinct so that the three worlds of desire, form, and formless world of pure spirit in the ten directions appear like a jewel on one's own palm. The substance of *Irwŏn*, as the realm of nirvāṇa, is devoid of arising and ceasing or birth and death; the principle of its function is the causal law of karmic retribution. These two aspects of *Irwŏn*, being based on each other, have formed a perfect circle (*SS* I: 1).

Another attribute of *Irwŏn* is that the creative transformation of true void cum marvelous existence freely conceals and reveals itself through all things in the universe throughout vast *kalpas* without beginning (*CN* pt. 2, chap. 1, sec. 1). This view is elaborated on by Sot'aesan in his writing of "the Vow to *Irwŏnsang*" as follows (*CN* pt. 2, chap. 1, sec. 4):

> *Irwŏn* is the ineffable realm of samādhi, the realm that transcends being and nonbeing, and birth and death. It is the noumenal realm of heaven and earth, parents, brethren, and laws; the original nature of all buddhas, patriarchs, ordinary people, and sentient beings.

Irwŏn can manifest itself in permanence and impermanence. Viewed as permanent, it unfolds itself to be as spontaneous and natural as the endless world of nature. Viewed as impermanent, it manifests itself as numberless worlds through the formation, abiding, disintegration, and void of the universe and the birth, old age, illness, and death of all beings. In accordance with the functions of their minds and bodies, it lets the four forms of birth[26] change their destinies through the six realms of existence,[27] promoting or demoting, and letting favors arise in harm or harm in favors (*CN* pt. 2, chap. 1, sec. 4).

Sot'aesan's world view is expressed in Buddhist terms though he used the term *Irwŏn* instead of *Dharmakāya* Buddha as the absolute reality of the universe. However, he identifies *Irwŏnsang* with *Dharmakāya* Buddha as the model of triple discipline, leading from the above world view to his soteriology:

> In order to be promoted and favored rather than demoted or harmed, we, deluded beings, vow that we shall sincerely discipline ourselves to keep our mind and body perfectly, to know facts and principles perfectly, and to use our mind and body perfectly by modeling ourselves on this *Dharmakāya* Buddha, *Irwŏnsang*, so that we may be endowed with the great power of *Irwŏn* and unified with the noumenal nature of *Irwŏn* (*CN* pt. 2, chap. 1, sec. 4).

According to Chŏngsan, "being endowed with great power of *Irwŏn*" means that we gradually attain the three great powers of concentration, wisdom, and morality by disciplining ourselves with the threefold practice of spiritual cultivation, enquiry into facts and principles, and careful choice in *karmic* action. By disciplining ourselves with the threefold practice, we protect our mind and body from disturbances, delusions, and errors, eventually attaining the three great powers as immovable as a steel pillar. It also means that we can go through the six paths freely delivering all sentient beings with the three great powers. With a wholehearted concentration of mind, one can employ at will the awesome power of heaven and earth. What is meant by "being unified with the noumenal nature of *Irwŏn*"? It means that, upon attaining the three great powers of *Irwŏn*, we practitioners enter the perfect and complete samādhi that is devoid of wicked thoughts and foolish imagination in quietude on the one hand. On the other hand, we have the utterly fair and unselfish mind, the one mind of no disturbance in any affair while in motion. Only if one has perfected the two modes of *Irwŏn*, can one be said to have reached the Buddhahood.[28] Thus the heart of the Won Buddhist practice lies in being enlightened to the truth of *Irwŏnsang* and thereby reflecting on it when one uses one's six senses (eye, ear, nose, mouth, body, and mind) as perfectly as *Dharmakāya* Buddha, *Irwŏn*. For instance, one can realize nirvāṇa by reflecting on one's *Irwŏn* (empty and calm, numinous awareness) in a condition which makes one greedy, angry, or deluded.

In the section "Practice of *Irwŏnsang*," Chŏngsan spelled out how to discipline oneself with *Irwŏnsang*, which is paraphrased as follows. One should take the faith in the truth of *Irwŏnsang* as the standard of practice in order to be enlightened to it; one cannot be enlightened to it without having faith in it. By being enlightened to it, one is to know, nourish, and use one's original mind, which is as perfect, complete, and impartial and unselfish as *Irwŏn*, namely, Prajñā-wisdom. Prajñā-wisdom is the functioning aspect of *Dharmakāya* of one's own nature, and it is by the light of this wisdom that one can save oneself from drowning in the misery-sea of greed, anger, and delusions. Therefore, one should know, nourish, and use this wisdom upon being enlightened to one's own nature, *Dharmakāya, Irwŏn* (*CN* pt. 2, chap. 1, sec. 3).

Thus, the true religious practice begins with taking the truth of *Irwŏnsang* as the standard of moral perfection. The practitioner should discover the true *Irwŏn* through its symbol, *Irwŏnsang*; keep the true nature of *Irwŏn*; and apply the perfect mind of *Irwŏn* to daily affairs so that the truth of *Irwŏnsang* can be reflected in daily life. If one disciplines oneself in the truth of *Irwŏnsang* for a long time, one will attain the great emancipation like Lao Tzu's, the great enlightenment like the Buddha's, and the great Mean like Confucius's. These are the ultimate goals of practice in Won Buddhism.

Dharmakāya Buddha, *Irwŏn*, is approached through the dual paths of religious worship and practice, which are explicated in terms of the fourfold beneficence and threefold practice respectively.

The reason for taking *Irwŏn*, *Dharmakāya* Buddha, as the object of religious worship is that it is the fundamental source of the fourfold beneficence to which one owes one's own existence. Hence, the actual religious worship of *Dharmakāya* Buddha, *Irwŏn*, lies in being aware of and requiting the fourfold beneficence. Thus, one of the salient features of Won Buddhism is expressed in the motto: *Be Aware of Beneficence and requite it!* One of the main causes of human misery, individual or collective, is the resentment against others among individuals, families, societies, and nations. Resentment arises in one's heart when one is not aware of one's indebtedness to the source of one's own life, which is recognized as beneficence. More precisely, beneficence is that without which one cannot exist. One cannot exist and preserve one's life without heaven and earth. One could not have been brought into this world without one's parents. One could not survive where there are no other human beings, animals, and plants. And one cannot live in peace without the laws of moral cultivation for individuals, of managing a household, of regulating a society, of ruling a nation, and of keeping the world peace.

The Four Beneficent Sources of Human Life

Sot'aesan had recognized the four beneficent sources of human life, viz., heaven and earth, parents, brethren, and laws, as the manifestation of *Dharmakāya* Buddha, *Irwŏn*. Thus, *Irwŏn* is the fundamental source of the "fourfold beneficence" (K. *saŭn*) (*CN* pt. 2, chap. 2) as well as the original nature of all buddhas. Therefore, the worship of *Dharmakāya* Buddha, *Irwŏn*, amounts to the worship of the fourfold beneficence. The true worship of *Dharmakāya* Buddha, however, lies in the requital of the fourfold beneficence. Each of the fourfold beneficence is expounded in terms of indebtedness, requital, and the result of requital and ingratitude as is briefly explained below.

1. Beneficence of Heaven and Earth (K. *ch'ŏnjiŭn*) (*CN* pt. 2, chap. 2, sec. 1)

It may sound unnatural to regard heaven and earth as the object of religious worship; however, it will not take long for one to realize that human life is impossible if there is no air, water, or earth. Heaven and earth provide us with the universal beneficence of nature, which Sot'aesan identified with the essence of *Dharmakāya* Buddha. All living beings owe their lives to the way and virtue of heaven and earth. The automatic rotation of the grand framework of the universe is in accordance with the way of heaven and earth and the result of their rotation is their virtues. The virtues of heaven and earth are exemplified in the brightness of the sun and the moon, thanks to which we can discern and know a myriad of things; and the favors of the wind, clouds, rain, and dew, thanks to which a myriad of things are nurtured and we are able to survive off their products.

In the ways of heaven and earth are eight moral characteristics, from which eight moral maxims are derived for humans to follow. The ways of heaven and earth are (i) extremely bright, (ii) extremely sincere, (iii) extremely fair, (iv) reasonable and natural, (v) vast and limitless, (vi) eternal, (vii) with no good or evil fortunes, and (viii) not harboring the idea of favor done to others.[29] The way to requite the beneficence of heaven and earth lies in one's moral cultivation by modeling oneself after their ways. One can form one body with heaven and earth in virtue if one practices the eight virtues, viz., wisdom (brightness), immortality (eternity), imperturbability in face of one's good or ill fortunes, and genuine benevolence (not abiding in the idea of favors done to others). Once one has perfected one's moral character with these virtues, one's moral influence on other sentient beings will be like that of heaven and earth.

Ingratitude to heaven and earth, on the other hand, brings on heavenly punishment. Although heaven and earth are empty and silent to one's deeds, unexpected hardships and sufferings in life and sufferings caused by one's deeds are due to ingratitude. If one does not model oneself after the ways of heaven and earth, one will (i) be ignorant of facts and principles, (ii) lack sincerity, (iii) be either excessive or deficient, (iv) be unreasonable, (v) be partial, (vi) be ignorant of the transformation of the phenomenal world, of the principles of birth, old age, illness and death, (vii) be ignorant of good and ill fortunes, and the ups and downs of the world. When one renders favors to others, one will be (viii) attached to the idea of having done so, covertly praising oneself and overtly boasting.

2. Beneficence of Parents (K. *pumoŭn*) (*CN* pt. 2, chap. 2, sec. 2)

The Confucian moral duty of filial piety as heavenly moral principle is identified as the essence of *Dharmakāya* Buddha. This is an aspect of Sot'aesan's synthesis of central tenets of Confucianism and Buddhism. One is indebted to one's parents in the following three ways. (i) One owes one's body to one's parents which is the basis of all facts and principles of life; (ii) with unlimited love and sacrifice, one's parents have raised and protected one until one grows to be self-reliant; and (iii) one's parents have taught one one's duties and responsibilities to human society.

As the way of requiting the beneficence of parents one should follow the following four maxims. (i) Follow the way of moral discipline (threefold practice) and the ways of humanity (requital of beneficence); (ii) Support your parents faithfully as much as you can when they lack the ability to help themselves, and help them have spiritual comfort; (iii) In accordance with your ability, protect the helpless parents of others as your own during or after the lifetime of your parents; (iv) After your parents are deceased, enshrine their pictures and biographical records and remember them.

If one is filial, one's own offspring will be as one's offspring follows one's own example. If one protects the helpless parents of others as far as possible, one will be helped and protected when one becomes helpless. If, however, one does not requite the beneficence of parents, one's own offspring will follow one's example and one will be condemned by those who believe in the morality of filial duty. Moreover, one will be deserted throughout many lives by other people when in need of help in accordance with the causal law of *karmic* retribution.

3. Beneficence of Brethren (K. *tongp'oŭn*) (*CN* pt. 2, chap. 2, sec. 3)

Sot'aesan identifies the beneficence of brethren or fellow beings as essence of *Dharmakāya* Buddha, not because they are endowed with Buddha-nature, but because it is impossible for one to live without it. The term 'brethren' here designates, besides one's own siblings and compatriots, all people, animals, and plants. One owes one's life to brethren in this sense of the term. People of different occupations help one another by exchanging products on the principle of mutual benefit and thus are indebted to one another.

The moral maxim for requiting the beneficence of brethren requires people of all occupations to exchange what they can offer with others on the principle of mutual benefit based on fairness. If people requite the beneficence of brethren by honoring the principle of mutual benefit based on fairness, they will be blessed in paradise. If, however, people become ungrateful to one another, violating the principle of mutual benefit based on fairness, they will drive themselves to hate and abhor one another and make themselves mutual enemies, causing quarrels among individuals, ill-will among families, antagonism among societies, and war among nations.

4. Beneficence of Laws (K. *pŏmnyurŭn*)(*CN* pt. 2, chap. 2, sec. 4)

Sot'aesan identifies laws as emanating from *Dharmakāya* Buddha. By the term "laws" are meant (i) religious and moral teachings that sages show for us to follow, (ii) the laws with which people of all occupations direct and encourage us to preserve our lives and advance our knowledge, and (iii) judicial institutions that help punish injustice and preserve justice and help discriminate right from wrong and good from evil. Thus, the term "laws" covers religious and moral principles, social institutions and legislation, and civil and penal laws. The connotation of the term "laws" is the principle of fairness for human justice. One owes one's existence to laws in this sense of the term.

The basic moral principle for requiting the beneficence of laws is as follows. If one is indebted to the prohibition of certain things by the laws, one ought not to do them; and if one is indebted to the encouragement of certain things by the laws, then one ought to do them. One ought to learn and practice as the way of requiting the beneficence of laws: (i) the way of individual moral cultivation, (ii) the way of regulating one's family, (iii) the way of harmonizing the society, (iv) the way of governing the state, and (v) the way of putting the world at peace as an individual and as a member of a family, society, nation, and the world.[30]

Why one should requite the beneficence of laws is explained simply in terms of blessings and punishment. If we are grateful to the beneficence of laws, we will be protected thereby. If, however, we are ungrateful to the beneficence of laws, that is, we do not requite it, we will be punished, bound, and restrained. However, unless one is edified to be a benevolent and wise person capable of changing hell into paradise, the ideal cannot be realized. Being fully aware of this problem, Sot'aesan has provided a way of transforming deluded and selfish beings into living buddhas through the threefold practice.

We have seen that practice of *Irwŏnsang* lies in being enlightened to the truth of *Irwŏnsang* and thereby knowing, nourishing, and following one's original nature, namely, Prajñā-wisdom when one uses one's six senses. The three aspects of practice, namely, knowing, nourishing, and following one's original nature, *Dharmakāya*, *Irwŏn*, take the central tenet of the Won Buddhist religious practice called threefold practice.

The three modes of one's original nature are concentration, wisdom, and morality as Huineng (638–713), the sixth patriarch of Chan Buddhism, said,

"When the mind ground is free from evil, that is morality (*śīla*) of one's own nature. When the mind ground is free from disturbance, that is the concentration (*samādhi*) of one's own nature. When the mind ground is free from delusions, that is the wisdom (*prajñā*) of one's own nature."[31] Thus, keeping the morality, concentration, and wisdom of one's own nature is called the threefold learning or three studies in Buddhism. This teaching has its origin in the Buddha's eightfold noble path, which consists of (i) right view, (ii) right thought, (iii) right speech, (iv) right action, (v) right livelihood, (vi) right effort, (vii) right mindfulness, and (viii) right concentration. These are summarized into the triple discipline, viz., wisdom (i, ii), morality (iii, iv, v), and concentration (vi, vii, viii). It should be noted that the eightfold path of the Buddha was taught as the way of delivering sentient beings from the sea of misery to a happy land.

The Threefold Practice in Won Buddhism

The threefold practice in Won Buddhism has its root in Sot'aesan's insight of concentration, gnosis, and careful choice, which he identified with the Buddhist triple discipline. However, it is thoroughly renovated and reformulated as the way of realizing Buddhahood in this very life. In other words, one can solve the problems of life and death by achieving the goal of the threefold practice, which is to attain Buddhahood. The three parts of the threefold practice are like the three legs of a tripod; one cannot stand alone without the support of the other two.

1. Cultivation of Spirit (K. *chŏngsin suyang*) (*CN* pt. 2, chap. 4, sec. 1)

In order to maintain the mental state of samādhi, serene reflection, or quiet illumination, which is free from disturbance, one must do spiritual cultivation. By spirit is meant the mental state which, being clear and calm, is devoid of discrimination or attachment to anything, or clear awareness in the tranquility of no thought. This is the substantial aspect of one's own nature, *Dharmakāya* of one's mind. By cultivation is meant nourishment of the clear and calm spirit by removing internal discrimination or attachment and by keeping the mind from external disturbance.

If one's spiritual power is so weak as to lose one's mental poise in adverse conditions, one cannot but suffer. We live in a world where our mind can easily be disturbed by such adverse conditions. If one is blinded by vehement desire, anger, or delusions, one loses the dignity and integrity of one's personality, thus drowning in the sea of misery. One ends up with ruining one's family and disgracing oneself. Suffering from agony and delusion or from vexation and anxiety, one may end up feeling sick of life, falling into despair, having a nervous breakdown, becoming mentally deranged, or even committing suicide in extreme cases. Thus, the purpose of spiritual cultivation is to attain the spiritual power so that one's mental poise in any adverse condition should be as immovable as a huge mountain and as serene and calm as the empty sky. The way of cultivating the spirit lies in seated meditation and repeated intoning of *Namo Amitābha* (*CN* pt. 3, chap. 3).

2. Inquiry into Facts and Principles (K. *sari yŏn'gu*) (*CN* pt. 2, chap. 4. sec. 2)

The functioning aspect of *Dharmakāya* of one's nature is wisdom. Wisdom in primitive Buddhism meant methodic contemplation on the basic elements of the universe, thereby realizing, for example, the emptiness of one's own ego or self, which was explained in terms of the five aggregates (*skandha*), viz., body, feelings, perceptions, dispositions, and consciousness. In the Mahāyāna wisdom literature, wisdom meant the realization of the emptiness of these aggregates and the rest of the elements.

In Won Buddhism a great importance is placed on seeing into one's own nature, since one will be unable to subdue and annihilate the three poisons of vehement desire or greed, anger or hatred, and delusions or foolishness in one's mind unless one is enlightened to one's own nature, *Dharmakāya* Buddha, *Irwŏn*. However, Won Buddhism does not encourage one to spend a lifetime or even years sitting in meditation in order to attain the great enlightenment. It teaches a practical way via an inquiry into facts and principles.

By facts are meant rightness, wrongness, gain, and loss in human affairs. By principle is meant the first metaphysical principle of the universe, viz., the principle of ultimate reality and its phenomenal appearance, and the principle of existence and nonexistence of all things in the universe. By existence and nonexistence are meant the cycles of the four seasons, the atmospheric phenomena of winds, clouds, rain, dew, frost, and snow; the birth, old age, illness, and death of all things; and the transformation of rising and falling, and prosperity and decline. By inquiry are meant studies and investigations.

Why does one need to inquire into facts and principles? The answer is that one can save oneself from drowning in the sea of misery only if one attains a thorough knowledge of facts and principles as defined above. If one acts as one pleases without knowing rightness, wrongness, and gain and loss in human affairs, whatever one does will lead to transgression and suffering. If one lives without knowing the principle of the ultimate reality and its phenomenal appearance and the change of existence and nonexistence, one will suffer because one will not know the cause of the unexpected joys and sorrows, and one's thoughts will be hurried and narrow-minded. Nor will one understand the principle of birth, old age, illness, and death, and the causal law of *karmic* retribution. One will be unable to distinguish truth from falsehood, falling into falsehood and eventually facing the ruin of one's family and disgracing oneself. Thus the purpose of inquiring into the unfathomable principles of the universe and complicated human affairs lies in attaining the ability to analyze and pass prompt judgment on practical daily affairs. One cannot live a perfect life without such ability.

Thus the Won Buddhist's way of attaining wisdom by inquiring into facts and principles is quite different from the traditional Buddhist's way of attaining wisdom by awakening into one's own original nature, although a Won Buddhist is also advised to meditate with Sŏn/Zen conundrums daily. The training subjects for inquiry into facts and principles are the study of scriptures, giving lectures, discussions, and meditation with a Zen conundrum (K. *ŭidu*),[32] the principle of nature and metaphysical first principle of the universe, and keeping a diary for a fixed term (*CN* pt. 3, chap. 2).

3. Careful Choice in Karmic Action (K. *chagŏp ch'wisa*) (*CN* pt. 2, chap. 4, sec. 3)

The third aspect of the practice of *Dharmakāya* is to follow one's original nature, namely, Prajñā-wisdom, which is perfect, complete, impartial, and unselfish. Being enlightened to one's original nature, however, is a necessary but not a sufficient condition for realizing Buddhahood for one may be unable to follow one's original nature, namely, Prajñā-wisdom while using one's six sense organs because of one's habit-force, even though one has seen into one's original nature. Thus, one needs gradual cultivation upon sudden enlightenment. This requires one to train oneself in choosing justice and forsaking injustice while creating karma through thinking, speaking, and acting. This practice can be called careful choice in *karmic* action (K. *chagŏp ch'wisa*) since *karma* creation (K. *chagŏp*) means the operation of the six sense organs, viz., eyes, ears, nose, tongue, body, and mind and careful choice (K. *ch'wisa*) means taking what is right and forsaking what is wrong.

The powers of spiritual cultivation and inquiry into facts and principles will be complete only if one attains the power of right conduct or the ability to create the right karma; otherwise, one's moral cultivation will be like a fruit tree with good roots, branches, leaves, and flowers without any fruit. Depending on what kind of *karma* one creates, one creates a heavenly world or a hell no matter where one lives. An evil karma follows oneself wherever one goes like a shadow until one wears it out completely. Good karma, too, follows one wherever one goes until it is exhausted.

We human beings do not always do good although we know it is preferable and cannot always sever ourselves from evil although we know we should, so that we discard a tranquil paradise and enter a perilous sea of misery. We do so because either we do not always know right from wrong in adverse conditions, or we cannot control the burning greed, or we are pulled by the habit-force, which is as unyielding as iron and rock. Thus, we aim at changing the detestable sea of misery into a paradise by training ourselves to create good karma and keep evil karma from being created. For this purpose the practitioner practices keeping a daily diary, which involves checking the ten, twenty or thirty precepts of prohibition (*CN* pt. 3, chap. 11), carefulness, and deportment. As an important way of dissolving evil karma, the practice of repentance is strongly suggested (*CN* pt. 3, chap. 8).

Concluding Remarks

To the question how much Sot'aesan owed to the ancient sages for the composition of the doctrine, Chŏngsan said that Sot'aesan's creation was primary and his adoption of ancient sages' teachings was secondary. To the question of Sot'aesan's affinity to the Buddha Śākyamuni, Chŏngsan wrote on the granite monument for Sot'aesan under the title, "The Epitaph on the Sacred Monument of Grand Master Sot'aesan who attained the Consummate Enlightenment,"

> As the four seasons keep rotating and the sun and the moon alternate illuminating in the universe, myriad things attain the way of coming into being. As buddhas succeed one after another and sages transmit the laws from one to the other, sentient beings receive the beneficence of deliverance. This is the natural law of the universe. Ever since the Buddha Śākyamuni opened his order at Gṛdrakuta, his teachings passed the period of orthodoxy and vigor, and the period of semblance, finally reaching the period of decline and termination. The correct way was not followed in the last period while the world was full of false doctrines; the spirit lost its power to the material, which was ruling the world. Consequently the bitter seas of misery where sentient beings were tormented got deeper and deeper; this was the occasion for Grand Master Sot'aesan, our savior, to come to this world again.[33]

On January 22, 1962, Chŏngsan on his deathbed said, "We are people who did practice and public service together for many previous lives, and are not the people who have met for the first time in this order. We are the people who will frequently meet again and work together in the future."[34] In Won Buddhism Sot'aesan and Chŏngsan are believed as new advent of the Buddha Śākyamuni and Mahākāśyapa together for opening a new order for the new era. Thus, the question whether Won Buddhism is a sect of Korean Buddhism is answered with the view that Won Buddhism is a new Buddhism; it is not a branch of old tree of Buddhism, it is a new seedling of the religion of enlightenment (Buddhism).

When Sot'aesan established a new Buddhist order, he synthesized mainly the two moral systems of Buddhism and Confucianism by reforming and renovating some of the central tenets of both systems so that the religious and moral teachings of both systems could be made relevant to the new era. He derives moral duties from the way we are indebted to the fourfold beneficence and uses the religious force to help us put our hearts into the moral duties, saying that a reverent offering to Buddha is none other than the requital of the fourfold beneficence. Since the moral duties to requite the fourfold beneficence are mostly Confucian, and thus this-worldly, and since the fourfold beneficence is identified with the essence of *Dharmakāya* Buddha, Sot'aesan is suggesting that we practice the two teachings integrated into our daily life. In this way Sot'aesan has synthesized the two apparently opposing moral systems into a new ethico-religious system of Won Buddhism.

The essence of the Confucian moral teaching is *ren* (benevolence) and *yi* (righteousness), which Sot'aesan acknowledged as the leading moral principle (*SS* I: 5). Now, the essential principles of the requital of the beneficence of heaven and earth and that of parents are "harboring no false idea upon rendering favors to others" and "protecting the helpless," respectively. And these two moral virtues cannot be practiced unless one genuinely loves others or "cannot witness the suffering of others" or "does not do to others what one does not like oneself," which is the essence of the Confucian moral virtue of r*en*. The essential principles of the requital of the beneficence of brethren and that of laws are "the way of mutual benefit" and "the way of eradicating injustice and maintaining justice," respectively. In these two ways is reflected the Confucian moral virtue of righteousness. Since the fourfold beneficence is the essence of *Dharmakāya* Buddha, one's act of beneficence requital is none other than making an offering to the Buddha.[35] The central moral principles of the Confucian ethics are synthesized as the essential ways of beneficence requital, which in turn is none other than worshipping Dharmakāya Buddha. Thus, the two ethico-religious principles of Buddhism and Confucianism have been synthesized in the doctrine of Won Buddhism, blunting the sharp edge of the neo-Confucian criticism of Buddhism.

Notes

1. For the reason why Sot'aesan quit the learning, see Bongkil Chung, *The Scriptures of Won Buddhism with an Introduction* (Honolulu: University of Hawai'i Press, 2002) p. 33. This work contains translations of two books: the *Canon* and the *Scripture of Sot'aesan*. Henceforth, note the following indications: *SS* for the *Scripture of Sot'aesan* and *CN* for the *Canon*. Citations from these works will be marked in the text with these

abbreviations followed by section numbers. When a reference is made to the whole volume, *The Scriptures of Won Buddhism* will be used.

2. For a detailed description of Sot'aesan's activities after the enlightenment, see *The Scriptures of Won Buddhism,* pp. 38–47. It should be noted here that Sot'aesan ushered in Chŏngsan at age 18 as the chief legislator or "the mother of Dharma" of the doctrine of the new religious order he was establishing.

3. Sot'aesan surveyed: The Four Classics and the *Xiaojing* (The Book of Filial Piety) of Confucianism; The *Jingangjing* (The Diamond Sūtra), The *Sŏnyo* (The Essentials of Zen), The *Pulgyo taejŏn* (Complete Works of Buddhism), The *P'alsangjŏn* (The Eight Aspects of the Buddha's Life); *Yinfujing* (The Book of Secret Planning), *Yushujing* (The Book of Jade Hinge) of Daoism; The *Tonggyŏng taejŏn* (The Canon of Eastern Learning) and *The Kasa* (Hymns of Ch'ŏndogyo); The Old and New Testaments of Christianity.

4. It was offered on the 6th, 16th, and 26th days of every month with ten days of preparation. The nine disciples offered separately on the nine mountain tops that surround Kiryong ri, Sot'aesan's birthplace.

5. This volume contains three books. Book 1 is the only new writing done in Korean vernacular by The Society for the Study of Buddha-dharma and books 2 and 3 are collections from Buddhist scriptures in Chinese with Korean translations. The *Wŏnbulgyo kyojŏn* published in 1962 is a new compilation of the Won Buddhist scriptures, book 1 of which is a redaction of the book 1 of 1943 edition and the newly compiled *Taejonggyŏng* (the scripture of Sot'aesan). Part 1 "On Renovation" of the *Chŏngjŏn* (1943) was redacted as sections of Chapter 1 of *the Scripture of Sot'aesan.*

6. See the *Scripture of Sot'aesan* I: 15–19.

7. *Kanhwa Sŏn* is a meditation practiced with an essential point in a *kongan* story.

8. "The reality body of the Buddha is inconceivable;/ Formless, signless, without comparison,/ It manifests material forms for the sake of beings./ In the ten directions they receive its teachings,/ Nowhere not manifested" (*Huayan wujiao jiguan*, *T* 1867.45.513, English translation by Thomas Cleary, "Cessation and Contemplation in the Five Teachings of the *Huayan*" in *Entry into the Inconceivable: An Introduction to Hua-yen Buddhism* (Honolulu: University of Hawai'i Press, 1983), p. 68. Also see *Mohe jiguan T* 1911.46.75b, "Vairocana Buddha is ubiquitous; how can you say that objects of vision and thought are not true dharmas? This is the truth of neither being nor nonbeing."

9. *The Scripture of Sot'aesan* II: 15.

10. Robert E. Buswell, Jr., *The Zen Monastic Experience*, pp. 220–222. "But when Korean meditation monks who are training in the kanhwa technique routinely admit that they expect it will take upwards of twenty years of full time practice to make substantive progress in their practice, there seem to be valid grounds for question how subitist in practice the Sŏn tradition really is" (p. 220).

11. *Liuzu tanjing, T* 2008.48.342b; English translation by Wing-tsit Chan, *The Platform Scripture* (New York: St. John's University Press, 1963), p. 59.

12. See Heinrich Dumoulin, *Zen Buddhism: A History* (New York: Macmillan, 1988), p. 172.

13. The four cardinal virtues in the Confucian ethics have their ground in the human nature which is good according to Mencius. "The feeling of commiseration is

the principle of benevolence [*ren*]. The feeling of shame and dislike is the principle of righteousness [*yi*]. The feeling of modesty and complaisance is the principle of propriety [*li*]. The feeling of approving and disapproving is the principle of knowledge" (*Mengzi*, bk. 2, pt. 1, ch.5; English translation by James Legge, *The Works of Mencius* [Oxford: Clarendon Press, 1895], pp. 202–203).

14. *Yuanren lun*, *T* 1886. 45. 708c17; For English translation, Peter Gregory, trans., *Inquiry into the Origin of Humanity* (Honolulu: University of Hawai'i Press, 1995), p. 117.

15. For a detailed exposure of the problems in the 1962 edition, see *The Scriptures of Won Buddhism*, Appendix I.

16. Regrettably, the general principle of beneficence requital is replaced with the four essentials for social reformation in the 1962 edition of *Wŏnbulgyo kyojŏn*, making the path of faith impossible to approach.

17. Mubi Sŭnim, *Kŭmganggyŏng ogahae* (Korean Vernacular Translation of the Five Masters' Interpretation of the Diamond Sūtra) (Seoul: Pulgwang ch'ulp'anbu, 1992), p. 65.

18. *T* 2076.51:244c, "Huijong, seeing a monk coming, draws a circle with his hand, and writes the character 'sun' in it; the monk gives no response"; see Heinrich Dumoulin and Ruth Fuller Sasaki, *The Development of Chinese Zen* (New York: The First Zen Institute of America, 1953), p. 19.

19. For a detailed history of the origination and development of the circular symbol, see Robert E. Buswell, Jr., "Ch'an Hermeneutics: Korean View," in Donald S. Lopez, Jr., ed., *Buddhist Hermeneutics* (Honolulu: University of Hawai'i Press, 1988), pp. 248–250.

20. *The Dharma Words of Master Chŏngsan* I: 2.

21. *Kŭmgansan ŭi chuin* (The Owner of Mt. Diamond) (Iksan, Korea: Wŏlgan Wŏn'gwangsa, 1990), p. 357. This volume contains the unedited sayings of Sot'aesan; the *Scripture of Sot'aesan* in *the Scriptures of Won Buddhism* is an edited and canonized version of what is in this version. Sot'aesan's original writing contains "Mind-Buddha *Irwŏnsang*"; the edited version (both 1943 and 1962 editions) contains "*Dharmakāya* Buddha *Irwŏnsang*."

22. *Kŭmgangsan ŭi chuin*, p. 345; *The Scripture of Sot'aesan* II: 6.

23. Pak Chŏnghun, ed., *Hanuran hanich'i e* (Unitary Principle within One Fence) (Iri: Wŏnbulgyo ch'ulp'ansa, 1982), pp. 212–19.

24. Pak Chŏnghun. *Chŏngsan chongsa chŏn* (A Biography of Master Chŏngsan) (Iksan: Wŏnbulgyo ch'ulp'ansa, 2002), p. 291.

25. Chinul says that one's own nature is true *Dharmakāya* and numinous awareness is true Buddha. See *Susim kyŏl*, *T* 2020.48.1006c; Buswell, *The Korean Approach to Zen*, p. 165. The rendering of *yŏngji* (C. *lingzhi*) as "numinous awareness" is Buswell's. See Peter N. Gregory, *Inquiry into the Origin of Humanity*, p. 179.

26. Viviparous, as with mammalia; oviparous, as with birds; moisture or water born, as with worms and fishes; metamorphic, as with moths from chrysalis, or with *devas*, or in hells, or the first beings in a newly evolved world.

27. Hells, hungry ghosts, animals, malevolent nature spirits, human existence, and deva existence.

28. O Sŏnmyŏng, *Chŏngsan chongsa pŏpsŏl* (Dharma Sermons of Master Chŏngsan) (Iksan, Korea: Wŏlgan Wŏn'gwangsa, 2000), pp. 402–403.

29. The ways of heaven listed here reflect the ways of Confucian heaven expounded in the *Zhongyong* (Doctrine of the Mean). See James Legge, *The Analects, Great Learning, & Doctrine of the Mean* (Oxford: Clarendon Press, 1893), pp. 413–22 (*Doctrine of the Mean,* chaps. 20–26).

30. This clearly reflects the Confucian moral and political agenda explicated in the *Daxue* (The Great Learning). See Legge, *The Confucian Analects, Great Learning, & The Doctrine of the Mean*, pp. 356–359.

31. *T* 2007.48.342b; Wing-tsit Chan trans., *The Platform Scripture*, p. 109. The word 'ground' is added to Chan's translation.

32. Twenty cases of *kongan* are adopted in Won Buddhism. See the *CN* pt. 3, chap. 5.

33. *The Dharma Words of Master Chŏngsan* I: 17.

34. *The Dharma Words of Master Chŏngsan* XV: 37.

35. This is the crux of Sot'aesan's synthetic renovation of the two ethico-religious systems; unfortunately the "essential principles of beneficence requital" in the Doctrinal Chart in the 1943 edition has been replaced with "Four Essentials" in the 1962 edition.

4

Yi Nŭnghwa, Buddhism, and the Modernization of Korea

A Critical Review[1]

Jongmyung Kim

Introduction

This essay examines Yi Nŭnghwa's (1869–1943) role in the modernization of Korea in the early twentieth century. The primary concern of this essay will be to assess Yi's literary activities and his view of Buddhism based on two of his major works, *Paekkyo hoet'ong* (Harmonization of All Religions) and *Chosŏn Pulgyo t'ongsa* (A Comprehensive History of Korean Buddhism, hereafter, History of Korean Buddhism). Yi Nŭnghwa considered Buddhism a useful teaching that could be adapted for different ideologies, including democracy, individualism, socialism, and cosmopolitanism. Yi discovered the potential for harmonization between traditional Buddhism and the modernization of Korea. His publications on Buddhism and active social engagement were expressions of his goal, which was the modernization of Korea.[2] In this context, one can even claim that although his publications focused on Buddhism, Yi was in fact more interested in the modernization of Korea than in Buddhism itself.[3]

The first section of this essay addresses Yi's literary activities. The next section examines Yi's view of Buddhism as a religion, a system of thought, and the epitome of Korean culture as expressed in his works. The third section evaluates the role of Yi's literary activities and his view of Buddhism in the process of Korea's modernization. This essay concludes that while Yi did not play a substantial role in his day owing to the limits of his literary activities and thought, he made a significant contribution to the formation of the modern form of Buddhist Studies in Korea and, by extension, of Korean Studies in general.

Yi Nŭnghwa's Literary Activities

Considered a "pioneer of Korean Studies" and the "father of Religious Studies in Korea," Yi Nŭnghwa was a prolific writer who left behind more than ten book-length publications and 230-plus articles, all of which focus on religion and Korean society. He lived during the period of Japanese occupation (1910–1945), and his scholarship was a product of his time. Two opposing evaluations of Yi have appeared in Korean academe: To some, Yi Nŭnghwa was pro-Japanese; to others, he was a nationalist. Scholars have assessed Yi's scholarship along these two lines. The argument that Yi was a Japanophile prevented his scholarship from being assessed duly.[4] However, Yi's personal career indicates that he was not actively pro-Japanese except for his participation as a contributor to the compilation of the *Jōsen shi* (History of Korea),[5] which was sponsored by the Japanese Government General in Seoul. On the contrary, he emphasized national consciousness by calling attention to the significance of the myth of Tan'gun, the legendary founder of ancient Korea, in his writing of *History of Korea*,[6] hence the evaluation of his scholarship in the context of national consciousness.[7]

It was not until the 1980s that Korean scholars began to pay attention to Yi's scholarship, especially in the fields of folklore, history, and religion.[8] However, an in-depth study of Yi's scholarship was still lacking. Although the focus of his scholarship centered on Buddhist Studies, the Buddhist circles of Korea became interested in his scholarship only in recent years. In addition, no substantial research on his *magnum opus*, *History of Korean Buddhism*,[9] has yet been done.[10]

Yi's scholarship can be divided into two phases; the dividing line falls in the early 1920s. From 1912 to 1922, Yi devoted himself to the research of Buddhism; from 1922 until his death in 1944, he focused on religious history and social history. The intellectual atmosphere during his time in Korea was complex. Western civilization was infiltrating Korean society, and new religions, including Christianity, were on the rise; whereas traditional religions, represented by Confucianism and Buddhism, were in decline. Politically, Korea was under Japanese colonial rule. Yi's scholarly concern went through an evolution. He began his scholarship by focusing on the Chinese classics, and then moved on to foreign languages, including English, Japanese, Chinese, and French. Subsequently, he turned toward Buddhist Studies, the religious history of Korea,[11] and, finally, the social history of Korea.[12]

The majority of Yi's works are related to Buddhism, totaling more than 140 texts. He began studying Buddhism in 1900 at the age of 32.[13] Yi's initial contact with Buddhism occurred while reading *Perfect Enlightenment Sūtra* (C. *Yuanjuejing*)[14] and *Record of Pointing to the Moon* (C. *Zhiyuelu*), which led him to recognize the profundity of Buddhist teachings and inspired him to embrace Buddhism. Of Yi's works on Buddhism, the most noteworthy are *Harmonization of All Religions* and *History of Korean Buddhism.* While the former represents his religious pluralism, the latter manifests his view of Buddhism.

Published in 1912, *Harmonization of All Religions* was the first of Yi's works. It marked the starting point of his research on the history of Korean religions, including Buddhism.[15] *Harmonization of All Religions* was also the first of its kind in Korea to deal with world religions from a comparative perspective,[16] thus attempting to harmonize all religions in Korea.

Harmonization of All Religions is composed of two parts: "Comparison of Religions" and "Correction of the Misunderstanding of Buddhism." Part One consists of thirteen chapters and compares Buddhism with eleven other religions: Philosophical Taoism (K. *Togyo*), Religious Taoism (K. *Kwisin sulsu chi kyo*), Religion of the Immortals (K. *Sinsŏn chi kyo*), Confucianism, Christianity, Islam, Brahmanism, Religion of the Ultimate Reality (K. *T'aegŭkkyo*), Religion of Belief in Tan'gun (K. *Taejonggyo*), and Religion of the Heavenly Way (K. *Ch'ŏndogyo*). Chapters 12 and 13 of Part One are significant for their discussion of Yi's approach to religion and his Buddhist thought. Part Two attempts to correct the false impressions that the Korean people had about Buddhism, including its nature, ethics, and practices.[17]

After Yi Nŭnghwa published *Harmonization of All Religions* in 1912, he commenced writing a comprehensive history of Korean Buddhism. With a collection of data from 1907,[18] and published in 1918 totaling 2,300-odd pages, *History of Korean Buddhism* is organized as follows. Volume 1 deals with the chronological history of Korean Buddhism from its initial period in the fourth century to his day. The greater part of this volume is concerned with Buddhist events, including the state-sponsored Buddhist rituals, Buddhist works of art, and biographies of eminent Sŏn masters in India, China, and Korea. Volume 2 describes the origin of Korean Buddhism with a focus on Sŏn Buddhism. Volume 3 is an encyclopedia of Buddhism that deals with 200 items relevant to Korean Buddhism.

Yi Nŭnghwa's View of Buddhism

In *Harmonization of All Religions* and *History of Korean Buddhism*, Yi discusses Buddhism as a "religion," a system of thought, and national culture. Yi considered Buddhism to be the oldest among the world's religions.[19] Buddhism, in his view, was the only religion that both the king and the people in Korean history had respected over the past 1,500 years.[20] However, he viewed Buddhism as only one of many religions in Korea. *Harmonization of All Religions* manifests this point:

> There are now tens of major religions and not a few were founded by the Korean people. . . . All teachings (lit. "all roads") were derived from one principle (lit. "one round circle"). People do not know this and discriminate their way from others' while saying that their way is right, but others' paths are wrong. . . . Therefore, Confucian scholars argue that the right way is Confucianism, Buddhist followers say that it is Buddhism, and other religious adherents also maintain that their religion is the orthodox way. I only wish that when people discuss the notions of mind and nature, they will make a right conclusion through a comparison between their own and others. . . . I understand the essential ideas of all religions in Korea from the comparative perspective and harmonized them on the basis of their textual evidence.[21]

It is obvious from the above passage that Yi viewed all religions in Korea as essentially the same in the sense that they were all derived from one principle. In this regard, his approach to Buddhism is characterized by the theory of harmonization of all religions in Korea.[22] The most important part of *Harmonization of All Religions* is Yi's discussion of Buddhism, comparing it with Confucianism and Christianity. Yi's comparison between Buddhism and Confucianism focuses on issues of filial piety, the afterlife, original nature, and the middle path. In his comparison between Buddhism and Christianity, Yi deals with commandments, karmic retribution, and liberation. He does not admit the religiosity of Confucianism; he considers it to be just a political thought, an ethical system, and a philosophical discourse. He also argues that the evil practices of Confucianism and its control of freedom of thought caused Korea to fall behind the times. Furthermore, his criticism of Confucianism led him to conduct research in the field of Korean Studies,[23] including Korean Buddhism. In contrast, he viewed Christianity as supplementary to the advanced Western cultures. The increasing influence of Christianity on Korean society expedited his research on Korean Buddhism.

Yi Nŭnghwa was specially attracted by the Buddhist concept of the mind, nirvāṇa, the true nature, the five aggregates, the six consciousnesses, the seven elements of existence, the twelve abodes of sensation, the eighteen realms of sense, and the schools of meditative Buddhism and doctrinal Buddhism. In response to what he considered people's misunderstanding of Buddhism, Yi contended that Buddhism is not nihilism; meditation is the right approach to enlightenment; and not all monks adopted clerical marriage and meat-eating. He also emphasized that Buddhism did not teach miracle-making or divine response; Buddhism is both religion and philosophy; and the notions of Buddhist paradise and hell are just skillful means. In defending Buddhism against public misunderstanding, Yi's goal was not to evaluate the merits and shortcomings of the religions in Korea, but to argue for Buddhism's place as a utilitarian religion in Korean society. He contended that Buddhism was the best tool for the modernization of Korea.

Yi was particularly interested in the Buddhist concepts of the mind, non-duality, and the principle of equality. Among the Buddhist schools, his main interest lay in Sŏn Buddhist thought. As for the mind of Buddhism, Yi said, "Christianity and Confucianism are acceptable. However, I was most infatuated with Buddhism which teaches that everything depends on one's mind and self-nature."[24] The concept of the mind is a theoretical foundation on which Yi based the superiority of Buddhism over other world religions. *Harmonization of All Religions* reveals that the concept of heaven is one of the major criteria Yi employed to evaluate the religions in Korea.

In the book, Yi classifies heaven into four categories: the physical heaven, the heaven of controlling power, the heaven of fortune, and the heaven of principle. Yi viewed Confucianism as pertaining to four types of heaven, whereas Christianity, Islam, Brahmanism, the Religion of Belief in Tan'gun, the Religion of the Divinity, and the Religion of the Heavenly Way focus on the heaven of controlling power. In contrast, Yi contends that the Buddhist heaven signifies the heaven of heavens[25] because, according to Buddhism, even the notion of heaven is none other than the representation of one's self-nature. Yi's recognition of self-nature led him further toward the non-duality of all existence in essence.

The *Perfect Enlightenment Sūtra*, the first Buddhist book that Yi read, impressed him considerably. He was particularly fascinated with the following passages in this scripture: "All hindrances are none other than final enlightenment. Both discriminative thought and non-discriminative thought are nirvāṇa. . . . Both wisdom and delusion are prajñā. Both bodhisattvas and heretics equally pursue enlightenment. The realms of ignorance and of thusness are not different."[26] The non-dual mode of thinking expressed in this passage constitutes an important part of his Buddhist thought. Another concept Yi found valuable in Buddhism is the principle of equality. Yi said: "The 'Buddha' means an enlightened one and the 'teaching' signifies the senior's instruction to the junior. Who is the senior? He is the Buddha. Who are the juniors? They are sentient beings. . . . [In essence,] a Buddha is an ordinary person and an ordinary person is a Buddha."[27]

For Yi, in its essence, there is no distinction between the enlightened Buddha and ignorant sentient beings: All sentient beings have Buddhahood in their original nature. Yi found in the Buddhist principle of equality the potential to overcome the exclusivist attitude of Confucianism and carry out the modernization of Korea. In this sense he contended that the Buddhist principle of equality shared a common idea with Western democracy.[28]

Yi argued that genuine Buddhism meant the harmonized form of Sŏn Buddhism and doctrinal Buddhism.[29] However, his primary concern was with

Sŏn Buddhism, which was a recurring theme in his major works on Buddhism, including *History of Korean Buddhism*, and the majority of his essays.[30] For instance, issues relevant to Korean Sŏn Buddhism, including the development of the Chogye-jong after Chinul, occupy the greatest part of Volume 3 of *History of Korean Buddhism*.[31] In Volume 2 of *History of Korean Buddhism*, Yi seeks to identify the origin of Korean Buddhism[32] primarily by focusing on the dharma lineage of Korean Sŏn Buddhism as represented by eminent masters, including Chinul (1158–1210), the philosophical founder of Korean Sŏn Buddhism, and Hyujŏng (1520–1604). Yi's emphasis on Korean Sŏn Buddhism is also continued in Volume 3, where the content of *History of Korean Buddhism* is summarized.[33]

Yi viewed Korean Buddhism as the epitome of Korean culture. In his preface to *History of Korean Buddhism*, Yi states:

> The history of twelve Buddhist schools and the pedigree of nine hundred temples were buried in oblivion and thrown away into the dust. Those who have ears do not listen to and those who have eyes do not look. Though untalented, I am concerned about this. Despite my ignorance, I made up my mind to write this book [*History of Korean Buddhism*].[34]

In his epilogue to *History of Korean Buddhism*, Chang Chiyŏn (1864–1921), an influential journalist, states, "Korean Buddhism has a long history. However, extant Buddhist materials are not many and the majority of them were even lost. . . . Shocked by these facts, Yi Nŭnghwa wrote this book [*History of Korean Buddhism*]."[35] In his commentary to the *History of Korean Buddhism*, Cho Myŏnggi (1905–88), a noted scholar of Buddhism, also claims, "After the Japanese annexation of Korea in 1910, Yi Nŭnghwa came to devote himself to conducting research and collecting historical data . . . which proves that his primary concern was with indigenous Korean culture." In other words, Yi's intention to preserve Buddhist culture was one of his major motives for writing the *History of Korean Buddhism*. For Yi, monastic structures, Buddhist publications, the names of famous places and mountains,[36] the Korean alphabet, and folk festivals were representative of Korean Buddhist culture.[37]

Yi Nŭnghwa and Korean Modernization

Yi's aim in publishing books and essays was to promote Buddhism, and his target audience was the general public. However, his intention of propagating Buddhism was not fulfilled in the context of multireligious circumstances. In addition, his works, mostly written in classical Chinese, were hardly accessible to his target audience, who could not read classical Chinese. Consequently, Yi's writings could not play a substantial role in the modernization of Korea in the colonial context, despite his aspiration to employ Buddhism for that reason. Yi's ultimate goal of studying Buddhism was to write a Buddhist history of Korea. However, such an effort was not unique to Yi, but common to his contemporaries and, by extension, to his Asian counterparts of the time. During the latter half of the nineteenth and the first half of the twentieth centuries, most Buddhists in China, Japan, Sri Lanka, and Korea faced similar political and social changes due to imperialist expansion. Adopting the notion of "modernism" from Western liberalism, Korean Buddhists carried out reforms by responding to the general movements of modernization and nation-building, thus embarking on reforms in order to make Buddhism socially viable. Two major concerns of Korean Buddhist reformers were "identity" and "responsiveness." They tried to promote the traditional identity of the Korean people by producing books on Korean Buddhist history and constructing a sectarian identity that was distinct from that of Japanese Buddhism.[38] They also wished to show the practicality of Buddhism in contemporary society.[39]

One noticeable aspect of Yi's relationship with Buddhism lies in the fact that he was a lay devotee. The reform movements of Korean Buddhism in his day were primarily led by reform-minded monks, including Han Yongun (sobriquet: Manhae, 1879–1944), a representative monk-reformist, within the monastic communities.[40] The failure to involve the laity in various programs of reform was indeed one of the limitations of the process of modernization in Korean Buddhism.[41] Even Han Yongun was not an exception. The main purpose of Han's representative work, *Treatise on the Reform of Korean Buddhism*, was to reform the Buddhist communities, which did not include the lay circle.[42] This was one of the major aspects of Buddhist reform in Korea that set it apart from its counterparts in other regions of Asia, where the laity played a vital role. Unlike his fellow Buddhist scholars, Yi never joined a monastery and remained a lay Buddhist throughout his life. Yi was also the only layperson to undertake the editorship of Buddhist magazines.[43]

Yi was exceptional in leading Buddhist reform as a layperson; however, his efforts to promote Buddhism for the modernization of Korea fell short of achieving the desired goal. Like other Korean Buddhists, except for Han Yongun,[44] Yi uncritically adopted a nationalist stance amid the social changes and did not seriously consider how to locate nationhood within Buddhist teachings. Yi was the editor-in-chief of many Buddhist magazines, including the *Pulgyo chinhŭnghoe wŏlbo* (The Monthly of the Association for the Promotion of Buddhism).[45] Research has indicated that early Buddhist journals were instrumental in the propagation of Japanese colonial rule.[46] In addition, the Buddhist reform movement in Korea made notable changes after the March First Independent Movement of 1919. Before the March First Movement, the majority of Buddhist leaders conceded to colonial rule.

Often based on Japanese sources, Yi's works on Buddhism were mainly published before 1919, which also limited the possible role that Yi's writing could play in the process of Korea's modernization. Yi's works were aimed to evangelize Buddhism. The title of the *Harmonization of All Religions* indicates that Yi intended the book to be "a must for the transmission of the Way [Buddhism] in its offering of a comparison of different scriptures [of all religions in Korea]." His *History of Korean Buddhism* was also published with the same goal. Yi argues, "I am a Buddhist. Therefore, I want to respond to anti-Buddhists. Though it took the form of history, the *History of Korean Buddhism* is, in fact, written for propagation."[47]

Yi made a great effort to promote Buddhism in Korean society.[48] Yi's reform movement is referred to as the "Buddhist movement for the laypeople" (K. *kŏsa Pulgyo undong*). However, Yi was subject to the same limitations as other Korean Buddhists of the time in that he was not able to materialize the idea in the context of Korea and its modernization.[49] One of the reasons for Yi's failure had to do with the language he used. As noted above, the majority of Yi's works were written in classical Chinese; the main body of the *Harmonization of All Religions* was composed in classical Chinese, except the particles, and the *History of Korean Buddhism* was written entirely in classical Chinese. Yi justified the use of classical Chinese with the claim that it was used to transmit the historical data in their original form.[50] However, he also mentioned that the Korean version of historical data was too secular to be used.[51] Yi may not be blamed for his exclusive use of classical Chinese in his works given that his fellow Koreanists, such as Pak Ŭnsik (1859–1925) and Sin Ch'aeho (1880–1936), who emphasized the exclusive use of the Korean alphabet, also wrote in classical Chinese. Yi also emphasized the importance of the Korean alphabet as an essential part of Korean culture, an issue to which we will return later. Writing in classical Chinese caused a great hindrance to the promotion of Buddhism in sending out messages to his target audience. Who, then, was his target audience?

In his epilogue to the *History of Korean Buddhism*, Chang Chiyŏn states, "Eight or nine out of ten people are illiterate. Shocked by this fact, Yi Nŭnghwa wrote this book [*History of Korean Buddhism*]."[52] According to this quotation, the target audience of the *History of Korean Buddhism* was the ordinary people of Korea, who were illiterate. The majority of laypeople in his day were old women and children,[53] who could not read classical Chinese. If so, contrary to his wish, the influence of Yi's *History of Korean Buddhism* on them was almost nonexistent. Then, could his works, including the *History of Korean Buddhism*, exert a significant influence on a small number of intellectuals, including Buddhist monks, who numbered only five to six thousand at the time?[54] The answer is also negative. What was the influence of his works on Sŏn practitioners? Sŏn monks were few in number in Yi's day[55] and did not show much interest in doctrinal teachings because they were still influenced by the Sŏn adage that Sŏn does not depend on words and letters.

One area in which *Harmonization of All Religions* did play a significant role has been modern Korean Buddhist scholarship. *History of Korean Buddhism* has helped to pave the road to an objective and scientific study of Korean Buddhism, and hence has played a decisive role in the modernization of Buddhist Studies in Korea.[56] *History of Korean Buddhism* has also had a great deal of influence on Japanese scholars' understanding of Korean Buddhism, as demonstrated in Japanese publications, including *Richō Bukkyō* (Buddhism of the Chosŏn Dynasty, 1929) and *Jōsen Zenkyōshi* (History of Korean Sŏn Buddhism, 1930).[57] *History of Korean Buddhism* still serves as a textbook for the study of Korean Buddhism in contemporary Korea.[58]

Harmonization of All Religions has its own limitations: It neglected the issues of Buddhist rituals and organization, and in some places, showed biased views toward Buddhism.[59] *History of Korean Buddhism* has some limits as well: It is primarily a collection of data on Korean Buddhism; some of its parts are filled with Yi's personal speculation and do not provide any supporting textual evidence.[60] Yi could be accused of having accepted the Japanese scholars' biased views of Korean history. In short, Buddhist monks, the intellectuals, and the ordinary people of his time found Yi's publication mostly unappealing or even unacceptable, and thus they failed to have any substantial influence on the process of Korea's modernization in the colonial context.

Yi believed that Korean Buddhism played a significant role in the course of Korean history. However, he was also aware that Buddhism was not in a respectable condition in his time, which he considered to be a result of the anti-Buddhist policy of the Chosŏn government. The changing circumstances in Japanese Buddhist circles and the rise of Christianity in Korea also expedited his effort to conduct research on Korean Buddhism as a religion, a system of thought, and a national culture.

Yi identified himself as a Buddhist, but still advocated religious pluralism, which makes him unique among the scholars of his day. His theory of harmonization of all religions in Korea is different from the kind of harmonization that developed in East Asian traditions. The theory of harmonization in the history of East Asian Buddhism developed after the eighth century in China; it changed from focusing on the unity of meditation and the doctrine of Buddhism to harmonization between Buddhism and Confucianism, and again to harmonization among Confucianism, Buddhism, and Taoism. The theory of harmonization is considered an important aspect of Korean Buddhism.[61] Wŏnhyo (617–86) has been regarded as the first Buddhist who harmonized doctrinal disputes in the Buddhist history of Korea, and critics consider him the pioneer of the theory of harmonization in Korea.

After Wŏnhyo, the harmonization theory in Korean Buddhism developed primarily in two directions: The first emphasizes the harmony between the different Buddhist schools; the second focuses on the harmony between Buddhism and other religious and philosophical systems. The Korean Buddhists during the Koryŏ period (918–1392) were more concerned with the harmonization between meditation and doctrine in the Buddhist circles, whereas during the Chosŏn period (1392–1910), the theory of unity between Confucianism and Buddhism, or among the three religions of Buddhism, Confucianism, and Taoism, was most visible.

Even though Yi emphasized the harmony among different religions, he did not think that all religions were equal in every aspect. For Yi, Buddhist doctrines and their functions far surpassed those of other religions. Of the Korean religions, his primary concern was with Buddhism, Confucianism, and Christianity.[62] Yi evaluated them as follows: Confucianism was the most inferior religion, Christianity was superior to Confucianism, and Buddhism was the most sophisticated of the three. This was the same for his evaluation of the three religions in terms of their potential contributions to the modernization of Korea.[63]

The harmonization theory that developed in the history of Korean Buddhism was a product of the religious situation of the times as well as the non-dogmatic character of Buddhist thought itself. Yi's attempt was also a response to the religious conditions of his time.[64] Although he considered Buddhism the best of all the religions in Korea, Buddhism was in decline in his day. In such a context, Yi authored *Harmonization of All Religions* with the purpose of propagating Buddhism while emphasizing its supremacy. Nevertheless, we are left with little textual evidence that his wish was fulfilled during his lifetime. In addition, when the March First Movement of 1919 broke out against Japanese colonial rule, and thirty-three people signed the Declaration of Independence, all of the signatories were religious adherents, but of the thirty-three, only two, Han Yongun and Paek Yongsŏng (1864–1940), were Buddhists. In contrast, about half of the signatories were Christians. This is one incident which reveals that even though Yi evaluated Buddhism as the best religion, the religion's role in Korean society in his time was rather questionable.

Given that it was not until modern times that religious pluralism infiltrated the mainstream of religious studies in the world, Yi's approach to religious harmonization shed new light on the study of religion in Korean scholarship. This is more significant in that Yi paved the road to the objective study of Buddhism in Korea based on Spenserian social Darwinism and comparative methodology. He also proposed the potential for the scientific study of religion through religious phenomenology and a historical approach to religion.

Yi's Buddhist thought is characterized by the concepts of self-nature and non-duality, the theory of equality, and an emphasis on Sŏn Buddhism. However, the notion of self-nature failed to be linked to social activities and the realization of non-duality was difficult in a context where nationalism and imperialism were dominating society and the international scene. The doctrines of self-nature and non-duality serve as the basis of the Buddhist concept of equality, which Yi considered the essence of Buddhism. His approach to the issue of Buddhist equality is quite different from that of Han Yongun. Like Yi, Han also viewed the principle of equality to be an essential teaching of Buddhism. According to Han, equality produces the idea of freedom and the ignorance of equality leads to oppression. Han regarded the loss of Korea's sovereignty to be a result of social inequality and Japan's annexation of Korea to be a violation of the liberty and equality of the Korean people. With the rise of the March First Movement of 1919, Han's Buddhist ideas of equality developed into a concrete program for the independence of Korea.[65] However, unlike Han, Yi failed to transform his understanding of Buddhist equality into a practical social theory; instead, his major interest remained with Sŏn Buddhism.

Harmonization of All Religions reveals that Yi was familiar with both Theravāda and Mahāyāna canonical texts. Yi also felt that Sŏn Buddhism and doctrinal Buddhism coexisted in his era. He attempted to identify the Korean lineages of doctrinal Buddhism with a focus on the Flower Garland School (K. *Hwaŏmjong*).[66] However, Yi was more interested in Sŏn Buddhism than doctrinal Buddhism. Actually, Yi's Sŏn-oriented reform movement of Korean Buddhism was characteristic of his Buddhist thought.[67] Yi regarded the Linji lineages as the orthodox line of Sŏn Buddhism and identified Imjejong, or the Imje School, as a Korean version of the Linji school of Chan in ninth-century China. He emphasized the idea that the Imje School had an inseparable relationship with the internal and external situation of Korean Buddhist circles in his day.

Korean Buddhism of Yi's day had more doctrinal features than meditative ones. Moreover, for him, Sŏn Buddhism was not in a position to exert a strong influence on Korean society during his time.[68] Nevertheless, Yi prioritized Sŏn Buddhism, and his emphasis on it is presumed to be a product of external influence. Before the twentieth-century Asian reform movements, including the Buddhist Theosophical Society in Sri Lanka in 1980, the exclusive attention to meditative experience was unprecedented, and Buddhist meditation moved into the spotlight as Buddhism began to participate in broad social concerns during contemporary Buddhist reform movements. In Japan, Zen was presented as a remedy to the one-sided emphasis on rationality and empiricism.[69] Likewise, Yi claimed Sŏn Buddhism was the original sect of Korean Buddhism as a way of preventing subjugation to Japanese Buddhism; as a result, Yi's interest in Buddhist meditation emerged as his way of Buddhist social engagement.

However, Yi's exclusive emphasis on Sŏn Buddhism seems not to have elicited a positive response from Korean intellectuals during the process of Korean modernization.[70] For example, the Flower Garland School played a significant role in the history of Korean Buddhism. Wŏnhyo and Ŭisang (625–702), the founders of the Korean version of the Flower Garland School, were ardent scholar-monks of doctrinal Buddhism. Their tradition was transmitted to Chinul, Hyujŏng, and his successors.[71] In addition, doctrinal Buddhism still flourished during Yi's time. Han Yongun also stated that one of reasons for the decline of Buddhism in his day was that there was an overemphasis on doctrinal Buddhism, which was inclined to exegetical studies. Han thus emphasized Sŏn Buddhism. In case of Han, however, the emphasis falls equally on doctrinal training and Sŏn Buddhist meditation, whereas Yi was primarily inclined toward Sŏn Buddhism. Han's integration of meditative Buddhism and doctrinal Buddhism characterized his Buddhist thought,[72] and he presented the simultaneous practice of the two as the core of Buddhism. Han's integration format provided the doctrinal foundation for the unification movement of the monastic communities during the colonial period.[73]

Yi's emphasis on Sŏn Buddhism was in line with the trends of his time. Concerned about the rise of Christianity, Korean Buddhists developed their reform movements primarily within the framework of the Sŏn tradition,[74] and an emphasis on Sŏn Buddhism was common among Korean Buddhists at that time.[75] In his approach to Sŏn Buddhism, Yi was particularly interested in the dharma lineage of Korean Sŏn Buddhism. A question has been raised recently concerning the validity of the dharma lineage theory proposed by Yi and others. Issues involved in the discussion of the dharma lineage of Korean Sŏn Buddhism include that of continuity. That is, the origin of the Chogye Order goes back to the Koryŏ period, and the Order was re-established in 1938. Whether the current Chogye Order is the same as the one established during the Koryŏ dynasty is a question that requires further discussion.[76] At least one can say that the attempt to understand the current Chogye Order as the direct descendent of the Chogye Order of the Koryŏ dynasty has much to do with the ideological motivation to create an orthodox lineage of the school.[77]

Yi's major contribution to Korean Buddhism is in his role as a pioneer of modern Korean Buddhist scholarship. Modeling his study of Korean Buddhism on the issues of the periodization of Buddhist history, discourses on the dharma lineages, subitist-gradualist debates, and the different types of meditation, Korean Buddhism launched a modern approach to scholarship, taking those issues as the object of scholarship. Another of Yi's contributions has been his keen attention to Buddhist cultural heritage in Korea. Yi recognized the importance of Buddhist material culture, including *Sŏkkuram* (The Stone Cave Grotto), *Changgyŏnggak* (The Storage Hall for the *Tripiṭāka Koreana*), and *Hunmin chŏngŭm* (or *Han'gŭl*, the Korean alphabet), as well as Buddhist publications.[78] Yi showed special interest in the Korean alphabet. His discussion of the Korean alphabet in the *History of Korean Buddhism* is the most comprehensive account of any topic discussed in the book, comprising sixty-seven pages in classical Chinese. It deals with related issues, including the history of the creation of the Korean alphabet, a grammatical comparison among Korean, Japanese, Mongolian, and Chinese, and a discussion of the origin of the Korean alphabet, and its vowels and consonants. Through a close analysis of the Korean language, Yi argued that the Korean alphabet originated from Sanskrit, a topic that is still being debated among Korean linguists.

Conclusion

This essay aimed to examine Yi Nŭnghwa's role in the process of modernization of early twentieth-century Korea, when it was under Japanese colonial rule. Yi was a prolific writer and left behind voluminous writings with a focus on Buddhism. Despite his ambition to change the acceptance of Buddhism among the Korean people and thus employ Buddhism as a major tool for the modernization of Korean society, his Buddhist thoughts did not materialize into social action; and his works, written in classical Chinese, could not appeal to his target audience because they were not familiar with the language. Yi also conceded to the Buddhist policy of the Japanese colonial government and lived his life as an active Japanophile in his later career.[79] Nevertheless, Koreans owe the methodology of and source materials for modern Buddhist studies in Korea to Yi, and by extension, Korean studies in general. Yi created a bridge between pre-modern and modern forms of scholarship in his handling of the data, methodology, and content of his writings. In this sense, Yi Nŭnghwa deserves the title of "pioneer," as he established modern Buddhist scholarship in Korea.[80] Yi Nŭnghwa can also be considered a "pioneer" of Korean Studies and the "father" of religious studies in Korea.

Notes

1. I would like to thank an anonymous reader and Professor Pankaj N. Mohan of Sydney University in Australia for their reading of this paper and providing valuable comments.

2. Yi Chaehŏn, "Kŭndae Han'guk Pulgyohak ŭi sŏngnip kwa chonggyo insik—Yi Nŭnghwa wa Kwŏn Sangno rŭl chungsim ŭro" (The Establishment of Buddhist Studies and Religious Consciousness in Modern Korea—Focusing on Yi Nŭnghwa and Kwŏn Sangno). Ph.D. dissertation, Han'guk chŏngsin munhwa yŏn'guwŏn, 1999, pp. 111–112.

3. Yang Ŭnyong, "Yi Nŭnghwa ŭi Han'guk Pulgyo yŏn'gu" (Yi Nŭnghwa's Study of Korean Buddhism), *Chonggyo yŏn'gu* 9 (1993): 45–65, p. 51.

4. According to Pori Park, except for Yang Ŭnyong, Buddhist scholars of Korea did not include Yi Nŭnghwa as a Buddhist reformer. See Pori Park, "The Modern Remaking of Korean Buddhism: The Korean Reform Movement During Japanese Colonial Rule and Han Yongun's Buddhism (1879–1944)." Ph.D. dissertation, University of California, Los Angeles, 1998, pp. 19–20.

5. Yi Chaehŏn, "Yi Nŭnghwa yŏn'gu ŭi hyŏnhwang kwa kwaje" (Current Status and Issues of the Study of Yi Nŭnghwa), *Han'guk chonggyo sa yŏn'gu* 7 (1999): 5–28, pp. 24–25.

6. Sin Kwangch'ŏl, "Yi Nŭnghwa ŭi chonggyohak chŏk kwanjŏm" (Yi Nŭnghwa's View of Religious Studies), *Chonggyo yŏn'gu* 9 (1993): 173–198, pp. 193–194.

7. Kim Chongsŏ, "Hanmal, Ilche ha Han'guk chongyo yŏn'gu ŭi chŏn'gae" (The Development of the Study of Korean Religion at the End of the Chosŏn Dynasty and

under Japanese Rule), *Han'guk sasang sa taegye* (Compendium of the Intellectual History of Korea), vol. 6 (Sŏngnam, Korea: Han'guk chŏngsin munhwa yŏn'guwŏn, 1993), 243-314, p. 298.

8. Sin, "Yi Nŭnghwa ŭi chonggyohak chŏk kwanjŏm," p. 187.

9. *Tan'gyŏng* (Platform Sūtra, 1939) and the *Chosŏn Pulgyo ponmal* (The Cause and Effect of Korean Buddhism, u.d.) are two more extant works on Buddhism composed by Yi Nŭnghwa.

10. Yi, "Yi Nŭnghwa yŏn'gu ŭi hyŏnhwang kwa kwaje," p. 6.

11. Except for the *Harmonization of All Religions* and the *History of Korean Buddhism*, his extant works on religion include *Chosŏn Togyo sa* (A History of Daoism in Korea), *Chosŏn Kidokkyo kŭp oegyo sa* (A History of Christianity and Diplomacy in Korea), and *Chosŏn musok ko* (A Study of Shamanism in Korea).

12. Yi Nŭnhgwa's extant works on the history of Korean society include *Chosŏn haeŏhwa sa* (A History of the Professional Female Entertainers of Korea). See Yi, "Yi Nŭnghwa yŏn'gu ŭi hyŏnhwang kwa kwaje," p. 27.

13. Yang, "Yi Nŭnghwa ŭi Han'guk Pulgyo yŏn'gu," pp. 50–51.

14. For the importance of this scripture in Korea and research on it, see A. Charles Muller, *The Sutra of Perfect Enlightenment: Korean Buddhism's Guide to Meditation* (Albany: State University of New York Press, 1999).

15. Sin, "Yi Nŭnghwa ŭi chonggyohak chŏk kwanjŏm," p. 196.

16. Yi, "Kŭndae Han'guk Pulgyo hak ŭi sŏngnip kwa chonggyo insik," p. 86.

17. Yi Nŭnghwa, *Paekkyo hoet'ong* (Harmonization of All Religions) (Seoul: Poryŏn'gak, 1973), pp. 56–80.

18. Yi Nŭnghwa, *Chosŏn Pulgyo t'ongsa e ch'wihaya* (About a Comprehensive History of Korean Buddhism). *Chosŏn Pulgyo ch'ongbo* (The Journal of the Collection of Korean Buddhism) 16 (August 1917). *Han'guk Pulgyo chapchi ch'ongbo* (The Journal of the Collection of Korean Buddhist Magazines) 14: 346–55, p. 347.

19. Sin, "Yi Nŭnghwa ŭi chonggyo hak chŏk kwanjŏm," p. 187.

20. Yang, "Yi Nŭnghwa ŭi Han'guk Pulgyo yŏn'gu," pp. 61–62.

21. Yi Nŭnghwa, *Paekkyo hoet'ong sŏ* (Preface to the Harmonization of All Religions), in *Paekkyo hoet'ong* (Preface to the Harmonization of All Religions) (Seoul: Poryŏn'gak, 1973).

22. Yang Ŭnyong. "Yi Nŭnghwa ŭi hangmun kwa Pulgyo sasang" (Yi Nŭnghwa's Scholarship and Buddhist Thought), in *Sungsan Pak Kilchin Paksa kohŭi kinyŏm: Han'guk kŭndae chonggyo sasang sa* (Pak Kilchin Festschrift: Intellectual History of Modern Korean Religions) (Iri, Korea: Won'gwang taehakkyo ch'ulp'anbu, 1984), 437–465.

23. Yi, "Yi Nŭnghwa yŏn'gu ŭi hyŏnhwang kwa kwaje," pp. 16–17.

24. Yi, *Chosŏn Kidokkyo kŭp oegyo sa* (A History of Christianity and Diplomacy in Korea) (Seoul: Chosŏn Kidokkyo ch'angmunsa, 1928), p. 60. This was the same for Han Yongun, Yi's contemporary and the representative figure in the reform movement of Korean Buddhism.

25. Yi, *Paekkyo hoet'ong*, pp. 56–57.

26. Yi, "Kŭndae Han'guk Pulgyohak ŭi sŏngnip kwa chonggyo insik," p. 86.

27. Yi, "*Chasŏ*" (Preface), *Chosŏn Pulgyo t'ongsa*, vol. 1, p. 1.

28. Yi, "Kŭndae Han'guk Pulgyo hak ŭi sŏngnip kwa chonggyo insik," pp. 76–86.

29. Yi, "Kŭndae Han'guk Pulgyo hak ŭi sŏngnip kwa chonggyo insik," pp. 102–103. Han Yongun argued that meditative practice (*Sŏn*) and doctrinal study (Kyo) should be equally emphasized. For a detailed account of Han's integration of Sŏn and Kyo, see Park "The Modern Remaking of Korean Buddhism," pp. 162–200.

30. Yang, "Yi Nŭnghwa ŭi Han'guk Pulgyo yŏn'gu," p. 64.

31. Yi, *Chosŏn Pulgyo t'ongsa*, pp. 336–377.

32. Yang, "Yi Nŭnghwa ŭi Han'guk Pulgyo yŏn'gu," p. 8–59; Yi, "Kŭndae Han'guk Pulgyo hak ŭi sŏngnip kwa chonggyo insik," p. 102.

33. Yang, "Yi Nŭnghwa ŭi Han'guk Pulgyo yŏn'gu," pp. 63–64.

34. Yi, "*Chasŏ*," p. 1.

35. Yi, "*Pal*" (Epilogue), *Chosŏn Pulgyo t'ongsa*, vol. 2, p. 1.

36. Yi Nŭngwha said, "The famous mountain Kŭmgang was named after the abode of a bodhisattva and the Tripiṭāka Koreana preserved in Haein Monastery is the dharma treasure of the world" (Yi, "Chasŏ," p. 1).

37. Yi Nŭnghwa, "Tangok p'ogyo sŏl" (A Discussion of Propagation at the Buddhist Paradise and Hell). *Chosŏn Pulgyo ch'ongbo* (The Journal of the Collection of Korean Buddhism) 16 (1919). *Han'guk Pulgyo chapchi ch'ongbo* (The Journal of the Collection of Korean Buddhist Magazines) 15: 373–777.

38. Park, "The Modern Remaking of Korean Buddhism," pp. 4–26.

39. Park, "The Modern Remaking of Korean Buddhism," p. 102.

40. Park, "The Modern Remaking of Korean Buddhism," pp. 17–19.

41. Park, "The Modern Remaking of Korean Buddhism," pp. 89–93.

42. Park, "The Modern Remaking of Korean Buddhism," pp. 138–143.

43. Park, "The Modern Remaking of Korean Buddhism," p. 85.

44. Han Yongun was a unique Buddhist thinker who attempted to appropriate the modern social involvement and nationalism from a Buddhist standpoint and his reform ideas became the main source of reference for the monastic reforms (Park, "The Modern Remaking of Korean Buddhism," pp. 27–29).

45. Park, "The Modern Remaking of Korean Buddhism," pp. 76–95.

46. Henrik H. Sørensen, "Korean Buddhist Journals during Early Japanese Colonial Rule," *Korea Journal* 30, no. 1 (January 1990): 17–27, p. 23.

47. Yi, "*Chasŏ*," p. 1.

48. Han Yongun also pointed out that the lack of propagation of Buddhist teachings contributed to the decline of Buddhism in Korea (Park, "The Modern Remaking of Korean Buddhism," p. 142).

49. Han Yongun was also deeply concerned until his death in 1944 with the development of Buddhism for the masses (K. *minjung Pulgyo*). However, he failed in bringing the Buddhist movement into his contemporary (Park, "The Modern Remaking of Korean Buddhism," p. 151).

50. Yi, "*Pŏmnye*" (Legend), *Chosŏn Pulgyo t'ongsa*, vol. 1 p. 1.

51. Yi Kwangnin and Sin Yongha, *Saryo ro pon Han'guk munhwa sa: kŭndae p'yŏn* (A Cultural History of Korea Seen through Source Materials: the Modern Period) (Seoul: Ilchisa, 1984), p. 58.

52. Yi, "*Pal*," p. 1.

53. Park, "The Modern Remaking of Korean Buddhism," p. 93.

54. Robert E. Buswell, Jr., *The Zen Monastic Experience: Buddhist Practice in Contemporary Korea* (Princeton, NJ: Princeton University Press, 1992), p. 27.

55. The number of Sŏn monks has increased since then. However, they still do not exceed ten percent of the total number of monks in contemporary Korea.

56. Yi, "Yi Nŭnghwa yŏn'gu ŭi hyŏnhwang kwa kwaje," p. 15.

57. Yi, "Kŭndae Han'guk Pulgyo hak ŭi sŏngnip kwa chonggyo insik," p. 104.

58. Yang, "Yi Nŭnghwa ŭi Han'guk Pulgyo yŏn'gu," p. 56.

59. Yi, "Kŭndae Han'guk Pulgyo hak ŭi sŏngnip kwa chonggyo insik," p. 90.

60. Yi, "Kŭndae Han'guk Pulgyo hak ŭi sŏngnip kwa chonggyo insik, p. 105.

61. However, criticism of the theory of harmonization as a characteristic feature of Korean Buddhism also exists. For this, refer to Jae-Ryong Shim, *Korean Buddhism: Tradition and Transformation* (Seoul: Jimmoondang Publishing Company, 1999), pp. 147–157.

62. Yi, "Kŭndae Han'guk Pulgyo hak ŭi sŏngnip kwa chonggyo insik," p. 13.

63. Yi, "Kŭndae Han'guk Pulgyo hak ŭi sŏngnip kwa chonggyo insik," pp. 56–57.

64. Sin, "Yi Nŭnghwa ŭi chonggyo hak chŏk kwanjŏm," p. 181.

65. Park, "The Modern Remaking of Korean Buddhism," pp. 150–164.

66. Yi, "Kŭndae Han'guk Pulgyo hak ŭi sŏngnip kwa chonggyo insik," p. 103.

67. Yang, "Yi Nŭnghwa ŭi hangmun kwa Pulgyo sasang," pp. 437–465; Yang, "Yi Nŭnghwa ŭi Han'guk Pulgyo yŏn'gu," pp. 63–64.

68. Yi Nŭnghwa attributed the decline of Sŏn Buddhism of Korea primarily to the unhindered action of Kyŏnghŏ (1846–1912), who has been credited as a revivalist of modern Korean Sŏn Buddhism (Yi, *Chosŏn Pulgyo t'ongsa*, pp. 962–963).

69. Park, "The Modern Remaking of Korean Buddhism," pp. 9–16.

70. This was the same for Man'gong (1876–1946), an eminent Sŏn master in Yi Nŭnghwa's time, who paved the way to Sŏn exclusivism in the Buddhist circles of Korea. See Kim Jongmyung, "Man'gong ŭi Sŏn sasang: t'ŭkching kwa yŏkhal" (Man'gong's Approach to Zen: Its Characteristics and Role). *Chonggyo yŏn'gu* 34 (Spring 2004): 203–332.

71. As a response to the strong influence of the Flower Garland School in the later period of Chosŏn Korea (1392–1910), discourses on the types of Sŏn Buddhism developed among scholar-monks, even including Confucian scholars. For this refer to Kim Jongmyung, "Ijong Sŏn . samjong Sŏn nonjaeng" (Discourses on the Types of Sŏn Buddhism), in Yi Hyogŏl, et al., *Nonjaeng ŭro ponŭn Pulgyo ch'ŏrhak* (Buddhist Philosophy Seen through Discourses) (Seoul: Yemun sŏwŏn, 1998), 224–261.

72. Park, "The Modern Remaking of Korean Buddhism," p. 191.

73. Park, "The Modern Remaking of Korean Buddhism," pp. 165–167.

74. Yi, "Kŭndae Han'guk Pulgyohak ŭi sŏngnip kwa chonggyo insik," p. 37.

75. Han Yongun also attempted to restructure Korean Buddhism by giving priority to Sŏn Buddhism (Park, "The Modern Remaking of Korean Buddhism," p. 139).

76. Keel Hee-Sung, "Han'guk Pulgyo ŭi chŏngch'esŏng t'amgu: Chogyejong ŭi yŏksa wa sasang ŭl chungsim ŭro hayŏ" (The Chogye Order and the Search for the Identity of Korean Buddhism), *Han'guk chonggyo yŏn'gu* 2 (June 2000): 159–93.

77. For the discussion of the issue, see Pak Haedang, "Chogyejong ŭi pŏpt'ong sŏl e taehan kŏmt'o" (A Critical Research on the Dharma Lineage of the Chogye Order), *Chŏrhak sasang* XI (December 2000): 43–62.

78. Sŏkkuram and Changgyŏnggak were designated by the UNESCO as world cultural heritage in 1995, *Hunmin chŏngŭm* and the Zen text, *Paegun hwasang ch'orok*

pulcho chikchi simch'e yojŏl (Excerpts from the Pointing Directly to the Essence of the Human Mind by the Monk Paegun), as the Memory of the World in 1997 and 2001, respectively.

79. Ch'oe Pyŏnghŏn, "Ilbon ŭi kangjŏm kwa Pulgyo" (Japanese Control of Korea and Buddhism), *Pulgyo p'yŏngnon* 17 (Winter 2003): 268–93.

80. Yi, "Kŭndae Han'guk Pulgyohak ŭi sŏngnip kwa chonggyo insik," pp. 90–91.

5

Gendered Response to Modernity

Kim Iryŏp and Buddhism[1]

Jin Y. Park

Discussions of Buddhist modernity in Asia have frequently characterized the phenomenon with the emergence of nationalism, mass-proselytization, lay Buddhist movements, and the influence of political situations such as imperialism, communism, and colonialism, to name a few.[2] The modern period in Korean Buddhism was the time for reform.[3] Whether it takes the form of a revival of Zen tradition or a proposal for a total reform of traditional Buddhism,[4] Buddhist modernity in Korea began with a strong desire to repeal the suppression of Buddhism during the Chosŏn Dynasty.[5] In the process of transformation, Korean Buddhism faced the issue of nationalism and colonialism.[6] It had also become evident that there was a need to translate the language of Buddhist scriptures into Korean, to reconsider the strict demarcations between clergy and laities, and to revisit the meaning of Buddhist practice in the environments of modern time. What these descriptions suggest is that Buddhism's encounters with modernity in Korea have been understood mainly in connection with the political situation. The primacy of political situation in the understanding of modern Korean Buddhism inevitably marginalizes the experience, which, at first glace, is not understood as directly related to the politics of the time. One such area has been the role of gender in Korean Buddhism's encounters with modernity.

In this essay, I consider Kim Iryŏp's (1896–1971) Buddhism revealed through her life and thoughts as another expression of Korean Buddhism's encounter with modernity. The questions I attempt to answer in this essay are as follows: What was the role that Buddhism played in the construction of woman's identity at the dawn of the modern period in Korea? Which aspects of Buddhism made an appeal to a woman who was searching for her identity and independence? How would this consideration of the role of gender change our view about modern Korean Buddhism?

This essay unfolds in three parts. The first two sections discuss Kim Iryŏp's life before she joined the monastery as a case study of a Korean woman's encounter with modernity; the third section investigates Kim Iryŏp's Buddhist thought and the position of Buddhism in her philosophy; the final section considers the complex synergy in the play of gender, modernity and Buddhism in Kim Iryŏp's writings.

Love and Modernity

Kim Iryŏp's first publication as a Buddhist nun appeared in 1960, when she was sixty-four, under the title *Silsŏngin ŭi hoesang* (Memoir of the One who Has Lost the Mind), better known by its subtitle, *Ŏ'nŭ sudoin ŭi hoesang* (A Memoir of a Practitioner).[7] More than a half of this book consists of her letters to ex-lovers. These letters were again reprinted in her second publication, *Ch'ŏngch'ŭn ŭl pulsarŭ'go* (Having Burned out the Youth, 1962). Both the first and second books became bestsellers and were credited with having converted many women to Buddhism. Readers of these books, however, might experience some uneasiness. The nature of this uneasiness is somewhat different from the uncanny feeling one frequently encounters in reading the paradoxical and unconventional language in Zen writings. In considering the reason for the uneasy feeling, one might realize that it has to do the content of these books: The main parts of both publications deal with Kim Iryŏp's love affairs.

Reading a love story of a Zen teacher in a first-person narrative is not a common experience, even when the love story takes the format of a reflection thirty years after the affairs came to an end. Despite some uncomfortable feelings readers might have as they read the details of Kim Iryŏp's love stories, according to Kim, these books were written for the purpose of proselytization.[8] In her third and last publication, entitled *Haengbok kwa pulhaeng ŭi kalp'i esŏ* (In Between Happiness and Misfortune, 1964), Kim Iryŏp assumes the role of a counselor by providing her advice about love for all those who suffer from both happy and unhappy experiences caused by love.

Love stories have rarely been a topic of discussion in Korean Buddhism. The love story between Wŏnhyo (617–686) and Princess Yosŏk in the seventh century and various versions of love affairs in the life of Zen master Kyŏnghŏ (1849–1912) in the modern period could be among the most well-known love stories in the history of Korean Buddhism. The case of Kim Iryŏp is different from either of these situations in several ways. Both Wŏnhyo's and Kyŏnghŏ's love stories were recorded by a third person, and not presented as first-person narratives. Also, in both cases, their love affairs have been frequently interpreted as a higher level of action, even when the affair literally meant a violation of precepts. Some claim that their love affairs cannot be reduced to mere love stories or sexual relationships because those affairs represented the free spirit of the enlightened mind. It remains debatable whether Wŏnhyo's and Kyŏnghŏ's love stories represent unobstructed actions of the enlightened mind, as some claim,[9] or whether the narratives of unobstructed love affairs are themselves symbolic gestures designed to create a Zen ideology of the unobstructed mind.[10] What is important for our discussion is that Kim Iryŏp's love stories have been presented and interpreted in a context which is totally different from Wŏnhyo's and Kyŏnghŏ's cases.

Beginning from early on in her career as a writer and New Woman until after she joined the monastery, Kim Iryŏp's meditations on love continued to appear in her writings until the last publication mentioned above. Why, some might ask, was love such an important issue to Kim Iryŏp? In order to answer this question, we need to understand the meaning of love in the cultural context of Korea during the early twentieth century. Scholarship on Korean modernity and New Women at the beginning of the twentieth century in Korea has revealed that love, to the New Women (of whom Kim Iryŏp was one of central figures), had a special meaning which reflected the spirit of the time.[11]

The New Woman (K. *sinyŏsŏng*) is a term that became popular in the 1920s in Korea as a woman's magazine called *Sinyŏja* (New Women) appeared in 1920. The definition of New Women is still debatable. In general, the expression was used to refer to women who "were educated and became aware of gender equality, who possessed determination that was much stronger than Old Women and whose capacity to carry out the determination was outstanding."[12] They were also characterized as women "who were aware of the value of their existence and their historical responsibilities as women and who tried to realize them."[13] Unlike the traditional image of women in Korea, which emphasized the role of women as mother and wife, the ideal image of women proposed by New Women emphasized social and political involvements in their activities. In sum, compared to Old Women, New Women emphasized: "first, economic independence; second, rationalization and simplification of family system; third, rejection of male dominated traditional thoughts; fourth, a call for the stronger awareness of women's responsibility and duties; fifth, campaigns by women's organization and female students for Old Women so that they can become aware of various women's issues including health and child-education."[14]

For New Women, love had a special meaning as an expression of their rights. To them, falling in love was correlative with being modern; it was also synonymous with exercising the idea of woman's freedom. Falling in love and having love affairs were understood by New Women to be manifestations of their freedom, which can further be explained as aspects of the dawning of modernity in Korea. Modernity in the West began with the discovery of human beings. The right of a human being to make decisions as an independent individual has been emphasized in various aspects of modernity. Liberal love that was understood as an expression of an individual's feelings toward another individual emerged as one major venue for the New Women in Korea to declare their individuality.

That the idea of liberal love was understood in connection with gender equality, and thus to be equated with modernization, is well articulated in the newspaper articles and journal essays published at the turn of the century. For example, as early as 1896, the *Tongnip sinmun* (*The Independent* [Newspaper]) called for the equality of men and women and considered gender equality as one requirement for the creation of a civilized society: "Women are not lower than men in any respect; however, men look down upon women because men have failed to become civilized and thus do not think logically and humanely; instead, relying only on their physical power, men have suppressed women. How can they be different from barbarians?"[15] Gender equality here is identified with civilization; it represents rational thinking of the civilized being, which the bilingual newspaper *Tongnip sinmun* contrasts with the barbarian practice of gender discrimination.[16] This line of argument accords with the New Women's claim that liberal love affairs are manifestations of individuals' freedom and, thus, of women's liberation, which is further characterized as a feature of a modernized and civilized society. Kim Iryŏp's life before she joined the monastery presents a good example of this logic of love as understood by a New Woman who considered herself to be intellectually challenging the traditional value system of her society.

Kim Wŏnju, as she was known before taking the pen name Iryŏp, was born in northern Korea in 1896, the daughter of a Christian pastor. According to her memoir, her mother was a rather active woman who did not have much interest in the traditional woman's roles, such as cooking and sewing, but was good at managing household finances.[17] As the oldest daughter of a family with five children, Kim Wŏnju had to take care of her siblings from a very early age. Her parents had an unusual zeal for education. Without concern for villagers' criticism, her mother pledged to Kim Wŏnju that she would be educated like any male child.[18] Kim Iryŏp's biography shows that the education at Ehwa Haktang (1913–1918) and subsequent study in Japan (1919–1920) had a great influence on her awareness of the gender discrimination in Korean society.[19] After Kim Iryŏp came back from Japan, she launched a literary magazine *Sinyŏja* (New Women), which is considered to be the first magazine in Korea run by women for women for the purpose of the liberation of women.[20]

What is notable in the life story of Kim Iryŏp is the change in her attitude toward love and morality. In her autobiographical essay, Kim Iryŏp states that she grew up with a strong belief in the existence of a God-given moral system of good and evil and the existence of heaven and hell in the afterlife. As a Christian, she also had a strong belief that Christians go to heaven, whereas nonbelievers burn in hell. With such a belief, as early as the age of eight, she imagined her future as a missionary to the land of nonbelievers to whom she would send the words of God and save them from the fires of hell.[21] However, Kim Iryŏp's Christian faith wavered over time as she began to have doubts about various aspects of the Christian doctrine.[22] Some believe that her doubts about Christianity began and were intensified as she experienced a series of deaths in her family. One of her sisters died in 1907[23]; her mother died right after she gave birth to a boy in 1909, and the newborn baby died several days later. Her father died in 1915 when Kim Iryŏp was twenty. When her half sister, who was the only immediate family member left to Kim Iryŏp after the death of her father, died in 1919,[24] she became a complete loner in the world.

By 1920, it was clear that Kim Iryŏp no longer considered herself a Christian.[25] Around that time, her sense of morality turned drastically away from the Christian-based morality to a radical idea, which she called the "Sinjŏngjoron" (New Theory of Chastity), to which we will return shortly. In her essay "Naŭi aejŏng yŏkchŏng" (The Path of My Love Affairs), Kim Iryŏp explains how much this new idea about a woman's chastity deviates from the moral code in which she used to believe. She explains that, having believed in Jesus since she was a child, she had thought that having a sexual relationship before marriage or having an affair with a man other than one's husband was a guaranteed path to hell.[26] However, beginning around 1918 and continuing for about a decade, Kim Iryŏp's life was a series of affairs without marriage, with a married man, or in a married life without love. She married three times, divorced three times, and gave birth to a son out of wedlock.[27] People might have different positions regarding Kim Iryŏp's life and its ethical implications; however, regardless of one's views on these issues, one cannot deny that Kim Iryŏp's life and the change in her attitude toward morality were strongly influenced by her search for an independent identity and freedom, which was in turn heavily colored by her awareness of the gender discrimination in her society. A review of Kim Iryŏp's publications during the 1920s supports this claim.

Gender and Creation of a Modern Self

Kim Iryŏp's writings span from the 1920s to the 1960s and cover many different genres, including poetry, fiction, essays, and Buddhist writings, as she journeys through a panoramic life as a young female writer, feminist activist, and Zen Buddhist nun. What strikes readers in examining the bulk of Kim Iryŏp's writings is the consistency of her message despite the contradictions on the surface. Her writings and her life represent her long search for a self, for freedom to find herself, and meditations on the nature of that self. That her search for self and freedom was closely related to the issue of gender is well-articulated in her writings published during the 1920s.

In a newspaper article published in 1927, titled "Na ŭi chŏngjogwan" (My View on Chastity), Kim Iryŏp openly criticizes the centuries-old practice of the double standards placed upon chastity and declares what is known as a "New Theory of Chastity." In a conventional sense, "chastity" is a virtue that has been applied exclusively to women. Society demands a woman to be faithful to one man, whereas men are allowed to have relationships with more than one woman. In her challenge to the norms of her society, Kim Iryŏp finds this traditional concept of chastity one of the most visible realities of gender discrimination in Korean society, as she states:

> In the traditional concept of chastity, chastity was materialized and thus a woman with a past was treated as if she has become stale and had no freshness. In other words, when a woman had a sexual relationship with a man, she was treated as if her chastity had been lost. Chastity in this case was viewed like a broken container made of jewels.
>
> However, chastity is not such a static entity. . . .
>
> Even when a person had affairs with several lovers in the past, if the person possesses a healthy mind, is able to completely clean up from the memory whatever has happened in the past, and is capable of creating a new life by fully devoting herself/himself to the new lover, such a man or a woman possesses the chastity which cannot be broken.[28]

Later in the same essay, Kim Iryŏp emphasizes the importance of the new concept of chastity for the creation of a new woman, a new man, and eventually a new history:

> We, new women and new men, who want to do away with all the conventions, traditions, concepts and who are determined to bring attention to a new and fresh concept of life, cannot but strongly resist, among other things, the traditional morality on sex, which has ignored our personalities as well as our individual characteristics.[29]

Kim Iryŏp's idea of chastity was first introduced around 1920 when she was running a society for New Women known as Ch'ŏngt'aphoe (Society for the Blue Tower). This new idea of chastity was Kim Iryŏp's declaration of freedom as she states, "Human beings are free from the time they are born. The freedom to love, freedom to get married, and freedom to get divorced, are all sacred; to prohibit this freedom is a bad custom of an underdeveloped [society]."[30] In another essay, entitled "Uri ŭi isang" (Our Ideals), published in 1924, Kim Iryŏp repeats her ideas on love and chastity:

> Without love, there cannot be chastity. Chastity does not mean morality toward one's lover that can be imposed from outside; it is the passion representing the maximum harmony of affection and imagination for one's lover; it is a feeling related to one's original instinct which cannot be demanded without love. . . . Chastity then is not something fixed . . . but that which is fluid and that which can always be renewed. Chastity can never be identified with morality; it is the optimum state of one's sense of affection . . . .[31]

Whether it was practical in Korean society at that time to declare such a radical view on chastity or whether her concept of chastity had achieved its goal as an agenda to promote women's positions in that society is not a question that can be answered with a simple yes or no. Superficially speaking, Kim Iryŏp's personal life can be taken as a demonstration of her own view on chastity. One can even say that such a seemingly licentious life was an expression of freedom, from Kim Iryŏp's perspective. However, if that told Kim Iryŏp's whole story, she might not have had to resort to Buddhism. It is in this context that we can explain the role Buddhism played in Korean women's struggle to create a new vision for women at the dawn of the modern period.

When Kim Iryŏp developed her view on chastity, she was bold and strong. However, soon after she published the essay "My View on Chastity" in 1927, she declared that she had given up on love, a statement which was received with ridicule by the public.[32] The society would not accept Kim Iryŏp's decision to join the monastery and tried to interpret her tonsure as nothing other than reactionary. An interview appearing in the literary magazine *Kaebyŏk*'s January 1935 issue is suggestive not only of people's curiosity about the reason for Kim Iryŏp becoming a nun but also of the image of Buddhist nuns at the time. The first question asked by a reporter reflects people's speculation that Kim Iryŏp had left the secular world and joined the monastery in order to escape a certain scandalous incident in her life. The reporter asked:

> "It appeared to us that you had had a happy life in Sŏngbuk-tong and how did you end up getting a divorce?" Iryŏp: "That was to devote myself to Buddha-dharma." I [reporter]: "Do you mean that there was no problem between you and your husband?" Iryŏp: "There was absolutely nothing like that. Our marriage was extremely satisfactory. [We] were very happy." I [reporter]: "How then was a divorce possible? Did you divorce then, as you mentioned earlier, in order to perfect the Buddha-dharma?" Iryŏp: "Yes, that was so." [33]

Was Kim Iryŏp's tonsure reactionary, as some people interpreted it, or was it based on her determination to fully devote her life to the teachings of the Buddha, as Kim Iryŏp claimed?[34] In order to answer this question, we should further consider following questions: What did Kim Iryŏp expect from Buddhism, if her joining the monastery was *not* a mere escapism from her failed marriages and love affairs? Was Buddhism able to offer, both in terms of monastic life and in its philosophy, what she was looking for? Also, if Buddhism was able to offer what a New Woman at the beginning of modern time searched for, can Buddhism play the same role for women in our time?

Before we answer these questions, let us briefly consider the logic of liberal love which was the foundation of Kim Iryŏp's thought in her pre-monastic life. What is striking about the role of the liberal concept of love and love affairs is that, to the New Women who embraced this liberalist view of individual identity, love was not only a concept but also a reality for their liberation. For New Women, "free love" represented a concrete reality of a woman's rights to make decisions in her own life. Freedom to make her own decision in the selection of her spouse and in the nature of the relationship with her spouse meant, to New Women, a full-scale challenge to the concept of a woman that their society had held for centuries. Those representatives of the New Women in the early twentieth century—Na Hyesŏk, who was the first female artist in western painting; Kim Myŏngsun, the first woman writer; and Yun Simdŏk, the first female singer—all embraced liberal love as an act of claiming their individuality, independence, and gender equality, and eventually all became victims of their own actions because of the gap between their ideal and the norms of the society. Their failure, however, was caused as much by the resistance of their society as by their inability to see the limitations of the ultimate value they imposed on love. These women failed to see that the idea of free love itself was a cultural product, not a timeless, universal truth. Hence, it could not be the only ultimate manifestation of individuality and freedom for which these New Women so desperately searched.

Ch'oe Hyesil, the author of *Sinyŏsŏngdŭrŭn muŏsŭl kkumkkuŏtnŭn'ga?* (What Did New Women Dream About?), made this point succinctly in her investigation of different responses to the theme of love as it appeared in Korean literature published in the 1910s and the 1930s. Ch'oe states: "In the 1910s, to get involved with a love affair itself represented the spirit of the time, whereas in the 1930s, a love affair had already diminished into a personal issue, at best, and, at worst, was related to an immoral action."[35] This passage not only confirms the special function that love and love affairs played in Korean society in the process of modernization, it also claims that "love" is not a homogenous universal feeling that human beings experience, nor does it have a consistent form independent of the fashion of changing times; rather, it is culturally and socially bound in its meaning and in the form of its manifestation. Elevating the meaning of love as a lever for their agenda of gender equality, the New Women were blind to this fact, for which they had to pay a dear price.

In the essays that describe her state just before she joined the monastery, Kim Iryŏp more than once expresses her disillusionment with the idealized concept of love. Unlike the eternal value she imposed on love, Kim Iryŏp confesses, love was also subject to changes. The limitations of the reality of love she was facing, Kim Iryŏp seemed to realize, were the limitations of her own freedom.

Modern Self and Buddhist Self

Reflecting upon the time when she joined the monastery, Kim Iryŏp states that she felt a sense of urgency. She describes this urgency as the "need to survive." This was the topic of the dharma talk Zen Master Man'gong (1871–1946) gave to her when she became his disciple: "When one leaves the secular world and joins the monastery, the study for the person is 'to survive.' "[36] The existential urgency expressed by Man'gong as grounds for Buddhist practice becomes a major theme of Kim Iryŏp's Buddhist thoughts. Kim Iryŏp explains this awareness of existential reality as a desperate desire to become a "human being."[37] And to become a human being, for her, was to find a real "I." Time and again in her Zen writings, Kim Iryŏp meditates on the meaning of this "I."

The importance of finding the real "I" in Kim Iryŏp's thoughts is also reflected in her evaluation of her own time. Kim Iryŏp characterizes her time as a period when people have lost their selves. In an essay entitled "Narŭl irŏbŏrin na" ('I' who Have Lost 'Me'), Kim Iryŏp addresses this fundamental problem by raising the question of the meaning of being a human and being a true "I" as a groundwork for one's attitude toward life:

> Since life is a matter about which everyone has his or her concerns, different people have different positions from different perspectives. However, before we discuss issues related to the life of a human being, it is important for us to think about whether "I" am a human being. . . .
>
> The standard of value regarding existence is determined by whether "I" am a being who has "my" life at "my" disposal. . . . When we say "I," this "I" has meaning only when this "I" is free to handle her own life. By the same token, only the life in which this "I" is free to handle her life can be called a "life of a human being." In our lives, however, the "I" is far from being free in various aspects of life, so why do we still call it "I" and pretend as if "I" am "I?"
>
> If we actually live our lives as free beings, how can we have all those complaints and dissatisfactions? . . . Moreover, if we are really

free beings in this life . . . why are we still being bound by time and space and unable to free ourselves from the birth and death of this body?[38]

The fact that one exists within the boundary of the finite being and thus is subject to the reality of birth and death as well as to various dissatisfactions caused by one's limited capacity is evidence to Kim Iryŏp of the limits of human existence. Such a limited being cannot be the owner of the "I" because the subject of actions by nature should be one who is in charge of those actions. The small "I" (K. *soa*) is the name Kim Iryŏp gave to the being who is subject to the limitations of the finite being, including birth and death. Kim Iryŏp compares the small "I," which is the everyday "I" in the saṃsāra, to the ripples in the ocean which are always subject to changes. Behind and below ripples, Kim Iryŏp claims, should exist the source and origin of life, the life which Kim Iryŏp calls the big "I" (K. *taea*) which is free from changes of birth and death.

The Buddha, to Kim Iryŏp, is another name for this ocean in which the small "I" joins the big "I" and thus realizes the foundation of its own existence. To her, the Buddha is the original name of the universe in which "the state of the universe (before thoughts arise) and the creativity of reality (after thoughts arise) become united."[39] Kim Iryŏp clarifies:

The Buddha is a single representative of this and that, yesterday and today, and you and me. In other words, it is the unified "I." The Buddha then is another name for "I."

The Universe is the original body of this "I"; hence ten thousand things are all "my"-self. The ten thousand things being "my"-self, only the being who is capable of exerting the capacity of the ten thousand things can be endorsed as a being who has attained the full value of its existence.

In life, beings possess the right to absolute equality. Because of that, whatever position a being is in or whatever shapes a being's body takes, if the being can manage his or her own life, the being takes the most valuable position in the standard of [existential] value.[40]

The being which "takes the most valuable position in the standard of existential value" is the being who possesses the "original spirit" (K. *ponjŏngsin*). Kim Iryŏp contends that only the being who keeps the original spirit can maintain a life of a human being:

Only when one finds the original spirit of human beings which is non-existence (K. *mujŏk chonjae*) and only when one is able to use

> it at one's disposal, do the human beings' lives open up. When that happens, one becomes an independent being who is not swindled by environments, and, thus, whenever, wherever, and with whatever shape of a body one lives one's life, whatever kind of life it might be, one finds nirvāṇa.[41]

Kim Iryŏp equates this original spirit with self-identity (K. *cha'a*), creativity (K. *ch'angjosŏng*), Buddha-nature (K. *pulsŏng*), truth, and original heart (K. *ponmaŭm*), which she further describes as "the identity of all beings' existence and pre-existence which cannot be described or named."[42] She describes all the beings of the world as parts of this original existence.

The theory of "no-self" constitutes one main feature of Buddhist philosophy. The Buddhist emphasis on the lack of any permanent, independent entity which can define one's existence does not deny the existence of a phenomenal "I." In an ultimate sense, Buddhist no-self can be understood as an attempt to liberate one from the limits of "I," which is confined in the boundary of the independent self. Kim Iryŏp, like many Buddhist thinkers before her, interprets this unbounded extension of one's self by breaking up the temporary and illusory boundaries created by the small "I" as the ultimate teaching of Buddhism. This is the universal "I," Kim Iryŏp believes—the ocean below the ripples on its surface, which is the "such-ness" of one's existence, as is repeatedly emphasized in Zen tradition.

What attracts our attention in Kim Iryŏp's approach to Buddhism is a consistent emphasis on the idea of the "I"—what Kim Iryŏp defines as the big "I"—after the breakdown of the small "I." Whereas Buddhist writings frequently attempt to avoid underscoring the "I" because of the danger of reifying the little "I," Kim Iryŏp explicitly emphasizes the fact that the Buddhist theory of no-self *is* the theory of self, with a note that this self is the universal self without boundaries. The importance of Buddhist teaching to Kim Iryŏp, then, lies not so much in the removal of the self as in liberating the self from the boundaries imposed on it, be they social, biological, or merely illusory. Hence, Kim Iryŏp declares: "To take refuge in the Buddha is to take refuge in one's self."[43]

As a New Woman, she declared the new concept of chastity, and demanded freedom as the inborn right of an individual. As a Buddhist nun, she was still searching for freedom as an existential right of a human being. It is in this context that we identify the function of Buddhism in Kim Iryŏp's life and thoughts. Unlike the common claim that Kim Iryŏp's Buddhist phase was in stark contrast to her pre-monastic life, we see here that Buddhism provided Kim Iryŏp with a way to continue her pursuit of freedom and self-identity by expanding her challenge to the existing mode of thinking in her time and society.

In her autobiographical essay, Kim Iryŏp states that all the paths she had taken in her life were ways to find her identity:

> Now I realize that as I walked through the different paths of love, literature, and freedom, though it was not clear to me at that time, in my subconscious, my mind which struggled to reach the life of a human being was also undertaking [the teaching of] "I need to survive" as I practice it now [as a Buddhist nun].[44]

In her pre-monastic life, and in the monastic setting as well, the theme of self-identity in Kim Iryŏp's writing was expressed through "love, literature, and freedom." In the aforementioned interview with the reporter from the *Kaebyŏk* magazine in 1935, Kim Iryŏp was asked whether she was still writing after she joined the monastery, to which she responded, "One should not, when one's thought is not ripe."[45] When asked whether she intended to open up a new horizon in her writing when her practice became mature, Kim Iryŏp relied, "Yes, like Śākyamuni Buddha. . . ." Kim Iryŏp came back to the world of letters in the 1960s and became a productive writer until her death in 1971. She also explicitly declared that she became a nun in order to find the source of her writing so that she could write the most appealing works.[46] These responses confirm that Kim Iryŏp's way to Buddhism was not a disconnection from her previous life as a writer and New Woman who looked for freedom and personal identity, but a continued path to search for them.

Kim Iryŏp considered the final stage of her Buddhist practice a returning to the world as a "great-free-being" (K. *taejayuin*):

> As a school student grows up to be an adult in a society, a nun completes the education at a monastery and becomes able to lead a life free from the idea of purity and impurity. Thus she becomes an independent mind—the mind before a thought arises—which is not being manipulated by environments. She can come back to the secular world in which she leads a life free from good and evil, beauty and ugliness, heaven and hell. This is the liberated person. The final winner is the great-free-being (K. *taejayuin*) who is bound by nothing.[47]

In this passage, one can hear the echoes of Kim Iryŏp's search for freedom in her pre-monastic life. Was Kim Iryŏp able to complete her search for identity and freedom as a Buddhist nun? The question should remain unanswered at this point. However, without answering this question, we can still tell that her Buddhism offers us several points which we need to consider for a comprehensive understanding of modern Korean Buddhism. In the following section, I will discuss three aspects of Kim Iryŏp's Buddhism in relation to the contemporary Buddhist discourse. The first is the meaning of Kim Iryŏp's Buddhism in understanding Korean Buddhism in the modern period; the second is the challenge Kim Iryŏp's

Buddhism presents to us as to the binary postulation between modernity and tradition; and the third is the understanding of Kim Iryŏp's Buddhism in the context of recent efforts to create a Buddhist feminist discourse.

Buddhism, Modernity, and Gender

Korean Buddhism in the first half of the twentieth century can be broadly categorized into two aspects: The first is a revival of Sŏn/Zen tradition, and the second is Buddhist reform movements. The former has been represented by Zen Masters Kyŏnghŏ (1849–1912), who has been credited as a revivalist of Korean Zen Buddhist tradition, and his disciples including Man'gong (1871–1946), Hanam (1875–1951), and Suwŏl (1855–1928), to name a few. Representative figures for the latter include Paek Yongsŏng (1864–1940), Han Yongun (1879–1944), and Pak Chungbin (1891–1943). The revival of Zen Buddhism is characterized with the revival of Kanhwa Sŏn (or Kanhua Chan) tradition (the Zen of observing a critical phrase), which was established in Korea by Pojo Chinul (1158–1210) in the thirteenth century. Hwadu/Huatou meditation (or meditation with a critical phrase) played a central role for the practice and subsequent attaining of enlightenment for the Zen masters mentioned above. For the reformists, the issue of bringing Buddhism back to the life-world of people emerged as one main agenda for their reform of Buddhism. Translation of Buddhist scriptures, lay Buddhist movements, and reinterpretation of Buddhism in the context of modern time became part of their Buddhist narratives. For both reformists and Zen masters, colonial reality of Korea and Japanese Buddhist influence on Korean Buddhism during and after the colonial period (1910–1945) had been a frequent theme of their Buddhism.

Visibly invisible in this picture of modern Korean Buddhism are women practitioners and female teachers. The invisibility of women in the discussions of modern Korean Buddhism, however, does not mean that women did not exist in Korean Buddhist tradition. As we examined in Kim Iryŏp's case, women speak a different language in their relation to Buddhism. Women's relation to Buddhism is different because their "social ontology" is different. By "social ontology," which I borrowed from Charles W. Mills, I mean the way one's existence is defined by one's social environments. In the case of Kim Iryŏp, her social ontology is defined by a gendered society that takes the male discourse as the genderless normative, as the racial world of the whites universalizes the colorless normative in a colored society.[48]

With these ideas in mind, if we compare Kim Iryŏp's Buddhism with that of the male teachers of her contemporaries, we find visible differences between the two. First, even though Kim Iryŏp was a disciple of Zen Master Man'gong and strongly advocated Zen Buddhism, she did not spend much time discussing the

Kanhwa Sŏn tradition, nor did she emphasize the Zen style of communication, which is very much visible among the male Zen masters of her time. Miriam L. Levering pointed out that Zen Buddhist discourses of equality are charged with the rhetoric of masculine heroism and thus implicitly demand women practitioners to take on masculine qualities if they want to embody Buddhist teaching at all.[49] In this context, the essays Kim Iryŏp published in three volumes during the 1960s provide examples of Zen writing that does not display the masculine rhetoric and that discusses women's experience of Buddhism in a socio-cultural and historical context of modern Korea in which Kim Iryŏp lived her life.

Second, despite the utter differences in appearance, Kim Iryŏp's writings served one of the goals of Korean Buddhist reformists: the idea of bringing Buddhism back to the everyday lives of people from its seclusion on the mountainside. Whereas male Buddhist masters' writings project to achieve this goal by focusing on the translation of Buddhist sūtras into vernacular Korean and a reinterpretation of Buddhist doctrines to make it accessible by the general public, Kim Iryŏp's writings served this function by offering Buddhist interpretations of the life as experienced by a woman in Korean society.

Third, in Kim Iryŏp's writings, colonial reality and activities for independent movements in Korea, which usually takes a central role in many of Korean Buddhist discourses in her time, is not highlighted. Secondary sources on Kim Iryŏp testify that she was an active participant in the socio-historical reality of Korea. For example, Ch'oe Eunhŭi, a reporter of *Han'guk ilbo*, requested from Kim Iryŏp the details of her activities at the March First Movement.[50]

We can say that gender was one major factor that produced these differences between Kim Iryŏp's Buddhism and that of her male contemporaries. Kim Iryŏp's Buddhism also makes us aware of the need to revisit the binary formula between tradition and modernity. During the 1920s, when Kim Iryŏp published her literary works and her thoughts on women's liberation, Kim Iryŏp's thought demonstrated a clear tension with traditional value systems. Her view on women's chastity exemplifies the challenges New Women brought against the tradition. From the viewpoint of these women, overcoming the traditional system was necessary in order to achieve a humane and free life, and Kim Iryŏp positioned herself at the forefront of such social changes. However, in her case, Buddhism eventually became a major route to pursuing her goal. When one is faithful to the binary postulation of the tradition versus modernity, with the acceptance of modernity in the context of Korea, the person is not likely to go to the mountainside to become a Buddhist nun. She would change her hairstyle, adopt a new fashion, wear makeup, and come to the city in which newly emerging cafés attract newly styled human beings called modern girls and modern boys.[51] Kim Iryŏp was arguably a leading figure among this newly emerging group before she became a nun. However, if we understand, as I have demonstrated in this essay, Kim Iryŏp's life as a nun was a continued path in her search for identity and freedom which she pursued as a New Woman in her pre-monastic life, Buddhism is not that which stands at the opposite end of modernity but that which can provide a philosophical foundation to pursue the goal initiated by the modernist spirit.

Finally, Kim Iryŏp's life and thought presents to us a potential function Buddhism can play for the creation of a Buddhist feminist discourse. Recent Buddhist scholarship on the relationship between gender and Buddhism has illuminated the complex role gender has played in the development of Buddhism. Research shows that, even though Buddhist traditions have displayed a patriarchal position in their literature and monastic systems, this does not necessarily prove that the fundamental teachings of Buddhism are patriarchal or that the tradition is irreparably sexist.[52] The fact that Kim Iryŏp's journey to Buddhism created a fundamental change in the philosophical horizon of her views on women's liberation proffers the possibility that Buddhism can contribute to the feminist discourse in our time.

Notes

1. A version of this paper appeared in *Korea Journal* 45, no. 1 (Spring 2005): 114–141.

2. See Steven Heine and Charles S. Prebish, eds., *Buddhism in the Modern World: Adaptations of an Ancient Tradition* (Oxford, London: Oxford University Press, 2003). Also see Ian Harris, ed., *Buddhism and Politics in Twentieth-Century Asia* (London and New York: Pinter, 1999).

3. For the discussion of the reform of Korean Buddhism at the beginning of the twentieth century, see Kim Kyŏngjip, *Han'guk Pulgyo kaehyŏngnon yŏn'gu* (A Study on the Reform Theories of Korean Buddhism) (Seoul: Chin'gakchong, 2001).

4. Han Yongun is a representative example of this case. See Pori Park, "The Modern Remaking of Korean Buddhism: the Korean Reform Movement during Japanese Colonial Rule and Han Yongun's Buddhism (1879–1944)." PhD dissertation, University of California, Los Angeles, 1998. A more radical challenge can be found in new Buddhist movements such as Won Buddhism. See Kwangsoo Park, *The Won Buddhism (Wŏnbulgyo) of Sot'aesan: A Twentieth-Century Religious Movement in Korea* (San Francisco-London-Bethesda: International Scholars Publications, 1997); Bongkil Chung, *The Scriptures of Won Buddhism: A Translation of the Wŏnbulgyo kyojŏn with Introduction* (Honolulu: University of Hawai'i Press, 2003).

5. See Yang Ŭnyong, "Kŭndae Pulgyo kaehyŏk undong" (Buddhist Reform Movements in Modern Korea), *Han'guk sasangsa taegye* (Compendium of the Intellectual History of Korea), vol. 6 (Pundang, Korea: Han'guk chŏngsin munhwa yŏn'guwŏn), 129–175.

6. See Robert E. Buswell, Jr. "Imagining 'Korean Buddhism,'" in Hyung Il Pai and Timothy R. Tangerlini, eds., *Nationalism and Construction of Korean Identity*, Korea

Research Monograph (Berkeley: Institute of East Asian Studies, 1998), 73–107; Henrik H. Sørensen, "Buddhism and Secular Power in Twentieth-Century Korea," in Ian Harris, ed., *Buddhism and Politics in Twentieth-Century Asia*, 127–152; Jae-Ryong Shim, "Buddhist Responses to the Modern Transformation of Society in Korea (Vitality in Korean Buddhist Tradition)," *Korea Journal* 33, no. 3 (Autumn 1993): 50–56.

7. The subtitle, *A Memoir of a Practitioner*, became used as a title of the book because the expression "the one who has lost the mind" in Korean also means the one who went crazy. I will follow this convention from now on in referring to this volume.

8. Kim Iryŏp, *Silsŏngin ŭi hoesang: Ilmyŏng ŏ'nŭ sudo'in ŭi hoesang* (Memoir of the One who Has Lost the Mind; also known as A Memoir of a Practitioner) (Yesan, Korea: Sudŏksa, 1960), p. 3 and p. 199. Ha Ch'unsaeng, the author of two volume compilation of the life of Korean nuns in modern time, also evaluates Kim Iryŏp's publications in the 1960s as an expression of "a bodhisattva's ultimate action of searching for bodhi and its practical phase of helping sentient beings, which is the source-power of [Kim Iryŏp's] mass-proselytization" (*Kkaedarŭn ŭi kkot: Han'guk Pulgyo rŭl pinnaen kŭnse piguni* [The Flowers of Enlightenment: Buddhist Nuns in Modern Time who Have Lightened up Korean Buddhism] [Seoul: Yŏrae, 1998–2001], vol. 1, p. 79. All the quotations from Korean sources in this essay including those from Kim Iryŏp's works are my translations.

9. Kim Iryŏp herself also mentioned that Wŏnhyo's activities are not a violation of precepts as unenlightened people tend to see it but are examples of the unobstructed action of love. See Kim Iryŏp, "Chilli rŭl morŭmnida" (I Do Not Know the Truth), *Mi'rae'se'ga taha'go namdorok* (Until the Future Life Comes to an End and Even Afterwards), vol. 1 (Seoul: Inmul yŏn'guso, 1974), p. 326.

10. For example see Bernard Faure, "Random thoughts: Wŏnhyo's 'Life as thought' " *Pulgyo yŏn'gu* 11/12 (November 1995): 197–223.

11. See Ch'oe Hyesil, *Sinyŏsŏng tŭrŭn muŏsŭl kkumkkuŏtnŭn'ga?* (What Did New Women Dream About?) (Seoul: Saenggak ŭi namu, 2000); Kim Chinsong, *Sŏure ttansŭhorŭl hŏhara: kŭndaesŏng ŭi hyŏngsŏng* (Allow Dance Halls in Seoul: the Formation of Modernity) (Seoul: Hyŏnsil munhwa yŏn'gu, 1999); Mun Okp'yo, ed., *Sinyŏsŏng: Han'guk kwa Ilbon ŭi kŭndae yŏsongsang* (New Women: Images of Modern Women in Korea and Japan) (Seoul: Ch'ŏngnyŏnsa, 2003); Kwŏn Podre, *Yŏnae ŭi sidae: 1920 nyŏndae ch'oban ŭi munhwa wa yuhaeng* (The Age of Love Affairs: the Culture and Fashion in the Early 1920s) (Seoul: Hyŏnsil munhwa yŏn'gu, 2003).

12. Yi Paeyong, "Ilje si'gi sinyŏsŏng ŭi yŏksajŏk sŏnggyŏk" (Historical Characteristics of New Women during the Japanese Colonial Period), in Mun Okp'yo, ed., *Sinyŏsŏng*, 21–50, p. 22.

13. Yi, "Ilje si'gi sinyŏsŏng ŭi yŏksajŏk sŏnggyŏk," p. 22.

14. Yi, "Ilje si'gi sinyŏsŏng ŭi yŏksajŏk sŏnggyŏk," p. 23.

15. *Tongnip sinmun*, 21 Apr. 1897. Quoted in Kim Chinsong, *Sŏure ttansŭhorŭl hŏhara*, p. 203.

16. *Tongnip sinmun*, 26 May 1899. Quoted in Ch'oe Hyesil, *Sinyŏsŏngdŭrŭn muŏsŭl kkumkkuŏtnŭn'ga?*, p. 33. The *Tongnip sinmun* continued its support for gender equality emphasizing the importance of education for women. The trend was reinforced with the establishment of the institution for the education of women. Ehwa Haktang opened the institution in 1886 and was followed by Chŏngsin yŏhakhyo (1887) and others.

17. Kim Iryŏp's life is reflected in many of her writings. The most comprehensive material is a collection of her autobiographical essays under the title "Chilli rŭl morŭmnida." These essays were originally published in *Yŏsŏng tonga* (Dec 1971–June 1972). Also see "Iryŏp sojŏn: naŭi ipsan'gi" (A Short Biography of Iryŏp: a Story of My Joining the Monastery) in *Miraese'ga taha'go namdorok*, vol. 1, 256–265.

18. Kim Iryŏp, "Chilli rŭl morŭmnida," p. 266.

19. It is still debatable whether women's movements in Korea in 1920s and 1930s were closely related to those in Japan. (For the discussion of the issue, see Mun Okp'yo, ed., *Sinyŏsŏng: Han'guk kwa Ilbon ŭi kŭndae yŏsŏngsang*.) However, in the case of Kim Iryŏp, it seems clear that she was influenced by women's movements in Japan, which she learned during her stay in Japan. One evidence of this is the name, Ch'ŏngt'aphoe (Society for the Blue Tower), a women's forum she organized during the time of her editorship of the magazine *Sinyŏja* (New Women). The name clearly reflects that of a radical feminist magazine in Japan named *Seitō* (Blue Stockings; K. *ch'ŏngt'ap*) (Kim Iryŏp, "Chilli rŭl morŭmnida," p. 298). The first issue of the magazine *Seitō* came out in 1911 in Japan. It was at the gathering of the Society for Blue Tower that Kim Iryŏp first expressed her idea on chastity.

20. *Yŏja'gye* (Women's World), first published in 1917, precedes *Sinyŏja*, whose first issue came out in 1920. However, *Sinyŏja* was the first to be published for the liberation of woman.

21. Kim Iryŏp, "Chilli rŭl morŭmnida," p. 268.

22. Kim Iryŏp's criticism of Christianity and her endorsement of Buddhism appear a number of times in her essays. See especially "Ssi sŏnsaeng e ge" (To Mr. C) in *Ŏ'nŭ sudo'in ŭi hoesang*, 72–83 (Also reprinted in *Ch'ŏngch'un ŭl pulsarŭ'go* [Having Burned out the Youth, 1962] [Seoul: Kimyŏngsa, 2002], 210–234) and "Aem ch'in'gu ŭi pyŏnjirŭl ilggo" (After Reading a Letter from M) in *Ŏ'nŭ sudo'in ŭi hoesang*, 161–169 (Also reprinted in *Ch'ŏngch'un ŭl pulsarŭ'go*, 236–253).

23. For the occasion, Kim Iryŏp wrote a poem, "Tongsaeng ŭi chugŭm" (The Death of My Sister), which has been considered the first modern-style poem in Korea.

24. Kim Iryŏp, "Tongsaeng ŭi chugŭm" (The Death of My Sister), *Sinyŏja* 3 (May 1920). Reprinted in *Miraese'ga taha'go namdorok*, 390–398. (This is an essay, not the poem under the same title as referred to in the note above.)

25. It is not clear exactly when she turned away from Christianity and when she began to consider herself a Buddhist. In her essay, Kim Iryŏp states that she was an atheist for about ten years before she encountered Buddhism ("Chilli rŭl morŭmnida," p. 329) and she considers 1927, when she met Paek Sŏnguk and began to publish her works in the magazine *Pulgyo*, as the time she became a Buddhist ("Chilli rŭl morŭmnida," pp. 424–435).

26. Kim Iryŏp, "Naŭi aejŏng yŏkchŏng" (The Path of My Love Affairs), in *Haengbok kwa pulhaeng ŭi kalp'i esŏ* (In Between Happiness and Misfortune) (Seoul: Whimun ch'ulp'ansa, 1964), p. 21.

27. See Kim T'aesin, *Rahula ŭi sa'mo'gok* (Songs of Rahula Yearning for His Mother) (Seoul: Han'gilsa, 1991), an autobiography by an alleged son of Kim Iryŏp. Despite the author Kim T'aesin's claim that Kim Iryŏp is his mother, the disciples of Kim Iryŏp at Kyŏnsŏng Hermitage at the Sudŏk Monastery still challenge the idea, according to an

informal conversation I had in July 25, 1996 with Kyŏngwan, a second-generation dharma disciple of Kim Iryŏp.

28. Kim Iryŏp, "Na ŭi chŏngjo'gwan" (My View on Chastity), *Chosŏn ilbo*, 8 Jan. 1927. Reprint in *Kkosi chimyŏn nuni siryŏra* (As Flowers Wilt, So Do Tears Well Up) (Seoul: Osangsa, 1985), 117–120, p. 117.

29. Kim Iryŏp, "Na ŭi chŏngjo'gwan," p. 119.

30. Kim Iryŏp, "Chilli rŭl morŭmnida," p. 298.

31. Kim Iryŏp, "Uri ŭi isang" (Our Ideals), *Pu'nyŏ chigwang* (The Light of Women) (July 1924). Reprinted in *Kkosi chimyŏn nuni siryŏra*, 81–86, p. 82. For a list of Kim Iryŏp's publications in the literary magazines and newspapers during the 1920s and up to 1935, see Chŏng Yŏngja, "Kim Iryŏp munhak yŏn'gu" (A Study on Kim Iryŏp's Literature), *Suryŏn ŏ'munhakchip* 14 (1987): 1-26, pp. 4-6.

32. Kim Iryŏp, "Chilli rŭl morŭmnida," p. 320.

33. *Kaebyŏk*. "Sakpal ha'go sŭngbok ibŭn Kim Iryŏp yŏsa ŭi hoe'gyŏn'gi" (An Interview With Tonsured Ms. Kim Iryŏp in a Nun's Robe) (January 1935): 12–17, p. 13–14.

34. In her autobiography, Kim Iryŏp, looking back this period, actually mentions that her love for her husband gradually deteriorated. See for example, Kim Iryŏp, "Chilli rŭl morŭmnida," p. 320

35. Ch'oe Hyesil, *Sinyŏsŏngdŭrŭn muŏsŭl kkumkkuŏtnŭn'ga?*, p. 101. In this investigation, Ch'oe compares the different reactions to two major novels by Yi Kwangsu (1892–1950): *Mujŏng* (1917) and *Yujŏng* (1933). As representative works by Yi during the first half of the twentieth century, both novels deal with love. Ch'oe asks why the former has been evaluated for its representation of modernity whereas the latter has been treated as nothing more than a "mere" love story, even though both deal with love. The quotation was her answer to the question.

36. Kim Iryŏp, "Chilli rŭl morŭmnida," pp. 321–322.

37. Kim Iryŏp, "Chonggyo ŭi mokjŏk" (The Goal of Religion), in *Iryŏp sŏnmun* (Zen Writings by Iryŏp) (Seoul: Munhwa sarang, 2001), p. 79.

38. Kim Iryŏp, "Na rŭl irŏbŏrin na," in *Iryŏp sŏnmun*, p. 54.

39. Kim Iryŏp, "Pulgyo esŏ'nŭn woe chŏnghwa undong'ŭl irŭk'yetnŭn'ga?" (Why Did Buddhism Launch a Purification Movement?), in *Ŏ'nŭ sudoin ŭi hoesang*, 156–160, p. 156.

40. Kim Iryŏp, *Ŏ'nŭ sudoin ŭi hoesang*, p. 156.

41. Kim Iryŏp, "Saengmyŏng" (Life), p. 5; also see Kim Iryŏp, "Pulgyo wa munhwa" (Buddhism and Culture) in *Ŏ'nŭ sudoin ŭi hoesang*, p. 16.

42. Kim Iryŏp, "Saengmyŏng," p. 7.

43. Kim Iryŏp, *Ŏ'nŭ sudoin ŭi hoesang*, p. 30.

44. Kim Iryŏp, "Chilli rŭl morŭmnida," p. 330.

45. *Kaebyŏk*, "Sakpal ha'go sŭngbok ibŭn Kim Iryŏp yŏsa ŭi hoe'gyŏn'gi," p. 16.

46. Kim Iryŏp, "Hanjari ŭi toep'uri" (Repetition of the Same Place), *Miraese'ga taha'go namdorok*, p. 486.

47. Kim Iryŏp, "Pulgyo esŏ'nŭn woe chŏnghwa undong'ŭl irŭk'yetnŭn'ga?," pp. 156–157.

48. Charles W. Mills, "Non-Cartesian *Sums*: Philosophy and the African-American Experience," in *Blackness Visible: Essays on Philosophy and Race* (Ithaca and London: Cornell University Press, 1998), p. 12.

49. Miriam L. Levering, "Lin-chi (Rinzai) Ch'an and Gender: The Rhetoric of Equality and the Rhetoric of Heroism," in José Ignacio Cabezon, ed., *Buddhism, Sexuality and Gender* (Albany: State University of New York Press, 1992), 137–156.

50. Kim Iryŏp, *Iryŏp sŏnmun*, p. 239.

51. Once again, readers are referred to recent publications on modernity in Korea. See note 11.

52. See Rita Gross, *Buddhism after Patriarchy: A Feminist History, Analysis, and Reconstruction of Buddhism* (Albany: State University of New York Press, 1994).

Part Two

Revival of Zen Buddhism in Modern Korea

6

Mirror of Emptiness

The Life and Times of the Sŏn Master Kyŏnghŏ Sŏngu[1]

Henrik H. Sørensen

Introduction

Sŏn Buddhism (C. Chan; J. Zen) is the dominant form of Buddhism in modern Korea. The developments—historically as well as doctrinally—leading up to the current situation began more than twelve hundred years ago during the Silla dynasty (c. 300–936). In the course of its long history, the Korean Sŏn tradition has experienced several periods of prosperity as well as periods of decline. The two periods in which the tradition prospered the most were the first flowering during the late Unified Silla–early Koryŏ, covering roughly the years 800–960 AD, and the second period corresponding to the second half of the Koryŏ, i.e., c. 1200–1392 AD. During the following Chosŏn dynasty, a period in which Confucianism dominated the kingdom politically and ideologically, Buddhism and Sŏn with it experienced lengthy periods of upheaval and persecution, but never to such an extent that the existence of the religion was in serious danger of becoming extinct. In this period Sŏn experienced brief periods of prosperity, the most successful being the first half and the final decades of the sixteenth century. Despite its long history, Korean Sŏn Buddhism eventually entered a period of decline after the seventeenth century; more significantly, the first half of the nineteenth century marked an all-time low in its fortunes. The late Chosŏn decline of Sŏn Buddhism was not a result of Confucian persecution or other external factors, but chiefly came about due to internal problems. In particular, the lacking practice of Sŏn meditation combined with a general lack of competent leaders would appear to have been main contributing factors.[2]

This essay is devoted to a discussion of the significance and role of the late Chosŏn monk Kyŏnghŏ Sŏngu's (1849–1912) life, including the type of Sŏn Buddhism he taught and his writings, as well as his over-all importance for the development of Korean Sŏn Buddhism during the first half of the twentieth century.[3] Kyŏnghŏ is among the few important Sŏn Buddhist leaders in the Korea of the second half of the nineteenth century. His rise to eminence took place at a time when the Chosŏn dynasty was in rapid cultural and political decline after almost 600 years of constricting domination by Confucian ideology. Moreover, Kyŏnghŏ's greatest contribution to Korean Buddhism rests on the facts that he revived traditional Sŏn training and was the teacher of several of the most influential Sŏn monks who rose to prominence during the first half of the twentieth century. Today the legacy of Kyŏnghŏ and his disciples can still be felt in Sŏn Buddhist circles in Korea.

Kyŏnghŏ's Life

According to Manhae Han Yongun's biographical introduction, Kyŏnghŏ was born in a village near Chŏnju, North Chŏlla Province, on August 24, 1849.[4] He was of the Song family, but exact details are not given. Judging from context, however, we may conclude that he came from a rather poor peasant family. He lost his father at an early age and traveled with his mother to Seoul, where both settled. Perhaps out of necessity, he entered the Ch'ŏnggye Temple located in the Kwangju area at the age of nine as a novice under a monk called Kyehŏ (n.d.). From the Yearly Account of Sŏn Master Kyŏnghŏ Sŏngu (*Kyŏnghŏ Sŏngu Sŏnsa Yŏnbo*), we learn that he received the *śrāmanera* (K. *sami*) ordination the same year (*KP* 735–45). In the temple he was given a basic education and, at age fourteen, was taught Confucianism by a visiting scholar. The combined study of Buddhism and Confucianism made Kyŏnghŏ a man of letters, an achievement that marked an important turning point in his life.

When he was ordained he received the dharma-name Sŏng'u, later styling himself Kyŏnghŏ. When Kyeho eventually returned to secular life, Kyŏnghŏ went to continue his studies under Master Manwha (n.d.), a scholar-monk who headed the lecture-hall at Tonghak Temple in Mt. Kyeryong. Kyŏnghŏ was then fourteen years old. Under Manhwa's guidance, the young monk progressed rapidly in his studies of Buddhist philosophy, becoming the *sūtra*-master of the temple at the young age of twenty-three.

Traveling to Seoul in early 1879 to visit his former teacher Kyehŏ, who had returned to lay-life, Kyŏnghŏ was forced by heavy rains to seek shelter in a village ravaged by an epidemic. Unable to lend any assistance to the suffering villagers,

Kyŏnghŏ realized the bitterness of suffering in the world and concluded that his scholarly knowledge could help neither himself nor others. Downcast, he returned to his temple. Later accounts tell us that he was so ashamed of himself that he covered his head with a large, hollowed-out gourd. After his return to the Tonghak Temple, Kyŏnghŏ disbanded his followers and confined himself to intense Sŏn meditation working with the *kongan* "Before a donkey has left, a horse arrives."[5] During his stay in his retreat, he ate only once a day and never lay down to sleep, sitting continuously in meditation. One day, after a long period of hard practice, he experienced a major enlightenment by which he realized the eternal truth behind the scriptures. It is said that what occasioned his breakthrough was when somebody outside his meditation room mentioned the *kongan*, "a cow without nostrils." This event took place late in November, 1879 (*KP* 662–65). Following his spiritual awakening, Kyŏnghŏ went to the Ch'ŏnjang Temple. Here he received dharma-transmission from the Sŏn Master Yŏngun (b. 1783), an eleventh-generation successor in the direct line of Hyujŏng (1520–1604) also known as Great Master Sŏsan. At age thirty-three, Kyŏnghŏ succeeded Yŏngun as spiritual leader (K. *pangjang*) of the temple. He lived for a number of years in Ch'ŏnjang Temple in semi-seclusion instructing a handful of disciples.

In 1882, Kyŏnghŏ set out on a pilgrimage to the famous temples of Korea with the aim of restoring the practice of Sŏn Buddhism, which had deteriorated severely among Korean Buddhists during the nineteenth century. His travels took him to such temples as the Haein Temple, the Pŏmŏ Temple, the Sŏgwang Temple, the Songgwang Temple, and the Mahayŏn Temple among others.[6] Kyŏnghŏ's pilgrimage for the revival of Sŏn Buddhism fell into three parts. The first, which took him to all the important Buddhist centers in the southeastern part of the country, took place between 1882 and 1900. The second, from 1900 to 1904, brought him to the major temples in the southwestern part of the peninsula including the temples in Mt. Chiri, while the last leg of his long "tour" took him to the northeastern part of Korea. Here he visited and stayed in a number of the famous temples in the area covered by Mt. Kŭmgang. Wherever he went, disciples flocked to him as he advocated the practice of Sŏn as the fountainhead of Buddhism.

During his years of preaching and traveling around the country, Kyŏnghŏ attracted a number of eminent monks. Among the most prominent of these were Suwŏl Ŭmgwan (1855–1928), Hyewŏl Hyemyŏng (1861–1937),[7] Man'gong Wŏlmyŏn (1872–1946),[8] and Han'am Chungwŏn, all of whom later became leading masters in the Korean Sŏn Buddhist tradition. Kyŏnghŏ never lost his fondness for the Buddhist scriptures, though he was mainly interested in their practical application, and on one of his sojourns in Haein Temple, he had several sets of the Buddhist canon printed directly from the famous set of wooden blocks stored there. Because of the popularity his vigorous teaching style and unconventional nature garnered him among the common people, Kyŏnghŏ caused Buddhist doctrines and the practice of Sŏn meditation to flourish anew. Breaking with the established tradition of reserving Sŏn practices for members of the saṅgha only, Kyŏnghŏ sought to teach these practices to the laity as well. By 1905 his popularity had reached such dimensions that he was in constant demand for lecture tours. Being a modest man, he naturally felt ill at ease over the commotion he was evoking and decided to "go underground." Suddenly nobody knew where he was, for he had moved in secret to the northern part of the country. Here he adopted the name "Academician Pak" (Pak Chinsa) and lived incognito as a Confucian scholar in retirement. Wearing a topknot and teaching the local people, he did not shrink from eating meat or drinking wine. It was in this period that he established himself as an accomplished calligrapher and *kŭm* player (*KP* 743). In that period he signed his poems and songs with the styled name Nanju (Orchid Island) (*KP* 743). Although the standard Buddhist explanation for Kyŏnghŏ's "retirement" was a wish to live his last years as a hermit in obscurity, it is possible that the political situation of that time may have played a considerable role in his decision to retreat from "the world." As is well known, Korea's time as an independent kingdom was swiftly running out, and the general unrest in the country brought about by fighting between the Japanese army and the so-called Righteous Army of royalist Koreans must have complicated Kyŏnghŏ's touring. After his sojourn in the north, Kyŏnghŏ returned to Mt. Kap where he lived in a small hermitage for the rest of his life. He passed away without any signs of illness on April 25, 1912. He was subsequently cremated by his close disciples (*KP* 744). For some strange reason there is no record of the existence of either a memorial stele or a *śarīra-stūpa* for Kyŏnghŏ. The reason for this anomaly is not known. However, several ancestor portraits of him are known to exist, including a *t'aenghwa* kept in Pŏmŏ Temple near Pusan.

Kyŏnghŏ's Buddhist Thought

For an understanding of Kyŏnghŏ's thought as it appears in his extant writings, it is preferable to take his *Odoga* (Song of Enlightenment) as our point of departure.[9] The *Odoga* was written at Kyŏnghŏ's mother's house the year following his spiritual awakening at the hermitage on Mt. Kyeryong. The work is called a song (K. *ka*), but actually is in prose-form, following the tradition of *gātha*-writing as it developed in China during the Tang dynasty (618–907). In its style and content, the *Odoga* has much in common with such celebrated Chan songs as the *Xinxin ming* (On Faith in the Mind) traditionally attributed to Sengcan (d. 606), the third Chinese patriarch of Sŏn Buddhism, and Yongjia's (665–713) *Zhengdao ge* (Song of Attaining the Way). Below follows the most essential passages from the *Odoga*:

The beauty of the mountain is Mañjuśrī's eye,
And the sound of water Avalokiteśvara's ear.
When I hear the bellowing of the ox and the neighing
Of the horse, then I hear the speech of Samantabhadra.
All the Changs and Yis are fundamentally Vairocana.
Buddhas and patriarchs, Sŏn and doctrinal Buddhism,
How can they differ, but through the discrimination of men?
The stone man plays the flute and the wooden horse nods the time.
Ordinary people do not know their self-nature, but say,
"The highest plane is not my lot" (*KP* 48–9).

In this passage, Kyŏnghŏ describes his realization of the perfect, all-embracing, and penetrating *dharmadhātu*, in which all dualities are coexistent and in which every sentient being is a Buddha. The doctrine through which Kyŏnghŏ here expresses his practical understanding can be in the *Avataṁsaka sūtra*, which discusses the interpenetration of the absolute (K. *li*) with the relative (K. *sa*). In this vision of totality, the narrow and dualistic splitting of Buddhism into sects or creeds is a fabrication of deluded minds. The actions of the stone man and a wooden horse are Kyŏnghŏ's way of demonstrating the absolute reality beyond the calculations of the rational mind. Here, that reality is presented in the form of a typical *kongan*. Concerning this statement, Kyŏnghŏ's expression resembles that of the Chinese Chan Master Dongshan (807–869), who in his *Baojing sanmei ge* (Song of the Precious Mirror Samādhī) gives the following description: "The wooden man starts singing/the stone woman gets up to dance!"[10]

This type of phrase is quite standard in Sŏn Buddhism, occurring constantly in the various *kongan* collections. From this statement on absolute reality, Kyŏnghŏ goes on to lament the fact that people generally do not care about realizing their own true nature, again a standard Sŏn precept, but excuse themselves and thereby ignore their own potential for enlightenment. Further on in the *Odoga*, Kyŏnghŏ elaborates on his own experience of enlightenment:

A man jokingly said, "A cow without nostrils,"
And upon hearing that, I was awakened to my original Mind.
Names and forms became empty like space,
Dwelling in stillness, constantly emitting light.
Henceforth there was one single smell,
And instantly one thousand realizations,
And behind my head the spiritual form of the Diamond World.
The four great elements and the five skandhas constitute this pure body.
The highest paradise is the hell of boiling cauldrons and cold water;
The Lotus World is the hell of sword-trees and sword-mountains,
And the land of the dharma-nature is a heap of rotting manure.

> The great thousandfold worlds are an anthole or
> The eyelash of a mosquito; the Trikāya, the four wisdoms,
> Emptiness, and all things and sensations are fundamentally
> The heavenly truth (*KP* 50).

Here we are presented with the essentials of Kyŏnghŏ's realization. Referring to a "cow without nostrils," the words that triggered his enlightenment, he proceeds to a detailed account of his enlightened vision. The main focus is on non-duality, illustrated by the identity of phenomena attributed to saṃsara and nirvāṇa. Kyŏnghŏ gives a lengthy account of this identity and takes the reader on a tour of the Buddhist cosmos. In saying that the land of dharma-nature and a heap of dung are the same, he is almost echoing the words of Yunmen (864–949), Chinese Chan master who, when asked about the Buddha, replied, "A shit-wiping stick!" Clearly, Kyŏnghŏ's choice of words reflects the same uncompromising experience of non-duality and totality connected with the realization of *dharmakāya*. The filthiest thing is really pure, and the most minute particle is huge.

The keynote to Kyŏnghŏ's thought, and Sŏn in general, is mind (K. *sim*). In his own words, it is "original mind" (K. *ponsim*). In East Asian Mahāyāna, the meaning of the mind generally has two aspects: the samsaric, deluded mind of most beings, encompassing all modes of discursive mental activity; and the absolute mind or Buddha-nature, which is identical with *dharmakāya*. As such it is perceived as being transcendental, all-encompassing, and all-penetrating. As Kyŏnghŏ himself says, fundamentally these two aspects are the same, for the absolute mind is the cause-ground for both delusion and enlightenment. Moreover, in his *Ilchin-hwa* (Discourse on a Dust Mote), a dharma-talk, Kyŏnghŏ says: " 'The Three Realms are nothing but Mind,' and there is another saying by the men of old that goes: 'The wind in the branches and the moon's shining on the hillside reveal the True Mind. Yellow flowers and emerald bamboo brightly display the wonderful dharma' " (*KP* 90).

The doctrine underlying the first quotation originally comes from the *Daśabhūmika sūtra*, an early Mahāyāna text that later was incorporated into the *Avataṁsaka sūtra*. In time it became an essential part of the *tathāgatagarbha*-doctrine through Vasubandhu's (fl. third century) commentary, the *Daśabhūmika-sūtra-śāstra*, and the important *Dasheng qixin lun* (Treatise on the Awakening of Faith in Mahāyāna). Kyŏnghŏ uses the quotation to explain the dual functioning of the mind as being both the cause-ground from which the phenomenal world arises and, at the same time, absolute reality, or *dharmakāya*. The second quotation describes the enlightenment potential inherent in all phenomena, that is, the fundamental "reality" of the objective world. This mind, or absolute reality, cannot be attained through study or cultivation but will be experienced if one returns to one's own mind, which is identical with the mind of all Buddhas. In his *Yŏ Tŭng'am hwasang* (For Ven. Tŭng'am), we find Kyŏnghŏ quoting the Sixth Patriarch Huineng:

> The Sixth Patriarch said, "If the former thought is deluded, it is that of a living being, and if the latter thought is awakened, it is that of a Buddha."[11] Men of old said, "When a dragon transforms itself, it does not change its scales. When ordinary people return to the Mind, they become Buddhas without having to change their appearance."[12] Therefore this dharma-door, highly honored and respected, the hundred thousand samādhi and the limitless wonderful principles, all remain with a worthy person. Any thought becomes dust to the mind (*KP* 126).

The Buddha Mind is not something one obtains through practice; it has always been there. As one attains enlightenment, the obscuring clouds of ignorance are transformed into Prajñā (K. *hye*), i.e., wisdom, and the practitioner realizes that he or she has been a Buddha all along. This essential Mind doctrine in Sŏn is traditionally attributed to Bodhidharma (d.c. 530), and can be found expressed in the *gātha* "A transmission outside the scriptures/No dependence on the written word/Directly pointing to the mind of man/Looking into one's own nature and attaining enlightenment."[13]

Because returning to one's own Buddha nature has never been easy, the Sŏn tradition has upheld certain requirements toward this end. Of great importance in Sŏn practice is the development of a correct attitude toward, and faith in, one's own Buddha-nature. Quoting from Chinul (1158–1210) in his exhortation to Ven. Tŭng'am, Kyŏnghŏ says:

> Those who enter into training must take a step forward. The first thing to do is to set up a true foundation. To have faith in the Five Vows, and the Ten Wholesome Acts, the Twelvefold Chains of Cause, and the Six Perfections, all these are not the true cause. To have faith in the fact that one's own mind is the Buddha and not give rise to one single doubt concerning this until three long kalpas have become empty—if such a faith is attained, then that is the true foundation (*KP* 111).

According to Kyŏnghŏ and Chinul, the faith in the fact that one's own mind is originally the Buddha is the basis for enlightenment. When the proper foundation has been established, the Sŏn practitioner must endeavor to return to his true nature and not concern himself with anything else. Kyŏnghŏ stresses this in his exhortation to the assembly of monks, *Sijung* (Instructing the Assembly), as follows:

> Those who enter into the practice of Sŏn are not dependent upon a fixed abode. They ought only to concern themselves with looking back into their own "house and finding its master." When that has

> been accomplished, their understanding will not be hindered by externals nor affected by life and death. High and superior, clear and distinct, calm and composed, neither bound nor liberated, without defilements nor nirvāṇa. One wears clothes all day, but without wearing a stitch to one's name, and to have food every day, but never eating a single grain of rice,[14] up to the point where happiness and unhappiness and the boundary between life and death has been dissolved (*KP* 93–94).

In Sŏn training, the most important thing is to return to one's true nature. When that has been done, the individual naturally will unite with the Way, and will no longer be affected by external conditions, whether favorable or adverse. The discriminating consciousness will cease to operate, and saṁsara and nirvāṇa will be empty words. The Sŏn adept conducts his daily affairs without any clinging, eating his fill and wearing his clothes with no ado. In this way, he will attain to a transcendental state of being while still remaining in the world, thereby exemplifying the bodhisattva ideal of "being in the world but not of the world." The key words here are forbearance and non-attachment.

The actual process by which the Sŏn practitioner returns to his true nature is via the *kongan* meditation technique. As Kyŏnghŏ's own experience had shown him, the practice of meditation was indispensable, and he gave detailed instructions on this topic to his followers. The most prevalent Sŏn practice in Korea since the time of Chinul was the *hwadu* investigation. *Hwadu* literally means "the head of the word" but actually implies the "head of the thought." A *hwadu* is the quintessential part of a *kongan*, i.e., the real object of contemplation. The famous "Mu" *kongan* illustrates this point more clearly: "Once, as a mangy dog was passing by, a monk asked Zhaozhou (778–897), "Does a dog have the Buddha-nature?' Zhaozhou answered, "Wu!' "

The single word *wu* (K. *mu*) is the focal point, i.e., the *hwadu* of the "case." By constantly concentrating one's whole being on this "single word" (K. *kanhwa*), the meditator is supposed to be able to return to his "true mind."

Kyŏnghŏ continues his discussion of the *hwadu* practice in his *Yŏ Tŭng'am hwasang*:

> Sometimes investigating the *hwadu* is like going against a current under full sail. At times the *hwadu* seems distant and without taste; sometimes the mind is hot and sluggish. But then on the other hand, this is not really anybody else's affair. There is nothing to do but take a firm grip on the *hwadu* and do the extraordinary. The correct thing is to collect one's energy neither too quickly nor too slowly. Be alert and tranquil, firm and continuous. Your breathing must be regular, and you must be neither hungry nor satiated, with

> your nose level and eyes [half closed]. Be in a harmonious frame of mind and keep your back straight; then no obstructions can arise. The life of a human being is like a horse racing past a chink in a wall, or like the morning dew. Surely it is as agile as a lantern swaying in the wind (*KP* 292c).

Here we are given straightforward instruction in Sŏn meditation, with Kyŏnghŏ outlining various obstacles the practitioner is likely to encounter on the path, as well as ways to overcome them. The encouragement ends with a typical Buddhist warning about the evanescence of life, as a means to induce people to do their best toward the attaining of enlightenment. Kyŏnghŏ's admonition seems to echo the Buddha's *gātha* at the end of the *Vajracchedika sūtra*: "All dharmas are like a dream, like an illusion, like a bubble and a shadow. They are like the dew and the lightning. Thus ought you to view them."[15]

Not all of Kyŏnghŏ's teachings were formulated in the medium of classical Sino-Korean. Several of his more popular tracts were written in Korean (Han'gŭl). There are several reasons for this. First, there were many semiliterate people among his lay-followers for whom mastery of literary language was too far away. Second, Kyŏnghŏ seems to have been interested in reaching as many people as possible—monastic and lay alike—with his instructions in Sŏn practice. Hence, we find an extensive use of Korean or combined use of Chinese characters (K. *hanja*) and the Korean language in a number of his writings on Sŏn practice. I have singled out one piece, the *Chung norŭt hanŭn pŏp* (How to live as a monk; or Method of accomplishing the important affair) (*KP* 148–54) as representative for this type of his output. A central passage from the work follows:

> In order to awaken to the [true] mind, one must [first] understand that this body is no more than a dead corpse, and that in the final sense this world is nothing but a dream. The life-span of man corresponds to be leaving in the evening of the very same day you have arrived in the morning. At times one may be reborn in one of the hells, at times in the realm of animals and sometimes in the realm of hungry ghosts. [In all those cases] one will be subjected to great pain and suffering.
>
> Since this is true, one should not concern oneself with the worldly life. Simply investigate and observe your mind carefully at all times. What does that which is now seeing, hearing and thinking look like? Does it have a form or not? Is it big or small? Is it yellow or green? Is it bright or dark?
>
> Investigate and observe this matter carefully. Let your investigation and observation [of it] become like that of a cat catching a mouse, like a hen brooding on her eggs, or like a very hungry, and old, cun-

> ning rat which gnaws through a bag of rice. Cause your investigation and observation to become one-pointed and do not let it go.[16] Keep it before you by giving rise to the doubt and by questioning yourself. Do not let the [feeling of] doubt dissipate while you are going about your daily affairs, and do not let go of the investigation [of the *hwadu*] even while you are not doing anything in particular. By practicing diligently and sincerely in this way, the moment of awakening to your own mind will eventually come about (*KP* 148).

Kyŏnghŏ is here following earlier masters of Korean Sŏn to the point. His line and argumentation, even the words and images he uses, are part and parcel of the Sŏn tradition. Given that the central part of the above excerpt has been lifted almost verbatim from Hyujŏng's (1520–1604) *Sŏn'ga ku'gam* (Tortoise Mirror of the Sŏn School), a manual for beginning Sŏn practitioners, it is obvious that Kyŏnghŏ was paying special attention to new converts and trainees.

An essential part of Sŏn training is the *mundap,* a dialogue between a master and his advanced disciples, where the disciples are invited to test their attainment against that of their master. An interesting section in the *Kyŏnghŏ pŏbŏ* (Kyŏnghŏ's Dharma Discourses) gives an insight into a *mundap* over which Kyŏnghŏ presided:

> Opening the assembly for Sŏn instruction, someone said, "What are the conditions of true entering [into the Way] and true illumination [of the Mind]?" The master said, "Clouds gather around South Mountain, rain falls on North Mountain!" Someone else asked, "What are the principles of the Way?" The master answered, "They may be compared with the looper caterpillar; when it moves one foot, every last foot turns [with it]." Someone asked, "How does one attain enlightenment (K. *kyŏnsŏng*)?" The master said, "Go away and wait for the void to speak!" (*KP* 141)

In the *mundap,* the Sŏn master is in the position of "killing" or "bestowing life." Or, according to Linji (d. 867), one of Kyŏnghŏ's spiritual forefathers, the master is able to "take away the man but not the object, or to take away the object but not the man, to take away both the man and the object, and to take away neither man nor object."[17] This means that the Sŏn master can use any means he finds useful in bringing the disciple closer to enlightenment. Sometimes the master proceeds by encouragement or by scolding, and sometimes by being unapproachable or "steep as a cliff." Through his seemingly opaque and irrational answers, Kyŏnghŏ attempted to shock his disciples out of their ordinary conceptual frame of mind and induce them to enter the non-dual; that is, as it is sometimes expressed in Sŏn, "to take a leap from the top of a hundred foot-high pole."[18]

Another *mundap* from the *Kyŏnghŏ pŏbŏ* shows Kyŏnghŏ in action against an equally enlightened master, the hermit T'aep'yŏng (n.d.):

> The venerable T'aep'yŏng, who was living on Mt. Kyeryong, heard of the Master's great reputation and accordingly went to pay him a visit at the Pusŏk Temple [where Kyŏnghŏ was staying]. When he arrived, T'aep'yŏng entered [the hall] and enquired of the master, "What is the meaning of the Patriarch's coming from the West?" The master struck him with his staff. The hermit then said, "You strike me and I accept your striking me, but as regards the Patriarch's coming from the West, it is far from the meaning!" Kyŏnghŏ thereupon said, "What then is the meaning of the Patriarch's coming from the West?" The hermit then struck him with his staff. The master said, "The lion bites the man, the Korean black dog pursues a ghost." The hermit said, "The grace of the dharma is boundless!" The master laughed and returned to his room (*KP* 146–147).

Here T'aep'yŏng bests Kyŏnghŏ in the *mundap* exchange, using the classic Sŏn trick of first rejecting and then accepting. Laughingly, Kyŏnghŏ demonstrates his understanding in the statement about the lion and the dog, which is then matched by T'aep'yŏng. This example of *mundap* can also be seen as a demonstration of "killing and bestowing life." We note that the old *kongan* about the meaning of "Bodhidharma's coming from the West" was still very much in use in Kyŏnghŏ's era, thus demonstrating the timeless spirit of Sŏn. The most striking feature of Kyŏnghŏ's teaching is his strong sense of orthodoxy and indebtedness to the tradition. Even in cases where he does not explicitly cite a traditional authority, his statements always accord with the standard tenets of Sŏn Buddhism. As we also saw in the *mundap* exchanges above, their contents and form are strictly traditional and could well have taken place 600–700 years earlier. Kyŏnghŏ's thought, and the type of Sŏn he expounded, can therefore safely be called a product of the established tradition of Korean Sŏn Buddhism.

Teaching Monks and Laymen

Among Kyŏnghŏ's achievements while traveling through Korea to propagate Buddhism was his founding of a number of Buddhist societies primarily for laypeople. The establishing of such societies for the practice of the dharma has a long history in East Asia and can be traced at least as far back as the fifth-century Chinese monk Huiyuan (344–416), who founded the famous White Lotus Society on Mt. Lu in Southern China. One of the characteristics of these Buddhist societies or clubs is the equal status of the laity and saṅgha members, with the greatest emphasis given to joint efforts toward some exalted spiritual goal. Kyŏnghŏ's societies were primarily concerned with the revival and cultivation of Sŏn Buddhism, which had fallen into disfavor during the latter half of the Chosŏn dynasty.[19] Not only were monks and nuns again inspired to practice meditation, but the practice of Sŏn also came into vogue among lay Buddhists. The following excerpt is from Kyŏnghŏ's *Kyŏltong su chŏnghye tongsaeng tosol sŏngbul tong kwa kyŏlsa mun* (Upon the Establishment of a Society for the Cultivation of Samādhi and Prajñā, for Being Reborn in the Tuṣita Heaven and to become a Buddha) (*KP* 202–245):

> For those who have correct views, I ask you from now on to reform. The World Honored One has said, "Rely on the dharma and not on the person, rely on the whole teaching and not on the partial one." Now when reading such Mahāyāna *sūtras* as the *Avataṁsaka*, the *Saddharmapundarikā*, the *Shoulengyan jing* (Pseudo-*Śūraṅgama*), the *Yuanjue jing* (Scripture of Perfect Enlightenment), the *Vimalakīrtinirdeśa*, the *Mahāparinirvāṇa*, and all the Mahāyāna *śāstras* by men such as Aśvaghosa, Nagārjuna, Asaṅga, and Vasubandhu, and all the recorded sayings of the Sŏn school, the *Zongjing lu* (Records of the [Chan] School's Mirror) and the *Yŏmsong*, and when taking [all these] into account, at what place has it not been possible for living beings of the recent age to have access to the words of the true and right Way? (*KP* 210)

Here Kyŏnghŏ points out that there is an enormous amount of material for a Buddhist to study, but there is no excuse for anybody being unfamiliar with the doctrines. At the same time he demonstrates his own extensive learning by reeling off the names of most of the important texts of the Korean Buddhist tradition, all of which he is supposed to have known. All beings are able to enter into Sŏn practice regardless of sex, age, or intelligence, because all are endowed with Buddha-nature. In the next excerpt, Kyŏnghŏ addresses the members of the society:

> If there are men of common views and abilities, it is not a question of whether a person is a monk or a layman, male or female, old or young, wise or stupid, noble or mean, and it is not a question of whether he is intimate or rejected, distant or near, separated from or together [with his family], first or last—all are eligible to enter [into the Way]. This is because all the people have a limitless treasure-house that is no different from the Buddha. It is only those who in successive *kalpas* have not met with the advice of good friends that must crawl through the Threefold Worlds, careering through the

> Four Modes of rebirth." Not only is it thus, but it is like an extensive illusion equal to the [story about] the prodigal son who left from his home village, with transmigrating souls being carried from one obstacle to the next, enduring many sufferings, until one day after ten thousand births and deaths their hearts and minds torn asunder by each misconception, not realizing the reason for their deficient lives. Alas! How can they partake of tea and food, and not seek a way out? (*KP* 219–220)

It is possible for all living beings to attain liberation precisely because they all possess the potential for enlightenment. Only those who purposely reject their own true nature are bound to endure the sufferings of saṁsāra and will be unable to enter the Way. In this admonition Kyŏnghŏ repeats the standard Buddhist warning to those who refuse to work for their own awakening, thereby incurring bad karma that they will endure in life after life.

The rules of the society are appended to the end of the address. Most of these rules are in the form of commandments or vows, but some are more explicatory in nature. Rules 1 and 5 follow:

> One must reflect over the speed with which impermanence operates—that "birth and death are great matters"—and diligently cultivate samādhi and prajñā. To not diligently cultivate these while still searching for the fruits of Buddhahood amounts to rejecting practice and seeking rebirth as before; it is like wanting to go south with the shaft of one's cart pointing north. Do not grasp illusory existence, mistaking it for a whole lifetime. [. . .]
>
> 5. Those who truly cultivate samādhi and prajñā but do not wish to be reborn in the Tuṣita heaven will be allowed into the society. Those who can truly practice samādhi and prajñā but wish to go to Sukhāvatī for rebirth will likewise be admitted as members of the society (*KP* 229–230).

In the first rule, Kyŏnghŏ emphasizes the doctrine of impermanence, perhaps the most essential of all Buddhist doctrines. Next, he stresses the importance of the dual practice of samādhi and prajñā, thus revoking Chinul's celebrated regulations for the Sŏn community he established at Songgwang Temple.[20] For Kyŏnghŏ, this practice was basic and the real cause for rebirth in Tuṣita and his rule shows that, even when occupied in practices belonging to the devotional and other-worldly tradition in Buddhism, he gave central importance to Sŏn practice. Kyŏnghŏ further stresses this view in rule 5 when he says that samādhi and prajñā actually have priority over rebirth in the Tuṣita heaven, and adds that it does not really matter in which paradise one wishes to be reborn as long as one cultivates samādhi and prajñā. It is obvious that Kyŏnghŏ was not interested in the afterlife, but was only concerned that his followers wholeheartedly practice meditation and acquire wisdom. Further, Kyŏnghŏ disapproved of the dualistic splitting of the Buddhist community into monk and layman, whereby saṅgha members lived a life of purity and meditation free from the "dust of the world," whereas the laity led a worldly life within the realm of illusion. Even though he guarded and respected the code of discipline, he did not consider significant the differences between ordained members of the saṅgha and those who only kept the lay vows. What mattered to him was whether a person had faith in his potential as a buddha, and whether he practiced meditation accordingly. Where the laity previously had been delegated a secondary, albeit important, role as faithful donors and superstitious believers, they now were given direct access to the treasures of Sŏn Buddhism. By stressing the practice of Sŏn meditation among the laity, Kyŏnghŏ not only gave Korean Buddhism a long-needed rejuvenation, but also brought the ordained and unordained members of the saṅgha closer together.

In order to stimulate Sŏn training, Kyŏnghŏ compiled a manual for his disciples. This work, the *Sŏnmun ch'waryŏ* (Essential Selections for Sŏn Buddhists; hereafter *Essential Selections*),[21] consists of a number of the most important Chinese and Korean Chan/Sŏn texts and excerpts (see appendix at the end of this chapter). It is interesting to see that Kyŏnghŏ selected many of the early Chinese Chan texts, many of which were written and collated during the Tang dynasty. The *Essential Selections* is also significant for showing the great importance Kyŏnghŏ placed on the Sŏn teachings of Chinul, and as many as five of Chinul's works have been included. Naong also figures prominently in the *Essential Selections,* whereas the teachings of T'aego Pou and his lineage of orthodox Imje Sŏn have been largely ignored. The exact reason for this is not known, but it is possible that the more aggressive Sŏn style represented by Pou may not have appealed to Kyŏnghŏ whose own style was more ecumenical and struck a balance between Sŏn and doctrinal Buddhism.

It is unclear when Kyŏnghŏ compiled the *Essential Selections*, but it was probably done during his final years in seclusion on Mt. Kap. For some reason, the work was not published until many years after his death, but we must suppose that he taught on the basis of the texts it contains. The *Essential Selections* would in time become an important resource for students of Sŏn in Korea, and it remains so up to this very day.

Kyŏnghŏ's Poetry

Though Kyŏngho was in every sense of the word a man of the Buddhist tradition, he can also be seen to have displayed considerable originality in his poetry.

Schooled in classical Chinese, he must have mastered—or at least been familiar with—the standards of Chinese poetry. However, though he adopted the forms of four or eight lines with seven characters to a line (K. *ch'irŏn yul*) or four or eight lines with five characters to a line (K. *oŏn yul*), with occasional rhymes, he did not always follow the traditional rules of Chinese poetry. His poems generally follow the free tradition of the Buddhist *gātha*. The informal song such as represented by the *Odoga*, his main work, relates more to the tradition of folk singing. It also appears to have been a form he favored as it allowed for greater freedom and creativity (*KP* 501–556). Because we have already just seen an example of Kyŏnghŏ's use of the *ka*, I have excluded further examples from the selection that follows.

Enlightenment Poem

When I heard someone say, "A cow without nostrils,"
I suddenly realized that the Three Thousand Worlds are my home.
In the sixth month on the road under Mt. Yŏnam
A carefree wanderer sings the song of the Great Peace (*KP* 53–54).

This poem is found appended to the *Odoga* in both collections and recaptures the moment of Kyŏnghŏ's awakening. Entering the all-embracing state of enlightenment, he rejoices over the success of his practice that has enabled him to truly return to his "old home." The "Great Peace" (K. *t'aepyŏng*) mentioned in the poem denotes nirvāṇa.

The Old Road

The old road never changes;
Very quietly it removes itself from the affairs of the world.
What comes out of the gates of Shaolin
Has no intention of giving birth to affirmation and negation (*KP* 318).

This poem pays homage to the Sŏn tradition and its founder, Bodhidharma. Here the poet says that ever since the transmission of Sŏn Buddhism in China, its teaching has come down to his time unchanged. The characteristic of the "old road" is that it uses the non-dual approach to pass beyond the world of dust, or saṁsāra.

No Mind

Sitting on the white stones by the green pines,
How can I break these heavy thoughts?

With one stroke I return to my dwelling place
The flying birds likewise have no-mind (*KP* 317).

Here Kyŏnghŏ tells us that even he, an enlightened master, might sometimes find his mind crowded by habitual thought patterns. However, as soon as the adept, through awareness and strength of will, returns to the original state of being where no illusions arise, thoughts vanish of themselves like birds flying through the sky.

Not Two

Who will consider wrong the teaching of non-duality?
On an autumn day the wild geese fly south.
This is real alternation,
For in spring they surely will return north again (*KP* 324).

The subject of this poem again is non-duality. Here Kyŏnghŏ tries to show how the decay and regeneration of the phenomena of the world take place through the alternation of the seasons as illustrated by the migrating geese. According to the philosophy of *yin* and *yang*, the contraction and expansion of the universe follow a fixed pattern of mutual interdependence. However, these dual functions are the active expression of one undivided whole, the Way.

The Dance of the Cranes

To be aware of the causes of birth and death is a great affair.
The ten thousand phenomena can be swept away at once by a single wind.
Today I sit together with the clouds;
On the four peaks the cranes dance, returning home (*KP* 322–323).

The poet opens his poem with a reminder of the rapid passing of life, and then parallels this grave image with that of a carefree Sŏn hermit dwelling at ease in the mountains. The poem can be seen as consisting of two seemingly distinct halves, one representing saṁsāra, the other nirvāṇa. However, we already know that Kyŏnghŏ did not consider these two as essentially antithetical. We therefore may take his poem as a demonstration of *upāya* intended to turn people away from worldly pursuits and toward enlightenment. More than mere highlights in the poet's vision, the cranes symbolize long life and prosperity, by-products of enlightenment.

A Joyful Mind

Ten years within the Empty Gate,
Naturally forgetting the world of cause and effect—

Beautiful flowers bloom all over the ground.
The radiant moon hangs in the blue sky;
A multitude of streams return to the oneness of the sea.
Ten thousand shapes arrive at perfect emptiness.
Cultivating today joyfulness and wisdom
The Mirror Mind reflects distant and near (KP 337).

Here Kyŏnghŏ celebrates his tenth anniversary as a member of the "unborn" (K. *pulsaeng*). By powerful Buddhist symbols, he strives to convey an enlightened vision of oneness and totality. The moon and the sea reflect One Mind, or *dharmakāya*, as the origin of all phenomena. The mirror, also a symbol of Buddha Mind, illustrates the functioning of the awakened mind. To an enlightened person, all things are seen for what they are; that is, he knows that they are fundamentally unborn and not different from his own mind.

Gradual Practice and Instantaneous Enlightenment

In Mt. Kyeryong, searching for the subtle reality,
The ten thousand forms individually strike the eye anew.
Sitting in meditation hidden from the view of the world by clouds and mist,
Picking up the water-moon heightens the spirit even more.
Who would say that the schools are dormant today?
And yet, how many years of hard work [before I attained this liberation]?
The Buddha Hall is brightly lit, the altar as well.
To establish the true dharma requires the sincere mind of men (*KP* 369).

This poem deals with the classic paradox of gradualism and subitism in Sŏn Buddhism. An unenlightened person finds cultivation essential to the attainment of enlightenment but, when seen from the enlightened point of view, neither cultivation nor realization exists. The picking up of the "water-moon" is a symbolic description of Kyŏnghŏ's enlightenment. Generally it is impossible to pick up a reflection from the surface of a body of water, yet this is precisely what happens at the moment of enlightenment—the attaining of the unattainable. On the relative level, gradual practice is necessary because it creates a foundation for the instantaneous realization of the absolute.

Samādhi and Prajñā Temple

Living in seclusion on the peak of Mt. Tŏksung,
In the temple of samādhi and prajñā,

Time is of no account.
Through the fact of continuous practice in the meditation hall,
From the past down to the present,
The "cypress tree mind" is emptied of anxieties of distant *kalpas*.
Instead of honor and riches, the mountain stream rushes past my door.
As opposed to the king's capital,
I have the white drifting clouds above.
All the officials, dressed-up like butterflies
Are True Suchness.
From today onwards,
I also will go through life dragging my tail (*KP* 384).

When practicing meditation in the mountains far from the trouble-filled world, the hermit enjoys a tranquility and serenity beyond time. Instead of honor and wealth, the mountain dweller partakes of the surrounding and permeating natural harmony. In the last lines, Kyŏnghŏ ironically acknowledges his own growing reputation as a master of Sŏn and compares himself with the court officials in their ceremonial robes.

Spring of Great Peace

Brilliant spring of great peace,
Take a look at the hundred new plants.
On Mt. Kyeryong rain fell last night,
Lightly moistening the dust (*KP* 321).

Here again we find Kyŏnghŏ rejoicing over his attainment of enlightenment. On the surface there is nothing spiritual about this poem. It resembles any other nature poem. From the context, however, we know that the "Spring of Great Peace" was of immense importance in Kyŏnghŏ's development as a religious leader. The exuberance of spring, when myriads of plants awaken from their winter slumber and unfold their leaves, is compared to the profundity and depth of the enlightenment experience, in which all one's latent potential is aroused and brought to fulfillment. The following poem also concerns nature, though from a somewhat different perspective.

Spring Insects

The autumn wind is cold and again even colder,
At midnight I cannot sleep.
It is because of the insects' sad singing,
That I shed tears on my pillow (*KP* 318).

When autumn comes around and the temperature drops, insects die. In Korea, the "death songs" of many insects can be heard clearly on an autumn night. Reflecting on the eternal truth of the evanescence of life, Kyŏnghŏ is deeply moved. This poem is interesting because it reveals the humaneness and emotional heart of this otherwise austere Sŏn master. Also, the poem in question is much closer to the traditional Chinese style of nature poetry.

Sleeping

My head slumps, and I tend to fall asleep.
Seeing that apart from sleep there is nothing else—
Seeing that,
My head nods, and I fall asleep again (*KP* 316).

In this poem, Kyŏnghŏ spoofs the notorious "meditation killer"—sleep. In Sŏn Buddhism, sleep is generally considered one of the greatest obstacles to sound practice because it robs the mind of clarity and continuity. We might imagine Kyŏnghŏ sitting in meditation and surrendering to the demon of sleep, but clearly he has already gone beyond the dualistic notions of practice and no-practice and nods happily in his "awakened-sleep." His attitude can be compared with that of the Chinese Chan master Baozi Wenqin (fl. 10th cent.):

Drinking tea, eating rice,
I pass my time as it comes.
Looking down at the stream, looking up at the mountains,
How serene and relaxed I feel indeed![22]

In the Sŏn tradition, it is customary for a master to write a death poem just before dying.[23] The death poem generally serves to express the constant mind of the master, and to deliver his final statement of the Sŏn dharma to the disciples, in which he summarizes the basic characteristics and purport of his teaching. Needless to say, many of these death poems display strong eccentric and original traits. Kyŏnghŏ followed this custom, and his death poem epitomizes a life of transcendental communion with the Way:

Death Poem

The Mind Moon alone is perfect,
Its brilliance swallows the ten thousand shapes.
The brilliance and the objects are both forgotten,
So what shall I call this? (*KP* 745)

The Buddha Mind includes all phenomena. In the depth of samādhi any notion of self and others is completely dissolved leaving no room for this and that. In these, his last words, Kyŏnghŏ shows the same strength and radical Sŏn spirit that has been apparent in his previous writings, amply demonstrating an unending state of nirvanic existence.

Kyŏnghŏ also left behind a lengthy poetical piece, the *Kŭmgang san yusan ka* (Song on Roaming in the Diamond Mountains), in which he combines the appreciation of nature and historical spots with Buddhist ideology and imagery. This monumental piece consists of one hundred and seventy-five, four-line verses and describes Kyŏnghŏ's impressions while visiting the Diamond Mountains (Mt. Kŭmgang) in Kangwŏn Province. The *Kŭmgang san yusan ka* contains a multitude of historical and cultural elements including the author's wish to see the birth of the Koryŏ kingdom, the Diamond Mountains as a Buddha land, topographical details, and observations including the famous temples and hermitages of the mountain which are all treated together with abbreviated accounts of the stories or famous persons connected with their respective histories. That Kyŏnghŏ was both an astute and interested observer of Buddhist culture as well as of Buddhist history is reflected throughout the song.

In describing the sights of Chang'an Temple, one of the major temples in the Diamond Mountains, Kyŏnghŏ provides us with historical information on the treasures kept there as follows:

> Entering the Taeungbo Hall,
> The two-storied, bright-colored Kŭmbŏp Hall,
> With the Tathāgatas of the Three Times and the Six Bright Bodhisattvas.
> Divine they are in their perfect and complete forms.
> In the Sasŏng Hall are the Sixteen Holy Ones,
> Which were made by the Patriarch Naong.
> The characters on the hanging [sign-] board
> are divine wonders.
> With the name itself well preserved,
> Although it has still not been placed inside a pavilion (*KP* 521).

These passages almost sound like a historical narrative with their factual information and vivid images. The information on the temple's halls and treasures, including the celebrated images made by Naong, show Kyŏnghŏ as an astute observer and narrator.

However, this monumental work is foremostly a poetic celebration of the Diamond Mountains as a holy Buddhist realm, something which is abundantly clear as we read on in the verses:

> Munp'il Peak's wonderful form stands outlined,
> [And] with Sejon Peak it makes a pair.

The two hermitages Pogwang and Poun,
[Where] the scripture for invoking the [name of] the Buddha can be
seen,
Is then reached.
The Kŭmgang Cave and the Saja Cave,
Above the clouds rise the dharma,
At Munsu Hermitage,
One by one, when seeking these locations out,
[One realizes that] their names are not mere legend,
But actual facts, indeed . . . (*KP* 541).

In contrast to the description of the wonders to be seen in Chang'an temple, Kyŏnghŏ here celebrates the beauty of the peaks and hermitages of the Outer Diamond Mountains. Moreover, this passage almost reads like a tour-map. The *Kŭmgang san yusan ka* is in effect a poetic tour-guide to the scenic and historical spots in the Diamond Mountains. Following Kyŏnghŏ, many Korean monks of the early twentieth century would also leave poetic impressions as well as accounts of their visits to Mt. Kŭmgang.

Conclusion

Kyŏnghŏ might not be considered an innovator of Korean Buddhism in the same manner as Manhae Han Yongun or the immigrant Japanese Buddhist priests. One reason for Kyŏnghŏ's popularity and apparent success in reviving Sŏn Buddhism in Korea must be seen in the light of the scarcity of enlightened masters who could set a strong example. Kyŏnghŏ was such a master, and it was precisely because of his obvious authority and charisma that he could act as a magnet and rallying point for the saṅgha. What appears to have been a characteristic of his was the dedicated interest he took in teaching the dharma to the laity, something that must have been a novelty to most Koreans at the time. Not only did he teach laymen, but he also encouraged them to practice Sŏn meditation, which previously had been of concern only to monks and nuns. Kyŏnghŏ used many means to induce the common people to practice Buddhism. Through his popular poems and songs echoing Buddhist truths, he encouraged the laity in every way. When teaching Buddhist doctrines, he did not limit himself to formal preaching, but adopted the manner and garb of a Confucian scholar to teach the illiterate in local country schools. In establishing Buddhist societies open to both priests and the laity, Kyŏnghŏ contributed greatly to the Buddhist revival in Korea during most of the twentieth century. However, his greatest achievement was to bring Buddhism "down from the mountains" and back into the cities, thereby bridging the perennial gap between the saṅgha and the general population.

Kyŏnghŏ most certainly was not an unlettered or ignorant Sŏn monk, but on the contrary a well-read and thoroughly educated man. Throughout his writings, an abundance of references to the *sūtras*, *śāstras*, and the classic Sŏn collections clearly demonstrates his broad knowledge. At the same time, the consistent absence of Confucian ideology in Kyŏnghŏ's teaching seems odd, given the position of Confucianism as the state ideology during the Chosŏn dynasty. Most likely Kyŏnghŏ consciously sought to keep his Buddhism aloof from Confucianism, which, after all, represented the philosophy of the corrupt upperclass whose influence and dominance had placed Korean Buddhism in the shadow for more than 500 years.

Kyŏnghŏ's poetry allows for a good insight into his personal universe, displaying both humor and originality. Often by using traditional Buddhist images, he communicates the message of the truth beyond phenomena. It can well be said that his poems convey the same teachings as his traditional and formal writings, but in a more easygoing and carefree manner.

Kyŏnghŏ's merit did not lay in innovation. His revitalization of Korean Buddhism and of Sŏn in particular was completely in accord with the most fundamental Oriental mode of thought when facing the problem of historical development: looking back before going ahead. Kyŏnghŏ's achievements were founded on a reaffirmation of the tradition through his own wholehearted dedication to and personification of its essential values. The importance of Kyŏnghŏ's life and thought for the renaissance of Korean Buddhism during this century can still be felt, since a large number of monks of the present generation trace their line back to him.

Appendix

The Contents of the *Sŏnmun ch'waryo*

1. The Seven Buddhas of the Past.
2. Illustrated accounts of the Thirty-three Sŏn Patriarchs[24]
3. *Xuemai lun* (Treatise on the Blood Arteries) attributed to Bodhidharma
4. *Guanxin lun* (Treatise on Mind-Contemplation) attributed to Bodhidharma
5. *Sixing lun* (Treatise on the Four Cultivations) attributed to Bodhidharma.
6. *Prajñāpāramita sūtra*
7. *Wuxing lun* (Treatise on Awakening to [One's Own] Nature) attributed to Hongren (601–674), the Fifth Patriarch
8. *Cuishang cheng lun* (Treatise on the Highest Vehicle)
9. *Wanling lu* (The Wanling Record) compiled by Pei Xiu (797–870)

10. *Chuanxin fayao* (The Dharma Essential Methods on the Transmission of the Mind) compiled by Pei Xiu
11. Dharma Discourses (K. *pŏbŏ*)[25]
12. *Chanjing yu* (Words of Chan Admonition) by Wuyi Yuanlai (fl. 15th century)
13. *Susim kyŏl* (Secrets on Mind Cultivation) by Chinul (1158–1210)
14. *Chinsim chiksŏl* (A Straight Talk on the True Mind) by Chinul.
15. *Chŏnghye kyŏlsa mun* (Text for the Society of Samādhī and Prajñā) by Chinul
16. *Wŏndon sŏngbullon* (Treatise on the Complete and Sudden Attainment of Buddhahood) by Chinul
17. *Kanhwa kyŏrŭiron* (Treatise on Resolving Doubts about Observing the *Hwadu*) by Chinul
18. *Sŏnmun pojang rok* (Records from the Precious Treasury of Sŏn Buddhism) attributed to Ch'ŏnch'aek (1228–?)
19. *Sŏnmun kangyo chip* (Essential Collection of the Outline of Sŏn Buddhism)[26]
20. *Sŏn kyo sŏk* (An Explanation of Sŏn and Doctrinal Buddhism) by Hyujŏng
21. *Zixing zhenfo jie* (Gathā on the True Buddha of the Self-nature) attributed to Huineng (638–713)
22. *Wuzong jiafeng* (The Family Styles of the Five Schools). Compiler unknown.
23. *Xinxin ming* (Inscribed on the Mind of Faith) attributed to Sengcan (d. 606)
24. *Yongjia dashi zhengdao ge* (The Great Master Yongjia's Song on Attaining the Way) by Xuanjue
25. *Zuochan yi* (The Performance of Seated Meditation) by Changlu Zongze (fl. 11th century)
26. *Shiniu tu* (The Ten Ox Pictures) by Kuoan (fl. 12th century)

Notes

1. This chapter is partly based on my early work, "The Life and Thought of the Korean Sŏn Master Kyŏnghŏ," *Korean Studies* 7 (1983): 9–33.

2. For a presentation of various aspects of Chosŏn dynasty Buddhism, see Takahashi Toru, *Richō bukkyō* (Buddhism under the Yi Dynasty) (Tokyo, 1929) (reprint Poryŏn'gak, 1972). Although somewhat biased in its description of late Chosŏn Buddhism, it contains a wealth of useful information. See also the more recent survey by Kwon Kee-jong, "Buddhism undergoes Hardships: Buddhism in the Chosŏn Dynasty," in *The History and Culture of Buddhism in Korea*, ed. The Korean Buddhist Research Institute (Seoul: Tongguk University Press, 1993), 169–218. For a discussion of the anti-Buddhist policies of the Chosŏn government throughout lengthy parts of the dynasty, see the excellent study by John Jorgensen, "Conflicts between Buddhism and Confucianism in the Chosŏn Dynasty: A Preliminary Survey," *Pulgyo yŏn'gu* 15 (1998): 189–242.

3. Biographical entry in *Han'guk Pulgyo inmyŏng sajŏn* (The Korean Buddhist Biographical Dictionary), comp. Yi Chŏng (Seoul: Pulgyo sidaesa, 1993), pp. 144b–5a. Kyŏnghŏ's writings can be found in the *Kyŏnghŏ pŏbŏ* (Kyŏnghŏ's Dharma Discourses; hereafter indicated as *KP*, and will be marked in the text followed by page numbers), ed., Kyŏnghŏ Songu Sŏnsa Pŏbŏ Chip Kanhaeng Hoe (Seoul: Inmul yŏn'gu, 1981). This compilation constitutes the single-most important source on Kyŏnghŏ's life and brand of Sŏn Buddhism.

4. The main source on Kyŏnghŏ's life is the *Sŏnsa Kyŏnghŏ hwasang haengjang* (Circumstances of the Activities of the Late Ven. Kyŏnghŏ) (*KP* 654–91), written in 1931 by Hanam (1876–1951), one of his main disciples. The other major source is the *Kyŏnghŏ sŏnsa yakpo* (Abbreviated Account of [the Life of] the Sŏn Master Kyŏnghŏ) (*KP* 692–98), written by Han Yongun (1879–1944) as part of his compilation of some of Kyŏnghŏ's writings, the *Kyŏnghyŏ chip* (Collected Writings of Kyŏnghŏ). Lastly we have a modern account, the *Kyŏnghŏ Sŏngu sŏnsa nyŏnbo* (The Yearly Account of [the Life of] the Sŏn Master Kyŏnghŏ Sŏngu) (*KP* 736–47). *Kyŏnghyŏ chip* was originally published in 1942, and was later reprinted by Poryŏngak, Seoul, 1979. See also the more recently published version of *Kyŏnghŏ chip* in *Han'guk Pulgyo chŏnsŏ* (Complete Works of Korean Buddhism; hereafter *HPC*), vol. 11, ed., Han'guk Pulgyo Chŏnsŏ P'yŏnch'an Wiwŏn hoe (Seoul: Tongguk taehakkyo ch'ulp'anbu, 1992), 587b–701. This is directly based on the surviving manuscripts, but deviates greatly from the original compilation published by Han Yongun. It appears that Han Yongun actually considered himself a follower of Kyŏnghŏ's. Given the fact that he did not join the Buddhist *saṅgha* as a novice until 1905, and that Kyŏnghŏ passed away in 1912 after having lived in retreat for several years, it is questionable just how much relationship there was between the two, if any at all. Given the opportunistic nature of Han Yongun, I suspect that he had ulterior motives in claiming a spiritual link with Kyŏnghŏ, something which may have been motivated by his otherwise rather loose association with the latter's disciple Man'gong.

5. This saying comes from the entry of Lingyun Zhiqin (n.d.) in the *Jingde chuandeng lu* (Records of the Transmission of the Lamp from the Jingde Period). *T* 2076.51. 285b.

6. The *nyŏnbo* gives a full list of the temples Kyŏnghŏ visited on his pilgrimage. See *KP* pp. 738–41.

7. The *nyŏnbo* states that Hyewŏl Hyemyŏng became a disciple of the master in 1890. See *KP* p. 739.

8. Man'gong Wŏlmyŏn became a disciple in 1898. See *KP* p. 739.

9. For a pioneering study of Kyŏnghŏ's Sŏn thought, see Yi Sŏngt'a, "Kyŏnghŏ ŭi Sŏn sasang (Kyŏnghŏ's Sŏn Thought)," in *Sungsan Pak Kilchin paksa hwagap kinyŏm: Han'guk Pulgyo sasang sa* (Festschrift in Commemoration of Professor Sungsan Pak Kilchin's 60th Birthday: The History of Korean Buddhist Thought) (Iri, Korea: Wŏn'gwang taehakkyo ch'ulp'ansa, 1975), 1103–20.

10. *T* 1986.47. 515ab.

11. See the *Liuzu dashi fabao tan jing* (The Dharma Platform Scripture of the Sixth Patriarch, the Great Master), *T* 2008.48.350b.

12. I have been unable to identify the source for this quotation.

13. See D. T. Suzuki, *Essays in Zen Buddhism, First Series* (London: Rider, 1949), p. 176; and Heinrich Dumoulin, *A History of Zen Buddhism* (Boston, MA: Beacon Press, 1971), p. 299, note 1.

14. This passage is quoted almost verbatim from Yunmen's biography in *T* 2076.51.356c.

15. *T* 235.8.752b.

16. Compare with *HPC* 7, pp. 636c–7a.

17. *Chodang chip* (Taipei: Guangwen Shuji, 1973), p. 487a. Reprint of Haein Temple original blocks.

18. This saying, which later was widely used in Sŏn Buddhism, originated with Changsha Jingcen (n.d.), a disciple of *Nanquan Puyuan* (748–835). It can be found in the former's biographical entry in *T* 2076.51.274b.

19. See Yi Sŏngt'a, "Kyŏnghŏ sidae ŭi Sŏn kwa kyŏlsa (Sŏn Buddhism at the Time of Kyŏnghŏ and Its Societies)," in *Chinsan Han Kidu paksa hwagap kinyŏm: Hanguk chonggyo sasang ŭi chae chomyŏng* (Festschrift for Chinsan, Dr. Han Kidu: Further Elucidation on the Thought of Korean Religion), vol. 1., comp. Chinsan Han Kidu Paksa Hwagap Kinyŏm Nonmunjip Kanhaeng Wiwŏn Hoe (Iri, Korea: Wŏn'gwang taehakkyo ch'ulp'an'guk, 1993), 425–36.

20. *HPC* 4, pp. 698a–708a. For the full translation of this text, see Buswell, *The Korean Approach to Zen*, pp. 96–134.

21. *Sŏnmun ch'waryo*, comp. *Kyŏnghŏ Sŏngu hyŏnt'o* (Seoul: Poryŏnggak, 1982).

22. Taken from Suzuki, *Essays*, p. 264.

23. For a collection of these death poems from Chinese and Japanese Chan/Zen masters, see *Zen Poems of China and Japan: The Crane's Bill*, eds., Lucien Stryk, Takashi Ikemoto, and Taigan Takayama (New York: Anchor Press, 1973), pp. 19–27, 63–76.

24. This is the mythological lineage of Indian and Chinese patriarchs believed to constitute the transmission of the Chan dharma from Śākyamuni to Huineng. Appended is a portrait of the Korean master T'aego Pou, an important Sŏn master in the Linji/Imje tradition.

25. Consisting of twelve excerpts from various texts on Sŏn/Chan practice. With the exception of two text-excerpts by the Korean Sŏn master Naŏng, all the other are by Chinese Chan masters from the Linji School.

26. This text consists of a dialogue between the Sŏn master Ch'ŏngp'ung (n.d.) and the monk Howŏl (n.d.) on the major Sŏn doctrines taught in the Imje tradition.

7

Sŏn Master Man'gong and Cogitations of a Colonized Religion

Mu Soeng

This essay seeks to examine the life of Buddhist monk, Man'gong (1872–1946), during the Japanese occupation of Korea (1910–1945), and his prominent role in the struggle against the attempted colonization of Korean Buddhism. This role becomes quite significant when we consider that the occupying Japanese authorities had made a concerted effort to restructure the basic institutions of Korean Buddhism and remake them in the image of Japanese temples run by married clergy. The age-old Buddhist tradition of Korea, embedded largely in the ascetic mountain monk paradigm, was in danger of losing its basic identity along with the rest of the institutions of Korean society. Any resistance to the brutal occupation was not without a great degree of personal danger to the resisters. Man'gong, as the leader of a handful of Buddhist monks to offer such resistance, thus became, in turn, one of the iconic figures of revived Buddhism after the Japanese occupation ended in 1945. Much of Man'gong's fame also derives from the fact that he was very active in support of nuns, who had traditionally been shunned by the Korean Buddhist establishment. His role is thus not only personal and heroic, but also historical within the context of modern Korean Buddhism.

One has to appreciate that the moniker, "Hermit Kingdom," was actually based on Korea's self-imposed isolation from the rest of the world from early 1600s to 1850s. This period, which marks the second half of Korea's Chosŏn dynasty (1392–1910), is signified by a neo-Confucian ascendancy that sought to bring an end to Buddhism's long-held place in Korean society.

Korean Buddhism during the Late Nineteenth and Early Twentieth Centuries

Although in China Buddhism never became a state religion—except for few isolated regional rulers—it permeated and inserted itself into the life of the peasantry to the extent that it could not be rooted out by any edict of the imperial court. The Confucian mandarins at the court could, and did, regulate the conduct of urban temples, especially in regional centers, but China is a huge country with an overwhelming farming population. The Chinese, moreover, had a long history of harmonizing and synthesizing the teachings of Confucianism, Daoism, and Buddhism. It paid political dividends for Chinese elite to tolerate Buddhism at the peasantry level while collaborating with urban temples to make sure that they were never a political threat. After the great persecutions of 845–47, there is a general absence of any extended persecution of Buddhism in China as it got reshaped as a folk religion without any overt power base.[1]

Although the Song dynasty in China (960–1279) saw the emergence of neo-Confucianism, it was also a period of "Three Learnings" where all three religions could dialogue with and tolerate each other. This unfortunately did not happen in Korea, which had a long history of Buddhism being the state religion under the unified Silla period (668–935) and the succeeding Koryo dynasty (936–1392). Korea is a small country, much of it too rugged for habitation. For whatever historical and psychological reasons, Confucian elite in Korea did not engender the same degree of tolerance for either Buddhism or Daoism as did their counterparts in China. The result was a rigid, intolerant Confucian orthodoxy in power in the wake of Japanese invasions in 1592 and 1598.[2]

During this period (from 1600s on) the policies of neglect and repression of Buddhism that had been well-established prior to Japanese invasions were resumed. Only a handful of *sūtra* monks and temples remained in cities (to perform Buddhist ceremonies for rites of passage when no comparable Confucian ceremonies were available). Zen (Sŏn) monks retreated to their small practice communities in the mountains and countryside. A ban was imposed in 1623 that prohibited non-authorized monks from entering the city gates of Seoul, the capital, except in the case of either parent's death. "Buddhist temples seem to have been offered some mild form of protection during the reign of king Chŏngjo (r. 1777–1800). After that it was a time once again of benign neglect."[3]

It is not without irony that the foundations for a revival of Buddhism in modern Korea were laid under pressure from the Japanese who, as occupying authority from 1910–1945, would undertake a systematic effort to dilute and marginalize the traditional forms of Korean Buddhism. King Kojong (r. 1864–1906), under increasing pressure from Japan to become a vassal state, acceded to the request, in April, 1895, by Japanese priest, Sano Zenrei of the Nichiren sect, to repeal the ban on monks' entry into the capital city. Under further pressure from

Japanese Buddhist establishment, he agreed to allow the monks to live and build their temples in the capital. There was a meeting in Seoul in 1896 of all Japanese and Korean Buddhists in which it was formally agreed that Japanese Buddhism had a right to propagate its brand of Buddhism in Korea.

It was against this background that the role played by the monk Kyŏnghŏ (1849–1912) becomes quite pivotal in the revival of Korean Buddhism. I have discussed this role at length in my book on the history of Korean Buddhism.[4] The fact that, after his awakening experience, Kyŏnghŏ became the first monk of any note to travel throughout the country to reestablish and rebuild the old training centers is a turning point in modern Korean history. He presided over numerous assemblies, corresponded extensively with his followers, and established several Buddhist societies that included laypeople along with monks and nuns. In short, he set up his own life and activities as a model for future generations of Korean monks and nuns to follow. Among his immediate disciples, no one took to this model with greater enthusiasm than Man'gong.

It must also be noted here that, as dynamic a personality as Kyŏnghŏ was, his historic role was without doubt facilitated by the disempowerment of the anti-Buddhist Confucian establishment under encroaching Japanese political pressures. It was a time of transition and turmoil, and Kyŏnghŏ was the right man at the right time to bring his singular personality into the mix to revive the moribund Korean Buddhist establishment with new vigor. Kyŏnghŏ's historical role was further cemented by the activities of his major disciples who have also been discussed in my book on Korean Buddhism.[5]

Sŏn Masters Man'gong and Kyŏnghŏ

Man'gong is generally considered to be the most prominent of Kyŏnghŏ's disciples. Unfortunately, not much verifiable material about Man'gong's life has been published in Korean or English languages. Whatever material is available in either language comes from the oral tradition where hagiographical elements inevitably creep in. It might have been possible to construct a more fully fleshed-out portrait of the person behind the stories had someone been able to talk to his immediate disciples, none of whom is alive today. The material contained in my book comes from the oral tradition, and many of these stories are shared across the broad spectrum of modern Korean Buddhism. Similar stories circulate about other disciples of Kyŏnghŏ. There have been recent attempts by scholars at Dongguk University in Korea to recover and translate the letters these disciples wrote to each other in 1930s and 40s, and it may be that through these letters we may get a more nuanced picture of Korean Buddhism than is currently available.[6]

The prominence of Man'gong is not difficult to explain. During the years of Japanese occupation Man'gong and Pang Hanam, another of Kyŏnghŏ's disciples, ran the two most influential meditation centers in Korea—Man'gong at Sudŏk-sa, and Hanam at Sangwŏn-sa. They became the role models for their contemporary monks and nuns for living a life of strict *vinaya* (the monastic rules) as well as intensive meditation practice in formal retreat settings.

In popular Korean Buddhist imagination, the two monks are linked like twins. Scholars and practitioners of Korean Zen consider Hanam a towering summit in the north, and Man'gong a peak rising in the south. Since the Silla period, the mountains in the Kangwŏn region, which included Odae mountain where Hanam's Sangwŏn-sa was located, and Sŏrak mountain had been called the "northern" mountains—henceforth the doctrine of Hanam, which flourished in the northern part, was called the "Northern School." Man'gong, who resided in Chŏnghae-sa in Yesan, South Ch'ungch'ŏng Province, and who exerted a far-reaching influence on the southern district, was regarded as leader of the "Southern School." A visitor to both temples observed:

> The atmosphere at Han Am's Sangwon temple was candid and tranquil and the master preached Sŏn Buddhism with a high regard for Scriptural Buddhism, never neglecting all the precepts required of a Buddhist. Han Am may be compared to an icy brook running through a wintry valley or to buds sprouting from a withered branch, while Mang Gong's Jeung-hae temple was noisy with the whisperings of secular visitors. The latter was elegant and refined in his outward appearance while equipped with the courage and dignity of a fierce beast.[7]

While Hanam was content to almost never leave his temple and let the world come to him, Man'gong was much more active in visiting other temples and taking on the unofficial role of the "spiritual head" of Korean Buddhism. Indeed there are those who believe that in some areas his contributions outstrip those of Kyŏnghŏ.

Kyŏnghŏ died shortly after the formal annexation of Korea by the Japanese in 1910. The issues of reviving Korean Buddhism that Man'gong and other disciples of Kyŏnghŏ had to deal with in 1920s through 40s were much more magnified and confrontational with a colonial power who sought not only to dominate the country but also to remake Korean Buddhism in its own image. The struggle was simultaneously within the Buddhist saṅgha to reform itself from the inside out as well as against pressures from the Japanese Buddhist establishment for (a) institutionalizing a married clergy to replace the traditional ascetic, celibate monastic culture, and (b) the creation of a "parish priest" model along the lines of Soto Zen and Pure Land priests in Japan. Added to this volatile mix were conversion efforts by evangelical Christianity and the emergence of new lay-oriented religious movements such as Won Buddhism founded by Sot'aesan. The reform movements within the Buddhist saṅgha were championed by monks like Han Yongun (1879–1944), also known as Manhae, who sought to modernize the traditional saṅgha through a revision of nearly all facets of Korean Buddhism, "including the understanding and purpose and duty of Korean Buddhism, the education of the members of the saṅgha, the practice of meditation, doctrinal learning, recitation, ritual, monastic organization, ethics, the question of celibacy, economy, and temple management."[8]

Han Yongun was vociferously denounced by his colleagues as a self-aggrandizing and collaborating monk, and the reforms he sought were stillborn. Today he is known more as a great Korean patriot rather than a reform monk. Nonetheless, it was the milieu in which Man'gong negotiated his own role as a spokesperson for the traditional, celibate, monastic saṅgha. He was born in 1872 and became a novice-monk as a young boy. We do not have any details about his family or boyhood, but it seems reasonable to speculate that he came to the temple as an orphan. For several years, he studied sūtras at Tonghak-sa.[9]

One day, when Man'gong was thirteen years old, there was a ceremony to mark the end of a three-month retreat and the beginning of "free" time. Among those present was Kyŏnghŏ who happened to be visiting the temple at the time. Kyŏnghŏ had been a former lecturer on sūtras at this temple and had attained his great awakening there in 1879. As part of the ceremony, the Abbot gave a talk, saying:

> You must all study very hard, learn Buddhism, and become like great trees, from which temples are built, and like large bowls, able to hold many good things. The *sūtra* says, "Water becomes square or round according to the shape of the container it is put in. In the same way, people become good or bad according to the friends they have." Always have the Buddha in mind and keep good company. Then you will become great trees and containers of Dharma. This I sincerely wish.[10]

Everyone was filled with admiration at the abbot's understanding of the dharma. Kyŏnghŏ was then asked to give a talk. He said:

> All of you are monks. Monks are free of petty personal attachments and live only to serve other people. Wanting to become a great tree or a container of dharma will prevent you from becoming a true teacher.
>
> Great trees have great uses; small trees have small uses. Good and bad can all be used in their own way. None are to be discarded. Keep both good and bad friends. You mustn't reject anything. This is true Buddhism. My only wish for you is that you free yourselves from all conceptual thinking.[11]

No one was more impressed by Kyŏnghŏ's talk than the thirteen-year-old Man'gong. As Kyŏnghŏ was walking out of the Dharma room, Man'gong ran after him and pulled at his robes. Kyŏnghŏ turned around and asked, "What do you want?"

"I want to be your student. Please take me with you."

Kyŏnghŏ tried to make him go away, but Man'gong would not leave. Finally, Kyŏnghŏ said, "You are still only a child. You are not capable of learning Buddhism yet."

Man'gong said, "People may be young or old, but is there youth or old age in Buddhism?"

"You bad boy!" exclaimed Kyŏnghŏ. "You have killed and eaten the Buddha! Come along now."

So, he took Man'gong to Ch'ŏnjang-am; and left him there under the care of monk T'aehŏ. He also gave Man'gong a *kongan* to work on, "Ten thousand dharmas return to One; where does the One return to?"

For the next five years, Man'gong worked on his *kongan* day and night. At last when he was at Pongok-sa, he sat facing the wall meditating on this *kongan* for several days, forgetting even to eat and sleep. Then one night when he opened his eyes, a large hole appeared in the wall in front of him. He could see the whole landscape! Grass, trees, clouds, and the blue sky appeared through the wall with total clarity. He touched the wall. It was still there, but it was transparent like glass! He looked up, and he could see right through the roof. At this Man'gong was filled with an inexpressible joy. Early the next morning, he went to see the resident Zen Master. He rushed into the interview room and announced, "I have penetrated the nature of all things. I have attained enlightenment."

"Oh, have you?" said the master. "Then what is the nature of all things?"

Man'gong said, "I can see right through the wall and the roof, as if they weren't there."

The master said, "Is this the truth?"

"Yes. I have no hindrance at all."

The master took his Zen stick and gave Man'gong a hard whack on the head. "Is there any hindrance now?"

Man'gong was astonished. His eyes bulged, his face flushed, and the wall became solid again. The master said, "Where did your truth go?"

"I don't know. Please teach me."

"What *kongan* are you working on?"

"Where does the One return?"

"Do you understand One?"

"You must first understand One. What you saw was an illusion. Don't be led astray by it. With more hard work on your *kongan*, you will soon understand."

Man'gong came out of the interview room with renewed determination. For the next three years, he continually meditated on his *kongan*. Then one morning that was no different from other mornings, he heard the words during the Morning Bell Chant, "If you wish to understand all Buddhas of the past, present and future, you must perceive that the whole universe is created by the Mind alone." Hearing these words, Man'gong's mind opened up. He understood that all the Buddhas dwell in a single sound. He clapped his hands, laughed and sang the following verse of enlightenment:

The true nature of empty mountain is beyond the millions of years and
past and future.
White cloud, cool wind, come and go by themselves endlessly.
Why did Bodhidharma come to China?
The rooster cries before dawn and then the sun rises over the horizon.

About a year later, there was an important ceremony at the temple. Kyŏnghŏ was specially invited and was present. Man'gong went to his room thinking, "This Zen Master and I are the same. We have both attained enlightenment. He is Buddha, so am I. But since he was my first teacher I will bow to him, just as an ordinary monk does."

After Man'gong had bowed, Kyŏnghŏ said, "Welcome. It's been a long time since I've seen you. I heard that you have attained enlightenment. Is that true?"

Man'gong said, "Yes, Master."

"Wonderful. Now let me ask you a question."

Kyŏnghŏ picked up a fan and a writing brush and put them in front of Man'gong. "Are these the same or different?"

Without hesitation, Man'gong said, "The fan is the brush; the brush is the fan."

For the next hour, with grandmotherly compassion, Kyŏnghŏ tried to teach Man'gong his mistake. But Man'gong wouldn't listen. Finally, Kyŏnghŏ said, "I have one more question for you. In the burial ceremony, there is a verse that says, 'The statue has eyes, and its tears silently drip down.' What does this mean?"

Man'gong was stunned. He could find nothing to say. Suddenly, Kyŏnghŏ shouted at him, "If you don't understand this, why do you say that the fan and the brush are the same?"

In great despair, Man'gong bowed and said, "Forgive me."

"Do you understand your mistake?"

"Yes, Master. What can I do?"

"Long ago, when Zen Master Choju (Ch. Zhaozhou; J. Joshu) was asked if a dog has the Buddha-nature, he said, 'No!' What does this mean?"

"I don't know."

Kyŏnghŏ said, "Always keep this mind that doesn't know and you will soon attain enlightenment."

So, for the next three years, Man'gong did very hard training. One day, he heard the great temple bell ring and understood Choju's answer. He returned to Kyŏnghŏ, bowed, and said, "Now I know why the Bodhisattva faces away: because sugar is sweet and salt is salty." Kyŏnghŏ then acknowledged Man'gong's breakthrough awakening.

Man'gong became a famous Zen Master after he received transmission from Kyŏnghŏ. He came to Tŏksan in 1905 and built a small hermitage there. Soon he became the Zen Master at nearby Sudŏk-sa, a small but ancient monastery on that mountain. His fame spread and soon several hundred practitioners gathered to learn from him over the following years.

Man'gong became a pioneer in teaching Zen Buddhism to laypeople and to nuns. This was a radical departure for his time since the traditional Zen communities, in banishment from the cities, had been insular and had not much in contact with the society at large. We have seen earlier how Kyŏnghŏ pioneered the model of a new Zen master who traveled throughout the country and also helped the establishment of Buddhist societies that included laypeople as well as monks and nuns. Man'gong took to this model with great dynamism and commitment.

There was a constant stream of visitors to his mountain temple. Since all these people could not be accommodated in the temples around Sudŏk-sa, Man'gong built a temple called Chŏnghae-sa (Samādhi and Prajñā Temple) further up on the mountain for the training of his senior students. During his lifetime, Sudŏk-sa became a magnetic center for Korean Zen monks, and it is said that there was hardly a Zen monk in Korea who did not come to pay his respects to Man'gong. For Man'gong, following the model set up by Kyŏngŏ, rigorous training by monks and nuns in the Zen hall (Sŏnbang) did not preclude extended interaction with laypeople. There were periods for secluded training, but there was also time for extended interaction with visiting laypeople as well as travel to other parts of the country to give lectures to Buddhist assemblies.

In 1920 he established Sŏnhakwŏn (Society for the Study of Zen), which allowed laypeople to practice and study Zen alongside monks and nuns. This society became a significant presence in the revival of Korean Buddhism from that time on. The society continues today in some kind of quasi-legal status within the larger Chogye Order, and many people still look upon it as a living legacy of Man'gong for purity of practice.

Man'gong established a nunnery, called Kyŏnsŏng-am, in Tŏksan in the vicinity of Sudŏk-sa, for his student-nuns. Here hundreds of nuns came to train under him. Today, Kyŏnsŏng-am has a new building on the same site and is the largest training center for Zen nuns in Korea. Four of Man'gong's twenty-five Dharma heirs were nuns. Of these, the best known was the nun

Iryŏp (1896–1971), a long-time abbess of Kyŏnsŏng-am. Other notable nun-heirs were Pŏphui (d. 1975) and Mansŏng (1897–1975). All of these nuns and their students have played a crucial role in the development of nuns' saṅgha in Korea in modern times. Today, the nuns outnumber the monks and uphold the most rigorous standards for meditation practice and ethical conduct.

Sŏn Master Man'gong and Cogitation of Buddhism in Colonized Korea

Man'gong won everlasting fame, not only among Korean Buddhists, but amongst Koreans in general, when he challenged the authority of the Japanese government for its interference in the affairs of Korean Buddhism. After the Japanese had taken formal control of Korea in 1910, they initiated a number of policies to subvert Korean Buddhism. Among these policies were: merging the Buddhists of Korea under Japanese Buddhist schools, a centralized head temple system controlled by the Japanese, and changing the *vinaya* (monastic) rules for the monks permitting marriage, eating meat, and consuming alcohol. The monastic rules had been changed in post-Meiji Japan, and a married clergy had become the norm. Up until 1904, Korean (and Chinese) monks had followed the celibacy rule; to change this basic structure meant a dilution of traditional Korean Buddhism. Indeed, within a generation or so, the married clergy outnumbered the traditional celibate monks.[12]

The attempt at centralization consisted of a supreme patriarch, with spiritual authority over 32 regional head temples (K. *ponsa*), each with its own abbot, and 900 local temples (K. *malsa*). In theory, the 32 abbots were elected by the local temples in the region, and the supreme patriarch was elected by the 32 abbots. But each one of them had to be approved by the Japanese authorities. Before this attempt by the Japanese, there had been no central organizational authority in Korean Buddhism and each temple saw itself as autonomous answering to its own lineage. Now all of the abbots of 32 temples had to come to Seoul each year to meet the Japanese governor for New Year's "greetings."

On March 11, 1937, Man'gong and 30 other abbots met with the Japanese governor, Minami Jiro, for his annual pep talk. The celibate monks of the Zen and *sūtra* schools had been talking to each other about a merger and forming a single entity with the avowed aim of managing the affairs of Korean Buddhism with a single voice. The Japanese government naturally saw these negotiations as a threat to their own attempt to create a married clergy, which was to be their instrument for the control of Korean Buddhism.

At the 1937 meeting, it seems, the subtle pressures of the past became more explicit. A statement was made by the governor which said, "Korean Buddhism would do much better to follow Japanese Buddhism and cooperate with it." Suddenly, Man'gong got up from his seat and strode over to where the governor was.

With his fist, he struck the governor's table and gave out a deafening Zen shout, "Katz!" Then he said, "The universe of the Ultimate Truth was originally clear and empty. Where did the mountains, rivers and earth come from?" Man'gong continued to speak to the shocked governor and the abbots, "For what reason should Korean Buddhism follow Japanese Buddhism? Any person who forces the monks to break their precepts will go straight to hell." To many observers, it was the turning point in the self-renewal of Korean Buddhism and a unified Chogye Order was formed in 1941 that continues today as the largest of Buddhist sects in Korea.

As mentioned earlier, Man'gong had spent some twenty years before the 1937 meeting traveling to most temples in Korea, teaching there, and generally taking on the leadership role in the revitalizing effort of Korean Buddhism. The oral material of the period strongly indicates that political dissidents and resisters were constantly in touch with Man'gong and other prominent monks. Even when the Japanese secret police was suspicious of such visits, nothing came of it for these visits could always be justified as a student visiting his teacher. Any account of how active Man'gong was in his advisory role to political dissidents is unfortunately lost now with the passing of the older generation of monks.

His collaboration with Yongsŏng (1864–1940), another prominent figure in modern Korean Buddhism, is well-known. Both repeatedly encouraged Korean monks to strengthen their traditional spirit and resist Japanese attempt to subvert it. Not much has been preserved to show how various Zen teachers might have encouraged the resistance against the Japanese, though it is reasonable to assume that they did not do so in public assemblies for fear of being spied upon. The oral tradition, however, suggests that Zen monks were part of an informal network of dissenters and subversives. Yongsŏng became an active participant and took part in the now-famous nationwide demonstration against Japanese occupation on March 1, 1919. He was put into prison for his role.

Sŏn Master, Sŏn Stories

Man'gong spent the later years of his life in a small hut at Chŏnghae-sa, and lived there alone with an attendant to take care of his needs. The name of the hut was "Hut for Turning the Disk of the Moon" (K. *Chŏnwŏlsa*). Today, there is a beautiful pagoda on the way up the mountain from Sudŏk-sa to Chŏnghae-sa in Man'gong's memory. The calligraphy on the pagoda reads, "The whole world is a single flower" (K. *segye ilhwa*).

On the last day of his life, it is said, he washed himself and sat on his meditation cushion. Looking in the mirror, he pointed at himself and said, "Well, the time has come when I have to take leave of you!" Saying this, he roared with laughter and breathed his last.

As with other Zen masters, the exchanges between Man'gong and his students have become the lore of modern Korean Buddhism, especially for Zen monks. These exchanges serve as teaching devices and are the repository of the mind-to-mind wisdom tradition that Zen tradition thrives on. Some of them are recorded here:

One evening, Man'gong's attendant turned on the lamplight. The lamplight was reflected in the window. Seeing this, Man'gong first asked the attendant, pointing to the lamp, "Is this lamplight correct?" then pointing to the reflection, "Is that lamplight correct?"

The attendant immediately turned off the lamplight and asked, "Old teacher, what will you do?"

Without speaking, Man'gong turned on the lamplight and lifted it to its stand.

Once a scholar came to visit Man'gong and asked, "What is the teaching of Buddha?"

Man'gong said, "It's in front of your eyes."

The scholar asked, "If it's in front of me, why can't I see it?"

Man'gong said, "Because you have you. So you cannot see."

The scholar asked, "Do you see?"

Man'gong answered, "There is only you. But you cannot see. Besides that, there is me. So it's even more difficult to see."

Then the scholar asked, "If there is no you, and there is no me, then who can see?"

Man'gong said, "No you, no me. . . . Then who wants to see?"

The scholar remarked, "No matter how valuable the gold dust is, it will still hurt when it gets into your eyes."

One day, Man'gong and Suwŏl, also a dharma successor of Kyŏnghŏ, were sitting together and having a conversation. Just then, Suwŏl picked up a bowl containing browned rice, a Korean delicacy and a favorite snack, and said, "Don't say this is a bowl of browned rice. Don't say this is not a bowl of browned rice. Just give me one word."

Man'gong reached over, took the bowl from Suwŏl and threw it out of the window.

Suwŏl was very pleased, "Very good. That's wonderful."

Once Man'gong received a letter from a lay practitioner asking, "Respectfully, I ask you, teacher: I don't understand what Buddha attained when he saw a star on the morning twilight of April 8 (traditionally celebrated as the day of Buddha's enlightenment). What is the meaning of his experiencing spiritual awakening?"

Man'gong commented, "Sand fell down into the eyes."

A monk once made a circle in the air and asked Man'gong, "Why is it that all the monks of the world between the sky and the ground cannot get into the middle of this circle?

Man'gong also made a circle and said, "Why is it that all the monks cannot go out from the middle of this circle?"

Man'gong once said, "People live with the hope that good things will come to them, but they don't know that when you get a good thing you get a bad thing. As you study the Way, give up [the idea] of being human. Become deaf, deformed and blind, and stay away from all other [external] things. Then Big I will be naturally realized."

The following two exchanges have been used since Man'gong's time as *kongans*:

One afternoon, Man'gong was eating watermelon with a group of other monks. Suddenly, he heard the shrill chirrup of a cicada—"mei-mei-mei-mei-mei . . ." from the trees and said loudly, "Anybody who can catch this cicada and bring it to me will not have to pay the price of a piece of watermelon. If you cannot catch it, then you have to pay me three coins. Everybody say something, now!"

Someone pretended to catch the cicada, someone made the shrill chirrup of the cicada, someone shouted "Katz," someone hit Man'gong on the back and said, "I caught the cicada!"

Man'gong did not accept any of these answers and said, "Everybody give me three coins."

Just then, the monk Kŭmbong drew a circle in the air and said, "There is no Buddha in this circle. There is no circle in the Buddha."

Man'gong said, "Kŭmbong! You too. Give me three coins."

If you were there, what could you have done?

Once, at the end of a summer retreat, Man'gong slowly came into the dharma room, looked around at those gathered and said, "Today is the last day of the summer retreat. Everybody did very well. But I alone was without work. So I set a fishing trap, and today one fish has been caught in the net. Come, speak. How will you save the fish?"

A participant stood up and moved his mouth [like a fish].

Man'gong, seeing this, slapped his own knee and shouted,

"That's correct! Caught one fish!"

Then another participant tried to say something. Immediately Man'gong hit his knee and said, "Right! I have caught one more fish."

To any answer, Man'gong gave the same response.

The largest collection in English language of anecdotes about Man'gong, and poems written by him is contained in *The Whole World is a Single Flower* by Zen Master Seung Sahn. The material comes from the oral tradition and may have changed in re-telling, but it still gives a nuanced portrait of a Zen master in 1930s and 40's Korea.

Today, video pictures of monks from various factions within the Chogye Order fighting each other in pitched battles with baseball bats or more lethal instruments are a regular staple of television news in Korea. It is the same Chogye Order for whose revitalization Man'gong and other luminaries of his generation devoted their entire lives. Perhaps these are the pruning of a religion that has become forgetful of the struggles undertaken by Man'gong, Kyŏnghŏ, and others to save it from being obliterated by a colonizing power. It certainly does not honor the memory of those who made so many sacrifices.

Notes

1. Kenneth Chen, *Buddhism in China* (Princeton, NJ: Princeton University Press, 1964), pp. 232–233.
2. Henrik H. Sørensen, "Buddhist Spirituality in Premodern and Modern Korea," Takeuchi Yoshinori, ed., *Buddhist Spirituality II* (New York: Crossroad Publishing Company, 1999), 109–133, p. 109.
3. Mu Seong, *Thousand Peaks: Korean Zen-Tradition and Teachers* (Cumberland, RI: Primary Point Press, 1991), p. 162.
4. Mu Seong, *Thousand Peaks*, pp. 162–178.
5. Mu Seong, *Thousand Peaks*, pp. 179–196.
6. See, for example, Chong Go, "A Study of the Letters of Korean Seon Master Hanam," Master's Thesis, Dongkuk University, Seoul, Korea, 2002.
7. Mu Seong, *Thousand Peaks*, p. 189.
8. Sørensen, "Buddhist Spirituality in Premodern and Modern Korea," p. 120.

9. The information about Man'gong's life and activities that follows is taken from Mu Seong, *Thousand Peaks*, pp. 179–196.

10. Seung Sahn, *Dropping Ashes on the Buddha* (New York: Grove Press, 1976), p. 163.

11. Seung Sahn, *Dropping Ashes on the Buddha*, pp. 163–164.

12. Mu Seong, *Thousand Peaks*, p. 177.

8

Sŏn Master Pang Hanam

A Preliminary Consideration of His Thoughts According to the Five Regulations for the Saṅgha[1]

Patrick R. Uhlmann

Pang Hanam (1876–1951) played a prominent role in the making of modern Korean Buddhism. One of Kyŏnghŏ's main disciples, Hanam is widely perceived as an awakened Sŏn master and teacher who furthered the revival of Korean Sŏn practice.[2] During the last two decades of his life, Hanam also was one of the representative spiritual leaders of Korean Buddhism, elected and reconfirmed as Supreme Patriarch of the Chogye Order and its antecedent institutions.[3] His approach to Buddhist thought and practice undeniably influenced the fabric of modern Korean Buddhism.

Despite this, however, Hanam remains to this day a relatively unknown figure. For decades, the concern to preserve his legacy and memory was limited to his immediate disciples.[4] Until recently, Hanam likewise was a marginal figure in academia, mentioned only casually and cursorily in general works on Korean Buddhism.[5] Thus, the prevailing perception of Hanam in Korean society remains mainly informed by popular accounts and novels.[6]

Facing the challenges of modernity, Hanam reasserted the vitality and pertinency of the Korean Sŏn tradition by putting it into practice.[7] The Five Regulations for the Saṅgha (K. Sŭngga och'ik; henceforth Five Regulations) is Hanam's guideline of practice. They include (1) Sŏn; (2) recitation of the Buddha's name (K. *yŏmbul*); (3) scriptural studies (K. *kan'gyŏng*); (4) rituals (K. *ŭisik*); and (5) safeguarding the monastery (K. *suho karam*).[8]

The following discussion attempts to delineate Hanam's approach to Buddhism according to the five topics of his Five Regulations, and thereby to describe his overall view of the Korean Buddhist tradition.

Sŏn is listed as the first and most important item among the Five Regulations, the "fundamental concern" of practitioners for whom "in order to attain Buddhahood, it is necessary to pass through the gate of Sŏn."[9] Hanam's own journey through "the gate of Sŏn" was a process characterized by three awakening experiences. His first two awakenings occurred in 1899, at the age of twenty-three, merely two years after he had become a monk. His first awakening had been triggered by reading a passage from Chinul's *Susimgyŏl* (Secrets on Cultivating the Mind) and his second one occurred upon hearing Kyŏnghŏ quoting a passage from the *Diamond Sūtra*.[10] Although Kyŏnghŏ had sanctioned his second awakening, Hanam realized a decade later that he had yet to achieve his final awakening.[11] In Spring 1910, Hanam came across a scriptural passage he could not comprehend and which confused his mind.[12] Hanam promptly withdrew to a remote mountain hermitage for intense practice. There, in the winter of the same year, he experienced his third, sudden, and final awakening while kindling a fire.[13]

The trajectory of Hanam's awakening experiences is influenced by and similar to those of Chinul and Kyŏnghŏ. Hanam's first awakening attests the persistent influence of Chinul's writings since the early days of his monastic training.[14] Chinul underwent three awakening experiences without the physical presence of a teacher. Hanam similarly had three awakening experiences triggered by the reading or hearing of Buddhist texts. While his final awakening was not catalyzed by a text, it was nevertheless the perplexity he experienced upon reading a text that motivated him to seek a final breakthrough. Although Hanam achieved his second awakening under Kyŏnghŏ, both his first and—perhaps even more significantly—his final awakening occurred without a teacher.

Hanam was likewise profoundly influenced by Kyŏnghŏ, under whose guidance he studied for five years—a relatively short period if compared to that of Man'gong who attended Kyŏnghŏ for two decades. Together with Man'gong, Hanam is considered Kyŏnghŏ's foremost disciple who promoted the Sŏn renaissance initiated by Kyŏnghŏ.[15] It was Kyŏnghŏ's acknowledgement of his second awakening that established Hanam's reputation as an accomplished Sŏn practitioner and secured him continuous requests from several monasteries to supervise their Sŏn centers.

Paradoxically, Hanam's third awakening simultaneously seems to deemphasize and reinforce Kyŏnghŏ's influence on him. On the one hand, it supersedes the second awakening by invalidating its finality and thus weakening Kyŏnghŏ's sanction thereof. On the other hand, it was precisely by following Kyŏnghŏ's own behavioral model that Hanam achieved his final awakening.

Renowned for his erudition, Kyŏnghŏ initially pursued a successful career as *sūtra*-lecturer at several monasteries. However, upon accidentally venturing into a village ravaged by an epidemic, he suddenly realized that his textual knowledge could not remedy the suffering of the world. This prompted him to disband his entourage of disciples and to commit himself exclusively to intense and solitary practice until he eventually achieved awakening.

Upon experiencing his aforementioned perplexity, Hanam emulated Kyŏnghŏ's example by abruptly disbanding the gathering of monks in the meditation hall and withdrawing into the seclusion of a remote mountain hermitage where he achieved his third and final awakening. Thus, although Hanam's final awakening supersedes the one he had achieved under Kyŏnghŏ, it was accomplished by following Kyŏnghŏ's example.

It is precisely because he achieved a final awakening "independently" from Kyŏnghŏ—an awakening not certified by Kyŏnghŏ (whose exact whereabouts at that time were unknown) or, for that matter, any other Sŏn master—while at the same time emulating Kyŏnghŏ, that Hanam can be considered as his genuine disciple.

According to traditional Chan/Sŏn discourse, a master can only point the way to a disciple, ultimately it is up to the disciple to achieve awakening for and by himself. Hanam himself refers to this point when he expressed his gratitude to Kyŏnghŏ for not having exposed the ultimate truth to him.[16] On the other hand, and again consistent with Chan/Sŏn discourse, Kim T'anhŏ, Hanam's biographer and main disciple, asserted that "Hanam's third awakening was not different from his second one."[17] The deep impact of Chinul and Kyŏnghŏ permeates Hanam's approach to Sŏn practice and his literary production, which, from a traditional point of view, is considered to be anchored in, and effluent from, his awakening.

Hanam's approach to Buddhist practice in general, and Sŏn in particular, is characterized by a tendency to harmonize different—and at times conflicting—points of views, a reliance on extensive textual knowledge, and a thorough and consistent emphasis on the primacy of practice, which are distinctive attributes of Chinul and Kyŏnghŏ's versions of Sŏn.

In one of his earliest writings, Hanam provides a basic definition of Sŏn.[18] Significantly enough, he does so by referring to Sŏn as Sŏn *practice* (K. *ch'amsŏn*). Hanam proceeds by dividing the term *ch'amsŏn* in its two constituents "ch'am" and "sŏn," explaining both characters individually, but in a way that manifests their interrelatedness and inseparability. Referring to Bodhidharma's definition of Chan (K. Sŏn) as the Mind, the Buddha, and the Way, Hanam defines "Sŏn" as the mind of sentient beings (K. *chungsaengsim*). Hanam further elaborates on the mind of sentient beings in terms of its pure and defiled aspects, following the well-known model occurring in the *Awakening of Faith in the Mahāyāna*.[19] Perhaps more original is his discussion of the character "ch'am" (literally, "to investigate" or "to practice"), which he associates with the character "hap" (literally, "to merge with" or "to accord with"). Hence, for Hanam, practice means to correspond and conform to one's own nature—that is, to sustain and cultivate one's pure mind and not seek anything outside of it. A Sŏn practitioner should be firmly convinced of his own mind as being the Buddha, the dharma, and, as such, not differing from the stage of final awakening.[20] Hanam underlines this point by quoting Chinul's criticism of any practice based upon the presupposition that the ultimate truth ("Buddha"/"dharma") is to be found outside of oneself ("mind"/"nature") as being absurd as "trying to make rice by boiling sand."[21] Interestingly, it was exactly this passage that had triggered Hanam's first awakening.

Like most Sŏn masters since Chinul, Hanam advocates *hwadu* (C. *huatou*) investigation as the primary method of Sŏn practice. Accordingly, he urges practitioners to select and adhere to a *hwadu*. However, unlike most Sŏn masters, who exclusively advocated the practice of a particular *hwadu* as being superior to all others, Hanam recommends different *hwadu* as being equally effective.

Hanam's lack of sectarian concerns, a characteristic concomitant with his inclusive and harmonious approach, is manifested throughout his writings, in which he frequently refers to Chinese and Korean Chan/Sŏn masters of different lineages and representing different points of views.

The primacy of practice in Hanam's thought implies that his approach to Buddhism translates as a *modus operandi*. This is exemplified in his dealing with the controversy between "observing the *hwadu*" (K. *kanhwa*) and "looking back on the radiance of the mind" (K. *panjo*). While reminiscent of the alleged opposition between Dahui and Hongzhi or the Linji and Caodong schools in Song China, this issue emerged in Korea as a serious problem only during the period of Japanese colonialism, resulting from the influence of the Sōtō and Rinzai schools. The approach of *kanhwa* was mainly advocated by the Rinzai school, whereas that of *panjo* was promoted by the Sōtō school. These sectarian approaches were disseminated among certain Korean monks—through Japanese proselytism in Korea or Korean monks who had studied in Japan—and fueled polemic disputes in Sŏn centers as to which approach was the most adequate for Sŏn practice (See *HIBL* 54–55).

Hanam observes that this dispute is a modern phenomenon, caused by "some" practitioners who exclusively assert the superiority of either *kanhwa* or *panjo* and criticize their opponents as relying on dubious sources. According to Hanam, the "ancient masters" did not differentiate between *kanhwa* and *panjo*, and therefore the question of which of these two approaches is the superior one is ultimately a non-issue. He emphasizes that the real issue consists in achieving awakening through genuine practice. Whether or not one's awakening experience can be qualified as being "thorough," "ultimate," or "profound" depends on whether one's practice is genuine or not. In other words, awakening and its qualities are primarily determined by how genuinely the practitioner either investigates the *hwadu* or looks back on the radiance of the mind. *Kanhwa* and *panjo* are merely specific methods of practice, skillfull means, to which the criteria of "profound" or "shallow" do not apply.

According to Hanam, monks exclusively advocating either *kanhwa/hwadu* or *panjo* do so because, upon having experienced a minor realization, they become satisfied and do not persevere in their practice any further. Convinced of their method as the superior one, they become oblivious of the limitless number of skillful means of the Buddhas and patriarchs, and thus are no longer able to apply these for the benefit of other sentient beings.

Hanam recognizes the value of both *hwadu* and *panjo* methods.[22] He identifies the problem as residing not with the method, but with the practitioner, that is, those practitioners who one-sidedly and exclusively cling to a single method. Hanam advises practitioners to abstain from creating or adhering to antagonistic point of views concerning the true dharma of the Buddhas and patriarchs, as this would merely create hindrances for their own practice. He emphasizes that the issue of *panjo* versus *kanhwa* is irrelevant for a Sŏn practitioner, since genuine practice (literally: "practice according to truth") is like a fireball burning the face of those who approach it (*HIBL* 57). The Buddha-dharma has no point at which any conceptual understanding can be attached.

Hanam's emphasis on practice in his discussion of the *hwadu-panjo* controversy is consistent with his definition of Sŏn as *ch'amsŏn*, Sŏn as practice. As such, Sŏn practice is "nothing extraordinary" and can be cultivated by anybody: "wise and fools, of high and low status, old and young, male and female" alike (*HIBL* 94–95). Difficulties merely result from the lack of conviction and the power of one's vow (*HIBL* 95).

As an advocate of "sudden awakening and gradual cultivation" (K. *tono chŏmsu*) Hanam specifically emphasizes the necessity of continuous diligent practice even after having achieved awakening. In a letter to Kyŏngbong, he admonishes that "One has to be even more cautious after having achieved awakening than before achieving it. This is because before awakening one knew what one had to do. But after awakening, if one does not practice with diligence or lapses into indolence, then one will wander between birth and death, forever, with no hope of escape."[23] To underline this point, Hanam quotes Dahui, that is, to be more precise, he quotes Dahui as quoted by Chinul: "Often people with sharp spiritual faculties can break through this matter [of life and death and achieve sudden awakening] without expending a lot of effort. Then, thinking that it is easy, they do no longer practice. Thus, after the passage of many days and months, they will be caught forever by Māra."[24]

In the same letter, Hanam refers to the example set by "ancient masters, who, after having achieved awakening, hid their traces, concealed their names, and lived retired on mountains for the rest of their life, nurturing the sacred embryo" as an appropriate way of life for "us who are living in the degenerate age of the dharma."[25] Hanam equally observes that these masters spent the rest of their life without ever leaving the mountains. This letter, written two years after his arrival at Sangwŏn-sa, reflects Hanam's firm intention to spend his remaining life there, committed to assiduous practice and following the tradition of "ancient masters." With the exception of rare and poorly documented short trips, he actually spent the last twenty-seven years of his life at Sangwŏn-sa.[26] Under his supervision, the meditation hall of Sangwŏn-sa evolved into a major Sŏn center, attracting a great number of monks who gathered there to practice under Hanam's strict but solicitous guidance.[27]

The daily schedule of the meditation hall during retreats consisted of approximately fourteen hours of Sŏn practice: from 3:00 to 6:00, from 8:00 to 11:00, and from 13:00 to 21:00.[28] Monks were expected to observe a regimen of strict silence and exclusive Sŏn practice. In contrast to prevalent usage at other monasteries, the monks at Sangwŏn-sa were served only two meals a day, in the morning and at noon. Although prevented by a chronic gastrointestinal disease from practising Sŏn with other monks in the meditation hall, Hanam reportedly practised Sŏn "all the time" in his room, sleeping only three to four hours a day.[29]

Hanam identifies the pursuit of conceptual understanding and the failure of putting one's acquired understanding into practice as the main problem of Sŏn practitioners. He addresses the futility of conceptual knowledge in Sŏn practice by paraphrasing a passage from Chinul: "[T]he path is originally impeccable, and has neither direction nor position. Thus it truly cannot be studied. If one studies the path while passions still exist, one will only become deluded to the path."[30] Hanam then elaborates that "[t]he issue depends merely with the sincerity of a single thought-instant of the individuals in question. There is hardly anybody who does not understand the path. But even though they understand the path, they do not put their understanding into practice. Therefore they move far away from the path."[31]

Far from discarding all forms of conceptual knowledge, Hanam emphasizes the necessity to put into practice what one knows. In other words, knowledge or understanding is useful only to the extent that it is actually put into practice.

Perhaps the most succinct and distinctive formulation of Hanam's understanding of Buddhism is expressed in a title given to one of his published interviews: "The essence of Buddhism is genuine practice"; or more literally: "The teachings of the Buddha are found in actual practice."[32] Therein, Hanam points out that people of "nowadays" have considerable knowledge but that their practice is not concomitant with it; that is, there is excessive knowledge and insufficient practice. He repeatedly emphasizes practice as the most central aspect of Buddhism.[33] In another article, Hanam formulates this problem as the following question: "Why is it that although the verbal teachings of the sages and saints are published in books, read, heard, recited, and memorized by people, there are only a few who actually put them into practice?"[34]

According to Hanam, the main reason for this problem is that practitioners think only of learning extensively, thereby distracting their mind and objective, which results in their failure to realize what is essential (*HIBL* 147–48). As a solution, he suggests that practitioners learn a few things, but make sure to practice them well. A practitioner should select a short and convincing passage from the verbal teachings, i.e., from Buddhist texts, keep it in mind as a lifelong teacher, and truly practice accordingly.

Hanam is convinced that if a practitioner, although he may not "gain the fame of a learned scholar," perseveres without retrogressing, he will obtain "a genuine benefit regarding the fundamental issue" and, ultimately, his wisdom will expand and "naturally" reach the level of sages and saints (*HIBL* 148). In a dharma-lecture intended to convey a "straight shortcut to the essential," Hanam illustrates how practitioners—those monks "committed to the gate of the Buddha and the domain of the patriarchs"—should exclusively focus on whatever practice they are engaged in: He refers to the attitude displayed by a cat implementing to catch a mouse, which consists of assuming an immovable posture and being focused on straightforwardly observing the mouse (*HIBL* 148–49).

Hanam's approach to Sŏn emphasizes practice over method and, therefore, is not limited to the equally valued methods of either "investigating the *hwadu*" or "looking back on the radiance of the mind," nor does it preclude doctrinal studies. Its broad and inclusive characteristics are also manifested in the way he handled controversial issues between Sŏn on the one hand, and *yŏmbul* and scriptural studies on the other. Hanam's approach appears even more distinctive since it incurred criticism from other Sŏn practitioners in his time.

Yŏmbul (Recitation of the Buddha's Name)

The most articulate formulation of Hanam's approach to *yŏmbul*, the practice of recollecting the Buddha's name, occurs in his preface to the name-list of those monks who undertook the winter retreat in the Sŏn Center at Manil-hermitage, Kŏnbong-sa (*HIBL* 334–40).

In 1921, the abbot of Kŏnbong-sa and the majority of resident monks resolved to abolish the "Association for Reciting the Buddha's Name" at Manil-hermitage, and to replace it with an "Association for Sŏn Practice."[35] To ensure a smooth transition, the abbot invited Sŏn practitioners from all over Korea to undertake the winter retreat at the hermitage. Complying with the request that he supervise the retreat, Hanam, through his presence, contributed to the prestige of the newly opened Sŏn center as well as to the Sŏn renaissance initiated by Kyŏnghŏ.

The wholesale abolishment of the recitation of the Association for Reciting the Buddha's Name caused resentment among a considerable number of monks and Hanam apparently felt compelled to convey his approach to the *yŏmbul* practice in a dialogue with an anonymous monk who confronts him with the pertinent question: "The ancient masters said that the recitation of the Buddha's name and Sŏn practice are originally not two separate practices. Why is it then that now the Association for Reciting the Buddha's Name has been abolished and replaced by a center for Sŏn practice?" (*HIBL* 338).

Hanam's response consists in acknowledging the non-duality of the recitation of the Buddha's name and Sŏn practice while at the same time also justifying the abolishment of the Association of Reciting the Buddha's Name at Kŏnbong-sa and, by implication, the abolishment of the associations in other monasteries as well. His main argument rests on the assumption that current practices of the recitation of the Buddha's name are a degeneration or a misunderstanding of its original form. In Hanam's view, *yŏmbul* originally refers to the "recollection" and not the "recitation" of Buddha's name. Hence, he criticizes *yŏmbul* as "recitation" as being completely different from and even antagonistic to Sŏn practice, and then he proceeds to arguing that *yŏmbul* as "recollection," not as "recitation," is identical to Sŏn.

If through *yŏmbul* a practitioner seeks rebirth in Pure Land, this presupposes the tangible existence of a pure land and, by implication, the existence of an impure land where the practitioner is currently located. This kind of *yŏmbul* (*yŏmbul* as recitation) not only causes the practitioner to posit a dichotomy between pure and impure lands, but also induces him to perceive himself as inherently being an ordinary sentient being, a form of existence contrasting with and opposed to that of the Buddha. As a result, *yŏmbul* (as recitation of the Buddha's name) produces duality, rather than overcoming it. In contrast, Sŏn practice (K. *ch'amsŏn*) establishes from its inception, through the initial activation of the *bodhicitta*, that one's mind *is* indeed the Buddha. By means of one single thought, the practitioner destroys the ignorance accumulated during aeons. Hence, the dichotomy between ordinary sentient beings and the Buddha, or between pure and impure lands, is absent in Sŏn practice. From this viewpoint, therefore, *yŏmbul* as a recitation of the Buddha's name promotes duality whereas Sŏn overcomes it.

Hanam explains that the non-duality of *yŏmbul* (as a recollection of the Buddha's name) and Sŏn lies in the fact that both practices cut off all forms of the dualist mode of thinking. He illustrates his argument by quoting T'aego Pou (1301–1382) and Naong Hyegŭn (1320–1376), the two most influential Sŏn monks in the late Koryŏ dynasty.

According to T'aego, the correct practice of *yŏmbul* consists of recollecting that one's own nature is identical to the Buddha Amitābha. This recollection has to be maintained, like a *hwadu*, thought-moment after thought-moment, at all times of the day and in all postures (walking, sitting, standing, or reclining). Eventually, assiduous and continuous practice will cause the flow of mind and thoughts to be suddenly cut off and bring about the manifestation of Buddha Amitābha's true body.[36] Sharing a similar view, Naong urges the practitioner to keep in mind that Buddha Amitābha is located in a place where thoughts are exhausted and absent.[37]

Hanam, retrospectively, approved the abolishment of the *yŏmbul* association at Manil-hermitage as an appropriate measure, criticizing, if not condemning, its *yŏmbul* practitioners as outwardly seeking rebirth in the Pure Land while being oblivious of their own nature as being inherently identical to Amitābha or the Pure Land. He accentuates his criticism by quoting a passage from Chinul which states that those practitioners who fail to achieve the samādhi of oneness through *yŏmbul* recollection merely visualize Amitābha's "appearance or invoke his name with feelings that arise from views and craving. After days or years, they often end up being possessed by *māras* and demons. They wander around in madness, they wander aimlessly, all their practice having been in vain."[38]

According to Hanam, the main criterion for differentiating between correct and "degenerated" *yŏmbul* is whether the practitioner seeks inside or outside of his mind. Correct *yŏmbul* and Sŏn are identical practices in the sense that both focus on one's mind.

Besides orthopraxy, adherence to tradition was a further criterion in Hanam's evaluation of *yŏmbul* practice. An adequate example thereof occurs in his reply to a letter from the monk Powŏl Sŏng'in.[39] Probably opposed to the abolition of the *yŏmbul* association at Manil-hermitage, Powŏl refers to the Silla dynasty monk Palching (?–785), considered as the founder of the first *yŏmbul* association, Manil yŏmbul hoe, at Kŏnbong-sa and portrayed as having been miraculously flown to the Pure Land together with thirty-one *yŏmbul* co-practitioners.[40]

In his reply, Hanam recognizes the "auspiciousness" of Palching's *yŏmbul*, but cautions that "nowadays, such an auspicious event can hardly be discussed with people lacking wisdom" (*HIBL* 226). Hanam seems to postulate a difference between *yŏmbul* as a time-honored tradition and the modern and "degenerate" practice thereof. The absence of a criticism of Palching's practice, whose traditional depiction is similar, if not identical, to *yŏmbul* as "seeking outside one's mind," suggests that instead of differentiating between *yŏmbul* as "recollection" and *yŏmbul* as "recitation," Hanam may be implicitly criticizing a modern version of *yŏmbul* informed by *nenbutsu* as propagated by Japanese Pure Land schools in Korea.[41]

Scriptural Studies

Texts played a prominent role throughout Hanam's life, influencing both his thought and practice. An anecdote relates that, as a child enrolled in the village school, Hanam read about the Heavenly Emperor who ruled the world in primordial times. When he asked who preceded the Heavenly Emperor, his teacher mentioned Pan Gu, the cosmic man who parted heaven from earth.

When Hanam again inquired who preceded Pan Gu, his teacher was unable to reply. Thereafter, Hanam spent "over a decade reading the Chinese classics without finding a satisfactory answer to this question" (*HIBL* 449–450). Thus, Hanam's spiritual quest had already begun in his childhood, triggered by a doubt catalyzed by the reading of a text. Texts also played a role in the subsequent occurrences that lead him to his awakening experiences.

Hanam's affinity with texts and predilection to textual knowledge was further mediated by Kyŏnghŏ, who himself had devoted the first decade of his monastic career to the assiduous study of Buddhist, Confucian, and Daoist texts, including the *Daodejing* and *Zhuangzi*.[42] The legacy of Hanam's extensive textual knowledge and scriptural studies, ascribed to his early education and Kyŏnghŏ's influence, extended far beyond the limits of the Buddhist curriculum—Hanam did lecture on Daoist texts during Sŏn retreats—and was subsequently inherited by Kim T'anhŏ, one of his main disciples.

Scriptural studies or "*kan'gyŏng*" (literally, "reading *sūtras*"), the third item in Hanam's Five Regulations, are paraphrased as the study of the Tripiṭaka or "the words of the Buddhas and patriarchs" and as a prerequisite for monks in order to educate sentient beings (*HIBL* 29). Although Hanam probably would subscribe to such a normative interpretation, for him, texts and the study thereof represent much more than mere expedients for proselytism: they assume an instrumental, if not essential, function in Sŏn practice and in achieving awakening.

Hanam advises practitioners to "adopt the expedient words and phrases of the ancient patriarchs as one's teacher and friend" (*HIBL* 232–34). Referring to Chinul, who regarded the *Platform Sūtra of the Sixth Patriarch* and Dahui's *Epistles* as his lifelong teachers and friends, Hanam states that he himself considers Dahui's *Epistles* and two of Chinul's works, *Excerpts from the Dharma Collection and Special Practice Record with Personal Notes* and *Resolving Doubts about Observing the Hwadu,* as the most essential writings and the living words of the patriarchs. He wrote to Kyŏngbong that, "If these [texts] are always on your desk and if, from time to time, you compare your experiences with what is written in them, then your practice during this one life will be mostly free of transgressions. I also gain strength from these."[43]

For Sŏn practitioners, Chan/Sŏn texts function as valuable auxiliary devices both for their descriptive and prescriptive aspects. Hanam specifies that these texts must be considered as "living words" and admonishes practitioners against becoming attached to them. Texts, i.e., written or spoken words, cannot substitute genuine practice, as a practitioner achieves awakening only through realizing the sublime [one's true nature] for himself. From this viewpoint, words, even "true words," have no connection with one's practice and should not become the object of attachment.[44] Hanam elaborates this point with the illustration that "if someone wants to write down the truthful words of the Buddhas and

Patriarchs, even using the entire water of the ocean as ink will not be enough to complete this task. Genuine cultivation does not necessitate many words" (*HIBL* 119). However, avoiding attachment does not imply any disregard for the written word: Hanam himself used to preserve, if not to treasure, the letters of his extensive correspondence with monks and laypeople alike.

As the supervisor of the Sŏn center at Sangwŏn-sa, Hanam combined scriptural studies with Sŏn practice. His dharma-lectures, especially those he held once every five days during Sŏn retreats, manifest his erudition of Buddhist scriptures. Hanam also edited, punctuated, and published several authoritative texts, namely, the *Brahma-net Bodhisattva Precepts Sūtra* (*Pŏmmang posalgye-kyŏng*), the *Five Commentaries on the Diamond Sūtra* (*Kŭmgang-kyŏng oga-hae*), and the *Dharma Lectures of Pojo Chinul* (*Pojo pŏbŏ*).

Not surprisingly, Hanam viewed the *Diamond Sūtra,* Kumārajīva's translation of the *Vajracchedikaprajñāpāramitā Sūtra,* as a primary text to be studied, that is, "received, kept, read, and recited" by Sŏn practitioners. Hanam frequently lectured on this text during Sŏn retreats, but, because of its difficult content, or "deep meaning," he encouraged monks also to study the *Five Commentaries.* It was upon the request of his disciples and co-practitioners that he produced a punctuated recension of the *Diamond Sūtra* and its commentaries. Hanam apparently urged every monk at the Sŏn center to accurately copy his recension by hand—even after its printed publication.

During leisure time, especially during summer and winter retreats, Hanam lectured on the *sūtra* by reading the text aloud while the monks repeated and committed it to memory. Hanam thus made scriptural studies virtually a part of the daily curriculum of the Sŏn center at Sangwŏn-sa.

By far the most important punctuated recension produced by Hanam was that of Chinul's works.[45] The first of its kind and frequently reprinted, this recension promoted a renewed interest in Chinul's works and thought among Korean monks. It furthermore reflects Hanam's life-long indebtedness to Chinul, who inspired his inclusive and conciliatory approach to Buddhist practice in general and Sŏn in particular. Hanam's series of lectures on Buddhist sūtras and Sŏn texts—not to mention Daoist scriptures—was a rare, if not unique, occurrence in Korean Sŏn centers during that period. A considerable number of Sŏn monks exclusively advocated an anti-textual approach to Sŏn and categorically discarded other Buddhist practices, including doctrinal studies, *yŏmbul*, and rituals. Hanam's use of texts as supporting and/or being concomitant with Sŏn practice incurred him the criticism and opposition from monks adhering to what they considered to be a "pure" form of Sŏn practice.

The events surrounding Hanam's recension and publication of Chinul's collected works provide ample evidence of such criticism. When Hanam presented his recension to the monks practicing Sŏn under his guidance at Sangwŏn-sa, he was criticized for having done so by at least one of them. Probably anticipating more widespread criticism, Hanam wrote a preface in which he relates:

> Among the co-practitioners, someone said: "The recondite purpose of Bodhidharma's coming from the West has nothing to do with words and letters. How can it be right to promote the ignorance of those who nowadays are cultivating the mind, by having them to memorize words and follow phrases?" I replied: "If one is only attached to texts and words and does not truly cultivate, even if he has read the entire Tripiṭaka, he will end up being possessed by māras and demons. A true practitioner knows at a word how to return home. All of a sudden, he will open the proper eye, and even street gossip and noisy talk will turn out to be a skillful explanation of the essential element of the dharma. How much more so is this then the case with the direct shortcut admonition of our patriarch [Chinul]?" Therefore, I will not be dissuaded either by derision or grudge, but I will put all my energy in this enterprise [of publishing Chinul's works] and will have my co-practitioners of Sŏn to study his works at all times, so that they grasp the profound meaning and consider Chinul's works as the proper eye of the teachings for entering the path.[46]

This lengthy quotation demonstrates Hanam's emphatic justification of scriptural studies, his firm resolution to publish Chinul's works, and his intention to declare them as required readings for the monks' training at his Sŏn center. As Hanam's preface was published in the year following his nomination as the Supreme Patriarch of the Chogye Order, his promotion of scriptural studies was, by implication, a message directed to all, or at least a larger audience of, Korean monks.

Rituals

As the fourth item of Hanam's Five Regulations, rituals were understood as being the external manifestation of the Buddhist teachings, religious performances for the education of sentient beings, and provided with the specification that "without rituals, religion cannot exist" (*HIBL* 27–30). However, this interpretation of rituals as primarily addressing lay concerns reflects more the understanding of his disciples than that of Hanam himself. Throughout his career, Hanam promoted and performed rituals, fully aware of their intrinsic value for the monastic community as well. His dwelling at Sangwŏn-sa, a sacred place of pilgrimage and object of ritual worship, further predisposed and promoted his involvement with rituals. Located on the Odae Mountains, Sangwŏn-sa is renowned as the repository of the Buddha's relics brought back from China by the Silla dynasty monk Chajang (ca. 590–658) and as the place where the Bodhisattva Mañjuśrī had repeatedly manifested himself.

In 1930, Hanam was elected as "master of ceremonies" of the "Association for Praising and Worshiping the Stūpa containing the relics of Śākyamuni's Vertex on Odae Mountain" established by Yi Chonguk, the abbot of nearby Wŏljŏng-sa.[47] The association's goal was to promote the Odae-Mountain as a Buddhist holy site and to bring Wŏljŏng-sa and other temples out of insolvency and debts. Its members included high-ranking Japanese officials of the government-general from which Yi Chonguk succeeded in obtaining help for solving the insolvency of Wŏljŏng-sa. On the other hand, the association also served to mobilize Korean Buddhists to comply with Japanese colonial policies. Apparently, Hanam, in contrast to Yi Chonguk, skillfully avoided getting involved in pro-Japanese policies or statements, and his engagement in this association was motivated by a genuine concern to assist Yi Chonguk in restoring the finances of Wŏljŏng-sa, the head-temple to which Sangwŏn-sa was subordinated. Hanam took his function as "master of ceremonies" seriously and ascertained that a fixed amount of yearly revenues were allotted for incense-burning and rice-offering to the stūpa of Śākyamuni's relics, located five *li* above Sangwŏn-sa.[48] His *Eulogy of Bodhisattva Mañjuśrī*, a text to be recited within a larger ritual context, suggests Hanam's involvement with the promotion and performance of rituals for Mañjuśrī.[49] Hanam's most relevant contribution to rituals is his *Liturgy for the Minor Ceremony of Prostration and Repentance* (*So yech'am mun*), a simplified version of a longer text, the *Liturgy for the Great Ceremony of Prostration and Repentance* (*Tae yech'am mun*).[50] This ceremony was performed fortnightly in Buddhist monasteries, and consisted of elaborate and numerous sets of full prostrations and liturgical repetitions. Apparently concerned that the full-scale performance was too lengthy and "ineffective" because of its superfluous and redundant repetitions, Hanam compiled a simplified version of the liturgy, which still preserved the solemnity of the performance. Although his version has been "widely circulated, adopted and practiced until today," Hanam was not the only monk to propose a shortened liturgy of this ritual. The fact that he did so indicates that Hanam shared the concern voiced by other contemporary and prominent monks—including Han Yongun, Kwŏn Sangno, and An Chinho—for the simplification, standardization, and unification of Buddhist rituals.[51] Besides revealing Hanam's involvement with the ongoing discourse on rituals, this text is also relevant because through it and its performative enactment, Hanam asserts, reinforces, and even imposes, his view on Buddhist lineages, which assigns a predominant position to Chinul and deemphasizes that of T'aego.[52]

Hanam considers rituals as an inalienable dimension of Buddhist monastic life and as belonging to the repertoire of activities that monks should be proficient in performing. He repeatedly invited monk-experts in Buddhist music

(K. *ŏsan*) and liturgical dance (K. *pŏmp'ae*) to impart their skills to the monks at Sangwŏn-sa (*HIBL* 29).

Hanam extensively praises the filial piety of monks, particularly the performance of memorial services for one's Sŏn master(s) and secular parents. He repeatedly expressed his intention to perform or attend such services at different monasteries, although his poor health ultimately prevented him from traveling. Hanam regularly performed memorial services at Sangwŏn-sa, including elaborate services lasting up to seven or more days (*HIBL* 291).

Rituals for one's parents and teachers involved copious food-offerings necessitating a considerable amount of money. Considering the harsh economical conditions of most Korean monasteries at the time, and the notoriously precarious situation of Sangwŏn-sa, Hanam's praise for monks who secured and provided the necessary money for such rituals corroborates the degree of importance that he attributed to the performance of rituals.

Hanam's appreciation of rituals also includes what has sometimes been derogatorily labeled as "popular" or "non-buddhist" practices, such as the worship of the Big Dipper (K. *ch'ilsŏng*) and the Mountain God (K. *sansin*).[53] Because of his emphasis on the primacy of practice, Hanam considers even "popular" practices as conducive to spiritual development, provided that the practitioner performs them earnestly. He argues that "because Buddhism is tolerant and embracing other religions, there is no need to assert that one has to exclusively believe in Buddhism alone."[54] Hence, even individuals praying for worldly benefits at shrines dedicated to the Big Dipper or the Mountain God, located within or near the compounds of Buddhist monasteries, eventually will be induced "naturally," in *illo tempore*, to believe in Śākyamuni.[55]

Since the late Chosŏn dynasty, numerous mutual aid associations were established in various monasteries, involving monks and laypeople alike. A considerable number of these associations were named "Big Dipper Mutual Aid Association" (K. *ch'ilsŏng kye*) because their members regularly performed rituals for the Big Dipper. In his preface to the regulations of the "Big Dipper Mutual Aid Association" at Songna-sa, Hanam portrays such practices in a positive light.[56] Certainly, the "popular" rituals performed by these associations did not decrease Hanam's support.

Safeguarding the Monastery

"Safeguarding the monastery" (K. *suho karam*) is explained as an activity that monks should engage in when they are not involved in "religious" practice, that is, Sŏn, *yŏmbul*, studying *sūtras*, or performing rituals. Although, almost deceptively, listed as the last of Hanam's Five Regulations, "safeguarding the monastery" certainly should not be considered as a subsidiary or secondary activity less important than the antecedent four items. "Safeguarding" here specifically refers to the restoration or rebuilding of monasteries whose function consisted in providing an institutional basis for Buddhism, without which the monastic community could not survive, let alone engage in the above-mentionned "religious" activities at all.

Since the late Chosŏn dynasty, the monastic community had primarily subsisted secluded in and confined to mountain temples, many of which had fallen into decay as a consequence of the deprivation of state support. Hence, "safeguarding" the restoration and rebuilding of monasteries, was a critical issue for the revival of Buddhism and the Sŏn renaissance initiated by Kyŏnghŏ and furthered by Hanam, Man'gong, and other monks. The particular significance that Hanam attributed to "safeguarding the monastery" is manifested in his own biographical trajectory, as well as in his praise of monks who did so and his stern admonitions to those who did not. His refusal to abandon Sangwŏn-sa, first during the North Korean invasion and later when the South Korean military threatened to destroy the monastery, attests the extent of Hanam's adamantine resolution to "safeguarding the monastery," possibly even at the cost of his life. For Hanam, however, "safeguarding" primarily meant to protect the monastery from "internal" enemies: mismanagement and corruption by Buddhist monks.

The "head-temple system" (K. *ponsan chedo*) and the "temple ordinance" (K. *sach'allyŏng*) promulgated by the Japanese colonial authorities granted abbots the power to buy and sell monastery land as they pleased, without being required to consult and obtain the consent of their monastic community. Mismanagement and fraud by these abbots, who were turned into minor capitalists, caused the financial ruin of a considerable number of monasteries and the forfeiture of their landholdings. This was also the predominant situation in the Odae Mountains, where the insolvency of Wŏljŏng-sa onerously impacted its branch temple, Sangwŏn-sa. Hence, Hanam had to confront the consequences of mismanagement at the very least since his arrival at Sangwŏn-sa, where the acute shortage of food compelled resident monks to grow potatoes and chestnuts, barely sufficient for eating twice a day. Facing this severe deprivation, Hanam reportedly said: "Śākyamuni ate only once a day, we eat twice a day. Thus we should be thankful and practice diligently."[57] Moreover, he interpreted the lack of evening meals as being appropriate and beneficial for Sŏn practice, since customary mealtime could be used for further practice and a moderately empty stomach induced a sound sleep.[58] While displaying the imperturbable attitude of a charismatic Sŏn master, Hanam, in his subsequent writings, strongly admonished monks against corruption and mismanagement of monastic assets. It is conceivable that Hanam had moved to Sangwŏn-sa upon the request of Yi Chonguk, and with the intention of "safeguarding" it. At any rate, Hanam's presence at Sangwŏn-sa certainly contributed to Yi Chonguk's enterprise to bring nearby Wŏljŏng-sa out of insolvency and to (re-)establish the Odae Mountains as a prominent Buddhist stronghold. Hanam's solemn dedication to the practice and teaching of Sŏn attracted a large group of disciples, and Sangwŏn-sa soon evolved into a renowned Sŏn center, although Hanam never assumed its abbotship.

The close connection and cooperation between Hanam and Yi Chonguk ensued from the proximity of their respective abodes (Wŏljŏng-sa and Sangwŏn-sa), their function as highest representatives of the Chogye Order (Hanam as its Supreme Patriarch, Yi Chonguk as its General Managing Director), and their common concern with "safeguarding" monasteries. Hanam esteemed Yi Chonguk for his skillful management in resolving the bankruptcy of Wŏljŏng-sa as a monk devoted to the ideal of "safeguarding the monastery" and thus recommended him to the Japanese authorities for the post of General Managing Director (K. *ch'ongmu wŏnchang*) of the Chogye Order.

Within the corpus of Hanam's extant writings, however, it is Yi Chonguk's teacher, Sŏn master Sŏrun Pong'in, who most adequately illustrates the paragon of a monk "safeguarding the monastery." Sŏrun not only made substantial donations to monasteries and hermitages, but also founded new Sŏn centers and provided them with a secure economic basis. Some of his activities, which are centered in Kangwŏn Province, are detailed in the records that Hanam compiled upon the request of several recipient monasteries.

Sŏrun's restoration of Puryŏng-sa also included the establishment of a Sŏn center. He assigned land to the exclusive use by the Sŏn center, in order to ensure its perpetual existence and functionality. He also established religio-economic associations such as Yŏmbulhoe, Ch'ilsŏnggye and Hwaŏmhoe, involving monks and laypeople, which provided additional financial support to the monastery (*HIBL* 350–360). Subsequently, Sŏrun established a Sŏn center at Ose Hermitage. In establishing Sŏn centers (referred to as *sŏnhoe* or *sŏnwŏn*), Sŏrun was concerned with providing them with sufficient sources of financial revenues for securing their continuous subsistence and independent management. He hoped to accomplish this by allotting a fixed amount of land and its yearly revenues to the exclusive use by, or for, these Sŏn centers (*HIBL* 365–367).

Sŏrun also pioneered and substantially contributed to the restoration of the economic basis of Sangwŏn-sa. In 1928, two years after Hanam's arrival, he sent sufficient rice supplies to ensure that its monks could complete the summer retreat. Sŏrun continued providing supplies for retreat periods in subsequent years and, in 1932, he donated paddy fields and their yearly revenues to the monastery (*HIBL* 364). Besides immediate relief, Sŏrun's financial assistance had the long-term objective of securing a permanent economic basis and the self-sufficient management of monasteries and hermitages. Hanam held Sŏrun in high esteem not only for his engagement in "safeguarding the monastery," especially concerning Sangwŏn-sa, but also because he most adequately corresponded to Hanam's image of the ideal Buddhist monk.

Sŏrun's "safeguarding the monastery" involved the establishment of Sŏn centers, halls for *yŏmbul* practice, associations for scriptural studies, and the securing of funds for the performance of rituals. In other words, Sŏrun directly or indirectly promoted all activities subsumed in Hanam's Five Regulations.[59]

A monk involved in all activities delineated in the Five Regulations must correspond to, and have the qualities of, both a dedicated religious practitioner and a manager of moral integrity. Perhaps none other than Hanam himself as Sŏn Master and the Supreme Patriarch of the Chogye Order most effectively embodied and combined the ideal of monk and manager.

Hanam's concern with management is reflected in some of his writings and in the way he administered the Chogye Order. In donation records, he meticulously details the date, sort (land, victuals, or money), exact quantity, and anticipated use of donations that have been made to a specific temple or hermitage. Hanam concludes these records with severe admonitions to the current and future resident monks against the fraudulent management and misappropriation of monastic property. In his donation record for Sangwŏn-sa, Hanam warns monks against ignoring the opinion of their colleagues and using their power to defraud the monastery's assets or revert them to other temples. He explicitly states that he wrote this record to warn the monks in charge of managing the monastic assets against squandering or diverting these for individual profit and to remind them of the ineluctable and dire consequences of the law of karmic retribution. In addition, he emphasizes the necessity for accurate and honest management in order to ensure that the Sŏn center at Sangwŏn-sa will not be abolished in the future (*HIBL* 364). In his donation record for Ose Hermitage, Hanam specifies that disregard for the law of karmic retribution by abbots or incumbents of "three duties" (K. *samjik*) results in "falling into hell" or "the three evil destinies of rebirth" (*HIBL* 367). In his epitaph for Puryŏng-sa, Hanam addresses those who are (or will be in the future) "attached to selfish desire, use their connections with powerful individuals to abolish the Sŏn center and dissipate the assets of the monastery," warning that they will, "because of the gravity of their fault, inevitably fall into the evil destinies of rebirth. May this warning frighten those concerned" (*HIBL* 360).

"Safeguarding the monastery" was a primary concern for Hanam, since corrupt monks in administrative positions not only could ruin the entire monastery, but also threatened the subsistence of Sŏn centers, and, by implication, the Sŏn renaissance.[60] Hanam was convinced that the revitalization and preservation of the Korean Sŏn tradition could be achieved only if he and his colleagues, besides arduous Sŏn cultivation, were also actively engaged in preventing corruption and mismanagement of these Sŏn centers.

As the first Supreme Patriarch (K. *chongjŏng*) of the Chogye Order, Hanam had to "safeguard," or manage, what was, and still remains, despite its schism, the preeminent institution of Korean Buddhism. Most accounts on Hanam refer to him as the Chogye Order's first Supreme Patriarch, but they scarcely consider the implications of such a position. The idyllic portrayal of Hanam as having delegated all business matters concerning the Chogye Order to others, and as being exclusively dedicated to the practice and teaching of Sŏn at Sangwŏn-sa, far away from the secular world, is no longer tenable.

Although Hanam assumed the position of Supreme Patriarch under the condition that he not be required to move from Sangwŏn-sa to Chogye Order Headquarters in Seoul, this does not imply that he disregarded the responsibilities incumbent with his position. Obviously, Hanam delegated much of his responsibilities to the headquarters in Seoul, where the *de facto* management of the Chogye Order was carried out by its General Managing Director Yi Chonguk, whose nomination Hanam had supported and approved, and by his associates. However, Hanam kept himself informed on current affairs and exercised his authority. Once a month, a delegation from Chogye Headquarters brought to Sangwŏn-sa documents that needed Hanam's signature and approval. Hanam reportedly was able to handle all the paperwork by merely staying up all night.[61] Thus, although he delegated much of his authority and devoted a rather limited amount of time to bureaucratic paperwork, Hanam remained truthful to his principle that whatever task one is engaged in, one has to perform well.

As mentioned above, Hanam's concept of "safeguarding the monastery" had implications for the revival of Buddhism in general, and the Sŏn renaissance in particular. In a sense, Hanam's appointment as Supreme Patriarch of the Chogye Order coincided with his concern for the future of Korean Buddhism, both in its spiritual and institutional aspects. He was convinced that the future of Buddhism and the Chogye Order (prosperity, stagnation, or decline) strictly depended upon the principle of karmic retribution, i.e., "one reaps what one sows."[62] Similar to his admonitions against misappropriating monastic assets, here too, Hanam's reference to karmic retribution was primarily addressed to monks. That is, the future of the Chogye Order and of Buddhism primarily depends on whether monks, and only secondarily also laypeople, do engage in genuine and diligent practice, rather than on the surrounding socio-political factors. Therefore, for Hanam, the impending issue was ultimately reducible to practice, whose primacy he consistently and repeatedly emphasizes.

Hanam was convinced that as long as Buddhists, both monks and laypeople, were earnestly committed to practicing Sŏn, *yŏmbul*, *kan'gyŏng*, or any activity subsumable within the Five Regulations, they would motivate other individuals in their vicinity, "in cities and mountains alike," to begin practicing as well. This increasing number of practitioners will cause a renewed flourishing of Buddhism in Korea. There is, as such, no necessity for proselytizing by "delivering speeches or giving lectures," as the Buddha-nature is inherent in everyone and anybody can make the decision to practice.[63] According to Hanam, there is ultimately no propagation of Buddhism outside of one's own practice.

Conclusion

Throughout his life, Hanam remained firmly and profoundly convinced that the most important fundamental and essential issue for himself and for other Buddhists consisted in focusing on genuine practice. Although Hanam, as a Sŏn master, primarily emphasized Sŏn cultivation, he also recognized, in conformity with the time-honored tradition he valued so much, both the legitimacy and pertinency of other categories of practice, as recorded in his Five Regulations for the Saṅgha, namely, the recollection of the Buddha's name, scriptural studies, performance of rituals, and protecting the monastery. Hanam considered, and demonstrated by his own example, that these practices were intrinsically connected with, and auxiliary to, the cultivation of Sŏn.

Notes

1. This paper was written in 2006 and therefore does not reflect the findings of Korean scholarship directly or indirectly related to Hanam published after 2006.

2. This perception is articulated in the recurrent saying "Man'gong in the South and Hanam in the North," (K. *nam Man'gong puk Hanam*), referring to Kyŏnghŏ's two foremost disciples promoting his Sŏn renaissance, the first at Tŏksung-san in the southern Ch'ungch'ŏng Province, the second at Sangwŏn-sa on Odae-san in the northern Kangwŏn Province.

3. Since his early career, Hanam had served as supervisor of the meditation hall (K. *chosil*) at several monasteries, including T'ongdo-sa (1905–1910), Kŏnbong-sa (1921–1922), Pong'ŭn-sa (ca. 1923–1926), and Sangwŏn-sa (1926–1951). His career as a high-ranking representative of Korean Buddhism began in 1929 with his election as one of the seven patriarchs (K. *kyojŏng*). He was elected during the Plenary Assembly of Korean Buddhist Monks (Chosŏn Pulgyo sŭngnyŏ taehoe), although he did not attend the meeting. In 1934, he was appointed as vice chairman of the *Sŏn hakwŏn*. In 1936, he was elected as the Supreme Patriarch of the Chogye Order (then known under its official designation as Pulgyo Chogyejong), and in 1941, as Supreme Patriarch of the newly founded *Chosŏn Pulgyo Chogyejong*, a post he held until the end of the Japanese occupation in 1945. In 1948, Hanam was elected as the second patriarch (K. *kyojŏng*) of the Chogye Order, whose designation meanwhile had been renamed to *Chosŏn Pulgyo* tout court. Again, in 1949, Hanam was elected as Supreme Patriarch of what is still known as the Chogye Order (*Chogyejong*). As the schism into Chogye and T'aego Order had not yet occurred, Hanam's position as Supreme Patriarch virtually represented Korean Buddhism in its entirety.

4. Hanam's stūpa and stele were erected at Sangwŏn-sa in 1959. His main disciple Kim T'anhŏ (1913–1983) composed Hanam's epigraph and biography, the latter first published in 1966. After T'anhŏ's death, the monk Myŏngjŏng published Hanam's extant writings as *Collected Works of Hanam*. The discovery of further texts motivated Hyegŏ, Tanhŏ's disciple, to form an association of Hanam's disciples, which published

Hanam's One Bowl of Records (*Hanam Ilballok*; henceforward *HIBL*, and marked in the text followed by page numbers) in 1995, and an expanded edition thereof in the following year. See Hanam Taejongsa Munjip P'yŏnch'an Wiwŏn Hoe, ed., *Hanam Ilballok: Hanam Taejongsa Pŏbŏrok* (Hanam's One Bowl of Records: The Recorded Dharma-lectures of Great Patriarch Hanam) (Seoul: Minjoksa, 1996). [Second revised and enlarged edition; first published in 1995].

The compilers of the *HIBL* did not include, nor refer to, any of the pro-Japanese articles that are claimed to be authored by Hanam. Hanam's autobiographical record, or at least a version thereof, was discovered in 2001. The manuscript, titled *Ilsaeng p'ae'gwŏl* (A Life of Blunders), provides a brief description of Hanam's awakening process. Most probably, it is a copy made by Kim T'anhŏ between 1945 and 1950 of a non-extant original written by Hanam in late 1912. For a reprint of the manuscript with a vernacular Korean translation, see Yun Ch'anghwa, "Hanam ŭi chajŏnjŏk kudogi *Ilsaeng p'ae'gwŏl*" (*Ilsaeng p'aegwŏl*, Hanam's Autobiographical Account of his Search for the Path), *Pulgyo p'yŏngnon* 5, no. 4 (Winter 2003): 294–306. Much of Hanam's literary production, which probably could substantially augment and corroborate the autobiographical informations of the *Ilsaeng p'aegwŏl*, was destroyed during the conflagration of Sangwŏn-sa in 1947.

5. This situation began to change with the pioneering work by Kim Hosŏng, which includes, among others, "Hanam ŭi Toŭi-Pojo pŏpt'ong sŏl: 'Haedong ch'ojo e tae haya' rŭl chungsim ŭro" (Hanam's View on the Toŭi-Pojo Dharma-lineage: Focusing on "Regarding the First Patriarch of Korea"), *Pojo sasang* (1988): 401–416; and "Hanam sŏnsa: Pojosŏn kyesŭnghan chongmun ŭi sŏnjisik" (Sŏn Master Hanam: A Kalyāṇamitra of the [Chogye] Order who Inherited Pojo's Sŏn") in *Hanguk Pulgyo inmul sasang-sa* (History of Thought in Korean Buddhism Based upon Individuals) (Seoul: Minjoksa 1990), pp. 462–473. The bulk of Kim's research on Hanam has been edited as a monograph, *Pang Hanam sŏnsa: Chogye-jong ch'odae chongjŏng* (Sŏn Master Pang Hanam: The First Supreme Patriarch of the Chogye Order), (Seoul: Minjoksa, 1996). For a review thereof, see Masŏng's "Pang Hanam sŏnsa rŭl ilggo" ("Having read [Kim Ho-sŏng's] 'Sŏn Master Pang Hanam' ") in *Sŏnu Toryang* 8 (March 1996), pp. 279–283. Further contributions were made by Ch'oe Sudo, a third-generation disciple of Hanam, focusing on pedagogical aspects of Hanam's thought: Ch'oe Sudo (Ilgwan), "Hanam sŏnsa ŭi Pulgyo kyoyuk sasang"("A Study of Sŏn Master Hanam's Thought about Buddhist Education"), MA thesis, Dongguk University, Seoul, 1994; and by Brian K. Zingmark, a disciple of Hyegŏ, who made the first study on Hanam available in a Western language, an in-depth examination and translation of Hanam's epistolary documents: Brian K. Zingmark (Chong Go) "A Study of the Letters of Korean Sŏn Master Hanam," MA thesis, Dongguk University, Seoul, 2002. The quotations from Hanam's letters made in this essay rely upon Zingmark's translations, although occasional emendations were made when deemed appropriate in order to reflect Hanam's Sino-Korean original.

Coinciding with a renewed interest in modern Korean Buddhism, including its institutional aspects, several scholars have begun to discuss Hanam's role within the Chogye Order, his relations with Yi Chonguk, Kim T'anhŏ, and Japanese colonial policies. See Pak Hŭisŭng, "Chosŏn Pulgyo Chogyejong ŭi chuyŏk yŏn'gu: chongjŏng kwa chongmu ch'ongjang ŭl chungsim ŭro" (A Study on the Leading Figures of the Chosŏn Buddhist Chogye Order: Focusing on its Supreme Patriarch and its General Manager), *Chŏngt'ohak yŏn'gu* 4 (2001): 249–276. On Hanam's relation with T'anhŏ, see the following two articles by Kim Kwangsik, "Odae-san sudowŏn kwa Kim T'anhŏ: chŏnghye kyŏlsa ŭi hyŏndaejŏk pyŏnyong" (The Center for Cultivation at Odae Mountain and Kim T'anhŏ: the Modern Transformation of the Samādhī and Prajñā Community), *Chŏngt'ohak yŏn'gu* 4 (2001): 177–226; as well as his "Kim T'anhŏ ŭi kyoyuk kwa kŭ sŏnggyŏk," (Kim T'anhŏ's Education and its Characteristics), *Chŏngt'ohak yŏn'gu* 6 (2003): 213–243. See also the paper presented by Hyegŏ, "Samhak kyŏmsu wa Sŏn-kyo yunghoe ŭi Hanam sasang" (Hanam's Thought of Simultaneous Cultivation of Three Teachings and Harmony of Meditational and Doctrinal Schools), at the First Seminar on the Premodern and Modern Intellectual History of the Chogye Order, Dongguk University, Seoul, Korea, September 17, 2004.

6. See, for example, Yun Ch'ŏnggwang, *Bibissi inki pangsong p'ŭro kosŭng yŏljŏn 15. Hanam k'ŭn sŭnim: pa'guni e murŭl tamgo tallyŏ kanuna* (Popular Broadcasting Programs of the BBS [Buddhist Broadcasting System]: the Lives of Eminent [Korean] Monks, vol. 15: Eminent Monk Hanam: "You Fill a Basket with Water and are Running Around") (Seoul: Uri ch'ulp'ansa, 2002). A significant number of oral anecdotes on Hanam circulating among his first- and second-generation disciples awaits and requires systematic transcription and publication. The most popular of them have been published in editions of limited scholarly value, which omit clarification of sources and provenance. The problem of having scarce and fragmentary biographical information available, in contrast with a plethora of popular accounts, has been pointed out by Kim Hosŏng and is emblematic of many modern Korean monks. For recent efforts at implementing such fragmentary material with oral history, see Yongmyŏng, *Isibi-in ŭi chŭngŏn ŭl t'onghae pon kŭn hyŏndae Pulgyo sa* (Modern Korean Buddhism as Seen by Twenty-Two Witnesses) (Seoul: Son'u Toryang, 2002). On the significant function of oral history for the study of modern Korean Buddhism, see Kim Kwangsik's article, "Kusulsa yŏn'gu ŭi p'iryosŏng: kŭn-hyŏndae Pulgyo ŭi kongbaek ŭl meuja" (The Necessity of Studying Oral History for Filling up the Gaps in the History of Premodern and Modern [Korean] Buddhism), *Pulgyo p'yŏngnon* 5, no. 2 (June 2003): 217–234.

7. Kim Hosŏng and Hyegŏ discuss Hanam's thought according to the traditional threefold training, consisting of perfect conduct (Sk. *śīla*), meditation (Sk. *samādhī*), and wisdom (Sk. *prajñā*). Hanam, and most other Sŏn masters as well, certainly valued these categories, but since he apparently did not explicitly refer to them in his own writings, it is perhaps more, or at least equally, meaningful to attempt at delineating his thought according to the Five Regulations that he actually enunciated.

8. Hanam formulated this set of five practices, known as the *Five Regulations for the Saṅgha*, shortly after his arrival at Sangwŏn-sa in 1926, where he spent the rest of his life (*HIBL* 27–30). These Five Regulations not only characterize Hanam's own practice, but also that of the numerous monks who came to practice Sŏn under his guidance. It is possible and probable that Hanam formulated similar regulations, earlier versions or variations thereof, when he previously acted as the supervisor of Sŏn centers at other monasteries, notably those of T'ongdo-sa (from 1905 to 1910), Kŏnbong-sa (around 1921), and Pongŭn-sa (around 1923 until his departure for Sangwŏn-sa in 1926). Hanam's earliest extant piece of writing is the "Standards to be Observed in Sŏn Centers" (Sŏnwŏn kyurye) (*HIBL* 31–36) compiled for the winter retreat at Manil-am, Kŏnbong-sa, in 1921. Although this text is primarily concerned with the efficient administration of a Sŏn center, and not Buddhist practice *per se*, it still manifests Hanam's predilection for laying out regulations in written form.

That the Five Regulations characterized Hanam's approach to Buddhist practice appears from the fact that they were mentioned in the same order, albeit with a slightly different wording, nearly two decades later in "O'in suhaeng i chŏnjae ŏ kyŏlsim sŏngbyŏn" (The Success of Our Practice Entirely Depends on the Determination of the Mind), an article published in 1944 in *Sin Pulgyo* 56: 2–4. This article is beset with phrases supporting Japanese colonial policies, but its authorship, although attributed to Hanam, remains dubious—and probably was written by Hŏ Yŏngho. If originally written by Hanam, the printed version of the article probably had undergone heavy revision. But even if Hanam was not involved in any sense with the production thereof, this article remains relevant because it, in that case, indicates that whoever authored it, referred to Hanam's Five Regulations in order to add credibility and authenticity to the article.

9. *HIBL* 28. Strictly speaking, only the Five Regulations have been formulated by Hanam and, as such, written with black ink on a tablet suspended on the wall in the meditation-hall at Sangwŏn-sa. The explanations and elaborations following each single regulation have been subsequently recorded by his disciple(s). The compilers of the *HIBL* do not provide clarification as to whether—and if so, to what degree—these elaborations reflect Hanam's oral expositions.

10. See *Ilsaeng p'ae'gwŏl* for Hanam's own account of his awakening experiences. The passage from the *Susimgyŏl* is found in *Pojo chŏnsŏ* (The Complete Works of Pojo [Chinul]), Pojo sasang yŏn'guwŏn, ed., (Chŏlla namdo, Korea: Puril ch'ulp'ansa, 1989), p. 31; for an English translation thereof, see Robert E. Buswell, Jr., *The Korean Approach to Zen: The Collected Works of Chinul* (Honolulu: University of Hawaii Press, 1983), p. 140–141. The passage from the *Diamond Sūtra* occurs in the *Jingang boruo boluomi jing, T* 8. 235. 749a 24–25; for an English translation thereof and the poem Hanam composed upon his first awakening (*HIBL* 453), see Zingmark, p. 24.

11. Perhaps more important than this exchange between Kyŏnghŏ (quoting the *Diamond Sūtra* and thereby catalyzing Hanam's awakening) and Hanam (achieving the awakening experience and responding with a poem) was the subsequent recognition of Hanam's awakening as a social fact. Kyŏnghŏ, in the presence of the congregation of monks, quoted a passage from Gaofeng Yuanmiao's (1238–1295) *Essentials of Chan* (C. *Chanyao*) and asked whether someone could explain its meaning. Hanam was the only monk who provided a satisfactory answer. The next day, Kyŏnghŏ ascended the Dharma-platform and, (in a formal setting) addressing the congregation, said "Hanam's study had already surpassed the stage of 'opening the mind,' " thereby recognizing and sanctioning Hanam's awakening. See Kim T'anhŏ, "Hyŏndae Pulgyo ŭi kŏin: Pang Hanam" (A Giant of Modern Korean Buddhism: Pang Hanam) in *Han'guk ŭi in'gan-sang 3, chonggyoga sahoe pongsaja p'yŏn*. (The Portrayal of Korean People, vol. 3: Religious Figures and Figures in Public Service) (Seoul: Singu Munhwasa, 1966), pp. 3–342. Reprinted in *HIBL* 449–462, p. 453.

12. According to his biography, the passage in question occurs in the *Record of the Transmission of the Lamp*, but I have so far not been able to trace it in the literature.

13. For Hanam's poem composed after his final awakening, see *HIBL* 457; English translation in Zingmark, pp. 25–26. The *Ilsaeng p'aegwŏl* places this event in 1912.

14. Hanam became a monk at Changan-sa, a large monastery located in the Diamond Mountains, under Haengnŭm Kŭmwŏl, an otherwise unknown Sŏn Master, who soon advised him to move to nearby Sin'gye-sa for the study of Buddhist texts. It was there that Hanam began reading Chinul's works, and most likely also Chinul's biography.

15. Hanam attended Kyŏnghŏ from 1899 to 1904, and Man'gong attended Kyŏnghŏ from 1884 to 1904. Hanam's status as one of Kyŏnghŏ's foremost disciples is exemplified by the fact that he was entreated by Kyŏnghŏ to travel along with him to the North (*HIBL* 455), and later also by Man'gong's request that he compiled Kyŏnghŏ's Account of Conduct (*HIBL* 322).

16. In his *Account of Conduct of Venerable Kyŏnghŏ*, Hanam wrote: "Although I was dull-witted, I early on met and listened to his [Kyŏnghŏ's] profound words, but the reason why I venerate our departed master [Kyŏnghŏ] even more is that he did not thoroughly expose [the ultimate truth] for me. Therefore how could I dare to forget the kindness of the Dharma [i.e., my indebtedness to Kyŏnghŏ's teaching]" (*HIBL* 320).

17. Kim T'anhŏ, "Hyŏndae Pulgyo ŭi kŏin: Pang Hanam," p. 338 (*HIBL* 456). The recently discovered *Ilsaeng p'aegwŏl* contains the same statement. This would imply that, if granted that Hanam himself wrote these words (which remains to be proven), he himself denied the difference between his second and third awakening. It seems rather probable that T'anhŏ and/or Hanam wanted to deemphasize this difference out of respect for Kyŏnghŏ.

18. *Sŏn mundap isibil-jo* (Twenty-one Sŏn Questions and Answers) composed in 1921 (or 1922) at Manil-am, Kŏnbong-sa (*HIBL* 37–69). As one of Hanam's earliest and longest extant writings, this text is presented by the compilers of the *HIBL* as the "most systematic" description of Hanam's Sŏn thought (*HIBL* 37). However, in his discussion of Hanam's style of Sŏn, Kim Hosŏng does not refer to this text, but instead focuses on *Ch'amsŏn e taehaya*, an article published by Hanam in 1932.

19. The two aspects of the mind of all sentient beings refer to, first, the pure mind (K. *chŏngsim*) which corresponds to the essence of true suchness without outflows (K. *muru chinyŏ*), and, second, the defiled mind (K. *yŏmsim*) which is defiled by ignorance and its products, namely, the three poisons (greed, hatred, and delusion).

20. When referring to practitioners, this paper consistently uses the masculine pronoun. While Hanam did not discriminate against female practitioners or nuns, his audience was *de facto* masculine.

21. *Susimgyŏl* (Secrets on Cultivating the Mind), *Pojo chŏnsŏ*, p. 31; English translation in Buswell, *The Korean Approach to Zen*, pp. 140–141.

22. In a later text, *Ilchinhwa* (One Dust Mote Talk), published in *Sŏnwŏn* 1 (October 1931): 14–15; reprinted in *HIBL* 90–97. Hanam also characterizes Sŏn practice in terms of "looking back on the radiance of the mind" (*HIBL* 94).

23. *Letter to Kyŏngbong* dated the 7th day of the 3rd month of 1928 (*HIBL* 230–31); adaptation of Zingmark's English translation, pp. 131–132. Hanam's letters to Kyŏngbong represent the largest bulk of his extant private correspondence. Hanam composed this letter in reply to Kyŏngbong who informed him that he had achieved awakening in the winter of 1927. Kyŏngbong (1892–1982) has kept a meticulous diary covering sixty-seven years of his life since he was eighteen and he also preserved his correspondence with Hanam and other eminent monks of his time. Kyŏngbong's records thus are an invaluable source for documenting the history of modern Korean Buddhism. See Myŏngjŏng, ed., *Samsogul ilji* (Samsogul Diary) (Yongsan, Korea: Kŭngnak sŏnwŏn, 1992).

24. *HIBL* 230; *Pojo chŏnsŏ*, p. 38; Buswell, *The Korean Approach to Zen*, p. 148; *T* 1998.47.920a. This passage reveals that Hanam quoted Dahui not directly from Dahui's

works, but because he found this passage—and was impressed by it—while studying Chinul's works.

25. *HIBL* 230; Zingmark, p. 131.

26. Hanam himself acknowledged that he left the Odae Mountains twice: to go to Seoul to get his teeth fixed and to travel to Pulguk-sa. See Yamashita Shinichi, "Ikeda Kiyoshi keimu kyokuchō Hō Kangan zenji wo tou" (Director of the Bureau for Police Affairs Ikeda Kiyoshi visits Sŏn Master Pang Hanam), *Chōsen bukkyō* 101 (Aug. 1934): 4–5. As Zingmark points out, Kyŏngbong recorded in his diary that Hanam came to visit him in 1931 for two days (Zingmark, 37–38).

27. Sōma Shōei, "Hō Kangan zenji o tazunete" (Meeting Sŏn Master Pang Hanam), *Chōsen bukkyō* 87 (April 1933): 14–19. Sōma portrays Hanam as being focused on supervising the practice of [younger] monks, displaying a great care toward them. Hanam's care is also exemplified in his epistolary correspondence with younger monks. See, for example, his *Reply (2) to T'anhŏ's letter* (*HIBL* 219).

28. This and the following description of practice at the Sŏn center of Sangwŏn-sa relies on the account—the earliest of its kind—by Sōma Shōei, a Japanese monk of the Sōtō school, who undertook the winter retreat at Sangwŏn-sa from December 1932 to Spring 1933. Sōma was fluent in conversational Korean as he previously dwelled in different Korean monasteries for four years. When he arrived at Sangwŏn-sa, the retreat had already begun and strict regulations prohibited any late-coming monk to join the retreat. Hanam made an exception for him, perhaps because he came with a recommendation letter from Yi Chonguk.

29. Sōma, "Hō Kangan zenji o tazunete," p. 17.

30. The passage paraphrased by Hanam occurs in Chinul's *Excerpts from the Dharma Collection and Special Practice Record with Personal Notes* (*Pojo chŏnsŏ*, p. 162; Buswell, *The Korean Approach to Zen*, pp. 336–337). Chinul himself likewise quoted this passage from Dahui's *Recorded Sayings* (*T* 1998.47.918b).

31. *Reply (2) to T'anhŏ's letter* (*HIBL* 219); English rendering following Zingmark's excellent translation (p. 111).

32. Hō Kangan, "Bukkyō wa jikkō ni ari" (The Essence of Buddhism Lies in Genuine Practice, 1936), pp. 227–29; article reprinted in *Kŭndae Pulgyo kit'a charyo*, vol. 2 (*Han'guk kŭnhyŏndae Pulgyo charyojip*, vol. 64) (Seoul: Minjoksa, 1996), pp. 233–35. Despite being attributed to Hō Kangan (i.e., Pang Hanam) this article in Japanese actually is a summary of an interview with Hanam on the 28th of October, the identity of the interviewer(s) is not mentioned; for the sake of simplicity, this article is henceforth referred to as Hō Kangan.

33. Because the article was not written by Hanam himself, the degree to which it reflects Hanam's words remains open to question. However, as Hanam's emphasis on practice is ubiquitously manifested in his other writings, especially in his article "Myop'osŏ" (Like a Cat Catching a Mouse), *Kŭmgang-jŏ* 22 (1937): 50–51 (reprinted in *HIBL* 144–50) published the following year, this interview can be considered as a succinct rendering of his position. On the other hand, it is possible, and probable, that the compiler(s) of the interview additionally emphasized "practice" in order to induce monks and laypeople to comply with Japanese colonial politics, notably the Campaign for Development of Spiritual Fields (K. *simjŏn kaebal undong*) which was strongly promoted between 1935 and 1937.

34. Pang Hanam, "Myop'osŏ"; reprinted in *HIBL* 147.

35. The "Association for Reciting Buddha's Name at Manil-hermitage," known as *Yŏmbul-manirhoe*, had been established in 1881 by Manhwa Kwanjun (1850–1919), a monk who significantly contributed to the rebuilding of Kŏnbong-sa after its conflagration of 1878. In 1913, the decision was made to convert all Buddha-name-recitation Halls of each main monastery and affiliated monasteries into Sŏn-halls, the only exception being Kŏnbong-sa's Manil-am. The *Yŏmbul-manirhoe* was thus the last to be abolished.

36. *T'aego Pou hwasang ŏrok* (Dharma Records of Master T'aoego Pou), *HPC* 6. 679c.

37. *Naong hwasang ŏrok* (Dharma Records of Master Naong), *HPC* 6. 728a.

38. Pang Hanam. "Sŏnjung panghamnok sŏ" (*HIBL* 339); This passage occurs in Chinul's *Encouragement to Practice: The Compact of the Samādhi and Prajñā Community* (*Kwŏnsu chŏnghye kyŏlsa mun*) (*Pojo chŏnsŏ*, p. 27; Buswell, *The Korean Approach to Zen*, p. 122). It is interesting to note that, in handling the issue of yŏmbul, Hanam does not confine himself to quoting Chinul, who also wrote a text on this issue, the *Essentials of Pure Land Practice* (*Yŏmbul yomun*) (*Pojo Chŏnsŏ*, pp. 413–16), but also quoted other eminent monks from the Koryŏ dynasty, T'aego Pou and Naong Hyegŭn. This shows that while Chinul is his main source of inspiration, Hanam tends to make use of a broad spectrum of references in dealing with whatever issue is at hand.

39. Pang Hanam. "Reply to Venerable Powŏl's Letter" (*HIBL* 225–26). Although undated, this letter must have been written while Hanam supervised the Sŏn Center at Manil-hermitage, since its recipient, Powŏl Sŏngin, died in 1924.

40. The content of Powŏl's letter can be inferred from Hanam's reply to it. It was from Palching's "Gathering for practicing *yŏmbul* for ten thousand days" (K. *Yŏmbul manirhoe*) that Manil-hermitage derives its name. On Palching and the tradition of ten thousand days *yŏmbul* gatherings, see Han Pogwang, "Manil yŏmbul kyŏlsa ŭi sŏngnip kwa kŭ yŏkhal"(The Formation and Role of the Community for the Recitation of Buddha's Name for Ten Thousand Days), *Chŏngt'ohak yŏn'gu* 1 (1998): 51–72; on the *yŏmbul manirhoe* at Kŏnbong-sa, see his "Kŏnbong-sa ŭi manil yŏmbul kyŏlsa" (The Community for the Recitation of Buddha's Name for Ten Thousand Days at Kŏnbong-sa), *Pulgyo hakpo* 33 (1996): 73–95. Han Pogwang, however, does not refer to Hanam or the circumstances surrounding the abolition of *yŏmbulhoe* at Kŏnbong-sa.

41. The influence and impact of the Japanese Pure Land schools in Korea awaits extensive inquiry. Proselytizing of the Jōdo school began approximately in or after 1897 with the arrival in Seoul of superintendent *daisōjō* Nogami Unkai. In 1906, a newly promulgated regulation made it possible for Korean monasteries to become affiliated with, and managed by, Japanese temples, and a considerable number of major monasteries became thus closely connected with the Jōdo and Jōdoshin schools. See Kang Sŏkju and Pak Kyŏnghun, *Pulgyo kŭnse paegnyŏn* (The Recent History of Korean Buddhism in the Last Hundred Years) (Seoul: Minjoksa, 2002) [Revised edition, first published in 1980, henceforth referred to as Kang and Pak], pp. 26–30. It is not difficult to assume that Korean monks who visited and/or studied in Japan under the aegis of Pure Land schools, as well as those who were proselytized by the same in Korea, must have been influenced in their *yŏmbul* practice by *nenbutsu*.

42. Hanam refers to and praises the thorough erudition of his teacher in his *Account of Conduct of Venerable Kyŏnghŏ* (*HIBL* 297–325; esp. p. 315).

43. *HIBL* 233; English translation by Zingmark. p. 135.

44. "Letter to Kyŏngbong" dated the 13th day of the 9th month of 1930 (*HIBL* 248–250). In this letter, Hanam quotes an "ancient master,"—i.e., Quanhuo Yantou (828–887)— saying "What comes in through the gate is not the family treasure" and admonishes Kyŏngbong: "If you merely try to practice spiritual cultivation by clinging to words, then words are just words and you are you. Like oil just sits on water, you will not be able to achieve the level of awakening where all delusions are suddenly and thoroughly destroyed" (adaptation from Zingmark, p. 147). Hanam's warning against attachment to words—written words—is also expressed in his published articles, such as "Ch'amsŏn e taehaya" (On Sŏn Cultivation), *Pulgyo* 100 (October 1932): 35–37; reprinted in *HIBL* 107–120.

45. Alternatively titled as *Dharma-discourses of Pojo [Chinul]*, Hanam's recension included five of the eight works by Chinul, as well as his epitaph. See Pang Hanam, ed., *Koryŏguk Pojo sŏnsa ŏrok* (*Recorded Sayings of Sŏn Master Pojo [Chinul] of the Koryŏ State*) (Kangwŏn-do, Korea: Wŏljŏng-sa, 1937); and also his "Koryŏguk Pojo Sŏnsa ŏrok ch'anjip chunggan sŏ" (Preface to the Reprint of the Complete Works of the Recorded Sayings of Sŏn Master Pojo [Chinul] of the Koryŏ State) in *Pojo chŏnsŏ*, p. 429; *HIBL* 331–33.

46. "Koryŏguk Pojo Sŏnsa ŏrok ch'anjip chunggan sŏ," p. 429; *HIBL* 331–33.

47. Sōma wrote that Hanam had been at Sangwŏn-sa for nine years without ever leaving the mountain "and protected the relics of Buddha's vertex" (Sōma, "Hō Kangan zenji o tazunete," p. 17). Besides his miscalculation—Hanam had been at Sangwŏn-sa for seven years only when Sōma wrote his account—Sōma portrays Hanam as being tied to a particular place, which he definitely was not: in several of his letters, Hanam repeatedly expressed his intention to travel to other monasteries, among other things, for the performance of Buddhist rituals. Sōma's reference to Hanam as the protector of the Buddha's relics refers to his function as "master of ceremonies" of the "Association for Praising and Worshiping the Stūpa Containing the Relics of Śākyamuni's Vertex on Odae-Mountain" (*Odae-san Sŏgjon chŏnggol t'abmyo ch'an'ang hoe*).

48. See Pang Hanam. "Odaesan Sangwŏn-sa Sŏnwŏn hŏndap yakki" (Brief Record of the Donation of Paddy Fields to the Sŏn Center at Sangwŏn-sa in the Odae Mountains), *HIBL* 361. Hanam was not the only individual promoting Sangwŏn-sa as sacred space. Kyŏngbong, for example, also sent a group of lay-donors affiliated with T'ongdo-sa on a pilgrimage to Sangwŏn-sa. In a "Letter to Kyŏngbong," dated the 20th day of the 4th month of 1937 (*HIBL* 264–65), Hanam mentions that this group remained several days at Sangwŏn-sa praying for (worldly) happiness (*HIBL* 265).

49. The extant and undated version of Hanam's "Munsu posal ch'an" (Eulogy of Bodhisattva Mañjuśrī), *HIBL* 193–94, is a copy made by Kim T'anhŏ.

50. Although not dated, Hanam's "So yech'am mun" (Liturgy for the Minor Ceremony of Prostration and Repentance), *HIBL* 370–373, was probably composed after 1930, the year Hanam published his article "Haedong ch'ojo e taehaya" (Concerning the First Patriarch of Korea[n Sŏn]), *Pulgyo* 70: 7–10, in which he formulated his view on the Patriarchs and Dharma-lineage(s) of the Korean Buddhist tradition. The twelfth and last part of the liturgy in fact depicts Hanam's version of the Korean Sŏn patriarchs and lineage(s).

51. It is thus possible that Hanam planned or produced recension of other liturgical texts as well. An Chinho also included a "Liturgy for the Minor Ceremony of Prostration and Repentance" in his widely acclaimed *Sŏngmun ŭibŏm* (Manual of Buddhist Rituals). See An Chinho, *Sŏngmun ŭibŏm* (1937) (Seoul: Pŏmnyunsa, 2000); pp. 13–38

(first volume). For Han Yongun's criticism of this and other rituals, see his *Chosŏn Pulgyo Yusillon* (Treatise on the Reformation of Korean Buddhism), written in 1910 but published in 1913; reprinted in *Han Yongun chŏnjip* (Collected Works of Han Yongun), vol. 2: 33–125 (esp. pp. 102–106).

52. Hanam advocated Toŭi as the first patriarch of Korean Sŏn and Chinul as its "revitalizing patriarch." Perhaps more pronounced, and certainly more articulated, than this liturgy is the article he published on this issue in 1930: *Haedong ch'ojo e taehaya* (Concerning the First Patriarch of Korean Sŏn), *Pulgyo* 70: 7–10 (847–851; *HIBL* 74–89). Contrary to prevalent views, which either asserted T'aego or Chinul as the first patriarch of Korean Sŏn, Hanam advocated Toŭi and criticised T'aego. The issue was closely linked with the identity of the Chogye Order. Hanam considered that the Chogye Order "originated" when Toŭi introduced Sŏn from China and was not established only after Chinul—as has been first asserted by Yi Nŭnghwa. Further, by pointing out inconsistencies in the lineage of T'aego, known for having introduced Linji Chan in the late Koryŏ, Hanam was able to differentiate between the Chogye Order and a putative Linji or Imje Order, which could be associated with the Japanese Rinzai school. From this point of view, Hanam's Toŭi-Chinul Dharma-lineage was an assertion of a long and independent tradition of Korean Sŏn. For a detailed discussion of Hanam's lineage theory, see Kim Hosŏng, "Hanam ŭi Toŭi-Pojo pŏpt'ong sŏl: 'Haedong ch'ojo e tae haya' rŭl chungsim ŭro" (Hanam's View on the Toŭi-Pojo Dharma-lineage, focusing on "Regarding the First Patriarch of Korea"), *Pojo sasang* 2 (1988): 401–416.

53. Hō Kangan, "Bukkyō wa jikkō ni ari," p. 229; *Han'guk kŭnhyŏndae Pulgyo charyojip*, vol. 64, p. 235.

54. Hō Kangan, "Bukkyō wa jikkō ni ari," p. 229; *Han'guk kŭnhyŏndae Pulgyo charyojip*, vol. 64, p. 235.

55. Hō Kangan, "Bukkyō wa jikkō ni ari," p. 229; *Han'guk kŭnhyŏndae Pulgyo charyojip*, vol. 64, p. 235.

56. Interestingly, unlike his criticism of *yŏmbul* as a practice of "seeking outside one's mind," Hanam, far from voicing any objections against worshiping the Big Dipper or the Mountain God, benignly viewed these associations promoting such practices. See his "Kangnŭng-gun Yŏngok-myŏn Songna-sa ch'ilsŏnggye sŏ" (Preface to the Ch'ilsŏng Mutual Aid Association at Songna-sa, County of Kangnŭng, Subcounty of Yŏngok), *HIBL* 368–369. Hanam also referred to such an association established by Sŏrun (*HIBL* 350).

57. Sōma, "Hō Kangan zenji o tazunete," p. 6.

58. Sōma, "Hō Kangan zenji o tazunete," p. 16.

59. Hanam mentions that in 1918, as a part of his project to restore Puryŏng-sa, Sŏrun printed "Mahāyāna sūtras" and "Recorded Sayings of the Patriarchs" and established a *hwaŏmhoe* the following year (*HIBL* 359).

60. Hanam's concern for Sŏn centers whose existence was being threatened by mismanagement is also expressed in his "Chogye-chong T'oeun Wŏnil Sŏnsa pimyŏng pyŏng sŏ" (Preface and Inscription to the Stele of Sŏn master T'oeun Wŏnil of the Chogye Order, *HIBL* 347–349) which he compiled in the third month of 1943. Hanam points out that Wŏnil's (1877–1939) last words were an admonition to his disciples that the assets he had secured for Chikji-sa, especially the food supplies (K. *sŏllyang*), be never diverted to other ends (*HIBL* 349).

61. As pointed out by Pak Hŭisŭng, Hanam delegated the management of the Order's affairs to Yi Chonguk and Chogye Headquarters in Seoul, but reserved for himself

the right to make and approve—or reject—the final decisions. (Pak Hŭisŭng, "Chosŏn Pulgyo Chogyejong ŭi chuyŏk yŏn'gu," p. 263. Pak's information also relies on the interviews he conducted with Pogyŏng Hŭit'ae, a second-generation disciple of Hanam and direct disciple of T'anhŏ).

62. In a "Letter to Kyŏngbong" dated the 26th day of the 3rd month of 1949, Hanam expressed himself as follows: "As the superintendent of the Dharma [i.e., the supreme patriarch] I cannot help but being concerned about the prosperity or decline of the [Chogye] Order as well as about the prosperity or stagnation of the Buddhist Dharma. However, the outcome of these matters happens according to the principle that one reaps what he sows [what one acts, that is what he gets]. So why worrying or lamenting about them?" (*HIBL* 288).

63. Hō Kangan, "Bukkyō wa jikkō ni ari," p. 228; *Han'guk kŭnhyŏndae Pulgyo charyojip*, vol. 64, p. 234.

9

Zen Master T'oe'ong Sŏngch'ŏl's Doctrine of Zen Enlightenment and Practice

Woncheol Yun

Introduction

This essay investigates T'oe'ong Sŏngch'ŏl's (1912–1993) theory of "sudden enlightenment and sudden practice" (K. *tono tonsu*) based on his theory of Three Gates and its implication in Sŏngch'ŏl's view on *hwadu* (C. *huatou*) meditation. Through a series of publications and lectures, Sŏngch'ŏl presented a "radical subitist" theory of Buddhist soteriology as the authentic form of Zen practice. By so doing, he challenged the traditional position of Pojo Chinul (1158–1210), who has been credited as the systematizer and re-founder of the Chogye Order, to which Sŏngch'ŏl served as the Supreme Patriarch from 1981 until his death in 1993. Whereas Chinul advocated the doctrine of "sudden enlightenment and gradual practice" (K. *tono chŏmsu*), Sŏngch'ŏl claimed that this doctrine is "heretical" and that only the doctrine of "sudden enlightenment and sudden practice" represents authentic Zen soteriology. Sŏngch'ŏl contended: "Enlightenment is achieved all at once, and the whole spiritual development or cultivation is also achieved all at once without any gradual process."[1]

The Theory of Sudden Enlightenment and Sudden Practice

One of the most important concepts in Sŏngch'ŏl's Zen theory can be found in his concept of *kyŏnsŏng* (seeing through one's nature). Following the famous Zen adage, "Pointing straight to the human mind, discovering the [self-] nature is realization of the Buddhahood," the Sixth Patriarch Huineng confirmed the "sudden" doctrine as the most authentic Zen ideology. Sŏngch'ŏl considers *The Platform Sūtra of the Sixth Patriarch* as the *locus classicus* of the concept of "discovering the self-nature."[2] Sŏngch'ŏl defines *kyŏnsŏng* as "insight into the True Suchness of self-nature."[3] "The True Suchness of self-nature," or "the self-nature that is True Suchness," refers to the original innate Buddha-nature within oneself.

Since Sŏngch'ŏl insists that discovering the self-nature is the same as realizing one's original perfect Buddhahood, and that it is the only authentic Zen Buddhist enlightenment, he can be said to present an absolutist interpretation of the concept "discovering the nature."[4] Sŏngch'ŏl insists that one can discover the self-nature only when *all* false thoughts have been eliminated. In order to explain this, he repeatedly uses the simile of clouds and the sun:

> Although the sun of the wisdom of True Suchness is always illuminating the dharma world with its limitless rays, sentient beings are not able to see it because the dark clouds of the three fine and six coarse kinds of ignorance cover it. As the bright sun shines when clouds disappear and the blue sky is uncovered, the great perfect enlightenment is attained and the original [self-] nature that is True Suchness is seen completely when all false thoughts up to the three most infinitesimal ones are extinguished without remainder (*SC* 7).

The state from which false thoughts, the primary feature of sentient beings, are all eliminated must be that of Buddha. Therefore, Sŏngch'ŏl regards the ultimate Zen Buddhist ideal as none other than "discovering the self-nature." Citing various classical texts, Sŏngch'ŏl notes:

> Hereby, it is made clear that, on the basis of the authentic explanations in such perennial paradigms of Buddhist teachings as *Zongjing lu, The Treatise on the Awakening of Mahāyāna Faith, The Nirvāna Sūtra,* and *Yogācārabhūmi-śāstra*, to discover the [self-nature is to [realize] no-mind (K. *musim*), in which the false thoughts have been completely extinguished and the truth has been verified; or the Ultimate Enlightenment (K. *ku'gyŏnggak*), in which the [false thoughts up to the most] infinitesimal [ones] have been left far behind; and the Great Nirvāṇa (K. *tae yŏlban*), where defilements do not arise. It is unquestionable that discovering the [self-] nature is [realization of] the "Tathāgata ground" and Buddhahood (*SC* 20).
>
> Discovering the nature is none other than [the accomplishment of] the state of Tathāgata, Great Nirvāṇa, Buddhahood . . . and is thus the final ultimate goal of Buddhism (*SC* 21).

Sŏngch'ŏl asserts that the term "sudden enlightenment" in Zen Buddhism refers to none other than the "discovery of the self-nature." The clouds and the sun simile above allude to the meaning of the term "sudden." The term "sudden" here does not simply refer to a temporal instant. As Bernard Faure points out, it covers multiple "orders of mutually reinforcing . . . meanings," namely, being: (1) simultaneous, (2) absolute, and (3) immediate or not mediated.[5]

Sŏngch'ŏl's idea of the simultaneity of the "elimination of false thoughts," and of "the discovery of the self-nature," as explained through the simile of clouds and the sun, is grounded in the principle of the "middle path" (K. *chungdo*). Sŏngch'ŏl characterizes the principle of the middle path as "absolute negation and affirmation" or, "double negation and double affirmation." In his *Paeg'il pŏmmun* (One Hundred Days' Dharma Talk), Sŏngch'ŏl explains the middle path, focusing on the idea that absolute negation entails absolute affirmation.[6]

According to Sŏngch'ŏl, "discovering the self-nature" means that the attributes of sentient beings—especially, false thoughts and ignorance—have been absolutely negated. The Buddha Nature, which sentient beings have always had, without being aware of it, is to be affirmed through this negation. As the simile of clouds and the sun indicates, the negation and affirmation involved in the enlightenment experience coincide and are simultaneous with each other. The concept of simultaneity is based on the relationship between what is negated and what is affirmed, or the cover and the covered. The removal of the cover and disclosure of the covered must happen simultaneously, so that they actually constitute one single event.

The second layer of the meaning of "sudden" in the expression "sudden enlightenment" coincides with "absolute" or "perfect" enlightenment. Sŏngch'ŏl repeatedly emphasized that "discovering the self-nature" is no less than realizing one's own original perfect Buddhahood. For Songch'ŏl, the removal of ignorance and the disclosure of the Buddha Nature can not be done partially but only completely, if the term "enlightenment" is to be applied to those experiences. Sŏngch'ŏl states:

> [D]iscovering the self-nature, in the authentic transmission of the dharma from the buddhas and patriarchs, refers to the enlightenment of perfect and sudden verification . . . [whereby] ignorance is permanently severed. Therefore, great masters of the legitimate transmission have never accredited "discovering the self-nature" and "enlightenment of the mind" to anything other than the [experience of] perfect verification that comes as the fruition of Marvelous Enlightenment (K. *myo'gak*) (*SC* 29).

According to Sŏngch'ŏl then, when it comes to the experience of Zen Buddhist enlightenment, there are only two categories of beings, namely, buddhas and sentient beings. Sŏngch'ŏl asserts that there are no beings in between, insofar as enlightenment is concerned, for partial enlightenment should not be recognized in Zen Buddhism.

This theory is grounded in the absolute mutual exclusiveness of sentient beingness and Buddhahood. More specifically, it is based on an absolute, ungraduated distinction between the unenlightened and enlightened states. Explaining passages from the *Nirvāṇa Sūtra*, where some bodhisattvas, such as Mañjuśrī, are said to have discovered the self-nature, and where Buddha is called "great *śramana*," "great *Brahman*," or "great sentient being," Sŏngch'ŏl notes:

> Although the world-honored ones who have attained authentic enlightenment, that is, the *tathāgatas* who have accomplished the fruition [of buddhahood], and the bodhisattvas of great power, may be called great brahmans or great sentient beings, they are distinguished from ordinary brahmans or sentient beings because of their authentic enlightenment. Whatever they may be called, it does not change the fact that they have attained the right awakening. Therefore, even when a *tathāgata* or world honored one who has clearly seen the Buddha Nature is called a bodhisattva in skill-in-means, it does not make any difference to the fact that he is a *tathāgata* or world honored one who has clearly realized the Buddha Nature (*SC* 59f.).

Sŏngch'ŏl insists that no compromise should be made regarding the concept of enlightenment and states that the difference between enlightenment and non-enlightenment is like the difference between "gold and sand" or "a gem and a pebble" (*SC* 29, 154). Hence the core of his message: "The only authentic Zen enlightenment is the complete experiential verification (K. *wŏnjŭng*)" (*SC* 28).

According to Sŏngch'ŏl, enlightenment should not be confused with any experience that falls short of the absolute perfection of Buddhahood. Hence, he notes that even the Bodhisattvas of Great Freedom (K. *Chajae posal*), who have reached the eighth consciousness, who have the wisdom of nondiscrimination and act without expectation of reward, are far from enlightenment because they have not yet completely discovered the self-nature, due to the ignorance they have, however infinitesimal it might be (*SC* 38, 254, and *passim*). He also notes that the Equal Enlightenment (K. *tŭnggak*) attained in the tenth bhūmi, which is the highest status a bodhisatta reaches, is not the "discovery of the self-nature," nor is it authentic enlightenment for the same reason (*SC* 8, 13, and *passim*).

Sŏngch'ŏl's absolutist notion of enlightenment, with the criterion of "discovering the self-nature," has been criticized as being reification, objectification, alienation, or idolization of enlightenment as a transcendental, mystic, or supernatural state.[7] However, it should be noted that "discovery of self-nature," which Sŏngch'ŏl claims Buddhist enlightenment is all about, refers to the actual experience of awakening to *one's own original Buddhahood*, not to the attainment of a certain object that has been alien, so far, to the subject. One of the most essential premises of Zen Buddhism is non-duality and Zen Buddhist tradition has been characterized by its iconoclasticism based upon that premise of non-duality. Sŏngch'ŏl's views are obviously grounded in that tradition despite his expression of them in dualistic language. Although Sŏngch'ŏl himself often uses such terms as "absolute," it is inappropriate to impose dualistic meanings of words on his Zen Buddhist discourse regarding enlightenment.

This uncompromising distinction between enlightenment and non-enlightenment should be understood in terms of the principle of the middle path, which Sŏngch'ŏl regards as the very essence of Buddhism. Contrary to the implication of eclecticism or compromise that the term "middle" has in its ordinary usage, the Buddhist term "middle," in the principle of the middle path, implies absolutism, as its definition "absolute negation and absolute affirmation" suggests. Negation and affirmation can be truly one and the same only at the point of absolute extremity. Sŏngch'ŏl does not directly refer to the concept of the middle path in *Sŏnmun chŏngno*, but one can safely say that the repudiation of any middle position between enlightenment and non-enlightenment, which Sŏngch'ŏl expresses persistently in this book, is based upon this principle.[8]

Sŏngch'ŏl's absolute distinction of sentient beings and Buddha, based upon sentient beings' reality of non-enlightenment, presupposes absolute identification of them based upon the principle that all sentient beings, without exception, have the Buddha-nature and thus are already Buddhas. The reverse is also true: his absolute identification of sentient beings and the Buddha presupposes the undeniable reality that sentient beings have not realized their Buddhahood and thus need, for that realization, actual experience of enlightenment of "discovering the self-nature." It should also be noted that this absolutist notion of enlightenment, according to the criterion of "discovering the self-nature," serves as the ground for Sŏngch'ŏl's repudiation of the theory of "sudden enlightenment and gradual practice," which calls for further need of practice after "enlightenment."

The third meaning of "sudden" as "immediate" again stems from the absolute distinction between sentient beings' and the Buddha's states. According to Sŏngch'ŏl, what characterizes sentient beings is false thoughts and ignorance. As explained in the simile of clouds and the sun, it is the clouds of ignorance that hinder "discovering the self-nature" and thus enlightenment. Therefore, no aspect of false thoughts can mediate enlightenment. False thoughts are what should be eliminated for enlightenment, not what can mediate enlightenment.

This impossibility of mediation seems to be best explained in terms of the theory of Two Truths, that is, *paramārtha-satya* (the absolute truth) and *saṃvṛti-satya* (the relative truth). Nāgārjuna characterizes the theory of Two Truths as a pedagogical device:

By the two truths
Buddha's teachings are given:
Saṃvṛti-satya and *paramārtha satya.*
Those who do not know the difference
Of these two truths
Do not know the deep truths of Buddhism.
Without depending upon the *saṃvṛti-satya,*
The *paramārtha satya* cannot be expressed.
Without knowing the *paramārtha satya,*
No one enters nirvāṇa.[9]

Although it is inevitable that the absolute truth must be expressed in terms of the relative truth, the only "truth" the relative truth can be said to contain is that it is a useful expression of the absolute truth, or that it is a good skill-in-means. No matter how useful a certain skill-in-means may be for an immediate purpose, its status as relative truth does not change. Furthermore, at the point where the relative truth hinders the disclosure of the absolute truth because of sentient beings' tendency to idolize and thus to mistake what is provisional for the absolute, or in Buddhist terms, to become attached to the provisional, the provisional should be eliminated so that there will be no mediation resulting in the disclosure of absolute truth in a causal sequence. All mediation should eventually be avoided because mediation itself is *the* hindrance. Sŏngch'ŏl notes:

> The teaching of sudden enlightenment and discovery of the self-nature, which the preceding buddhas and succeeding patriarchs transmitted one another from mind to mind, is the pulse of buddhas and patriarchs and the marrow of the right teaching. All other various teachings are no more than skill-in-means for convenience and temporary expedients designed to guide people. Therefore when [we] take the standpoint of the orthodox way of teaching, [we] should reject them as false teachings. If [a teacher] mistakes expedient expectations designed for skill-in-means as the true teaching and thus does not discard but attaches himself to them, sentient beings would be bound to those tentative expedient explanations and unable to return to the truth. Therefore [I] reject them ardently and advocate the correct way of the teaching (*SC* 79).

Such a denial of mediation has made Zen Buddhism a strongly iconoclastic tradition. One of exemplary expressions of the iconoclastic spirit of Zen is the phrase, "When you meet the Buddha, kill the Buddha; when you meet the patriarch, kill the patriarch."[10]

Among all the different kinds of mediation, it is intellectuality and language that have been most emphatically refuted in the Zen Buddhist tradition. Sŏngch'ŏl follows that tradition faithfully throughout *Sŏnmun chŏngno*, and dedicates three chapters (the thirteenth through the fifteenth) to criticizing the theory of "sudden enlightenment and gradual practice" on the basis that it is grounded in, and gives validity to, the "intellectual understanding" (K. *chihae*).

Sŏngch'ŏl maintains that "discovering the nature" is the absolute removal of sentient beings' discriminating tendencies and the realization of one's own original perfect Buddhahood. Sŏngch'ŏl uses the ideals of no-thought (K. *mu'nyŏm*) and no-mind (K. *musim*), as conceptual tools to equate "discovering the self-nature" with the realization of the original perfect Buddhahood.

Sŏngch'ŏl defines no-thought or no-mind simply as the absence of false thoughts as he states: "Since all false thoughts are severed without remainder, it (discovering the self-nature) is called no-thought or no-mind"(*SC* 7). Here "false thoughts" refers to discriminating tendencies and habits.[11] Other popularly used synonyms for false thoughts are ignorance (K. *mum'yŏng*; Sk. *avidyā*) and defilement (K. *pŏnnoe*; Sk. *kleśa*). The discriminating tendencies are both the product and the producer of karma while, at the same time, they are karma. Therefore, in a broad sense, "false thoughts" indicate the whole sequence of karma. In this sense, Sŏngch'ŏl notes that "mind" or "thought" is the fundamental disease of all sentient beings, regardless of whether it is the mind or thought of heretics, ordinary people, saints, sages, or bodhisattvas (*SC* 8).

Sŏngch'ŏl asserts that no-thought or no-mind is the ultimate core of all Zen Buddhist teachings, since the realization of the original perfect Buddhahood is nothing but attaining the state of no-thought and no-mind. He states, "The difference between sentient beings and all the Buddhas lies in that of having thoughts (K. *yu'nyŏm*) and having no thoughts (K. *mu'nyŏm*)" (*SC* 78).

Referring to *The Treatise on Awakening Mahāyāna Faith*, Sŏngch'ŏl notes that there are two categories of ignorance or false thoughts: (1) those with discrimination; and (2) those without discrimination (*SC* 36). The former are called "coarse and heavy" false thoughts, and the latter "infinitesimal" ones. As shown in the chart below, there are six kinds of coarse ignorance and three kinds of infinitesimal ignorance, though Sŏngch'ŏl himself does not enumerate all of them. Sŏngch'ŏl's defines the "discovering the self-nature" or enlightenment in terms of no-mind as follows:

> To extinguish all false thoughts all at once, including those of the three infinitesimal and the six coarse kinds; and to become thoroughly enlightened to the original self-nature that is True Suchness, which has been permanently abiding without any change; in a word, to extinguish the false and verify the truth—this is the discovery

of the self-nature which is the same as [realization of] the ultimate no-mind (*SC* 11).

Following Fazang's explanation in *Dasheng qixinlun yiji* (The Doctrinal Explication of The Treatise on Awakening Mahāyāna Faith), Sŏngch'ŏl correlates coarse ignorance with the sixth consciousness and infinitesimal ignorance with the eighth consciousness, or *ālaya-vijñāna*. Furthermore, again following Fazang, he correlates infinitesimal or "fundamental" ignorance with the eighth through the tenth *bhūmis* and coarse, false thoughts to the seventh *bhūmi* and lower status. Sŏngch'ŏl's explanations of the six coarse and three infinitesimal kinds of ignorance can be put into the following scheme:[12]

<table>
<tr><td rowspan="3">"Root" or Infinitesimal Ignorance</td><td>Mark of Karma</td><td>Tenth Bhūmi</td><td rowspan="3">Eighth Consciousness
Bodhisattvas with the freedom of autonomy
No discrimination</td></tr>
<tr><td>Mark of Subject</td><td>Ninth Bhūmi</td></tr>
<tr><td>Mark of Object</td><td>Eighth Bhūmi</td></tr>
<tr><td rowspan="6">"Branch" or Coarse Ignorance</td><td>Mark of Cognition</td><td rowspan="6">Seventh Bhūmi</td><td rowspan="6">Sixth Consciousness
Discrimination</td></tr>
<tr><td>Mark of Continuation</td></tr>
<tr><td>Mark of Attachment to Projection</td></tr>
<tr><td>Mark of Scheming Names</td></tr>
<tr><td>Mark of Arousal of Karma</td></tr>
<tr><td>Mark of Suffering in the World of Karma</td></tr>
</table>

By introducing this scheme, Sŏngch'ŏl attempts to demonstrate that even the bodhisattvas of the tenth *bhūmi*, who are in the state of highest freedom, Equal Enlightenment and Adamantine Samādhi, have not yet completely realized no-thought or no-mind. Sŏngch'ŏl insists that they are not different, insofar as enlightenment is concerned, from any other sentient being. He is claiming that no credit should be given to them at all regarding enlightenment, let alone to beings of a lower "status."

The praxiological message Sŏngch'ŏl wants to deliver through this absolutist claim is clear: The Ultimate Enlightenment or Accomplishment of Buddhahood is in principle a matter of "all or nothing"; and the standard of enlightenment should not be compromised, since even the slightest compromise would be fatal to the endeavor. Later, we will examine just how the belief that enlightenment is a matter of "all or nothing" has been the driving force for the vigorous brand of practice in the Zen monastery tradition, especially with regard to *Kanhwa Sŏn*, or *kongan* meditation. For Sŏngch'ŏl, to be content with less than "all" is to lose the most essential force in Zen practice. Sŏngch'ŏl considers the theory of "sudden enlightenment and gradual practice" to be the ultimate example of the kind of compromise that is responsible for depriving many Zen practitioners of this driving force, hence his criticism of it in his writings and sermons.

As a creterion to determine the individual practitioner's distance from Ultimate Enlightenment and thus evaluate the status of the practitioner with regards to the infinitesimal and coarse ignorance and their corresponding bodhisattva *bhūmis*, Sŏngch'ŏl employs a paradigm known as the principle of Three Gates (K. *samgwan*). Three Gates are (1) "to keep integrity in an awakened state, whether moving or staying still" (K. *tongjŏng iryŏ*); (2) "to keep integrity while dreaming" (K. *mongjung iryŏ*); and (3) "to keep integrity while in a dreamless sleep" (K. *sungmyŏn iryŏ*). Referring to the Chapter of the Ten Bhūmis in the *Huayan jing* (The Flower Ornament Sūtra) and to the *Shizhu jing* (The Ten Bhūmis Sūtra), Sŏngch'ŏl explains that the first and the second states correspond to the seventh *bhūmi*, where coarse ignorance has been eliminated. The third state corresponds to the eighth through the tenth *bhūmis* and the "Buddha Ground" (K. *pulchi*) (*SC* 108–110).[13]

Furthermore, Sŏngch'ŏl notes that there are two different kinds of the third state, namely, "keeping integrity even in the deepest sleep" and "keeping integrity in the True Suchness." The former is the state of the bodhisattvas in the eighth through the tenth *bhūmis*, which is also called "keeping integrity in no-inscription (K. *mu'gi*; Sk. *avyakśita*)." The latter is the state of the Buddha, which is also called the "permanent abidance in the True Suchness" (*SC* 108, 112). Sŏngch'ŏl insists that only the latter is truly permanent abidance in the ultimate no-mind, although sometimes the term "no-mind" also applies to some and not to the true, ultimate no-mind of Buddhahood (*SC* 112). Here, Sŏngch'ŏl is emphasizing the need for unceasing practice (with uncompromising self-examination of one's own level according to the criterion of "keeping integrity," even for those in the state of the tenth *bhūmi*, let alone those in the lower states.

Some scholars question how consistent Sŏngch'ŏl's subitist claim is with regard to the hierarchy of practitioners' levels. And I have to admit that Sŏngch'ŏl did make seemingly contradictory statements: On the one hand he seems to allow for the gradual advancement toward the ultimate achievment in one's practice; on the other, he seems to deny it. For example, while explaining the relationship between different *bhūmis* and various levels of "keeping integrity," S'ŏngch'ŏl states:

> "Discovering the self-nature" means that [a person of] Equal Enlightenment completely severs, with [his] adamantine mind, the eighth

> consciousness [or *ālaya vijñāna*], which is the most infinitesimal thought, and enters the Marvelous Enlightenment. This is also called "sudden enlightenment" (*SC* 78).

In this passage, and on many other occasions, Sŏngch'ŏl undoubtedly admits to a process of climbing up different levels of achievement in Zen practice. Also, he does describe "sudden enlightenment" in such a way as to limit it, though not exclusively, to the removal of the last layer of ignorance that remains after the long struggle of a practitioner going up through the *bhūmis* to the eighth *bhūmi*.[14] Nonetheless, more often that not, Sŏngch'ŏl denies the need to go through hierarchical steps to reach enlightenment:

> When false thoughts have all perished, one completely discovers one's self-nature. To discover the self-nature completely is the right enlightenment and [realization of] no-thought. Then one suddenly enters into the Buddha Ground, which is Ultimate Enlightenment, *without going through the hierarchy of different levels* (*SC* 80, emphasis added).

Although these two statements appear to contradict each other, they both may find appropriate places in Sŏngch'ŏl's theory. First, as mentioned earlier, the meaning of the term "sudden" should not be confined to its ordinary sense of a temporal "rapidity," but should include the other meanings that have been discussed. Sŏngch'ŏl's statements may be reworded into the following two principles: (1) Differences among the hierarchical levels and the efforts made to climb the ladder of levels are significant in the world of sentient beings; however, (2) they are not significant at all in light of the most essential difference in Zen soteriology, namely, the difference between enlightenment and non-enlightenment, or between Buddha and sentient beings. The point Sŏngch'ŏl wants to make most emphatically is that soteriological endeavors carried out under the first principle can be fully retained only when that endeavor is uncompromisingly based upon the second principle.

Therefore, the term "sudden practice," in Sŏngch'ŏl's theory, does not mean that there is no need for effort, or that no human effort can have value in terms of realizing enlightenment. On the contrary, Sŏngch'ŏl's theory emphasizes unceasing, uncompromising, vigorous practice. Wŏnyung, one of Sŏngch'ŏl's disciples, notes: "The term 'sudden practice' indeed is an expedient expression coined to indicate that there is no need for practice after sudden enlightenment."[15] The term "sudden practice" does not address the issue of whether enlightenment is attained with or without arduous efforts. It just indicates that: (1) Enlightenment should be absolutely perfect so that there is no need of practice aimed at further enlightenment; and (2) the idea of advancement along the hierarchy of different levels of achievement is not only meaningless in regard to the fundamental difference between enlightenment and non-enlightenment, but also may be fatal to the ardor for practice, because it tends to generate a compromising attitude toward practice by arousing contention with achievement lesser than perfection.

As explained thus far, the primary meaning of the term "sudden" in the "sudden enlightenment" of Sŏngch'ŏl's theory is "perfection" rather than "temporal rapidity." The term "sudden practice" should be understood in the same way. Although the latter meaning is also crucial in Sŏngch'ŏl's use of the term "sudden," it should be understood in light of the terms "perfect" and "immediate" (i.e., not mediated). Therefore, Sŏngch'ŏl's first principle, as stated above, is not necessarily gradualist, and his theory as a whole is not necessarily self-contradictory.

Sŏngch'ŏl's primary concern lies in emphasizing the importance of the practitioner's unceasing and uncompromising efforts to practice. As for the integrity that should be kept, whether in dreams or in the deepest sleep without dreams, it is undisrupted concentration that is being emphasized. Regarding this point, Sŏngch'ŏl cites *Huayan jing*, which states, "Bodhisattvas in the seventh *bhūmi* practice the wisdom of skill-in-means and the superb truth. They abide firmly [in that practice] without disruption [at any occasion]. They never stop [that practice] even for one single thought-moment" (SC 110). Furthermore, in citations regarding Dahui Zonggao, it is stated that Dahui could not maintain *dhyāna* and control over himself once he fell asleep, and failed to keep integrity. He continued vigorous practice until he attained Ultimate Enlightenment.[16] Thus, the notion of the Three Gates in Sŏngch'ŏl's theory primarily serves as a criterion for self-examination, preventing premature abatement of vigorous practice.

In addition to the principle of the Three Gates, Sŏngch'ŏl introduces the principle of the "revival from death" to emphasize the importance of undisrupted practice. Since Zen practice centers on the endeavor to stop the sequence of thoughts and thus to attain "no-thought" or "no-mind," Zen practitioners are apt to fall into the state of "completely lifeless quiescence" and to be content there. The danger of this is inherent in the ideal of "no-thought" or "no-mind" itself, since that ideal requires *elimination* of "thoughts." Furthermore, the state of no-mind is primarily described in negative or passive terms such as "no-act," (K. *muwi*), "no-affair" (K. *musa*), or "no-arising" (K. *musaeng*).

One of the most popular expressions for the elimination of thoughts is "severing both the previous and the subsequent phrases [of thoughts]" (K. *chŏnhujedan*), that is, a "disconnection of the sequence [of thoughts]."[17] Disconnecting the sequence of thoughts can be said to be the primary visible goal of Zen practitioners who devote themselves to the "no-thought" or "no-mind" practice. On many occasions, it is understood to be the same as "discovering the self-nature," or attaining Ultimate Enlightenment:

> If not a single thought arises, both previous and subsequent phases [of the karmic process of thought-arising] are cut off. Then the illumining essence becomes independent, and object and self become one. [Such a person] straightforwardly reaches the origin of the mind, has nothing to know or attain, does not make any [discriminative] choice, nor has anything to confront or to practice.[18]

Regarding the above citation, Sŏngch'ŏl states: "When all thoughts are quiescent, the True Suchness of self-nature is thoroughly verified. This is called 'discovering the nature,' 'sudden enlightenment,' or 'accomplishment of buddhahood' " (*SC* 119).

However, on other occasions, especially in the context of admonishing against contentment with "complete lifeless quiescence," resulting from the complete elimination of "thoughts," Sŏngch'ŏl makes it clear that the "disconnection of the sequence [of thoughts]" is not all that is required for the attainment of Buddhahood. Sŏngch'ŏl cites the following passage from *Guzun suyu lu* (Record of the Old Masters' Sayings):

> Nowadays, many people in general take it as the ultimate state to be quiescent in body and mind, to sever the preceding and succeeding [phases of thought] and to be always in respite so that [in the moment of] one thought ten thousand years pass. Yet they do not know that this prominently marvelous state (K. *sŭngmyo kyŏnggye*; C. *shengmiao jingjie*) hinders them so that the right view of themselves cannot come forth nor can the wondrously penetrating brightness be revealed.[19]

Sŏngch'ŏl notes that this "prominently marvelous state" is taken as a lifeless state in Zen tradition (*SC* 116). He also notes that there are two different levels of "death" in Zen practice, namely, that of the seventh *bhūmi*, and the "great death" of the eighth and upper *bhūmis*:[20]

> There are two kinds of "prominently marvelous state," where not a single thought arises and both the previous and subsequent phases of the thoughts are severed: the "samādhi of no-thoughts" in the seventh *bhūmi* and the "samādhi of the complete extinction" in the eighth *bhūmi* . . . (*SC* 121).

> The state of no-inscription (K. *mu'gi*) of the *ālayavijñāna*, in which the sixth consciousness with coarse and heavy false thoughts has been completely extinguished, is the "great death." . . . To attain the great revival from the depth of the great death of the tenth *bhūmi* is the

> "true great death" (K. *chindaesa*) in which even the non-inscription of the *ālayavijñāna* has been permanently obliterated . . . (*SC* 124).

Sŏngch'ŏl states that only the great revival from the great death is the state in which one truly discovers one's self-nature, the Ultimate Marvelous Enlightenment, or the attainment of Buddhahood. He characterizes the "revived" states as the "great functioning with the whole existence" and describes it as the workings of the "wisdom of the great mirror," "permanently illuminating while permanently quiescent," and "brightly penetrating both in and out" (*SC* chapters 10–12). From this characterization of the "revived state," one may construe the nature of the "prominently marvelous state." Although it is described as a state of "no-mind," it falls short of full Buddhahood, because it lacks active functioning. The reason for this lies in the fact that all the media for activities available to the practitioner as a sentient being—represented by "thoughts"—are eliminated while the alternative, that is, Buddha's way, is not yet attained.

Sŏngch'ŏl's emphasis here is again on the need for continuous practice with undiminished vigor, regardless of the levels of the practitioner's achievement, until the final ultimate enlightenment is attained. What he most emphatically admonishes against is for a practitioner to be content with one's own state prematurely. Being content with a state other than Buddhahood is idealizing what should be eliminated, or "mistaking an enemy for one's dear son" (*SC* 175). Sŏngch'ŏl cites a passage from *Biyan lu* (Blue Cliff Record) and warns against this in a strongly iconoclastic tone: "Even the Buddhas, or the most renowned patriarchs of the past, had not reached this state of extreme depth where one goes through a great death and then revives from it. Even Śakyamuni or Bodhidharma should doublecheck."[21]

In addition to his insistence on the point that even the "prominently marvelous state" should not be settled for, Sŏngch'ŏl puts particular emphasis on the role of masters, especially with regard to the final breakthrough that will take place through the revival from "death." In Sŏngch'ŏl's Zen practice, having one's state checked by one's master is as indispensable as recognizing that one should go through self-examination according to the criterion of the Three Gates. Sŏngch'ŏl cites Dahui's famous episode as an exemplary instance that demonstrates the indispensable role of a master in encouraging a practitioner not to stop short of enlightenment and guiding him out of the state of "death." Sŏngch'ŏl notes:

> After one has attained the state of "keeping integrity whether awakened or sleeping," he should acquire thorough penetration [into the truth], without remainder, in order to discover the self-nature completely. Due to differences in opportunity and levels of ability, some may have attained only incomplete penetration. That is why

> you cannot be sure until you consult a master with right eyes and get his "recognition" (*SC* 113).

Although Sŏngch'ŏl does not explicitly state the reason why a master's guidance is indispensable, we can construct a possible explanation. Once one has reached the state of virtual "no-mind" by "severing both the preceding and the succeeding phases" of the sequence of thoughts, and is able to "keep integrity even in the deepest sleep without dreams," then all the media available to a sentient beings are eliminated. Even the criterion of the Three Gates is not meaningful anymore, for both Buddhahood and the eighth to the tenth *bhūmis* surpass the highest criterion. It is at this point that only a master (the enlightened person, in principle) knows whether his disciple has attained the final fruition of Buddhahood or is still in the lifeless side of "no-mind."

Many modern Buddhist scholars approach the master-disciple relationship in the Zen Buddhist tradition from a sociological perspective and consider it the result of hierarchies in the social power structure, or the patriarchal system of a society in general. Such an approach implies that behind the apparent religious authority of Zen masters there are only sociological factors at work. In many cases, sociological factors are taken as the only *real* rationale for the relationship, and the authority of Zen masters regarding religious truth is taken as an institutionalized disguise of the true rationale. Faure states:

> The definition of masters and disciples, and of what is supposed to be transmitted through them, is primarily social. Despite the constant reference to ultimate truth, it does not acquire its validity from some extra-social criterion but is closely related to status. . . . Chan masters . . . are not masters because they have realized the truth and can now teach it (although, of course, this may be the case); rather, they can teach the truth because, having been socially defined as Chan masters, what they teach has the performative power of being the truth. . . . [T]he "master function" is a "position" determined by the discourse; it is a function (and not a pure origin) of discourse. In this sense, its performative power required a broad social consensus.[22]

This perspective can be a powerful tool for the analyses of many features of Zen Buddhist institution, for it is beyond doubt that sociological, political, and economic factors constitute a large portion of the rationale for the master-disciple relationship in Zen Buddhism. However, it is doubtful whether it provides an access to a proper understanding of the concern in religious *sui generis* without committing the fallacy of reductionism. It also should be noted that the Zen masters' role in the context of soteriological endeavor and the soteriological rationale behind the relationship, as Sŏngch'ŏl emphasizes, is actually working effectively as primary momentum and vector in the actual scenes of Zen practice—even in the phases, like that of "great death and great revival," where those "outside" factors, such as socio-political or economic concerns, hardly have relevance; whereas, the practitioner's concern for enlightenment experience assumes overwhelming primacy.

The Sudden Enlightenment and Kongan (Encounter Dialogue) Practice

In his Introduction to *Sŏnmun chŏngno*, Sŏngch'ŏl insists that *kongan* or *hwadu* meditation is the best way to "discover the self-nature" and attain enlightenment. We will not get into the details of the meaning of various *kongans*, or whether Sŏngch'ŏl's claim is valid; our discussion will focus on the relevance of Sŏngch'ŏl's emphasis on *kongan* meditation to his theory of Zen practice and enlightenment. In what follows, we will examine Sŏngch'ŏl's emphasis on *kongan* study in terms of its relation to the following: (1) the notion of "no-mind"; (2) his insistence upon constant and undisrupted practice; and (3) the final examination for the "seal of recognition" (K. *in'ga*) of enlightenment given by the master to a disciple.

To be noted here is that Sŏngch'ŏl's emphasis of *kongan* stems from the self-imposed identity of Chogye Sŏn as the Korean version of the Chinese Linji Chan tradition that developed into *gong'an Chan* at the hands of Dahui Zonggao. Sŏngch'ŏl's discourse on Zen practice and enlightenment is basically within this tradition. Although some of the more fundamental issues Sŏngch'ŏl raises may also be relevant to a broader context of Buddhism, his emphasis on *kongan* study should be considered almost exclusively within this context.

First, Sŏngch'ŏl's emphasis upon *kongan* meditation is much related to the doctrine of "no-mind." One of the essential principles of the doctrine of "no-mind" is "no-reliance" (K. *musoŭi*), the focal point of *kongan* meditation. The principle of "no-reliance" is particularly important when distinguishing between two possible kinds of *kongan* meditation: (1) the examination of *kongan* as "live words" (K. *hwalgu*); and (2) the examination of *kongan* as "dead words" (K. *sagu*). This distinction does not refer to two different kinds of *kongans*, but to two different modes of examining *kongan*. Examination of *kongan* as "live words" denounces any reliance on frames of reference including conceptualization because these words are considered to be products of the discriminating consciousness of sentient beings. Whereas, if one attempts to understand the "meaning" of *kongan* relying on one's intelligence, one is examining that *kongan* as "dead words." Hence, examination of *kongan* as "dead words" is also called the "study of meaning" (K. *ch'amŭi*):

> "Live words" refer[s] to the Buddha-Patriarchs' succinct and straight vignettes or phrases, which are beyond sensory perception, false

conception and discriminating consciousness. Language and cognition do not work there. There is no place for reasoning, wording or meaning to function [in the study of "live words"]. [The "live words"] have neither a taste, nor a clue to approach them with. . . .

[Study of] "dead words" refers to the operation of language and reasoning, that is, "intellectual or conceptual understanding."[23]

Pojo Chinul (1158–1210) introduced *kongan* practice to Korean Buddhism. Sŏngch'ŏl praises Chinul's distinction of "live words" study from "dead words" study, while criticizing him for having accepted the latter as a legitimate, although lower-level, way of studying *kongan*. Chinul calls the latter the way of "complete and sudden faith and understanding," and the former the way of "shortcut."[24] Chinul explains the differences as follows:

> From the standpoint of complete and sudden faith and understanding, these ten defects of knowledge and conceptual understanding are conditionally arisen from the true nature also and cannot be grasped or rejected. Nevertheless, as this approach permits acquired understanding and thought via words and meaning, understanding and conceiving, a beginning student is able to receive it in faith and keep it respectfully. But from the standpoint of the shortcut approach, once there is an intimate realization of the true nature and secret conformity with it, neither the way of words nor the way of meaning exist any longer, for this approach does not allow acquired understanding or thought.[25]

The reason that *kongan* study is employed in Zen Buddhism, resulting in the establishment of the so-called *kanhwa Sŏn*, or *gong'an Chan* tradition, is because it is believed to be the most effective way to practice "no-mind" that does not rely on any sentient beings' ways of thinking, particularly their discriminating thoughts. In other words, *kongan* study is designed to bring about in the unenlightened mind a state close to the enlightened mind, or, "no-mind":

> Until enlightenment to the self-nature is attained, [*hwadu* plays] the role of a point on which a practitioner is to concentrate her/his consciousness in meditation practice, and of a weapon with which s/he is to expel all the discriminative attachment and false awareness. Therefore, however convenient and superb "live word" a *hwadu* may be, it also belongs to the realm of false ideas until enlightenment is realized. It should be discarded when enlightenment is attained, in the same way that you should leave the raft behind once you have crossed the river. However, the spiritual state of a *kongan* practitioner

> is closer to the "right thought" than any other unenlightened state of mind. It is because the practitioner is only holding the *kongan* without activating discriminating tendencies. . . .[26]

Thus the rationale for Sŏngch'ŏl's emphasis on *kongan* study can be found in the unique function it has in Zen practice of "no-mind," which he claims is exactly what Zen enlightenment is all about.

Secondly, Sŏngch'ŏl's emphasis on *kongan* study can be explained in relation to his insistence upon undisrupted and constant practice. Wŏnyung notes that continuous concentration with utmost devotion is the essence of *kongan* study, citing Boshan Wuyi (1575–1630):

> What is most important in [*kongan*] study is devotion. Boshan said: "This single word 'devotion' is the most important essence of [*kongan*] study. The word 'devotion' has the strongest power." One should just immerse oneself in questioning *hwadu,* as devotedly as a cat watches a mouse, waiting for a chance to catch it, as a traveler misses home, as a widow takes care of her only son, or as a starving person wants a bowl of rice. There is no other way for it than diligence.[27]

This emphasis on constant devotion is related to the nature of *hwadu* study as "questioning" meditation. To study "live words" is defined as formulating "a lump of doubt," not doubt about the meaning of the words or parables given as *hwadu*, but pure doubt, without an object. Wŏnyung notes: "The emphasis upon questioning meditation on *hwadu* becomes even stronger after Dahui. So much so that constant and unbroken questioning became the very essence of *hwadu* study, and *hwadu* study without questioning but with just concentration became "dead word" study."[28]

Sung Bae Park explains the "questioning" meditation in terms of the dynamics of the faith-doubt dialectic:

> Since most practitioners cannot reject the patriarchal faith that "I am Buddha," yet must also confess that "I am not Buddha," an inner conflict between these two poles of faith and doubt or affirmation and negation is created. How can this be resolved?
>
> . . . [T]he Ch'an tradition invented the practice of questioning meditation, which resolves this inner contradiction not by emphasizing one pole or the other, but by activating and intensifying the polarity through a process of unbroken questioning.[29]
>
> Resolving the problem with "yes or no" or, in other words, by making the choice of "one pole or the other," is the discriminating mind's mode of functioning. One may say that *kongan* study is

> designed to make the unenlightened mind work in a nondiscriminating (enlightened) mode by "activating and intensifying the polarity." The popular description of the ultimate state of mind in *kongan* study, namely, "Only the lump of doubt exists, nothing else," refers to the extreme intensity and continuity of questioning undisrupted by the discriminating tendencies of the unenlightened mind.

Therefore, as soon as the slightest amount of discriminating functioning, above all intellectual discerning, is activated, *kongan* study is ruined. This is why "any interpretation of the *kung-an*, no matter how precise or beautiful it may be, is useless for the questioning meditation itself and can even be an obstruction."[30] Referring to the exemplary *kungan* of *wu*, or "No!" stemming from Zhaozhou's anecdote, Park notes:

> For the *kung-an* meditation it is crucial to maintain a constant, unbroken questioning of *wu*. The key to the *kung-an* is not the word *wu*, but the active process of questioning itself, i.e., "Why? Why? Why? . . . Ultimately, the purpose of the questioning meditation is to 'cast away [one's] discriminating mind,' as Wu-men declares. . . ."[31]

Sŏngch'ŏl's strong emphasis upon constant and uncompromising practice can be understood in terms of the nature of *kongan* study as explained above.

The third rationale of Sŏngch'ŏl's emphasis upon *kongan* study can be found in the unique role *kongan* plays as the "official" criterion for the seemingly arbitrary procedure of examining the progress of one's practice. In order to attain the "seal of recognition" of enlightenment, a practitioner must pass the examination given by his master with *kongan* in "question and answer" session (K. *mundap*). The master discerns whether the disciple "has broken" the *kongan* through the "question and answer" session, which is the "official" criterion of enlightenment. Hence *kongan* is called "the barrier set up by Chan masters" (K. *chosagwan*).[32]

Wŏnyung, referring to the etymological meaning of the term *kongan*, likens the significance of *kongan* to that of official public regulations:

> The term "*kongan*" means "official documents of government offices." The official documents of government offices contain public regulations designed to be applied to everybody fairly. The regulations Zen masters impose on practitioners should be publicly fair without intervention by the slightest private element. . . .
>
> In secular society, people mandate the judiciary to make fair decisions on right and wrong according to law. Zen practitioners mandate decisions on enlightenment to "good advisers." The "good

> adviser" examines with *kongan* whether the practitioner's eyes are open or not.[33]

It is only the master who is able to determine a disciple's state and pass the sentence of further practice. This is especially true for those who are in the state of "great death," because the ultimate criterion of self-examination, i.e., the Three Gates, is already fulfilled. Furthermore, it is only an enlightened person who is able to recognize the practitioner's enlightenment. That recognition should not be made arbitrarily and *kongan* functions as the "public" criterion for it.

The Nature of Enlightenment and the Limits of Gradualism

One of the characteristics of Zen Buddhism is its belief that enlightenment can be attained by anyone here and now. This belief stems from the creed that all sentient beings are already Buddhas and that enlightenment is all about discovering one's own original nature, which is True Suchness. Hence, Zen Buddhism uses plain terms, not sophisticated philosophical ones, to describe the enlightened state, such as "peaceful and leisurely spirit," "undisturbed quiescence," "no-attainment," "no-act," or "no-affair." Sŏngch'ŏl uses the term "no-thought" or "no-mind" as a shorthand for all these terms, and characterizes the post-enlightenment state as "preservation of no-mind":

> If [one] attains the state of no-mind where all thoughts perish, [he] does not have any activity or event but is only leisurely and quiescent. A master of the Tao who places himself in this state of great respite, is peaceful and leisurely in both body and mind even when in the bustle of a large crowd. As a drop of poisoned water takes away life immediately, activation of a single most infinitesimal thought makes one's own nature obsolete. But once [no-mind is] attained, [it is] attained forever. It always stays the same without change, so that not even one single infinitesimal thought arises. To stay leisurely and free in this state of great quiescence is what the masters with right eyes do after enlightenment (*SC* 89f.).

This characterization of enlightenment implies no further need for practice after the realization of Buddhahood, thus negating the theory of "sudden enlightenment and gradual practice." This negation is a logical corollary of his definition of "enlightenment" as "realization of perfect Buddhahood" and also his unspoken definition of "practice" as "sentient beings' efforts *for the purpose of* attaining enlightenment." Furthermore, Sŏngch'ŏl asserts that the state of no-thought or no-mind entails the perfect wisdom that enables the enlightened person "to have insight both in and out" (K. *nae'oe myŏngch'ŏl*) and "to be always illuminating the world while completely quiescent" (K. *sangjŏk sangjo*) (*SC* chapters 10–12).

Two questions may be raised regarding such a notion of the enlightened state: (1) On what grounds can it be said that, once one attains enlightenment, one "always stays the same without change" in that enlightened state? and, (2) How are two seemingly incompatible qualities (i.e., complete quiescence and the active functioning of perfect wisdom), actualized simultaneously? Sŏngch'ŏl himself does not give a direct answer to either of these questions. However, we will take the liberty of constructing possible answers on the basis of our understanding of the context of Sŏngch'ŏl's doctrine.

As for the first question, we may consult the *Treatise on the Awakening of Mahāyāna Faith*, in which two types of Buddhist faith are addressed: that is, "retrogressive backsliding faith" (K. *t'oesin*) and "unretrogressive or nonbacksliding faith" (K. *pult'oesin*). The former corresponds to "doctrinal faith" (i.e., the faith that "I can become Buddha"), and the latter to patriarchal faith (i.e., the faith that "I am already Buddha").[34] Doctrinal faith, grounded in the dichotomy between sentient beings and Buddhahood, as perceived by the sentient beings' dualistic way of thinking, is always vulnerable to retrogression:

> [F]rom the conventional Buddhist perspective, especially the gradual[ist] tradition of doctrinal faith, a truly nonbacksliding or unretrogressive faith is not possible. Why is this so? From the gradual[ist] point of view, faith is a function of will and intellect. Consequently, since the human intellect can assent to falsehoods and the human will is fallible, it is always possible to backslide; belief can turn to doubt, resolve can weaken, vows and precepts can be broken.[35]

Thus, seen from the perspective of doctrinal faith, there is a difference in the strength of faith, and also a difference in the levels of advance toward the goal of becoming a Buddha.

In contrast, patriarchal faith cannot be perfect until one actually becomes a Buddha. To claim that "I am Buddha" before actualizing Buddhahood through the enlightenment experience is either fraud or self-deception. True patriarchal faith is not a function of sentient beings' mind, as the conventional meaning of the term "faith" indicates, but the content of enlightenment.

The content of Buddhist enlightenment has been described by the concepts of "dependent origination" and "emptiness." Buddhahood, or enlightenment, is equal to the realization of the ontological truth that everything in the world, including oneself, is conditioned (or dependently originated), and thus "empty." Park notes:

> In the *Majjhima-nikāya* the Buddha is recorded as saying: "Those who see 'dependent origination' will see the dharma; those who see

> dharma will see 'dependent origination.' " In the *Samyutta-nikāya* the Buddha said, "Those who see the dharma will see me; those who see me will see the dharma." When we combine these two statements, we arrive at the understanding that Buddha is the world of dependent origination, i.e., the way all dharmas arise through conditional coproduction. Therefore, "I am Buddha" must also mean "I am dependent origination."[36]

In this context, "discovering one's own original Buddha-nature," that is, confirming that "I am Buddha," which is the Zen Buddhist definition of enlightenment, is the same as the confirmation that "I am dependent origination." By the very definition of the term "dependent origination," the awakening of the ontological truth of "dependent origination" requires a nondiscriminating way of thinking. Once there is no discrimination, especially between Buddhahood and sentient beings, the concept of "retrogressing or backsliding into a sentient being" is obsolete. Park's explanation of the irreversibility of patriarchal faith, as follows, can be directly applied to Sŏngch'ŏl's idea of "discovering the self-nature":

> The immovability and irreversibility of patriarchal faith are derived from the fact that one is ontologically grounded in Suchness or dependent origination.
>
> In other terms, patriarchal faith can be understood as a function of One Mind, i.e., the mind of nondiscrimination and nonthought. As soon as one returns to One Mind, one no longer discriminates between sentient beings and Buddhas or between enlightenment and nonenlightenment, but instead directly cognizes the world of emptiness and dependent origination. Backsliding is not possible in a mind free of discriminating thoughts. Since no distinctions are made, there is nowhere to backslide to and no one to backslide. Thus, since patriarchal faith is ontologically grounded in dependent origination as a function of One Mind, it is not subject to backsliding in any way whatever.[37]

The faith that "I can become Buddha" presumes an awareness that "I am not Buddha now." Both the will to believe the Buddhist teaching that it is possible for sentient beings to become Buddha, and the awareness that one is not yet Buddha, are grounded in discriminative thinking. Even when one has determined to follow patriarchal faith, the discriminative awareness that "I am not Buddha 'yet' " cannot but arise until he truly confirms the faith that "I am already Buddha," or, until he "*discovers* the self-nature." However, once this faith has been confirmed, the confirmation cannot be cancelled, since it consists of the complete nullification of any discrimination which would make such a cancellation possible.

The second question is related to another characteristic of Zen Buddhist soteriology, namely, its tendency to put exclusive emphasis on enlightenment without much discussion of the phenomenal reality of sentient beings. In terms of *ti-yong*, or "essence-function" construction (a unique East Asian conceptual tool used to explain a world full of dichotomy and dualistic phenomena from a non-dualistic perspective), such a tendency can be characterized as a *ti* (essence) oriented attitude, without paying attention to *yong* (function). Not only Zen Buddhism but East Asian religious thoughts in general have had the same tendency.

One product of *ti* oriented tendency is the notion that *yong* will be automatically perfected when *ti* is perfected. This is why we cannot find one example of Sŏngch' ŏl's writings of how an enlightened person functions in the actual world, except for such general and vague notions as "always illumining while permanently quiescent." This exclusive concern with *ti* and apparent lack of concern with *yong* is both a strong point and a weak point of Zen Buddhism in modern secular society, where the concern with *yong* prevails. It is a strong point because it gives Zen the potential to promote a fundamental rectification of the "materialist" trend of human civilization. It is a weak point because it is difficult in modern secular culture for an ideology to be persuasive without presenting a realistic vision of the *yong* aspect of life.

Sŏngch'ŏl grounds his repudiation of the gradualist theory of "sudden enlightenment and gradual practice" on two principles: (1) the difference between "realization awakening" (K. *chŭngŏ*) and "understanding-awakening" (K. *haeŏ*); and (2) "the lineage of the authentic transmission of dharma."

In Sŏngch'ŏl's criticism of the gradualist theory of "sudden enlightenment and gradual practice," the most important issue is the meaning of "sudden enlightenment." Although the term "sudden enlightenment" is used in both gradualist and subitist theories, it has very different meanings in each theory. Also, the different views of *practice*, expressed as "sudden practice" and "gradual practice," are derived from the different meanings of "sudden enlightenment."

As explained thus far, in Sŏngch'ŏl's theory the term "sudden enlightenment" refers to Ultimate Marvelous Enlightenment, which is realized only through complete experiential verification. Claiming that one has realized "sudden enlightenment" means that one has eliminated all defiling false thoughts and verified one's original perfect Buddhahood. In this sense, "sudden enlightenment" is understood as identical to accomplishment of the highest ideal of Buddhism, called nirvāṇa or *anuttara samyak sambodhi* among other terms. Hence, once "sudden enlightenment" is attained, there should be no need for practice with the purpose of attaining further enlightenment. Furthermore, Sŏngch'ŏl insists that nothing less than such final enlightenment should be considered to be "sudden enlightenment."

The gradualist notion of "sudden enlightenment," however, does not necessarily refer to "enlightenment by verification," but includes "understanding-awakening." Guifeng Zongmi, the systemizer of gradualist Zen soteriology, notes: "[Among the various combinations of] sudden or gradual enlightenment and practice, 'sudden enlightenment and gradual practice' refers to understanding awakening."[38] He compares "sudden enlightenment to sunrise or the birth of a baby," and "gradual practice" to the clearing of fog by the sun beams or the growth of a baby.

The focal point of the gradualist theory is that one must first have "understanding-awakening" in order to have right faith and do right practice until reaching final "enlightenment by verification."[39] Zongmi states: "The theory that one must first attain sudden enlightenment and only then can gradually practice is grounded in the notion of 'understanding-awakening.' Therefore it is said in *Huayan jing*: 'After accomplishing right awakening at the moment of the initial arousal of the mind [of faith], one goes through the three sage stages and ten saint stages, accomplishing them one by one.' "[40] It seems that the core didactic message of such a gradualist program of practice and enlightenment places the same amount of emphasis on steadfast practice as Sŏngch'ŏl's. However, the gradualist view and that of Sŏngch'ŏl sharply contrast each other with regard to whether or not "discovering the nature" refers to sudden enlightenment as initial understanding-awakening, or as Ultimate Marvelous Enlightenment, after which practice is obsolete. Chinul explains "sudden enlightenment and gradual practice" as follows:

> When the ordinary man is deluded, he . . . does not know that his own nature is the true dharma-body; he does not know that his own numinous awareness is the true Buddha. He looks for the Buddha outside his mind. While he is thus wandering aimlessly, the entrance to the road might by chance be pointed out by a wise advisor. If in one thought he then follows back the light [of his mind to its source] and sees his own original nature, he will discover that the ground of this nature is innately free of defilement, and that he himself is originally endowed with the non-outflow wisdom-nature which is not a hair's breadth different from that of all the Buddhas. Hence it is called sudden awakening.
>
> Next let us consider gradual cultivation. Although he has awakened to the fact that his original nature is no different from that of the Buddhas, the beginningless habit-energies are extremely difficult to remove suddenly and so he must continue to cultivate while relying on this awakening. Through his gradual permeation, his endeavors reach completion. He constantly nurtures the sacred

> embryo, and after a long time he becomes a saint. Hence it is called gradual cultivation.[41]

With the term "discovering the self-nature," Chinul obviously refers to the initial arousal of faith based upon "understanding-awakening." However, it does not seem that the "understanding-awakening" Chinul equates with "sudden enlightenment" and "discovering the self-nature" is simply "intellectual understanding" (K. *chi-hae*) as Sŏngch'ŏl claims. In Chinul's system, obviously influenced by the *Huayan* concept of the equality of the initial arousal of faith and Ultimate Marvelous Enlightenment, "understanding-awakening" is, rather, complete enlightenment, even though defilements may still be intact. For Chinul, enlightenment is not a matter of removing defilements completely. Initially, for Chinul, defilements are not something to be removed. Instead, the fact that defilements are an unavoidable condition of sentient beings is something to be awakened to. Chinul assigns the work of removing defilements to the post-enlightenment task of perfecting initial enlightenment into Ultimate Marvelous Enlightenment. The popular saying among Korean Buddhists, "In attaining enlightenment, it does not matter whether defilements are intact or not," is based upon such a notion of enlightenment.

Nonetheless, Sŏngch'ŏl criticizes Chinul's notion of enlightenment as belonging to scholastic Buddhist philosophy (K. *kyo*), or more precisely, Huayan philosophy, and not orthodox or authentic Zen doctrine. Sŏngch'ŏl claims that "understanding-awakening" is an experience which is absolutely different from discovering the self-nature and thus attaining sudden enlightenment as understood as Ultimate Marvelous Enlightenment, or realization of one's original perfect Buddhahood. According to Sŏngch'ŏl, enlightenment must be the complete removal of defilements.

Furthermore, Sŏngch'ŏl insists that "understanding-awakening" is that which should be removed in order for the practitioner to discover the self-nature. Sŏngch'ŏl points out that "understanding-awakening" does not remove the coarse and heavy false thoughts, let alone the infinitesimal ones. He identifies "understanding-awakening" with "intellectual understanding," and thus considers it to be a product of false thoughts stemming from "sensory (karmic) habits" (K. *chŏngsŭp*) (*SC* 159–172). Therefore, he notes that to practice on the basis of "understanding-awakening" is like "jumping into the fire holding an armful of wood" (*SC* 175).

The subitist and gradualist theories share the same didactic message about the crucial importance of steadfast practice, but are grounded in two completely different praxiologies. The subitist theory claims that one should not rely on anything that belongs to "mind" or "thought," whereas the gradualist theory allows for this. The subitist theory insists that one can never extinguish defilements by *employing* the ways of sentient beings but, rather, only by *removing* them, whereas the gradualist theory insists it is not only possible, but in fact necessary to use the ways of sentient beings. One can say that the subitist theory focuses on "principle" (K. *li*), "essence" (K. *ch'e*), and "absolute truth" (K. *chinje*), whereas the gradualist theory focuses on "phenomena" (K. *sa*), "function"(K. *yong*), and "conditioned truth" (K. *sokche*).

Conclusion: The Lineage of the Authentic Transmission of Dharma

Zen Buddhism traditionally places much emphasis on the symbiotic relationship between enlightened masters and their disciples. The relationship has been represented in such traditional lore as the "direct transmission of dharma from mind to mind" and the inheritance of robes and bowls used by previous masters as a "seal of recognition." Chinese Buddhist hagiographers have painstakingly written down, and even concocted, the "history of transmission records," a "history of mind-to-mind transmission" of the enlightenment experience from the Śākyamuni Buddha to his chief disciple Mahākāśyapa, and from Mahākāśyapa down through the twenty-eight successive patriarchs in India, and in China, from Bodhidharma through Huineng, the sixth patriarch.

In developing his doctrine of Zen practice and enlightenment, and his criticism of gradualist theory, Sŏngch'ŏl relies heavily on the notion of "the legitimate lineage of the authentic transmission of dharma." He considers the Linji Chan tradition, from which the Chogye order in Korean Buddhism identifies itself as being descended, to be the orthodox form of Zen Buddhism, and he claims that the theory of "sudden enlightenment and sudden practice" is its authentic doctrine. On the basis of these premises, Sŏngch'ŏl repudiates the gradualist theory of "sudden enlightenment and gradual practice" as heretical and labels its advocates, specifically Shenhui, Zongmi, and Chinul, as "heretics."

Although Sŏngch'ŏl takes the Linji line of Zen lineage as representing the "orthodox" Zen tradition, he also cites many Zen masters of other lineages as "masters with right eyes." He was able to do this because he used two criteria for orthodoxy, namely, legitimate lineage and subitist doctrine. On the one hand, Sŏngch'ŏl attempted to prove that subitism is the "orthodox" Zen soteriology and gradualism is "heretical" by presenting prominent Zen masters, especially those in the Linji line, as examples of the "legitimate lineage of the transmission of truth." On the other hand, he believed subitist doctrine to be a crucial quality of "masters with right eyes," so that he cited the writing of Zen masters outside of the Linji lineage as well.

It should not be difficult to see that his emphasis on the notion of "legitimate lineage" and related "orthodoxy" claims are the aspect of his theory that has been most criticized by scholars. However, as these scholars with critical views are also aware, the doctrinal points Sŏngch'ŏl attempts to underscore with these notions are of more crucial importance than his historical claims.

Notes

1. T'oe'ong Sŏngch'ŏl, *Paeg'il pŏmmun* (One Hundred Days Sermons), vol. 2 (Seoul: Changgyŏnggak, 1992). pp. 317–318 and *passim.*

2. Even though the term "true nature" (C. *zhenxing*) appears in some versions of the Fifth Patriarch Hongren's (601–674) *Treatise on the Essentials of Cultivating the Mind*, it is considered to have been inserted at a later date. See Chŏng Sŏngbon, *Chungguk Sŏnjong ŭi sŏngnipsa yŏn'gu* (A Study of the History of the Establishment of Chinese Chan Schools) (Seoul: Minjoksa, 1991), p. 283.

3. Sŏngch'ŏl, *Sŏnmun chŏngno* (The Correct Path of the Zen School) (Seoul: Pulgwang, 1981), p. 2 and *passim.* Citations from *Sŏnmun chŏngno* will be marked in the text with an abbreviation *SC.*

4. Paul Demiéville points out that subitism is absolutism by its nature ("La pénétration du bouddhisme dans la tradition philosophique chinoise," p. 31. Cited in Bernard Faure, *The Rhetoric of Immediacy: A Cultural Critique of Chan/Zen Buddhism* [Princeton, NJ: Princeton University Press, 1991], p. 34).

5. Faure suggests "fast," "absolute," and "immediate" (*The Rhetoric of Immediacy*, p. 33). I prefer "simultaneous" to "fast" because the term "fast" may be mistaken to mean that an ongoing human effort in practice is not necessary, and this is not an appropriate understanding of Sŏngch'ŏl's theory. Rolf A. Stein also translates "*tun*" as "simultaneous" ("Sudden Illumination or Simultaneous Comprehension," in Peter N. Gregory, eds., *Sudden and Gradual: Approaches to Enlightenment in Chinese Thought* [Honolulu: University of Hawaii Press, 1987], 41–65). Faure's "absolute" has the same connotation as "perfect." However, I chose the latter to avoid implication of transcendence or mystification.

6. Sŏngch'ŏl, *Paeg'il pŏmmun,* vol. 1, pp. 55–57, 60, 62–64, 76–83.

7. Pŏpsŏng, "Kkadarŭm ŭi ilsangsŏng kwa hyŏngmyŏngsŏng" (Enlightenment as Routine and Revolution), *Ch'angjak kwa pip'yŏng* 82 (Winter 1993): 329–340.

8. The term "middle path" appears on two occasions in *Sŏnmun chŏngno,* in citations from the *Nirvāna Sūtra.* However, the essence of this principle is prominent throughout this book, especially in the 9th through the 12th chapters.

9. *Madhyamakakārikā* 24. English translation by Kenneth K. Inada, "The Metaphysics of Buddhist Experience and the Whiteheadian Encounter," p. 146. Recited from Sung Bae Park, *Buddhist Faith and Sudden Enlightenment* (Albany: State University of New York Press, 1983), pp. 49f.

10. *Linji lu, T* 1985.47.500b22–23.

11. Park, *Buddhist Faith and Sudden Enlightenment,* p. 81.

12. For the names and characteristics of the "marks," see *Dasheng qixinlun, T* 1666.32.577a7–21; English translation by Yoshito S. Hakeda, *The Awakening of Faith* (New York: Columbia University Press, 1967), pp. 44f.

13. There is an unclear part in Sŏngch'ŏl's citations and explanations. Earlier in *Sŏnmun chŏngno,* he cites a passage from Fazang's *Dasheng qixinlun yiji,* which states: "The last of coarse ignorance, the mark of Cognition, is severed in the seventh *bhūmi*" (*SC* 40). There Sŏngch'ŏl makes the following comment: "The seventh *bhūmi* of Huayan, which keeps integrity even when dreaming, is still in the realm of the six kinds of coarse ignorance. . . . The eighth *bhūmi* does not have the six kinds of coarse ignorance, and the Buddha Ground does not have the three kinds of infinitesimal ignorance" (*SC*

40f). Now Sŏngch'ŏl says that a bodhisattva in the "samādhi of no marks" of the seventh *bhūmi* keeps integrity even when dreaming "because the coarse and heavy false thoughts are overcome" (*SC* 110). To be consistent, it seems that two different states in the same seventh *bhūmi* must be distinguished: the one before all the coarse ignorance is severed; and the other in the "samādhi of no marks" where there is no coarse ignorance. If so, this distinction would be important to Sŏngch'ŏl's theory because it would represent the borderline between the two kinds of "keeping integrity even when sleeping." However, Sŏngch'ŏl does not make further mention of this.

14. Sŏngch'ŏl does not intend to limit the availability of "sudden enlightenment" exclusively to a certain *bhūmi*. Referring to the episode of Dahui Zonggao's (1089–1163) enlightenment from *Dahui yülu* (*T* 1998.47.883a17–b16), Sŏngch'ŏl notes that it is possible to jump from the seventh *bhūm*i directly into the ultimate state as Dahui Zonggao said (*SC* 121).

15. Wŏnyung, *Kanhwa Sŏn: Sŏnjong tonbŏp sasang ŭi parŭn ihae* (Kanhua Zen: Correct Understanding of Zen Subitism) (Seoul: Changgyŏnggak, 1993), p. 237.

16. *Dahui Pujue Chanshi zongmen wuku T* 1998B.47.953b15–22; *Dahui pujue chanshi yulu*, *T* 1998.47.936a5–26; *Sŏnmun chŏngno*, pp. 105–107.

17. *Dasheng qixin lun* explains the sequence of thoughts by employing the *Abhidharma* theory of the "four marks": arising, abiding, changing, and ceasing. Elimination of "false thoughts" is achieved by disconnecting this sequence. See *Dasheng qixin lun, T* 1666.32.576b18–c4, 577b18–23; Hakeda, *The Awakening of Faith*, p. 39; and Park, *Buddhist Faith and Sudden Enlightenment*, pp. 81f.

18. *Jingde chuandeng lu* 29 (*T* 2076.51.459b29–c2). Cited in *Sŏnmun chŏngno*, p. 119 (the location is erroneously specified as the fascicle 30 of *Jingde chuandeng lu*).

19. *Guzun suyu lu* 44, *ZZ* 1315.68.296a8–11; *Sŏnmun chŏngno*, p. 116.

20. As can be seen in the second of the following citations, Sŏngch'ŏl seems to propose one more type of death, which can be said as the "true great death"; the true great death, however, can be understood as the Budddhahood attained through a revival from the "great death."

21. *Biyan lu*, *T* 2003.48.179b2–5; *Sŏnmun chŏngno*, p. 128.

22. Faure, *The Rhetoric of Immediacy*, p. 22.

23. Wŏnyung, *Kanhwa Sŏn*, p. 76. Since Sŏngch'ŏl does not provide detailed theoretical explanation of *kongan* study in his writings, except for emphasizing its importance in Zen practice, it is difficult to present his own definition of it. However, Wŏnyung, one of Sŏngch'ŏl's disciples and current Head Master of Haein Monastery Zen Center, offers us help in this book with the subtitle, *Sŏnjong tonbŏp sasang ŭi parŭn ihae* (Correct Understanding of Zen Subitism). This book can reasonably be considered to contain accurate reflections of Sŏngch'ŏl's views on the subject.

24. Chinul, *Kanhwa kyŏrŭi ron* (Resolving Doubts About Observing the Hwadu), *HPC* 4.733a15–18; English translation by Robert E. Buswell, *The Korean Approach to Zen: The Collected Works of Chinul* (Honolulu: University of Hawaii Press, 1983), p. 240.

25. Chinul, *Kanhwa kyŏrŭi ron*, *HPC* 4.733a22–b3; Buswell, *The Korean Approach to Zen*, p. 240.

26. Wŏnyung, *Kanhwa Sŏn*, pp. 86f.

27. Wŏnyung, *Kanhwa Sŏn*, p. 138. Boshan's words are from *Boshan chanjing yu*, ZZ 1257.63.757c1.

28. Wŏnyung, *Kanhwa Sŏn*, p. 103.

29. Park, *Buddhist Faith and Sudden Enlightenment*, pp. 66f.

30. Park, *Buddhist Faith and Sudden Enlightenment*, p. 76.

31. Park, *Buddhist Faith and Sudden Enlightenment*, p. 76.

32. *Wumen guan*, *T* 2005.48.292c22; Wŏnyung, *Kanhwa Sŏn*, p. 74.

33. Wŏnyung, *Kanhwa Sŏn*, pp. 73f.

34. Park, *Buddhist Faith and Sudden Enlightenment*, pp. 43f.

35. Park, *Buddhist Faith and Sudden Enlightenment*, p. 44.

36. Park, *Buddhist Faith and Sudden Enlightenment*, p. 25.

37. Park, *Buddhist Faith and Sudden Enlightenment*, p. 45.

38. Guifeng Zongmi, *Yuanjue jing da shou* (Great Commentary on the Sutra of Perfect Enlightenment), *ZZ* 243b.9.334c8–9.

39. However, most scholars participating in the sudden/gradual debate overtly or implicitly deny "enlightenment by verification" as an experiential reality.

40. Zongmi, *Chanyuan zhuquan jidu shou, T* 2015.48.407c18–21.

41. Chinul, *Susim kyŏl* (Secrets on Cultivating the Mind), *HPC* 4.709c13–710a3; Buswell, *The Korean Approach to Zen*, p. 144.

10

Sŏn Master Daehaeng's "Doing without Doing"

Chong Go

Introduction

Sŏn Master Daehaeng is one of the most influential Buddhist teachers in Korea today. As a traditional Buddhist nun in a patriarchal society, she founded a temple, Hanmaum Seon Center (K. *Hanmaŭm sŏnwŏn*), which has grown to 25 Korean and international branches, and has more than 30,000 families registered as members. In addition to being the teacher of over 150 ordained nuns and monks, Daehaeng Sŭnim[1] has played a major role in supporting the Bhikkuni Sangha of Korea.

Born in 1927 during the Japanese occupation of Korea, Daehaeng Sŭnim witnessed the suffering of a great many people, which gave rise to an intense questioning about the meaning of life and why beings suffer. This led to a deep enlightenment experience at an early age, followed by decades spent applying and testing her understanding. She lived in the mountains for years at a time, sustained by whatever was at hand. Although she became well-known as a healer, Daehaeng Sŭnim has said that what she was really trying to do was to help people awaken to their fundamental nature, their Buddha-nature, and its inherent ability. It was this goal that led her to establish the first Hanmaum Seon Center in 1972, which has since grown into one of the foremost Buddhist organizations within the Chogye Order (Jogye Order) of Korean Buddhism and in Korean Buddhism itself.

One of the most striking things about Daehaeng Sŭnim's role in modern Korean Buddhism is her ability to reach out to a wide range of people, many of whom previously had little or no interest in Buddhism. Korean visitors to Daehaeng Sŭnim's temple are often struck by the large numbers of men and teenagers. At many temples in Korea, the only laypeople to be seen are middle-aged and elderly women; there are very few laymen, and almost no teenagers. In contrast, Hanmaum Seon Center's laymen's organization and youth group are among the largest and most active in Korea.

Daehaeng Sŭnim has been able to reach so many people in large part because she teaches spiritual cultivation in such a way that anyone can practice, regardless of their occupation, age, or gender. She points directly to one's inherent Buddha-nature, teaching people how to make this the focus of their spiritual practice throughout all aspects of their lives. She reminds them of the innate ability and wisdom within each one of us, and through detailed teachings shows people how to rely upon this. Everything that arises during one's daily life becomes part of one's spiritual practice and provides a chance to grow spiritually. The effect of these teachings is that anyone can immediately begin changing his or her life.

In contrast, the more commonly taught methods of spiritual practice such as *hwadu* meditation, reciting the Buddha's name, and, to a lesser extent, prostrations are all limited by time and place. For example, *hwadu* meditation is generally restricted to ordained monks and nuns in meditation halls or hermitages, while prostrations and chanting are ideally done at a temple. Further, during *hwadu* meditation, one is only practicing while "holding" the hwadu, and when one's chanting and prostrations stop, so does one's practice.

All of this was contrary to what Daehaeng Sŭnim had awoken to. She perceived that one's Buddha-nature was the true source of all one's thoughts and actions. Thus, every single aspect and every single moment of one's life was the manifestation of truth and the Buddha-dharma. Nothing in one's life was separate from the truth. One's Buddha-nature was there even in the midst of suffering and deluded acts. Thus, for Daehaeng Sŭnim, spiritual cultivation must begin and end with one's inherent Buddha-nature and include absolutely everything that arises within the course of daily life.

To this end, Daehaeng Sŭnim teaches people to have faith in their inherent Buddha-nature and to entrust it with whatever confronts one. Next, one must continue to observe while going forward and experimenting. One experiments with letting go and relying upon their fundamental nature, and one experiments with applying the experiences that result. All the while, one continuously lets go of the things one knows and the things one doesn't know. This also includes all concepts of self and other.

As Daehaeng Sŭnim talks to people about this process of spiritual practice, she often emphasizes the necessity of "doing without doing" (K. *ham i ŏpsi handa*). Without this, she warns, it will be difficult to make progress in one's spiritual practice. As she explains this expression, its meaning can perhaps best be translated as "doing without any thought of doing;" that is, there is no thought of being a doer in one's actions. Daehaeng Sŭnim goes on to use this expression in two different contexts. The first context of "doing without doing" is as a description of our fundamental reality, where the dualistic concepts of "you" and "I" are naturally not present. The second, and more emphasized, context of "doing without doing" is as a method of spiritual practice, where one strives to let go of the thoughts of a separate doer.

This essay will first examine "doing without doing" as a natural state. Next, in order to understand "doing without doing" as a spiritual practice, and why it is important, it will be necessary to examine the effects of the concept of self. Special attention will be paid to the labeling effects of the thought of "I." The last section of this essay will look at "doing without doing" as a method of spiritual practice in which one lets go of thoughts of "I" and the sense of a separate self that is the source of one's actions. By doing this, one moves into harmony with the fundamental nature of reality.

"Doing without Doing" as an Expression of Fundamental Reality

The first context in which Daehaeng Sŭnim uses "doing without doing" is as an expression of the fundamental reality of our world, where everything is naturally functioning together without the mistaken view of a separate doer. In this state, all beings are sharing the same life, the same mind, the same body; we work together as one and share all things. An important point of this aspect of "doing without doing" is that it describes a state that is happening naturally, without a conscious effort on the part of the individual.

This level of functioning is important because it represents the fundamental nature of reality, where all lives and things are always functioning together non-dually, as one. Thus, if one is in harmony with this state, wisdom, understanding, and spiritual development become much more attainable. On the other hand, if one is behaving contrary to this fundamental state of "doing without doing," then everything in one's life becomes much more difficult, not to mention attaining wisdom and understanding.

People who awaken to this state are aware of differences and distinctions, such as of self and others, but they are able to see them for what they truly are: illusions.[2] They do not cling to these distinctions, nor do these distinctions lead to attachment or aversion. All beings are interconnected, but at the same time, each has its own unique role to play.

The natural state of "doing without doing" can be viewed from many different perspectives. For example, sometimes Daehaeng Sŭnim describes it in terms of the inherent oneness of all life:

> No matter where you go, it is all one monastery, one place for spiritual practice. "One" means the whole. The foundation of the

> entire universe is connected to the foundation of human being's minds. Both the realm of the living and the realm of the dead are contained within this world, and, through this foundation, all of the consciousnesses of both realms are directly connected. Thus all lives are sharing the same life, working together, sharing the same body, and manifesting together while sharing everything.[3]

All beings are sharing everything and manifesting together, so, from the perspective of the foundation, there is no "you" or "I" that could be separated out and called an unchanging self.

In the next example, Daehaeng Sŭnim continues this same theme, emphasizing that even the body is a collection of lives working all together: "Inherently, people release everything. Why? Our bodies are full of lives that all work together, so they all are empty. Why? There's not a single thing that 'you' do, there's nothing that 'you' alone see. There's nothing that 'you' hear by yourself, nothing that 'you' alone say. There is no single thing that you can claim to do by yourself."[4]

This idea that there is no separate and unchanging self is directly related to the idea of emptiness. Emptiness, as Daehaeng Sŭnim describes it, is not a state where nothing exists; instead, emptiness is a state where everything is always changing and manifesting every instant. It is empty because there is nothing that one can single out and say "this is." Thus, any labels such as "me" or "I" will always be inadequate and incomplete. Daehaeng Sŭnim explained this in the context of giving:

> When you give something to others, just give it without any thought of giving, and move on. Just live like this. Once you give something, that's all. Let go of any thought about having given something. Why? Because "I" doesn't exist. . . . What people call "I" is always changing and never remains the same for even an instant, so it is said that "I" is empty. Everything in our life is empty, everything changes every moment.[5]

Everything is interconnected and working together, without a separate "you" or "I," but, through ignorance, beings give rise to thoughts of self and labels of "I," which hinder their perception of the true nature of reality. Thus, people mistakenly base their actions on a dualistic worldview and behave in ways that are contrary to their true nature, and so fall into suffering.

The concept of self, or "I," is often described in Buddhism as a false construct that arises from various aggregates, but it is also a process of labeling that forms our image of ourselves, reinforces dualistic thinking, and reduces our awareness of the ever-changing nature of reality.

What people usually think of as self, or "I," is considered by Buddhist teachings to be a false entity. Traditionally, it is described as a false sense of self that arises from the combination and interaction of the five aggregates: form, feeling, perception, volition, and consciousness. The purpose of this description is to show people that what is thought of as "I" is not a fundamental entity, rather, it is something that is always changing and has no fixed basis. By understanding that "I" is not an inherent entity, people would be able to free themselves from all clinging related to the idea of a separate self

However, the concept of "I" can also be viewed as a labeling process. When people use phrases such as "I did . . . ," "____ is happening to me," or "she did . . . ," while conforming to conventions of language, they are also creating labels that simplify and constrain much more complex events. It appears that most of what people think of as their self is actually comprised of these labels that they have made. Further, the effects of these labels on people's psyche are immediate and far-reaching. By using "I" to label the things in their lives, people are creating a sense of duality between themselves and their environment. They are also immobilizing the events and people in their lives, and they are even creating their own future.

One of the major effects of thinking in terms of self and other is to create and reinforce subtle impressions of separation and difference, which can have a profound effect upon one's consciousness and behavior. When one labels people, or describes events in terms of self and other, one is creating a subtle image that one's self and all other beings are each fundamentally separate and distinct. "I" becomes separate from "you." The corollary of "I did . . . ," is "you didn't do . . ." When one thinks "he did . . . ," the associated implication is "he didn't. . . ." "She is in Seoul," implies that she exists at only one place and time, which is different from where the speaker exists.

This sense of separateness and duality has many implications. First, it is contrary to what Buddhism describes as a fundamental truth of the universe, that all beings are interconnected. It also has the effect of negating the law of cause and effect, which can be seen as another way of describing the interconnectedness of all things and life: What one does to someone else, one also does to one's self. A dualistic view of the world around them leads people to believe, even if they are only semi-aware of it, that they will not be truly affected by what they do to others.

Dualistic thinking may also work to reinforce materialistic thinking. Daehaeng Sŭnim always emphasizes that this world is the combination of the visible and invisible, which are always functioning together. However, if one is unaware of the invisible connection, then one cannot help but rely almost exclusively upon the physical senses. In a world seen and defined through only the senses, phenomena also appear separate and distinct from one another. Further, because one only perceives the material aspects of the world, material objects assume much greater importance. However, the more one pursues material things, the more unhappy and dissatisfied one will feel, because the fundamental, immaterial relationship between all lives and things is not reflected in one's thoughts and actions. Ultimately, the dualistic perspective of self and other causes suffering because one's perceptions are out of harmony with the underlying reality.

Thoughts of self and other also cause people to immobilize and narrowly define their views and experiences. When someone makes statements such as "I did . . ." or "she is . . . ," they are creating a label that describes their perception of what happened or who someone is. This label is a device that makes understanding easier by simplifying much more complex events, but this also means that the label is usually inaccurate to some degree because it cuts away all other interpretations and depth.

One immediate effect of labeling in general is to remove all other viewpoints and create the impression that the event or person is unchanging. People carry those labels around long after the events that inspired them have passed. In terms of one's psychic reality, the other person or event remains unchanging. Also, using the word "I" time after time creates the impression of something unchanging. This perception, that something is still the same as it was, is contrary to the principle that each and every thing is in a state of constant change. Furthermore, these kinds of fixed views make it harder for the objects of one's labels to change and grow because one still treats them as they once were. How to overcome these and other problems related to the construction of "I" will be addressed in the third section of this essay, " 'Doing without doing' as a Method of Spiritual Cultivation."

There are two additional problems with labeling things in terms of "I" or "you": labels are usually based upon memories, which are not very reliable; and the labels used can also alter one's memories of the event. People usually treat the labels they use as if those labels were an exact record of what happened or is happening. However, those labels are themselves usually memories or based upon other memories. Research in the field of cognitive psychology has shown that there is no such thing as static, long-term memory. The memory of an event is not an unchanging record of the event, as is often thought. Instead, the memory is constantly reinterpreted and re-encoded each time it is recalled. For example, in a study about the dependability of eyewitnesses,[6] researchers showed students a film of a low-speed car accident. Later, one group was asked how fast the cars were going when they *smashed* into each other, and one group was asked how fast the cars were going when they *hit* each other. Although both groups saw the same film, the group that had read the word *smashed* in the question always estimated that the cars were moving faster than did the group that read the word *hit*. Thus, the label that was applied to the event changed the memory of it. This study led to many others that showed the same effect: Memory is a reinterpretative process, not a photographic image of an event. In this sense, memory is what we remember of the stories we tell ourselves. It could even be said that the label we apply to something becomes the memory.

Labels such as "you" and "I" affect people's perceptions and judgments by creating the impression that things are unchanging and by altering one's memories so that they become more similar to the labels that were used. The implication that the use of labels such as "you" and "I" have formed and reformed our memories, and thereby our perceptions of reality, is significant in itself. However, it is even more important in light of Daehaeng Sŭnim's teaching that everything follows mind.

On one level, this teaching is similar to the common understanding of the Yogācāra (Consciousness Only) School, which says that we create our reality through our reactions to the subjective interpretations and thoughts we carry around. For example, if I'm offended by someone and give him the label, "he's a jerk," that often becomes the label that I carry around for long afterward. The next time I meet him, I'll be tempted to treat him badly, or with resentment. Being treated like this, he is more likely to respond in kind. This kind of negative label creates a vicious cycle of reactive behavior, which creates an unpleasant environment. On the other hand, if I interpret his behavior positively, this breaks the cycle of reactive behavior. This is probably one reason why Daehaeng Sŭnim always teaches people to interpret things positively. She gives many examples of how to view situations like this in more positive terms, for example, "I also behaved like that when I didn't know any better," and "This is my true self trying to teach me." By changing one's perceptions, one changes one's reactions to the world around oneself and thereby changes one's environment.

The idea that everything follows mind can be understood solely in terms of individual psychological processes. However, Daehaeng Sŭnim also uses it to mean that things are much more directly created by mind—that the thoughts and intentions one gives rise to directly affect others and the world around oneself. Daehaeng Sŭnim often emphasizes that the intentions and thoughts one gives rise to can manifest in, and change, the material world. This is possible because of the fundamental non-duality of all things. Because every single life and thing are all connected, including both visible and invisible realms, what happens at one place or time affects everything else.

We can see examples of this interconnectedness all around us: the mother who suddenly knows that her child is in trouble somewhere; the strong positive effects on cancer patients who visualize their NK cells eating cancer cells; people's ability to affect what number a computer randomly generates, the effects of prayer groups on people's health, and so forth. According to Daehaeng Sŭnim's teachings, all these examples can be explained by knowing that both the living and dead, the past, present, and future, together with all visible and invisible realms are all connected through the fundamental one mind. Daehaeng Sŭnim often emphasizes that when we input a thought into our foundation, our One Mind, it can be communicated anywhere and it can manifest into the material realm.

The implications of the labeling effects of "I," together with the principle that everything follows mind, are quite significant. Essentially, how one thinks about oneself can have a strong effect on her or him and the world around that individual. It can even be said that one's thoughts create the world in which one exists. This is a key point of Daehaeng Sŭnim's teachings: The mind gives rise to matter, not the other way around. Although matter can affect mind, fundamentally matter arises because of a previous thought or intention. A particularly relevant example of how thoughts affect one's world can be seen in the effect of self-statements.

Self-statements are the self-descriptive statements that one tells oneself over and over. Sometimes they are positive statements, but more often they are negative. The strong effect these have on people has been well documented by psychologists for many years, but their effects become even more significant in light of the idea that everything follows mind. Not only can they affect one's psychological processes, but because of the fundamental non-dual connection of all things, they can also directly affect people and things outside oneself. Further, repeated self-statements work to freeze, or immobilize, that condition, rather than allowing it to change freely.

Daehaeng Sŭnim sometimes gives the example of someone who keeps repeating to herself: "I have cancer." By repeating this, it is as if instructions are being sent to all the lives in the body that this is the state of health one is supposed to have, and so they work to make it so. If someone says, "I'm no good," others may also pick up on this statement and treat one accordingly. According to the principle of non-duality, the effect of this self-statement arises not only from its effects on psychological processes or body language, such as one's deportment or interpersonal style, but also from one's direct connection with others.

In addition to self-descriptive statements, the statements one tells one's self about others can also affect the world around them. For example, Daehaeng Sŭnim said that if one often thinks negatively about the leader of a country, then through the fundamental connection of all lives, this thought will have an influence upon that leader. She said that those thoughts will make him more likely to behave according to people's opinion of him, and will also make it harder for him to change. Daehaeng Sŭnim said that it is important to raise positive energy for the leaders, because whatever energy is directed at them will return back to the general public. The more people in a society or nation who think this way, the stronger the effect. Similarly, Daehaeng Sŭnim said that if the general level of thought in a society is negative, that will work to push a country into a more negative situation. If many people in a society think in a positive way, this also directly influences its society. She compared this effect to an election: Whichever side has the most votes wins.

Aside from the direct interpersonal influences, people are directly affected through the unseen connection that all beings share. This effect can manifest across all aspects of a society: social, political, and economic. Again, it must be stressed that this effect is not just the result of interpersonal relations, it works through all visible and invisible realms and has a generalized effect. This is one reason why Daehaeng Sŭnim always emphasizes that people should interpret and view things in a positive and constructive manner.

The strong effect of one's thought upon one's life and surroundings has been recognized and used in many different settings. Two examples can be seen in prayer groups and cognitive behavior therapy. In prayer groups, groups of people are asked to pray for the well-being of a particular person, who is usually a stranger and often in a distant location. Many people have found that this type of group prayer was beneficial, even for people who at the time did not know they were the object of a group's prayer.[7] These effects have been experienced by people and groups across religions, and from a Buddhist perspective this is relatively easy to explain: All life is connected through a common, inherent foundation.

Of all the psychotherapy methods, those based upon cognitive behavior therapy are generally considered to be the most effective and produce the fastest results. As shown with techniques such as affirmations, cognitive behavior therapy works to change one's life and environment by changing one's thought habits. For example, such a technique trains a person to recognize the habit of saying "I'm no good" and then to counter it with a positive statement, such as "I'm not very good at playing the piano now, but if I practice I will improve," or "I may not be very good at math, but there are lots of other things I'm good at." By changing their thoughts, people change their outlook on the world.

However, even the best of these methods still view the world in terms of an individual self, in terms of "I." They fail to address the fundamental limitations of the construct of "I," so their ability to help people is accordingly limited.

"Doing without Doing" as a Method of Spiritual Cultivation: Letting Go of Thoughts of "I"

When Daehaeng Sŭnim uses the expression "doing without doing," generally she uses it to describe a method of spiritual cultivation in which one actively lets go of all thoughts related to the mistaken view of a separate doer, i.e., "I," "me," or "mine."

By letting go of thoughts of "I," and practicing "doing without doing," one is able to overcome the limitations inherent in the construct of "I." Letting go of the thoughts of "I" dissolves the persisting labels and dualities that "I" creates, and allows things to change and grow naturally. One's actions and thoughts naturally move into harmony with the fundamental nature of reality, which in turn makes awakening and true spiritual development possible. About this, Daehaeng Sŭnim said:

> The essence of mind cannot be described with words, and its functioning penetrates everything . . . You must discard the illusion of "I." If you discard this illusion, all difficulties will subside. Your worries will disappear. But if you do not discard these persistent thoughts of "I did" or "I must live," which are based upon your concepts of the material world, you cannot die. This does not mean the death of the body. It means instead that you harmonize yourself with the truth, the truth in which everything flows, constantly changing from one form to another.[8]

Daehaeng Sŭnim's teachings about letting go of thoughts of self and others contain several elements. The most essential elements of letting go of "I" are awareness and faith in one's inherent foundation. Because one has faith that one's foundation is taking care of things, it is possible to let go of thoughts of self, of "I," and instead rely upon one's foundation. Sometimes she compares the practice of letting go of "I" to dying, and at other times she emphasizes the importance of changing one's thinking and not blaming others.

However, "doing without doing" is not about trying to repress thoughts; it is about handling those thoughts wisely once one becomes aware of them. For example, when someone realizes that they have been caught up in the thoughts of "I" and "you," one thing that they can do is to simply end that chain of thought. As with speaking, when we think we often have a choice about which topics we pursue and in what framework we view them. We can decide that we are not going to indulge in that line of thought and are going to just stop following it, or we can choose to interpret events in a way more consistent with the fundamental nature of reality.

The act of letting go can be simple or complex, and what works for one person may not work for another; but two of the most essential elements are simply awareness and belief. One must be aware of the thoughts one has in order to recognize their patterns. Without awareness, it is impossible to recognize when you are caught up in dualistic thoughts of self and other. Without some level of belief in your inherent foundation, it is hard to let go of all that you have thought of as "me."

In Daehaeng Sŭnim's teachings, belief in one's foundation is the basis of all letting go. Because one truly knows that it is one's foundation that is doing all the things in one's life, one naturally lets go and entrusts everything to it. To those who have truly experienced their foundation, even the thoughts of "letting go" or "not letting go" do not arise.

Daehaeng Sŭnim teaches people that all beings are inherently endowed with a fundamental nature, a fundamental mind that is directly connected to all things and functions non-dually with them all.

> Everything in the universe is directly connected to the mind of human beings, and so every single thing works together with mind. If you truly awaken to this, you will realize that your inherent nature is intrinsically pure, that your mind is inherently endowed with everything and that it is complete as it is, and you will also realize that you can freely send out and take in anything through mind. All of these things will naturally become clear to you. No one else can take this away from you and no one else can give it to you.[9]
>
> Throughout the universe there is a fundamental, infinite energy upon which all things depend. The ability and potential of every single thing in the universe arises from and returns to this energy. Regardless of what people think, or how things may appear, everything is continuously functioning like this. Every single thing continuously revolves around this fundamental energy, transcending time and space.[10]

This foundation is the source of all ability and wisdom, and is within us. It is not what people think of as "I," but it is also not separate from us. When we entrust it with everything that confronts us, it can melt down all hardships and obstacles, and provide wisdom and show us the path. Because people have lost sight of this, Daehaeng Sŭnim uses many expressions to describe it: foundation, mind, Buddha-nature, fundamental mind, the captain, *chuin'gong* in Korean, inherent nature, and others. However, as Daehaeng Sŭnim says, this fundamental nature includes the functioning of all visible and invisible realms, the past, present, and future, and is beyond any explanations or descriptions. Through this foundation, all beings share the same life, the same mind, the same body, work together as one, and share all things together. Thus, how could any part be separated into "you" and "I?"

If someone truly knows this foundation, he or she automatically entrusts it with whatever arises in life. It is not a question of doing or not doing; the individual just knows that whatever he or she encounters is part of and being done by the foundation. However, even if someone does not completely perceive this foundation for him- or/herself, if each one tries to sincerely entrust thoughts of "I" and "you" to it, then he or she still moves in harmony with the foundation.

"Dying" is one expression that Daehaeng Sŭnim uses to describe this whole-hearted entrusting of everything to one's foundation:

> You should entrust everything—solitude, poverty, loneliness, anxiety, and illness—that comes up in your life to your foundation and live

> freely. Entrusting everything is letting go of everything. This is the way to die. The phrase "First, you must die!" means unconditionally releasing everything, without any excuses or reasons, including both what you understand and what you don't understand. When things go well, you should release them with gratitude. When things don't go well, you should also release them with the faith that, "Only the foundation can solve this and lead me in the right direction. Because nothing is fixed, even this can change." You should keep letting go like this. For it is only by dying unconditionally that you can discover your true self, your eternal root.[11]

Dying is a good way to describe letting go, because by completely giving up this "I," I am also giving up the things that I think of as my own. It means letting go of all of the labels of "I" or "you" that one has carried around. As seen above, what people often call their self or "I," consists of the collection of labels including "I" and "you." In terms of loss, death is the ultimate loss of everything we possess. If one lets go of the "my" in "my house" or "my body," then one is also letting go of the sense of possession and ownership. Although this may seem frightening, Daehaeng Sŭnim teaches that one does not lose anything fundamental; instead, all one loses is the fixed concepts and opinions that one has falsely taken refuge in. In fact, when one is able to let go of the labels, "I" and "you," Daeheang Sŭnim emphasizes, one actually feels freer and happier, because one has freed oneself from the boundaries created by these concepts of "I," and "you."

Letting go of "I" and practicing "doing without doing" can be applied to every aspect of our lives. There's no aspect of our lives in which we do not bring the concept, "I." For example, Daehaeng Sŭnim has said the following about reading books and "doing without doing":

> I never say to throw away books, but I do suggest not to read books that can cause attachments to outside things. Read those books that focus on the inside, read them while you do not read. Do you know the meaning of reading while not reading? It means: you do not read; you just do errands. What you read, what you know, what you experience, can be used by the captain when you release them. The captain can use them when the captain controls all unenlightened beings within your body. That's why you just do errands. You do errands and just provide what you read and know to the inside and the captain uses them to control unenlightened beings within the body, then the unenlightened lives within the body all function together as one.[12]

This quote contains a good example of how practitioners can overcome mistaken views by changing their understanding of what they are experiencing, i.e., understanding that " 'I' does not do things; 'I' is merely running errands for one's foundation."

When trying to let go of thoughts involving "I," it can sometimes be very helpful to view the situation from another perspective, that is, to change the way we think about it. Daehaeng Sŭnim gives various examples of this that are directly related to "doing without doing" and letting go of "I." For example, if one finds oneself thinking, "I did . . ." one should change such a mode of thinking into "That was done by the foundation." "She did," can also become "inherently all beings share the same life, the same mind, the same body, work together as one, and share everything all together." The thought, "I'm sick," can become "this is my foundation teaching me," or "Even this illness came from my foundation, so my foundation will take care of this body." Random or embarrassing thoughts can also be interpreted as "even this thought comes from my foundation." Blame and resentment of others can be transformed through the thought, "all minds and my mind are one mind," or "only the foundation can make our relationship harmonious." "It's his fault," can also become "that happened because I lacked wisdom," or, "I also behaved like that once when I didn't know any better."

The effects that arise from changing one's interpretations and perspectives are due to the principle that everything moves according to how we think. For example, if we view something as suffering, then that is all we'll experience. Whereas, if one views it as a lesson, one starts seeing things one can learn from, and one begins to realize how one has made a contribution to the happening of that situation. Far deeper experiences and paths can be revealed, if one realizes that what one calls suffering arises based upon one's preferences. The dualistic mind tries to flee from what it dislikes, i.e., suffering, and wants to cling to what one considers pleasant and enjoyable. When one entrusts to one's foundation everything that comes to oneself, both good and bad, success and failure, one comes to understand both sides of things, even seen and unseen realms. This is possible because one's thoughts and attitude are in harmony with one's fundamental nature, which inherently includes both sides of everything. These thoughts are not just psychological processes; each one is also fundamentally true: Everything *is* being done by one's foundation, all minds and "my" mind *are* one mind, "I" *also* behaved like that when "I" didn't know any better, that *did* happen in order to teach "me" (because my purpose for being born is to learn and spiritually evolve). Even if someone has not yet deeply awakened to their inherent, fundamental nature by changing their thoughts into harmony with that nature, it is much easier for them to grow and develop and awaken to their fundamental nature.

Not blaming others is an aspect of Daehaeng Sŭnim's teachings that is especially relevant to the idea of "doing without doing." Of all of her teachings, not blaming others is one of the most strongly emphasized. Blaming others for the things we experience in our lives is probably one of the most spiritually corrosive things we can do. By blaming others for the things in our lives, we are behaving in direct opposition to two fundamental Buddhist truths: nonduality and cause and effect.[13]

Blaming others seems to be one of the most severe forms of creating dualities. Not only does it establish a "me" as opposed to "you," blaming also greatly reinforces these dualities by the assignment of an action, usually, "He did ____ to me." Describing oneself as the victim of other's actions also seems to create a strong emotional response. This may be a manifestation of the body's "fight or flight" response, but it also provides an interesting example of how everything follows mind. The moment one silently repeats those statements of blame, one can feel their effects: One feels tense, angry, or resentful. One's body is reacting immediately to one's thoughts. On the other hand, if one repeats to oneself the phrase, "All minds and my mind are one mind," one immediately feels more calm and peaceful. Further, changing one's thoughts in this manner prevents the feelings of resentment that would have otherwise arisen the next time one meets that person.

By denying one's role in the situation one faces, blaming others also denies the law of cause and effect. This has implications that affect us immediately and directly. First, if one lives while ignoring the law of cause and effect, one is going to end up causing oneself and others a great deal of suffering. In other words, one suffers because one's own thought, speech, and actions have violated the principles of one's fundamental nature as well as the norms of society. Second, by avoiding responsibility for what one has done, the person also prevents herself from learning and growing. If one refuses to acknowledge the results of one's own actions, then there is no possibility of learning from those experiences and moving beyond that level of development. By blaming others we are denying our fundamental connection with all other beings, and thereby reinforcing our sense of duality; we are also denying the law of cause and effect. As we deny our role in creating the world we live in, we strangle our spiritual growth and development. This is why blaming others is something that people interested in spiritual cultivation must overcome at all costs.

Conclusion

The goal of Daehaeng Sŭnim's teachings is to help people to awaken to their inherent nature for themselves. To this end, Daehaeng Sŭnim often uses the expression "doing without doing" to describe a method that has the effect of helping people attune themselves to their inherent nature. Inherently, everyone and everything is living in this natural state of "doing without doing," where everything is interconnected as one. The problem is that people have lost sight of this, and thoughts of self and other work to maintain this ignorance. These thoughts create and reinforce dualistic perspectives, immobilize our perceptions, and falsely define our world. However, through the elements of "dying," belief in our foundation, changing our thinking, and not blaming others, this spiritual practice of "doing without doing" allows us to overcome the hindrances that the mode of thinking "I" has created. In this manner, we are able to move into harmony with our fundamental nature, making spiritual growth and awakening possible.

When compared to traditional explanations of similar ideas such as "no-mind"(K. *musim*) and "no-thought"(K. *mu'nyŏm*), Daehaeng Sŭnim's teachings of "doing without doing" are accessible to nearly everyone and easy to put into practice. This is a core element of Daehaeng Sŭnim's teachings—putting one's understanding into practice. She emphasizes the necessity of applying and experimenting with what one understands, and observing the results with a settled mind while letting go of any attachments. In this way everyone can realize the ultimate meaning of "doing without doing."

Notes

1. "Sŭnim" is the respectful term of address for a Buddhist nun or monk in Korea.

2. Daehaeng Sŭnim explains that, while a conventional awareness of self and others is present, one is nonetheless aware of the fundamental non-dual nature of things.

3. Daehaeng Sŭnim, Hyewon Sŭnim, eds., "Hŏgongŭl kŏtnŭn kil," (Walking on Emptiness), *Chŏnggi pŏphoe* (Third Sunday Dharma Talk), vol. 2 (1999), p. 381.

4. Dharma talk by Daehaeng Sŭnim on May 21, 1995.

5. Daehaeng Sŭnim, *The Furnace Within Yourself* (Anyang, Korea: Hanmaum International Culture Institute, 2004), p. 59.

6. Elizabeth L. Loftus and John C. Palmer, "Reconstruction of Automobile Destruction: An Example of the Interaction between Language and Memory," *Journal of Verbal Learning and Verbal Behavior* 13 (1974): 585–589.

7. There has been some research to determine the effectiveness of prayer groups, most notably "Does Prayer Influence the Success of in Vitro Fertilization–Embryo Transfer?" by K. Y. Cha, D. P. Wirth, and R. A. Lobo, *The Journal of Reproductive Medicine* 46, no. 9 (Sept. 2001): 781–787; and Larry Dossey, M.D., *Healing Words* (New York: Harper Books, 1993). However, this introduces another problem, that is, whether it is appropriate to make science a standard by which we judge religion. As anyone who has studied in an advanced scientific field has discovered, science has fundamental limitations when trying to measure things outside the phenomenal realm. The things that science understands are far outnumbered by the things it doesn't understand and can't explain. Thus, it seems like a mistake to make science the standard by which we judge the truth of the spiritual and of religion.

Regarding criticism of studies of prayer groups, there have been some legitimate criticisms about the way some studies were done and the credibility of certain researchers. However, there also seems to be a reluctance to examine topics like prayer groups, in part, because the topic departs from the received views of scientific fields. Also, most prayer groups presuppose the existence of a supreme being, and this may be the cause of further opposition to studies of these groups.

8. Daehaeng Sŭnim, *Walking without a Trace* (Anyang, Korea: Hanmaum International Culture Institute, 2001), p. 9.

9. Daehaeng Sŭnim, *The Furnace Within Yourself*, p. 25.

10. Daehaeng Sŭnim, *Mind, Treasure House of Happiness* (Anyang, Korea: Hanmaum International Culture Institute, 2003), p. 21.

11. Daehaeng Sŭnim, *To Discover True Self, "I" Must Die* (Anyang, Korea: Hanmaum International Culture Institute, 2002), p. 23. Daehaeng Sŭnim sometimes further describes the process of enlightenment as dying three times. She describes it as "stages that are not stages," where individuals first sees their true nature, next they realize that they and everything else are not two, and third, they are able to manifest non-dually with any thing or place. Throughout this process one must let go again and again of what one has experienced.

12. Dharma talk by Daehaeng Sŭnim on July 1, 1994. See also Daehaeng Sŭnim, *No River to Cross* (Boston: Wisdom Publications, 2007), pp. 72–73.

13. It should be noted that not blaming others does not mean that we abuse or debase ourselves, or encourage others to do so. We look at why something happened, acknowledge the part we played, and see what we can learn from what happened and then try to apply that.

Part Three

Religion, History, and Politics

11

The Japanese Missionaries and Their Impact on Korean Buddhist Developments (1876–1910)[1]

Vladimir Tikhonov

This work deals with the interactions between the Japanese Buddhist missionaries and the Korean monkhood in the turbulent early modern period of Korean history, which began with the conclusion of Korea's first "unequal" treaty with Japan in 1876 and ended with Japanese annexation of the whole country in 1910. As Korea was peripherized and increasingly drawn into Japan's fledgling sphere of influence in East Asia, modern Japanese Buddhism became a reference model for the Korean monks who tended now to view Japan as their "protector" in practice and an ideal of "Buddhism-friendly" modernity in theory. In fact, even before the Japanese intrusion, Korean Buddhism was struggling to readjust its hitherto subjugated social position proportionally to the level of wealth and influence of richer monasteries, and to provide important religious and ideological background for Korea's first generation of modern reformers in the 1880s. But the Japanese missionaries managed to quickly appropriate the nascent discourse of "Buddhist modernity" in Korea and turn it into a tool of co-opting Korean Buddhist clergy for its own political purposes. While a partial or full loss of nationalistic credentials was a logical result of this process for the Buddhist community, its unequal alliance with the invaders/colonizers might be also understood as perhaps an unavoidable result of the combination of traditional Confucian oppression and new Christian anti-Buddhist attitude.

With the gradual weakening of neo-Confucian orthodoxy and the growth of the *Sirhak* (Practical Learning) movement, long-absent interest in Buddhism started to develop among the minority of more open-minded Confucian scholars, with famous calligrapher and writer Kim Chŏnghŭi (1786–1856; known as "the Vimalakīrti of the Eastern State") typifying the new generation of the literati more open to Buddhist ideas.[2] The gradual decline of *yangban* (gentry)-centered class system and consequent increase in the social position of traditional urban "middle-class" groups (K. *chungin*), who remained in closer contact with Buddhist circles, enabled some non-*yangban* lay Buddhists (Yu Taech'i, an Oriental medical doctor of *chungin* background; O Kyŏngsŏk, a *chungin* interpreter; and others) and even Buddhist monks to play prominent roles in the early radical "Enlightenment" (K. *kaehwa*; Westernization-oriented reformist) movement in 1870 to 1884.[3] Younger *yangban*-progressives (especially Kim Okkyun), who were guided by *chungin* Yu Taech'i (?–1884) and Buddhist monk Yi Tongin (?–1881) into a new and unknown world of modernity, seem to have even conceived of Buddhism as a substitute for outdated neo-Confucian ideas—as an ideological tool for making society more equal.[4] In their case, their deeply interested attitude toward Buddhism was also strengthened by their experiences in Japan, where they could see how Buddhism successfully endeavored to transform itself to better suit the realities of Meiji era "civilization and progress." In Kim Okkyun's case, his Buddhist devotion was remembered long after his death: On the twenty-third anniversary of his assassination, memorial services were held in a Japanese temple and in the Kakhwangsa Temple in central Seoul. The readers of Government–General-run *Maeil Sinbo* (March 28, 1916) were reminded also that Kim Okkyun had recommended meditation practice to his high-positioned Japanese friends, Inukai Tsuyoshi (1855–1932), a well-known party leader and future prime minister, being one among them.[5] Another prominent leader of the "radicals" of the 1870–1880s, Pak Yŏnghyo (1861–1939), though not very religious personally, recited the memorial speech in that temple ceremony.[6] It is interesting to point out also that one of Kim Okkyun's pennames, "Kogyun" (literally meaning "old bamboo sheath"), dates back to one of the nicknames of Mengshan De-I (1231–1308), a Yuan Dynasty Chan Buddhist monk whose works were widely read in Korea.

So, Buddhism, after a long break, again became, at least partially, what it was before the start of neo-Confucian persecutions under the Chosŏn kings: that is, it became an important actor not only on an economical but also on an ideological stage. In the atmosphere of the renewed interest in Buddhism and its proponents on the part of fledgling progressive circles, it was only natural that some socially engaged monks would have made certain efforts to establish contact with supposedly more "advanced" foreigners to benefit the objects of the "progressive's" interest. Those foreigners were first and foremost Japanese due to the relative absence of serious linguistic and religious barriers. With their common knowledge of the classical Chinese language and Buddhism, the Japanese people facilitated the communication. Such efforts would naturally have been expected by the monks' progressive *yangban* allies, who inherited from their *Sirhak* predecessors a much more open and interested attitude to Japan than that typical of contemporary Chosŏn society as a whole. As the analysis of their reports shows us, the younger *yangban* members (mostly moderate progressives) of the 1881 Courtiers' Observation Mission to Japan perceived Meiji Japan more as a possible (although very controversial) model of partly successful "self-strengthening" and as a victim of the West's high-handed "gunboat diplomacy" than as a threat to Chosŏn's sovereignty.[7]

At the same time, the socio-political and economic character of those first modern encounters between the representatives of the two long-separated branches of East Asian Buddhist tradition was necessarily shaped by the new position of Japan versus Korea as the newest (and the only in East Asia) member of the "European club" of supposedly "civilized" capitalist nations striving, in anticipation of Western competition, to carve out its own colonial and semi-colonial "sphere of influence" while simultaneously ruining the traditional "tributary" international order of the region. Korea—along with Taiwan, the first candidate for adding to Imperial Japan's "modern" political and economic peripheral dependency zone, for obvious geographical and political reasons—after the signing of the unequal Kanghwa Treaty (1876), was exposed to both the economic penetration of Japanese goods (in fact, mostly European goods shipped by Japanese traders) and the religious, cultural, and ideological penetration of the "ideological apparatus" of the Meiji state. By the latter, I mean both the dominant ideological paradigm of the Meiji state (the idea of the superiority of "modernized" Japan to its still "barbaric" and "feudal" neighbors, and the belief in the necessity of Japanese "guidance" over them for the sake of their "de-barbarization") and the concrete ideological institutions (Buddhist missions, modern style "Enlightenment" [K. *kyemong*] schools, etc.) whose aims were, with full use of Japan's newly acquired comparative economic advantage, to make the Korean counterparts internalize this paradigm, willingly acknowledging the inferior position of Korean periphery to the Japanese "core."

In the process of imposing Japan-centered and Japan-designed schemas of a "modernized East Asian community" on the Korean progressives, the Japanese took full advantage of the ambiguity of the latter's own blueprints for Korean "Enlightenment" (a result of the long political and cultural isolation of Korea from the developing world capitalist system), as well as Japan's deeper, older, and wider mastery of Europe-related knowledge and skills. As a result, from the beginning of the 1880s, the positive, but vague interest toward Japan likely inherited from later *Sirhak* thinkers was, in the cases of key early radical "Enlightenment" leaders (first and foremost, Kim Okkyun, Pak Yŏnghyo, and Yu Taech'i), gradually replaced with almost unquestioned acceptance of general Meiji ideological paradigm, together with firm and complicated economic and political ties of highly unequal nature. In a sense, early radical "Enlightenment" leaders were "peripherized" and "marginalized" by the Japanese "core" even before the same fate befell the rest of the country in the process of annexation. Due to a fateful combination of the early radical Enlightenment leaders' keen interest in Buddhism (stemming largely from *Sirhak* roots), increased social and economic activities of Korean Buddhist community, the Japanese strategy of using Buddhist missionaries for the sakes of East Asian expansion,[8] several progressive Korean monks were already under Japanese influence by 1879–1880.

Among those progressive monks, Yi Tongin is the best known, largely due to his exceptional closeness to Kojong in January–March of 1881 (unthinkable for a "lowly" Buddhist monk in the neo-Confucian polity) and the diversity of his diplomatic assignments. Still, he definitely was not the only Korean Buddhist monk deeply influenced by the Japanese missionary enterprise and the role of Buddhism in Meiji "civilization and progress" project. In a way, he was one of the first representatives of the whole generation of socially active Buddhist monks whose views and behavior were completely changed by their contacts with the Japanese Buddhist missions.

Serious enhancement of Buddhism and the Buddhists' political, social, and cultural roles in Korea seems to have drawn attention of the Meiji government and has influenced its decision to actively utilize the services of Japanese Buddhist missionaries with a view to win over the sympathies of Korean Buddhist circles and use the latter as a tool for imperialist penetration on the Peninsula. In mid-1870s, when Japan started its intrusion into Korea with the signing of the Kanghwa Treaty and the subsequent opening of Pusan to the Japanese, most Japanese Buddhist sects, and especially the Higashi Honganji branch of the Amidaist Shin sect were greatly pleased with the end of the persecutions of early Meiji period, and were more than ready to support the governmental policies through missionary work and international propagation of Japanese Buddhism, both to the Christians of the West and the Buddhists of China and Korea. In the case of the Higashi Honganji branch, it showed rare enthusiasm in the participation of the Meiji government efforts to colonize Hokkaido, even in the darkest days of the persecution of 1868–1872, striving to prove its adherence to the largely traditional idea of the "non-duality of the defense of the state with the protection of Buddha-Dharma."[9] So, it came as no surprise that Honganji administrative head, Kennyo, instructed by then-Home Minister Ōkubo Toshimichi and Foreign Minister Terajima Munenori, quickly dispatched priest Okumura Enshin to open a missionary center (J. *betsuin*, literally "branch temple") in Pusan in October 1877, almost immediately after Pusan was opened to the Japanese.

The space for the "branch temple" was gladly leased by Japanese consular authorities inside the consulate's building—the doctrine of "non-duality of royal and Buddhist law" to which Okumura explicitly subscribed seemingly could work in ways profitable for the missionary enterprise. The officially stated aim of the opening of the center was to propagate Buddhism among the Japanese residents of Pusan, but the real intention of Okumura and his superiors was to forge the relations with the Korean progressives inclined towards Buddhism and, ultimately, to utilize the progressives' interest in Meiji reforms in the course of penetration into Korea.[10] Chairman of the House of Peers Duke Konoe Atsumaro, known later for his Pan-Asianist activities in China, instructed Okumura's superiors in the following way on the historical importance of their mission in Korea:

> Recently, various Western states are paying close attention to the Eastern affairs, and, if we will not establish long-term strategy now, the consequences would be difficult to cope with. As the advanced state of the East, our country should show an example of altruistic care about others, and, for this sake, the negative feelings about Japan spread among the Chinese and Koreans have to be cleared away, and the states of the East have to be induced to the closest cooperation. But government alone cannot manage to do all these things. That is why it is necessary to borrow the strength of religion and education.[11]

As can be seen, the Buddhist mission was to play an important role in the overall design of Japan's continental mission, often described in the terms of Pan-Asianist rhetoric.

From the very beginning, apart from approximately 300-odd Japanese residential populace of that open port, the main object of Okumura's missionary efforts were Korean monks through whom he was going to establish a Japanese Buddhist presence in Korean religion, culture, and even politics. The unusual interest toward the Japanese monks among Koreans was palpable as soon as the mission was began. Almost every day, Okumura had up to 8 to 10 (and, on some days, even up to 50) Korean visitors, laymen and monks, to treat to tea, Chinese poetizing, "brush conversations" in classical Chinese on Meiji Japan's recent affairs, and even explanations of Amitaist doctrines. For example, one frequent visitor was the famous Pŏmŏsa preceptor, monk Honhae (Buddhist name, Ch'anyun [?–1912]—the teacher of Kim Kuha and Pak Poryun, two noted preceptors of the colonial period). He made his first visit to Okumura on February 9, 1878 (almost immediately after the opening of the mission), and then made repeated visits in June and December of 1878, exchanging expensive gifts with the Japanese. That Japan was radically changing was more or less understood by the Koreans from Pusan and its vicinities who could witness Japan's formidable gunships in Pusan harbor and the new Westernized uniform of military and consular officials.

For many of the better-educated Koreans, these changes looked like one of the possible examples Korea, threatened by what was perceived as unremitting Western attempts at political and religious subversion, could eventually refer to. And for Buddhists, especially the monks relegated to the lowest social status by the neo-Confucian orthodoxy, a much more elevated standing of their Japanese counterparts (visibly protected and revered by the consular officials) and, by extension, Meiji patterns of incorporating religion into the modernization project in general made them objects of envy as well. In such an atmosphere of strong and growing interest to the perplexing yet enviable transformation of the neighboring country, it hardly seemed a surprise that very soon a special category of Koreans who are willing to study Japanese and immerse themselves deeper into the Japanese Buddhist milieu emerged. For the ones whose interest could be satisfied by learning on the spot, in 1879 Okumura set up a language school in which Koreans were taught Japanese and students from Japan could pick up some Korean.[12] The students were provided with highly rewarding employment as well—as the consulate and mission acted in the close cooperation, Japanese-speaking Korean disciples of Okumura could be used as interpreters by the consular officials.[13] In such a way, a distinctive Japanese–Korean Buddhist milieu was formed in Pusan from the end of the 1870s, a precedent that set an example for the future attempts to transplant Japanese Buddhist patterns onto Korean and Chinese soil. At the same time, those most enthusiastic about learning both "the state of the world" and the situation of the much-better-positioned Japanese saṅgha were provided with opportunities to cross the sea and enter the Buddhist and political world of Japan. The opportunities looked even more precious since the Korean monks had been prevented from sustaining their time-honored tradition of pursuing the knowledge and experience overseas for the last five centuries due to the neo-Confucian oppression of Chosŏn rulers. As the knowledge of Japan was soon urgently demanded by the radical reformers that grouped around Kim Okkyun, those monks who dared the voyage to Japan rapidly found themselves in the center of stormy and violent political events.

As Im Chongguk, one of the pioneers of research on pro-Japanese collaboration-related issues in modern South Korea, mentions in his writings, the first Korean monk to leave for Japan and study there was a certain Kim Ch'ŏlju, a Kyŏngju native who, with Okumura's help, managed to smuggle himself into Japan in December of 1878 by posing as Japanese (because Koreans still were not permitted to travel to Japan privately). He was accepted into the Shin sect, re-ordained, and permitted to study, but could not achieve much before his early death in 1879.[14] I was unable to fully corroborate this information, for Korean sources for Buddhist history for that period are sketchy at best, and, among the Japanese documents, only Okumura's diary briefly mentions Kim Ch'ŏlju's trip to Japan and his death of mental illness.[15] This first trip—and we can imagine how many difficulties and dangers it entailed—was actually the beginning of a totally new chapter in Korea's recent Buddhist history. Travels to Japan, just as peregrinations in China in good old days, were to contribute greatly to Korean Buddhism's transformation into a faith better able to fit itself to the changed regional environment.

Okumura's other victory also came in 1878, when a young and energetic Korean monk, Yi Tongin, came to his missionary center. This incident is much more verifiable. According to Okumura's diary, one of the first encounters with the Korean monk took place on December 9–11, 1878, when three days were cheerfully spent in "brush conversation" about how "to protect the state and restore Buddhist sect." Very similar questions about Chosŏn's preposterous isolation and Chosŏn Buddhism's pitiful position were customarily asked to Okumura by many other Korean monks during that period, as Okumura's diary shows. We have the reasons to surmise that state protection (i.e., political matters) was a much more important topic for those talks than Buddhist sectarian matters, for, as Okumura said afterward "[Yi Tongin] always spoke of the political matters and, while explaining international relationship, never mentioned Buddhism." He also "earnestly requested" to be allowed to see a Japanese military vessel. This wish was realized on December 11, 1878. Yi was also accompanied by above-mentioned Kim Ch'ŏlju. After this, Yi Tongin took his leave from the mission. He seems to have been remembered by Okumura with considerable respect and interest: The latter characterized Yi as a man who "always was concerned with the love of his country and protecting the [Buddhist] law." This standardized phrase could only mean that Okumura and his superiors approved of Yi Tongin's political views and wished to use the Korean monk in the framework of their religious structure, in full accordance with the sect's doctrine of the "inseparable nature of the protection of the [Buddhist] law and protection of the country."

The opportunity to do so presented itself very soon. In the intercalary lunar month (between March and April), 1879, Yi Tongin went to Okumura's mission again, and, by Okumura's recommendation, held important talks with the newly appointed Japanese Minister to Korea, Hanabusa Yoshimoto (1842~1917), who was on his way to Seoul. Yi Tongin went back to Seoul in early summer, but soon, in mid-June, returned to Okumura's mission, and started decisive talks on the undertaking an illegal trip to Japan similar to Kim Ch'ŏlju's.[16] What were the reasons for Yi's interest in such an adventure?

According to Okumura's diary (June 1879, first decade), Yi Tongin was trusted and "promoted to the responsibility" by the "revolutionary party members," Kim Okkyun and Pak Yŏnghyo. This was due to the monk's "patriotic" and "dharma-protecting" intentions, as well as his views on the "decay of the fortunes" of Chosŏn state, all of which were in full harmony with the ideas of the Enlightenment leaders. The trust of the "revolutionary leaders" seemed to have been deep indeed, for Yi Tongin could shock Okumura by showing him four approximately 6-centimeter-long rods of pure gold and explaining that Kim and Pak had given Yi the precious metal for travel expenses.[17] At this point, we encounter an important question: (1) Was Yi Tongin acquainted with the would-be Enlightenment leaders, Kim and Pak, before the beginning of his contacts with the Japanese, or (2) did he contact the *yangban* leaders of the incipient Enlightenment movement after already having Japanese connections, perhaps in the position of a possible bridge-builder between the reformist nobles and the Japanese? In the former case, we can speak about Yi (an Enlightenment neophyte) trying, from the very beginning, to make inroads into the outer world for the benefit of his group. However, in the latter case, we have grounds to possibly characterize the bridge-building between the Seoul *yangban*s and the Japanese missionaries as self-seeking middleman acts of an entrepreneurial treaty-port resident. This latter view has some support by the fact that Yi's trip to Japan was sponsored by the Seoul circle of would-be revolutionaries and was, as we will see later, also a very profitable commercial enterprise. In this case, Yi may be compared to another famed *kŏgan* (middleman) of the time, Song Pyŏngjun (1857–1925), who, from 1877, managed a money-lending business and trade enterprise in Pusan on behalf of Ōkura Kihachirō (1837–1928), a well-known figure in the Meiji business world. Although arriving later than Yi Tongin, Song Pyŏngjun also managed to build very close relationships with Kim Okkyun and Pak Yŏnghyo, serving as their informal adviser in Japan-related matters from 1882.[18]

For several reasons, I am inclined to agree with Yi Kwangnin in assuming that, unlike Song Pyŏngjun, Yi Tongin's ideological connections and bonds of personal loyalty with his Seoul sponsors were extremely deep.[19]

First, according to the papers of Sir Ernest M. Satow (1843–1929)[20] (the Second Secretary at the British Legation in Tokyo) dated May 12, 1880, the first time the two met, Yi Tongin explained that his Japanese name, Asano, meant "Korean savage." Such cultural self-effacement shows Yi to be a person of very unorthodox thinking, considering the standards of intense cultural pride (bordering on self-aggrandizement) typical of the educated mainstream of the 1870s. Self-denigration such as this was only possible in the heterodox *Sirhak* milieu; similar self-critical expressions can be found in books by Pak Chiwŏn (1737–1805) and Pak Chega (1750–1805) when unfavorably comparing Chosŏn with Qing culture, a social issue that undeniably influenced Kim Okkyun's circle. In refutation of traditional ideas of cultural superiority, Yi Tongin seems to have been incomparably more radical than even Pak Kyusu (1807–1876), the famous mentor of Kim Okkyun's circle. Pak considered Korea's erstwhile honorary name, "The Land of Rituals and Righteousness," to be shamefully Sino-centric and "hardly suitable for pronouncing proudly in the world."[21]

Second, Yi Tongin was a staunch supporter of development and commercial exploitation of Chosŏn's mineral and botanical recourses (gold, coal, ginseng) through the improvement of communications and trade. He stressed this at his second meeting with Satow on May 15, 1880, and in his speech to the Rise Asia Society (*Kōakai*) in April of the same year. The issue was first addressed by the *Sirhak* thinkers (especially influential was Pak Chega) in the late eighteenth and early nineteenth centuries and, afterward, enjoyed popularity in the Enlightenment circle.

Third, if Yi Nŭnghwa's information is to be believed, Yi Tongin's friend and fellow traveler, Paektamsa monk T'ak Chŏngsik, first met Kim Okkyun at the Hwagyesa temple, which was very close to Yi Tongin's home, Samsŏngam (affiliated with Hwagyesa from 1884 and his residence before moving to Pŏmŏsa).[22] If true, the Buddhist connection between Yi Tongin and Kim Okkyun (an avid and sincere lay believer) is also worth considering.[23]

In a nutshell, Yi Tongin's connection to Kim Okkyun and Pak Yŏnghyo seems to have been based on ideological affinity, and possibly also personal loyalty and religious sympathy. The trip was undertaken not only for commercial gain (although this aspect was also quite important), but, as Yi Tongin said to Okumura, basically for "inspecting Japan's situation and contributing to Chosŏn's changes." In other words, it was a "reconnaissance mission" of sorts, prompted and sponsored by the Kim Okkyun/Pak Yŏnghyo circle. In Yi Tongin's case, the history of modern Korean Buddhism directly touches upon the crucial moment of Korea's early modern history, that is, the building of close relationships between Korea's first reformist radicals and the Meiji elite, which, in time, developed into intellectual and material dependence of the former on the latter.

Yi Tongin's first place of residence (from June 1879 until April 1880) was the Honganji temple in Kyoto. After having secretly sailed to Japan in June 1879, Yi Tongin was immersed in the study of the Japanese language and was busy inspecting various aspects of Japanese society. He did find time, however, to send a letter of gratitude (with an elegant classical Chinese poem on Buddhist topics) to Okumura on November 13, 1879, and to purchase newly-printed books on modern subjects for Kim Okkyun and Pak Yŏnghyo. These books were delivered by Okumura himself in May 1880, when Okumura went back to Chosŏn. After Okumura arrived in Honganji on March 19, 1880, Yi Tongin was quickly reordained as a Shin sect novice (April 5, 1880), taken to Tokyo (April 6, 1880), and introduced to the dignitaries at Foreign Ministry (April 9–11, 1880). On the same trip, he also met Fukuzawa Yūkichi (1835–1901) and other important personalities interested in "Korean reforms." In more realistic terms, Okumura most likely wished to make the Koreans follow the Japanese model of reform in close subservience to the Japanese government. As is well known, while he was living at the Asakusa branch temple of the sect in Tokyo, on August 11, 1880, Yi Tongin won the confidence of Kim Hongjip (1842–1896), an important member of the "moderate reformist" group who came on a mission to the Meiji government and who stayed in the same Asakusa branch temple.[24]

Yi Tongin's circle of Japanese contacts was fairly wide as well, which is hardly surprising. As the first Korean studying in Meiji Japan, he would be a legitimate object of interest for groups of diverse orientations. But the group that left written traces of its contacts with Yi Tongin was the Rise Asia Society, known as the first institutional proponent of Pan-Asianist ideology in Japan. The Society, organized several months after Yi Tongin arrived in Japan in 1880, consisted largely of the followers of a popular politician, Ōkuma Shigenobu (1838–1922). Ōkuma wrapped their ambitious expansionist designs in the florid banner of "defending the Three States of East Asia from the Western encroachments" and "promoting the solidarity between the peoples of the same culture." This was basically grounded in the *idée fixe* of obtaining equality with and possibly even superiority over the Western powers by carving Japan's own "sphere of influence" in the adjacent region in the same imperialistic fashion. Ōkuma's ideas were largely based on the Social Darwinist perspective of inevitable racial rivalry as an ultimate manifestation of the struggle for survival. This was solidly grounded in the superiority complex of "modernized" Meiji Japan toward its supposedly "less advanced" neighbors, now considered to be the natural objects of Japan's own civilizing mission. These ideas were later summarized in 1885, in a somewhat more radicalized form, by Tarui Tōkichi in his *Daitō Gappō-ron* (Theory of the Unification of the Great East), which envisioned future Japanese colonization of Korea and expansion into China.

The activity of Yi Tongin in the Rise Asia Society, as judged by the text of his presentation to a session of that Society printed in "Kōakai hōkoku" (May 1880),[25] demonstrates unusually strong political ambitions. Bluntly criticizing Queen Min's circle for its total monopolization of state power and extremely inefficient decision-making and policy implementation, Yi Tongin suggested that, in order to achieve the Meiji ideals of *fukoku kyōhei* (wealthy nation and strong military), Korea should repair the roads so as to guarantee unimpeded transport of Japanese merchandise from the treaty ports to the hinterland. He also felt Korea should borrow from the Japanese government to develop mining and reclaim new land. Another idea Yi Tongin mentioned in his presentation to the Society, and later strived to implement, was to send several dozen Korean students to Japan to study subjects ranging from accounting to diplomacy, for Japan was "to be taken as example, model, and the guiding spirit for Korean reforms." (In this he was partially successful; the 1881 "Courtiers' Observation Mission" to Japan was largely the result of his efforts.) The conclusion of this presentation was that only a "brotherly" Japan would be able to "defend" Korea from "humiliations by the West," and that it was much more ethical to share the profits of development with Japanese "brethren" than with Western "aliens." His plans for Korean reform financed by the Japanese were to take place as an immediate program of action by Kim Okkyun's group (which tried hard to secure a loan from Japan, but without much success), and his Pan-Asianist inclinations foretold the emergence of a large and important stream in Korea's modern thought. For Buddhist and non-Buddhist alike, Pan-Asianism was to become the battle cry for very diverse groups of varying political leanings, both pro- and anti-Japanese.[26]

His pioneering trip to Japan, and his subsequent relationship with the Japanese (primarily, Okumura), enriched Yi Tongin and his Korean associates. In particular, the rich and entrepreneurial *chungin* physician, Yu Taech'i, benefited not only intellectually, but also economically. During his first trip to Japan, Yi Tongin used his time to buy many modern goods, including glasses, matches (which were unknown before in Chosŏn Korea), spyglasses, lamps, watches, calico, and photographs of stately European buildings (partly received as gift from Satow). These goods were partly for resale in Seoul, and partly as presents to the leaders of the Enlightenment circle, who, as expected, commissioned more goods from the entrepreneurial monk and prepaid the order.[27]

Satow's papers also give reason to think that he, the English diplomat who assiduously studied Korean with Yi Tongin's help, commissioned the Korean monk to bring more Korean vernacular books to him in Japan, and gave him money for that purpose.[28] Truly large-scale trade between the Enlightenment circle and its Japanese sponsors started after Yu Taech'i was introduced to Okumura through a letter from Yi Tongin, dated October 4, 1880. From Yu Taech'i's letters to Okumura (dated October 6 and November 1, 1880, lunar calendar), we know the Korean physician loaned the necessary capital for launching trade with the Japanese from Okumura, and had to pay monthly interest on the loan through his trade associate, Yi Taedong from Wŏnsan. Through Okumura, Yu Taech'i shipped cows' bones to Japan, where they were used for making fertilizer and special ointments; he received shipments of Western calicos from the Japanese for sale to Korean retailers.[29] The trade continued well into 1881, largely conducted on the Korean side by Yu Taech'i's son-in-law, Kim Ch'anghŭi. Yu's exports, sold in Nagasaki through Okumura's friends, were chiefly Korean honey, silks, and beans; the imports were goods mostly manufactured in Europe (chiefly in Britain). Also, during his visits to Japan, Yi Tongin was of considerable help in conducting the trade. The value of the goods traded in this fashion (of course, without paying taxes to the Korean government, in violation of the contemporary rules on taxing Korean merchants in treaty ports) in one year amounted to approximately 5,000 *nyang*—an enormous sum at that time.[30] Yu Taech'i (seemingly in an attempt to collect money for planned political actions by his *yangban* associates in the Enlightenment circle) imported European goods through Japanese middlemen, and exported chiefly Korean natural products; his trade activity can be defined, with certain reservations, as an early form of "comprador capitalism." This was typical for the areas affected by the rapid expansion of the Europe-centered capitalist system in the late nineteenth century. Yi Tongin's contacts with William Keswick (1834–1912), the Yokohama representative of the famous British firm, Jardine, Matheson & Co,[31] as well as his attempts to arouse Satow's personal interest in the Korean ginseng trade,[32] obviously were aimed in making this kind of comprador trade more profitable for the Korean side by circumventing the Japanese intermediaries and buying the European manufactured goods directly from European wholesalers. This was the idea Yi Tongin formulated in his conversation with Satow himself.[33]

Still, the absence of treaties with European powers and the general low level of European commercial interest left Yu Taech'i and Yi Tongin with the Japanese who were the only accessible partners for the comprador trade in Korean resources. In this respect, Yi Tongin's propensity to out-Japanize the Japanese in the talks on Korean Enlightenment at the Rise Asia Society are, in large part, explainable by this peculiarity of his socio-economic standing: his and Yu Taech'i's planned illegal comprador trade with the Japanese depended completely on Japanese loans and on Okumura's cooperation as intermediary. With perhaps an element of excessive speculation, Yi Tongin's views on Korean reforms (centered on the development of exportable recourses, Japanese trade, loans, and education) can be understood as a very crude draft of the political program of incipient Korean pro-Japanese comprador capital. Indeed, it can be seen as the first plan of "dependent development" in modern Korean history.

Was it an accident that, paradoxically, a monk, discouraged (at least in principle) by his vows from any profit-seeking activities, became not only one of the first known comprador traders of modernizing Korea but also the first known ideologue of Korea's dependent modernization? Given the extent of trade activities and property accumulation by the biggest and richest Korean temples of the period, the fact that a monk, Yi Tongin, spearheaded the development of inescapably unequal trade with Japan seems rather understandable. Having been deprived of most of their landholdings by the neo-Confucian reformers of the early Chosŏn period, the larger temples were able to regain significant wealth in the eighteenth and nineteenth centuries, amidst general development of internal trade and exchanges.[34] For one example, the temple of Pŏmŏsa, with which Yi Tongin was apparently affiliated for at least at some period of his life, was among the largest and richest in the southern provinces. In 1871, the temple possessed about 1,300 *majigi* (*turak*) of fields, plus approximately 2,000 *majigi* owned by various affiliated hermitages. The wealth was chiefly amassed by donations of the fields for conducting posthumous sacrificial services (K. *chejŏn*), as well as donations by temple-affiliated popular devotional guilds (*Mit'agye* and *Ch'ilsŏnggye*, among others) and commercial services for the peasantry (rice-milling, etc.).[35] The rich temple was keenly interested in enhancing the social status of the Buddhist community in order to save it from the depredations of local officialdom. This can be seen, for example, from a tale popular among Pŏmŏsa monks at that time, about a monk whose good deeds culminated in allowing a tiger to devour his body, following the example of Buddha's self-sacrifice, which "helped him to be reborn as a high official who came to the temples to protect them from corrupt and greedy local clerks."[36] The accounts of the newly acquired semi-official status of Meiji Buddhism as the "state-protecting native religion" were obviously fascinating for Pŏmŏsa's monastic populace. It comes as little surprise that revered Pŏmŏsa monks were prominent among the first visitors to Okumura's nearby mission, one example being Honhae's visits that were mentioned above. A monk from another large and rich temple, Yujŏmsa, not only visited Okumura, but also overtly asked him on August 3, 1880, "to help Korean monks in their predicament."[37] Obviously, the richer clergy of certain larger temples in the early 1880s came to see comprador connections with Japanese interests, whether commercial, political, or ideological, and open protection by the Japanese state, as a good method to defend and expand their own sphere of commercial activities. More helpless than any other commercially-active group in the face of official extortion, rapacity, and greed, the trading, land-owning monks, fettered by their low status, had the keenest interest in finding outside protection. The position of compradors working for Japan's interests, once the latter were dominant in Korea, suited them well.

On returning to Korea on September 28, 1880, Yi Tongin, as Kim Hongjip's *protégé*, was influential in conducting negotiations with Qing and Japanese representatives. He actively participated in preparations for establishing diplomatic relationships with the United States. Yi played a crucial role in introducing young Korean radical reformers to Okumura, who then served as one of the main middlemen in their relations with Japanese diplomats and traders, Fukuzawa (who became their ideological mentor), and the Rise Asia Society. Yi also played a pivotal role in preparing a large Korean inspection mission to Japan (Courtiers' Observation Mission) in 1881. Still, Yi's perceived failure to secure the purchase of a gunboat from Japan, and important differences in foreign policy between himself and Kim Hongjip, prompted Kim Hongjip's followers to arrange Yi's assassination. On May 9, 1881, Okumura received letters informing him that his outstanding *protégé* had disappeared.[38] In Chosŏn Korea, a monk's life was not worth much and was not firmly protected by either law or custom. This was one of the cardinal reasons why Yi and other reformist monks had no compunctions about their pro-Japanese stance. In addition, Yi Tongin's predisposition to vanity and bragging, as well as his love of bombastic and careless talk, could also have contributed to his untimely death. For example, Yi proudly presented himself as the "king's secret emissary to Japan" to the jail warders in Tongnae, who arrested him on espionage charges on December 18, 1880. At the second meeting with Satow, he told the British diplomat that the Korean government should be overthrown. Kim Hongjip and other key figures in Korean diplomacy had many reasons to fear a possible leaking of state secrets by such an emotional and impulsive monk.[39]

After Yi's disappearance, contacts of the Kim Okkyun-led radical reformist group with the Japanese followed the path designed by Yi. They secured the Japanese loans, imported Japanese technology and arms, and introduced early Meiji ideas to the country. By doing so, the youthful "radicals," knowingly or unknowingly, were laying the cornerstones of the future dependent development of Korean polity and economy inside Japan's sphere of influence. The episode of a monk whose position was lowest in the social hierarchy having a meteor-like career on the basis of his connections to Japanese Buddhist missionaries and his network of personal connections built in Japan shows that the impact of Japanese missionary enterprise was not limited to Buddhism per se. Native collaborators of the Japanese Buddhist missionaries in Korea could at times exert enormous influence on the society groping for changes and reforms, not unlike the cases of missionary natives and converts wherever Western Christian missions were found. However, the episode underlined the dangers of this missionary connection as well: Neither Yi's comprador-like entrepreneurial activity nor his Pan-Asianist or social reformist ideas could be considered properly Buddhist or monastic. When later, under Japanese rule, the temples became units of market economy and their abbots (who were like quasi-capitalists in monastic robes) were obliged in the later 1930s to follow Japan's official Pan-Asianist and militarist propagandist lines as well, the extent of these dangers became fully known. Modernity promised legal equality and state protection to the downtrodden Korean monks, but it also threatened them with adulteration of their disciplinarian traditions and time-honored ways of temple life. In fact, the search for modern Buddhism that is able to encompass the whole wealth of pre-modern regional tradition does not seem to have been successful.

Yi Tongin was by no means alone. In fact, in 1880–1881, a group of Korean monks keenly interested in cooperating with the Japanese and willing to receive a Japanese education and eventually being re-ordinaned, gathered in Pusan around Okumura. The group's well-known political representative was Paektamsa monk Kakchi, also known as Mubul. He was commonly referred to by his lay name, T'ak Chŏngsik, perhaps because of his activities behind the scenes of the Korean-Japanese collaboration. There were also Korean-British and Korean-Chinese relationships, and they did not have an explicitly Buddhist character, to say the least. As mentioned above, T'ak Chŏngsik first encountered Kim Okkyun in Hwagyesa temple. On obtaining the trust of the latter, T'ak built close contacts with Okumura as well and went to Japan, probably illegally, in April or May of 1880 to join Yi Tongin in his Asakusa quarters. He returned to Korea through Wŏnsan on June 25, 1880, met Okumura there, and the next day headed for Seoul, his likely aim being to meet Kim Okkyun and report to him about the situation in Japan.[40] When Yi Tongin was given a secret mission to again go to Tokyo to begin the backstage negotiations through Chinese diplomats for concluding a Korean-American treaty, he was again followed by T'ak Chŏngsik.

Now holding official permits to travel abroad, T'ak and Yi left Wŏnsan on November 4, 1880, after long talks with Okumura and the Japanese consul.[41] In Japan, the duo parted ways. Yi spent a month in Tokyo busying himself with meeting English and Chinese diplomats and then went back to Korea on December 18. He was briefly imprisoned on his arrival in Pusan by the local authorities and even threatened with death, and only the interference of his highly connected

Seoul friends saved his life, but this was an omen of the misfortune that was to befall him soon. At the same time, T'ak prolonged his sojourn in Japan, teaching Korean to W. G. Aston (1841–1911), then-British Consul in Kobe. He also met Yi Tongin's old acquaintance Ernest. M. Satow in Tokyo and held meetings with Chinese diplomats stationed in Tokyo about the prospects of establishing Korean-American relationships.

After Yi Tongin disappeared, T'ak informed both English diplomats of the incident and collected money from them, obviously believing that Yi had been simply detained somewhere and not killed, and that his freedom could be bought. According to Satow's papers, 200 yen donated by him was used by T'ak to buy mechanical watches, which were sent to Pusan in an attempt to gain the favor of those who, he thought, were holding Yi. T'ak apparently believed that Yi had been again imprisoned in Pusan, following the pattern of his brief detention there in December 1880. By July 1881, T'ak seems to have recognized that Yi Tongin had been assassinated and not simply detained, and he returned the 200 yen to Satow, to the great surprise of the latter. One reason for his noticeable solvency may have been the job he secured in 1881 as a Korean language teacher in the Tokyo School of Foreign Languages (established in 1873), with a monthly salary as high as 200 yen. When Kim Okkyun, T'ak's patron, came to Japan for the first time in April 1882 and stayed there until August, T'ak's knowledge of Japanese and his connections with the network of governmental and diplomatic officials helped Kim meet the country's notables, including the members of the Rise Asia Society and the famous educator Fukuzawa Yukichi. A year later, on Kim Okkyun's request, T'ak undertook a trading adventure, attempting to transport to Kobe the timber from Ullŭngdo Island, but he died on February 9, 1884, in Kobe due to a sudden illness. His death was widely reported in Japanese and Korean newspapers, and his lavish funeral in the Asakusa branch temple was attended by Kim Okkyun, who came for the third time to Japan to negotiate procurement of a loan for Korean reforms, following up on an idea first proposed by Yi Tongin.[42]

While the commercial project with Ullŭngdo timber did not succeed in earning Kim Okkyun's party the extra funds it needed for the planned *coup d'état* against the Seoul conservatives, T'ak still rendered Kim's party an invaluable service. The gunpowder the party used for the abortive *Kapsin coup d'état* in October 1884 was procured by T'ak through resident Westerners in Japan.[43] That a monk became engaged in the armament trade shows very well the contradiction Korean Buddhism encountered on the threshold of modernity. The struggle for Meiji-inspired reforms promised the monks a significant improvement in their status, but it involved them inescapably in very serious breaches of traditional monastic rules. Collaboration with the Japanese missionaries and Japan-inspired reformers led to the significant forfeiture of their religious authority by the activist monks and seriously changed the overall atmosphere in a number of temples.

In the 1880s, the penetration of Japanese Buddhist sects into Korea accelerated even further. Shin sect's monopoly in the Korean missionary field was broken in 1881 when the Nichiren sect built its temple called Myōkaku-ji (K. Myogaksa) in Pusan; in the next year, the same sect's Wŏnsan temple was erected as well.[44] Led by Arai Nissatsu (1830–1888), the Nichiren sect, which was officially recognized in 1876, was known as one of the leading proponents of the modernized version of state-protecting Buddhism theories. Arai turned Nichiren's dogma upside down, claiming that converting rulers into the right teaching would not lead to the great pacification of the world, but, on the contrary, the pacification by the lay rulers was the main prerequisite for establishing the right teaching.[45] No wonder the sect he led aspired to render service to the Meiji state by actively participating in propagating its virtues abroad. His missionary ambitions may also have reflected the desire to establish his sect's legitimacy in the face of its failure to unify all the groups claiming to be in the lineage succession from Nichiren.[46] Not to be defeated in the competition with Arai's sect, the Shin sect built its Inch'ŏn branch temple in 1885 to augment its existing Korean facilities in Pusan and Wŏnsan.[47] Then, Korea's capital became the place of their missionary rivalry. A Shin branch temple was established there on the Japanese settlement territory in 1890, and, interestingly enough, the Shin missionaries felt proud that their new temple stood exactly where Katō Kiyomasa's armies were based during the Japanese invasion of Korea from 1592 to 1598. The Nichiren sect based its Korean activities in Seoul the same year.[48] While Korean monks and nuns were still barred from legally entering the capital, their Japanese colleagues were able to build their temples there, and the obvious ability of the Japanese Buddhist establishment to obtain such momentous concessions from the Korean state certainly strengthened pro-Japanese inclinations in Korean Buddhist circles.

In the beginning of the 1894–1895 Sino-Japanese War, Seoul was occupied by Japanese troops, and the country as a whole was placed under the pro-Japanese Kim Hongjip cabinet (July 1894). After that, Japanese Buddhist activities in the capital became even more aggressive, the Nichiren sect being the acknowledged leader of this unprecedented charge. Believing that "granting an unparalleled favor to the feeble and impotent" Korean monks would convert them into Nichiren sect followers, Sano Zenrei (1859–1912), a ranking monk of the sect, was dispatched to Korea, and he succeeded, with strong support of the Japanese Consulate, in persuading Kim Hongjip to have the throne remembered by allowing Korean monks to enter the capital. Finally, King Kojong granted them permission on March 29, 1895.[49] Once the main symbol of the suppression of Buddhism by the Confucian state was eliminated under the Japanese influence, the prestige of Japanese monks soared sky-high in the eyes of their Korean counterparts. Now Korea's downtrodden Buddhists found themselves in the more elevated position their Japanese colleagues had enjoyed for two decades.

Predictably, the response of Korea's activist monks to the "unparalleled favor" bestowed on them by Sano was euphoric. The entrepreneurial Japanese monk was inundated with written and oral congratulations and thanks. A typical example is the letter of gratitude sent by Ch'oe Ch'wihŏ (Buddhist name: Sangsun), a well-known, educated monk who then resided in Suwŏn's large Yongjusa temple:

> We, monks, used to live as the basest and lowest in this country, and were prohibited from entering the capital for the last five hundred years. Amidst our usual melancholy, by a lucky incident, the friendship with neighboring [Japanese] state became strengthened, and You, respected preceptor, came from afar to compassionately bestow a great favor upon us. You allowed us, Korean monks, to throw off the 500 years-old humiliation, so that we can see the royal capital now. All of us, monks of this country, feel gratitude to You, and wish to use the opportunity to visit the capital in order to pay You our highest respect. (. . .)[50]

From a modern nationalist position, Ch'oe Ch'wihŏ's belief in the good intentions of the Japanese missionaries looks naïve at best or like a symptom of the deplorable lack of national consciousness that some might view as treason.[51] But we should remember that, strictly speaking, the formation of modern nationalism did not begin until the 1890s, and this ideology was not yet a dominant element in Korea's popular consciousness. Therefore, Japanese monks could be seen, first and foremost, as representatives of the same religious and cultural tradition, their obvious foreignness and political agenda notwithstanding. Moreover, modern nationalism's representative champions in the 1890s were American-educated Christian converts who regarded Buddhism as nothing more than an obstacle to Korea's participation in a Christian Western civilization. Their mouthpiece, a bilingual newspaper in vernacular Korean and English, *Tongnip sinmun* (*The Independent*, founded on April 7, 1896),[52] reduced Buddhism to the level of folk superstition. The following is a typical description:

> People usually believe in absurdities and long for unreasonable things once they lack knowledge. That is why female and male shamans, geomantic teachers and Buddhist monks are able nowadays to charm and captivate commoners into giving them money, luring weak-hearted womenfolk and absurdity-believing males into wasting their property in serving evil spirits. People are deceived just because they are ignorant. [. . .] Instead of wasting property by treating evil spirits so well, should we not rather use it to help the poor, to build a hospital for the ill or to build a school for educating the people?

> [. . .] We are not going to reprimand the female and male shamans, Buddhist monks and geomancy masters, but just warn them, thinking that they themselves are doing all this out of ignorance; once they understand that all those things are empty absurdities useless for the people, they will also stop believing in them. [. . .][53]

At the same time, the newspaper touted Christianity as the "religion of the strongest, richest, most civilized, advanced and blessed in the world."[54] Given the exclusivist religious attitude of the earliest Christian nationalists in Korea, it does not seem strange that Korean monks preferred receiving "favors" from their Japanese colleagues to accepting the "modern" version of Koreanness as advocated by the likes of *Tongnip sinmun*. In addition, the more moderate version of nationalism promoted by the reformist Confucians who published *Hwangsŏng sinmun* (Imperial Capital Newspaper, established as a daily on September 5, 1898), used Buddhist imagery in their florid editorials, but they too regarded Buddhism as an impediment to civilization. The age-old Confucian disregard of the "parasite" monks was added to the modern Orientalist view of Buddhism as "too abstract, mystic, and non-practical." One example of this view can be found in a lengthy article ambitiously entitled "The Origins of the Religions of All the States in East and West" (August 22, 1902) in which the writer approvingly cited the following Western judgments of Buddhism:

> Buddhism is just as full of empty, needless talk, as Islam is fond of using arms for the sake of its propagation. [. . .] All Buddhism is reducible to the idea of emptiness, while Christianity advances the belief in the only God. [. . .] There are some useful points in the Buddhist teachings of unselfishness and consideration, but, apart from the simple ethics, it is simply one big mistake. Once all humanity follows its dogma, it will soon become extinct. [. . .] Buddhist texts, such as *Flower Garland Sutra* or *Lotus Sutra* [. . .], are just full of absurd stories. [. . .][55]

Written off by both radical and moderate nationalists as a "superstition," a "vestige" of the "uncivilized" past, Buddhists would not be invited to participate in the nationalist anti-Japanese resistance. In contrast, the Meiji regime of the 1890s elevated the Buddhist sects into "truly Japanese, patriotic denominations" and gave them ample chances to serve the Empire, which attracted the Korean monks' interest and caused them to see this as an example of "Buddhism-friendly" modernity.

Korean monks' distrust of the nationalist modernity projects associated with Christian reformers was also carefully instigated by some of the Japanese Buddhist missionaries who were anxious to win the confidence of the Korean Buddhist public and raise additional funds at home through inciting the fear of the Christian threat in Korea. From the Japanese perspective as well, the topic was more than timely, given that the 1890s were marked by strenuous efforts in some institutional Buddhist circles to emphasize the unpatriotic and foreign nature of Christianity, and, by contrast, the loyalty of Buddhism as a native creed was emphasized.[56] For example, Katō Bunkyō, a noted Nichiren sect preacher with plentiful Korean experience[57] exploited the theme in the following way in his treatise *Chōsen Kaikyō ron* ("On Commencing the Preaching in Korea"), published in 1900:

> Recently, concurrent with the decay of Buddhism, Christian encroachment is becoming more and more severe every day, churches being built now in every important place in the country. They build schools, educate the children, help the poor, provide philanthropic medical aid, and earn the admiration of the Koreans by many other methods. Now they are welcomed virtually everywhere, the number of their churches having reached more than 300, and the number of their converts exceeding 540,000. Recently, the number of conversions was so high that the converts, as a kind of special race, can use the church for exerting decisive influence on the administration and judiciary. Even criminals, once they converted, can punish provincial officials under the missionary protection. [. . .] If that will continue for ten more years, Christianity will necessarily become Korea's religion. It is not only deplorable for the Buddhists, but also deeply related to Korea's independence and development. It clearly indicates that the crusaders are going to seize the whole world. Although we, the religious folk, are not supposed to speak on the state diplomatic matters, [. . .] why should the strengthening of Korea's independence be the exclusive domain of politicians only?[58]

It is clear that Katō's data, which he used to point out the threat of a Christian takeover in Korea, were grossly exaggerated, to say the least. Russia's authoritative *Opisanie Korei* (Description of Korea), printed in the same year as Katō's treatise, put the number of Korean Christians at around 30,000, only 777 of whom were officially baptized Protestants. Even if one takes into account the 3,000 students of Protestant-run schools, most of whom were not baptized and were not necessarily interested in religion *per se,*[59] the talk of Korea becoming a Christian state in ten years should have seemed far-fetched. However, playing on the fears about a growing Christian influence at the point when the Japanese-Russian tensions around Korea were steadily growing—Russia being a Christian power[60]—certainly was a winning maneuver. Missionary activities in Korea continued to be actively sponsored by the parent sects in Japan and vigorously supported on the ground by Japanese diplomats.

Christian missionaries were recognized by the Japanese Buddhist preachers in Korea as both competitors and reference models. By the beginning of the twentieth century these missionaries controlled some of the best modern schools in Korea, but Japanese Buddhist sects were contemplating advancement in the same direction. The above-cited *Chōsen kaikyō gojūnen shi* (1927) by the Amidaist Shin sect explained the principles of Japanese Buddhist educational work in Korea in those days in the following way:

> In order not to be mistrusted by Koreans, we used first to employ at least one Korean teacher and never demanded any tuition fee. We also provided the students with paper, ink and brushes, and, in addition to the traditional subjects, gradually introduced arithmetic, geography, history and so on, finally coming up to the religious and ethical instruction. [. . .] In cooperation with Korean provincial governors and other officials, we tried to provide best possible conditions for our Korean students and then could choose the best among them.[61]

The first Japanese missionary schools targeting Korean students made their appearance in the late 1890s. A veteran of a Korean mission, Okumura, was personally involved in setting up his sect's Kwangju missionary center (J. *fukyōshō*) with the help of a generous Foreign Ministry subsidy. Having secured the willing cooperation of Yun Ungnyŏl (1840–1911), a famous military reformer with strong pro-Japanese sympathies[62] and then governor of Chŏlla province, Okumura took two of his most promising local aides, Ch'oe Kanjin and Ch'oe Sep'al, on a grandiose Japanese tour, entirely financed by his sect in 1898. This pilgrimage seems to be among the first in the series of Japanese observation tours (K. *sich'al*) by Korean Buddhists, monks, and lay folk that, in the long run, contributed immensely to the remolding of Korean Buddhism along Meiji patterns. In addition, the establishment of the Shin sect missionary centers with schools attached continued. Mokp'o (1898) and Chinnamp'o, which were located in the vicinity of Pyongyang (1900), were their next targeted areas.[63] However, as soon as Korea fell under Japanese protection with the humiliating protectorate treaty that was forced on King Kojong on November 17, 1905, Japanese influence over Korea's indigenous Buddhist establishment was strong enough that missionary schools could be built in a much more effective way. Korea's own local modern Buddhist educational institutions were, in reality, sponsored and directed by Japanese advisers. Three months after Korea was made a protectorate, in February 1906, a group of younger activist Korean monks, led by the residents of wealthier monasteries in the vicinity of Seoul, organized the Buddhist Study Society (Pulgyo Yŏn'guhoe), which proclaimed Japanese Amidaism as its doctrinal base and invited Inoue Kenshin, a Japanese Jōdo sect preacher, to be its advisor. The Jōdo sect was administratively independent from the Shin sect and was its rival. As soon as the society was formed, it petitioned the Interior Ministry (K. *Naebu*) for permission to establish a modern Buddhist school. On February 19, the permission was given, and then the initiators urged every temple of importance in the country to send two young monks to study the "freedoms and rights theories of our times" in the new school. On April 10, the school was named Myŏngjin hakkyo (School of the Advancement in Enlightenment), which could easily be associated with Meiji, literally meaning "enlightened rule," and on May 8, it opened its doors. A new epoch of modern Buddhist education, molded along Japanese lines, began.

How were the studies organized in this new Buddhist school? Originally, the length of the course was set at two years, but it was extended to three years beginning in 1909. Thirty-five monks whose ages ranged from thirteen to thirty were selected as the first students to learn Japanese, the basics of sports, world history, and biology, in addition to the traditional Buddhist subjects. The monks followed a standard modern curriculum arranged along the Japanese lines, with two semesters a year, vacations, and a uniform dress code. When a monk graduated, his employment in a traditional monastic teaching institution (K. *kangwŏn*) was usually arranged, and the constant stream of Myŏngjin graduates was considered to be an important tool for the modernization and "Japanization" of Korea's provincial monastic educational system. One graduate of the school was Kim Yŏngsu (1884–1967; monastic name: P'ogwang), one of the leading Buddhist historians and theoreticians of the colonial time. He recalled that the school was basically geared to giving promising young monks beginner's training in modern subjects through courses constructed by Meiji Japanese Buddhists. Interestingly enough, one of the most important subjects was land surveying and measurement techniques. Buddhist temples were beset with greedy officials and local worthies watching for an opportunity to enrich themselves at the expense of monastic landholdings, so they needed well-qualified land surveyors who were able to advocate their causes in courts. Guest speakers were a regular feature of the school, and among them was such leading figure of pro-Japanese modernizing elite as Yun Hyojŏng (1858–1939), a prominent leader of various progressive societies of the 1900s.[64] Myŏngjin School, headed in 1906–1907 by one of the principal Buddhist activists of the period, Hong Wŏlch'o (1858–1934), had some of the most prominent Buddhist reformers, such as Han Yongun (Manhae; 1879–1944) and Kwŏn Sangno (1879–1965), among its first graduates.

Han Yongun was in charge of the land-surveying course beginning on December 10, 1908, and was known for his enthusiasm for this rather mundane pursuit. Wŏlch'o himself was among the first to profit from the newly-acquired expertise in land surveying: He was able to win a court case in autumn 1908, defeating those who wished to deprive his Suguksa temple (established in 1900 in Koyang county, Kyŏnggi province) of its land. On June 25, 1907, control over the school had been assumed by Yi Hoegwang (1862–1933), a monk of explicitly pro-Japanese political orientation, and the school was exposed to nationalist criticism. Renamed the Buddhist Pedagogical Institute (Pulgyo Sabŏm Hakkyo) in April 1910, the school eventually became the Buddhist Dongguk (Tongguk) University, the main center of Buddhist education and research in South Korea today.[65]

After Myŏngjin School had pioneered the way, modern Buddhist schools mushroomed in all corners of the country, showing evidence that the view of Christian nationalists about the incompatibility of Buddhism and civilization was misleading. The nationalist press was obliged to report on Buddhist progress in enlightenment. For example, *Taehan Maeil Sinbo* (Korean Daily News; founded on July 18, 1904) reported on November 27, 1906, on the establishment of one of the first provincial Buddhist schools: "In Yongjusa temple near Suwŏn, a monastic school named *Myŏnghwa* (Enlightened Changes) was established with more than 50 students. [. . .] A Japanese named Kimura Tanpaku was appointed as the Japanese language instructor [. . .]."[66] Teaching Japanese to Koreans was a ubiquitous sign of modernity in the 1900s, and admiration of the Meiji experience in Buddhist circles was especially visible. Some of the newly established provincial schools were run cooperatively by a Korean temple and a Japanese sect. For example, the T'ongdosa's Myŏngjin School was administered by the temple and the Jōdo sect. The following laudatory report was published December 21, 1906:

> Abbot of Sŏgwangsa temple in Anbyŏn county, Southern Hamgyŏng province, Kim Sŏgong [. . .], turned his attention towards reforms and progress, and, in order to educate the younger monks in the province's temples, established a branch of Myŏngjin School in his temple. He employed a Japanese teacher and shows diligence in the educational matters. In our country too, the monks are advancing forward![67]

That monks were "advancing forward" in Meiji Japan was hardly news to the contemporary Korean readership, but the fact that their Korean admirers were diligently following the same methods was clearly deemed newsworthy and praiseworthy. An even stronger appreciation of the monks' self-reforming efforts is shown in *Taehan Maeil Sinbo*'s report on a school called Kyŏnghŭng hakkyo that was launched in Mun'gyŏng through the cooperative efforts of several local temples on January 10, 1907:

> Abbots of several Northern Kyŏngsang province temples, including Kwŏn Hwaŭng from Taesŭngsa and Kim Wŏlhyŏn from Kimnyongsa in Mun'gyŏng, Kim Ch'wisŏn from Namjangsa in Sangju, Yun P'oun from Yongmunsa in Yech'ŏn, Kim Tamhwa from Kwanghŭngsa in

> Andong have been practicing compassionate deeds and aspiring to perfect themselves for quite a long time already. They turned their attention to the differences between today's epochal demands and those of the past and showed their enthusiasm for the new learning. In order to develop the education of younger monks, they established, by the common efforts of the temples from eight local counties, Kyŏnghŭng School in Taesŭngsa temple and made it a branch school of Myŏngjin School, which lies outside Seoul's Great Eastern Gate. There are numerous reports that they employ teachers and recruit students now. Indeed, the torch of Korean Buddhist wisdom, once extinguished, is kindled once again! Everybody praises it.[68]

As we can see, the Japanese model, advice, and tutelage inspired Korean monks to pursue their own agenda of modernization, and with visible success. By 1910, most major provincial temples possessed their own "new learning" schools. Some of the most ambitious graduates of these schools, who were capable of speaking Japanese and willing and able to continue their studies in Japan, soon formed the new intellectual core of Korea's changing Buddhist community. The foundations of the early colonial Buddhist discourse that began in 1910 and largely identified modernity and progress with Japanization were laid during the brief but eventful period of 1906–1910 when Korea's modern Buddhist education came into being.

Buddhist efforts to come to terms with modern education, however tinged with the emulation of Meiji models, are mostly praised by today's South Korean historians, almost in the same way they were lauded by the nationalist press a century earlier. However, Japanese influence that penetrated the Korean monastic community, namely Japanese involvement in the temple administration and pan-national Buddhist organizations, is condemned by the same historians. Such condemnation is understandable, as the Japanese missionary efforts to take control of Korean Buddhist organizations were undeniably a part of the colonizing process as a whole, in the same way Western Protestant activities in the Middle Eastern Arabic Christian communities in the nineteenth and early twentieth centuries were indisputably connected to the imperialistic plans of European powers. However, from a contemporary Korean Buddhist perspective, Japanese organizational penetration did have another side as well. Many monks simply did not know any other method to defend their property against the rapacity of the corrupt local officials, and others sincerely believed, very much in the spirit of the 1900s enlightenment movement, that the enlightened foreign tutelage would usher them into a brighter future.

The Korean state's attempts to build an administrative network that would protect and control the religion were mostly short-lived and unsuccessful. In 1902, for example, the State Bureau of Temples (K. *sasa kwallisŏ*) was set up with one national head temple (Wŏnhŭngsa near the Great Eastern Gate in Seoul, soon to be used as the seat of the Myŏngjin School) and sixteen provincial head temples were officially designated, but the system proved ineffective and was abolished in two years. In the meantime, cases of infringement against temples and their property were constantly on the rise. In February 1906, several temples in the Diamond Mountains (Kŭmgangsan) suffered from the encroachment of mine developers, and in February of the next year, the governor of Northern P'yŏngan province deprived Myohyangsa temple of its paddies under the pretext of returning them to the state. At the same time, Kŏnbongsa became a site of heated battles between Japanese troops and Confucian Righteous Army guerillas and suffered great losses.[69] In the atmosphere of chronic lawlessness and fear, an increasing number of temples quite understandably attempted to formalize their ties with Japanese Buddhist sects in the hope that such an arrangement would prevent future intrusions.

As soon as the Japanese Resident-General allowed Japanese Buddhist sects to assume trusteeship over Korean temples in November 1906, his office was flooded with applications. The Amitaist Ōtani sect, a keen rival of the Shin sect that had begun a missionary enterprise in Korea, succeeded in getting permission to assume the trusteeship over four temples, including Chikchisa temple in Kimch'ŏn county, Northern Kyŏngsang province. However, its applications to administer other temples, such as the land-rich Pŏmŏsa, were turned down, obviously because there was a concern about a possible nationalist reaction. Statistics on the number of applications for trusteeship by other Japanese sects are hard to find, but some sources claim that more than 100 Korean temples attempted to find a Japanese protector. Applications were made with the understanding that the Korean applicants were going to follow the doctrine and ritual of the Japanese protector sects, but Japanese administrators evidently had no illusions concerning the motives of the Koreans who turned to their Japanese colleagues for help. Takahashi Tōru (1878–1967), a famous scholar who was an official intimately involved in the religious policies of the Japanese administration, confidently maintained that Korean monks appealed for trusteeship in order to (1) protect their property from the rapacity of the officialdom and Confucian gentry, and (2) ensure Japanese army protection against foraging and pillage by the Confucian Righteous Army guerillas.[70] Whatever the underlying reasons were, the visible enthusiasm the Korean abbots showed for joining the Japanese sects stimulated Japanese missionaries to go even further. They started planning a wholesale alliance between Korean Buddhism as a whole and one of the Japanese sects involved in missionary undertakings. The main obstacle they envisioned was not Korean resistance but the unsolvable and potentially disastrous inflammable issue of what sect would ultimately get the immense trophy.

On March 6, 1908, Yi Hoegwang, one of the highest authorities in doctrinal Buddhism at that time, a person who was unofficially known as a "great doctrinal preacher" (K. *taekangbaek*) and acting director of Myŏngjin School, was elected as the spiritual head (K. *taejongjŏng*) of the newly created Wŏnjong (Complete Order) Order by 52 representatives of the main Korean temples. The name Wŏnjong refers to the Buddhist doctrine of complete, harmonious, non-obstructive totality (K. *wŏnyung muae*). The Wŏnjong Order was supposed to become Korea's first pan-national Buddhist association with the mission to implement civilization and a progressive agenda in the Buddhist community and protect the interests of the temples. Wŏnhŭngsa, the site of Myŏngjin School and the symbol of Korean Buddhist modernization, was chosen as its headquarters. The Buddhist Study Society was dissolved so that its activists could continue their service in the new organization. The formation of Wŏnjong was given mostly positive publicity, seen as one more progressive step in Korea's religious community, but what surprised some contemporaries was Yi Hoegwang's choice of Japanese advisor for the new organization. That choice was Takeda Hanshi (1863–1911), a Sōtō sect priest, who made his first Korean trip in 1890, but not as a missionary. Takeda Hanshi was at that point a free-wheeling nationalist activist (K. *chisa*; J. *shishi*), aspiring to make a contribution to Japan's continental expansion. After that, as a member of Gen'yōsha, a Pan-Asianist and extremely nationalist organization, he was part of Japanese intelligence efforts during the troublesome years of 1894–1895 and was tarnished by his participation in, among other adventures, the brutal assassination of Korea's Queen Min (Empress Myŏngsŏng) in late 1895.[71] Takeda was also an advisor to the strongly pro-Japanese Ilchinhwoe, established in November 1905, and a personal friend of its leader Yi Yonggu (1868–1912). The fact that he was chosen to advise the newly established Korean Buddhist order Wŏnjong meant that it would be politicized, and not in the way the Korean nationalist press and even a significant portion of the monks would wish.

Suspicions aroused by Takeda's appointment were soon strengthened. Aptly utilizing some minor incidents that occurred between Amitaist Shin and Jōdo missionaries and Korean monks, Takeda successfully persuaded Yi Hoegwang and his closest aides that only Sōtō Zen School could provide a really congenial protectorate for Korean Buddhism, which had been historically focused on meditation rather than the Amitaist faith. As Korea's annexation was officially declared in August 1910, new allies started to realize their plans. In October, Yi Hoegwang crossed into Japan and began negotiations with the head of the Sōtō sect, Ishikawa Sodō, which resulted in the two men forging an agreement that was marginally better for the Korean side than the original draft presented by the Sōtō sect. The agreement, which stipulated that the Wŏnjong was to be advised by the Japanese and to provide everything necessary for the Japanese to proselytize in Korea, was signed on October 6, 1910. The incident generated protests by some of the young Buddhist progressives involved in Wŏnhŭngsa affairs. On the surface, their reasons for protesting were purely doctrinal. The Korean Sŏn School was proud of its Linji (d. 866) and its Mazu (709–788) *dharma* lineage, whereas the Sōtō lineage derived from the Caotong school, which belonged to the rival Shitou (700–790) line. Because no nationalistic arguments surfaced, the Japanese administration had no reasons to suppress this Buddhist anti-Yi Hoegwang protest movement, and in the end assumed a compromising posture. The protestors realized that the agreement practically reduced Korean monks to the unenviable role of being local aides for the Sōtō sect's proselytizing efforts and deprived Buddhism in Korea of the last vestiges of any national or traditional legitimacy. Protestors built their own alternative Imjejong (Linji Order) as a Korean pan-national Buddhist organization and eventually obtained some success, albeit partial. The Japanese Government-General refused to recognize the agreement and issued its own "Decree on Temple [Administration]" (June 3, 1911), which laid the foundation for direct control of the colonial administration over Buddhist affairs. Disillusioned, Takeda died in oblivion the same year. Meanwhile, Yi Hoegwang remained popular and influential enough to be appointed as abbot of Haeinsa, one of the biggest temples in the country.[72] One of the most ambitious plans of the Japanese Buddhist missionaries in Korea failed, but it did leave its imprint on early colonial Buddhist community. The Sōtō sect remained an important model for Korean colonial Buddhists as a source of modern education, doctrinal and ritual materials, and inspiration.

All in all, the Japanese Buddhism during the period of 1876–1910, through its active and largely successful missionary undertakings, did become Korean Buddhists' "significant other." By 1910, Japanese Buddhism was the yardstick by which Korean Buddhists began to measure themselves; it was the model many chose to follow when it came to the educational and social activities of the modern kind; and it was the unchallenged supplier of modern education and knowledge for Korea's Buddhist circles. Japanese Buddhism succeeded in leading Korea's activist monks into identifying it with "Buddhist modernity" and believing that, for Buddhists, the ways of Meiji were those of progress and civilization. The tendency to design Korea's modernity along the line of Meiji experience, which was quite strong in Korea's early modern enlightenment discourse in general, reached its peak inside the Buddhist community. The fledgling nationalist aspirations of the 1900s were not totally alien to Buddhism but certainly were secondary to the mainstream belief in the worth of Meiji enlightenment. The subjunctive mood is hardly of any use in historical studies, but even if Korea would not have been fully colonized by Japan, Japanese influence on Korean Buddhist developments could have been crucial anyway, judging from the degree to which Korean Buddhism was already influenced by the Japanese missionary undertakings before 1910.

Notes

1. A version of this paper appeared in *International Journal of Buddhist Thought & Culture* 4 (February 2004): 7-49.

2. Han Kidu, "Chosŏn hugi sŏn Pulgyo ŭi hŭrŭm" (The Currents in Sŏn/Zen Buddhism in Late Chosŏn Period), *Sŏn kwa tongbang munhwa* (Chan and Oriental Culture) (Seoul: Korean Association for Buddhist Academic Exchanges, 1994), 243–262.

3. Yu Yŏngik, *Han'guk kŭnhyŏndae sa ron* (On Modern and Contemporary Korean History) (Seoul: Ilchogak, 1992), pp. 92–93.

4. Hwang Sŏnmyŏng, *Chosŏnjo chonggyo sahoe sa yŏn'gu* (The Research on Religious and Social History of the Chosŏn Dynasty) (Seoul: Ilchisa, 1992), p. 321.

5. Sŏnu Toryang Han'guk Pulgyo kŭnhyŏndaesa yŏn'guhoe, ed., *Sinmun ŭro pon Han'guk Pulgyo kŭnhyŏndaesa* (The Modern and Contemporary History of Korean Buddhism Seen through Newspapers) (Seoul: Sŏnu Toryang ch'ulp'anbu, 1999), pp. 529–530.

6. Sŏnu Toryang Han'guk Pulgyo kŭnhyŏndaesa yŏn'guhoe, ed., *Sinmun-ŭro pon Han'guk Pulgyo kŭnhyŏndaesa*, p. 533.

7. Hŏ Tonghyŏn, "1881 nyŏn chosa sich'aldan ŭi hwaldong e kwanhan yŏn'gu" (A Study of the Activities of the Courtiers' Observation Mission of 1881), *Kuksagwan nonch'ong* (The Journal of the National History [Compilation] Committee), vol. 66 (1995), 27–41.

8. Closely paralleling is the Western use of Christian missionaries in colonial undertakings; see Ch'oe Pyŏnghŏn, "Ilche Pulgyo ŭi ch'imt'u wa singminji Pulgyo ŭi sŏnggyŏk" (The Penetration of Japanese Imperial Buddhism and the Character of the Colonial Buddhism), *Chesamch'a hwant'aep'ŏngyang han'gukhak kukche hoeŭi. Han'gukhak nonch'ong* (Seoul: Organizing Committee of the 3rd Pacific and Asia Conference on Korean Studies, 1996), pp. 97–98.

9. Brian Victoria, *Zen at War* (New York: Weatherhill, 1997), pp. 16–17.

10. Chŏng Kwangho, *Kŭndae Hanil Pulgyo kwan'gyesa yŏn'gu* (A Study of the History of Korean-Japanese Buddhist Relations in Modern Times) (Inch'ŏn, Korea: Inha taehakkyo ch'ulp'anbu, 1994), p. 94.

11. Higashi Honganji Administration, ed., "Chōsen kaikyō gojūnen shi" (The Records of 50 Years [after] Commencing Mission to Korea, 1927), *Ilbon Pulgyo kaegyo charyo* (Materials on the Commencement of Japanese Buddhist Mission in Korea), in *Han'guk kŭnhyŏndae Pulgyo charyo chŏnjip,* vol. 62 (Seoul: Minjoksa, 1996), pp. 235–236.

12. Higashi Honganji Administration, ed., "Chōsen kaikyō gojūnen shi," p. 324.

13. Han Sŏkhŭi, *Ilche ŭi chonggyo ch'imnyak sa* (The History of Japanese Aggression in Religious Sphere) (Seoul: Kidokkyomunsa, 1990), p. 29.

14. Im Chongguk, "Ch'ogi chonggyo ch'imnyak kwa ch'inilp'a" (The Early Stage of Religious Aggression and Pro-Japanese Group), *Inmulgye* 64 (1989), p. 153.

15. Okumura Enshin, "Chōsen koku fukyō nisshi" (Diary of the Prozelytizatiaon of Korea, 1897), *Ilbon Pulgyo kaegyo charyo,* in *Han'guk kŭnhyŏndae Pulgyo charyo chŏnjip*, vol. 62, p. 402.

16. Vladimir Tikhonov, "The First Stages of Yi Tongin's Career (1878–1880): The forerunner of dependent development?" *Sunggyun Journal of East Asian Studies* 2, no. 1 (2002): 210–233, pp. 215–216.

17. Okumura, "Chōsen koku fukyō nisshi," pp. 403–404.

18. Information on Song can be found in Kuzuu Yoshihisa, ed., *Tōa senkaku shishi kiden* (Stories and Biographies of Pioneer Eastern Asian Adventurers) (Tokyo: Hara Shobō, 1935–1938), pp. 317–318.

19. Yi Kwangnin, *Kaehwadang yŏn'gu* (Research on the [Late Chosŏn] Enlightenment Movement) (Seoul: Ilchogak, 1973), pp. 22–23.

20. The excerpts from the papers of E. Satow related to Yi Tongin (mostly letters to W. G. Aston, then British Consul in Kobe) are published under the title "Yi Tongin e kwanhan Satow ŭi munsŏ" in *Sahak yŏn'gu* 31: 121–135. Originals are kept in the PRO (London), ser. 30–33 (the letters to W. G. Aston: P.R.O.302, 3).

21. Han'guk hak munhŏn yŏn'guso, ed., *Pak Kyusu chŏnjip* (Complete Works of Pak Kyusu) (Seoul: Asea munhwasa, 1978), vol. 2, pp. 558–559.

22. Yi Nŭnghwa, *Chosŏn Pulgyo t'ongsa* (A Comprehensive History of Korean Buddhism), (Seoul, 1917), vol. 2, p. 899.

23. Hwagyesa was known in the late 19th century as a temple closely connected to the royal family. Its Myŏngbujŏn (The Underworld Pavilion, the pavilion dedicated to the "10 kings of the underworld") possesses a calligraphic hanging board by Kojong's father, Taewŏn'gun (1820–1898) and the mineral springs in the temple area are famous as the place favored by Taewŏn'gun for his rest. Taewŏn'gun was also known as one of the sponsors of the temple's reparation in 1866; other sponsors included Queen Dowager Cho of the mighty P'ungyang Cho clan. See Seoul t'ŭkpyŏlsi, ed., *Hwagyesa: Silch'ŭk chosa pogosŏ* (Hwagyesa: Survey Report) (Seoul: Seoul t'ŭkpyŏlsi, 1988), pp. 47–53. Hwagyesa's prominence in court life evidently made the temple a favored destination for the elite reformers, who reportedly used to visit it, primarily for rest and recreation. One of Kim Okkyun's youthful followers, Ch'a Hongsik (1866–1884), later executed for his part in the abortive Kapsin Coup, was said to have originally been a Hwagyesa monk who met Kim when the latter came to rest in the temple for ten days. On having become Kim's personal servant and follower, Ch'a even followed him during his trips to Japan, serving as a cook. See: *Ch'uan kŭp Kugan* (Investigation and Trial Documents, 1601–1892) (Seoul: Asea munhwasa, 1978), p. 604.

Thus, it seems quite probable that the first meeting between Kim Okkyun and Yi Tongin could have taken place in Hwagyesa during one of the former's trips there.

24. Tikhonov, "The First Stages of Yi Tongin's Career (1878–1880)," p. 222.

25. "Kōakai hokoku," vol. 4 (May 14, 1880) in Yi Kwangnin, *Han'guk kaehwa sa ŭi chemunje* (The Issues in Korean Enlightenment History) (Seoul: Ilchogak, 1986), pp. 3–14.

26. On the role of Pan-Asianism in the history of modern Korean thought, see: Yi Kwangnin, "Kaehwagi ŭi han'gugin ŭi Asia yŏndae ron" (Korean Views on Asian Solidarity in the Enlightenment Period). *Kaehwap'a wa kaehwa sasang yŏn'gu* (Studies on Enlightenment Movement and Enlightenment Thought) (Seoul: Ilchogak, 1989), pp. 138–155.

27. Kim Tot'ae, *Sŏ Chaep'il paksa chasŏjŏn* (Autobiography of Dr. Sŏ Chaep'il) (Seoul: Posŏnsa, 1948), p. 60–64.

28. Satow's letter dated July 19, 1880.

29. The letters are currently in Kim Ŭihwan's private collection (Han Sŏkhŭi, trans., *Ilche-ŭi chonggyo ch'imnyak sa*, p. 45).

30. Han, *Ilche-ŭi chonggyo ch'imnyak sa*, pp. 46–47.

31. Satow's papers, May 20, 1880.

32. Satow's papers, May 15, 1880.

33. Satow's papers, May 15, 1880.

34. Chŏng Kwangho, *Han'guk Pulgyo ch'oegŭn paengnyŏnsa p'yŏnnyŏn* (Chronological History of the Latest One Hundred Years of Korean Buddhism) (Inch'ŏn, Korea: Inha taehakkyo ch'ulp'anbu, 1999), p. 139.

35. Chŏng, *Han'guk Pulgyo ch'oegŭn paengnyŏnsa p'yŏnnyŏn*, pp. 376, 396.

36. Chŏng, *Kŭndae Hanil Pulgyo kwan'gyesa yŏn'gu*, p. 23.

37. Chŏng, *Han'guk Pulgyo ch'oegŭn paengnyŏnsa p'yŏnnyŏn*, p. 4.

38. Okumura, "Chōsen koku fukyō nisshi," pp. 433–434.

39. Some popular authors of the colonial period tended to consider Yi's sudden disappearance an assassination by the conservative officials.

40. Okumura, "Chōsen koku fukyō nisshi," p. 410.

41. Okumura, "Chōsen koku fukyō nisshi," p. 421.

42. Yi Kwangnin, "T'ak Chŏngsik ron" (On T'ak Chŏngsik), *Kaehwagi yŏn'gu* (Study on the Reform Movement Period) (Seoul: Ilchogak, 1994), pp. 69–83.

43. Kim Okkyun, *Kapsin Illok* (The Diary of Kapsin [Coup], 1885) (Seoul: Kŏn'guk taehakkyo ch'ulp'anbu, 1977), p. 78.

44. Kwŏn Sangno, *Chosŏn Pulgyo yaksa* (A Brief History of Korean Buddhism) (Seoul, 1917), p. 249.

45. Ignatovich, A. N., Svetlov, G. E., Ignatovich, A. N., Svetlov, G. E., *Lotos i politika* (The Lotus and the Politics) (Moscow: Mysl', 1989), p. 139.

46. On Arai's activities, see also James Edward Ketelaar, *Of Heretics and Martyrs in Meiji Japan: Buddhism and its Persecution* (Princeton, NJ: Princeton University Press, 1990), pp. 174–191.

47. Chŏng, *Kŭndae Hanil Pulgyo kwan'gyesa yŏn'gu*, p. 55.

48. Higashi Honganji Administration, "Chōsen kaikyō gojūnen shi," pp. 214–218.

49. Pak Kyŏnghun, "Buddhism in Modern Korea," *Korea Journal* 21, no. 8 (1981): 32–40, p. 34.

50. Chŏng, *Kŭndae Hanil Pulgyo kwan'gyesa yŏn'gu*, p. 59. Afterwards, in February 1912, Ch'oe Ch'wihŏ contributed quite an adulatory description of Japanese Government-General's activities in Korea to the first issue of *Chosŏn Pulgyo wŏl'bo* (Korean Buddhist Monthly). He wrote that the Governor-General's "bright policy" was to "revitalize our land, politics, livelihood, and ethics," and especially to "benefit our religion, downtrodden for centuries." See *Chosŏn Pulgyo wŏl'bo* [1912], *Han'guk kŭnhyŏndae Pulgyo charyo chŏnjip*, vol. 1, pp. 38–39. Ch'oe Ch'wihŏ is also credited with authorship of one of the well-known Buddhist didactic songs of the early modern times, *Kwiilga* (The Song of Revert to the Oneness), where early modern ideas of "national duty" of "raising the country through promotion of scholarship and enterprise" are ultimately subjected to the "oneness" of Buddhist ideals. See Im Kijung, *Pulgyo kasa wŏnjŏn yŏn'gu* (A Study on the Originals of Buddhist Lyrics) (Seoul: Tongguk taehakkyo ch'ulp'anbu, 2000), pp. 1041–1042. Ch'oe Ch'wihŏ's readiness to accept the Meiji version of modernity as the most favorable for the fortunes of Korean Buddhists seems to be rather typical of the educated activist monks of the period.

51. That is how Im Hyebong appraises it in his popular review (Im, *Pulgyo kasa wŏnjŏn yŏn'gu*, pp. 62-63).

52. On the early nationalism of the 1890s, see, for example, Vipan Chandra, "Sentiment and Ideology in the Nationalism of the Independence Club (1896–1898)," *Korean Studies* 10 (1986): 13–34.

53. Editorial, Korean edition, May 7, 1896, in Sŏnu Toryang Han'guk Pulgyo kŭnhyŏndaesa yŏn'guhoe, *Sinmun ŭro pon Han'guk Pulgyo kŭnhyŏndaes*, vol. 2, pp. 61–62.

54. Editorial, Korean edition, January 26, 1897, in Sŏnu Toryang Han'guk Pulgyo kŭnhyŏndaesa yŏn'guhoe, *Sinmun ŭro pon Han'guk pulgyo kŭnhyŏndaes,* vol. 2, pp. 63–64.

55. Sŏnu Toryang Han'guk Pulgyo kŭnhyŏndaesa yŏn'guhoe, *Sinmun ŭro pon Han'guk pulgyo kŭnhyŏndaes,* vol. 2, p. 100.

56. Notto Thelle, *Buddhism and Christianity in Japan: from Conflict to Dialogue* (Honolulu: University of Hawai'i Press, 1987), pp. 194–214.

57. In 1898, he established Kokoku-ji (K. Hoguksa [Temple for the Protection of the State]) in Seoul. See Chŏng, *Han'guk Pulgyo ch'oegŭn paengnyŏnsa p'yŏnnyŏn,* p. 190.

58. Katō Bunkyō, "Chōsen kaikyō ron" (On Commencing the Preaching in Korea, 1900), in *Han'guk kŭnhyŏndae Pulgyo charyo chŏnjip,* vol. 62, pp. 485–486.

59. See Korean translation of *Opisanie Korei* (1900) (Russian Ministry of Finances, 1984, pp. 383–387).

60. On the growth of anti-Russian mood and cautious attitude toward other "European" (German, American) activities in Korea in the Japanese military milieu of the later 1890s–early 1900s, see Moriyama Shigenori, *Kŭndae Hanil kwan'gye sa yŏn'gu* (Research on the History of Modern Korean-Japanese relationship 1987), trans. Kim Semin (Seoul: Hyŏnŭmsa, 1994), pp. 74–85.

61. Higashi Honganji Administration, ed., "Chōsen kaikyō gojūnen shi," p. 242.

62. Shin sect monks saved his life in 1882, helping him to flee to Japan during the *Imo* Soldiers' Mutiny.

63. Higashi Honganji Administration, ed., "Chōsen kaikyō gojūnen shi," pp. 243–246, 252.

64. Chŏng Yŏnghŭi, *Kaehwagi chonggyogye ŭi kyoyuk yŏn'gu* (Study of Religious Education of the Early Modern Reform Period) (Seoul: Hyean, 1999), pp. 117–120.

65. Chŏng, *Kaehwagi chonggyogye ŭi kyoyuk yŏn'gu,* p. 123.

66. Sŏnu Toryang Han'guk Pulgyo kŭnhyŏndaesa yŏn'guhoe, *Sinmun ŭro pon Han'guk Pulgyo kŭnhyŏndaesa,* vol. 2, p. 141.

67. Sŏnu Toryang Han'guk Pulgyo kŭnhyŏndaesa yŏn'guhoe, *Sinmun ŭro pon Han'guk Pulgyo kŭnhyŏndaesa,* vol. 2, p. 141.

68. Sŏnu Toryang Han'guk Pulgyo kŭnhyŏndaesa yŏn'guhoe, *Sinmun ŭro pon Han'guk Pulgyo kŭnhyŏndaesa,* vol. 2, p. 143.

69. Chŏng, *Kŭndae Hanil Pulgyo kwan'gyesa yŏn'gu,* pp. 146–147.

70. Takahashi Tōru, *Richō Bukkyō* (Osaka: Osaka Hōbunkan, 1929), p. 919.

71. Nam-lin Hur, "The Sōtō Sect and Japanese Military Imperialism in Korea," *Japanese Journal of Religious Studies* 26 (1999): 107–134.

72. Pak Kyŏnghun, et al., *Kŭndae Han'guk Pulgyo saron* (On the History of Modern Korean Buddhism) (Seoul: Minjoksa, 1992), pp. 103–118.

12

Minjung Buddhism

A Buddhist Critique of the Status Quo—Its History, Philosophy, and Critique

John Jorgensen

History

In the dawn of October 27, 1980, the peace of the Buddhist headquarters and over three thousand monasteries throughout South Korea was broken at 6.00 a.m. by the forced entry of martial law troops. They arrested conservative leaders and abbots, fifty-five monks in all, investigated ninety-eight others, and detained ten monks and eight laymen. This operation continued over four days. Some of those arrested were severely tortured and a few died. The abbot of Naksan Sa, Wŏnch'ŏl, died under the torture.[1] The reasons for this outrage, announced by the martial law authorities, were that they were "purifying" Buddhism by removing communists, hooligans, draft dodgers and plotters of factional discord, and that they were purging dissolute or "fake" monks, and confiscating ill-gotten funds from rituals and magic that were being used for private benefit or to fund campaigns to be appointed abbot. Under torture, some of the monks "revealed" that they had hoarded illegal funds of well over two trillion *wŏn*, but no charges were laid and the money was never returned. Some of the monks were also sent away for reeducation. The reputation of Buddhism was besmirched; it was labeled a hotbed of lawbreakers. Negative reports were placed in the compliant press around November 14 and 15, after the interrogations and searches had been completed.

The explanations for what Buddhists called the 10.27 or Kyŏngsin Persecution have been that it was an extension into Buddhism of the "social cleansing" that the military regime of Chun Doo-hwan (Chŏn Tuhwan) began after the May 17–18 Kwangju Massacre. This involved the arrest of political and labor leaders; the purge of bureaucrats, teachers, and above all, journalists; and the rounding up of beggars, gamblers, and prostitutes in August 1980, as many as forty-thousand people, who were arrested and imprisoned in forced labor camps for "reeducation" called the Samch'ŏng Education Brigades.[2] Some of the arrested Buddhists also ended up in these camps. A second theory was that the persecution was used to control and eliminate political activities by the religion, and to make Buddhism return to its former role of supporter of the state. Buddhism was singled out because it was a soft target, having no foreign constituency like the Catholics or Protestants, and because it had newly created a general administration for the Chogye Order, which had hoped to form an autonomous administration and so had not actively cooperated with the new military regime. The Secretary-General, Song Wŏlju, had been elected in the brief freedom of the interregnum between the assassination of the former dictator, Park Jung-hee (Pak Chŏnghŭi), and the coup d'état of Chun Doo-hwan (Chŏn Tuhwan). Moreover, there had been some disputes within the Order, all of which provided an excuse for intervention.[3] Others think the reason was to expropriate Buddhist property, for the Chogye Order had requested the abolition of the 1961 Buddhist Property Control Law, and this appropriation would be made easier by accusing the Order of corruption and concealment of wealth. The confiscated property could then be used to set up Chun's political party, the Minjŏng Tang (Democratic Justice Party). Perhaps, though, the real motivation was to divert attention away from the Kwangju Uprising.[4]

This persecution roused the Buddhist world from its lethargy and almost unconditional support of the military regimes through "state protection Buddhism" (K. *ho'guk Pulgyo*), for even conservatives had been arrested, interrogated, and tortured. Above all, it stimulated a radicalization of young monks and the Buddhist laity (I have seen nothing on the role of Buddhist nuns), and precipitated the scattered critics and students into a new movement that has been labeled Minjung Buddhism. It promoted an anti-Western sentiment, the feeling that the Presbyterian Chun Doo-hwan and right-wing Christians financed by U.S. sources had contributed to the persecution of Buddhism, and this was allied to the widespread, and not altogether unbelievable supposition, that U.S. military authorities had been complicit in the Kwangju Massacre. This feeling was extended into suspicion of the progressive, engaged Christian groups, who also had foreign support.[5] Ironically, Chun, after his resignation in 1988, retired with his wife into a Buddhist monastery, Paekdam Sa, with the protection of his successor, Roh Tae Woo (Nŏ T'aeu). Minjung Buddhists reacted to aggressive Christian proselytization by pastors who claimed Buddhism had no paradise, on the grounds of the distortion of Buddhist doctrine, that it violated ecumenical dialogue, and distracted from the task of national reunification. "The nation (K. *minjok*) must transcend religion."[6]

A *hwadu* (C. *huatou*), a topic of meditation, was made from the persecution, and demands were raised for an explanation of the events and punishments for the perpetrators, while young Buddhists questioned the relationship of the state and Buddhist Order that had been called "state-protection Buddhism." Even more, they called on people to be aware of the current circumstances and to work for Buddhist independence. This produced anti-government, pro-democracy, and anti-American attitudes.[7]

The military authorities were, however, not totally incorrect in their assumption about corruption and dissidents in the Buddhist Order. After all, corruption was a major criticism made of established Buddhism by the Minjung Buddhists, and several former student activists may have been hiding in the monasteries. A suspect could have been Yŏ Ikku (1946–), a student of Dongguk University (the main Buddhist university), who in 1974 was sentenced to fifteen years in prison for involvement in the "Democratic Student Alliance incident," but was released on an amnesty in 1975, and became a monk. However, by 1979, he had returned to the laity. Yet he was certainly involved with the Han'guk Taehaksaeng Pulgyo Yŏnhaphoe (National Federation for Buddhist Associations of Universities and Colleges) (hereafter University Buddhist Association), which had been the first group to sponsor the idea of Minjung Buddhism.[8]

Despite the overwhelming support by the Buddhist establishment for the regime of Park Jung-hee (r. 1962–1979), who made a public show of his protection of Buddhism by sponsoring the reconstruction of Buddhist sites such as Pulguk Sa in Kyŏngju and writing out name plaques for monasteries in his own calligraphy,[9] there were some dissident voices among Buddhists. One such example was Pŏpchŏng (1935–), a monk of Songgwang Sa, whose sermons and writings contained critical messages. The government silenced him and placed him under house arrest in a small hermitage,[10] because he had been the lone voice of Buddhism at the 1975 Citizens Conference for the Restoration of Democracy (Minju Hoebok Kungmin Hoeŭi).[11] Notably, Pŏpchŏng was allocated the study and teaching of early Buddhism in the Haein Ch'ongnim, that is, Haein Sa,[12] and the doctrines of early Buddhism were a prime inspiration and basis for Minjung Buddhism.

Before the persecution, some Buddhist intellectuals were interested in the *minjung* theme, which had been used to interpret the Tonghak Rebellion and the Christian mission in Korea. *Minjung* were the people who were the subject of history, the oppressed who resist in a utopian hope, and part of the nationalist struggle.[13] Minjung ideology entered into Christianity as Minjung Theology in the mid-1970s,[14] and into Buddhism, possibly through the 1910 *Pulgyo Yusin non* (On the Restoration of Buddhism) by Han Yongun (1879–1944). The University

Buddhist Association, in their criticism of established Buddhism, held a conference at Songgwang Sa in 1976 on Minjung Buddhism at which a paper, "Minjung Pulgyo ron" was delivered by Chŏn Ch'aesŏng. The point of the paper was to make Buddhism a *minjung* Buddhism, in which Buddhism served the oppressed and liberated them, but the paper contained no concrete proposals beyond the appeal to the compassion of the bodhisattva. Following the publication of this paper, in 1978 a Minjung Buddhism Research Society was formed, but this remained the domain of a few young laymen and not the monks.[15]

The millenarian or utopian aspect was found in the linkage of Maitreya with *minjung* aspirations, as was done by the monk poet, Ko Ŭn (1933–), who had been an abbot and was active in campaigns for human rights and democracy, and wrote a biography of Han Yongun. Ko wrote that Amitabha was the promise of paradise (Pure Land) after death, and so was a tool of the oppressors who used such false promises to lull the oppressed into passivity and resignation, whereas Maitreya promised a realizable paradise on earth.[16] Yŏ Ikku also published a book on the Maitreya scriptures, *Mirŭkkyŏng ŭi se'gye*,[17] in 1980, the same year Han Chongman, the editor, published a series of essays beginning with those by Han Yongun, titled *Han'guk kŭndae minjung Pulgyo ŭi i'nyŏm kwa chŏn'gae* (The Concepts and Development of Modern Korean Minjung Buddhism).[18] Although largely a series of essays on reformist movements, the final essay by P'yo Ilcho, "Mirŭk sin'ang kwa Minjung Pulgyo" (Maitreya Faith and Minjung Buddhism), claims that Maitreya represents a new motive force in history. He noted that the Tonghak Rebellion by farmers largely began in a region of deep Maitreya belief, where the Chŭngsan religion began, but that this belief was forced underground during the Japanese colonial period. However, now these new religious groups with a dream of a worldly utopia should be studied to aid in the revival of *minjung* culture.[19]

These essays, with reformist and slightly utopian meanings, were part of a gradual radicalization that was a product of indigenous Korean themes. Although some have considered that Minjung Buddhism was inspired by liberation theology, or suggested an influence from Southeast Asian Buddhism,[20] this seems unlikely. Rather, in this early stage, Minjung Buddhism was not characteristically Marxist in orientation, just as Minjung Christians claimed to be authentically Korean and not to have derived their ideas from Marxism.[21]

The initial responses to the 10.27 Persecution and to the military regime's continuing oppression of the people can be divided into two types: the attempt to "monasticize" (K. *sawŏnhwa*) society, and research on the social role of Buddhism. At the start of 1981, the monasticization or "Sanghacizing" (K. *sŭnggahwa*) movement began, and in October at Myogak Sa, a monastery of the Pur'ip Order of Buddhism, an order founded in 1965 based on the ideas of the *Lotus Sutra* that had a following of about 300,000 in 1993,[22] a symposium was held on the Sawŏnhwa Movement. The Chogye Order, the largest in Korea, which had been placed by the military authorities under the control of a "purification" committee, would not have been sympathetic, but the abbot of Myogak Sa had been a member of the University Buddhist Association. The Sawŏnhwa Movement intended to make the monasteries into centers for *minjung* activity through education and to prepare those who would lead the labor movement through the education of the poor and illiterate workers in night classes. The ideal was to realize a Pure Land on earth, with the model being the primitive Sangha of the time of the Buddha in which there were no classes or private property—a type of early communist society. This model, once properly established in the monasteries, could be extended to secular society through education, social work, and labor activism. Most of the monks involved were members of the Chogye Order, but the main center was Myogak Sa. However, some monasteries of the main cities were involved, thereby creating regional centers.[23]

This movement created the Munhwa Ch'ongnim Yŏrae Sa (Tathagata Company for Cultured Monasteries), a for-profit company, and out of their symposium formed the Yŏrae Sa Pulgyo Yŏn'guhoe, a research group. Their ideas were then published in the *Ch'ŏngnyŏn Yŏrae* (Young Tathāgata), a quarterly magazine. Stressing the inseparability of the Sangha and secular society, they analyzed society through social science methods, claiming that liberation was not just for individuals but for all suffering members of society. Sufferings, as in birth, illness, old age, and death, were not merely the results of individual past deeds, but also due to social action, for all existence is mutually dependent and related through the mechanism of dependent origination (*pratitya-sammutpada*). Joint karma was thus stressed as the basis of social practice.[24]

The authorities then moved, between the end of December 1981 and early 1982, to arrest over 130 members of the Sawŏnhwa Movement, defining it as a Buddhist socialist movement. The leader, Pŏb'u, was arrested in Chŏnju just as he was about to open a national federation of these educational institutes. He was sentenced to three years in prison, and two layleaders received a one-year sentence each. They were all convicted of violating the National Security Law and of introducing Southeast Asian Buddhist socialism into Korea.[25] It is not clear which Southeast Asian Buddhism was meant, but it probably did not refer to the Vietnamese United Buddhist Church led by Thich Nhat Hanh, which was neutralist, pacifist, and socially engaged, and had been suppressed by the Communist victors from 1976.[26] Rather, the charge may have been directed more at a misunderstanding of the theories of Buddhadasa Bhikkhu of Thailand and his notions of a Buddhist socialism or Dhammic socialism, which was underpinned by dependent origination but not by materialistic Marxism.[27] It appears that the authorities considered any social activism, even that meant simply to improve the lives of the poor, as the same as communism, and so the leaders of the Sawŏnhwa Movement were jailed as subversives.

However, this did not halt such activities, for although most of the leadership of the Sawŏnhwa Movement was from the University Buddhist Association, it had many talented members who turned to other means of realizing their goals.

The first method was to do research on and publish works about the relationship of Buddhism, society, and social welfare. The other was to organize calls for reform. Young monks formed several organizations in 1981 such as the Chŏn'guk Chido Pŏpsa Tan (National Corps of the Dharma Guidance Teachers) and the Ch'ŏng'nyŏn Sŭngga Yukhwa Taehoe. The latter was formed at the Chung'ang Sŭngga Taehak (Central Sangha College), which had been established at Kaeun Sa, one of the monasteries active in the Sawŏnhwa Movement, on January 10, 1980. This College was the outcome of a push from December 1976 to create an institute of higher learning for Buddhist clergy separate from Dongguk University, which had a conservative Sangha College or Department.[28] The Central Sangha College encouraged a greater solidarity among the young clerics, rather than the divisive forces dictated by parish and lineage loyalties. It permitted a wider reflection on Buddhism because it also taught non-Buddhist disciplines and hinted that they had more in common with lay universities, whose radical students at that time conducted large-scale, sometimes violent, demonstrations against the government. The young monks thus developed a greater empathy with the grievances of the university students, and began to study the problems of society. These Central Sangha College students henceforth became the core of the monk radicals and reformers.[29]

These Central Sangha College students formed the Chŏn'guk Ch'ŏngnyŏn Sŭngga Yukhwa Taehoe or National Young Monks' Conference for Six Harmonies in July 1981. The six harmonies are elements of the mutual respect of bodhisattvas and sentient beings. The bodhisattva will keep the same precepts as beings, see beings as the same as themselves, live with them, practice the same things, and be compassionate. The harmonies are harmonious respect in body (ritual), speech (in praises), mind (belief), precepts, views (on emptiness and the like), and beliefs or practice. This Conference sought means to resolve the problems of the Sangha via reform and to examine the social role of Buddhism. It called for an actualization of the Pure Land.

Research was prosecuted within the Chogye Order by the Chogyejong Chongch'aek Yŏn'guso (Research Center on Policy of the Chogye Order) under the monks Ch'ŏnjang and Chinhyŏng. They sought concrete measures to reform the Order. The Center in turn established the Pulgyo Sahoe Munhwa Yŏn'guso (Research Center for the Study of Buddhist Society and Culture) headed by Prof. Han Sangbŏm. Two of the research team, Yŏ Ikku and Chŏng Sŭngsŏk, prepared a plan that would divide the Order into practice clerics and propagation clerics, each with their own defined roles. The latter would be allowed to marry and eat meat, rather as Han Yongun had suggested back in 1910. However, when the scheme was publicized, the conservative leadership dismissed the proposal, for the plan contradicted the whole Purification Movement to eliminate Japanese influence that had resulted in the split of the T'aego Order from the Chogye Order.[30] The Chogye Order leadership had been members of the Purification Movement.

However, the Center for the Study of Buddhist Society and Culture exerted influence through the publications of its members. These books were then widely read by the reformist students of the University Buddhist Association and the Central Sangha College. The most important of these books were edited translations by Yŏ Ikku from Japanese works on Buddhism and society. These Japanese works by Takahashi Seiichi were *Shakaigaku to Gendai Bukkyō* (Sociology and Contemporary Buddhism), Sōbunsha, Osaka, 1976, and an essay, "Bukkyō shisō to gendai shakai" (Buddhist Thought and Contemporary Society). Both of the translations were banned by the government as prohibited publications. However, they succeeded in becoming the conceptual bases of Minjung Buddhism.[31] Takahashi's works, in turn, were heavily indebted to the Marxist Buddhism of Senoo Girō (1890–1961), the leader of the Shinkō Bukkyō Seinen Dōmei (New Buddhist Youth League) that was founded in 1931 and banned in 1935.[32] Because of the obvious Marxist content of Senoo's movement, and thus Takahashi's book, it was no surprise that Yŏ Ikku's book was banned. In the early 1980s, Marxist matter was very difficult to locate, and students, as I recall from personal experience, were even reading old Japanese works on Marxism that dated back to the Taishō era. Moreover, by 1983, the Center for the Study of Buddhist Society and Culture also published material on the educational systems of Buddhism in Southeast Asia.[33]

Despite such setbacks, the members of the Center attempted to unite the lay scholars with the monasteries of the Conference for the Six Harmonies at a meeting on July 17, 1983 at Pŏmŏ Sa just outside of Pusan. Titled the Chŏn'guk Ch'ŏngnyŏn Pulgyodo Yŏnhap Taehoe (National Buddhist Youth Federation Conference), it attracted over 1,700 people from many organizations including the University Buddhist Association, the Sŏngnimhoe from Dongguk University, and students of the Central Sangha College. It called for reform of the Buddhist Order, the promotion of democracy, unification, and autarky (K. *chuch'e,* normally rendered *juche* following North Korean usage). "Those who have fallen to the ground, stand up on that ground." It wanted knowledge of the contradictions of contemporary society and criticized Buddhism for its inability to change society. The participants felt a responsibility to overcome these contradictions through practical work and vowed to form a solidarity of young Buddhists, lay and cleric, to reform Buddhism, to realize a Minjung Buddhism, and to build a Pure Land of the Buddha. Kim Chihyŏng was elected as Conference chair, the deputy-chair was Sŏng'il. But while they were preparing plans for a nationwide organization and for execution of their ideas, a monk was murdered at Sinhŭng Sa on Mt. Sŏrhak on August 15 when one group was trying to occupy this rich monastery. A new abbot was being appointed, but the majority of resident monks objected. Members of the Conference were drawn into the debates over this event, interrupting their plans. On August 16, the Federation Conference met at Kaeun Sa, declaring that the Order should be "purified," and demanding that the

Chogye Order leadership resign. A hunger strike by five hundred of the reformists began, and the Chogye Order Council called an emergency conference in September. Twenty-five hundred monks and nuns attended, and the constitution was revised. The Emergency Order Administration (K. *pisang chongdan*) gave the progressives and reformists a chance to implement some reforms, such as provision for lay propagators and public management of monastery finances. But the conservatives, headed by the highest-ranking abbots, mounted a counterattack and attempted to hijack the reformist agenda. This led to the resignation of the highest spiritual authority, the Rev. Sŏngch'ŏl, on July 14, 1984. Furthermore, the emergency split the reformist camp into those who claimed the Order itself could reform Buddhism, and the radicals who stated that the Order had to be reformed from without with the assistance of the laity. Indeed, the split in the Order led to violence and the occupation of Chogye Sa, the headquarters of the Order, and to the movement of the emergency administration to Pong'ŭn Sa, illustrating the difficulties of reform from within or without.[34]

Such a discouraging turn of events led the progressives to form new organizations, such as the Minjok Pulgyo Yŏn'guso (National Buddhism Research Center) headed by Sŏngmun. This was made up of a group of young monks partly dependent on the established Order. The radicals gathered around Yŏ Ikku and founded the Minjung Pulgyo Undong Yŏnhap (Minjung Buddhism Movement Federation) (hereafter Minjung Buddhist Federation) on May 14, 1985. This latter was a union of about 180 laypeople and clergy, aiming at the autonomy of Buddhism, overcoming the military dictatorship, supporting workers and farmers, demanding a democratic constitution, gaining a fair distribution of wealth, and promoting traditional Korean culture and reunification. However, the government soon arrested 104 of the founders for being members of an illegal organization because it described Korean society as being in a vicious political circle, corrupt because of special privileges for monopoly capital and inequalities between regions and classes, all of which were threatening the livelihood of the *minjung*. These critiques were far more pointed than any made previously, and the membership was active in labor disputes, such as the June 1985 demonstration by the female workers of the Sŏngdo Textile Company. Its ideas were published in the journal of the Federation, the *Minjung pŏptang*.[35]

The Federation survived because of the so-called 1985 Spring, during which the Chun dictatorship attempted to boost its legitimacy by liberalization, lifting the ban on political activities, all of which enabled political parties, religious groups, labor unions, and students to unite and rally, thereby gaining support from the middle class against the dictatorship. In the election that ensued, opposition parties gained substantial, though not majority, support. This produced a demand for direct election of the president, and an eventually abortive debate began.[36] Students, more determined and radical than ever, in May 1985 formed the Sammintu (Struggle Committee for Minjung Democratization), which led street rallies and the anti-American sit-in occupation of the U.S. Information Service Library in Seoul. They claimed that the *minjung* were exploited by the military and capitalists, who were subservient to the United States. They demanded the overthrow of the regime and the withdrawal of U.S. forces, and even looked, foolishly, to North Korea as an independent Korean state upholding traditional values. Although they soon split into factions, their violent demonstrations and suicides by flames in protest began to alienate more moderate groups.[37] Many of this minority of students were Marxists, and the Minjung Buddhist Federation was clearly more like a Buddhist arm of this radical student movement.

The first issue of *Minjung pŏptang* did not blatantly present Marxist ideas, but the message was evident through some of the language and the woodcut-style images of flag-waving workers and the like. The fundamental premise of the Minjung Buddhist Federation was to sympathize with the suffering masses, as a quote from the *Vimalakīrti-nirdeśa Sūtra*, repeated several times, made clear: "When sentient beings are in pain, the Buddha is in pain,"[38] and, "Because sentient beings are distressed, the bodhisattva is distressed."[39] The second premise, as another quote from the same *sūtra* illustrates, was that the task of the bodhisattva or committed Buddhist is to liberate beings from that suffering by creating a utopia: "What is meant by saying that the land of sentient beings is the Pure Land of the bodhisattva? . . . Because we build a Buddha Land in order to save sentient beings, those who vow to build that Buddha Land do not do so in the empty sky, but do so among sentient beings."[40]

The third premise, as Ko Ŭn underlined, was that Buddhism has to be for all beings and not for itself, but that Korean Buddhism had failed in that task. Three headline sentences in bold type highlighted these points: "The ultimate aim of Buddhism is that the thing called Buddhism disappears completely. If Buddhism does not belong to all sentient beings and all *minjung*, how is it not the greatest nonsense in the universe? During our history, our Buddhism has not been a Minjung Buddhism, but has been the Buddhism of kings."[41]

Thus, Buddhism is an expedient means to rescue all beings from suffering, and a bodhisattva vows to save all suffering beings before entering nirvaṇa. Once that universal liberation is achieved, Buddhism is needed no longer. But if Buddhism fails to act on these ideas, it is humbug. In Ko Ŭn's opinion, Korean Buddhism has failed because it has been in the service of the rulers, a "state-protection Buddhism," and not in the service of the *minjung*. It should be something easy to understand, not hidden by obfuscation or mystification:

> What is Buddha? He is all freedom, total equality. All sentient beings possess the basic nature of Buddha equally. . . . Buddha is compassion. When the *minjung* and sentient beings as a whole love each other, that condition is the basis of Buddha. . . . Let us become Buddha and

> get rid of the thing called Buddhism. As long as there is the thing "Buddhism," this world will be in suffering. . . .[42]

The next task was to analyze the suffering of the *minjung* by examining the "intentional structures" in which they live. In ancient times, the structure was represtend by a slave society, then a feudal society of serfs and the like, and in modern times it is in a capitalist society. In such a society, the workers are the basic constituent, with farmers, poor urbanites, and others having significant places. The Korean *minjung*, it was claimed, are living in a mega-structure of capitalism in which the hegemonic powers have made Koreans the victims through a Cold War system that has tragically split the nation. The *minjung* are oppressed by the vicious circle of dictatorship and unjust distribution of wealth. They are dependent on foreign capital and technology, and with special privileges for the monopoly *chaebŏl* (plutocratic cartels) and a gigantic foreign debt burden of five billion U.S. dollars; this is threatening to bankrupt them. Low wages, social and regional inequality, and low grain prices threaten the very existence of the *minjung*. Moreover, the antinational education tainted by colonial hangovers and Cold War ideology, the servility (K. *sadaejuŭi*) to the West, and rampant commercialism have all corrupted the culture and mentality of the *minjung*. Historically, from the time of the opening of the ports to the May 1980 Kwangju Massacre, the *minjung* have been oppressed, the nation divided and at war. Therefore, the aims of the Minjung Buddhist movement are to "build a Buddha Land that will secure the peace and a genuine freedom, and the happiness of the humanity of this *Sahā* world that is full of suffering due to exploitation and oppression." To achieve this, radical Buddhists have to form a concrete Buddhist power that could liberate the *minjung*, build an autonomous and democratic Buddhism; reject an antidemocratic, antinationalist colonial and compromising education and toadying, commercial culture; and promote an autonomous (K. *juche*) national education and a true *minjung* culture. Politically, (we need) to overcome the vicious circle of dictatorship and to actualize a genuine democracy that makes the *minjung* the ruler (K. *chu'in*); economically to establish an autarkic economy based on benefit to the *minjung* and an equal and fair distribution of wealth. Moreover, we need to autonomously and peacefully overcome the division of the fatherland that can be said to be the intentional origin of our country's *minjung*, and achieve a national unification.[43]

Following this are more concrete analyses of South Korea's place on the international military and economic stage in the first half of 1985, and detailed appraisals of the situations of the workers' movements and the problems of farmers. In addition, there is a detailed report on the conditions of Sŏngdo Textiles and the textile industry.[44] The labor movement in 1985 was considered to have stagnated since the Kwangju Massacre, with the number of unionists declining. The union leaders had made errors of individual activism and "adventurism," and it rather had to be built on a scientific base. The subjective and objective conditions included the protectionism of the advanced countries, which created obstacles to the export-led growth promoted by the Korean government. This resulted in attempts at dumping products and a freeze on wages. Chaebŏl privilege had bankrupted the small to medium-sized businesses. Labor activists who objected had been "reeducated" and the labor movement suppressed. Therefore, the authors asserted that support be given to the student movement. Moreover, there needed to be a struggle against unfair actions and new unions, such as those of taxi drivers, had to be formed. Specifically, the unions had to be democratized and there had to be a fight for a wage rise.[45]

Minjung pŏptang reports countered the popular misconception that the life of farmers had improved, with villagers no longer fearing a grain shortage in Spring (K. *porit kogae*) and now owning radios, TVs, tractors and using chemical fertilizers. However, the price of farm products had fallen, farmers were restricted in obtaining side-jobs and were going bankrupt, leading to a rural exodus. Part of this was produced by the government policies of importing agricultural goods and the faulty policy of promoting speculative crops. Farmers were going into increased debt. Figures showed that since 1975 the purchase price of grain had fallen, and the cost of production of rice, for example, had increased over the price the farmers obtained. The losses in 1975 were 720 *wŏn* per 80 kg of rice, but by 1984 this loss had risen to 20,239 *wŏn*. The low grain price was being used to subsidize industrialization, just as had been done in Meiji Japan. On the other hand, excess agricultural production from overseas was being landed in South Korea, keeping the prices low. Similar problems existed in the cattle industry. In 1983, 30 percent of all cattle slaughtered were imported from North America and Australia. Bananas imported from the Philippines by the government for 4,608 *wŏn* per 12 kg were sold in the markets for 30,000 to 32,000 *wŏn*, but Cheju farmers could only sell at 40,000 to 50,000 won to recover the costs of production, meaning that they were taking huge losses, whereas the government was gaining a windfall of seven billion won per annum, which it said was being used to promote small to medium-sized businesses.[46] This analysis is partly backed by external researchers.[47]

The journal also reported some simple examinations of Buddhism in Southeast Asia. Regarding Vietnam it only mentioned the struggle against the United States and the Diem regime, etc., but it carries no mention of the communist victory and the subsequent oppression of the Buddhist Church.[48]

Similar themes continue on through the later issues of *Minjung pŏptang*, with investigations into the 10.27 Persecution,[49] and farming problems,[50] although fresh topics such as ecology and the environment, a history of religious responses to national contradictions since the Tonghak Rebellion, women in Buddhism, and the peasants and the Ullambana festival were featured. News of concern to the activists was also reported—items such as the illegal encroachment by a stone quarry on the land of Kwan'ŭm Sa in Pusan. An all-night demonstration by local residents occurred, but the police arrested women and the aged, even invading the women's rooms. However, the police did not prosecute the illegal quarry operators.[51]

At other times, the *Minjung pŏptang* reacted fiercely against the dictatorship's violations of human rights. At the end of 1985, a large number of students, youths, and workers were arrested and tortured on suspicion of being communist operatives. In particular, officers of the student movement, the Minjuhwa Ch'ŏngnyŏn Hyŏbŭihoe (Youth Council for Democratization) were brutally tortured with water and electricity. Their testimony came out in court.[52] This provoked a reflection on violence under the headline, "Denounce the anti-human anti-democratic violence of the Chun regime." While Buddhism is a doctrine of compassion, they wrote, contemporary Korean society had been overloaded by a culture of violence that despised compassion. Violence, the authors opined, has two categories: violence toward the self such as suicide; and violence toward others. Although Buddhism's basic spirit was compassion, it lacked the persuasive power to control the hooligans. To smash the evil and elucidate the good, Buddhism has to defeat the ideology that supports violence by making people aware of the truth and by defending the powerless. This may mean killing one evil being to save many innocent lives (K. *ilsal tasaeng*), but these actions must never be for personal benefit. Evil people who cannot be dissuaded from killing many people or harming them are called *icchantika*. As *icchantikas* lack the roots or capacity for good, no amount of compassion will halt their evil deeds, and so to kill them in defense of the masses is not a violation of the precepts. The authors ask rhetorically, do *icchantikas* exist in Korean society, in an age when many people were slaughtered in Kwangju in order to satisfy the desire for political power? This was clearly aimed at Chun Doo-hwan and his allies.[53]

While this violence may be justified by the bodhisattva out of compassion for the victim, the bodhisattva willingly takes the karmic consequences of the murder onto his own account as part of his vow to save all beings, even if it means falling into the sufferings of hell.[54] Of course, the danger in this was that Nation-Protection Buddhists under the previous Park regime had used this as a justification to kill (suspected) communists.[55]

The perception that the Minjung Buddhist Federation condoned violence was heightened when a number of its leaders were indicted and arrested for participating in major street demonstrations for workers' rights in Inch'ŏn. This also alienated them from established Buddhism. The leadership was accused of being the puppetmasters of the demonstrations. [56] However, the account in *Minjung pŏptang* has it that on May 3, 1986, at 2.00 p.m. in front of the Inch'ŏn Citizens Culture Hall, there was a gathering of the New Democracy Party calling for a change to the constitution. Attacked by the police, while they were dispersing, members of the Min T'ong Yŏn, workers, and students (more than fifty thousand people in all) from a distance began to vehemently protest with calls for the Americans to get out and for the overthrow of the current regime. The demonstrations spread and continued on until 10 o'clock at night, and there were violent clashes initiated by the police. Several hundred people were arrested. Later, several members of the Minjung Buddhist Federation were arrested, and a warrant was issued for Yŏ Ikku, who went into hiding. However, this was not the end of the demonstrations, for on June 13, in Seoul, members of the Minjung Buddhist Federation participated with Catholic students and some two hundred others in a demonstration, and a stone-throwing riot broke out. In July, on the centenary of the Korean church, women demonstrated against the use of sexual torture, and members of the newly formed Chŏngt'o Kuhyŏn Chŏn'guk Sŭnggahoe (National Sangha Association for the Realization of the Pure Land) participated.[57] The latter was formed on June 5, 1986 by 221 monks who had split from the Minjung Buddhist Federation, probably because of the arrest of many of the latter organization's leaders. These monks demanded a revision of the Korean constitution for direct presidential elections and democratization. The leaders and members were monks, which left the Minjung Buddhist Federation weakened and with a largely lay membership. The Chŏng'to Sŭnggahoe were active however, making many public declarations.[58]

The Minjung Buddhist Federation, despite this major setback, persisted; and members came to defend the case of a young woman whom they alleged was sexually tortured in the Inch'ŏn prison, putting out a lengthy indictment on July 5, 1986.[59] The Minjung Buddhist Federation was even further radicalized by these events, and its actions led to an unprecedented mobilization by large numbers of the monkhood at Haein Sa on September 7, 1986. This monastic conference was called to examine the torture of the female student leader the Minjung Buddhist Federation had defended, and to demand an investigation of the 10.27 Persecution and the abolition of laws discriminating against Buddhism. This conference was summoned by reformists and revolutionary young monks such as Sŏngmun, Myŏngjin, and Hyŏn'gi, together with the cooperation of some moderates. In response, over two thousand monks attended, and they demanded autonomy for Buddhism, the democratization of society, and an end to the oppression of Buddhism and to making monasteries into tourist areas. They also rejected the pressure for the liberalization of imports. The newly elected secretary-general of the Chogye Order, Rev. Ŭihyŏn, redefined "state-protection Buddhism" as Buddhism for the citizens and not for a specific regime. He also mentioned the previously taboo 10.27 Persecution, declaring it "an outrageous act of violence that allowed jackboots to trample the holy monasteries." The conference declarations were critical of the existing conservative Buddhism that was closely allied to the state, and added the voice of the Buddhist Order to the chorus calling for democratization, surprising many observers. The young turks had confronted the conservatives and won a temporary victory. This conference made Buddhists realize that the democratization of society and the movement for Buddhist autonomy were inseparable, and promoted reformist ideals.

Following the conference, streams of declarations of support were issued, and the next day students of the Central Sangha College began a sit-down demonstration to defend Haein Sa against the police. The students defied the police, who tried to remove banners from the students' buses, and conflict ensued, leading to arrests and injuries. This defense lasted eight days. While this was happening, at Kaeun Sa, next to the College, a pressure group was organized to have laws oppressing Buddhism rescinded, and another to investigate the Persecution was begun at Pong'ŭn Sa. The regime arrested the instigating monks of the Haein Sa Conference on charges of violating the laws against public assembly, which just added to anti-regime sentiment. Moreover, when the public realized that some of the generally conservative Buddhist hierarchy had participated in this event, and the incumbent secretary-general, Rev. Nŏgwŏn, only in the office for a brief moment, had resigned to allow a new executive to take office they gave support to the cause. However, there were questions by some conservatives about the violence between the young monks and students defending Haein Sa and the police. Others objected to the politicization (or rather, radicalization) of Buddhism.[60]

It was this issue of violence that heightened divisions, just as Minjung Buddhism seemed to be gaining concrete results. The ultra-conservatives said religion should be separated from politics, conveniently ignoring their own collusion with the military dictatorships and their condoning of violence against those suspected of leftist tendencies. Moderates agreed with many of the aims of Minjung Buddhism, but condemned violence as non-Buddhist. On the other hand, the Minjung Buddhists of the Minjung Buddhist Federation accepted violence as a means to counter oppression such as torture and the massacre of protesting civilians by the military.

During this late 1986–1987 period, the violence and sense of crisis mounted. In March 1986, a Marxist student group, the Minmint'u (acronym for Minjok Minjuhwa T'ujaeng Wiwŏnhoe: Anti-Imperialist Anti-Fascist National Democratic Struggle Committee) was formed, and in April 1986 the Chamint'u (acronym for Panmi Chajuhwa Panp'asho Minjuhwa T'ujaeng Wiwŏnhoe: Struggle Committee for Anti-American Anti-Fascist Democratization), even more radical, was formed; and some of its supporters burned themselves to death in protest against the dictatorship. At a joint demonstration at Kŏn'guk University in October 1986, there were 19,000 riot police in attendance, and 1,275 protesters were arrested. Then in January 1987, a student from Seoul National University was tortured to death, and in elections that same year the electors of the five largest cities rejected the government candidates.[61] On March 31, 1987, which was the the 49th-day memorial for the death of the student, Pak Chongch'ŏl, on March 31, 1987, the Minjung Buddhists confronted the dictatorship. Pak was a

Buddhist, and the Minjung Buddhists were reinvigorated due to this event. The recently weakened Minjung Buddhist Federation immediately published a new monthly "newspaper," the *Minjung Pulgyo*. On the front cover of the first issue (February 25, 1987) was a picture of the late student, and the majority of the issue concerns the torture of the "patriotic citizen." It also mentioned the arrest of the monk Chin'gwan and it calls upon readers to follow the example of the late student, who according to Buddhist theory will be reborn. The paper states that Pak's actions in attempting to alleviate the sufferings of others would result in an individual karma for Pak's rebirth and a joint karma. The paper claimed that Buddhism gives greater emphasis to joint karma, because it determines social relationships, and so it does not disappear with the death of the actor. The karma of Pak's death due to the structural contradictions of South Korea will thus produce a new karma, which is democratization.[62] In the following issue of March 31,1987, there was a report of the ceremony and the confrontation of monks, laymen, and riot police that occurred.[63]

On April 12, 1987, the Minjung Buddhist Federation opened its second general assembly and opposed the regime's constitution.[64] The paper proclaimed that its role was to report impartially and to counter the distorted accounts in the mass media about Minjung Buddhism and the movement for democratization.[65] Therefore, it tended not to carry articles on theory or matter with overtly Marxist content, although headlines read, "The outcry to overthrow the dictatorship shakes the whole country."[66]

On the other hand, another anniversary galvanized Minjung Buddhist activists. On May 18, 1987, some eighty Buddhists gathered at Wŏn'gak Sa in Kwangju to commemorate the dead of the Kwangju Massacre. Fifty police attacked the monastery, firing tear gas canisters into the monastery and its dharma hall. A number of monks were arrested and thirteen people were detained overnight. Some were injured. The following day, eighteen student members of the Sŏngminhoe of Dongguk University went on an indefinite hunger strike in response. Over seven hundred monks began sit-in demonstrations at many famous monasteries, and on May 27, a massive student demonstration was launched in Kwangju with over five thousand Buddhists, including over two hundred monks, denouncing the assault on Wŏn'gak Sa. At Kaeun Sa on May 31, the Minjung Buddhists held a conference against the suppression of Buddhism, with demands for the "overthrow of the military dictatorship."[67]

Although these events further divided the Minjung Buddhists from the conservatives, events were also favoring the Minjung Buddhists. In April 1987, the Chun regime suspended debate on constitutional revision that had been initiated in response to large anti-government demonstrations in February 1986. The Reunification Democratic Party was then established in May 1987, which led demonstrations for constitutional revision. Demonstrators were propelled by the revelation in May 1987 that another student was tortured to death. Clergy of all religions commenced hunger strikes and, starting June 10, demonstrations broke out. On June 26, 1987, a large Peace March in Seoul, with hundreds of thousands of participants—workers, radical students, and housewives—that could not be controlled by the police alone, convinced Roh Tae Woo, the successor nominated by Chun Doo-hwan, that concessions had to be made; the summer Olympics were due to be held in Seoul in 1988, and the government did not want any riots that would interrupt the games and damage its reputation. Roh pledged to make a democratic reform in which there would be direct election of the president, fair competition, amnesty for political prisoners, protection of human rights and the extension of habeas corpus, freedom of the press, and so on. On October 28, the National Assembly ratified a new democratic constitution for the Sixth Republic. This was followed by an election on December 16, 1987, and Roh Tae Woo was elected president because the opposition was split. But Roh received only 37 percent of the votes; Roh was associated with the Chun dictatorship and with the Kwangju Massacre.[68] The December elections divided Minjung Buddhists' support between different opposition candidates, but Buddhist participation rates in the campaigns were low. Following the elections, the Minjung Buddhist movement weakened, and they were increasingly criticized by conservative Buddhists, especially for their support of presidential candidate Kim Dae-jung (Kim Taejung) and for standing for elections themselves.[69]

Moreover, splits began to appear in the movement, and on March 25, 1988, moderate monks who had been part of the Emergency Administration of the Order of 1983 and the Haein Sa Conference of 1986, formed the Taesŭng Pulgyo Sŭnggahoe (Mahāyāna Buddhist Sangha Association). They aimed to unite monastic (mountain) and Minjung Buddhism, and called their Buddhism Minjok Pulgyo or "National Buddhism," thereby de-emphasizing Marxist ideas of class struggle and focusing on national issues. It was an attempt also to overcome the factional struggles, and, of course, was centered on the monkhood, unlike Minjung Buddhism, which was more lay-oriented.[70] This Sangha Association was concerned about reform of the Order and was led by Songsan, Myŏngjin, and Sŏngmun. It criticized Minjung Buddhism and called for a reinterpretation of Buddhist doctrine. Thus, it was more inward than outward in orientation. However, it lost some trust when leading members were drawn into a dispute over the abbotship of Pong'ŭn Sa. The Association's organizational base was weak and in March 1991 its activities came to an end, probably because it could not position itself firmly between the conservative controllers of the Order and the progressive activists.[71]

The Mahāyāna Sangha Association had put out the first issue of its journal, *Minjok Pulgyo*, in January 1989, under the editorship of Mog'u, a monk activist who had been a member of the Minjung Buddhist Federation. The journal's stated goal was liberation of the nation and unification, and it replaced an earlier journal called *Silch'ŏn Pulgyo* (Practice Buddhism).[72] However, the issue included articles by Yŏ Ikku, who had been in hiding since May 1986 because he was sought by the police for involvement in the Inch'ŏn riots, and had finally been arrested in October 1988. He was writing, with permission, from Inch'ŏn prison as an army monk.[73] The journal also contained an article by Hyŏn'gi, a leader of the Sangha Association. This article dealt with "practical Mahāyāna thought," with the subtitle, "In order to develop the Minjung Buddhist Movement in a Mahāyāna fashion." Another article by Kim Yŏngguk attacked "Official Buddhism" (i.e., pro-government Buddhism) and its anti-communist ideology. The journal also contained examinations of Buddhism in North Korea and the lessons to be drawn from the Pong'ŭn Sa dispute over the abbacy.

The last issue of *Minjung pŏptang* appeared in the middle of 1988, in a typescript form and clearly produced under straightened circumstances, as the correction of errors, Chinese characters, and English letters are handwritten. It opens with an apology for the lack of an issue since No. 4, which came out in mid-1986, stating that this was due to the "insincerity" of the Minjung Buddhist Federation, which came out of the involvement in the Inch'ŏn riots and the oppression that followed, with Yŏ Ikku being sought by the police for over two years. It also admits errors in making declarations of "critical support" in the presidential elections, and noted that some activists had made unilateral decisions that produced divisions and mutual recriminations. This led to a reorganization and the formation of the *Minjung Pulgyo* newspaper. The journal authors criticized their movement for romanticism, and called for a "thought struggle" to make Minjung Buddhism more scientific and practical. They described the presidential elections as fraudulent, with the government still in the hands of the military. They called for the "military fascists" to be investigated and punished for the Kwangju Massacre, and noted that issues 8 and 10 of the *Minjung Pulgyo* carried denunciations of Roh Tae Woo as responsible for the massacre and published a series of photographs of the massacre scene.[74] The massacre, at that time, was still a burning issue that was used to attack the military rulers and the incumbent president.

The *Minjung pŏptang* article, "Saeroun t'ujaeng ŭi kyŏrŭi rŭl tajimyŏ" (Press for a Resolution for a New Struggle), argued that the earlier issues of the journal had not contained a consistent philosophy for Minjung Buddhism, but simply used an unfiltered theory of social movements, which caused confusion and difficulties in practice. Moreover, the movement faced a hostile Order. They stated that the reforms initiated by the 1986 Haein Sa Conference had failed, despite the declaration of the Chogye Order secretary-general. This statement had eventually been withdrawn at the instigation of the pro-government faction, because of the "fascist regime which could not approve the autonomy of Buddhism." Members of the Order had been obsequious to the government and had disgracefully supported the defense of the old constitution. Even more damaging was that the secretary-general of the Order had publicly announced support for Roh Tae Woo in the election, totally in contradiction to the people's hopes. Thus the majority of monks were deemed conservative, antidemocracy, anti-*minjung* and antireform, and so allied with the ruling class. Some Buddhists even gained fascist military support for their candidacy in the elections to satisfy their individual desires in an anti-Buddhist fashion.

Because there were so many definitions of Minjung Buddhism, several positions are described, such as the socialist Buddhism of Southeast Asia in which the Buddhist spiritual realm is supplemented by the material world of socialism, with socialism a preliminary stage in the building of a Buddhist Pure Land. The other version of Minjung Buddhism is the attempt to base Buddhism on a dialectical materialism, or the separation by Takahashi Seiichi of individual salvation Buddhism from social salvation Buddhism. The task of this *Minjung pŏptang* was to elucidate the thought and philosophy of Minjung Buddhism, not in an academic way, but to strengthen the movement that had been weakened since the presidential election. To do this, they needed to attract the attention of the people.[75]

The content of one of the main essays about this thought is fundamentally Marxist. This development had been made easier because Roh permitted open discussion of Marxism, and *Das Kapital* was published in a full Korean translation in 1987.[76] Even works by Mao Tse-tung became available. However, the Minjung Buddhist Federation leadership wrote this article for members only, cautioning, "this article is not the official standpoint of the Minjung Buddhist Federation." It was meant to be a brief explanation of one aspect of Minjung Buddhism that was needed to present some of the theoretical problems.

The essay begins with a quote: "There can be no revolutionary movement without revolutionary theory." This premise is followed by a brief analysis of reform movements in Korea since the 1950s to the 1987 elections and their limitations. To illustrate the material relationship of theory and practice, it adopts Marxist-Leninism and *juche* philosophy as its most important philosophy. In Korea this theory, the authors state, is split between the orthodox National Liberation (NL) faction and the Constitutional Assembly (CA) group. After explaining the basics of Marxist-Leninism, in particular, class, dialectics, and historical materialism, it shifts attention to debates over Korean society between the communist factions. The NL faction emphasized *juche* philosophy, and described Korean society as a colonial, semi-feudal society (or semi-capitalist society), which has distorted the autonomy of the *minjung*. For them, there is no difference between neo-colonialism and the old colonialism. Thus, the South Korean government is a representative of the fascist imperialists. In these circumstances, the bases for revolution are the workers, farmers, and students, and for reunification one has to oppose America. This seems to be fundamentally a line adopted from North Korea. The CA faction opposed the NL faction in 1987. It analyzed South Korean society as a neo-colonial national-monopoly capitalism, and its theory of revolution is national democracy. Thus the South Korean government was relatively independent. The internal contradiction then is between the bourgeois and working classes, but the most significant immediate contradiction is between the military fascists and the *minjung*, with the revolutionary forces the workers, farmers, urban poor, and progressive youth. The task for them is to stress the hegemony of the working class and deny the national capitalists.[77] In defense of their position, the authors stated that "the Minjung Buddhist movement does not adhere to Buddhism itself, but tries to devote itself to historical laws of development" in an autonomous (K. *juche*) action to realize equality and freedom, and realize a Pure Land for all humanity.

Moreover, they dispute the criticism that they were merely stone-throwers in clerical garb, by stating that Christian clerics also fought to reform society. While admitting mistakes, they contest criticism that Minjung Buddhists were selective in attending only to the pain of the *minjung*, and not to that of all people (including the ruling class), by using the example of the KAL flight 858 bombing of November 29, 1987, by North Korean agents.[78] The workers' voices in this were lost, and the suffering of the *minjung* was misused by the military regime, who manipulated the incident to replace personnel. Roh Tae Woo, on the other hand, had used the 10.27 Persecution to eventually gain the presidency. So naturally, one sympathizes with the persecuted and denounces those who misuse the pain of the *minjung*. One must put greater emphasis on that than on the suffering of all, including the perpetrators of oppression. This is an objective practice, and not selectiveness, for one has to highlight the vileness of the dictatorship. The critics, the authors stated, had been silent in the face of the persecution,[79] and so were hypocritical in their stance.

These articles and the defensiveness they contain display a tinge of desperation, the feeling that perhaps the movement had lost momentum, and that internal divisions and the external improvements in conditions were bypassing the committed activists. Certainly, some of the criticisms made of them were hypocritical or in error, but the attempts to clarify their position, with an increasing adherence to Marxist doctrine, probably alienated some members, who seem to have drifted away and joined new movements.

However, the fully mature theory of Minjung Buddhism was published in November 1988 under the title *Minjung Pulgyo ch'ŏrhak* (Minjung Buddhist Philosophy) by Yŏ Ikku, although parts had been published earlier in 1987. This, and the series of essays published in January 1989 under the title of *Minjung Pulgyo ŭi t'amgu* (Explorations of Minjung Buddhism), marked the final thrust of Minjung Buddhism. Thereafter, the movement dissolved and diffused into various directions, and the Marxist theme was gradually eliminated as new moderate Buddhist organizations appeared and the South Korean political and economic conditions improved. The last issue of *Minjung Pulgyo* appeared on July 17, 1989. It was largely displaced by more moderate journals, such as

Chŏngt'o kuhyŏn (Realization of the Pure Land) (October 1988–September 1992) and *Taesŭng Pulgyo* (Mahāyāna Buddhism) (May 1988–March 1991), published by the Silch'ŏn Pulgyo Chŏn'guk Sŭnggahoe (National Sangha Association of Practice Buddhism).[80] These were publications of the Pulgyo Chŏngt'o Kuhyŏn Chŏn'guk Sŭnggahoe (National Sangha Association for the Realization of the Buddhist Pure Land) and the Taesŭng Sŭnggahoe (Mahāyāna Sangha Association), breakaways from the Minjung Buddhist Federation. The National Sangha Association of Practice Buddhism was founded in October 1992 as a reformist monastic movement, and was lead by Ch'ŏnghwa and Chisŏn, who had led the Sangha Association for the Realization of the Pure Land, which was disbanded in August 1992. By 1994 this National Sangha Association of Practice Buddhism was at the forefront of the reformist groups. It called for direct elections to the administration of the Chogye Order, and reform of the constitution. Another concern was pollution, and it attempted to establish "reformed monasteries."[81]

The rapidly increasing prosperity of ordinary South Koreans, the increasing democratization, the expanding middle class, the collapse of the Soviet Union and the retreat of communism, the commercialization of China, and the shocking realities of the North Korean regime, quickly removed the stimuli for the Minjung Buddhist movement. The movement petered out and the former activists moved into new spheres, such as the environment, social welfare, and monastic reform. Even the long-term dissident, Pŏpchŏng, became involved in the environmental movement.[82]

Evaluation

The Minjung Buddhist movement was short-lived, lasting a little over a decade. It was made up of a number of different organizations, all with slightly divergent objectives and means to attain those goals. Like the "engaged Buddhists" studied in the book edited by Christopher Queen and Sallie King, the Minjung Buddhists did shift the emphasis in Buddhist soteriology from the personal and otherworldly to social and this-worldly liberation, one in which the individual has less importance than society as a whole. Therefore, these movements concentrated on how to remedy the causes of worldly suffering and oppression by advocating democratization and using the modern methods of activism and sociological analysis.[83] To make these into Buddhist movements, they appealed to versions of early Buddhism, the bodhisattva conduct, and compassion. However, unlike the engaged Buddhists, the Minjung Buddhists did not rely on set scriptures or create new catechisms, nor were there only one or two leaders who were emulated or made the symbols of a new order. On the other hand, Minjung Buddhists, like the engaged Buddhists, attacked folk religion elements such as devotional piety or prayer, were highly educated, and stressed the liberation from all forms of oppression, especially that conducted by the state and ruling class.[84] However, the greatest similarity is with the New Buddhist Youth League (Shinkō Bukkyō Seinen Dōmei) of Japan (1931–1935). Both this and Minjung Pulgyo were short-lived movements largely based on Marxism mixed with elements of Buddhism that opposed military dictatorships, capitalism, and most forms of war.

The leader of the New Buddhist Youth League, Senoo Girō (1889–1961) had been raised in a Jōdo Shinshū household and so had a profound belief that he and most humans were evil and had to rely on an absolute power for salvation. However, he increasingly came under the influence of Nichiren's patriotism, and then he moved toward the advocacy of international cooperation based on ideas of interpenetration propounded by Tiantai Zhiyi (538–597) based on the *Lotus Sutra*. In 1924, Senoo became interested in socialism and Marxism because of his attempts to reconcile disputing landlords and tenants, believing that he could create peace through changing consciousness. The failure of that attempt opened his eyes to class conflicts and the injustice of the situation, which pushed him away from the Nichiren position and more toward a general or united Buddhism (J. *tsū Bukkyō*). He denied the notion of a savior and stressed the Buddha as a human being. Under the influence of Marxist atheism he came to study primitive Buddhism via the researches of Ui Hakuju, Kimura Taiken, and Oldenburg. Senoo then wrote on new Buddhism (J. *shinkō Bukkyō*) and the path to social revolution, stressing causation and the liberation through no-self and the collective, for we are all mutually reliant.

Rejected by his former Nichirenite colleagues, Senoo formed the New Buddhist Youth League through which he propounded a Buddhist dialectics that was supposedly superior to a merely materialist dialectics. However, it was a vague and immature ideology, containing its own theoretical weaknesses, which were compounded by Senoo's own high-handed administration of the league. For example, although Senoo opposed Japan's aggressive war, his was not a total pacifism, still allowing the concept of a just war on the behalf of oppressed. After he was imprisoned by the authorities, he underwent a "conversion" (J. *tenkō*), and during the height of the Pacific War he became a nationalistic supporter of the emperor-system and the war effort. At the end of the war he again preached pacifism and finally joined the Japanese Communist Party.

Although the flaws in Senoo's thought and his ideological reversals may have been peculiar to his personality and the features of Jōdo Shinshū and Nichiren thought, the theoretical problems displayed in his attempts to merge Buddhism and Marxism, and the practical problems of leadership of the league,[85] are very similar to those seen in Minjung Buddhism and suggest both a common origin and common issues. Thus, Matsuoka speaks of many of the problems of Senoo's thought as being largely due to the vagueness of his humanistic beliefs that prevented him from ultimately protecting human rights and dignity.[86]

Likewise, Minjung Buddhism was generally ill-defined. Some of the participants and critics have, however, identified a number of major (overlapping) characteristics. These are:

1. Engage in criticism of established Buddhism
2. Provide a new analysis of Buddhism in a social scientific fashion in order to socialize Buddhism and give it more social practice
3. Develop Buddhism in a *minjung* fashion and build a Buddhist Pure Land on earth
4. Change the contradictions in society and eliminate the dependency of the *minjung* by making the *minjung* the masters of their own destiny through democracy
5. Find the ideals of Buddhism in early or primitive Buddhism and convert Buddhism from an individual pursuit toward the compassionate benefit of others and social salvation.

The means to achieve this were to make people aware of the weaknesses of established Buddhism, such as the alliance with oppressive military regimes, the reliance on the income from prayer Buddhism that promised ill-informed believers that prayer and ritual could bring benefits, and the corruption of the undemocratic leadership. The Minjung Buddhists called for the independence and autonomy of Buddhism by a separation of Sangha and state, and the democratization of the Order and society as a whole. To alleviate the suffering of the people, they demanded reform or even a revolution in the political and economic spheres, and the engagement in a struggle against colonialist and ruling class oppression. This required an equitable distribution of wealth and the removal of privileges for the *chaebŏl*. They called for human rights to be respected, and for an end to pollution, nuclear proliferation, and war. Although generally pacifist, the Minjung Buddhists did not exclude violence and revolution to attain their goals when the oppression and violence of the ruling classes allowed no other alternative except subjugation. They therefore formed societies and clubs, largely independent of the established Order, to prosecute these aims.[87]

Hyŏn'ŭng wrote that the movement began because the originally self-sufficient monasteries that were feudal in practice had been rapidly drawn into the capitalist structures of South Korean society. Once relatively isolated, having no electricity and visitors only on rare occasions, the monasteries had been largely inward-looking and remote. However, as the parks around them were made into tourist areas, that isolation was ended and the state increasingly interfered with the management and property of the monasteries, making Buddhism subordinate to the ideology of the military regime. This distorted Buddhism, increasingly factionalizing and secularizing it. The context induced a rethinking of the role of Buddhism and called for more participation in society; it also produced an anti-capitalist reaction. However, in Hyŏn'ŭng's opinion, Minjung Buddhism failed to adequately integrate the ideals of primitive Buddhism with the bodhisattva conduct and Pure Land ideals of Mahāyāna. On the other hand, it achieved a number of positive results, such as redirecting Buddhists toward the need to help resolve the problems of people and toward working for an ideal society, in which "all beings are Buddha" and the means are those of the *paramitās* of *upaya* (appropriate action), or the means to bring one to the other shore, that is liberation. Minjung Buddhism shook Buddhism out of its lethargy of self-contentment or resignation to fate and the reliance on the vows of the bodhisattva to liberate all beings, by encouraging one to practice like a bodhisattva and vow to build a new society. Minjung Buddhism demonstrated that new society or Pure Land is not some transcendental world of the future, but a world of equality, peace, and freedom in the social community of the here-and-now. Furthermore, if such a society is to be achieved, the focus of Buddhist practice moves from the monastic Order to the bodhisattva, who does not distinguish between cleric and laity. This demanded more cooperation between the laity and the monks and nuns. Therefore, Buddhist practices had to extend beyond the monastery grounds into general society, into schools, companies, and hospitals. Minjung activists thus held practice sessions and seminars in the cities and villages, spreading the doctrine. Because of the relationship of capitalism and individualism based on greed and selfishness, the ideal society or Pure Land would have to be socialistic or communistic, like the primitive Sangha. After all, Buddhism teaches the elimination of desire and the doctrine of no-self (*anatman*). Of course, this placed Minjung Buddhism in opposition to the South Korean regime, monopoly capitalists, and the military and the foreign powers, in particular the United States.

This socialistic tendency implied a materialist worldview, one of objective materialism, in which historical analysis focuses on class struggle with an aim of the working class coming to rule. This, however, alienated many Buddhists because of its Marxist bias, contradicting the subjective or idealistic tendencies of the dominant Buddhist philosophy in South Korea. After all, communism was totalitarian and the official ideology of the enemy, North Korea. Yet many Koreans also wanted reunification. The emphasis on primitive Buddhism also alienated those who adhered to Mahāyāna Buddhism. Primitive Buddhism could be described as materialist, especially seen from the theory of *pratītya samutpāda* (dependent origination), whereas Mahāyāna was centered on the mind and idealism.[88]

Theory

The most complete statement of Minjung Buddhist philosophy is in Yŏ Ikku's *Minjung Pulgyo ch'ŏrhak*. Although it is not the place here to give a detailed account of the philosophy as a whole and criticisms of it, as for example in the mechanics of dependent origination or the critiques of Mahāyāna philosophy, an outline of some of Yŏ Ikku's ideas are appropriate, since he was the prime ideologist of the movement.

According to Yŏ, enlightenment or awakening in Buddhism is a release from all ideologies, which is freedom. The contradictions posited between mind and body, or ideal and reality in these ideologies, bind one to ignorance and eventually to suffering. Liberation then is an overcoming of the contradictions of self and society in particular. Buddhist idealists isolate a person's mind from its material environment; therefore, to concentrate practice on the mind does not lead to liberation. Our internal struggle with the self also involves society, for the existence of the individual is dependent on food, and the collective struggle over the production of food and its distribution involves us in history. Although the Buddha did not discuss this, he did note that enlightenment is a transformation of values, and must be a problem of life.[89] Idealists, such as most Mahāyāna Buddhists, live in society and take all its benefits, while opposing all reforms to society on the basis that the reformists are materialists. Yŏ claims that Buddhism is realist and objective, for truth cannot be subjective, as truth is not the value of the individual. We live in a web of unlimited connections and continuous flux, and so enlightenment can only result from a dialectic, and cannot be subjective. Yet truth located in historical context is only relative and subjective, and thus is not perfect, and requires continuous supplementation, which is dialectical. Buddhism, then, is neither naïve materialism nor idealism.[90]

All existence, including mind, is a product of the material elements of existence through continuously changing interactions of conditions. All conditions, in turn, are products of other conditions, which means there is continuous flux and so no permanent entities. That is the meaning of emptiness. There can be no permanent self in these conditions. The self is changing continuously, and is provisional. The attempt to grasp a permanent entity such as self results in ignorance. Ignorance can only be overcome by the analyses of existence and the overcoming of desire or self.

In this existence, actions result in a moral force or influence that affects later events. Because actions influence others, including the environment, and not just the actor, karma is both personal and shared or common. However, this karma is linked to rebirth, which Yŏ describes as simply a conjectural possibility.[91]

Desire itself is a deed or action, but not all desire is bad. Desire can be for the truth or judgment due to insight. If this desire did not exist, there would be no enlightenment or Buddhism. The overcoming of ignorance, the first element in the chain of dependent origination, requires a "scientific" understanding, and the Buddha taught such an understanding in a form of dialectical materialism in which objects always contain latent contradictions because they are mutually dependent. Thus, wisdom is contradicted by ignorance, and the transcending of this contradiction is enlightenment. Mahāyāna mistakenly became attached to wisdom and produced a metaphysics that served the upper classes. Mahāyāna, by emphasizing idealism, ignored the social realities and could not alter the status quo.[92]

Hwaŏm (C. Huayan), for instance, is in error by teaching that the material worlds of space and time are products of human consciousness, and, in the name of mutual interpenetration and dependence, glosses over the sufferings due to class difference and cannot challenge contradictions and discrimination, merely merging them into an undifferentiated harmony. It merely requires a change of attitude. So, for example, at the height of its influence, it did nothing to eliminate slavery.[93] Likewise, Sŏn (Chan/Zen) called for a transcendence of dualism through direct practice and was a form of subjective idealism. Therefore, it cannot explain the fundamental principles through direct speech, denies that humans can consciously know the objective truth through theoretical or scientific thought, and falls into the mire of mysticism. But the objective world exists beyond the mind, for it continues after the death of the mind. Such a subjective doctrine as Sŏn is in danger of solipsism, and Sŏn epistemology is contrary to science and early Buddhism. For this reason, Sŏn cannot effect social change. However, because Sŏn denied authority (even of the Buddha), internalized the Pure Land, and humanized the Buddha-nature, if it is allied with progressive and reformist thought, it could become revolutionary.[94] Although, as critics have alleged, this analysis is heavily reliant on the dogmatic assertions of the Chinese communist author, Ren Jiyu, other authors think the criticism of Sŏn is not fully accurate, and think there is a possibility for *minjung* liberation and Sŏn to be made compatible.[95]

Rather than subjective idealism, the aspect of Buddhism that is useful for society is that of dialectics, as in the famous Sŏn formulation in which at first mountains are mountains. Through negation, the statement is altered to state that mountains are not mountains, and concludes again with the statement that mountains are mountains, which describes the marvelous existence of true emptiness. One therefore cannot be attached to anything, even Buddhism, which is simply a raft. This dialectic applies to self and society, and shifts from saving oneself to liberating others, as self and society are non-dual. The mission of Buddhism is to perfect society and the individual through a dialectical struggle.

True Buddhism lives in society, but is not attached to any society. However, it is not satisfied with current society, and so is a philosophy of permanent revolution. Buddhism needs to remove class discrimination and move toward justice. Injustice is based on class rule in terms of economic relations, and class society is but one stage in history. The Buddha denied classes (more strictly, castes) through the teachings of dependent origination and no-self. The Sangha required total removal of class distinctions and differentiation by wealth. The only distinction was through seniority, otherwise all were equal. Even the Buddha was not the controller of the Sangha; he was merely its first member. One was not to be subordinate to others; one had to be an island unto oneself. Members of the Sangha then engaged themselves in self- and mutual-criticism, and there were to be no secret doctrines. Consequently, to perceive dependent origination was to see the dharma, and to see the dharma was to see Buddha.

Because of non-self, private possessions were meaningless. However, the origins of society lay in the desire for profit or excess production, and possessions lead to class formation. The idea of ownership cannot be eliminated without class struggle in society or the realization of *anatman* at the personal level. Therefore, Buddhism cannot approve of capitalist ideology and ethics that are based on desire and the expansion of private possession. Capitalism glorifies the rights of production and private possession, which are desires rooted in ignorance.

However, Buddhism did not maintain fully the property-less and classless nature of the early Sangha; and Buddhism gradually became an opiate, promising a Pure Land after death to the subject classes and attributing inequality to their bad karma in earlier lives. It became a doctrine of mental transcendence, and so sanctioned the ruling class status quo. Hwaŏm and Ch'ŏnt'ae (C. Tiantai), by equating all things with True Thusness (K. *chinyŏ*), allowed one deed to be equated with all deeds, or all dharmas with true reality (K. *chinsang*), thereby sanctifying evil realities—rationalizing away the inequalities of society in the name of harmony. Exploitation, inequality, and irrationality were not countered as a result, something contrary to the spirit of early Buddhism. Because of this evolution of Buddhism and society, in which class intruded into the Sangha and Buddhism compromised its ideals in conformity with state demands, one needs to have an historical perspective in applying Buddhist philosophy and social practice.[96]

Yŏ then attempts to apply modern science, such as quantum theory, beginning with energy, matter, and movement, to justify dialectical materialism, which is an organic relationship like the laws of dependent origination. He claims that there are always latent contradictions in their relations, negation, and affirmation, over time. Contradiction is the basis for movement, for change. To desire stasis, in Buddhist terms, is suffering. Humans suffer because they are conscious of that change, and of their relationship with Nature and their creation of a society to meet their physical needs through production. Disputes then arise over production, thereby generating the dialectics of history. Ideology is then built on those social relations, and on the material foundations of production. Thus, we are all individuals in a society and are part of the many aspects of class struggle, which is about economic relations and property ownership. Religion, including Buddhism, is part of the ideological superstructure.

Yŏ gives a classic Marxist analysis of society, in which progress is the transformation of the forms and relations of production. Conservatives try to retain the ruling class benefits, but as flux is universal and ineluctable, eventually a new ruling class and a new means of production emerges. Progressive movements mobilize the masses in the name of justice. Revolution is the ultimate form of change in class society, and is part of the dialectical laws of history. It is also liberation of the masses through historical actions that accord with the material conditions informed by ideology.

Early Buddhism largely agrees with this view, taking material objects and the mind as given. The Buddhist analysis divided existence into material and psychosomatic constituents, such as the four elements and five *skandhas*, which combined under various conditions. However, Buddha added the doctrine of karma to this. Hence, Buddhism does not deny the real world, and additionally recognizes a world of morality. Early Buddhism was a pluralistic materialism and took the world as a given, but Mahāyāna used the moral aspect to create a moral idealism and so projected the subjective onto the objective. Therefore Buddhism, as an ideological superstructure, is divided between materialism and idealism. Yet the Buddha had concentrated more on human suffering and the contradictions that caused the pain, and not on any ideological superstructure.

Suffering is due to ignorance, which is giving relative values to changing elements of existence and clinging to them as permanent. Release from ignorance leads to enlightenment and freedom. In this context, Yŏ glosses over Friedrich Engels on freedom, stating that it is based on the recognition of the natural necessity that rules us and our environment. Freedom then is a product of historical development, a sublation of what *is* into the practice of what *must be*.[97]

In Buddhism, the means of analysis lead from the contemplation of *dharmas* to *prajñā* and the extinction of ignorance. The Way is the practice of what ought to be, which is to change the present through compassion, an absolute, unconditioned love. Compassion then is the realization of what ought to be, a revolutionary practice. Because humans are social beings, one cannot remove ignorance and suffering from the individual alone. The world that ought to be is not just the world of the individual; it is also the world of all humans. Therefore, the greatest compassion is to build happiness for the entire world; that is the supreme action and correct action (K. *chŏngŏp*). The Buddha, through his realization, spent his life trying to actualize this by teaching and building the Sangha.

The basis of compassion is no-self, the emptiness that is the result of dependent origination. One's self is a provisional construct, conditioned by society. Buddha tried to develop compassion and good deeds in people through the doctrine of karma, a utilitarian and moral causation. However, it does not necessarily follow that a good deed will produce a good result, for there are many supplementary conditions. Rather, there is a potential for good results from good deeds. Morality was also described in terms of reincarnation. This links us all, humans and non-humans, collectively, which instinctively encourages a love of all beings via collective karma. But reincarnation was only a theory, a mere possibility extrapolated from the laws of movement, and of itself could not defeat blind desire. This morality still remains in the domain of relativity.

The absolute morality or good is a universal benefit. It is the practice of selfless, compassionate, revolutionary deeds, as in the vow of the bodhisattva not to enjoy the benefits of liberation until all beings have been saved. This proper practice moves from the relative morality of causation and reincarnation to the absolute morality of the bodhisattva.

Buddhists have to firmly establish the meaning of their own existence through practice, establish a social life in cooperation with others through proselytization, and must act to give peace to all others through movement. One has to gain freedom from one's bonds, cooperate with others with sympathy, and preach. Of course, there are two types of bonds: the bonds of frustration for the individual, and the bonds of social ignorance. One has to be released from both kinds of bond for genuine liberation to be achieved. The bodhisattva then, having removed the personal bonds, offers him- or herself to reform the social environment. This cannot be limited to a mental release, for where society is corrupt, one cannot remove the bonds merely by a mental transformation of oneself and call that enlightenment. That lacks a concrete reality. Thus a bodhisattva acts to achieve social and economic justice as well, basing this on an analysis of the relationships of material production as the starting point, and then acts in consciousness of the dialectical relation of practice and propagation. One cannot liberate beings by living in seclusion in the mountain monasteries; one must liberate the nation, the classes, and so on. The oppressors and exploiters have also to be liberated, but they first have to be made to see the errors of their ways and change their social roles. Minjung practice thus begins with the Buddha himself, who started the transformation with the creation of the Sangha.[98]

Yŏ's attention then turned to the role of the Minjung Buddhist movement in Korean society. In Korean Buddhism there are contradictions between prayer Buddhism and practical Buddhism, between state-protection Buddhism and Minjung Buddhism. These contradictions should be studied if the desired changes are to be implemented. Moreover, Buddhism is a social phenomenon, and if one only knows Buddhism, one falls into the egoism of faith. Without knowledge of Buddhist history, one falls into speculation, and if one does not know about society, Buddhism becomes a mere ism. Therefore, one has to understand Buddhism in the context of history and society, analyzed through the lens of dialectical materialism or class struggle, the base and the superstructure.

Yŏ's analysis of South Korean society is that it is a "neo-colonialist state-monopoly capitalist society," with a material base in the state-monopoly capitalists. Everything in the society is subordinated to capitalist ownership. The state, through violent oppression, preserves the ruling class, which encroaches on the capital of others to increase currency circulation. Thus, the South Korean state has nationalized businesses such as the railways, roads, and communications, and redistributed production by providing privileges to the *chaebŏl* in the form of monopolies. This had its origins in imperialism and the comprador capitalist bourgeoisie in alliance with foreign powers. These relations were transformed into neo-colonial relations starting in about 1950. The former colonial powers formally granted independence to the South Korean state, but retained some economic powers. The comprador capitalist class was strengthened in the 1960s via export-oriented industrialization, while the military dictatorships represented neo-colonial interests. Thus, democratic institutions were destroyed by the alliance of the capitalists and the military, producing acute contradictions in society.

As a consequence, the reform movement has to oppose the foreign powers and build autonomy, overthrow the dictatorship and aim for democratization, and finally reunify the fatherland. In that sense, the movement is also nationalistic but not nationalism in league with capitalism. Nationalist means alone will not remove the neo-colonialist condition, for that can only be achieved through class struggle. If the monopoly capitalists use nationalism, it will be to extend their monopolies and ally themselves with the foreign powers. The national liberation has to be through the *minjung* and democracy.

The *minjung*, who have always led the historical struggle, are not identical with the masses (K. *taejung*). The masses are an amorphous, unorganized, powerless group with no consciousness of solidarity. The *minjung*, in contrast, are politically active, with a base in historical experience. They are a subjective grouping with a purpose. Although scholars define *minjung* variously, they are a group with political awareness hoping to bring about change. They may come from different social backgrounds, but they share a common desire. *Minjung* are the production workers, urban poor, and progressive intellectuals, who wish to change society through building a democracy and the removal of the foreign powers. Tactically, *minjung* activists should try to bring the liberal forces into the fold in order to fight against the dictatorship. This means that there is a contradiction within the *minjung* movement itself between the progressive national capitalists and petty bourgeoisie, and the working class. The liberal forces have only a limited understanding of the movement, so the struggle for democracy then is only the first stage of the struggle, because liberal democracy supports private ownership of the means of production. Capitalist democracy and the proletarian dictatorship are both class dictatorship, or class oppression. The *minjung* are the majority, so true democracy must be ruled by the *minjung*.

Minjung Buddhism is based on the notion that sentient beings, and even insentient beings, are the masses that have to be universally saved by the Buddha's teaching, because the bodhisattva vows to liberate all beings. Even the earth is to be included, for when sentient beings die, their physical remains merge into and constitute soil. However, this salvation has to be achieved in stages over time, and so has to be selective at the start. The bodhisattva begins by saving the weak and the poor, gathering the good to his or her side, and countering the strong and evil. The practice of expedient means allows violence in the removal of exploitation and oppression. Minjung Buddhism, then, is a practice Buddhism *for* beings: a practice of dependent origination in concrete terms of social and historical conditions. Unlike the Buddhism *of* beings, which is universal, supra-historical and absolute, Minjung Buddhism is a Buddhism of expedient means, historically grounded, relative, and conditioned. The Buddhism of beings is that of the Buddha-nature. Minjung Buddhism is the realization in concrete terms of the principles of the Buddhism of beings, the practice rather than the theory. Where class understanding and religious doctrine conflict, class understanding must prevail, for religion is part of the superstructure, a mere reflection of the material base. A theory of "seeing one's nature and becoming Buddha" used in Sŏn Buddhism that has no connection with the social reality is merely an ideal, divorced from concrete, historical liberation. It is only in the mind, and so is just an expression of the ideological superstructure. In contrast, the bodhisattva vow of salvation of beings is a concrete liberation from actual conditions, which is the basis of the Minjung Buddhist movement. Ideals are only properly grounded in a scientific recognition of the social structures, or of the base, as reflected in one's own self. Minjung Buddhism is not an idealism, but is based on the early Buddhist philosophy of dynamism, with a motive in the dialectical ideals of Mahāyāna philosophy. It examines the weak points of dialectical materialism, such as the mental aspects, and perfects it with Buddhist philosophy. Therefore, it has to start from a progressive Buddhist intelligentsia, and leads to the building of a Buddha Land on earth.[99]

Critiques

This attempt to graft Buddhism and Marxism has been criticized by moderates and others. Hyŏn'ŭng, while recognizing the poverty of historical philosophy in Buddhism, thinks that Minjung Buddhism has yet to convincingly construct a Buddhist view of history. This is because it has merely grafted historical materialism onto Buddhism, and has not generated the view of history out of Buddhist thought and experience, ignoring much of Mahāyāna in the process. The exclusion of Mahāyāna led to a deficiency in doctrinal understanding, especially with relation to the view of reality, and to the description of Mahāyāna as merely conceptual or idealistic, or in the interpretation of the doctrine of dependent origination. Again, the inclination toward socialism requires some qualifications, for in Buddhist doctrine, one can detect both socialistic and capitalistic elements. Rather, these tendencies need to be harmonized and explained. Moreover, while the bodhisattva has the historical intention to rescue all beings, the arhat wishes to be free of history and oppression.[100]

Hong Sasŏng added that the violence that arose from the class struggle betrayed its base in Buddhist religious thought that has as its core compassion, which abhors violence. *Chŏlbok* (J. *shakubuku*), the notion that one suppresses and defeats evil people and counters contrary theories, therefore does not imply violence, such as that which broke out at the Haein Sa Conference. This violence was rejected by the majority of Buddhists.[101] Pak Kyŏngjun agrees, stating that revolution implies violence, as does class struggle, and that *chŏlbok* is not violence. However, he concedes that there is not an absolute prohibition on violence in Buddhism, giving examples of "selective killing" in the five precepts for the laity set out by Wŏn'gwang, but that was in different circumstances.[102] Yet the Minjung Buddhists apparently did not emphasize *chŏlbok*, probably because of the bad reputation of *shakubuku* as used in Nichiren Buddhism and by the Sōka Gakkai in particular. *Shakubuku* was aggressive proselytizing that some apologists dismiss as nonviolent, but the intolerance behind it crossed over into mental coercion and even physical violence.[103] Moreover, it is likely that Yŏ Ikku and others did not wish to openly acknowledge their debts, via Takahashi Seiichi, to Senoo Girō and the Nichiren socialism of the New Buddhist Youth League. Senoo also subscribed to the last resort of killing one to give life to the many in a violent revolution.[104] Nichiren Buddhism was deeply unpopular in Korea because of its intolerance of other creeds or forms of Buddhism, and its extreme nationalism. In 1963 the Korean National Assembly wanted to outlaw Sōka Gakkai as an anti-Korean organization, but it secretly proselytized. Sōka Gakkai worships Amaterasu Omikami and Hachiman Bosatsu as the foundation and protective gods of Japan. Moreover, Nichiren Buddhism was associated with Japanese imperialism and the repression of native Korean Buddhism during the Japanese colonial period.[105] Many even regard Nichirenism and Sōka Gakkai as non-Buddhist.[106]

Moreover, most Korean Buddhists rejected the idea of class struggle, for all sentient beings should be saved, the oppressed and the oppressor. One should not view anyone as an enemy, for their exploitative actions are products of ignorance.

Again, the Minjung interpretation of doctrine was considered too mechanistic, leading to distortions. In particular, the idea of the primitive Sangha as communistic was deemed simplistic, for according to some documents, one quarter of the joint property was to be invested in production. Also, the creation of a classless and equal society does not guarantee the liberation of the individual, despite appeal via the mutual dependency of society and individual through dependent origination.[107]

Others rejected the historical materialist interpretation of Buddhism as made by Ren Jiyu. For them, the mind-only doctrine and the like of Yogācāra and Hwaŏm is not a ruling ideology of subjective idealism, and Ren's interpretations are doctrinally superficial and procrustean.[108] Moreover, the Minjung Buddhist idea of enlightenment appears to be different from that of Buddhism. Enlightenment, in the objector's view, is not a dialectical progress, nor gradual progress, nor a social scientific knowledge. In particular, it is not a dialectical completion.

This formulation also leaves out meditation, a fundamental practice in Buddhism. Again, Pak disputes the Minjung Buddhist notion of the Pure Land, for the Land is not the perfection of society and is unrelated to a class(less) society. This is because the Pure Land is related to individual perfection.[109]

Another problem is the identity of the *minjung*, since the concept is not clearly defined. The identification of the revolutionaries with the bodhisattva is also rejected.[110] Some of these issues are related to the problems of the Minjung Buddhist movement itself, such as its weak subjectivity (K. *juch'esŏng*) as a Buddhist movement that seems to have left it subordinate to ordinary social movements; the arrogance of the leadership in assuming a superiority over established Buddhism, in an overbearing elitism; and an organizational egoism that led to factionalism and struggles for supremacy through undemocratic methods.[111]

Conclusion

Despite all these problems, which I have oversimplified here (with some problems in the criticisms also), and despite the dependency for much of the doctrine on the ideas of the Japanese Senoo Girō that was based in the situation of the imperialist Japan of the 1930s and on the simplistic analysis of Buddhism by Ren Jiyu, a communist propagandist, Minjung Buddhism had a number of achievements. Hong lists the outcomes as rousing established Buddhism from its lethargy and introducing a more critical outlook that gave greater focus on social problems. It made many realize that Buddhists had to become involved in social issues. This led more to oppose the antidemocratic forces, both in Korean society and within the Order itself. Even conservatives were drawn into some of the reform activities. Moreover, the use of a social science interpretation of Buddhist doctrine made some realize that Buddhist doctrine was not merely an academic or individual exercise, but was solely for the liberation of human beings. Therefore, Minjung Buddhism produced new viewpoints, such as putting Buddhist doctrines into historical context, highlighting the issue of individual suffering and its relation to social or joint suffering or release. It redirected attention back to some of the fundamental doctrines such as dependent origination. The movement also helped restore some of Buddhism's democratic capacity and its regaining of control over monastic property by asserting its independence from the state.[112]

Although a direct causal relation cannot be posited, the increased activism and participation in the democracy movement, in social welfare and proselytization through the media and modern technology that Minjung Buddhism stimulated, seems to have resulted in an increased following for Buddhism as a total and percentage of the South Korean population.[113] Minjung Buddhists, through their alliance at times with labor activists, radical Christians, and others, opened up further avenues for dialogue of Buddhists with other groups in society. Moreover, it opened up new routes for Buddhist input into social issues and debates. Minjung Buddhism made Buddhists aware of the issues of the environment, pollution, and the use of national parks. It highlighted the problems that result from an over-emphasis on exports, of trade liberalization, and monopoly or oligopoly capitalism. It confronted Buddhists with the realities of the inequities of society, and the label *minjung* drew Buddhism into a major theme of dissident South Korean discourse. On the other hand, the elitism and romanticism of the leadership, its failure to distinguish itself clearly from the totalitarian *juche* "thought" of North Korea, and the oppressive elements latent in its means toward liberation, alienated many. Yet it issued challenges that could not be simply ignored, thereby making Buddhism more self-conscious or mindful and aware of problems inherent in its own doctrines and practices. But once it had played its role, it disappeared, just as the Buddhism it came out of is meant to, and some of the conservative forces, such as prayer Buddhism and irrational views, have continued stronger than ever. However, Minjung Buddhism planted some ideas into the minds of engaged Buddhists that will continue to generate reforms and contestation of the practices of conservative Buddhism.

Notes

1. Tongguk taehakkyo sŏngnip tongmunhoe, comp., *Han'guk Pulgyo hyŏndaesa* (Seoul: Sigongsa, 1997), p. 598.

2. Bruce Cumings, *Korea's Place in the Sun: A Modern History* (New York: W. W. Norton, 1997), pp. 377–379; Stewart Lone and Gavan McCormack, *Korea Since 1850* (Melbourne: Longman Cheshire, 1993), pp. 155–157.

3. Kyoyug'wŏn Purhak yŏn'guso, *Chogyejong sa: Kŭn.hyŏndae p'yŏn* (Seoul: Taehan Pulgyo Chogyejong kyoyug'wŏn, 2001) (hereafter *CS*), pp. 254–256; see also Kim Chongch'an, "Minjung Pulgyo undong ŭi chŏn'gae kwajŏng" (The Process of the Evolution of Minjung Buddhism), in Pŏpsŏng et al., *Minjung Pulgyo ŭi t'amgu* (Seoul: Minjoksa, 1989), p. 184; Min Pul Yŏn (Minjung Buddhist Federation, 1985), "Tangsi ŭi Pulgyo sanghwang kwa chŏnmang—10.27 Pŏmnan ŭl chungsim ŭro" (The Conditions and Prospects of Buddhism of the Times—with a focus on 10.27 Persecution), *Minjung pŏptang* 2 (16 Oct. 1985): 76–77. This is included in the collection of materials published and reproduced by the Minjung Pulgyo Undong Yŏnhap 10-chu-nyŏn Ki'nyŏm Saŏphoe, *Minjung Pulgyo* (Minjung Pulgyo Undong Yŏnhap, 1995), continuous pagination. This book also includes reproduction of the newspaper, *Minjung Pulgyo*. All references to the journal and the newspaper are to this reproduction and follow its pagination.

4. *Minjung pŏptang* 1 (16 Oct. 1985), p. 77; Mun Chan Ju, "A Historical Introduction to Minjung Buddhism: A Liberation Buddhism of South Korea in 1980's," *Kankoku Bukkyōgaku Seminar* 9 (2003): 249–250. For the property law, see Henrik Sørensen, "Buddhism and Secular Power in Twentieth-Century Korea," in Ian Harris, ed., *Buddhism and Politics in Twentieth Century Asia* (London: Pinter, 1999), pp. 138–139.

5. Sørensen, "Buddhism and Secular Power in Twentieth-Century Korea," pp. 139–140. Sørensen notes Chun's Christian allegiances and states that the persecution was triggered by a layman burning himself to death at Hŭngnyun Monastery in Kyŏngju. This was on the same day that the persecution was launched. See Tongguk Taehakkyo sŏngnip tongmunhoe, comp., *Han'guk Pulgyo hyŏndaesa*, p. 598. For the conservative Christian links to the state, foreign missionaries, and tolerance of state violations of human rights as "nation protecting religion," see Kwang-ok Kim, "Ritual Forms and Religious Context," in Lewis R. Lancaster and Richard K. Payne, eds., *Religion and Society in Contemporary Korea* (Institute of East Asian Studies: University of California, Berkeley, 1997), pp. 218–219, 224–226.

6. "Pulgyo rŭl pibanghanda!" (Buddhism Slandered), *Minjung pŏptang* 1 (1985): 50–51.

7. *CS*, 256.

8. Hong Sasŏng, "Minjung Pulgyo undong ŭi p'yŏngka wa chŏnmang," (The Prospects and Appraisal of the Minjung Buddhist Movement), in Pŏpsŏng et al., *Minjung Pulgyo ŭi t'amgu*, pp. 101–102; entry for Yŏ Ikku in Han'guk Pulgyo Ch'ongnam p'yŏnch'an wiwŏnhoe, *Han'guk Pulgyo ch'ongnam* (Handbook of Korean Buddhism) (Seoul: Taehan Pulgyo chinhŭngwŏn, 1993), p. 663, which differs a little on dates.

9. "Pulguk Sa pog'wŏn Pulsa hoesang," *Pulgyo wa minjok chunghŭng* (Buddhism and the Restoration of the Nation) 1 (1974): 1–3.

10. Sørensen, "Buddhism and Secular Power in Twentieth-Century Korea," p. 139.

11. Hong, "Minjung Pulgyo undong ŭi p'yŏngka wa chŏnmang," p. 98; Kim, "Minjung Pulgyo undong ŭi chŏn'gae kwajŏng," p. 179.

12. *CS*, 240. A *ch'ongnim* is a training monastery.

13. Nancy Abelmann, "*Minjung* Theory and Practice," in Harumi Befu, ed., *Cultural Nationalism in East Asia: Representation and Identity* (Institute of East Asian Studies: University of California, Berkeley, 1993), pp. 139–142. Also see Sang-t'aek Yi, *Religion and Social Formation in Korea: Minjung and Millenarianism* (Berlin: Mouton de Gruyter, 1996), pp. 38–39.

14. Abelmann, "*Minjung* Theory and Practice," p. 148, on Christian poet Kim Chiha; Donald Clark, "History and Religion in Modern Korea: The Case of Protestant Christianity," in Lewis R. Lancaster and Richard K. Payne, eds., *Religion and Society in Contemporary Korea*, pp. 189–190.

15. Hong, "Minjung Pulgyo undong ŭi p'yŏn'gka wa chŏnmang," pp. 99–100; Mun, "A Historical Introduction to Minjung Buddhism," pp. 244–246.

16. Sang-t'aek Yi, *Religion and Social Formation in Korea: Minjung and Millenarianism*, p. 99. This essay by Ko Ŭn, "Mirŭk kwa Minjung," is dated 1979 in the collection, Kim Chiha et al., *Mirŭk sasang kwa Minjung sasang* (Maitreya Thought and Minjung Thought) (Seoul: Hanjin ch'ulp'ansa, 1988), pp. 51–93. For entry on Ko Ŭn, see *Han'guk Pulgyo ch'ongnam*, p. 610.

17. Referred to in Sang-t'aek Yi, *Religion and Social Formation in Korea: Minjung and Millenarianism*, p. 237.

18. Seoul: Han'gilsa, 1980.

19. P'yo, "Mirŭk sin'ang kwa Minjung Pulgyo," pp. 358–359.

20. Mun, "A Historical Introduction to Minjung Buddhism," p. 254, citing Mok Chŏngbae, "Yŏksa p'yŏn, Kŭn-hyŏndae," in *Han'guk Pulgyo ch'ongnam*, 105; Jae-ryong Shim, "Buddhist Responses to the Modern Transformation of Society in Korea," in Lewis Lancaster and Richard K. Payne, eds., *Religion and Society in Contemporary Korea*, p. 83.

21. Clark, "History and Religion in Modern Korea: The Case of Protestant Christianity," p. 190; Hwang P'ilho, "Haebang Sinhak kwa Minjung Pulgyo ŭi pigyo punsŏk" (Liberation Theology and Minjung Buddhism—a comparative analysis), in Pŏpsŏng et al., *Minjung Pulgyo ŭi t'amgu*, pp. 245–246. Hyŏn Yŏnghak considers that Minjung Theology dates only from 1979, cited in James T. Bretzke, "Minjung Theology and Inculturation in the Context of the History of Christianity in Korea," *East Asian Pastoral Review* 28 (1991): 119–120.

22. See *Han'guk Pulgyo ch'ongnam*, pp. 197–199, for Pur'ip jong.

23. Mun, "A Historical Introduction to Minjung Buddhism," p. 253; *CS*, 258; Hong, "Minjung Pulgyo undong ŭi p'yŏngka wa chŏnmang," p. 101; Kim, "Pan'gong ideorogi wa ŏyong Pulgyo," p. 182.

24. Kim, "Pan'gong ideorogi wa ŏyong Pulgyo," p. 183; Mun, "A Historical Introduction to Minjung Buddhism," pp. 253–254.

25. Mun, "A Historical Introduction to Minjung Buddhism," pp. 254–255; Hong, "Minjung Pulgyo undong ŭi p'yŏngka wa chŏnmang," p. 101; Kim, "Pan'gong ideorogi wa ŏyong Pulgyo," p. 183; *CS*, 259.

26. See Sallie B. King, "Thich Nhat Hanh and the Unified Buddhist Church of Vietnam: Nondualism in Action," in Christopher S. Queen and Sallie B. King, eds., *Engaged Buddhism: Buddhist Liberation Movements in Asia* (Albany: State University of New York Press, 1996), pp. 344–346, 353, 355–356.

27. Santikara Bhikkhu, "Buddhadasa Bhikkhu: Life and Society through the Natural Eyes of Voidness," in Queen and King, eds., *Engaged Buddhism: Buddhist Liberation Movements in Asia*, pp. 166–170, and Donald K. Swearer, "Centre and Periphery: Buddhism and Politics in Modern Thailand," in Ian Harris, ed., *Buddhism and Politics in Twentieth-Century Asia*, pp. 217–219, which also mentions activities of Buddhist layman Sulak Sivaraksa in the 1970s.

28. *CS*, 236, 259; Mun, "A Historical Introduction to Minjung Buddhism," p. 251.

29. Kim, "Pan'gong ideorogi wa ŏyong Pulgyo," pp. 185–186; Mun, "A Historical Introduction to Minjung Buddhism," p. 252.

30. Mun, "A Historical Introduction to Minjung Buddhism," pp. 255–256; CS, 259; Kim, "Pan'gong ideorogi wa ŏyong Pulgyo," pp. 187–188.

31. Mun, "A Historical Introduction to Minjung Buddhism," p. 257; Hong, "Minjung Pulgyo undong ŭi p'yŏngka wa chŏnmang," pp. 101–102; Yŏ Ikku, *Minjung Pulgyo ch'ŏrhak* (Seoul: Minjoksa, 1988), p. 74 note 38.

32. Cf. Chŏng Sŭngsŏk, "Tongnam A ŭi chinbojŏk Pulgyo undong kwa Minjung Pulgyo" (The Progressive Buddhist Movements of South-east Asia and Minjung Buddhism), in Pŏpsŏng et al, *Minjung Pulgyo ŭi t'amgu*, pp. 233–236; Shakai Mondai Shiryō Kenkyūkai, comp., *Bukkyō to Shakai undō: shūtoshite Shinkō Bukkyō Seinen Dōmei ni tsuite*, Shisō kenkyū shiryō, tokushū 52 (Kyoto: Tōyō bunkasha, 1972). This material was the report by the criminal investigation branch of the Ministry of Justice, a top secret

report by the thought police made in 1938. Indeed, Matsuoka Mikio, *Nichiren Bukkyō no shakaishisōteki tenkai: Kindai Nihon no shūkyōteki ideorogi* (Tokyo: Tokyo Daigaku shuppankai, 2005), p. 156, calls it a Buddhist Marxism in order to show the dominance of Marxism over Buddhism in Senoo's thought. For discussions of Senoo Girō, see Matsuoka Mikio, *Nichiren Bukkyō no shakaishisōteki tenkai,* chapter 4 and Inagaki Masami, comp., *Senoo Girō Shūkyō ronshū* (Collected Essays on Religion by Senoo Girō) (Tokyo: Daizō shuppan, 1975).

33. Kim, "Pan'gong ideorogi wa ŏyong Pulgyo," p. 188; Mun, "A Historical Introduction to Minjung Buddhism," p. 256.

34. Kim, "Pan'gong ideorogi wa ŏyong Pulgyo," pp. 187–190; Mun, "A Historical Introduction to Minjung Buddhism," pp. 258–261; CS, 259–264.

35. Hong, "Minjung Pulgyo undong ŭi p'yŏngka wa chŏnmang," pp. 103–104; Mun, "A Historical Introduction to Minjung Buddhism," pp. 261–262.

36. Doh C. Shin, *Mass Politics and Culture in Democratizing Korea* (Cambridge: Cambridge University Press, 1999), pp. 1–2.

37. Lone and McCormack, *Korea Since 1850*, pp. 160–161.

38. Yŏ Ikku, "Minjung Pulgyo undong ŭl ŏttŏk'e ihaehal gŏsin'ga" (How shall We Understand the Minjung Buddhist Movement?), *Minjung pŏptang* 1 (July 1985): 10.

39. "Min Pul Yŏn ŭi undong panghyang kwa kwaje" (The Topics and Directions of the Movement of the Minjung Buddhist Federation), *Minjung pŏptang* 1 (July 1985): 20.

40. "Min Pul Yŏn ŭi undong panghyang kwa kwaje," p. 21.

41. "Minjung pŏptang han malssŭm" (A Minjung Pŏptang Speech), *Minjung pŏptang* 1 (July 1985): 14–15.

42. "Minjung pŏptang han malssŭm," p. 15.

43. "Min Pul Yŏn ŭi undong panghyang kwa kwaje," *Minjung pŏptang* 1 (July 1985): 20–22.

44. "(Chu) Sŏngdo Sŏmyu ŭi pudanghaego, kangje sap'yo rŭl kobalhanda" (Complaint against the Unfair Dismissals and Forced Resignations of Sŏngdo Textiles), *Minjung pŏptang* 1 (July 1985): 42–45.

45. "85 nyŏndo sangban'gi nodong undong ŭi p'yŏngka" (Evaluation of the Workers' Movement of the Latter Half of 1985), *Minjung pŏptang* 1 (July 1985): 30–33, figures, 36.

46. "Nong'ŏp munje ran muŏsin'ga" (What are the Problems of Agriculture?), *Minjung pŏptang* 1 (July 1985): 37–39.

47. Robert E. Bedeski, *The Transformation of South Korea: Reform and Reconstruction in the Sixth Republic under Roh Tae Woo 1987–1992* (London: Routledge, 1994), pp. 89–90; Lone and McCormack, *Korea Since 1850*, p. 158.

48. "Hyŏndae Tongnam A ŭi Pulgyo" (The Buddhism of Contemporary South-east Asia), *Minjung pŏptang* 1 (July 1985): 53.

49. *Minjung pŏptang* 2 (October 1985): 74–93.

50. *Minjung pŏptang* 2 (October 1985): 104–113.

51. "Mubŏp chidae, Pusan Si Kwan'ŭm Sa ch'aesŏkjang" (A Lawless Zone: The Quarry at Kwan'ŭm Monastery, Pusan City), *Minjung pŏptang* 2 (October 1985): 142–143.

52. "Min Chŏng Ryŏn kanbudŭre taehan p'ongnyŏk haengsa wa yonggong chojak ŭi chinsang" (The Truth of the Fabrications of Pro-communism and the Violent Deeds against the Cadres of the Min Chŏng Ryŏn), *Minjung pŏptang* 3 (Feb. 1986): 199–201.

53. "Chŏn Chŏnggwŏn ŭi pan'in'ganjŏk panminjujŏk p'ongnyŏk ŭl kyut'anhanda!!," *Minjung pŏptang* 3 (Feb. 1986): 198.

54. Michael Zimmermann, "War," in Robert E. Buswell, Jr., ed., *Encyclopedia of Buddhism*, 2 vols, Macmillan Reference: New York, 2 (2004), p. 894, citing the *Bodhisattva-bhūmi* and *Nirvana Sūtra*.

55. Kim, "Pan'gong ideorogi wa ŏyong Pulgyo," 97–98; see *Pulgyo wa minjok chunghŭng* 1 (1974), 12, where Park Jung-hee is called an incarnation or substitute for a bodhisattva in his 1973 sponsorship of the reconstruction of Pulguk Sa, and Kim Haeun, "Pulgyo kŭn-kŭndaehwa ron," which justifies a war of defense by the idea of selective killing to avoid many victims as used by Sŏsan Hyujŏng in the Hideyoshi invasions, etc., in the same journal, pp. 195–196, 204–205.

56. Hong, "Minjung Pulgyo undong ŭi p'yŏngka wa chŏnmang," p. 104; Kim, "Pan'gong ideorogi wa ŏyong Pulgyo," p. 192; Mun, "A Historical Introduction to Minjung Buddhism," pp. 262–263.

57. "Min Pul Yŏn ilji," *Minjung pŏptang* 4 (August 1986): 278–279.

58. *CS*, 265; Mun, "A Historical Introduction to Minjung Buddhism," pp. 263–264; Hong, "Minjung Pulgyo undong ŭi p'yŏngka wa chŏnmang," p. 105.

59. *Minjung pŏptang* 4 (August 1986): 268–271.

60. *CS*, 265–267; Mun, "A Historical Introduction to Minjung Buddhism," pp. 264–265; Hong, "Minjung Pulgyo undong ŭi p'yŏngka wa chŏnmang," p. 105–106.

61. Lone and McCormack, *Korea Since 1850*, p. 161.

62. *Minjung Pulgyo* 1: 365–366.

63. *Minjung Pulgyo* 2: 369.

64. *Minjung Pulgyo* 3 (30 April 1987): 373.

65. *Minjung Pulgyo* 1: 365.

66. *Minjung Pulgyo* 4 (15 June 1987): 377.

67. *Minjung Pulgyo* 4 (15 July 1987): 380; Mun, "A Historical Introduction to Minjung Buddhism," pp. 266–267; Hong, "Minjung Pulgyo undong ŭi p'yŏngka wa chŏnmang," pp. 106–107; Kim, "Pan'gong ideorogi wa ŏyong Pulgyo," p. 192.

68. Shin, *Mass Politics and Culture in Democratizing Korea*, pp. 2–4; Lone and McCormack, *Korea Since 1850*, pp. 161–162; Cumings, *Korea's Place in the Sun*, pp. 387–388.

69. Mun, "A Historical Introduction to Minjung Buddhism," pp. 267–268; Hong, "Minjung Pulgyo undong ŭi p'yŏngka wa chŏnmang," pp. 107–108; Kim, "Pan'gong ideorogi wa ŏyong Pulgyo," p. 193.

70. Mun, "A Historical Introduction to Minjung Buddhism," p. 268; Hong, "Minjung Pulgyo undong ŭi p'yŏngka wa chŏnmang," pp. 108–109; Kim, "Pan'gong ideorogi wa ŏyong Pulgyo," pp. 193–194.

71. *CS*, 271.

72. Mog'u, preface, "Minjok haebang kwa t'ong'il ŭl wihayŏ" (For Liberation of the Nation/Volk and Unification), *Minjok Pulgyo*, ch'angganho (initial issue) (Seoul: Tonggwang ch'ulp'ansa, 1989), p. 5.

73. Mog'u, "Minjok haebang kwa t'ong'il ŭl wihayŏ," p. 7; see also *Minjung Pulgyo*, special issue (17 July 1989), p. 455. This was the final issue of the *Minjung Pulgyo*.

74. *Minjung pŏptang* 5: 295–297; *Minjung Pulgyo* (10 Dec. 1987), 393–394, 397–398, and (13 May 1988), 406–407.

75. *Minjung pŏptang* 5 (1988): 297–300.

76. Lone and McCormack, *Korea Since 1850*, p. 166.

77. "Undong ŭi kwahakhwa wa t'ong'il, tan'gyŏl ŭi munje—sasang t'ujaeng ŭl chungsimŭro" (Making the Movement Scientific and the Problems of Unification and Solidarity: with a focus on the Thought Struggle), *Minjung pŏptang* 5: 317–323.

78. For a description of the incident, see Don Oberdorfer, *The Two Koreas: A Contemporary History* (London: Little and Brown, 1997), pp. 183–188.

79. " 'Minjung Pulgyo ran muŏsin'ga' ŭi kisa naeyong kwa kwallyŏnhan panbak" (Refutation of the Content of the Article, 'What is Minjung Buddhism?'), *Minjung pŏptang* 5: 353–355.

80. Collected into two volumes under the heading, *Han'guk hyŏndae Pulgyo undongsa* (P'aju'gun, Korea: Tosŏ ch'ulp'ansa, 1996).

81. *CS*, 271–272.

82. Sørensen, "Buddhism and Secular Power in Twentieth-Century Korea," p. 143; *CS*, 288.

83. Christopher S. Queen, "Introduction: The Shapes and Sources of Engaged Buddhism," in Queen and King, eds., *Engaged Buddhism: Buddhist Liberation Movements in Asia*, pp. 10–11.

84. Queen, "Introduction: The Shapes and Sources of Engaged Buddhism," pp. 5–10.

85. Matsuoka, *Nichiren Bukkyō no shakaishisōteki tenkai*, chapter 4, "Senoo Girō ni okeru sensōkan no hensen to sono shisōteki haikei," pp. 138–198. There is a considerable literature on Senoo, the major studies being by Inagaki Masami, *Butsuda o seoite gaitō e: Senoo Girō to Shinkō Bukkyō Seinen Dōmei* (Tokyo: Iwanami shoten, 1974), and Senoo Tetsutarō and Inagaki Masami, comps., *Senoo Girō nikki* (Tokyo: Kokushokankōkai, 1974–1975).

86. Matsuoka, *Nichiren Bukkyō no shakaishisōteki tenkai*, p. 187.

87. Hong, "Minjung Pulgyo undong ŭi p'yŏngka wa chŏnmang," pp. 92–94; Pak Kyŏngjun, "Minjung Pulgyo i'nyŏm ŭi pip'anjŏk koch'al" (A Critical Examination of the Concepts of Minjung Buddhism), in Pŏpsŏng et al., *Minjung Pulgyo ŭi t'amgu*, pp. 133–134.

88. Hyŏn'ŭng, "Taesŭng Pulgyo ŭi silch'ŏn sasang: Minjung Pulgyo undong ŭi Taesŭngjŏk chŏn'gae rŭl wihayŏ" (The Practical Thought of Mahāyāna Buddhism: To Develop the Minjung Buddhist Movement in a Mahāyāna Fashion), *Minjok Pulgyo* 1 (1989): 120–127.

89. Yŏ, *Minjung Pulgyo ch'ŏrhak*, preface. Note that Nichiren discussed issues in terms of food and life and the sanctity of food. See Daniel B. Montgomery, *Fire in the Lotus: The Dynamic Buddhism of Nichiren* (London: Mandala, 1991), p. 143.

90. Yŏ, *Minjung Pulgyo ch'ŏrhak*, pp. 31–34.

91. Yŏ, *Minjung Pulgyo ch'ŏrhak*, pp. 35–54. This is a gross summary.

92. Yŏ, *Minjung Pulgyo ch'ŏrhak*, pp. 57–62.

93. Yŏ, *Minjung Pulgyo ch'ŏrhak*, pp. 103–105.

94. Yŏ, *Minjung Pulgyo ch'ŏrhak*, pp. 113, 123–127.

95. This issue is taken up in Hee-Sung Keel, "Zen and *Minjung* Liberation," *Inter-Religio* 17 (Summer 1990): 24–37. This debate demands further attention.

96. Yŏ, *Minjung Pulgyo ch'ŏrhak*, pp. 62–74.

97. Yŏ, *Minjung Pulgyo ch'ŏrhak*, pp. 141–174.

98. Yŏ, *Minjung Pulgyo ch'ŏrhak*, pp. 177–186.

99. Yŏ, *Minjung Pulgyo ch'ŏrhak*, pp. 187–214.

100. Hyŏn'ŭng, "Taesŭng Pulgyo ŭi silch'ŏn sasang," pp. 127–134.

101. Hong, "Minjung Pulgyo undong ŭi p'yŏngka wa chŏnmang," pp. 120–121.

102. Pak, "Minjung Pulgyo i'nyŏm ŭi pip'anjŏk koch'al," pp. 160–162.

103. Montgomery, *Fire in the Lotus*, pp. 185–189, 197.

104. Shakai Mondai Shiryō Kenkyūkai, comp. *Bukkyō to Shakai undō*, p. 342. It should be noted, however, that Senoo did differ in many aspects with Nichiren, although he adopted the idea of "killing one so that ten thousand can live" in 1931 as a means toward an ideal society, and he cited the *Nirvana Sutra* and *Renwang jing* as evidence that even Buddhism allowed for this killing to liberate the masses. This *issetsu tashō* (K. *ilsal tasaeng*) is said to have originated as a phrase with Nichiren, but after World War II the general consensus reached was that this was from a work falsely attributed to Nichiren, for elsewhere in genuine works Nichiren even opposed the use of military force against monks who violated the precepts, something the *Nirvana Sutra* permitted. See Matsuoka, *Nichiren Bukkyō no shakaishisōteki tenkai*, pp. 164–165.

105. Yi Kang'o, *Han'guk sinhŭng chonggyo ch'ongnam* (Handbook of Korean New Religions) (Seoul: Taehŭng kihoek, 1992), pp. 610–611, 641–642, 645 *passim*; for Nichirenite intolerance, see Montgomery, *Fire in the Lotus*, pp. 266–267.

106. Montgomery, *Fire in the Lotu*, p. 196.

107. Hong, "Minjung Pulgyo undong ŭi p'yŏngka wa chŏnmang," pp. 122–123.

108. For details, see Pak, "Minjung Pulgyo i'nyŏm ŭi pip'anjŏk koch'al," pp. 163–168.

109. Pak, "Minjung Pulgyo i'nyŏm ŭi pip'anjŏk koch'al," pp. 142–154.

110. Pak, "Minjung Pulgyo i'nyŏm ŭi pip'anjŏk koch'al," pp. 135–139.

111. Hong, "Minjung Pulgyo undong ŭi p'yŏngka wa chŏnmang," pp. 123–125.

112. Hong, "Minjung Pulgyo undong ŭi p'yŏngka wa chŏnmang," pp. 111–119.

113. Cf. figures in Yoon Yee-heum, "The Contemporary Religious Situation in Korea," in Lancaster and Payne, eds., *Religion and Society in Contemporary Korea*, p. 4; *Han'guk Pulgyo ch'ongnam*, p. 135.

13

Formation of Modern Buddhist Scholarship

The Cases of Pak Chonghong and Kim Tonghwa[1]

Sungtaek Cho

Introduction

With the collapse of the Chosŏn dynasty (1392–1910), during which Confucianism had been adopted as an overarching social system, anti-Buddhist policy began to make changes. Modern Korean Buddhism is generally regarded as having begun in 1895, the year marking the lifting of the measure prohibiting Buddhist monks from entering the capital city, through the help of Sano Zenrei, a Nichiren monk from Japan. With this, the monks were legally allowed to freely enter the capital city, marking the end of the long, dark years characterized by "mountain Buddhism" (K. *sanchung Pulgyo*). Although Buddhism was to be revived from the suppression that had lasted for about 500 years, the fact that this change came about not through the efforts of Korean Buddhism, but as a result of external power dynamics, especially through the Japanese monks, affected the direction and content of the modernization of Korean Buddhism in many ways to come in the following years.

From the standpoint of the Korean Buddhist community, Japanese Buddhism was both a model for its own modernization and an object of rejection to be avoided. Pressured to be differentiated from Chosŏn Buddhism that had been suppressed for long years on the one hand, and the need to overcome colonial Buddhism or so-called "Japanized Buddhism" on the other, Korean Buddhist society implemented many reform programs that sometimes conflicted with one another or produced contradictory outcomes within the community. For instance, some argued in favor of permitting monks to marry as a practical measure to modernize Buddhism, while others saw it as an element of "Japanized Buddhism" and urged stricter adherence to the rule of celibacy. In contrast to its dualistic attitude toward Japanese Buddhism, the Korean Buddhist community's response to "modernity" was consistently positive and proactive. It created many modern reform programs intended to place Buddhism in harmony with modern civilization, while at the same time reacted to the growing influence of Christianity, which had been exercising great influence on the modernization of Korean society at that time. Emphasis on active missionary work in the central city, the translation of Buddhist scriptures from classical Chinese into Korean (K. *han'gŭl*), and efforts to popularize Buddhism in general can all be viewed as the Buddhist community's attempts to adapt to a new religious environment that had come to be defined as "modern."

Most research on modern Korean Buddhism conducted both at home and abroad has dealt mainly with the Korean Buddhist community's response to the challenges posed by modernity and Japanese colonial Buddhism. One thing that has been overlooked in this is the influence of modern Buddhist scholarship. Although there had also been some scholarly works on Buddhist doctrines in traditional Buddhism, it was not scholarship in the modern sense but, rather, a "study of one's own sect," with a strong sectarian tendency. Early modern Buddhist scholarship originating in Europe was based on rigorous philological study of Buddhist texts and empirical historical research. East Asian Buddhism in the early modern period, which had followed the tradition of Mahāyāna Buddhism and Sŏn (Zen) Buddhism, revealed completely different aspects in the understanding of its own tradition, since modern European Buddhist scholarship was introduced in the early twentieth century. The most important difference between the traditional study of Buddhism and modern Buddhist scholarship lies in the emergence of Buddhist "scholars," some of whom are lay believers. Buddhist scholars were different from the scholar-monks in the traditional sense. In understanding their own tradition, the Buddhist scholars try to move away from the platform of traditional Buddhism and adopt an objective historical perspective, and their new understanding has had a lasting, if indirect, impact on the reform programs of modern Buddhism in East Asia.

In the case of Korean Buddhist society, modern Buddhist scholarship was introduced from Japan during the colonial period. The Buddhist scholars of the time, who were educated in the Western civilization adopted by Japan and its modern universities, identified the modernization of Buddhism with a new understanding of Buddhism based on modern scholarship. A good example is Kim Tonghwa (1902–1980), who will be discussed in this essay together with Pak Chonghong (1903–1976). Through a discussion of the orientation of Buddhist scholarship employed by these two figures, this essay tries to understand how the modern European Buddhist scholarship introduced to Korea from Japan during the colonial period was understood by Korean Buddhist scholars. Toward this end, I focus on how Kim and Pak understood the problem of "modernity" and how it influenced their understanding of Buddhism and Buddhist scholarship.

Pak Chonghong and Kim Tonghwa were pioneers in Buddhist scholarship in Korea after the liberation from Japanese colonization (1945), and their scholarly achievements continue to exert great influence on the Korean Buddhist community. As these two scholars are not the only ones who have left large footprints in the field of Korean Buddhist scholarship during the second half of the twentieth century, it is worth explaining the reasons why we chose these two figures for our investigation of the nature of Korean Buddhist scholarship. Both Kim and Pak have some similarities and differences that make them appropriate subjects for case studies. They were born nearly at the same time—in 1902 and 1903, respectively—when the political and economic invasion and exploitation of Korea by the West and nearby powers was underway in full force. Also, as colonial intellectuals, both of them experienced the conflicts of tradition and modernity, which had a significant influence on the formation of their scholarship on Korean Buddhism in particular and Buddhist thought in general.

In a strict sense, Pak Chonghong's expertise is in Western and Korean philosophies, rather than in Buddhist philosophy. The backbone of his scholarly world is modern German philosophy, especially Hegel and Heidegger. Yet, as he said, the primary motivation for his "philosophical activities" lay in understanding "the existence of myself, our time, this society and this country,"[2] which led him to search for the national and cultural identity of Korea in his exploration of Korean philosophy. His research of Korean Buddhism was part of his efforts to understand Korean philosophy per se, and in this process, Pak wanted to identify the originality of Korean Buddhism, which is distinct from that of India, China, and Japan.

Kim Tonghwa is different from Pak Chonghong in many aspects. Pak was trained in Chinese Confucian classics from childhood. In contrast, Kim became a Buddhist monk as a child, thus was exposed to Buddhism, and then later went to Japan for a college education where he was exposed to modern Buddhist scholarship. While Pak studied specifically Korean Buddhism as a part of Korean philosophy, Kim studied Buddhism in general, and his interest in Korean Buddhism was to place it within the broader context of pan-Buddhism, including Indian Buddhism.

It is true that modern European Buddhist scholarship brought a new perspective to the traditional understanding of this religion, and it broadened and enriched the realm of Buddhist studies in its relationship with various branches of the humanities developed in the West, such as philology, philosophy, theology, linguistics, archaeology, and religious studies. However, both the critical consciousness and perspective implicated in modern Buddhist scholarship are fundamentally founded on the Western colonial perspective toward the East. As Edward Said points out, the Western view of the East starts with the conception of the East as the Other, the unknown and the mystic, and thereby an object of interest and conquest. This conception of the East is imbued in its approach to Buddhism as well.[3] Needless to say, both Pak's philosophical orientation and his new approach to Korean philosophy and Korean Buddhism, as well as Kim's Buddhist scholarship, are based on the "modern scholarship" that emerged in Europe. It may not be fair to evaluate their scholarship from the post-colonial criticism of the close relationship between modernity and colonialism; they lived through the colonial period with a strong sense of national pride and responsibility for their native land. However, it is important to point out, not to personally criticize these two figures, but in order to diagnose the nature of modern Korean Buddhist scholarship, that the very beginning of modern Buddhist scholarship was anchored in the colonial reality.

Before we discuss some details about the scholarship of Pak and Kim, I would like to summarize several issues that have been raised until recent years over the identity of Eastern thought in the community of Korean scholars. For the last ten years or so, there has been active discussion over the conceptual definition and research methodology of Korean thought as well as East Asian thought. This arose partly as a result of reflection on Eurocentric world history and the universal mainstream of Western culture that has continued since the early modern period. Such an awareness stimulated scholars, and interest in Korean tradition gradually emerged. In addition, the growing trend of globalization began to foster a sense of crisis related to the cultural identity of Korea, which urges scholars to reappropriate traditional Korean thought. It is against this backdrop that Korean scholars found the Korean scholarship on Confucianism and Buddhism, which constituted the traditional thought of the East and together forms the main components of Korean thought,[4] particularly problematic.

One of the questions that arose in this context has to do with categorization. In other words: Is Eastern thought (K. *sasang*) a philosophy or not? This issue duly reflects the problematic relationship between East and West, especially in modern times, when Western imperialism and colonialism have imposed their socio-political and cultural systems on the Eastern world. The discussions over this issue among Korean scholars can be summarized into the following three groups.

First, for some scholars, especially those whose expertise lies in Western philosophical tradition, Eastern thought should be categorized as a religious thought (in the case of Buddhism) or a social ideology that deals with political systems and social structure (in the case of Confucianism), but it cannot be defined as a philosophy because it pursues individual cultivation and enlightenment (which applies to both Buddhism and Confucianism). This position considers philosophy a phenomenon of the Western world, which inevitably limits the scope of philosophy.

The second group of scholars claims that Eastern thought possesses many elements that can be considered philosophical and thus can be identified as a philosophy. In this case philosophy is defined as rational and logical arguments. This definition of "philosophy" also has its own limits. Many of the proponents of this definition still think of philosophy as based on the Western concept of philosophy and thus study Eastern thought only from a Western perspective. This is the group of people I criticize in the present article, with Pak Chonghong and Kim Tonghwa standing out as its most obvious representatives.

The third position on the relationship between "philosophy" and Eastern thought is often found among conservative scholars of Eastern thought. This position holds that Eastern thought cannot be measured by Western criteria; it claims that "East is East and West is West" and there is no need to evaluate Eastern thought with the categories developed in the West. According to the classification of Jae-ryong Shim, who was one of the leading scholars of Korean Buddhism, the so-called traditional Confucian teachers of the old days are part of this category.[5] Needless to say, the very attitude of this position forecloses any room for dialogue in the issue.

In addition to the relationship between "philosophy" and Eastern thought, another frequently discussed issue includes the question of the identity of Korean thought. That is, how do we define Korean thought? The most comprehensive definition of the concept of Korean thought is "thought by Koreans living in Korea." There seems to be an agreement that this definition is comprehensive enough. But the issue of the scope of Korean thought is still far from clear among Korean scholars. There are also gaps between the "reality" and "theory" behind the debates on the nature of Korean thought.

Yi Myŏnghyŏn, for example, wants to include "the fruits of Western philosophy, whose seeds were sewn from 1920 and on" within the scope of Korean thought or Korean philosophy.[6] Given that Buddhism and Confucianism were imported from outside and became "Koreanized" through a process of acculturation for a long period of time, it may not be impossible that Western philosophy has become "Koreanized" as a part of Korean thought. However, if we look at how the term "Korean thought" is used in an ordinary sense, only Confucianism and Buddhism, among various kinds of imported thought, are included within the definition of Korean thought. Many people use the term this way, and the academic curriculum in Korean universities is organized this way, as well. The specialty areas of those who are majoring in Korean thought are usually Buddhism, Confucianism, and Tonghak thought, as well as modern thinkers such as Sin Ch'aeho. People who specialize in Western philosophy agree to define Korean thought as "thought by Koreans living in Korea," but few seem to think that they are studying Korean thought, although they are Koreans and based in Korea.

The Case of Pak Chonghong

As a member of the first generation of modern Korean philosophers, Pak Chonghong made pioneering efforts to systematize Korean traditional thought such as Buddhism, Confucianism, and Tonghak in the context of Korean intellectual history as well as in the philosophical perspective. Despite those achievements, however, the research methodology on Korean thought that he tried to establish and his attitude toward it are quite problematic from today's perspective. Those problems can be identified as the very origin of the many problems surrounding scholarship on Korean thought today.

In his essay, "Preliminary Thoughts on the Study of Korean Thought" published in 1958, Pak notes that he deals with "the attitude and the scope of the study of Korean thought."[7] He adopts a comprehensive approach to the conceptual definition and scope of Korean thought, arguing that the thoughts of Koreans have to be Korean thought and that Korean thought is produced because Koreans live as Koreans, and it is taken up as a study for that very reason (*PCHC* 9). According to this conceptual definition of Korean thought, this is nothing other than the thought of "Koreans living in Korea." However, despite such a rather broad definition of Korean thought, he confines the scope of his research of Korean thought to traditional thought, especially Confucianism and Buddhism, and to some of the more recent evolution of Korean thought, including Sirhak (practical learning) and Tonghak (Eastern learning) thought. Pak's position contrasts with the positions of other Korean scholars who try to include "the fruits of Western philosophy, whose seeds were sewn from 1920 and on" within the boundary of Korean philosophical thought.

Pak claims that his research of Korean thought is only preliminary; hence, he does not offer any specific research methodology or stance for the study of Korean thought. But we can get a glimpse of his ideas about the research methodology of Korean thought through his remarks scattered throughout the essay.

First of all, Pak thinks of Korean thought as "thought that has Korean character." He asks himself, "If Korean art and music truly have reached a level praised by foreigners, then, would there not be something remarkable in the thought of Koreans who have produced and lived with such art and music?" (*PCHC* 10). Pak further notes that it is one major objective of the philosophers of Korean thought to find the characteristics of Korean thought that are unique to Korea. Applying the idea to the study of Korean Buddhist thought, he states that "it is expected that we can clarify the unique nature of Buddhist thought by studying and understanding Chinul's thought" (*PCHC* 14). In sum, he believes that the mission of Korean Buddhist scholarship and of Korean philosophy is to identify characteristics of Korean Buddhism that distinguish it from Buddhism of other regions. For him, studying Korean thought means finding Korean characteristics. For the theoretical basis of his research methodology to find Korean characteristics, he suggests regional variances in language. He notes, "The way Koreans think is limited by the structure of the Korean language. . . . It is language that mediates and links one's thought with one's life or one's foundation" (*PCHC* 16–17). He believes that different languages lead to different thought systems.

Yet the following problems can be pointed out in his methodological premise of divining the identity of Korean Buddhist thought through its characteristics.

First, a characteristic of something is what makes it distinguished from others, and at the same time, it should continue for a certain duration of time. An instant projection of a phenomenon devoid of a historical context cannot be a characteristic. Pak seems to believe that it is possible to infer the characteristics of Korean Buddhism inductively and, furthermore, by closely examining the Korean thought by studying the thoughts of those renowned scholar-monks in Korean Buddhist history, such as Sŭngnang (5th c.), Wŏnch'ŭk (613–696), Wŏnhyo (617–686), and Ŭich'ŏn (1055–1101). But I wonder whether the historical characteristics of Korean Buddhism running through Sŭngnang, Wŏnch'ŭk, Wŏnhyo, and others really exist, as Pak proposes.

Second, Pak maintains that "it is Ŭich'ŏn who widely spread the spirit of *hwajaeng* [reconciliation of doctrinal controversy], a tradition in Korean Buddhism, by promoting the importance of cultivating doctrine and contemplation" (*PCHC* 154). Here, Pak claims the theory of harmony to be the very characteristic that runs through Korean Buddhist thought from Wŏnhyo to Chinul and all the way down to the Chosŏn dynasty. However, I wonder whether that is really the case. Chinul does not even mention Wŏnhyo in his works, nor does he discuss harmony. Also, there are no dharma disciples or successors who inherited Wŏnhyo's Buddhist thought. In this case, can we still claim the theory of harmony, which has frequently been identified as the core of Wŏnhyo's Buddhism among contemporary Korean Buddhist scholars, to be the defining factor of Korean Buddhist thought?

Third, in asserting that "Koreans' talent and capacity of philosophical contemplation are displayed in the doctrinal development of Buddhist thought" (*PCHC* 206), Pak tries to prove their excellent ability for philosophical contemplation by demonstrating the extraordinariness and creative interpretations made by a few distinguished figures, including Sŭngnang, Wŏnch'ŭk, and Wŏnhyo (through comparison with their contemporaries in China). But the fact that only four or five people exercised influence on Chinese Buddhist society over the millennium from the import of Buddhism to Chinul's time shows the dearth of Korean Buddhist thought. Ironically, contrary to his intention, Pak's argument demonstrates the paucity of Korean Buddhist thinkers and poverty of Buddhist thought in Korea.

Fourth, though Pak says that he wants to closely examine the characteristics of Korean Buddhism, he does not conduct a comparative analysis alongside

Chinese and Indian Buddhism. He examines Wŏnhyo's thought in his commentary on *The Awakening of Faith in Mahāyāna*, but in many cases, he does not distinguish between the main ideas of *The Awakening of Faith in Mahāyāna* and Wŏnhyo's own thought. Even though *The Haedongso* (The Commentary of the East), which is Wŏnhyo's commentary on *The Awakening of Faith in Mahāyāna*, is a representative work of Wŏnhyo, it is essential to compare it with those of other commentaries for a better understanding of Wŏnhyo.

Fifth, by discussing the close relationship between language and philosophical characteristics, Pak argues that Korea had its own unique thought. But because East Asia had the common, intellectually mediating language of Chinese characters at the time, language seems to have functioned as a medium linking East Asia as a community of intellectual discourse rather than guaranteeing the development of the unique characteristics of Korean Buddhist thought.

Sixth, an element consistent in Pak's attitude in studying Korean traditional thought is a strong sense of nationalism. Although not negative in itself, nationalism, if excessively expressed, can do harm to one's academic perspective. He often mentions in his works that "We [Koreans] have something as good as the West." This may be an expression of his national pride and self-respect, but it also reveals his sense of Eastern inferiority to the West and obsession with modernization. This tendency is not observed solely in Pak; it is often present in the writings of Korean intellectuals produced from the liberation until the 1970s.

For Pak Chonghong, the main purpose of studying Korean thought is to identify its characteristics. This attitude is shared by many contemporary scholars studying Eastern thought in the East and the West, but the limits of that position are clearly visible. The concept of regional characteristics based on the unit of a nation-state such as Korea, China, or Japan has been created since modern times. Nations and regions as political units are old concepts coinciding with the history of war, whereas the concept of a nation as a cultural unit is a recent phenomenon. Pak tries to study Korean Buddhism through Wŏnhyo under the notion that he is a representative figure of Korean Buddhist thought. But it is historically more compelling to consider that Wŏnhyo's interest was not solely in Korean Buddhism, but also in joining the intellectual discourse in the pan-Buddhist area of his time, which included India and East Asia. This suggests that it might not be possible to identify regional characteristics of Korean Buddhism by studying Wŏnhyo or Chinul. One might even wonder whether it is possible at all since such an undertaking would have meaning only in a limited sense. The term "one hundred thoughts" in "the controversy of one hundred thoughts," which is Wŏnhyo's main object of *hwajaeng*, refers to the community of discourse on Buddhist thought encompassing East Asia at large, including China.

I am not saying that regional characteristics are not important in the study of Buddhism, or that regional characteristics are nonexistent. Actually, focus on regional characteristics in Buddhist scholarship began initially with Western scholars, who at first studied Buddhism as a part of regional studies. To me, the fact that Korean scholars of East Asian studies consider regional characteristics to be a main research topic shows that they are adopting the Western perspective of East Asian studies without criticism.

The Case of Kim Tonghwa

Unlike Pak Chonghong, who was not a Buddhist scholar in a rigorous sense and who studied Korean Buddhism as a part of Korean thought, Kim Tonghwa was a Buddhist scholar and studied Buddhism in general, without limiting it to Korean Buddhism. In this sense, criticism against Kim will be a criticism of Buddhist scholarship in Korea at large rather than directly of Korean Buddhism.

In his *Pulgyohak kaeron* (Introduction to Buddhist Studies), published in 1954, Kim discusses the conceptual definition and research methodology of Buddhist studies in detail. This work is the first modern-style introductory text and research manual of Buddhist studies in Korea, and even today it is widely read as an introduction to Buddhist studies. The book contains a great deal of Japanese Buddhist scholarship and scholarly achievements of his time, which is not a surprise, considering the author's educational background.

Japan adopted the culture and civilizations of Europe in the modernization process after the Meiji Reformation, and Japanese scholarship also followed this process. Skepticism about and even rejection of its own tradition by intellectuals were common phenomena in the modernization process in East Asia, and Japanese intellectuals were no exception. With the import of Western philosophy, a movement occurred in Japan to reject its own intellectual tradition on account of its being superstitious and unscientific. One of the traditions under criticism was Buddhism, which was regarded as irrational and superstitious in comparison to the rational scientific thought of the West.[8]

Ironic as it may sound, Buddhism forsaken by the Japanese was revived as Japanese Buddhist scholars imported it back from Europe. As Buddhism was discovered by Europeans as part of their colonial project to examine the culture of their colonies,[9] Europeans began to interpret Buddhism employing the methodology used in classical linguistics, religious studies, and philosophy, and Buddhism began to draw the attention of Japanese intellectuals as a scholarly discipline: Modern Buddhist scholarship emerged. Yet from the Western standpoint, modern Buddhist scholarship was analogous to Buddhism. The following statement by Sueki Takehiro shows very well how Eastern intellectuals viewed their tradition in early modern times and how they had come to accept their tradition reinterpreted from the Western standpoint:

> Extremely intellectual and intelligent elements are found in Indian thought. A good example is the Early Buddhism. Looking at the Early Buddhism of Shakyamuni in his lifetime, [one notices that] it is very different from the Buddhism we see and hear in Japan. Talking about Japanese Buddhism . . . [one finds that] it focuses mostly on emotion and intuition, lacking rationality. That is why many people tend to think that Buddhism is anti-rational thought. When I say that Buddhism is a rational thought system, most people are surprised.[10]

"Rationality of Early Buddhism" that Sueki Takehiro discusses is nothing but the Victorian perspective of British Buddhist scholarship, which is Buddhism reconstructed based on then-popular historicism and rationalism.[11] Under the influence of European Buddhist scholarship, Buddhism and Buddhist scholarship in modern Japan emphasized reason and the rationalist perspective, and attainment of objective truth by reason was proposed as a primary proposition of modern Buddhist scholarship.

The starting point of Kim's Buddhist scholarship is the attitude of the Japanese Buddhist scholars toward Buddhism in the early modern period. This can be seen in his assertion of the possibility of philosophical study of Buddhism. In his *Pulgyohak kaeron*, Kim divides Buddhist studies into three areas, namely, religious, philosophical, and ethical studies, and excludes discussions of Buddhist soteriology, including nirvāṇa or enlightenment, from the philosophical study of Buddhism.[12] Kim states:

> The doctrines of Buddhahood and nirvāṇa are both religious and subjective and relate to the doctrine of Buddhist cultivation. . . . When we say the Buddhist truth as the Jewel of Dharma, it means objective philosophical truth mainly. . . . It is subjectivity, but it is not a simple subjectivity, but subjectivity as an object of philosophy, i.e., objective subjectivity. If Buddhism is viewed simply as a religion, the truth in the Jewel of Dharma is actually unnecessary. Despite this, however, in reality the truth forms a large part of Buddhist doctrine, which is different from other religions.[13]

One cannot but wonder whether the so-called "objective philosophical truth," which Kim offers as the presupposition of philosophical study, is really the sole objective of philosophical discourse. Kim claims that because objective truth is the sole object of philosophical truth, "internal experience from enlightenment through nirvāṇa" is to be excluded from the philosophical truth of Buddhism. Indeed, this attitude is found in many Buddhist scholars today. For example, Sin O'hyŏn states in his essay "Wŏnhyo ch'ŏrhak ŭi hyŏndaejŏk chomyŏng" (Philosophy of Wŏnhyo from the Modern Perspective), "Of course, because our discussion intends to be thoroughly philosophical, we cannot discuss the doctrine of dependent origination and therefore, we cannot attempt a close examination of the loss of freedom and its recovery in causal relations. It is a matter of fact and cultivation, which is beyond the scope of philosophical analysis and explanation."[14]

Sin is not the only scholar who, under the name of a "philosophical approach to Buddhism," commits this fallacy of excluding internal experience such as "cultivation" and "enlightenment" as non-philosophical. On the basis of this attitude lies the conscious or unconscious presupposition that a thought system is entitled to be called "philosophy" only when it complies with the Western sense of the term. In Western philosophy, objective truth is conceived by reason and the focus is on the object of conception through abstraction from the conceiving subject. In Buddhism, the capacity of human consciousness in understanding truth is not limited to reason. Human consciousness has many levels and stages. Reason, from the standpoint of Western philosophy, is similar to the mental functions of the sixth and seventh consciousnesses in Buddhism, whereas the *a priori* universality of consciousness overlaps with some mental functions of the eighth consciousness (Storehouse consciousness).

The diverse stages of mind in Buddhism that are based on meditative experience have a hierarchical structure. In Buddhism, cultivation means transformation of the level of consciousness in understanding reality. Depending on the level or stage of consciousness, a corresponding reality unfolds. The two kinds of truth, ultimate truth and conventional truth, should be understood in such a way that an infinite range of experiences of diverse realities can be thought to lie between the two kinds, like the spectrum of a rainbow, rather than being two definite and separate stages of reality. The multilayered hierarchy of reality and the understanding of different levels of reality depending on one's level of cultivation are presupposed in the philosophy and religion of Indian origin. For example, Upaniṣad philosophy demonstrates the progression to the ultimate truth or the hierarchy of diverse realities. The ultimate reality called *ātman* is not understood through daily experiences, but experienced through a high level of cultivation.

After all, it can be said that the Buddhist philosophical system concerns the reality and consciousness unfolding diversely according to the level of cultivation. For instance, the expression that "every sentient being has the Buddha-nature" is not an expression of religious belief or a metaphysical thesis; it is an experienced reality reached through "enlightenment."

I think that it is improper to argue that the Buddhist doctrine of truth is the objective, philosophical truth as Kim does, or that objective truth is the sole object of the study of Buddhist philosophy, as Sin implies in his work. In the Buddhist doctrine of mind and reality as revealed in the changing levels of consciousness depending on one's cultivation, and the hierarchy of reality developing in correspondence to it, the premise of Western philosophy that objective truth is reached solely by reason loses its validity and legitimacy. The Buddhist believes that the experience of meditation, or samādhi, provides a more reliable foundation for epistemology than reason in daily life. The term "objectivity" in Western philosophy already presupposes "daily" and "rational" experience as opposed to the experience of "meditation." In this regard, Buddhist truth is not objective truth in the sense of Western philosophy because it is obtained from the experience of meditation and, ultimately, through enlightenment.

However, this does not mean that meditation or enlightenment experience is necessary to study Buddhism. This is only to point out that we need to understand that Buddhist texts are a verbalized record of the enlightenment experience, which is different from daily experience based on reason. In this regard, I have proposed "methodological agnosticism" as a method of studying Buddhism in another article.[15] Methodological agnosticism is a means to overcome the dilemma that, while Buddhist texts are records of enlightenment, scholars of Buddhism are not necessarily practitioners, nor can they proceed without being firmly grounded in reason. This approach presupposes a distinction between "rationality" and a "rationalistic approach." This requires that, while using rationality as the primary tool for scholarly study, we accept a certain realm, like enlightenment experience, as it is; in doing so, we deny our rationality access to it. In this way we may prevent the proper meaning of the Buddhist doctrine from being distorted.

Conclusion

In the Western intellectual history, it was reason that divided theology and philosophy. Since then, any attempt to define philosophy in the West had to be constantly conscious of theology, which traversed the realm of philosophy with ease. But philosophy has restricted its domain and narrowed its boundary of concern with a claim that certain issues or approaches cannot be "an object of philosophy." It is not the concern of this essay to take up the issue of the "definition" of philosophy itself. However, it is visible that the encounter between Eastern and Western philosophical worlds, through the examples of the Western category called "philosophy" and the Eastern thought system of "Buddhism," demonstrates the very limits of the commonsense definition of philosophy. It goes nearly without saying that when people in Korea say that traditional thought such as Buddhism and Confucianism are not philosophy, they are referring to Western philosophy in a very narrow sense. This very attitude reflects the power imbalance in the East-West encounter caused by Western imperialism and colonialism in early modern history. The problem of Buddhism as a philosophy, then, is a problem of historical reality, not of the nature of Buddhist philosophy or Eastern thought per se.

Korea had Buddhism but did not have Buddhist scholarship until modern times; there was a Buddhist scholarly tradition, but not scholarly discipline in the modern sense. Buddhist scholarship originating in Europe in the early nineteenth century was introduced to Korea through Japan and developed into its current form. Thus, it entirely reflects a Western-oriented worldview and a Western perception. From the liberation from colonization to the present, Korean scholars have uncritically followed that Buddhist scholarship without reflecting on the origin of the tradition. Now is the time to consider a new approach to traditional thought, including Buddhism. The new approach to Eastern thought must be, among other characteristics, wary of nationalistic tendencies, as displayed in the present case studies involving Pak Chonghong and Kim Tonghwa, and the related modernist need for it. Instead, it should proceed with a critical perspective.

Notes

1. An earlier version of this essay appeared in *Korea Journal* 45, no. 1 (Spring 2005): 5–28.

2. Quoted from Yi Namyŏng. "Yŏram ch'ŏrhak: hyangnaejŏk ch'ŏrhak kwa hyangoejŏk ch'ŏrhak ŭi chiphap ŭirosŏŭi Han'guk ch'ŏrhak" (Yŏram's Philosophy: Korean Philosophy as a Combination of Inward and Outward Philosophies). In Ch'ŏrhak yŏn'guhoe, ed., *Haebang 50 nyŏn ŭi Han'guk ch'ŏrhak* (Korean Philosophy during the 50 Years after the Liberation) (Seoul: Ch'ŏrhak kwa hyŏnsil sa, 1996), 11–26, p. 23.

3. See Edward Said, *Orientalism* (New York: Pantheon Books, 1978). See Philip Almond, *The British Discovery of Buddhism* (Cambridge: Cambridge University Press, 1988) for a more recent work on Buddhist scholarship. See also Jae-ryong Shim, ed. *Han'guk esŏ ch'ŏrhak hanŭn chasedŭl* (Philosophical Approaches in Korea) (Seoul: Jimmundang, 1986), pp. 319–342 on the Western view of Oriental philosophy.

4. See Shim, ed. *Han'guk esŏ ch'ŏrhak hanŭn chasedŭl* for various discussions on the research methodology of East Asian thought and philosophy.

5. Shim, ed. *Han'guk esŏ ch'ŏrhak hanŭn chasedŭl*, p. 228.

6. Yi Myŏnghyŏn, "Han'guk ch'ŏrhak ŭi chŏnt'ong kwa kwaje" (The Tradition and Tasks of Korean philosophy), in Jae-ryong Shim ed., *Han'guk esŏ ch'ŏrhak hanŭn chasedŭl*, p. 23.

7. Pak Chonghong, *Pak Chonghong chŏnjip* (Complete Works of Pak Chonghong), vol. 4 (Seoul: Hyŏngsŏl ch'ulp'ansa, 1982), pp. 9–19. Henceforth *PCHC*, and citations from this book will be marked in the text. Pak does not distinguish between thought and philosophy throughout the essay and uses them interchangeably.

8. As a matter of fact, many temples were forced to close down, and some had to close voluntarily with the banning of offerings. With the annexation of Korea to Japan in 1910, Japanese Buddhism entered Korea, and D. T. Suzuki introduced Japanese Zen Buddhism to the Western world. These can be seen as self-rescue measures of Japanese Buddhism to cope with a difficult time at home. See Robert Sharf, "The Zen of Japanese Nationalism," in Donald Lopez, ed., *Curators of the Buddha: The Study of Buddhism under Colonialism* (Chicago: University of Chicago Press, 1995), 107–160.

9. Early Buddhism, in particular, the Pāli Canon, formed the main current in England, while France was interested in Chinese Buddhism, reflecting its interest in China as a colonial market, and Italy in Tibetan Buddhism. See Almond, the *British Discovery of Buddhism.*

10. Sueki Takehiro, *Tōyō no gōri shisō* (Rationality in Eastern Thought) (Tokyo; Kodansha, 1970), p. 24.

11. See Sungtaek Cho, "Rationalist Tendency of Modern Buddhist Scholarship: A Revaluation," *Philosophy East and West* 52, no. 4 (October 2002): 426–440 for criticism of the rationalist approach to Buddhist scholarship and problems in the understanding of early Buddhism by English scholars during the Victorian period.

12. In *Pulgyohak kaeron* (Introduction to Buddhist Studies), Kim divides the areas of Buddhist scholarship as follows:

a. Teachings by the Buddha include: The Jewel of the Buddha, Study of the Founder, the Religious, Leaving suffering and achieving happiness, Beauty, Emotion, Buddhist sūtras, Study on meditation, and Faith;

b. Teachings on the Buddha, the Enlightened One, include: The Jewel of Dharma, Truth, the Philosophical, Transforming ignorance and unfolding enlightenment, Intellect, Buddhist commentaries, Study on wisdom, and Understanding;

c. Teachings on (achieving) Buddhahood include: Jewels of the Buddhist community, Ethics, the Ethical, Preventing unwholesome parts and cultivating wholesome parts, Goodness, Will, Buddhist book on discipline, Punishment, Practice (Kim Tonghwa, *Pulgyohak kaeron* [Introduction to Buddhist Studies] [Seoul: Paeg'yŏngsa, 1954], p. 7).

13. Kim Tonghwa, *Pulgyohak kaeron*, p. 90.

14. See Sin O'hyŏn, "Wŏnhyo ch'ŏrhak ŭi hyŏndaejŏk chomyŏng" (Philosophy of Wŏnhyo from a Modern Perspective), in Academy of Korean Studies, ed., *Wŏnhyo ŭi sasang kwa kŭ hyŏndaejŏk ŭimi* (Wŏnhyo's Philosophy and its Meanings from the Modern Perspective). (Sŏngnam, Korea: Chŏngsin munhwa yŏn'guwŏn, 1994), p. 174. Sin claims that "In the case of Wŏnhyo, the terms he uses are thoroughly philosophical as they are so much metaphysical and thus, Wŏnhyo's Buddhist thought can be properly understood only through a philosophical approach." I think that this is a misunderstanding of Wŏnhyo's thought and of Buddhism at the same time. His position is based on the assumption that cultivation cannot be an object of philosophical investigation. Sin O'hyŏn is not the only person who holds this view. Sin also notes in his essay that "The origin of philosophical knowledge is subjective experience.... However, because subjective experience has *a priori* universality beyond relative subjectivity, it must be distinguished from (Buddhist) wisdom mentioned earlier" (p. 73). I think that Sin has a wrong conception of "Buddhist wisdom." Furthermore, if subjective experience has (relative) objectivity, it is meant to emphasize the object of conception through abstraction of the object from the conceiving [conscious] subject. What is the *a priori* universality Sin assumes to exist? Is it not the ideology of Western philosophy, which he criticizes himself? I think it is the unity of the subject and the object that needs to be pursued. It does not matter whether it is called wisdom, pure experience, or *a priori* universality. Philosophical terms can be as ideological as any ideology since they are part of long history of philosophy, and a conceptual definition of a thing is, by nature, self-constraining. For instance, if I call the state of unity between the subject and the object "pure experience," it can be used as a

philosophical term distinctively from the term "pure experience" used in phenomenology. Regardless, the semantics of a term does not provide its conceptual definition.

On the importance of "cultivation/practice" in doctrinal or philosophical study of Buddhism, see Sungtaek Cho, "Pulgyo ŭi iron kwa silch'ŏn suhaeng: ch'ogi Pulgyo ŭi muaesŏl ŭl chungsim ŭiro" (The Theory and Cultivation in Buddhism: with a focus on the doctrine of not-self in early Buddhism), *Onŭl ŭi tongyang sasang* 8 (Spring/summer 2003): 163–189.

15. Sungtaek Cho, "Pulgyo ŭi iron kwa silch'ŏn suhaeng: ch'ogi Pulgyo ŭi muaesŏl ŭl chungsim ŭiro."

Bibliography

Abelmann, Nancy. "Minjung Theory and Practice." In Harumi Befu, ed. *Cultural Nationalism in East Asia: Representation and Identity*. Research Papers and Policy Studies 39. Berkeley: Institute of East Asian Studies, 1993, 139–165.

Almond, Philip. *The British Discovery of Buddhism*. Cambridge: Cambridge University Press, 1988.

An, Chinho 安震湖. *Sŏngmun ŭibŏm* 釋門儀範 (Buddhist Rituals, 1937). Seoul: Pŏmnyunsa, 2000.

An, Pyŏngjik 안병직. "Manhae Han Yongun ŭi tongnip sasang" 만해 한용운의 독립 사상 (Manhae Han Yongun's Thoughts on Independence). In Manhae Sasang Yŏn'guhoe, ed. *Han Yongun sasang yŏn'gu* 한용운 사상연구 (Studies on Han Yongun's Thought). Seoul: Minjoksa, 1980.

Bancroft, Anne. "Women in Buddhism." In Ursula King, ed. *Women in the World's Religions: Past and Present*. New York: Paragon House, 1987, 81–102.

Barnes, Nancy Schuster. "Buddhism." In Arvind Sharma, ed. *Women in World Religions*. Albany: State University of New York Press, 1987, 105–133.

Bedeski, Robert E. *The Transformation of South Korea: Reform and Reconstruction in the Sixth Republic under Roh Tae Woo 1987–1992*. London: Routledge, 1994.

Bielefeldt, Carl. "Ch'ang-lu Tsung-tse's Tso-Ch'an I and the 'Secret' of Zen Meditation." In Peter N. Gregory, ed. *Traditions of Meditation in Chinese Buddhism*. Studies in East Asian Buddhism 4. Honolulu: University of Hawai'i Press, 1986, 129–61.

Biyan lu 碧巖錄. *T* 2003.48.139a–292a.

Bretzke, James T. "Minjung Theology and Inculturation in the Context of the History of Christianity in Korea." *East Asian Pastoral Review* 28 (1991): 108–130.

Buswell, Robert E. Jr. (Bhikshu Hei Myong). "Korean Hua-t'ou Meditation: And Its Association With the Orthodox Indian Path," *Buddhist Forum Quarterly* 1, no.1 (1978–79): 27–35.

———. "The Pilgrimages of Hyangbong: Memoirs and Poems of the Kumgang Mountains." *Korean Culture* 11.4 (1990): 18–23.

———. "Imagining 'Korean Buddhism': The Invention of a National Religious Tradition." In Hyung Il Pai & Timothy R. Tangherlini, eds. *Nationalism and the Construction of Korean Identity*. Korea Research Monograph. Berkeley: Institute of East Asian Studies, 1998, 73–107.

———. "Buddhism under Confucian Domination: the synthetic vision of Sŏsan Hyujŏng." In Ja Hyun Kim Haboush and Martina Deuchler, eds. *Culture and the State in Late Chosŏn Korea*. Cambridge: Harvard University Press, 1999, 134–159.

———. "The Koryŏ Period." In Takeuchi Yoshinori, ed. *Buddhist Spirituality: Late China, Korea, Japan and the Modern World*. New York: The Crossroad Publishing Co., 1999, 79–108.

———. *The Formation of Ch'an Ideology in China and Korea*. Princeton, NJ: Princeton University Press, 1989.

———. *Tracing Back the Radiance: Chinul's Korean Way of Zen*. Honolulu: University of Hawai'i Press, 1991.

———. *The Zen Monastic Experience*. Princeton, NJ: Princeton University Press, 1992.

———. *P'aran nun sŭnim ŭi Han'guk Sŏn suhaeng ki* 파란눈 스님의 한국선 수행기 (A Blue-eyed Monk's Record of Practice of Korean Sŏn). Trans. Kim Jongmyung. Seoul: Yemun sŏwŏn, 2000.

———, trans. *The Korean Approach to Zen: The Collected Works of Chinul*. Honolulu: University of Hawai'i Press, 1983.

———, ed. *Religions of Korea in Practice*. Princeton, NJ: Princeton University Press, 2007.

Ch'oe, Hyesil 최혜실. *Sinyŏsŏngdŭrŭn muŏsŭl kkumkkuŏtnŭn'ga?* 신여성들은 무엇을 꿈꾸었는가? (What Did New Women Dream About?). Seoul: Saenggak ŭi namu, 2000.

Ch'oe, Namsŏn 崔南善. "Chosŏn Pulgyo: Tongbang munhwasasang e itnŭn kŭ chiwi" 朝鮮佛教: 東方文化史上에 있는 그 地位 (Chosŏn Buddhism: Its Place in Oriental Cultural History). *Pulgyo* (Buddhism) 74 (1930): 1–51.

Ch'oe, Pyŏnghŏn 최병헌. "Ilche Pulgyo ŭi ch'imt'u wa singminji Pulgyo ŭi sŏnggyŏk" 일제불교의 침투와 식민지 불교의 성격 (The Penetration of Japanese Imperial Buddhism and the Character of the Colonial Buddhism). *Chesamch'a hwant'aep'yŏngyang han'gukhak kukche hoeŭi. Han'gukhak nonch'ong* (The 3rd Pacific and Asia Conference on Korean Studies. The Collection of Korean Studies Papers). Seoul: Organizing Committee of the 3rd Pacific and Asia Conference on Korean Studies, 1996.

———. "Ilbon ŭi kangjŏm kwa Pulgyo" 일본의 강점과 불교 (Japanese Control of Korea and Buddhism). *Pulgyo p'yŏngnon* (Buddhist Review) 17 (Winter 2003): 268–93.

Ch'oe, Su-do (Ilgwan) 崔守道 (一貫). "Hanam sŏnsa ŭi Pulgyo kyoyuk sasang yŏn'gu" 漢巖禪師의 佛教教育思想 硏究 (A Study of Sŏn Master Hanam's Thought about Buddhist Education). MA thesis, Dongguk University, Seoul, 1994.

Ch'uan kŭp kugan 推案及鞫案, 1601–1892 (Investigation and Trial Documents, 1601–1892). Seoul: Asea Munhwasa, 1978.

Cha, K. Y., D. P. Wirth, and R. A. Lobo. "Does Prayer Influence the Success of in Vitro Fertilization–Embryo Transfer?" *The Journal of Reproductive Medicine* 46, no. 9 (Sept. 2001): 781–787.

Chan, Wing-tsit, trans. *The Platform Scripture*. New York: St. John's University Press, 1963.

Chandra, Vipan. "Sentiment and Ideology in the Nationalism of the Independence Club (1896–1898)." *Korean Studies* 10 (1986):13–34.

Chang, Garma C. C. *The Buddhist Teaching of Totality*. London: George Allen and Unwin, 1972.

Chen, Kenneth. *Buddhism in China*. Princeton, NJ: Princeton University Press, 1964.

Cho, Eunsu 조은수. "T'ong Pulgyo tamnon ŭl t'onghae pon Han'guk Pulgyosa insik: Han'guk Pulgyo rŭl tasi saenggak handa" '통불교' 담론을 통해 본 한국 불교사 인식: 한국 불교를 다시 생각한다. (The Understanding of the History of Korean Buddhism Seen through the Lenses of the Theory of Ecumenical Buddhism: Re-thinking Korean Buddhism). *Pulgyo p'yŏngnon* 6, no. 4 (Winter 2004): 30–51.

Cho, Sŭngmi 조승미. "Yŏsŏngchuŭijŏk kwanjŏm esŏ pon Pulgyo suhaengnon yŏn'gu: Han'guk yŏsŏng pulcha ŭi kyŏnghŏm ŭl chungsim ŭro" 여성주의적 관점에서 본 불교수행론 연구: 한국 여성 불자의 경험을 중심으로 (A Study on Buddhist Practice Seen from a Feminist Perspective: Focusing on the Experiences of Korean Buddhist Women). Ph.D. Dissertation, Seoul, Dongguk University, 2005.

Cho, Sungtaek 조성택. "Pulgyo ŭi iron kwa silch'ŏn suhaeng: ch'ogi Pulgyo ŭi muaesŏl ŭl chungsim ŭro" 불교의 이론과 실천수행: 초기 불교의 무애설을 중심으로 (The Theory and Cultivation in Buddhism: with a focus on the doctrine of not-self in early Buddhism). *O'nŭl ŭi tongyang sasang* 8 (Spring/Summer 2003): 163–189.

———, ed. *T'oeong S'ŏngch'ŏl ŭi kkaedrŭm kwa suhaeng-S'ŏngch'ŏl ŭi Sŏn sasang kwa Pulgyo sajŏk wich'i* 퇴옹성철의 깨달음과 수행-성철의 선사상과 불교사적 위치 (T'oe'ong S'ŏngch'ŏl's Enlightenment and Practice—S'ŏngch'ŏl's Zen Thoughts and his Position in the History of [Korean] Buddhism). Seoul: Yemun sŏwŏn, 2006.

———. "Rationalist Tendency of Modern Buddhist Scholarship: A Revaluation." *Philosophy East and West* 52, no. 4 (October 2002): 426–440.

Chodang chip 祖堂集. Taipei: Guangwen Shuji, 1973.

Chŏn, In'gwŏn, ed. 전인관. *Tongnip sinmun tasi ilggi* <독립신문> 다시 일기 (Re-reading the *Independent*). Seoul: P'urŭn yŏksa, 2004.

Chŏn'guk pigunihoe, ed. 전국비구니회. *Han'guk piguni ŭi suhaeng kwa sam* 한국 비구니의 수행과 삶 (Life and Cultivation of Korean Buddhist Nuns). Seoul: Yemun sŏwon, 2007.

Chŏng, Kwangho 鄭珖鎬. *Kŭndae Hanil Pulgyo kwan'gyesa yŏn'gu* 近代韓日佛教關係史研究 (A Study on the History of Korean-Japanese Buddhist Relations in Modern Times). Inch'ŏn, Korea: Inha taehakkyo ch'ulp'anbu, 1994.

———. *Han'guk Pulgyo ch'oegŭn paengnyŏnsa p'yŏnnyŏn* 韓國佛教最近百年史編年 (Chronological History of the Latest One Hundred Years of Korean Buddhism). Inch'ŏn, Korea: Inha taehakkyo ch'ulp'anbu, 1999.

Chŏng, Sŏngbon 정성본. *Chungguk Sŏnjong ŭi sŏngnipsa yŏn'gu* 중국 선종의 성립사 연구 (A Study of the History of the Establishment of Chinese Ch'an Schools). Seoul: Minjoksa, 1991.

Chŏng, Sŭngsŏk 정승석. "Tongnam A ŭi chinbojŏk Pulgyo undong kwa Minjung Pulgyo" 동남아의 진보적 불교운동과 민중불교 (Progressive Buddhist Movements in South Asia and Minjung Buddhism). In Pŏpsŏng et al, *Minjung Pulgyo ŭi t'amgu* 민중불교의 탐구 (Examination of Minjung Buddhism). Seoul: Minjoksa, 1989, 197–240.

Chŏng, Yŏnghŭi 鄭英熹. *Kaehwa'gi chonggyogye ŭi kyoyuk yŏn'gu* 개화기 종교계의 교육 연구 (A Study on the Education of Religious Organizations during the [Modern] Reform Period). Seoul: Hyean, 1999.

Chŏng, Yŏngja 정영자. "Kim Iryŏp munhak yŏn'gu" 김일엽 문학 연구 (A Study on Kim Iryŏp's Literature"). *Suryŏn ŏmunhakjip* 14 (1987): 1–26.

Chosŏn Pulgyo Wŏl'bo 조선불교월보 (Korean Buddhism Monthly, 1912) 1–6. Reprinted in *Han'guk kŭnhyŏndae Pulgyo charyo chŏnjip* 한국근현대 불교자료 전집 (Collection of Materials on Modern and Contemporary Korean Buddhism). Seoul: Minjoksa.

Chung, Bongkil, trans. *The Dharma Words of Master Chŏngsan*. Iksan: Won Kwang Publishing Co., 2000.

———, trans. *The Scriptures of Won Buddhism: A Translation of the Wŏnbulgyo kyojŏn with Introduction*. Kuroda Institute Classics in East Asian Buddhism. Honolulu: University of Hawai'i Press, 2003.

Clark, Donald. "History and Religion in Modern Korea: The Case of Protestant Christianity." In Lewis R. Lancaster and Richard K. Payne, eds. *Religion and Society in Contemporary Korea*. Institute of East Asian Studies. Berkeley, CA: University of California Press, 1997, 169–213.

Cleary, Christopher. *Swampland Flowers: The Letters and Lectures of Zen Master Ta Hui*. New York: Grove Press, 1977.

Cleary, Thomas. *Entry into the Inconceivable: an Introduction to Hua-yen Buddhism*. Honolulu: University of Hawai'i Press, 1983.

Cumings, Bruce. *Korea's Place in the Sun: A Modern History*. New York: W. W. Norton, 1997.

Daehaeng Sunim. *Walking without a Trace*. Anyang, Korea: Hanmaum International Culture Institute, 2001.

———. *To Discover True Self, "I" Must Die*. Anyang, Korea: Hanmaum International Culture Institute, 2002.

———. *Mind, Treasure House of Happiness*. Anyang, Korea: Hanmaum International Culture Institute, 2003.

———. *The Furnace Within Yourself*. Anyang, Korea: Hanmaum International Culture Institute, 2004.

Dai-Nihon zokuzōkyō 大日本続蔵経 (Continuation of the Tripiṭāka). Tokyo: Kokusho Kangyōkai, 1950–1990.

Dongguk Taehakkyo Pulgyo Munhwa Yŏn'guwŏn, ed. *Kŭndae tong Asia ŭi Pulgyo hak* 근대 동아시아의 불교학 (Buddhist Scholarship in Modern East Asia). Seoul: Tongguk taehakkyo ch'ulp'anbu, 2008.

———, ed. *Tong Asia ŭi Pulgyo, kŭndae waŭi mannam* 동아시아의 불교, 근대와의 만남 (Encounter of East Asian Buddhism with Modernity). Seoul: Tongguk taehakkyo ch'ulp'anbu, 2008.

Dossey, Larry. *Healing Words*. New York: Harper Books, 1993.

Dumoulin, Heinrich. *A History of Zen Buddhism*. Boston, MA: Beacon Press, 1971.

———. *Zen Buddhism: A History*, 2 vols. New York: Macmillan, 1988.

Dumoulin, Heinrich, and Ruth Fuller Sasaki. *The Development of Chinese Zen*. New York: The First Zen Institute of America, 1953.

Dushan 杜順. *Huayan wujiao jiguan* 華嚴五教止觀 (Cessation and Contemplation in the Five Teachings of the Huayan). *T* 45.1867. 509a–513c.

Faure, Bernard. *The Rhetoric of Immediacy: A Cultural Critique of Chan/Zen Buddhism*. Princeton, NJ: Princeton University Press, 1991.

———. "Random thoughts: Wŏnhyo's 'Life' as thought.'" *Pulgyo yŏn'gu* 11/12 (Nov 1995): 197–223.

Gregory, Peter, trans. *Inquiry into the Origin of Humanity*. Honolulu: University of Hawai'i Press, 1995.

Gross, Rita. *Buddhism after Patriarchy: A Feminist History, Analysis, and Reconstruction of Buddhism*. Albany: State University of New York Press, 1994.

Ha, Ch'unsaeng 하춘생. *Kkaedarŭm ŭi kkot: Han'guk kŭnserŭl pinnaen kŭnse piguni* 깨달음의 꽃: 한국 근세를 빛낸 근세 비구니 (Flowers of Enlightenment: Buddhist Nuns in Modern Time who Have Lightened up Korean Buddhism), 2 vols. Seoul: Yŏrae, 1998–2001.

Hakeda, Yoshito S., trans. *The Awakening of Faith*. New York: Columbia University Press, 1967.

Han, Chongman, ed. 한종만. *Han'guk kŭndae minjung Pulgyo ŭi i'nyŏm kwa chŏn'gae* 한국근대민중불교의 이념과 전개 (The Theory and Developments of Minjung Buddhism in Modern Korea). Seoul: Han'gilsa, 1980.

Han, Kidu 한기두. "Chosŏn hugi sŏn Pulgyo ŭi hŭrŭm" 조선 후기 선불교의 흐름 (The Currents in Sŏn/Zen Buddhism in Late Chosŏn Period). *Sŏn kwa tongbang munhwa* 선과 동방 문화 (Chan and Oriental Culture). Seoul: Korean Association for Buddhist Academic Exchanges, 1994.

Han, Pogwang 한보광. *Yongsŏng sŏnsa yŏn'gu* 용성 선사 연구 (A Study of Sŏn Master Yongsŏng). Seoul: Kamnodang, 1981.

———. "Kŏnbong-sa ŭi manil yŏmbul kyŏlsa" 건봉사의 만일 염불 결사 (The Community for the Recitation of Buddha's Name for Ten Thousand Days at Kŏnbong Monastery). *Pulgyo hakpo* 33 (1996): 73–95.

———. "Manil yŏmbul kyŏlsa ŭi sŏngnip kwa kŭ yŏkhal" 萬日念佛結社의 成立과 그 役割 (The Formation and Role of the Community for the Recitation of the Buddha's Name for Ten Thousand Days). *Chŏngt'ohak yŏn'gu* 1 (1998): 51–72.

———. "Yongsŏng sŭnim ŭi chŏnban'gi ŭi saengae—sanjung suhaenggi rŭl chungsim ŭro" 용성 스님의 전반기의 생애-산중 수행기를 중심으로 (The First Half of Master Yongsŏng's Life: focusing on the period of ascetic practices in mountains). *Taegak sasang* 1 (1998): 27–50.

———. "Yongsŏng sŭnim ŭi huban'gi ŭi saengae (2)—Taegak kyose ŭi hwakjang kwa haesan" 용성 스님의 후반기의 생애 (2)-대각 교세의 확장과 해산 (The Second Half of Master Yongsŏng's Life, 2: the Expansion of the Great Enlightenment Movement and its Dispersion). *Taegak sasang* 4 (2001): 9–72.

Han, Sŏkhŭi 한석희. *Ilche ŭi chonggyo ch'imnyak sa* 일제의 종교 침략사 (The History of Japanese Aggression in Religious Sphere). Seoul: Kidokkyomunsa Publishers, 1990. Trans. by Kim Sŭngt'ae from Japanese, *Nihon no Chōsen shihae to shukyō seisaku* 日本の朝鮮支配と宗教政策 (Japan's Occupation of Korea and Religious Policy). Tokyo: Miraisha, 1988.

Han, Yongun 韓龍雲. *Han Yongun chŏnjip* 韓龍雲全集 (Collected Works of Han Yongun). 6 vols. Seoul: Shin'gu munhwasa, 1980.

Han'guk hak munhŏn yŏn'guso, ed. *Pak Kyusu chŏnjip* 박규수 전집 (Complete Works of Pak Kyusu). Seoul: Asea munhwasa, 1978.

Han'guk hyŏndae Pulgyo undongsa 한국 현대 불교 운동사 (History of Buddhist Activism in Modern Korea), 2 vols. P'aju'gun, Korea: Tosŏ ch'ulp'ansa, 1996.

Han'guk Pulgyo Ch'ongnam P'yŏnch'an Wiwŏnhoe, ed. 한국불교총람편찬위원회. *Han'guk Pulgyo Ch'ongnam* 韓國佛教總覽 (Comprehensive Bibliography of Korean Buddhism). Seoul: Taehan Pulgyo chinhŭng wŏn, 1993.

Han'guk Pulgyo Chapji Ch'ongsŏ 한국 불교 잡지 총서 (Collection of Korean Buddhist Journals). 18 vols. Seoul: Poyŏn'gak, n.d.

Han'guk Pulgyo chŏnsŏ 韓國佛教全書 (Collected Works of Korean Buddhism). Seoul, 1979–1989.

Hanam Taejongsa munjip p'yŏnch'an wiwŏnhoe, ed. 漢巖大宗師文集編纂委員會. *Hanam ilballok: Hanam Taejongsa pŏbŏrok* 漢巖一鉢錄: 漢巖大宗師法語錄 (Hanam's One Bowl of Records: Recorded Dharma-lectures of Great Patriarch Hanam). Seoul: Minjoksa, 1996.

Harris, Ian, ed. *Buddhism and Politics in Twentieth-century Asia*. London and New York: Pinter, 1999.

Heine, Steven, and Charles S. Prebish, eds. *Buddhism in the Modern World: Adaptations of an Ancient Tradition*. Oxford and London: Oxford University Press, 2003.

Higashi Honganji Administration, ed. "Chōsen kaikyō gojūnen shi" 朝鮮開港五十年史 (The Records of 50 Years [after] Commencing Mission to Korea, 1927). *Ilbon Pulgyo kaegyo charyo* 일본 불교 개교 자료 (Materials on the Commencement of Japanese Buddhist Mission in Korea). In *Han'guk kŭnhyŏndae Pulgyo charyo chŏnjip*, vol. 62. Seoul: Minjoksa, 1996.

Hō, Kangan 方漢巖. "Bukkyō wa jikkō ni ari" 佛教は實行にあり (The Essence of Buddhism Lies in Genuine Practice). In *Kŭndae Pulgyo kit'a charyo* 近代佛教其他資料 (More Materials on Modern Buddhism), vol. 2. 1936, pp. 227–29 [233–34].

Hŏ, Tonghyŏn 허동현. "1881 nyŏn chosa sich'aldan ŭi hwaldong e kwanhan yŏn'gu" 1881년 조사시찰단의 활동에 관한 연구 (A Study of the Activities of the Courtiers' Observation Mission of 1881). *Kuksagwan nonch'ong* 국사관 논총 (The Journal of the National History [Compilation] Committee), 66 (1995).

Hong, Sasŏng 홍사성. "Minjung Pulgyo undong ŭi p'yŏngka wa chŏnmang" 민중불교 운동의 평가와 전망 (Evaluation and the Vision for the Future of Minjung Buddhist Movement). In Pŏpsŏng et al., *Minjung Pulgyo ŭi t'amgu* 민중불교의 탐구 (Examination of Minjung Buddhism). Seoul: Minjoksa, 1989, 89–127.

Huh, Woosung. "Manhae's Understanding of Buddhism." *Korea Journal* 40, no. 2 (Summer 2000): 65–101.

Hur, Nam-lin. "The Sōtō Sect and Japanese Military Imperialism in Korea." *Japanese Journal of Religious Studies* 26, nos. 1/2 (1999): 107–134.

Hwang, Chŏngsu (T'aejin) 黃貞洙 (泰震). "Kyŏnghŏ Man'gong ŭi Sŏn sasang: Tŏksungsanmun hyŏngsŏng ŭl chungsim ŭro" 鏡虛.滿空의 禪思想研究: 德崇山門形成을 中心으로 (Sŏn Thoughts of Kyŏnghŏ and Man'gong: focusing on the formation of the Tŏksung Faction). PhD dissertation, Seoul, Dongguk University, 1999.

Hwang, P'ilho 황필호. "Haebang Sinhak kwa Minjung Pulgyo ŭi pigyo punsŏk" 해방신학과 민중불교의 비교분석 (Comparative Analysis of Liberation Theology and Minjung Buddhism). In Pŏpsŏng et al, *Minjung Pulgyo ŭi T'amgu* 민중불교의 탐구 (Examination of Minjung Buddhism). Seoul: Minjoksa, 1989, 241–281.

Hwang, Sŏnmyŏng 황선명. *Chosŏnjo chonggyo sahoe sa yŏn'gu* 조선조 종교 사회사 연구(A Study on Religious and Social History of the Chosŏn Dynasty). Seoul: Ilchisa, 1992.

Hyegŏ 慧炬. "Samhak kyŏmsu wa sŏn-kyo yunghoe ŭi Hanam sasang" 三學兼修와 禪教融會의 한암사상 (Hanam's Thoughts on Equal Cultivation of Three Studies and the Integration of Zen and Doctrinal Teaching). A paper presented at the First Seminar on the Premodern and Modern Intellectual History of the Chogye Order. Seoul, Dongguk University, September 17, 2004.

Hyŏn'ŭng 현응. "Taesŭng Pulgyo ŭi silch'ŏn sasang: Minjung Pulgyo undong ŭi Taesŭngjŏk chŏn'gae rŭl wihayŏ" 대승불교의 실천 사상: 민중불교 운동의 대승적 전개를 위하여 (The Theory of Practice of Mahāyāna Buddhism: towards a Manahanist Evolution of the Minjung Buddhist Movement). *Minjok Pulgyo* 1 (1989): 120–138.

Hyujŏng 休靜. *Sŏn'ga kwigam* 禪家龜鑑 (Paragon of Zen Tradition). Seoul: Poyŏngak, 1978.

Ignatovich, A.N., Svetlov, G.E. *Lotos i politika* (The Lotus and the Politics). Moscow: Mysl', 1989.

Im, Chongguk 임종국. "Ch'ogi chonggyo ch'imnyak kwa ch'inilp'a" 초기 종교 침략과 친일파. (The Beginnings of Religious Aggression and Pro-Japanese Group). *Inmulgye*, 64 (1989).

Im, Hyebong 임혜봉. *Ch'inil Pulgyo ron* 친일 불교론 (On Pro-Japanese Buddhism) 2 vols. Seoul: Minjoksa, 1993.

Im, Kijung 임기중. *Pulgyo kasa wŏnjŏn yŏn'gu* 불교 가사 원전 연구 (A Study on the Originals of Buddhist Lyrics). Seoul: Tongguk taehakkyo ch'ulp'anbu, 2000.

Inagaki Masami, comp. *Senoo Girō Shūkyō ronshū* 妹尾義郎宗教論集 (Collected Essays on Religion by Senoo Girō). Tokyo, Daizō shuppan, 1975.

Jaffe, Richard M. *Neither Monk Nor Layman: Clerical Marriage in Modern Japanese Buddhism.* Princeton and Oxford: Princeton University Press, 2001.

Jingde chuandeng lu 景德傳燈錄. By Doayun 道原. *T* 2076.51.196–467.

Jorgensen, John. "Conflicts between Buddhism and Confucianism in the Chosŏn Dynasty: A Preliminary Survey." *Pulgyo yŏn'gu* 15 (1998): 189–242.

Kaebyŏk 개벽. "Sakpal ha'go sŭngbok ibŭn Kim Iryŏp yŏsa ŭi hoe'gyŏn'gi" 삭발하고 승복 입은 김일엽 여사의 회견기 (An Interview with Tonsured Ms. Kim Iryŏp in a Nun's Robe) (January 1935): 12–17.

Kang, Kŏn'gi, and Kim Hosŏng, eds. 姜健基. 金浩星. *Kkadarŭm: tono tonsu in'ga, tono chŏmsu in'ga* 깨달음: 돈오돈수인가, 돈오점수인가 (Enlightenment: Is it Sudden Awakening and Sudden Cultivation or Sudden Awakening and Gradual Cultivation?). Seoul: Minjoksa, 1992.

Kang, Man'gil. "Contemporary Nationalist Movements and the Minjung." In Kenneth Wells, ed. *South Korea's Minjung Movement: The Culture and Politics of Dissidence.* Honolulu: Univeristy of Hawai'i Press, 1995.

Kang, Sŏkju, and Pak Kyŏnghun 姜昔珠. 朴敬勛. *Pulgyo kŭnse paegnyŏn* 佛教近世百年 (Korean Buddhism during the Last Hundred Years). Seoul: Minjoksa, 2002.

Katō, Bunkyō 加藤文教. "Chōsen Kaikyō ron" 朝鮮開教論 (On Commencing the Preaching in Korea, 1900). *Ilbon Pulgyo kaegyo charyo* (Materials on the Commencement of Japanese Buddhist Mission in Korea). In *Han'guk kŭnhyŏndae Pulgyo charyo chŏnjip*, vol. 62. Seoul: Minjoksa, 1996.

Keel, Hee-Sung. *CHINUL: The Founder of the Korean Sŏn Tradition*. Berkeley Buddhist Studies Series. Seoul: Po Chin Chai Ltd., 1984.

———. "Zen and Minjung Liberation." *Inter-Religio* 17 (Summer 1990): 24–37.

———. 길희성.한국 불교의 정체성 탐구: 조계종 역사와 사상을 중심으로 하여 (The Chogye Order and the Search for the Identity of Korean Buddhism). *Han'guk chonggyo yŏn'gu* (Journal of Korean Religions) 2 (June 2000): 159–93.

Ketelaar, James Edward. *Of Heretics and Martyrs in Meiji Japan: Buddhism and its Persecution*. Princeton, NJ: Princeton University Press, 1990.

Kim, Chinsong 김진송. *Sŏule ttansŭhorŭl hŏhara: hyŏndaesŏng ŭi hyŏngsŏng* 서울에 딴스홀을 허하라: 현대성의 형성 (Allow Dance Halls in Seoul: the Formation of Modernity). Seoul: Hyŏnsil munhwa yŏn'gu, 1999.

Kim, Chongch'an 김종찬. "Minjung Pulgyo undong ŭi chŏn'gae kwajŏng" 민중불교운동의 전개과정 (The Process of the Evolution of Minjung Buddhism). In Pŏpsŏng, et al. *Minjung Pulgyo ŭi t'amgu*. Seoul: Minjoksa, 1989, 171–196.

Kim, Chongsŏ 김종서. "Hanmal, Ilche ha Han'guk chongyo yŏn'gu ŭi chŏn'gae" 韓末日帝下 韓國宗教研究의 展開 (The Development of the Study of Korean Religion at the End of the Chosŏn Dynasty and under Japanese Rule). *Han'guk sasangsa taegye* 韓國思想史大系 (Compendium of the Intellectual History of Korea) vol. 6. Sŏngnam, Korea: Han'guk chŏngsin munhwa yŏn'guwŏn, 1993, 243–314.

Kim, Haeun 김해은. "Pulgyo kŭn-kŭndaehwa ron" 불교 근근대화론 (Theory of Modern-Modernization of Buddhism). *Pulgyo wa Minjok Chunghŭng* 1 (1974): 165–210.

Kim, Hosŏng 金浩星. "Hanam ŭi Toŭi-Pojo pŏbt'ong sŏl: 'Haedong ch'ojo e tae haya' rŭl chungsim ŭro 漢岩의 道義－普照 法統說: '海東初祖에 對하야' 를 중심으로 (Hanam's view on the Toŭi-Pojo Dharma-lineage, focusing on [Hanam's article] 'Regarding the First Patriarch of Korea'). *Pojo sasang* 普照思想 2 (1988): 401–416.

———. "Hanam sŏnsa: pojosŏn kyesŭng-han chongmun ŭi sŏnjisik" 漢岩禪師: 普照禪 계승한 宗門의 선지식 (Sŏn Master Hanam: A kalyāṇamitra of the [Chogye] Order who inherited Pojo's Sŏn). *Han'guk Pulgyo inmul sasang-sa* 韓國佛教人物思想史 (An Intellectual History of Figures in Korean Buddhism). Seoul: Minjoksa, 1990, 462–473.

———. *Pang Hanam sŏnsa: Chogye-jong ch'odae chongjŏng* 方漢岩禪師: 조계종 초대종정 (Sŏn Master Pang Hanam: The First Supreme Patriarch of the Chogye Order). Seoul: Minjoksa, 1996.

Kim, Hyegong, ed. 김혜공. *Man'gong ŏrok* 만공어록 (Recorded Sayings of Man'gong). Korea: Sudŏk-sa, 1968.

Kim, Iryŏp 金一葉. "Tongsaeng ŭi chugŭm" 동생의 죽음 (The Death of My Sister). *Sinyŏja* 3 (May 1920).

———. "Uri ŭi isang" 우리의 이상 (Our Ideals). *Pu'nyŏ chigwang* (July, 1924).

———. "Na ŭi chŏngjogwan" 나의 정조관 (My View on Chastity). *Chosŏn ilbo* 8 (Jan. 1927).

———. *Silsŏngin ŭi hoesang: Ilmyŏng ŏ'nŭ sudo'in ŭi hoesang* 실성인의 회상: 일명 어느 수도인의 회상 (A Memoir of the One who Has Lost the Mind; also known as a Memoir of a Practitioner). Yesan, Korea: Sudŏksa, 1960.

———. *Ch'ŏngch'un ŭl pulsarŭ'go* 청춘을 불사르고 (Having Burned out the Youth, 1962). Seoul: Kimyŏngsa, 2002.

———. *Haengbok kwa pulhaeng ŭi sa'i esŏ* 행복과 불행의 사이에서 (In Between Happiness and Misfortune). Seoul: Whimun ch'ulp'ansa, 1964.

———. *Mi'rae'se'ga taha'go namdorok* 미래세가 다하고 남도록 (Until the Future Life Comes to an End and Even Afterwards), 2 vols. Seoul: Inmul yŏn'guso, 1974.

———. *Sudŏksa ŭi no'ŭl* 수덕사의 노을 (Sunset at the Sudŏk Monastery). Seoul: Pŏmusa, 1976.

———. *Kkosi chi'myŏn nuni siryŏra* 꽃이 지면 눈이 시려라 (As Flowers Wilt, So Do Tears Well Up). Seoul: Osangsa, 1985.

———. *Iryŏp Sŏnmun* 一葉禪文 (Zen Writings by Iryŏp). Seoul: Munhwa sarang, 2001.

Kim, Jongmyung 김종명. "Ijong Sŏn, samjong Sŏn nonjaeng" 이종선, 삼종선 논쟁 (Debate on the Types of Sŏn Buddhism). In Yi Hyogŏl, et al. *Nonjaeng ŭro ponŭn Pulgyo ch'ŏrhak* 논쟁으로 보는 불교철학 (Buddhist Philosophy Seen through Debates). Seoul: Yemun sŏwŏn, 1998, 224–61.

———. "Hyŏndae Han'guk sahoe wa sŭngga kyoyuk" 현대한국사회와 승가교육 (Modern Korean Society and Monastic Education). *Han'guk Pulgyohak* (Buddhist Studies of Korea) 28 (2001): 485–518.

———. *Han'guk chungse ŭi Pulgyo ŭirye: sasang chŏk pae'gyŏng kwa yŏksa chŏk ŭimi* 한국중세의 불교 의례– 사상적 배경과 역사적 의미 (Buddhist Rituals in Medieval Korea: Philosophical Background and Historical Significance). Seoul: Munhak kwa chisŏngsa, 2001.

———. "The *Tripiṭāka Koreana*: Its Computerizaion and Significance for the Cultural Sciences in a Modern Globalized World." In James Lewis and Amadu Sesay, eds. *Korea and Globalization: Politics, Economy, and Culture*. London: RoutledgeCurzon, 2002, 154–81.

———. "Chikchi ŭi Sŏn sasang kwa kŭ ŭiŭi" 직지의 선사상과 그 의의 (The Sŏn Thought of the *Paegun's Chikchi Excerpts* and Its Significance in East Asian Buddhism). *Yŏksa hakpo* 177 (March 2003): 33–65.

———. "Man'gong ŭi Sŏn sasang: t'ŭkching kwa yŏkhal" 만공의 선사상–특징과 역할 (Man'gong's Approach to Zen: Its Characteristics and Role). *Chonggyo yŏn'gu* 34 (Spring 2004): 203–32.

———. "Buddhist Soteriology in the Korean Context: Hyujŏng's Approaches to Enlightenment." In Torsten Larbig and Siegfried Wiedenhofer, eds. *Tradition and Theories of Tradition: An International Discussion*. Muenster, Germany: LIT Verlag, 2006, 78–108.

Kim, Kwang-ok. "Ritual Forms and Religious Context." In Lewis R. Lancaster and Richard K. Payne, eds. *Religion and Society in Contemporary Korea*. Institute of East Asian Studies: University of California, Berkeley, 1997, 215–248.

Kim, Kwangsik 金光植. "Ilje-ha Sŏnhak-wŏn ŭi unyŏng kwa sŏnggyŏk" 日帝下 禪學院 의 運營과 性格 (Managements and Characteristics of the Sŏnhak-wŏn during the Japanese Colonoialism). *Hanguk Tongrip undong-sa yŏn'gu* 한국독립운동사연구 (A Study on the History of Korea's Independence Movement) 8 (1994): 281–312.

———. *Yongsŏng* 용성. Seoul: Minjoksa, 1999.

———. "Odae-san sudo-wŏn kwa Kim T'anhŏ: chŏnghye kyŏlsa ŭi hyŏndaejŏk pyŏnyong" 오대산 수도원과 김탄허: 정혜결사의 현대적 변용 (The Center for Cultivation at Odae-Mountains and Kim T'anhŏ: a Modern Transformation of the Samādhi and Prajñā Community). *Chŏngt'ohak yŏn'gu* 4 (2001): 177–226.

———. "Kim T'anhŏ ŭi kyoyuk kwa kŭ sŏnggyŏk" 김탄허의 교육과 그 성격 (Kim T'anhŏ's Education and its Characteristics). *Chŏngt'ohak yŏn'gu* 6 (2003): 213–243.

———. "Kusul-sa yŏn'gu ŭi p'iryosŏng: kŭn-hyŏndae Pulgyo ŭi kongbaek ŭl meuja" 구술사 연구의 필요성 – 근 · 현대 불교의 공백을 메우자 (The Necessity of Studying Oral History: Let's Bridge the Gap in Modern and Contemporary [Korean] Buddhism). *Pulgyo P'yŏngnon* 5, no. 2 (June 2003): 217–234.

———. "Yi Sŏngch'ŏl ŭi Pulgyo kaehyŏkron" 이성철의 불교 개혁론 (Yi Sŏngch'ŏl's Theory of Buddhist Reform). In Sungtaek Cho, ed. *T'oe'ong S'ŏngch'ŏl ŭi kkaedarŭm kwa suhaeng* 퇴옹성철의 깨달음과 수행 (Enlightenment and Practice of T'oe'ong S'ŏngch'ŏl). Seoul: Yemun sŏwŏn, 2006, 216–265.

Kim, Kwangsik, and Yi Ch'ŏlgyo 金光植 李哲教. *Hanguk kŭnhyŏndae Pulgyo charyo chŏnjib* 韓國近現代佛教資料全集 (Collected Materials of Modern and Contemporary Korean Buddhism), 69 vols. Seoul: Minjoksa, 1996.

Kim, Kyŏngil 김경일. *Han'guk ŭi kŭndae wa kundaesŏng* 한국의 근대와 근대성 (Modernization of Korea and Modernity). Seoul: Paegsan sŏdang, 2003.

Kim, Kyŏngjip 김경집. *Han'guk kŭndae Pulgyo sa* 한국근대불교사 (History of Modern Korean Buddhism). Seoul: Kyŏngsŏwŏn, 1998.

———. "Kwŏn Sangno ŭi kaehyŏngnon yŏn'gu" 권상로의 개혁론 연구 (A Study of Kwŏn Sangno's Theory of Reform). *Han'guk Pulgyohak* 25 (1999): 401–427.

———. *Han'guk Pulgyo kaehyŏngnon yŏn'gu* 한국불교 개혁론연구 (A Study on the Reform Theories of Korean Buddhism). Seoul: Chin'gakchong, 2001.

———. "Kŭndae kaehwasŭng ŭi hwaldong kwa hyŏnsil insik" 근대 개화승의 활동과 현실 인식 (Activities of Modern Reformist Monks and Their Reality Consciousness). *Pojo sasang* 25 (Feb 2006): 463–490.

Kim, Okkyun 김옥균. *Kapsin Illok* 甲申日錄 (The Diary of the *Kapsin* [*Coup*], 1885). Seoul: Kŏn'guk taehakkyo ch'ulp'anbu, 1977.

Kim, Sut'ae 김수태. "Yi Nŭnghwa ui Han'guk Kidokkyo yŏn'gusa" 이능화의 한국기독교 연구사 (Yi Nŭnghwa's Study of Korean Christianity). *Chonggyo yŏn'gu* 9 (1993): 109–30.

Kim, T'aesin 김태신. *Rahula ŭi sa'mo'gok* 라훌라의 사모곡 (Songs of Rahula Yearning for His Mother), 2 vols. Seoul: Han'gilsa, 1991.

Kim, T'anhŏ 김탄허. "Hyŏndae Pulgyo ŭi kŏin: Pang Hanam" 現代佛教의 巨人: 方漢巖 (A Giant of Modern Korean Buddhism: Pang Hanam). Han'guk ŭi in'gan-sang, 3, chonggyo'ga sahoe pongsaja p'yŏn 韓國의 人間像3: 宗教家, 社會奉仕者 編 (The Character of Korean People, vol. 3: Religious Figures and Figures in Public Services). Seoul: Sin'gu munhwasa, 1966.

Kim, Tonghwa 金東華. *Pulgyohak kaeron* 佛教學概論 (Introduction to Buddhist Studies). Seoul: Paegyŏngsa, 1954.

———, ed. *Han'guk yŏktae kosŭng chŏn* 한국역대고승전 (History of Important Korean Monks). Seoul: Samsŏng misul munhwa chaedan, 1964.

Kim, Tot'ae 金道泰. *Sŏ Chaep'il paksa chasŏjŏn* 徐載弼博士自敍傳 (Autobiography of Dr. Sŏ Chaep'il). Seoul: Posŏnsa, 1948.

Kim, Yŏngguk 김영국. "Pan-kong ideorogi wa ŏyong Pulgyo" 반공이데올로기와 어용불교 (Anti-communist Ideology and Pro-state Buddhism). *Minjok Pulgyo* 1 (1989): 94–101.

King, Sallie B. "Thich Nhat Hanh and the Unified Buddhist Church of Vietnam: Nondualism in Action." In Christopher S. Queen and Sallie B. King, eds. *Engaged Buddhism: Buddhist Liberation Movements in Asia.* Albany: State University of New York Press, 1996, 321–363.

Ko, Ŭn 고 은. *Han Yongun p'yŏngjŏn* 한용운 평전 (Annotated Biography of Han Yongun). Seoul: Minŭmsa, 1975.

———. "Minjung Pŏptang han malssŭm" 민중법당 한말씀 (Talks from the Minjung Dharma Hall). *Minjung pŏptang* 1 (July 1985): 14–15.

———. "Mirŭk kwa Minjung" 미륵과 민중 (Maytreya and Minjung). In Kim Chiha et al. *Mirŭk sasang kwa minjung sasang* 미륵사상과 민중 사상 (Maitreya Thought and Minjung Thought). Seoul: Hanjin ch'ulp'ansa, 1988, 51–93.

Ku San. *Nine Mountains: Dharma Lectures of the Korean Meditation Master Ku San.* Korea: Song Kwang Sa Monastery, 1978.

Kŭmgansan ŭi chuin 금강산의 주인 (The Owner of Mt. Diamond). Iksan, Korea: Wŏlgan Wŏn'gwangsa, 1990.

Kwon, Kee-jong. "Buddhism undergoes Hardships: Buddhism in the Chosŏn Dynasty." In The Korean Buddhist Research Institute, ed. *The History and Culture of Buddhism in Korea.* Seoul: Dongguk University Press, 1993, 169–218.

Kwŏn, Sangno 權相老. *Chosŏn Pulgyo yaksa* 朝鮮佛敎略史 (A Brief History of Korean Buddhism). Seoul: Sinmun'gwan, 1917.

———. "Puljŏn Kwŏn Sangno kyosu wa Pang Hanam Sŏnsa ŭi sŏnjŏk mundap" 佛傳 權相老 敎授와 方漢巖 禪師의 禪的問答 (A Sŏn Dialogue between Professor Puljŏn Kwŏn Sangno and Sŏn Master Pang Hanam). *Pulgyo sibo* (Oct 1939).

Kyŏnghŏ chip 鏡虛集 (Collected Writings of Kyŏnghŏ). *HPC* 11.587b–701.

Kyŏnghŏ Sŏngu Sŏnsa Pŏbŏ Chip Kanhaeng Hoe, ed. *Kyŏnghŏ pŏbŏ* 鏡虛法語 (Kyŏnghŏ's Dharma Discourses). Seoul: Inmul yŏn'gu, 1981.

Kyoyugwŏn Purhak Yŏn'guso 교육원 불학 연구소. *Chogyejong sa: Kŭn.hyŏndae p'yŏn* 조계종사: 근현대편 (The History of the Chogye Order: the Modern and Contemporary Period). Seoul: Taehan Pulgyo Chogyejong kyoyugwŏn, 2001.

Lancaster, Lew, in collaboration with Park Sung-bae et al. *The Korean Buddhist Canon: A Descriptive Catalogue.* Berkeley, CA: University of California Press, 1979.

Lancaster, Lewis R., and Richard K. Payne, eds. *Religion and Society in Contemporary Korea.* Berkeley, CA: Institute of East Asian Studies, 1997.

Lee, Kyong-hee. *World Heritages in Korea.* Seoul: Hak Go Jae, 1998.

Legge, James, trans. *Confucian Analects, The Great Learning, & The Doctrine of the Mean.* Oxford: Clarendon Press, 1893.

———, trans. *The Works of Mencius.* Oxford: Clarendon Press, 1895.

Levering, Miriam L. "Lin-chi (Rinzai) Ch'an and Gender: The Rhetoric of Equality and the Rhetoric of Heroism." In José Ignacio Cabezon, ed. *Buddhism, Sexuality and Gender.* Albany: State University of New York Press, 1992, 137–156.

Linji lu 臨濟錄. *T* 47.1985. 496b–506c.

Loftus, Elizabeth L., and John C. Palmer. "Reconstruction of Automobile Destruction: An Example of the Interaction between Language and Memory." *Journal of Verbal Learning and Verbal Behavior* 13 (1974): 585–589.

Lone, Stewart, and Gavan McCormack. *Korea Since 1850*. Melbourne: Longman Cheshire, 1993.

Lopez, Donald, Jr., ed. *Buddhist Hermeneutics*. Honolulu: University of Hawai'i Press, 1988.

Luk, Chalres. *Ch'an and Zen Teaching*. Third Series. London: Rider, 1962.

———. *Practical Buddhism*. London: Rider, 1971.

———, trans. *Empty Cloud: The Autobiography of the Chinese Zen Master Hsü Yün*. Rochester: Empty Cloud Press, 1974.

Ma Myŏng 馬 鳴. *Han'guk Pulgyo sahwa* 韓國佛教史話 (A Narrative History of Korean Buddhism). Seoul: Kyŏngsŏwŏn, 1981.

Man'gong Mundo Hoe, ed. 滿空門徒會. "Man'gong Pŏbŏ: poryŏgo hanŭn chaga nugunya" 滿空法語: 보려고 하는 자가 누구냐 (Dharma Talks by Man'gong: who is trying to see?). Seoul: Myogwang, 1983.

Masŏng 마성. "Pang Hanam sŏnsa rŭl ilko" '방한암선사' 를 읽고 (Having Read [Kim Ho-sŏng's] 'Sŏn Master Pang Hanam'). *Sŏn'u toryang* 8 (March 1996): 279–283.

Matsuoka, Mikio 松岡幹夫. *Nichiren Bukkyō no shakaishisōteki tenkai: Kindai Nihon no shūkyōteki ideorogi* 日蓮仏教の社会思想的展開：近代日本 の 宗教的イテオロキ (Evolution of Nishiren Buddhism as a Social Theory: Religious Ideology in Modern Japan). Tokyo: Tokyo daigaku shuppankai, 2005.

Miller, Owen, and Vladimir Tikhonov. *Selected Writings of Han Yongun: From Social Darwinism to 'Socialism with a Buddhist Face.'* Honolulu: University of Hawai'i Press, 2008.

Mills, Charles W. "Non-Cartesian *Sums*: Philosophy and the African-American Experience," *Blackness Visible: Essays on Philosophy and Race*. Ithaca and London: Cornell University Press, 1998, 1–19.

Minjung Pulgyo Undong Yŏnhap 10-chu-nyŏn Ki'nyŏm Saŏphoe. *Minjung Pulgyo* 民衆佛教 (Minjung Buddhism). Korea: Minjung Pulgyo undong yŏnhap, 1995.

Mog'u 목우. "Minjok Haebang kwa T'ongil ŭl wihayŏ" 민족해방과 통일을 위하여 (Towards the Liberation of Korean People and Unification). *Minjok Pulgyo* 1 (1989): 5–9.

Montgomery, Daniel B. *Fire in the Lotus: The Dynamic Buddhism of Nichiren*. London: Mandala, 1991.

Moriyama, Shigenori 森山茂德. *Kŭndae Hanil kwan'gye sa yŏn'gu* 近代韓日關係史硏究 (Research on the History of Modern Korean-Japanese Relationship, 1987). Trans. from Japanese by Kim Semin. Seoul: Hyŏnŭmsa, 1994.

Mu Soeng. *Thousand Peaks: Korean Zen-Tradition and Teachers*. Cumberland, RI: Primary Point Press, 1991.

Mubi Sŭnim 무비스님. *Kŭmganggyŏng o'gahae* 金剛經五家解 (Korean Vernacular Translation of the Five Masters' Interpretation of the Diamond Sūtra). Seoul: Pulgwang ch'ulp'anbu, 1992.

Muller, A. Charles. *The Sutra of Perfect Enlightenment: Korean Buddhism's Guide to Meditation*. Albany: State University of New York Press, 1999.

Mun, Chan Ju. "A Historical Introduction to Minjung Buddhism: A Liberation Buddhism of South Korea in 1980's." *Kankoku Bukkyōgaku Seminar* 9 (2003): 239–270.

Mun, Okp'yo, ed. 문옥표. *Sinyŏsŏng: Han'guk kwa Ilbon ŭi kŭndae yŏsŏngsang* 신여성: 한국과 일본의 근대 여성상 (New Women: Images of Modern Women in Korea and Japan). Seoul: Ch'ŏngnyŏnsa, 2003.

Myŏngjŏng, ed. 明正. *Samsogul ilji* 三笑窟 日誌 (Samsogul Diary). Korea: Kŭngnak sŏnwŏn 1992.

———. ed. 明正. *Samsogul sosik* 삼소굴 소식 (News from the Samsogul Hermitage). Yangsan, Korea: Kŭngnak sŏnwŏn, 1997.

Naong hwasang ŏrok 懶翁和尙語錄 (Recorded Sayings of Master Naong). *HPC* 6.702b–729c.

Neumaier-Dargyay, Eva K. "Buddhist Thought from a Feminist Perspective." In Morny Joy and Eva K. Neumaier-Dargyay, ed. *Gender, Genre and Religion: Feminist Reflections.* Wilfrid Laurier University Press, 1995, 145–170.

No, Mirim 노미림. "Higuchi Ichiyou wa Kim Iryŏp ŭi yŏsŏngsŏng taejo" 樋口一葉와 金一葉의 여성성 대조 (Comparison of Femininity of Higuchi Ichiyou and Kim Iryŏp). *Ilŏ ilmunhak* 40 (2002): 141–165.

O, Chaeyŏng 오재영. "Pulgyo po'gŭp e taehan ŭigyŏn" 불교보급에 대한 의견 (My Thoughts on the Prozelitization of Buddhism). *Haedong Pulbo* 7 (1914): 562–571.

O, Sŏnmyŏng 오선명. *Chŏngsan chongsa pŏpsŏl* 정산종사법설 (Dharma Sermons of Master Chŏngsan). Iksan, Korea: Wŏlgan Wŏn'gwangsa, 2000.

Oberdorfer, Don. *The Two Koreas: A Contemporary History*. London: Little and Brown, 1997.

Odin, Steve. *Process Metaphysics and Hua-yen Buddhism*. Albany: State University of New York Press, 1982.

Oh, Bonnie B. C. "Kim Iryŏp's Conflicting Worlds." In Young-Key Kim-Renaud, ed. *Creative Women of Korea: The Fifteenth through the Twentieth Centuries.* Armonk, NY: M. E. Sharpe, 2004, 174–191.

Oh, Kang Nam. "A Study of Chinese Hua-yen Buddhism with Special Reference to the Dharmadhātu (Fa-chieh) Doctrine." Ph.D. Dissertation, McMaster University, 1976.

Okumura, Enshin 奥村圓心. "Chōsen koku fukyō nisshi" 朝鮮国布教日誌 (Diary of the Prozelytization in Korea). *Ilbon Pulgyo kaegyo charyo* 일본불교개교자료 (Materials on the Commencement of Japanese Buddhist Mission in Korea). In *Han'guk kŭnhyŏndae Pulgyo charyo chŏnjip*, vol 62. Seoul: Minjoksa, 1996.

P'yo, Ilcho 표일조. "Mirŭk sin'ang kwa Minjung Pulgyo" 미륵신앙과 민중불교 (Maitreya Faith and Minjung Buddhism). In Chongman Han, ed. *Han'guk Kŭndae Minjung Pulgyo ŭi i'nyŏm kwa chŏn'gae* 한국근대민중불교의 이념과 전개 (The Theory and Developments of Minjung Buddhism in Modern Korea). Seoul: Han'gilsa, 1980, 336–359.

Paek, Yongŏng 白龍城. *Yongsŏng taejongsa chŏnjip* 龍城大宗師全集 (Complete Works of the Great Master Yongsŏng), 18 vols. Seoul: Taegaksa, 1991.

Pak, Chaehyŏn 박재현. *Han'guk kŭndae Pulgyo ŭi t'ajadŭl* 한국 근대 불교의 타자들 (The Others in Modern Korean Buddhism). Seoul: P'urŭn yŏksa, 2009.

Pak, Chonghong 박종홍. *Pak Chonghong chonjip* 朴鍾鴻 全集 (Complete Works of Pak Chonghong), 7 vols. Seoul: Hyŏngsŏl ch'ulp'ansa, 1982.

Pak, Chŏnghun 박정훈. *Chŏngsan chongsa chŏn* 정산종사전 (A Biography of Master Chŏngsan). Iksan: Wŏnbulgyo Ch'ulp'ansa, 2002.

———, ed. *Hanuran hanich'i-e* 한울안 한이치에 (Unitary Principle within One Fence). Iri: Wŏnbulgyo ch'ulp'ansa, 1982.

Pak, Haedang 박해당. "Chogyejong ŭi pŏpt'ong sŏl e taehan kŏmt'o" 조계종의 법통설에 대한 검토 (A Critical Research on the Dharma Lineage of the Chogye Order). *Chŏrhak Sasang* 11 (December 2000): 43–62.

Pak, Hŭisŭng 박희승. Yije sŭngnyŏ ŭi ipsŏng ŭl hŏhami ŏttŏlrŏnjiyo 이제 승려의 입성을 許함이 어떨런지요 (How about Now Allowing Monks to Enter into the Capital?). Seoul: Tŭllyŏk, 1999.

———. "Chosŏn Pulgyo Chogyejong ŭi chuyŏk yŏn'gu: chongjŏng kwa chongmu ch'ongjang ŭl chungsim ŭro" 朝鮮佛敎曹溪宗의 主役 연구: 宗正과 宗務總長을 중심으로 (A Study on the Leading Figures of the Chosŏn Buddhist Chogye Order: Focusing on the Supreme Patriarch and General Manager). *Chŏngt'ohak yŏn'gu* 4 (2001): 249–276.

Pak, Kyŏnghun. "Buddhism in Modern Korea." *Korea Journal* 21, no. 8 (1981): 32–40.

Pak, Kyŏnghun, et al., ed. 박경훈. *Kŭndae Han'guk Pulgyosa ron* 近代韓國佛敎史論 (On the History of Modern Korean Buddhism). Seoul: Minjoksa, 1992.

Pak, Kyŏngjun 박경준. "Minjung Pulgyo i'nyŏm ŭi pip'anjŏk koch'al" 민중불교 이념의 비판절 고찰 (Critical Examination of Minjung Buddhist Ideology). In Pŏpsŏng et al. *Minjung Pulgyo ŭi t'amgu.* Seoul: Minjoksa, 1989, 129–170.

Pang, Hanam 方漢岩. "Ch'amsŏn e taehaya" 參禪에 對하야 (On Sŏn Meditation). *Pulgyo* 100 (October 1932): 35–37.

———. "Myop'osŏ" 猫捕鼠 (Like a Cat Catching a Mouse). *Kŭmgang-jŏ* 22 (1937): 50–51.

———. "Oin suhaeng i chŏnjae ŏ kyŏlsim sŏngbyŏn" 吾人修行이 專在於決心成辨 (The Success of My Practice Entirely Depends on the Determination of the Mind) *Sin Pulgyo* 56 (1944): 2–4.

———. "Taehoesojib ŭl t'ŭngmyŏng yŏbŏp kongŭi chŏngbŏp ŭl suji hara" 大會召集을 特命 如法公議 正法을 受持하라 (Special order for a general convocation: May the discussion be conducted according to the Dharma, may you be ever mindful of the True Dharma). *Pulgyo sinbo* 36 (October 1949): 1.

———. *Hanam ilballok: Hanam Taejongsa pŏbŏrok* 漢巖一鉢錄: 漢巖大宗師法語錄 (Hanam's One Bowl of Records: The Recorded Dharma-lectures of Great Patriarch Hanam). Ed. Hanam Taejongsa Munjip P'yŏnch'an Wiwŏn Hoe. Seoul: Minjoksa, 1996.

———, ed. "Koryŏguk Pojo sŏnsa ŏrok" 高麗國普照禪師語錄 (Recorded Sayings of Sŏn Master Pojo [Chinul] of the Koryŏ State). Kangwŏn-to, Korea: Wŏlchŏngsa, 1937.

Park, Jin Y. 박진영. "T'oe'ong Sŏngch'ŏl ŭi Pulgyo haesŏkhak kwa Sŏn Pulgyo yulli" 퇴옹성철의 불교 해석학과 선불교 윤리 (Zen Master T'oe'ong Sŏngch'ŏl's Buddhist Hermeneutics and Zen Buddhist Ethics)." In Sungtaek Cho, ed. *T'oeong Sŏngch'ŏl ŭi Kkaedrŭm kwa suhaeng-Sŏngch'ŏl ŭi Sŏn sasang kwa Pulgyo sajŏk wich'i* 퇴옹성

철의 깨달음과 수행–성철의 선사상과 불교사적 위치 (T'oe'ong Sŏngch'ŏl's Enlightenment and Practice—Sŏngch'ŏl's Zen Thoughts and His Position in the History of [Korean] Buddhism). Seoul: Yŏmun sŏwŏn, 2006, 19–47.

———. "Wisdom, Compassion, and Zen Social Ethics: the Case of Chinul, Sŏngch'ŏl, and Minjung Buddhism in Korea." *Journal of Buddhist Ethics* 13 (2006): 1–26.

———. " 'A Crazy Drunken Monk': Kyŏnghŏ and Modern Buddhist Meditation Practice." In Robert E. Buswell, Jr., ed. *Religions of Korea in Practice*. Princeton, NJ: Princeton University Press, 2007, 130–143.

———. "The Wŏn Buddhist Practice of the Buddha-Nature." In Robert E. Buswell, Jr., ed. *Religions of Korea in Practice*. Princeton, NJ: Princeton University Press, 2007, 476–486.

Park, Kwangsoo. *The Won Buddhism (Wŏnbulgyo) of Sot'aesan: A Twentieth-Century Religious Movement in Korea*. San Francisco-London-Bethesda: International Scholars Publications, 1997.

Park, Pori. "The Modern Remaking of Korean Buddhism: the Korean Reform Movement during Japanese Colonial Rule and Han Yongun's Buddhism (1879–1944)." Ph D dissertation. University of California at Los Angeles, 1998.

———. "Korean Buddhist Reforms and Problems in the Adoption of Modernity during the Colonial Period." *Korea Journal* 45, no. 1 (Spring 2005): 87–113.

———. "The Buddhist Purification Movement in Postcolonial South Korea: Restoring Clerical Celibacy and State Intervention." In J. Craig Jenkins and Ester E. Gottlieb, eds. *Identity Conflicts: Can Violence be Regulated?* New Brunswick, NJ: Transaction Publishers, 2007, 131–145.

Park, Sung Bae. *Buddhist Faith and Sudden Enlightenment*. Albany: State University of New York Press, 1983.

___ 박성배. "Tono tonsu ron" 돈오돈수론 (Theory of Sudden Awakening and Sudden Cultivation). *Paengnyŏn Pulgyo nonjip* 3 (1993): 201–254.

———. "Silla Buddhist Spirituality." In Takeuchi Yoshinori, ed. *Buddhist Spirituality: Late China, Korea, Japan and the Modern World*. New York: The Crossroad Publishing Co., 1999, 57–78.

Paul, Diana Y. *Women in Buddhism: Images of the Feminine in Mahāyāna Tradition*. Berkeley, CA: Asian Humanities Press, 1979.

Pojo sasang yŏn'guwŏn, ed. 普照思想硏究院. *Pojo chŏnsŏ* 普照全書 (Complete Works of Pojo [Chinul]). Chŏlla namdo, Korea: Puril ch'ulp'ansa, 1989.

Pŏpsŏng 법 성. "Kkadarŭm ŭi ilsangsŏng kwa hyŏngmyŏngsŏng" 깨달음의 일상성과 혁명성 (Enlightenment as Routine and Revolution). *Ch'angjak kwa pip'yŏng* 82 (Winter 1993): 329–340.

Pŏpsŏng, et al. 법 성. *Minjung Pulgyo ŭi t'amgu* 민중불교의 탐구 (Investigations of Minjung Buddhism). Seoul: Minjoksa, 1989.

Pulgyo chŏngjŏn 佛敎正典 (Correct Canon of Buddhism). Comp. Kim T'aehŭp. Seoul: Pulgyo sibosa, 1943.

Pulgyo kwan'gye tosŏ nonmun mongnok 불교관계 도서 논문 목록. Seoul: Taewŏnjŏngsa, 1986.

Queen, Christopher S. "Introduction: The Shapes and Sources of Engaged Buddhism." In Christopher S. Queen and Sallie B. King, eds. *Engaged Buddhism: Buddhist*

Liberation Movements in Asia. Albany: State University of New York Press, 1996, 1–44.

Red Pine [Porter, Bill]. *The Collected Songs of Cold Mountain*. Port Townsend: Copper Canyon Press, 2000.

Russian Ministry of Finances, ed. *Han'gukchi* 한국지 (Description of Korea, 1900). Trans. from Russian by Ch'oe Sŏn et al. Sŏngnam, Korea: Han'guk chŏngsin munhwa yŏn'guwŏn, 1984.

Said, Edward. *Orientalism*. New York: Pantheon Books, 1978.

Santikara Bhikkhu. "Buddhadasa Bhikkhu: Life and Society through the Natural Eyes of Voidness." In Christopher S. Queen and Sallie B. King, eds. *Engaged Buddhism: Buddhist Liberation Movements in Asia*. Albany: State University of New York Press, 1996, 147–193.

Sasaki, R. F. *The Development of Chinese Zen*. New York: First Zen Institute of America, 1953.

Schwartz, Benjamin. *In Search of Wealth and Power: Yen Fu and the West*. Cambridge, MA: Harvard University Press, 1964.

Seoul t'ŭkpyŏlsi, ed. *Hwagyesa: Silch'ŭk chosa pogosŏ* 화계사: 실측조사보고사 (Hwagyesa: Survey Report). Seoul: Seoul t'ŭkpyŏlsi, 1988.

Seung Sahn. *Dropping Ashes on the Buddha*. New York: Grove Press, 1976.

Shakai Mondai Shiryō Kenkyūkai, comp. 社会問題資料研究会. *Bukkyō to Shakai undō: shūtoshite Shinkō Bukkyō Seinen Dōmei ni tsuite* 仏教と社会運動： 主として新興仏教青年同盟について (Buddhism and Social Movements: Focusing on Young Adults Association of New Buddhism). Shisō kenkyū shiryō, tokushū 52. Kyoto: Tōyō bunkasha, 1972.

Sharf, Robert. "The Zen of Japanese Nationalism." In Donald Lopez, ed. *Curators of the Buddha: The Study of Buddhism under Colonialism*. Chicago: University of Chicago Press, 1995.

Shim, Jae-ryong. "Buddhist Responses to the Modern Transformation of Society in Korea (Vitality in Korean Buddhist Tradition)." *Korea Journal* 33, no. 3 (Autumn 1993): 50–56.

———. "Buddhist Responses to the Modern Transformation of Society in Korea." In Lewis Lancaster and Richard K. Payne, eds. *Religion and Society in Contemporary Korea*. Berkeley, CA: Institute of East Asian Studies, 1997, 75–86.

———. *Korean Buddhism: Tradition and Transformation*. Seoul: Jimmoondang Publishing Company, 1999.

———, ed. 심재룡. *Han'guk esŏ ch'ŏrhak hanŭn chasedŭl* 한국에서 철학하는 자세들 (Philosophical Approaches in Korea). Seoul: Jimmundang, 1986.

Shin, Doh C. *Mass Politics and Culture in Democratizing Korea*. Cambridge: Cambridge University Press, 1999.

Silch'ŏn Pulgyo Chŏn'guk Sŭnggahoe 실천불교전국승가회. *Han'guk hyŏndae Pulgyo undongsa* 韓國現代佛教運動史 (History of Engaged Buddhism in Modern Korea). P'aju'gun, Korea: Tosŏ ch'ulp'ansa, 1996.

Sim, Chaeyŏl, ed. 沈載烈. *Pojo pŏbŏ* 普照法語 (Pojo's Dharma Discourses). Seoul: Pusŏng Munhwasa, 1979.

Sin, Kwangch'ŏl 신광철. "Yi Nŭnghwa ŭi chonggyohak chŏk kwanjŏm" 이능화의 종교학적 관점 (Yi Nŭnghwa's View of Religious Studies). *Chonggyo yŏn'gu* 9 (1993): 173–98.

Sin, O'hyŏn 신오현. "Wŏnhyo chŏrhak ŭi hyŏndaejŏk chomyŏng" 원효 철학의 현대적 조명 (Philosophy of Wŏnhyo from a Modern Perspective). In Academy of Korean Studies, ed. *Wŏnhyo ŭi sasang kwa kŭ hyŏndaejŏk ŭimi* 元曉의 사상과 그 현대적 의미 (Wŏnhyo's Thought and its Meaning in Current Time). Sŏngnam, Korea: Han'guk chŏngsin munhwa yŏn'guwŏn, 1994.

Sin, Pongsŭng 신봉승. *Yi Tongin ŭi nara* 이동인의 나라 (Yi Tongin's Country), 3 vols. Seoul: Tongbang midia, 2001.

Smith, Kendra. "Sex, Dependency and Religion—Reflections from a Buddhist Perspective," in Ursula King, ed. *Women in the World's Religions: Past and Present*. New York: Paragon House, 1987, 219–231.

Sŏk, Myŏngjŏng, ed. 釋明正. *Kyŏnghŏ chip* 鏡虛集 (Collected Works of Kyŏnghŏ). Korea: Kŭngnak sŏnwŏn, 1990.

———, ed. *Hanam chip* 漢岩集 (Collected Works of Hanam). Korea: Kŭngnak sŏnwŏn, 1991.

Sōma, Shōei 相馬勝英. "Hō Kangan zenji o tazunete" 方寒巖禪師をたづねて (Meeting Sŏn Master Pang Hanam). *Chōsen bukkyō* 87 (April 1933): 14–19. (Korean translation, "Pang Hanam sŏnsa rŭl ch'ajasŏ," 방한암선사를 찾아서. *Taejung Pulgyo* [April 1994]: 80–83.)

Song, Hyŏnju 송현주. "Kŭndae Han'guk Pulgyo kaehyŏk undong esŏ ŭirye ŭi munje: Han Yongun, Yi Nŭnghwa, Paek Yongsŏng, Kwŏn Sangno rŭl chungsim ŭro" 근대한국불교 개혁운동에서 의례의 문제—한용운, 이능화, 백용성, 권상노를 중심으로 (Rituals in the Reform Movements of Modern Korean Buddhism: focusing on Han Yongun, Yi Nŭnghwa, Paek Yongsŏng, and Kwŏn Sangno). *Chonggyo wa munhwa* 6 (2000): 157–183.

Sŏng, Rakhŭi 성락희. "Kim Iryŏp munhangnon" 김일엽 문학론 (On Kim Iryŏp's Literature). *Ase'a yŏsŏng yŏn'gu* 14 (December, 1978): 307–326.

Song, Sŏkku 송석구. "Yi Nŭnghwa ŭi Yugyo yŏn'gu" 이능화의 유교연구 (Yi Nungwha's Study of Confucianism). *Chonggyo yŏn'gu* 9 (1993): 67–86.

Sŏngch'ŏl 性徹. *Sŏnmun chŏngno* 禪門正路 (The Correct Path of the Zen School). Seoul: Pulgwang, 1981.

———. "Pongamsa kyŏlsa" 봉암사 결사 (Compact Community at the Pongam Monastery). *Cha'girŭl paro popsida* 자기를 바로봅시다 (Let's Look at Ourselves Clearly). Seoul: Changgyŏnggak, 1987, 220–235.

———. *Paeg'il pŏmmun* 百日法門 (One Hundred Days Sermons) 2 vols. Seoul: Changgyŏnggak, 1992.

Sŏnmun yŏmsong yŏmsong sŏrhwa hoebon 禪門拈頌拈頌說話會本 (Assembled Edition of the Selected Songs of Sŏn Buddhism with Selected Songs). *HPC* 5.1a–925c.

Sŏnu Toryang Han'guk Pulgyo kŭnhyŏndaesa yŏn'guhoe, ed. 선우도량한국근현대사연구회. *Sinmun ŭro pon Han'guk Pulgyo kŭnhyŏndaesa* (新聞으로 본) 韓國佛敎 近現代史 (The Modern and Contemporary History of Korean Buddhism Seen Through Newspapers), 2 vols. Seoul: Sŏnu toryang ch'ulp'anbu, 1999.

Sørensen, Henrik H. "Korean Buddhist Journals during the Early Japanese Colonial Rule." *Korea Journal* 30, no. 1 (1990): 17–27.

———. "A Study of the 'Ox-Herding Theme' as Sculptures at Mt. Baoding in Dazu County, Sichuan." *Artibus Asiae* 51, nos. 3/4 (1991): 207–233.

———. "Buddhism and Secular Power in Twentieth-Century Korea." In Ian Harris, ed. *Buddhism and Politics in Twentieth Century Asia*. London and New York: Pinter, 1999, 127–152.

———. "Buddhist Spirituality in Premodern and Modern Korea." In Takeuchi Yoshinori, ed. *Buddhist Spirituality: Late China, Korea, Japan and the Modern World*. New York: The Crossroad Publishing Co., 1999, 109–133.

Stryk, Lucien, Takashi Ikemoto, and Taigan Takayama, eds. *Zen Poems of China and Japan: The Crane's Bill*. New York: Anchor Press, 1973.

Su'gyŏng 수경. "Han'guk piguni kangwŏn paltalsa" 한국 비구니 강원 발달사 (History of the Evolution of Seminaries for Buddhist Nuns in Korea). In Chŏn'guk piguni-hoe, ed. *Han'guk piguni ŭi suhaeng kwa sam* 한국 비구니의 수행과 삶 (Life and Cultivation of Korean Buddhist Nuns). Seoul: Yemun sŏwon, 2007, 15–51.

Sueki, Takehiro 末木剛博. *Tōyō no gōri shisō* 東洋の合理思想 (Rationality in Eastern Thought). Tokyo: Kodansha, 1970.

Suzuki, D. T. *Essays in Zen Buddhism*. First Series. London: Rider, 1949.

Swearer, Donald K. "Centre and Periphery: Buddhism and Politics in Modern Thailand." In Ian Harris, ed. *Buddhism and Politics in Twentieth-Century Asia*. London and New York: Pinter, 1999, 197–228.

T'aego Pou hwasang ŏrok 太古普愚和尙語錄 (Recorded Sayings of Venerable T'aego Pou). *HPC* 6. 669a–702a.

Taehan Pulgyo Chogyejong kyoyukwŏn Pulhak yŏn'guso, ed. *Pulgyo kŭndaehwa ŭi chŏn'gae wa sŏnggyok* 불교근대화의 전개와 성격 (Modernization of Buddhism: its Evolution and Characteristics). Seoul: Chogyejong ch'ulp'ansa, 2006.

T'aejin Sŭnim 태진스님. *Kyŏnghŏ wa Man'gong ŭi Sŏnsasang* 경허와 만공의 禪思想 (Zen Buddhist Thoughts of Kyŏnghŏ and Man'gong). Seoul: Minjoksa, 2007.

Taishō shinshū daizōkyō 大正新修大蔵経 (Tripitaka Compiled during the Taishō Period). Ed. Takakusu Junjirō et al. Tokyo: Taishō Issaikyō Kankōkai, 1924–1935.

Takahashi, Toru 高橋亨. *Richō Bukkyō* 李朝佛教 (Buddhism of the Yi Dynasty). Tokyo: 1929. Reprint, Seoul: Poryŏn'gak, 1972.

Tamamuro, Taijō, ed. 圭室諦成. *Nihon Bukkyō shi* 日本仏教史 (History of Japanese Buddhism), 3 vols. Kyoto: Hozokan, 1967.

Thelle, Notto. *Buddhism and Christianity in Japan: from Conflict to Dialogue*. Honolulu: University of Hawai'i Press, 1987.

Thurman, Robert A. F. *The Holy Teaching of Vimalakirti: A Mahayana Scripture*. University Park and London: Pennsylvania State University Press, 1976.

———. *Buddhism*. Three Parts. New York: Mystic Fire Video, 1999.

Tikhonov, Vladimir. "The First Stage of Yi Tongin's Career (1878–1880): the forerunner of dependent development?" *Sunggyun Journal of East Asian Studies* 2, no. 1 (2002): 210–233.

Tongguk Taehakkyo Sŏngnim Tongmunhoe, comp. 동국대학교성림동문회. *Han'guk Pulgyo hyŏndaesa* 韓國佛教現代史 (Modern History of Korean Buddhism). Seoul: Sigongsa, 1997.

Victoria, Brian Daizen. *Zen at War*. 2nd ed. Lanham, MD: Rowman and Littlefield, Inc., 2006.

———. *Zen War Stories*. London and New York: Routledge Curzon, 2003.

Wŏnyung 원융. *Kanhwa Sŏn: Sŏnjong tonbŏp sasang ŭi parŭn ihae* 간화선: 선종 돈법 사상의 바른 이해 (Kanhua Zen: Correct Understanding of Zen Subitism). Seoul: Changgyŏnggak, 1993.

Yamashita, Shinichi 山下眞一. "Ikeda Kiyoshi keimu kyokuchō Hō Kangan zenji wo tou" 池田淸警務局長 方漢巖禪師を訪ふ (Director of the Bureau for Police Affairs Ikeda Kiyoshi visits Sŏn Master Pang Hanam). *Chōsen Bukkyō* 101 (Aug 1934): 4–5.

Yang, Ŭnyong 양은용. "Yi Nŭnghwa ŭi hangmun kwa Pulgyo sasang" 이능화의 학문과 불교사상 (Yi Nŭnghwa's Scholarship and Buddhist Thought). *Sungsan Pak Kilchin Paksa kohui kinyŏm: Han'guk kŭndae chonggyo sasangsa* 숭산박길진박사고희기념 한국근대종교사상사 (Pak Kilchin Festschrift: Intellectual History of Modern Korean Religions). Iri, Korea: Won'gwang taehakkyo ch'ulp'anbu, 1984, 437–465.

———. "Yi Nŭnghwa ŭi Han'guk Pulgyo yŏn'gu" 이능화의 한국불교연구 (Yi Nŭnghwa's Study of Korean Buddhism). *Chonggyo yŏn'gu* 9 (1993): 45–65.

———. "Kŭndae Pulgyo kaehyŏk undong" 近代佛敎改革運動 (Buddhist Reform Movements in Modern Korea). In *Han'guk sasangsa taegye* 韓國思想史大系 (Compendium of the Intellectual History of Korea), vol. 6. Pundang, Korea: Han'guk chŏngsin munhwa yŏn'guwŏn, 1993, 139–65.

Yi, Chaehŏn 이재헌. "Yi Nŭnghwa yŏn'gu ŭi hyŏnhwang kwa kwaje" 이능화 연구의 현황과 과제 (Current Status and Issues of the Study of Yi Nŭnghwa). *Han'guk chonggyosa yŏn'gu* 7 (1999): 5–28.

———. "Kŭndae Han'guk Pulgyohak ŭi sŏngnip kwa chonggyo insik—Yi Nŭnghwa wa Kwŏn Sangno rŭl chungsim ŭro" 근대한국불교의 성립과 종교 인식-이능화와 권상로를 중심으로 (The Establishment of Buddhist Studies and Religious Consciousness in Modern Korea—Focusing on Yi Nŭnghwa and Kwŏn Sangno). PhD dissertation, Han'guk chŏngsin munhwa yŏn'guwŏn, 1999.

———. *Yi Nŭnghwa wa kŭndae Pulgyohak* 이능화와 근대 불교학 (Yi Nŭnghwa and Modern Buddhist Scholarship). Seoul: Chisik sanyŏpsa, 2007.

Yi, Chaehyŏng 李載炯. "Pulgyo kye ch'inil haengjŏk ŏttŏke pol kŏsin'ga, Chiam Yi Chonguk ŭl chungsim ŭro" 불교계 친일행적 어떻게 볼 것인가: 지암 이종욱을 중심으로 (What Should We Do with Pro-Japanese Activities of [Korean] Buddhists?—Focusing on Chiam Yi Chonguk). *Pulgyo p'yŏngnon* 4, no. 2/3 (Summer/Fall 2002): 302–328.

Yi, Chŏng, ed. 이정. *Han'guk Pulgyo inmyŏng sajŏn* 한국불교 인명사전 (Korean Buddhist Biographical Dictionary). Seoul: Pulgyo sidaesa, 1993.

Yi, Hyangsun 이향순. *Piguni wa Han'guk munhak* 비구니와 한국문학 (Buddhist Nuns and Korean Literature). Seoul: Yemun sŏwŏn, 2008.

Yi, Kang'o 이강오. *Han'guk sinhŭng chonggyo ch'ongnam*, 한국신흥종교총람 (Comprehensive Bibliography of New Religions in Korea). Seoul: Taehŭng kihoek, 1992.

Yi, Kwangnin 李光麟. *Kaehwadang yŏn'gu* 開化黨 硏究 (Study on the Enlightenment Party). Seoul: Ilchogak, 1973.

———. *Han'guk kaehwa sa ŭi chemunje* 韓國開化史의 諸問題 (Issues on Korean Enlightenment History), Seoul: Ilchogak, 1986.

———. "Kaehwagi ŭi Han'gugin ŭi Asia yŏndae ron" 개화기의 한국인의 아시아 연대론 (Korean Views on 'Asian Solidarity' in the 'Enlightenment' Period). *Kaehwap'a wa kaehwa sasang yŏn'gu* 開化派와 開化思想 硏究 (Studies on the Enlightenment Group and Enlightenment Thought). Seoul: Ilchogak, 1989.

———. "T'ak Chŏngsik non" 탁정식론 (On T'ak Chŏngsik). *Kaehwagi yŏn'gu* 개화기 연구 (Study on the Era of Enlightenment). Seoul: Ilchogak, 1994.

Yi, Kwangnin, and Sin Yongha 이광닌, 신용하. *Saryoro pon Han'guk munhwa sa: kŭndae p'yŏn* 사료로 본 한국 문화사: 근대편 (Cultural History of Korea Seen through Source Materials: the Modern Period). Seoul: Ilchisa, 1984.

Yi, Myŏnghyŏn 이명현. "Han'guk ch'ŏrhak ŭi chŏnt'ong kwa kwaje" 한국철학의 전통과 과제 (The Tradition and Tasks of Korean Philosophy). In Shim Jae-ryong ed., *Han'guk esŏ ch'ŏrhak hanŭn chasedŭl*, 19–36.

Yi, Namyŏng 이남영. "Yŏram ch'ŏrhak: hyangnaejŏk ch'ŏrhak kwa hyangoejŏk ch'ŏrhak ŭi chiphap ŭirosŏŭi Han'guk ch'ŏrhak" 열암 철학: 향내적 철학과 향외적 철학의 집합으로서의 한국철학 (Yŏram's Philosophy: Korean Philosophy as a Combination of Academic and Non-academic Philosophies). In Ch'ŏrhak yŏn'guhoe, ed. *Haebang 50 nŏn ŭi Han'guk ch'ŏrhak* 해방 50년의 한국 철학 (Korean Philosophy during the 50 Years after the Liberation). Seoul: Chŏrhak kwa hyŏnsil sa, 1996, 11–26.

Yi, Nŭnghwa 李能和. *Paekkyo hoet'ong* 百教會通 (Harmonization of All Religions, 1912). Trans. Kang Hyojong. Seoul: Unjusa, 1992.

———. Chosŏn Pulgyo t'ongsa e ch'wihaya 朝鮮佛教通史에 취하야 (About A Comprehensive History of Korean Buddhism). *Chosŏn Pulgyo ch'ongbo* 朝鮮佛教叢報 (The Journal of the Collection of Korean Buddhism) 16 (August 1917). *Han'guk Pulgyo chapchi ch'ongbo* 한국불교잡지총보 (The Journal of the Collection of Korean Buddhist Magazines) 14: 346–355.

———. *Chosŏn Pulgyo t'ongsa* 朝鮮佛教通史 (A Comprehensive History of Korean Buddhism, 1918), 3 vols. Seoul: Minsogwŏn, 2002.

———. "Tangok p'ogyo sŏl" 堂獄布教說 (A Discussion of Propagation at the Buddhist Paradise and Hell). *Chosŏn Pulgyo ch'ongbo* 朝鮮佛教叢報 (The Journal of the Collection of Korean Buddhism) 16 (1919). *Han'guk Pulgyo chapchi ch'ongbo* 한국불교잡지총보 (The Journal of the Collection of Korean Buddhist Magazines) 15: 373–7.

———. "Yŏsigwan" 如是觀 (The View of Thusness). *Chosŏn Pulgyo ch'ongbo* 朝鮮佛教叢報 (The Journal of the Collection of Korean Buddhism) 17 (1919). *Han'guk Pulgyo chapchi ch'ongbo* 한국불교잡지총보 (The Journal of the Collection of Korean Buddhist Magazines) 15: 447–56.

———. "Mansa malli rŭl chasim chasŏng e kuhagi wihaya" 만사만리를 자심자성에 구하기 위하야 (In Search of All Phenomena and All Principle from Self-mind and Self-nature). *Pulgyo* (September 1928): 60–62.

———. *Chosŏn Kidokkyo kŭp oegyosa* 朝鮮基督教及外交史 (A History of Christianity and Diplomacy in Korea). Seoul: Chosŏn Kidokkyo ch'angmunsa, 1928.

Yi, Sang-t'aek. *Religion and Social Formation in Korea: Minjung and Millenarianism*. Berlin: Mouton de Gruyter, 1996.

Yi, Sŏngt'a 이성타. "Kyŏnghŏ ŭi Sŏn sasang" 경허의 선사상 (Kyŏnghŏ's Sŏn Thought). *Sungsan Pak Kilchin paksa hwagap kinyŏm: Han'guk Pulgyo sasang sa* 숭산박길진박사 화갑기념 한국불교 사상사 (Festschrift in Commemoration of Professor Sungsan Pak Kilchin's 60th Birthday: The History of Korean Buddhist Thought). Iri: Wŏn'gwang taehakkyo ch'ulp'ansa, 1975, 1103–1120.

———. "Kyŏnghŏ sidae ŭi Sŏn kwa kyŏlsa" 경허시대의 선과 결사 (Sŏn Buddhism and Compact Community in Kyŏnghŏ's Time). *Chinsan Han Kidu paksa hwagap kinyŏm: Han'guk chonggyo sasang ŭi chae chomyŏng* 진산 한기두 박사 화갑기념 한국 종교 사상의 재조명 (Festschrift for Chinsan, Dr. Han Kidu: Further Elucidation on the Thought of Korean Religion). Ed. Chinsan Han Kidu Paksa Hwagap Kinyŏm Nonmunjip Kanhaeng Uiwŏn Hoe, vol. 1. Iri, Korea: Wŏn'gwang Taehakkyo Ch'ulp'an'guk, 1993, 425–36.

Yi, Taesŏk 이태석. "Yŏsŏng haebangnon ŭi nangmanjŏk chip'yŏng: Kim Iryŏp ron" 여성해방론의 낭만적 지평: 김일엽론 (Romantic Horizon of the Theory of Women's Liberation: the Case of Kim Iryŏp." *Yŏsŏng munhak yŏn'gu* 4 (2002): 177–201.

Yŏ, Ikku 여익구. *Mirŭkkyŏng ŭi se'gye* 미륵경의 세계 (The World of the Sūtra of Maitreya's Ascension). Seoul: Chiyangsa, 1986.

———. "Minjung Pulgyo undong ŭl ŏttŏk'e ihaehal gŏsinga," 민중불교운동을 어떻게 이해할 것인가 (How to Understand Minjung Buddhist Movement). *Minjung Pŏptang* 1 (July 1985): 10–13.

———. *Minjung Pulgyo Ch'ŏrhak* 民衆佛教哲學 (Philosophy of Minjung Buddhism). Seoul: Minjoksa, 1988.

Yongmyŏng 용명. *Isib'i-in ŭi chŭngŏn ŭl t'onghae pon kŭn hyŏndae Pulgyosa* 22 인의 증언을 통해 본 근현대불교사 (Modern Korean Buddhism as Seen by Twenty-two Witnesses). Seoul: Sŏnu toryang, 2002.

Yoon, Yee-heum. "The Contemporary Religious Situation in Korea." In Lewis R. Lancaster and Richard K. Payne, eds. *Religion and Society in Contemporary Korea*. Berkeley, CA: Institute of East Asian Studies, 1997, 1–17.

Yu, Beongcheon. *Han Yong-un and Yi Kwang-su: Two Pioneers of Modern Korean Literature*. Detroit: Wayne State University Press, 1992.

Yü, Chün-fang. "Ta-hui Tsung-kao and Kung-an Ch'an." *Journal of Chinese Philosophy* 6 (1979): 211–35.

Yu, Yŏnsik 유연식. *Han'guk kŭnhyŏndae sa ron* 한국근현대사론 (On Modern and Contemporary Korean History). Seoul: Ilchogak, 1992.

Yun, Ch'anghwa 윤창화. "Hanam ŭi chajŏnjŏk kudogi Ilsaeng P'aegwŏl" 漢岩의 자전적 구도기 一生敗闕 (Ilsaeng p'aegwŏl, Hanam's Autobiographical Account of His Search for the Path). *Pulgyo p'yŏngnon* 5, no. 4 (2003): 294–306.

Yun, Ch'ŏnggwang. 윤청광. Bibissi inki pangsong p'ŭro kosŭng yŏljŏn 15. Hanam k'ŭn sŭnim: paguni e murŭl tamgo tallyŏ kanuna BBS 인기방송프로 고승열전 15. 한암큰스님: 바구니에 물을 담고 달려가누나 (Popular Broadcasting Programs of the BBS [Buddhist Broadcasting System]: the Lives of Eminent [Korean] Monks, vol. 15: Eminent Monk Hanam: 'You fill a basket with water and are running around'). Seoul: Uri ch'ulp'ansa, 2002.

Zimmermann, Michael. "War." In Robert E. Buswells, Jr., ed. *Encyclopedia of Buddhism*, vol. 2. New York: Macmillan Reference, 2005.

Zingmark, Brian K. (aka. Chong Go 青高). "A Study of the letters of Korean Seon master Hanam." MA thesis, Dongguk University, Seoul, 2002.

Glossary of East Asian Characters

akch'wi konggyŏn 惡取空見
Arai Nissatsu (J) 新居日薩
Asakusa (J) 淺草
Asano (J) 朝野
Asano (J) 淺野
Baizhang Huaihai (C) 百丈 懷海
Baojing sanmei ge (C) 寶鏡三昧歌
Baozi Wenqin 報慈文欽
betsuin (J) 別院
Caodong zong (C) 曺洞宗
Bosha Wuyi (C) 博山無異
Boshan chanjing yu (C) 博山禪警語
ch'am 參
ch'amdoen malssŭm 참된 말씀
ch'amsaram 참사람
ch'amsŏn 慘禪
ch'amŭi 參意
ch'angjo 創造
ch'angjosŏng 創造性
ch'e 體
ch'ilsŏng 七星
ch'ilsŏnggye 七星契
ch'irŏn yul 七言律
ch'ŏch'ŏ pulsang 處處佛相
Ch'oe Ch'wihŏ 崔就墟
ch'ŏn 天
ch'ŏndang 天堂
Ch'ŏndogyo 天道教
Ch'ŏngdam青潭
ch'ŏnggyu 淸規

ch'ongmu wŏnjang 總務院長
Ch'ŏngnyŏn Yŏrae 靑年如來
Ch'ŏngt'aphoe 靑塔會
ch'ŏnha taejung 天下大衆
ch'ŏnjiŭn 天地恩
ch'ŏnma oedo 天魔外道
ch'ŏnsu ch'ŏnan kwanchaje posal kwangdae wŏnman muae taejabisim taedarani kyech'ŏng 千手千眼觀自在菩薩 廣大圓滿無碍大悲心大陀羅尼 啓請
Ch'ŏnt'ae 天台
Ch'oŭi Ŭisun 草衣 意恂
ch'ulse'gan 出世間
ch'wisa 取捨
cha'a 自我
chaebŏl 財閥
chagŏp 作業
Chajae posal 自在菩薩
Chajang 慈藏
Chamint'u 自民鬪
Chan (C) 禪
Chang Chiyŏn 張志淵
Changgyŏnggak 藏經閣
changjwa purwa 長坐不臥
Chanyao (C) 禪要
Chanyuan zhuquan jidu xu (C) 禪源諸詮集都序
chejŏn 祭奠
chib'a 執我
chihae 知解
Chikchisa 直指寺
chikjŏl pŏbmun 直截法門
chin 眞
chin'a 眞我
chin'yŏ 眞如
chinbo 進步
chindaesa 眞大死
*chinje*眞諦
chinsang 眞相
chinsim sŏngch'e 眞心性體
chinsim 眞心
chinsŏng 眞性
Chinul 知訥
chippŏp 執法
chisa 志士

chiŭn poŭn 知恩報恩
Cho Myŏnggi 趙明基
Cho P'oŭn pi 弔圃隱碑
choŏp 造業
Chodang chip 祖堂集
Chogye Sŏn 曹溪禪
Chogye-chong T'oeun Wŏnil Sŏnsa pimyŏng pyŏng sŏ 曹溪宗 退雲圓日禪師碑銘 幷序
Chogyejong 曹溪宗
chŏlbok 折伏
chŏm'o 漸悟
Ch'ŏndogyo 天道教
Chŏng Mongju 鄭夢周
chŏng'ŏp 正業
chŏngbŏp anjang 正法眼藏
chŏnggak chŏnghaeng 正覺正行
chŏnggwan 靜觀
Chŏnghyesa 定慧寺
Chŏngjo 正祖
Chŏngjŏn 正典
chongjŏng 宗正
Chŏngsan 鼎山
chŏngsim 淨心
chŏngsŭp 情習
Chŏngt'o Kuhyŏn Chŏn'guk Sŭnggahoe 淨土具現全國僧伽會
Chŏngt'ohak yŏn'gu 淨土學研究
chŏnhujedan 前後際斷
Chŏnwŏlsa 轉月舍
chosa 弔辭
chosagwan 祖師關
Chōsen Bukkyō (J) 朝鮮佛教
Chōsen Kaikyō ron (J) 朝鮮開教論
chosil 祖室
Chosŏn Kidokkyo kŭp oegyosa 朝鮮基督教及外交史
Chosŏn musok ko 朝鮮巫俗考
Chosŏn Pulgyo Chogye jong 朝鮮佛教曹溪宗
Chosŏn Pulgyo kaehyŏk an 朝鮮佛教改革案
Chosŏn Pulgyo Kaehyŏksillon 朝鮮佛教改革新論
Chosŏn Pulgyo kyehyŏk ron 朝鮮佛教開革論
Chosŏn Pulgyo ponmal 朝鮮佛教本末
Chosŏn Pulgyo sŭngnyŏ taehoe 朝鮮佛教僧侶大會
Chosŏn Pulgyo T'ongsa 朝鮮佛教通史

Chosŏn Pulgyo Yusillon 朝鮮佛教維新論
Chosŏn Pulgyo 朝鮮佛教
Chosŏn Sŏnjong chung'ang p'ogyo-dang 朝鮮禪宗中央布教堂
Chosŏn Togyosa 朝鮮道教史
Chosŏn 朝鮮
Chosŏn'gŭl Hwaŏm kyŏng 조선글 화엄경
chu'in 主人
chuch'e 主體
chuch'esŏng 主體性
chuin'gong 主人公
Chung norŭt hanŭn pŏp 중노릇 하는 법
chŭng'o 證悟
chungdo 中道
chungin 中人
chungsaengsim 衆生心
Chŭngsan 甑山
Chungwŏn 重遠
Daehaeng 大行
Dahui Zonggao (C) 大慧 宗杲
Daitō goho-ron (J) 大東合邦論
dao (C) 道
Dasheng qixinlun yiji (C) 大乘起信論義記
Daxue (C) 大學
Dongshan (C) 洞山
Fanwang jing (C) 梵網經
Fayan Wenyi (C) 法眼 文益
Fazang (C) 法藏
fukoku kyōhei (J) 富國强兵
Fukuzawa Yūkichi (J) 福澤諭吉
fukyōsho (J) 布教所
furei (J) 府令
Gaofeng Yuanmiao (C) 高峰 原妙
Genyōsha (J) 玄洋社
Guifeng Zongmi (C) 圭峰 宗密
Guzun suyu lu (C) 古尊宿語錄
hae'o 解悟
Haedong Pulbo 海東佛報
Haedongso 海東疏
Haeinsa 海印寺
hahwa chungsaeng 下化衆生
Hamhŏ Tŭkt'ong 涵虛得通
ham i ŏpsi handa 함이 없이 한다.

Hamhŏ Kihwa 涵虛 己和
Han Shan 寒山
Han Yongun 韓龍雲
Han'guk Pulgyo chŏnsŏ 韓國佛敎全書
Han'guk Taehaksaeng Pulgyo Yŏnhaphoe 韓國大學生佛敎聯合會
han'gŭl 한글
Hanabusa Yoshimoto (J) 花房義質
Hanam ilballok: Hanam Taejongsa Pŏbŏrok 漢巖一鉢錄: 漢巖大宗師法語錄
Hanam 漢岩
Hanam 漢巖
hanja 漢字
Hanmaŭm sŏnwŏn한마음 선원
Hanshan (C) 寒山
Hanŭnim 하느님
Hanyan (C) 寒巖
hap 合
Higashi Honganji (J) 西本願寺
ho'guk Pulgyo 護國佛敎
Hong Wŏlch'o 洪月初
Hongzhi (C) 洪州
Honhae 混海
honhap t'onghal 混合統轄
huatou (C) 話頭
Huayan (C) 華嚴
Huayan wujiao zhang (C) 華嚴五敎章
Huayanzong (C) 華嚴宗
Huineng (C) 惠能
Huiyuan (C) 慧遠
Hunmin chŏngŭm 訓民正音
hwadu 話頭
Hwagwawŏn 華果院
Hwagyesa 華溪寺
hwajaeng 和諍
hwalgu 活句
hwalsŏn 活禪
Hwangsŏng sinmun 皇城新聞
Hwaŏm ilsŭng pŏpkyedo 華嚴一乘法界圖
Hwaŏm 華嚴
hwaŏmhoe 華嚴會
Hwaŏmjong 華嚴宗
hwasaeng 化生
hyangho 鄉戶

hye 慧
Hyemyŏng 慧明
Hyewŏl 慧月
hyŏngmyŏngjŏk minjonggyo 革命的民宗教
Hyujŏng 休靜
Ilchinhwa 一塵話
Ilchinhwoe 一進會
ilchinsim taegwangmyŏngch'e 一眞心大光明體
ilsal tasaeng 一殺多生
ilsim 一心
Im Chongguk 林種國
Imjejong 臨濟宗
imo 壬午
imun dŭngdŭng 任運騰騰
in 仁
in'ga 印可
Inoue Kenshin (J) 井上玄眞
Inukai Tsuyoshi (J) 犬養毅
Irwŏn 一圓
Irwŏnsang e taehayŏ 一圓相에 대하여
Irwŏnsang 一圓相
Ishikawa Sodō (J) 石川素童
issetsu tashō (J) 一殺他生
jiao (C) 教
Jōdo (J) 淨土
Jōsen shi (J) 朝鮮史
Jōsen Zenkyō shi 朝鮮禪教史
juch'e 主體
Jūkō hōkoku taisei (J) 銃後報國體制
ka 歌
kaehwa 開化
kaehwadang 開化黨
kaemyŏng sidae 開明 時代
kakchi 覺地
Kakhae illyun 覺海日輪
Kakhwangsa 覺皇寺
kan'gyŏng 看經
Kang Ilsun 姜一淳
Kangnŭng-gun Yŏn'gok-myŏn Songna-sa ch'ilsŏng-kye sŏ 江陵郡 連谷面 松蘿寺 七星契序
kangwŏn 講院

Kangwŏn-to Uljin-kun Ch'ŏnch'uk-san Puryŏng-sa sajŏk pigi 江原道 蔚珍郡 天竺山 佛影寺 事蹟碑記
Kanhwa Sŏn 看話禪
kanhwa 看話
kapsin 甲申
karam suho 伽藍 守護
Katō Bunkyō (J) 加藤文教
Kegonshū (J) 華嚴宗
Kennyo (J) 嚴如
ki 起
Kim Ch'ŏlju 金鐵柱
Kim Chŏnghŭi 金正喜
Kim Hongjip 金弘集
Kim Okkyun 金玉均
Kim T'aehŭp 金泰洽
Kim Tonghwa 金東華
Kim Wŏnju 金元周
Kim Yŏngsu 金映遂
Kimura Taiken (J) 木村泰賢
Kōakai (J) 興亞會
Kogyun 古筠
bokjitgi 복짓기
Kojong 高宗
Kŏnbongsa 乾鳳寺
kongan 公案
kongju kyuyak 共住規約
Konoe Atsumaro (J) 近衛篤麿
kŏnpaeksŏ 建白書
ko-Pul kojo 古佛古祖
Koryŏ 高麗
Koryŏguk Pojo Sŏnsa ŏrok ch'anjip chunggan sŏ 高麗國 普照禪師語錄 纂集 重刊 序
Koryŏguk Pojo sŏnsa ŏrok 高麗國普照禪師語錄
kŏsa Pulgyo undong 居士佛教運動
ku'gyŏnggak 究竟覺
kubun t'onghal 區分統轄
Kŭmgang kyŏng o'gahae 金剛經五家解
Kŭmgang panya paramil-kyŏng chunggan yŏn'gi sŏ 金剛般若波羅蜜經 重刊 緣起 序
Kŭmgang san yusan ka 金剛山遊山歌
Kŭmganggyŏng 金鋼經

Kŭmgang-jŏ 金剛杵
Kŭmgang-san Kŏnbong-sa Manir-am sinsŏl sŏnhoe hu sŏnjung panghamnok sŏ 金剛山 乾鳳寺 萬日庵 新設禪會後 禪衆芳啣錄序
Kŭmsansa 金山寺
kuse chu'ŭi 求世主義
kwanje Pulgyo 官制 佛教
Kwanŭm posal 觀音菩薩
Kwanŭmchŏn 觀音殿
Kwiilga 歸一歌
kwisin sulsu chi kyo 鬼神術數之敎
kwisin 鬼神
Kwiwŏn chŏngjong 歸源正宗
Kwŏn Sangno 權相老
Kyehŏ 桂虛
kyemong 啓蒙
kyesu kwanŭm taebiju 稽首觀音大悲呪
kyo 敎
kyŏgoe Sŏn 格外禪
kyojŏng 敎正
Kyŏl tongsu chŏnghye tongsaeng tosol tongsŏng pulgwa kyŏlsa mun 結同修定慧同生兜率同成佛果結社文
kyŏn'gi 見起
Kyŏngbong 鏡峰
Kyŏnghŏ 鏡虛
Kyŏnghŏ Sŏngu Sŏnsa Yŏnbo 鏡虛惺牛禪師年譜
Kyŏnghŭng hakkyo 慶興學校
kyŏnghyŏn 境現
kyŏnsŏng 見性
Kyŏnsŏngam見性庵
li (C) 理
li (C) 禮
Liang Qichao 梁啓超
lingzhi (C) 靈知
Linji (C) 臨濟
Liuzu daxi fabao danjing (C) 六祖 大師 法寶 壇經
Lu (C) 廬
Maeil Sinbo 每日申報
malsa 末寺
Man'gong 滿空
Manhae 萬海
Manhwa 萬化
Manil yŏmbul hoe 萬日念佛會

manse chŏngbŏp 萬歲正法
Mazu (C) 馬祖
Mengshan De-I (C) 蒙山德異
Min Pul Yŏn 民佛聯
min 民
Minjok minjuhwa t'ujaeng wiwŏnhoe 民族民主化鬪爭委員會
minjok Pulgyo 民族佛教
minjok 民族
Minju Hoebok Kungmin Hoeŭi 民主回復國民會議
Minjuhwa Ch'ŏngnyŏn Hyŏbŭihoe 民主化青年協議會
Minjung Pŏptang 民衆法堂
minjung Pulgyo 民衆佛教
minjung 民衆
Minmint'u 民民鬪
Mit'agye 彌陀契
Mohe zhiguan (C) 摩阿止觀
mongjung iryŏ 夢中一如
mu 無
mu'gi 無記
mu'nyŏm 無念
mua ponggong 無我奉公
muja kongan 無字公案
mujŏk chŏngsin 無的精神
mujŏk chonjae 無的存在
mumyŏng 無明
mumyŏngp'ung 無明風
mundap 問答
munmyŏng sidae 文明 時代
Munsu posal ch'an 文殊菩薩讚
muru chinyŏ 無漏眞如
musa 無事
musaek chungsaeng 無色衆生
musaek yusang chungsaeng 無色有想衆生
musaeng 無生
musang chungsaeng 無想衆生
musim 無心
musisŏn much'ŏsŏn 無時禪無處禪
musoŭi 無所依
muwi 無爲
Muyung 無融
myogak 妙覺
Myōkaku-ji (J) 妙覺寺

Myŏngjin hakkyo 明進學校
Myŏngjŏng 明正
Myop'osŏ 猫捕鼠
nae oe myŏngch'ŏl 內外明徹
Naebu 內部
namu taejabi kwanseŭm 南無大慈悲觀世音
Nangbaek 朗伯
Nanquan Puyuan (C) 南泉普願
nanseang 卵生
Nanyang (C) 南陽
Nanyang Huizhong (C) 南陽慧忠
Naong hwasang ŏrok 懶翁和尙語錄
Naong Hyegŭn 懶翁 慧勤
nenbutsu (J) 念仏
Nichiren (J) 日蓮
nyang 兩
O Kyŏngsŏk 吳慶錫
o'ŏn yul 五言律
Odaesan Sangwŏn-sa Sŏnwŏn hŏndap yakki 五臺山上院寺禪院獻畓略記
Odoga 悟道歌
okhwang sangje 玉皇上帝
Ōkubo Toshimichi (J) 大久保利通
Ōkuma Shigenobu (J) 大隈重信
Okumura Enshin (J) 奥村圓心
Ōkura Kihachiro (J) 大倉喜八郎
ŏp 業
ŏsan 漁山
Ōtani (J) 大谷
P'alsangnok 八相綠
p'ogyosa 布敎師
p'yŏngdŭng chu'ŭi 平等主義
Paegun hwasang ch'orok pulcho chikchi simch'e yojŏl 白雲和尙抄錄佛祖直指心體要節
Paek Yongsŏng 白龍城
Paekkyo hoet'ong 白敎會通
Paekp'a Kŭngsŏn 白坡亘旋
Paektamsa 百潭寺
Pak Chega 朴齊家
Pak Chiwŏn 朴趾源
Pak Chonghong 朴鍾鴻
Pak Chungbin 朴重彬
Pak Kyusu 朴珪壽

Pak Ŭnsik 朴殷植
Pak Yŏnghyo 朴泳孝
Palching 發徵
panbon hwanwŏn 返本還源
Pang Hanam 方漢岩
pangjang 方丈
panjo 反照
pian (C) 邊
pisang chongdan 非常宗團
pŏbŏ 法語
Pogaesan 寶盖山
Pojo Chinul 普照 知訥
Pojo hu sisŏl Chogyejong 普照後施設曹溪宗
Pojo pŏbŏ 普照法語
pok 福
pokjitki 복짓기
Pŏmmang posalgye kyŏng 梵網菩薩戒經
pŏmnyurŭn 法律恩
Pŏmŏsa 梵魚寺
pŏmp'ae 梵唄
ponjŏngsin 本精神
ponmaŭm 본마음
pŏnnoe 煩惱
ponsa 本寺
ponsan chedo 本山制度
ponsan 本山
ponsim 本心
ponwŏn chinsŏng 本源眞性
Pŏphŭi 法喜
pŏpsinbul 法身佛
porit kogae 보릿고개
pulbŏp hwaryong 佛法活用
pulbŏp myŏlmang 佛法滅亡
pulchi 佛地
pulbŏp si saenghwal 佛法是生活
Pulbŏp Yŏn'guhoe 佛法研究會
Pulgapsa 佛甲寺
pulgong 佛供
pulgong 不空
Pulgyo Chinhŭnghoe Wŏlbo 佛敎振興會月報
Pulgyo Chogyejong 佛敎曹溪宗
Pulgyo chŏngjŏn 佛敎正典

Pulgyo P'yŏngnon 佛教評論
Pulgyo Sabŏm Hakkyo 佛教師範學校
Pulgyo sahoejuŭi 佛教社會主義
Pulgyo Sinbo 佛教新報
Pulgyo taejŏn 佛教大典
Pulgyo Yŏn'guhoe 佛教研究會
pulkak 不覺
pullip munja 不立文字
Pulpŏp myŏlmang sidae 佛法滅亡時代
pulsaeng 不生
pulsŏng 佛性
pult'oesin 不退信
pumoŭn 父母恩
qinggui (C) 淸規
Quanhuo Yantou (C) 全豁 巖頭
ren (C) 仁
Ren Jiyu (C) 任継愈
Renwang jing (C) 仁王經
Richō Bukkyō (J) 李朝佛教
S'ŏngch'ŏl 性徹
sa 事
sa'mujŏng 四無定
sabŏp 寺法
sach'allyŏng 寺刹令
sadaejuŭi 事大主義
saenghwal si pulbŏp 生活是佛法
sagu 死句
samgang oryun 三綱五倫
samgwan 三關
samhak 三學
sami 沙彌
Samil undong 三一運動
samjik 三職
Sammint'u 三民鬪
Samsip ponsa chuji hoeŭi so 三十本山住持會議所
Samsogul ilji 三笑窟 日誌
Samsŏngam 三聖庵
sanchung Pulgyo 山中佛教
sanggu pori 上求菩提
sangjŏk sangjo 常寂常照
sanjung suhaenggi 山中修行期
Sano Zenrei (J) 佐野前勵

sansin 山神
Sasa kwallisŏ 寺社管理署
sasa pulgong 事事佛供
sasang 思想
sa-Sŏn 死禪
saŭn 四恩
sawŏnhwa 寺院化
segye chuŭi 世界主義
segye kisi 世界起始
Seitō (J) 青鞜
Sengcan (C) 僧璨
Senoo Girō (J) 妹尾義郎
shakubuku (J) 折伏
shengmiao jingjie (C) 勝妙境界
Shenhui (C) 神會
shi (C) 事
shinkō Bukkyō (J) 新興仏教
Shinkō Bukkyō Seinen Dōmei (J) 新興仏教青年同盟
shishi (J) 志士
Shitou Xiqian (C) 石頭希遷
sich'al 視察
sijung 示衆
sim 心
simbul 心佛
Simjo manyuron 心造萬有論
simjŏn kaebal undong 心田開發運動
simsŏng 心性
Sin Ch'aeho 申采浩
Sin Pulgyo 新佛教
sin 神
Sin'gyo 神敎
sinjŏngjoron 新貞操論
sinmyo changgu taedarani 神妙章句大陀羅尼
Sinsŏn chi kyo 神仙之敎
sinyŏja 新女子
sinyŏsŏng 新女性
sirhaeng 實行
Sirhak 實學
So yech'am mun 小禮懺文
soa 小我
sok 俗
sokche 俗諦

Sŏkkuram 石窟庵
sŏllyang 禪糧
Sōma Shōei (J) 相馬勝英
Sŏn 禪
Sŏn'ga kwigam 禪家龜鑑
Sŏn'u Toryang 善友道場
sŏnbang 禪房
sŏndang 禪堂
Song Kyu 宋奎
Song Man'gong 宋滿空
Song Pyŏngjun 宋秉晙
Sŏngmun ŭibŏm 釋門儀範
sŏngni 性理
sŏnhoe 禪會
Sŏnjung panghamnok sŏ 禪衆芳啣錄序
Sŏnmun ch'waryo 禪門撮要
Sŏnmun sabyŏn manŏ 禪門四辨漫語
Sŏnmun yŏmsong 禪門拈頌
sŏnnong Pulgyo 禪農佛敎
Sŏnnum sugyŏng 禪門手鏡
sŏnwŏn 禪院
Sŏnwŏn kyurye 禪院規例
Sŏnwŏn 禪苑
Sŏnyo 禪要
Sŏrhak-san Ose-sa Sŏnwŏn hŏndap yakki 雪嶽山 五歲寺禪院 獻畓略記
Sŏrun Pong'in 雪耘奉忍
Sot'aesan 少太山
Sōtō (J) 曹洞
subo 受報
Sudŏksa 修德寺
Suguksa 守國寺
suho karam 守護伽藍
sŭngga och'ik 僧家五則
sŭnggahwa 僧家化
Sŭnggahoe 僧伽會
sŭngmyo kyŏnggye 勝妙 境界
sungmyŏn iryŏ 熟眠 一如
Sŭngnang 僧朗
Sunji 順之
sŭpsaeng 濕生
Susimgyŏl 修心訣
Suwŏl Ŭmgwan 水月 音觀
Suwŏl Yŏngmin 水月永旻

Suyang yŏn'gu yoron 修養硏究要論
T'aego Pou hwasang ŏrok 太古普愚和尙語錄
T'aego 太古
T'aep'yŏng 太平
t'aesaeng 胎生
T'ak Chŏngsik 卓挺埴
t'amjinch'i 貪嗔痴
T'oe'ong Sŏngch'ŏl 退翁 性徹
t'oesin 退信
tado 茶道
Tae yech'am mun 大禮懺文
tae yŏlban 大涅槃
taea 大我
taegak 大覺
Taegakkyo 大覺教
taegakchŏn 大覺展
T'aego Pou 太古普愚
T'aegŭkkyo 太極教
Taehan Maeil Sinbo 大韓每日申報
taehwal 大活
taejayuin 大自有人
taejŏkkwang sammae 大寂光三昧
Taejonggyo 大倧教
Taejonggyŏng 大宗經
taejongjŏng 大宗正
taejung kyohwagi 大衆教化期
taejung 大衆
taekangbaek 大講伯
taesa 大死
Taesŭng Pulgyo Sŭnggahoe 大乘佛教僧伽會
taiji (C) 太極
Takahashi Tōru (J) 高橋亨
Takeda Hanshi (J) 武田範之
Tan'gyŏng 壇經
Tarui Tōkichi (J) 樽井藤吉
tasinjŏn 茶神傳
ta-Sŏn ilmi 茶禪一味
tenkō (J) 転向
Terajima Munenori (J) 寺島宗則
Tiantai (C) 天台
ti-yong (C) 體用
T'oe'ong Sŏngch'ŏl 退翁性徹
Togyo 道教

tŏk 德
Tŏksan 德山
tono chŏmsu 頓悟漸修
tono tonsu 頓悟頓修
tono 頓悟
tonggu pulch'ul 洞口 不出
Tonghak 東學
tongjŏng iryŏ 動靜一如
tongp'oŭn 同胞恩
Toŭi 道義
tsū Bukkyō (J) 通仏教
tŭnggak 等覺
turak 斗落
Ui Hakuju (J) 宇井白寿
ŭibyŏng 義兵
Ŭich'ŏn 義天
ŭidu 疑頭
Ŭisang 義湘
ŭisik 儀式
Ullŭngdo 鬱陵島
Wangling lu (C) 宛陵錄
Wŏlmyŏn 月面
Wŏnbulgyo kyojŏn 圓佛教教典
Wŏnbulgyo 圓佛教
Wŏnch'ŏl 圓徹
Wŏnch'ŭk 圓測
Wŏnhŭngsa 元興寺
Wŏnhyo 元曉
Wŏnjong 圓宗
wŏnjŭng 圓證
Wŏnsang song 圓相頌
wŏnyung muae 圓融無礙
Wŏnyung 圓融
xin (C) 信
Xinxin ming (C) 信心銘
Yamakawa Jūen (J) 山川重遠
Yamashita Shinichi (J) 山下眞一
yangban 兩班
yanggu mugŏn 良久 黙言
Yangshan Huiji (C) 仰山慧寂
Yefu (C) 冶父
Yen Fu (C) 嚴復
yi (C) 義

Yi Hoegwang 李晦光
Yi Nŭnghwa 李能和
Yi Tongin 李東仁
Yi Yonggu 李容九
Yi Yŏngjae 李英宰
Yinbinshi wenji (C) 飲氷室文集
Yŏja'gye 女子界
yŏmbul 念佛
Yŏmbul manir hoe 念佛萬日會
Yŏmbul yomun 念佛要門
yŏmbulhoe 念佛會
yŏmbultang 念佛堂
yŏmgi 念起
yŏmsim 染心
Yŏmsong 拈頌
yŏn 緣
yŏn'gi 緣起
yong 用
yŏngji 靈知
Yongjia (C) 永嘉
Yongjusa 龍珠寺
Yu Taech'i 劉大痴
yu'nyŏm 有念
Yuanjue jing (C) 圓覺經
Yuanjue jing da shou (C) 圓覺經 大疏
Yujŏmsa 楡岾寺
yukjaju 六字呪
Yun Hyojŏng 尹孝定
Yun Ungnyŏl 尹雄烈
yungt'ong 融通
Yunmen (C) 雲門
yusaek chungsaeng 有色衆生
yusaek musang 有色無相
yusang chungsaeng 有想衆生
yusim 唯心
yusin 維新
Zen (J) 禪
Zhaozhou (C) 趙州
Zhengdao ge (C) 證道歌
zhi (C) 智
Zhiyi (C) 智顗
Zhiyuelu (C) 指月錄
zhong (C) 中

Zongjing lu (C) 宗鏡錄
Zongmi (C) 宗密

Contributors

Sungtaek Cho is Professor in the Department of Philosophy at Korea University, Seoul, Korea. He is a translator and editor of the fourth volume of the Wonhyo Translation Series, where he was the principle investigator and project manager from 1996 until 2002, when he moved to Korea University from State University of New York at Stony Brook. He is author of journal articles including "Selflessness: Toward a Buddhist Vision of Social Justice" (*Journal of Buddhist Ethics*, vol. 7), "Rationalist Tendency of Modern Buddhist Scholarship: A Revaluation" (*Philosophy East and West*, vol. 52:4) and "Buddhism and Society: On Buddhist Engagement with Society" (*Korea Journal*, vol. 42). He is currently Director of International Center for Korean Studies, Korea University.

Chong Go is an ordained Buddhist monk and a dharma student of Sŏn Master Daehaeng. A graduate of Dongguk University, his master's thesis topic was the letters and thought of Sŏn Master Hanam.

Bongkil Chung earned his Ph.D. at Michigan State University. He is a professor of philosophy at Florida International University. His major area of research is East Asian Mahāyāna Buddhist philosophy and Won Buddhist philosophy. Chung's publications include *An Introduction to Won Buddhism* (1993), *The Dharma-words of Master Chongsan* (2000), *The Scriptures of Won Buddhism with an Introduction* (2002), and numerous articles on Won Buddhism in international scholarly journals.

Woosung Huh is a professor in the Department of Philosophy at Kyunghee University, Seoul, Korea. He received his PhD in Philosophy from the University of Hawai'i, Manoa. He is author of *Gŭndae ilbon ŭi tu ŏlgul: Nisida ch'ŏrhak* (Two Faces of Modern Japan: Philosophy of Nishida, 2000), co-author of *In'gan iran muŏsin'ga* (What is a Man?, 1997), and author of articles including "The Philosophy of History in 'Later' Nishida: A Philosophic Turn" (*Philosophy East and West*, 1990), "Manhae's Understanding of Buddhism" (*Korea Journal*, 2000),

"Gandhi and Manhae: 'Defending Orthodoxy, Rejecting Heterodoxy' and 'Eastern Ways, Western Instruments' " (*Korea Journal,* 2001).

John Jorgensen is Senior Lecturer in the School of Languages and Linguistics at Griffith University in Australia. His research areas include Chinese and Korean Buddhism, Korean and Japanese new religious movements, and Tokugawa Buddhological and Indological scholarship. His publications include *Inventing Hui-neng* (Brill, 2005), "Conflicts between Buddhism and Confucianism in the Chosŏn Dynasty: A Preliminary Survey," and "Korean Buddhist Historiography: Issues from the Past for the Future."

Jongmyung Kim is Associate Professor of Korean Buddhism, Graduate School of Korean Studies, The Academy of Korean Studies, Sŏngnam, Korea. He is the author of *Han'guk ŭi segye Pulgyo yusan: sasang kwa ŭiŭi* (Korea's World Buddhist Properties: Thought and Significance, 2008), and *Han'guk chungse ŭi Pulgyo ŭirye* (Buddhist Rituals in Medieval Korea) and translator (into Korean) of Robert Buswell's *The Zen Monastic Experience.* Kim has also contributed a chapter or sections to *Buddhism: Introducing the Buddhist Experience, Tradition and Theories of Tradition, Korea and Globalization, T'oeong Sŏngch'ŏl ŭi kkaedarŭm kwa suhaeng* (Enlightenment and Practice of T'oe'ong S'ŏngch'ŏl), *Koryŏ sidae ŭi Pulgyo sasang* (Buddhist Thought of the Koryŏ Period), and *Nonjaeng ŭro ponŭn Pulgyo ch'ŏrhak* (Issues on Debate in Buddhist Philosophy), the *Encyclopedia of Buddhism* and *Great Thinkers of the Eastern World.*

Mu Soeng has been the director of the Barre Center for Buddhist Studies since 1992 where he teaches courses on Mahāyāna Buddhism and related areas. He was trained in the Korean Zen tradition and was a monk for twelve years. His most recent publication, *Trust in Mind: The Rebellion of Chinese Zen* explores the poem of the third patriarch of Chan Buddhism. His other publications include, *Thousand Peaks: Korean Zen—Tradition and Teacher, Heart Sutra: Ancient Buddhist Wisdom in the Light of Quantum Reality,* and *Diamond Sutra: Transforming the Way We Perceive the World.*

Jin Y. Park is Associate Professor of Philosophy and Religion at American University. Her book-length publications include *Buddhisms and Deconstructions* (2006), *Buddhism and Postmodernity: Zen, Huayan, and the Possibility of Buddhist Postmodern Ethics* (2008), *Merleau-Ponty and Buddhism* (co-edited, 2009), and *Comparative Political Theory and Cross Cultural Philosophy: Essays in Honor of Hwa Yol Jung* (2009). Park has also published a number of journal articles and book chapters on Zen and Huayan Buddhism, Buddhism and modernity in Korea, and Buddhist-postmodern comparative philosophy.

Pori Park is assistant professor of religious studies at Arizona State University. Her research interests include Buddhism, Korean religions, and the interaction between Buddhism, modernity, and nationalism. She has recently published "The Buddhist Purification Movement in Postcolonial South Korea: Restoring Clerical Celibacy and State Intervention," in *Identity Conflicts: Can Violence be Regulated?*, edited by J. Craig Jenkins and Ester E. Gottlieb (2007); "Buddhism in Contemporary Korea," in *Buddhism in World Cultures: Comparative Perspectives*, edited by Stephen Berkwitz (2006); and "Korean Buddhist Reforms and Problems in the Adoption of Modernity during the Colonial Period," *Korea Journal* 45/1 (Spring 2005).

Henrik Hjort Sørensen holds a PhD in Oriental Cultures and Languages. He has published numerous essays on Chinese and Korean Buddhism with special focus on Esoteric Buddhism and Buddhist material culture. Currently Sorensen is director of the Seminar for Buddhist Studies at the University of Copenhagen, Denmark.

Vladimir Tikhonov is Professor in the Department of Culture Studies and Oriental Languages at Oslo University in Norway. He is co-translator of *Selected Writings of Han Yongun: From Social Darwinism to 'Socialism with a Buddhist Face'* (2007) and author of numerous journal articles. His research interest includes history of Korean Buddhism, general history of Korea's ideologies, and, currently, Social-Darwinism as general East Asian ideological phenomenon.

Patrick R. Uhlmann is a PhD candidate at the University of California at Los Angeles. He is writing his doctoral dissertation on medieval East Asian Buddhism.

Woncheol Yun is Professor of Religious Studies at Seoul National University in Seoul, Korea. He earned his PhD from State University of New York at Stony Brook on the study of T'oe'ong Sŏngch'ŏl's Buddhist thought. His publication includes *Pulgyo sasang ŭi ihae* (Understanding Buddhist thought).

Index